KT-463-153

WORLD POVERTY

New policies to defeat an old enemy

Edited by Peter Townsend and David Gordon

First published in Great Britain in September 2002 by

The Policy Press
University of Bristol
Fourth Floor, Beacon House
Queen's Road
Bristol BS8 1QU
UK

Tel +44 (0)117 331 4054
Fax +44 (0)117 331 4093
e-mail tpp-info@bristol.ac.uk
www.policypress.org.uk

© The Policy Press 2002
Reprinted 2004

British Library Cataloguing in Publication Data
A catalogue record for this book is available from the British Library

Library of Congress Cataloging-in-Publication Data
A catalog record for this book has been requested

ISBN 1 86134 396 5 hardback
A paperback version of this book is also available

Peter Townsend is Professor of International Social Policy and Acting Director of the Centre for the Study of Human Rights at the London School of Economics and Political Science, and Emeritus Professor of Social Policy, University of Bristol and **David Gordon** is Professor of Social Justice and Head of the Centre for the Study of Poverty and Social Justice, and Director of the Townsend Centre for International Poverty Research, University of Bristol.

The right of Peter Townsend and David Gordon to be identified as editors of this work has been asserted by them in accordance with the 1988 Copyright, Designs and Patents Act.

All rights reserved: no part of this publication may be reproduced, stored in a retrieval system, or transmitted in any form or by any means, electronic, mechanical, photocopying, recording, or otherwise without the prior permission of The Policy Press.

The statements and opinions contained within this publication are solely those of the editors and contributors and not of The University of Bristol or The Policy Press. The University of Bristol and The Policy Press disclaim responsibility for any injury to persons or property resulting from any material published in this publication.

The Policy Press works to counter discrimination on grounds of gender, race, disability, age and sexuality.

Cover design by Qube Design Associates, Bristol.
Front cover: photograph supplied by Paul Grover.
Printed and bound in Great Britain by Hobbs the Printers Ltd, Southampton.

Contents

Notes on contributors

Sir Tony Atkinson is Warden of Nuffield College, Oxford University, past president of the International Economic Association and past president of the Royal Economic Society.

Jo Beall is Reader in Development Studies in the Development Studies Institute at the London School of Economics and Political Science. She has worked for the World Bank, UNDP, UN-Habitat, the OECD and the Department for International Development, UK. She has been a visiting professor in Colombia and has assessed poverty alleviation programmes in Pakistan. She has also been the regional gender expert on Southern Africa for the European Commission.

Owen Crankshaw is Associate Professor in the Department of Sociology at the University of Cape Town, South Africa. He is author of *Race, class and the changing division of labour under apartheid* (1996, Routledge). He has undertaken extensive social survey work for policy makers in South Africa as well as for the Department for International Development in the UK, the World Bank and the Mellon Foundation.

Kwabena Donkor worked recently as the Chief Executive Officer of a downstream state-owned oil company in Ghana. In the early 1990s he was a research assistant and taught at the University of Bristol, UK, where he gained his PhD, later published as *Structural adjustment and mass poverty in Ghana* (1997, Ashgate). His interests have been in third world development planning and administration, management development, strategic management, non-governmental organisations and poverty Alleviation. He is currently involved in consulting for NGOs, the public sector and international development agencies.

David Gordon is Professor of Social Justice and Head of the Centre for the Study of Social Exclusion and Social Justice and also the Director of the Townsend Centre for International Poverty Research, University of Bristol, UK. He combined his background in biology and geology with anti-poverty policy while helping to find safe water supplies in the South Pacific. He has researched and published in the scientific measurement of poverty, crime and poverty, childhood disability, area-based poverty measures, the causal effects of poverty on ill health, housing policy and rural poverty. He edited *Breadline Europe: The measurement of poverty* (with Peter Townsend, 2000, The Policy Press).

Athar Hussain is Deputy Director of the Asia Research Centre at the London School of Economics and Political Science. He has been engaged in research on China for almost twenty years and published widely on various aspects of the Chinese economy. His current research interests cover social security, urban and rural poverty and regional disparity. Together with a team of Chinese researchers, he recently finished a study of urban poverty for the Asian Development Bank.

Nazneen Kanji is Senior Research Associate at the International Institute for Environment and Development, London, and has worked extensively for the Department of International Development, the Swiss Agency for Cooperation and Development, the Norwegian Ministry for Foreign Affairs, UNCHS (Habitat) and various international NGOs in different African and Asian countries. Her research interests include the impact of structural adjustment policies on poverty at the household level; gender, livelihoods and social policy; and the influence of NGOs on anti-poverty policy processes. Her latest publication is *Poverty reduction: What role for the state in today's globalised economy?* (edited with Francis Wilson and Einar Braathen, 2001, Zed Press/CROP publications), which includes her chapter 'Poverty reduction and policy dialogue: the World Bank and the state in Zimbabwe, Zambia and Malawi'.

Sunil Kumar lectures on the MSc in Social Policy and Planning in Developing Countries at the Department of Social Policy, London School of Economics and Political Science. He is an urban social planner with interests in housing, poverty, livelihoods and institutions. He has undertaken work for the United Nations Centre for Human Settlements (UNCHS Habitat) and the UK Department for International Development (DFID). His latest research publication is entitled *Social relations, rental housing markets and the poor in urban India* (2001, LSE).

Jeanette E. Markle is a public policy researcher at the Project on Inequality and Poverty at the Commonwealth Institute in the US. She has been a research assistant on the Social Services Delivery Systems Project at the Institute for Urban Economics (IUE) in Moscow and an affiliate of the Washington-based Urban Institute. Earlier, she worked with the National Low Income Housing Coalition (NLIHC) in Washington, DC.

S.M. Miller is director of the Project on Inequality and Poverty (PIP) at the Commonwealth Institute in the US and Research Professor of Sociology at Boston College. He is the co-author of a forthcoming book on the politics of class and identity group respect. Trained in economics and concerned with organisational issues, he has been involved as an intellectual activist with governmental and non-governmental poverty and community action organisations in several countries. He is the co-founder and board member of the advocacy organisation, United for a Fair Economy. He also serves on the Scientific Board of the Comparative Research Programme on Poverty (CROP) in Bergen, Norway, and the board of directors of the Poverty and Race Research Action Council (PRRAC) in Washington, DC.

Susan Parnell is Associate Professor in the Department of Environmental and Geographical Sciences at the University of Cape Town, South Africa. She has taught at the School of Oriental and African Studies and has been a Visiting Fellow at Oxford University. She has participated in numerous international policy conferences and has done extensive consultancy work in the field of social development, working for national and local government departments in South Africa, as well as the Department for International Development, UK, and the UNDP.

Ladislav Rabušic is Associate Professor of Sociology at Masaryk University, Brno, the Czech Republic. He teaches courses on methods of social research, population studies, and ageing and society. His research interests include sociological aspects of Czech social policy. He has published on the ageing of society, poverty, and population trends both in Czechia and abroad, including a monograph *Ceská spolecnost stárne* (*'Czech society is ageing'*, 1995) and an edited book *Ceská spolecnost a seniori* (*'Czech society and the elderly'*, 1997). His latest book, on causes of Czech below-replacement fertility, is entitled *Kde ty všechny deti jsou* (*'Where have all the children gone'*, 2001).

Bernd Schulte is Research Fellow at the Max Planck Institute for International and Foreign Social Security Law, Munich, Germany. He has worked extensively with the European Commission and has published widely on constitutional questions of the development of social security and the welfare state in Europe.

Tomáš Sirovátka is Director of the Institute for Social Issues in the Faculty of Social Studies, Masaryk University, Brno, the Czech Republic. His recent research includes a national study of the links between the labour market and social policy, and studies of the effectiveness of income support schemes and active labour market policies, the legitimacy of social policy, and social assistance and income support policies in central European countries. His publications include a monograph *Marginalizace na pracovním trhu* (*'Labour market marginalisation'*, 1997), which focuses mainly on the consequences for the Czech Republic, and a book evaluating the recent developments of Czech social policy – *Ceská sociální politika na prahu 21. století: efektivnost, selhávání, legitimita* (*'Czech social policy on the eve of the 21st century: Effectiveness, failures, legitimacy'*, 2000).

Peter Townsend is Professor of International Social Policy and Acting Director of the Centre for the Study of Human Rights at the London School of Economics and Political Science. He is Emeritus Professor of Social Policy at the University of Bristol, UK. Since 1995 he has published reports on poverty, unemployment and health on behalf of the UN, UNDP, the EU, UNRISD and the Royal Danish Ministry of Foreign Affairs. He edited *Breadline Europe: The measurement of poverty* (with David Gordon, 2000, The Policy Press) and he has written a report for UNICEF on child poverty (with David Gordon and

Christina Pantazis, 2002). Currently he is convening a course on Child Rights and Child Poverty at the LSE.

Wim van Oorschot is Professor of Sociology at the Department of Sociology and the Tilburg Institute of Social Security Studies of Tilburg University, The Netherlands. His present research interests are social security policies and outcomes, and cultural aspects of welfare state change. He has published on (local) anti-poverty policies, labour market problems and policies, the history of social security, unemployment, pensions, benefit take-up and public opinion on the welfare state.

Jan Vandemoortele is Principal Adviser and Group Leader of the Social Development Group, Bureau for Development Policy, UNDP, New York. He was previously Director of Social Policy at UNICEF.

Acknowledgements

This book builds on a companion volume published just over a year ago – *Breadline Europe: The measurement of poverty*. That European book called attention to the vigour and originality of regional research into poverty. Among its prime features was evidence of the reconstitution of mass poverty in large parts of Eastern Europe. Because of the confusion that exists about meaning and measurement – some of it deliberately motivated to distract attention from failure to make sufficient inroads into the problem – a powerful case was put forward for the construction of a scientific measure of poverty itself.

This book takes up an international perspective, examines a considerable range of evidence from the poorer countries, including the most populous countries of the world, China and India, and pushes the analysis of poverty from measurement to the policies designed to alleviate it. The predominant concern is with the most populous and deprived regions of the world, growing inequality between rich and poor and the problems of global capitalism, but also the key roles of international agencies, transnational corporations and the politically dominant states. The leadership role of Europe is strongly represented. Indeed, some chapters (namely Chapters Five, Six and Seven) were, in their early form, presented as papers at six Economic and Social Research Council-funded conferences in Bristol, Budapest and London, between 1998 and 2000. We would like to thank those who contributed to this series of conferences, which helped to concert as well as communicate European approaches to dealing with many common problems of poverty. In particular we wish to thank Helen Anderson, Eldin Fahmy, Shailen Nandy, Christina Pantazis, Angela Aubertin, Karon Taylor, Jean Ingram, Remmy Ahmed, Sally Burrell, Alan Simpson, Tim Lang, Colin Hines, Richard Jolly, Meghnad Desai and Nancy Krieger for acts of generosity, patience and encouragement.

We have gained a lot from our contacts with international agencies, particularly the Division for Social Policy and Development of the UN, UNICEF, the UN University World Institute for Development Economics Research (WIDER), the Social Policy Research Centre of the University of New South Wales, the International Labour Organisation, the World Bank and UNRISD.

Special acknowledgement is due to WIDER and to Sir Tony Atkinson for permission to reproduce Chapter Two from the series of annual lectures arranged by WIDER, and to the Social Policy Research Centre of the University of New South Wales for permission to reproduce in Chapter One large parts of a lecture from their National Social Policy Conference in Sydney 1999. Thanks are due to Ashgate Press, for permission to reproduce passages from Kwabena Donkor's book *Structural adjustment and mass poverty in Ghana*.

We wish to thank the staff of The Policy Press, particularly Helen Bolton, Karen Bowler, Laura Greaves, Dawn Rushen and Dave Worth, for sympathetic and professionally adept handling of the problems of bringing an ambitious publication to fruition.

In relation to the chapters specified above we acknowledge too the financial support of the ESRC Seminar Series grant R45126470397 on 'Developing Poverty Measures'.

The human condition is structurally unequal

Peter Townsend and David Gordon

"I am often asked what is the most serious form of human rights violation in the world today and my reply is consistent: extreme poverty." (Mary Robinson, 2002)

In *Breadline Europe: The measurement of poverty* (Gordon and Townsend, 2000), we argued that the measurement and analysis of poverty could not be separated from the construction, or indeed the historical and contemporary responsibilities, of policies. They are driving causes of the human conditions and experiences making up 'poverty'. Yet poverty-diminishing or poverty-promoting policies are not generally identified as such, and their effects not precisely quantified. There is not much 'literature of inquiry' to trace the contribution of different policies to the overall extent of national and international, still less local, poverty. A growing awareness of this yawning gap in human knowledge led to the design of this book. Of course a single inquiry like ours cannot provide all the answers. Indeed, it cannot hope to provide much more than preliminary answers to questions about the distribution of poverty across the world and the trends taking place. Rather, this book can only represent a beginning – a point of departure – for resolute and determined programmes of research and analysis in many countries.

Our aim was to bring together research scientists and a range of information from across the world. In doing this we found that institutions had to be understood, and investigated, as agents directing and sponsoring policies that contributed to the changing extent and depth of poverty among people. These institutions include governments, but also other institutions. Many readers will no doubt be familiar with particular policies of particular governments that claim to reduce poverty. These include policies to improve or target benefits for poor people – such as allowances for children in families with low incomes, or new basic pensions for categories of the elderly population. Policies to get more people back into work, so that they can support themselves rather than become dependent on state benefits, provide another example. Inquiry can be made into the effects of such policies, whether intended or unintended. However, there are other state policies, for example those concerning tax (and especially those that concern tax indirectly) where the effects on poverty are neither clarified nor even appreciated as being relevant. Tax policies are a complex set that certainly addresses human welfare, and they turn on intentions to promote or restore equity – for example, between older people and the economically active population, or between families with and without children. There are many other state policies – such as charging for healthcare, adding or reducing subsidised public housing, imprisoning young delinquents, and establishing armed forces – that contribute to, or subtract from, the numbers in poverty. State policies also have to be traced through national, regional and local levels, and it is not easy to draw a distinction between state and council responsibility for local policies that increase or reduce local poverty. The social effects of each policy are relevant to the immediate or ultimate success in keeping the national rate of poverty low. What becomes important is the multiple effect of different state policies on trends in poverty.

The poverty-diminishing and poverty-promoting policies of institutions other than the state are even harder to identify. They include market institutions, companies and corporations, religious institutions and charitable or voluntary organisations. Sometimes the social policies of such institutions are declared – as in prospectuses, statements in constitutions or annual accounts, cherished historical accounts and everyday prayer and ritual. More often precise injunctions are open to interpretation, or are implied rather than textually expressed. A distinction must be made between institutionalised and personal forms of recommended or actual conduct. A distinction must also be made between institutional policies that have a short-term or immediate social effect, and those which encourage long-term forms of discrimination, caste or class. Sometimes, social institutions other than states act through governments or are subordinate to governments. At other times they act independently – with varying degrees of success.

This problem of identifying policy cause or responsibility is now being overshadowed by the rise of global institutions. Swift developments in the global market, the relationships between governments, the role of international agencies, and especially the rise in power of transnational corporations, are transforming the debate about poverty. Fifty-one of the world's largest economies are now corporations, and the rest nation states. Only 25 countries of the world are now listed as having larger Gross Domestic Product (GDP) than the total annual value of the sales of the world's biggest corporation, General Motors. Ten corporations (General Motors, Ford Motor, Mitsui, Mitsubushi, Itochu, Royal Dutch Shell Group, Marubeni Sumitomo, Exxon and Toyota Motor) have all bigger annual sales than the GDP of countries such as Malaysia, Venezuela and Colombia, and some of them more than Saudi Arabia, South Africa, Norway and Greece.

These three types of institutions (the richest governments, international agencies and largest corporations) are prime instigators or sponsors of the policies that deepen, perpetuate, or aim to reduce existing poverty and inequality.

The governments of the most powerful countries act both alone and in unison – through international agencies or as prompted by, or in deference to, the most powerful corporations, to influence terms of trade, overseas aid, the conditions for receiving loans and grants, and much else besides. These three structural forces invite scrutiny of their scope and changing functions. Their interrelationships invite closer study still. Until their responsibility for recent trends in the distribution of living standards can be pinpointed it will remain difficult to establish a baseline of cause and effect with which to prosecute the war on poverty.

The idea of these three 'transforming' the debate about poverty applies to the arguments they have put forward to reduce organised state welfare, progressive taxation, and employment rights, and to support actively privatisation. The question is whether this strategy has led to higher economic growth, with benefit to the poor (as is alleged), and to more of the poor acting successfully to surmount poverty. Much of the reliable evidence leads to contrary conclusions. The contributors to this volume make a case for an alternative strategy to do with:

- rights to employment and in employment;
- earnings and social security for a minimum livelihood;
- privatisation to be kept in better perspective by strong public sector services and genuinely democratic government;
- progressive versus regressive taxes;
- the realisation of human rights through improved international law; and
- better management and access to cash benefits as well as universal social services.

This would mean finding the right strategy for the big institutions of government and international government to take structural action to meet the immediate needs of the poor. This would not rule out the long-term changes that have to be introduced by countless organisations into institutions and community relationships, as well as individual acts, to meet the multiple effects of existing and transitional poverty. This alternative strategy demands hard investigation and advocacy.

The most powerful governments, together with the biggest international agencies and transnational corporations, comprise the forces that control the scale and character of social polarisation and poverty. To fulfil the anti-poverty goals that have been expressed, key economic strategies must be abandoned or substantially revised. The biggest problem faced by the six billion people of this world – the divisive effect of growing inequality and multiplying poverty – is becoming uglier each day. It is the lack of any framework of coordination between international and national action for the human good.

Policies must no longer be treated as measures designed, albeit inadequately, to improve the human condition, but rather as predominant causes of the deterioration of that condition. Many of them are instruments of control, even instruments causing lasting damage, and not just explicitly formulated legal or administrative remedies. Identifying which is which, and the scale and speed of their mixed effects, is *the* research task of the 21st century.

Yet the unintended good or bad effects of some policies, and the deeply structural and pervasive or inconsequential effects of others, is not considered or even seriously investigated in most scientific work. Science is expected to investigate conditions and draw weighty conclusions that are quite independent of the political process of managing and reacting to events. However, there are social scientists who are beginning to understand that this is only part of the scientific story. Taken to extremes, 'objectivity' can be artificial and thoroughly misleading. Prime or underlying forces are liable to be ignored. This happens when the only acceptable causes are believed to be specific or narrowly selective and not also general. Or it happens when what people, and especially leading political figures, believe is disregarded. The political process can shape the very survival of sections of a population as well as their impoverishment or prosperity.

This book asks this question: 'Are existing international and national policies likely to succeed in reducing poverty across the world?' It concludes that they are not; furthermore, a radically different international strategy, first and foremost, is needed. National policies can then adapt to fulfil the UN millennium objectives. An international policy manifesto is put forward to stimulate the present debate.

Policies intended to operate at different levels (international, regional, national and sub-national), and to include international agencies (such as the UN and the World Bank, national governments and groups of governments, and local and city authorities), are examined. The underlying assumptions in such policies of the causes and extent of poverty are brought to light and openly discussed. Key aspects of social policy, such as 'targeting' and means testing, deregulation and privatisation, are considered in detail, especially as they have been applied to certain countries of Europe, India, China and Sub-Saharan Africa.

The scope of the book is international and its focus is on anti-poverty policies rather than the scale, causes and measurement of poverty. It is divided into four parts:

- International anti-poverty policies: the problems of the Washington Consensus;
- Anti-poverty policies in rich countries;
- Anti-poverty policies in poor countries;
- Future anti-poverty policies: national and international.

International anti-poverty policies

The first part of this volume explains why a multiplication of international policies experienced mixed success in reducing poverty. Peter Townsend (Chapter One) gives a general account of trends in development from the 1960s, when poverty was placed at the forefront of international concern. The continued emphasis on economic growth by the Bretton Woods institutions has attracted increasingly critical attention. There is no evidence of marked change in the huge extent of poverty in the world. In some regions – especially Sub-Saharan Africa and the transitional economies of Eastern Europe and the republics of the former Soviet Union – it has increased noticeably. The partial shift of attention to 'social exclusion' has widened the understanding of the causes of poverty but not led to the mobilisation of effective action on the part of the international agencies or the most powerful states. What has been neglected is not so much the conditions of poverty or of exclusion, but rather those of acquisition and affluence at the other extreme of population experience, and the mechanics, or agents of the entire distribution. It is the phenomenon of 'social polarisation' that is attracting too little interest and yet is fuelling increasingly difficult and even dangerous as well as contentious social conditions. The focus of attention has to be turned to the prime institutions controlling this development, including the transnational corporations of the global market, the World Bank and the International Monetary Fund (IMF) and the countries of the G8 (Canada, France, Germany, Italy, Japan, Russia, the UK and the US). Thorough investigation of the phenomenon of social polarisation – a particularly marked feature of the modern world – is likely to reveal the need for the mobilisation of multiple strategies and policies leading to the establishment of an 'international welfare state'.

Tony Atkinson (Chapter Two) takes issue with two widely circulated assertions:

- that rising inequality is inevitable;
- that the 'Transatlantic Consensus', or the proposition that increased inequality in the US and high unemployment in Continental Europe are due to a shift of demand away from unskilled workers towards skilled workers, is an acceptable explanation of that growth.

He examines the determinants of what people receive in the market place and shows that the standard trade theory of the Heckscher-Ohlin kind is oversimplified and insufficient and questions the chief strategy of the Transatlantic Consensus. Instead he recommends an alternative approach. By examining trends in the whole range of earnings and of incomes after tax he points to the major role of government policies "in offsetting the rise in inequality of market incomes", although they had not more than partly offset that rise in most countries in the past two decades. First he shows how wage-bargaining and income policies can influence the wages dispersion itself. Then he calls attention to the varying importance in different countries of redistributive policies. Such policies have for many years exerted significant effects on the dispersion of after-tax incomes. Because economic growth has been uneven, he argues that major lessons can be learned from variations in policy that have caused, or are at least strongly correlated with, that differential growth. Newer economic theories place limits on previous assumptions about supply and demand, and help to explain why wage differentials continue to grow. Progressive income taxation and social transfers can substantially reduce the income inequalities that may arise in the market place.

In Chapter Three David Gordon describes how international social policy and academic research on poverty has changed in the last decade and, in particular, how a widening chasm is developing between the anti-poverty policies being advocated by UN agencies and those of the EU. Having outlined these two sets of policies, Gordon explains that they are underpinned by a diverging approach to the measurement of poverty: "Without good comparable measures of poverty, it will be impossible to determine if any anti-poverty policies are working effectively and efficiently". This chapter compares in detail the numbers living in poverty in different countries, criticises the poverty measures as well as the anti-poverty policies of the international financial agencies, and calls for a fresh international and scientific approach.

Anti-poverty policies in rich countries

How are anti-poverty policies being developed in the rich countries? A starting point is the US, undisputedly the most powerful country in the world. Mike Miller and Jeanette Markle (Chapter Four) focus on the change in US social policy from welfare to workfare and the importance of making improvements in the low-wage labour market in making this a successful transition. The political and social environment in which this transition is occurring includes two recent trends in US public policy: privatisation, and a general reduction in the role of the government (and the federal government in particular). A major difficulty in constructing effective social policy is the inadequate US measure of poverty. The enactment and evolution of the welfare programme as well as the causes of the dramatic 'reforms' of 1996 are traced. The 1996 legislation triggered the transition from an income maintenance approach under welfare, to one based on employment under workfare. The outcomes of the workfare programme, and the claims of its proponents and critics, are discussed. Since the programme must be reauthorised in 2002, the arguments likely to be the most prominent in public debate are summarised. If the situation of workfare participants and other low-income persons is to be improved, the chapter's authors argue, then the low-wage labour market must be better coordinated with strong social programmes. The private sector alone cannot provide a decent standard of living in its current form. Lessons can be drawn from the experience of the US by other nations grappling with similar issues.

The experiences of different European countries are then examined in turn. In Chapter Five Bernd Schulte explains what anti-poverty policies have been developed in Europe. He describes minimum incomes, access to the labour market and access to social services. He also describes the first, second and third European anti-poverty programmes from 1975 to 1994. Since the objective of the Treaty of Rome was to construct a European *Economic* Community little importance had been attached previously to common social policy. The first step was taken in the 1970s, by giving practical meaning to equal treatment for men and women in labour law and social security (laid down in Article 119 of the EEC Treaty). The intentions of the anti-poverty programmes were to stimulate political debate in the member countries, exchange information and experience of different policies, monitor poverty, and coordinate activities in the different countries to combat poverty. Income poverty remained the dominant feature of the conditions investigated, "because lack of financial means often leads to the lack of the other components of a decent life". By contrast, social exclusion was best understood as a denial of basic rights, or social citizenship. There was a tradition of relatively high public expenditure, strong fiscal policy and elaborate social insurance systems. For most member states, Schulte argues, "minimum-income schemes concern the most acute situation of lack of financial resources, but are not intended to cover all situations of poverty". Generally they were intended to be available for temporary benefit or as a "final safety-net mechanism" for a relative few in the population. Modern conditions seemed to have reduced the effectiveness of social security systems. There is a gap between the principles of equity or justice and the actual implementation of an administrative system of benefit. Apart from exchange of information and experience of national policies, there had to be a fresh look at regional policies. These included the introduction of the European Monetary Union (EMU) and the Euro (€), the European Employment Strategy and the Structural Funds.

Within Schulte's sketch of European social policies, the experiences of particular countries are then described in some detail. Tomáš Sirovátka, Wim van Oorschot and Ladislav Rabušic examine the legitimacy and support of social protection systems in the Czech Republic and the Netherlands. They take a close look at how the different economic and socio-political conditions of transformation in the two countries affect general citizen support. In the 1990s, social protection transformation policies in the Netherlands and the Czech Republic followed the same trend, aiming to restrict and control expenditure. The changes favour selection and the overall collective protection system guaranteed by the state is fading away. In both countries, the change has raised serious questions about conditions that make it – or do not make it – acceptable to the population.

The current Czech social protection system suffers from a very low legitimacy among Czech citizens. They expressed their most critical views when asked about benefits and parts of the system that target groups perceived as the most entitled to them, and whose claims were most restricted during the transformation. In the Czech Republic, this is the case with families that have children in particular. Introduction of means testing was to provide benefits to those who are entitled to them and need them. Citizens, however, perceive the system as unfair and as insufficient protection against poverty.

Chapter Seven describes the shift towards selective targeting of welfare in both Western and Eastern European countries in recent years. Wim van Oorschot critically discusses the pros and cons of means testing in relation to the broad aims of social policy: to do away with poverty, social injustice and dependency, and to integrate all groups and classes into society. He finds that means testing demotivates poor people from trying to be better-off, because of the effects of the poverty trap; that is, the high rates of marginal tax to which they are exposed. It provides major obstacles to social exchange and participation and creates ineffective delivery of social rights, since a substantial non-take up of benefits is inherent in the system. As van Oorschot explains, "It runs the risk of focusing too strictly on short-term economic interests at the cost of longer-term needs for social integration and participation". The quality of welfare for needy citizens is seriously endangered. Van Oorschot is concerned about the consequential risk of European welfare states moving themselves into "a vicious circle of ever-declining support for social protection and welfare provision".

Anti-poverty policies in poor countries

Anti-poverty policies in and for poor countries deserve even more intensive appraisal to find why they are failing to work. Compared with national action, international action attracts far less scrutiny than it should. This is partly because the international agencies and transnational corporations repeatedly offload responsibility onto states and local district councils. In this part, international and national anti-poverty policies are found to sit uneasily together. Kwabena Donkor (Chapter Eight) describes the ever-worsening situation in Sub-Saharan Africa, recording the weakest economic growth rates and development rates of all developing regions: "Mass poverty is of particular importance in Ghana and other developing countries. Mass poverty differs from case poverty where a relative few are poor in a generally affluent society. The term helps to direct attention to structural causes. With 'mass', poverty is the norm and not to be poor is the exception". In Ghana, 40% of the population were recorded as being in poverty in 1998-99 and 27% in extreme poverty.

Donkor argues that it is wrong to focus on the actions and responsibilities of individual governments. It was the role of global economic and political arrangements in the impoverishment of individuals, communities and nations that had to be given most attention. Poverty was "the by-product of colonialism and neo-colonialism of economic, political and social arrangements that in turn originated from capitalism and imperialism. It is therefore impractical, if not unethical, to attempt to separate national and individual poverty from world poverty since the two are intrinsically linked". During the 1980s structural adjustment programmes were 'imposed' on the African continent and at least 40 of the 56 countries were involved. These programmes of the World Bank and the IMF had "transformed the realism if not the interpretation of African political and social economy. This transformation – from devaluation and privatisation to cost recovery and deregulation – has been effected not only in the economic and social sphere but also the political". The ramifying social implications of this exercise of global economic and political power had not yet been grasped: "Symbiotic linkages between the ruling political and commercial classes in both the global metropolises and the Ghanaian periphery has relegated the mass of the people, who are outside these structures of linkage, to irrelevance in the distribution and ownership of resources". In the late

1980s the first instrument of poverty alleviation under adjustment was the Programme of Action to Mitigate the Social Cost of Adjustment (PAMSCAD). This was intended to be corrective action to mitigate the consequences of social adjustment. However, it turned out to be "a gargantuan fraud perpetrated on the poor of Ghana by the government and its international backers".

The World Bank's prescriptions for economic reform have been widely criticised in the context of structural adjustment policies and the deepening economic crisis in Africa. In Chapter Nine Nazneen Kanji examines the response of the Bank to growing criticisms, first taking the form of the Social Dimension of Adjustment (SDA) programme. This was a joint programme between the World Bank, the African Development Bank, United Nations Development Programme (UNDP) and bilateral donors. It emphasised 'social safety net' programmes and provided funding for the collection and analysis of data on poverty in individual African countries. Safety nets were identified as the third 'pillar' of the Bank's strategy for poverty reduction in its 1990 World Development Report (the other two being broad-based economic growth and human development). One increasingly popular instrument used by the donor agencies in delivering 'safety nets' are 'social funds'. These were designed to facilitate longer-term 'community-driven' development. They took many forms, including public work projects paying below-market wages to the long-term unemployed, and projects to extend primary education and healthcare facilities in places where the poorest groups in the population seemed likely to benefit disproportionately. However, questions had to be raised about the "negative and positive effects social funds can have on wider national policies and public sector performance". And second, it was difficult to make out the relevance of social funds to a multiple strategy to reduce poverty. Their scale and cost was small: "They are no substitute for wider economic and social policies which address the distribution of material and social assets in highly unequal societies and which do not rely on market-based mechanisms alone to reduce the unacceptable levels of poverty and deprivation which exist in Sub-Saharan Africa".

Any convincing account of policy effectiveness has to deal with *specific* policies in the developing countries. In Chapter Ten Jo Beall, Owen Crankshaw and Susan Parnell examine policies to improve urban water supply and sanitation in the poorest countries. As many as 1.1 billion people in the world lack safe water and 2.4 billion do not have access to adequate sanitation, with over 90% of them living in Asia and Africa. Johannesburg provides the case study. The city is posed with the challenge of meeting "the pressing service needs of burgeoning numbers of historically disadvantaged urban dwellers, without compromising the standards of services and supply to better-off rate-paying citizens". Difficulties in securing more resources from the rich city dwellers resulted from the latter being resistant to paying increased rates. And there were difficulties in securing outside resources because the policies promoted by international agencies depended on recovery of costs from users. The problems of service delivery spring in part from the history of apartheid and the perpetuation of many of the features of racial inequality as well as more recent patterns of differentiation and income inequality. When wages are extremely low or irregular and unemployment high, the introduction of charges or the raising of rents can mobilise hostility among large sections of the population. The problem of trying to improve hostels for migrant workers provides just one example. Although many have been refurbished and divided up into individual rooms or family accommodation they "are desperately over-crowded and the bathrooms and toilets lacking in maintenance. The limited ablution facilities, which are used by women and children as well as men, are associated with the worst humiliations of abject living conditions such as lack of privacy, hygiene and basic dignity". The case shows how the Johannesburg authority was trying to make the best of an inheritance of extreme inequality and the unrealisable expectations of both the majority of the South African population and the international financial agencies. Putting a policy focus on *basic* services might indirectly address urban poverty in the short and medium term and indeed be environmentally sound, but success, the authors argue, is likely to be frustrated in the longer term if issues of inequality and redistribution are not addressed.

The poverty of the masses in India has been of concern for generations. Sunil Kumar (Chapter Eleven) documents the mismatch between actual housing policies and the kind of policies needed to assist the poor in India. The case of the poor falls between two stools – they are excluded from formal housing processes, and are made insecure by the mechanisms that are supposed to serve them. "What is needed", writes Kumar, "is a radical rethink on how policy is formulated and implemented". The chapter draws on research in Bangalore (in Karnataka) and Surat (in Gujarat) to illustrate the broader policies required of the existing development agencies such as the World Bank, the Inter-American Development Bank and the UN Centre for Human Settlements (Habitat). Conditions in which a significant proportion of urban dwellers live without adequate housing and services – as in large parts of urban Africa – are often appalling. There is a top-down approach that focuses on conferring ownership rights without recognising that the difference and diversity of urban residents, within and between cities, requires a policy that is flexible and increases the housing options of the poor. In addition to action on material deprivation a housing policy which provides a range of tenure options and closely replicates informal mechanisms of delivery is what is needed. The difficulty lies in the ability of the institutions of the state to 'clone' such mechanisms primarily because they are intricately located within multiple social and political relationships. The faith placed in decentralisation, which aims to enable and facilitate local participatory decision making, is unlikely to have an impact unless local governments have greater and more transparent powers to make or influence policy. Despite India's long history of five-year planning there is little indication of a radical rethink on how policy is formulated and implemented.

In Chapter Twelve, Athar Hussain describes new research on urban poverty in China, which has the largest population in the world (although India is rapidly catching up). Information is drawn from the 1998 urban household survey of 17,000 households in 31 provinces, conducted by the National Statistics Bureau. The research team, made up of experts from China and from other countries, including the UK, decided to distinguish between a 'food poverty line' – defined by the average cost in different provinces for people among the poorest 20% of just buying enough food to provide the minimum necessary average of 2,100 calories per person per day – and (a higher) poverty line. The cost of meeting the poverty line was the cost of meeting the 'food poverty line' plus the cost of meeting other basic non-food needs. These were worked out using a regression exercise on the urban data and, just as food needs were calculated on the basis of an average of 2,100 calories per person, non-food needs were calibrated for different households in accordance with basic non-food expenditure of households just satisfying the criterion of spending on food to ensure a minimum of 2,100 calories. The national average food poverty line of ¥1,392 per month was estimated to be 32% lower in the province of Qinghai, at one extreme among the 31 provinces, and 69% higher in the province of Shanghai, at the other extreme. The general poverty line is smaller than the purchasing power parity equivalent of the World Bank's poverty standard of $1 per day. It produces an estimate for the whole of China of 4.7%, or 15 millions in poverty, when income is the standard, and 11.9%, or 37 millions in poverty, when expenditure is the standard. Where the exact poverty line is drawn matters in China because a large proportion of population has a very low income. Therefore, if the poverty line were drawn 50% higher than the very stringent threshold in fact adopted, the figure of 4.7% in poverty becomes 20% or nearly 90 millions in urban areas. It would be even higher if measures of the costs of subsistence, like that undertaken by the Institute of Forecasting of the Chinese Academy of Sciences and even by the National Statistics Bureau and the Ministry of Civil Affairs.

The key policies for the urban poor in China are the Minimum Living Standard Scheme (MLSS), a recent addition, and a longer-established social security package that includes social insurance. The MLSS began as a local initiative that was gradually extended to regions and then all urban areas. With the disappearance of the living allowance for laid-off employees by the end of 2003, the MLSS and unemployment insurance will be the "two last lines of defence against urban poverty". By the end of the 1990s 3.3 million registered unemployed, or 55% were receiving unemployment benefit; and 3 million of the 460 million urban population were recipients of the MLSS. Eligibility is restricted and special investigation of particular cities found that only about a quarter of those in poverty were receiving assistance.

In order to improve anti-poverty policies, China needs to extend publicly provided social assistance and social insurance and raise benefits; the administrative infrastructure needs to be greatly strengthened and poverty monitored more successfully, and the methods of financing benefits overhauled.

Anti-poverty policies have to be constructed to meet the needs of particular groups in populations – such as ethnic minorities, disabled people and older people – and not only populations as a whole. Discrimination has to be countered in its institutional and individual forms. Chapter Thirteen takes the example of old age and intergenerational solidarity. In the year 2000 there were about 550 million people aged 60+ throughout the world. This figure is expected to more than double by 2025, reaching 1.2 billion. Improvements in hygiene, water supply and control of infectious diseases have reduced the risk of premature death so that with the growth in numbers of older people policies for them are no longer assumed to be the prerogative of the industrialised countries only. The growth in life expectancy when accompanied by poverty is however a mixed blessing. While poor diet, ill health, inadequate housing, few material assets and minimal incomes are risks for the majority of the old in developing countries, their positive contributions to society tend to be overlooked. Jo Beall uses 1999 research to explore intergenerational relationships in South Africa to inform anti-poverty policies. She uses a concept of 'intergenerational solidarity' to reveal that older people act substantially on behalf of their families and communities, and have needs and rights in those situations that deserve to be more generally acknowledged and met. Crucially, they play a part in development that deserves to be understood and sustained – necessarily in part by adjuncts of structurally redistributive policies.

Future anti-poverty policies: national and international

The book's earlier analysis of social polarisation and persisting world poverty provides the case for the necessary replacement of existing national and international policies. This is urgent, if poverty is to be massively reduced in scale and at the speed declared in the year 2000 in the millennium development goals of the UN as well as statements by the World Bank and many of the leading governments, including the UK. In the final part of this book some of the key alternative policies, and general strategies, are considered. The first chapter (Chapter Fourteen) examines the influential role of the World Bank over the last 50 years in shaping approaches to poverty, and concludes that a major problem has been its avoidance of the obligation to adopt a core scientific measure of the phenomenon to facilitate comparison and the identification of the population groups who experience poverty in the worst forms. Another, related, problem has been avoidance of the obligation, accepted at the 1995 Copenhagen World Summit on Social Development, to monitor existing and newly introduced policies and measure their exact effects on the extent and severity of poverty. This applies to the components of the Bank's anti-poverty policies during recent decades. Structural action by the key institutional players – the transnational corporations and the governments of the most powerful nations, such as the G8 – working collaboratively as well as within existing and newly introduced international law, is the unknown factor. Unless that action materialises to meet universal rights and need for public services, satisfaction of the various international and national anti-poverty targets will be a dead letter.

The chapter concludes with a discussion of the ways in which an anti-poverty strategy may be improved, partly through the work of bodies other than the international financial agencies.

In Chapter Fifteen Jan Vandemoortele raises direct questions about alternative strategies and policies and calls for substantial action to meet the millennium development objectives. He argues that some of the global norms, and facts and findings on poverty, have led to two *incorrect* conclusions:

- that good progress is being made in reducing world poverty;
- that aggregate growth is the best way for reducing it further.

The chapter questions whether $1 per day is a valid gauge for monitoring global poverty, whether poverty statistics for China are unduly biasing global poverty trends, whether much of the debate on global poverty illustrates the fallacy of misplaced concreteness, whether equity is good for the poor, and whether there is a role for social policy. It concludes that equity matters for poverty reduction, based on the argument that if growth is good for the poor, but if inequality is harmful for growth (as most analysts now agree), then equity must be good for the poor. One argument concerns 'narrow targeting' of basic social services

> which has important hidden costs: (i) the cost of mis-targeting, due to the difficulty to identify the poor; (ii) cost of failing to reach the poor, as the non-poor seldom let subsidies pass by; (iii) cost of administering narrowly targeted programmes; control of mismanagement and petty corruption; (iv) cost of out-of-pocket expenses to document eligibility, which involves expenses such as bus fares; and (v) cost of non-sustainability.

There can be a profound loss of public support or confidence in the schemes.

Determined *regional* action may be one means of prompting the UN or the key powers in the world to act together to introduce more effective policies to reduce poverty. In Chapter Sixteen Tony Atkinson argues that the EU has reached a point in its development when a giant step can be taken to bring aid to the developing countries. In December 2001 the EU adopted a set of commonly agreed and defined indicators for social inclusion. These indicators cover financial poverty and its persistence, income inequality, low educational attainment, premature mortality and poor housing and will help to monitor action plans and judge progress towards Social Europe. They embody the objectives of the EU. Only weeks later the Euro (e) came into circulation so that 300 million people share a common currency as part of a monetary union. That total is soon likely to grow to 450 million. The two developments stand as testimony of what a region can elect to do.

This is therefore an ideal time, according to Atkinson, for the EU to take a major step on behalf of the poorest countries outside of it. A justifiable and affordable target could be agreed of providing official development assistance equal to 1% of Gross National Product (GNP). This would help to meet the millennium development goals agreed at the World Summit in September 2000. The EU and its member states already provide around half of all official international development aid. So far Denmark was the only country to have reached the target, but Sweden, the Netherlands and Luxembourg had exceeded or matched the post-war target of 0.7% of GNP. Other member countries were now in a position to agree, but also reach, the more ambitious but still entirely practicable target of 1%.

In their concluding chapter, Peter Townsend and David Gordon bring together the various strands of this volume's argument for a change of international policy direction if there is to be any realistic prospect of fulfilling the UN millennium development goals – to bring about a dramatic decline in the numbers in poverty. The evidence shows that a balance has to be struck between private and public sectors so that corporations accept clear social as well as market objectives, authorised by the major states acting together and the precepts of reformed international company law. The needs of the poor outside market activity will then be better recognised and compensated, and public provision of a minimum adequate income and universal basic social services will be accepted. Consequential steps to strengthen social insurance and other forms of guaranteed rights to an adequate income, and to strengthen different forms of redistributive aid within and between states would also need to be taken.

References

Robinson, M. (2002) 'Protecting human rights: the US, the UN and the World', speech in Boston, MA, 6 January.

Gordon, D. and Townsend, P. (eds) (2000) *Breadline Europe: The measurement of poverty*, Bristol: The Policy Press.

Part I
International anti-poverty policy: the problems of the Washington Consensus

Poverty, social exclusion and social polarisation: the need to construct an international welfare state

Peter Townsend

During the last half-century, the conventional wisdom has been that poverty can be diminished automatically through economic growth. This has got to change. During the next half-century, the world's most fundamental problem – as agreed by the biggest international agencies and a growing number of governments – is that wealth and poverty are becoming increasingly polarised, and that a different priority has to be followed.

Any resolution of this problem depends on connecting three concepts – *poverty*, *social exclusion*, and *social polarisation* – and bringing them into sharper and more distinguishable focus. Together they provide the basis for the scientific breakthrough to explain the problem, and develop the exact policies required to deal with it, as well as steer the international community away from impending disaster.

Poverty

Poverty was at the top of the agenda of problems formulated by Robert MacNamara, Director of the World Bank, at the end of the 1960s. Despite the mixed story since then (development, indebted nations, multiplying barbarism, extreme inequalities in living standards in the aftermath of the collapse of the former Soviet Union, the East Asian economic crisis, and much more besides), it has again risen for the last decade to the top of the Bank's agenda. From 1990 onwards, reports on the subject from the international agencies have multiplied. The number of general, country-specific and methodological reports issued by the Bank that may be said to be poverty-related threatens to swamp us all. The Bank's eagerness is supported by the International Monetary Fund (IMF) and other international agencies, especially the United Nations Development Programme (UNDP), and by non-government organisations, especially Oxfam (for example, see Oxfam, 1995; Guidicini et al, 1996; Oyen et al, 1996, among others). In 1989, John Moore, as Secretary of State in the Department of Social Security (DSS), stated that the problem did not apply to the UK (Moore, 1989). Early in 1999, Alastair Darling, Secretary of State in the

DSS, proudly announced a programme to undertake a poverty audit "and so place the problem at the top of the nation's agenda". Poverty is a recognised evil but has lacked precise agreed definition and a scientifically constructed remedy[1]. The US has its own definition and measure, which the international agencies do not relate to their priorities for development. Indeed, the amendments recommended by the National Academy of Sciences seems to have served the purpose of bolstering an independent American approach which is becoming highly sophisticated as well as impenetrable from outside (Citro and Michael, 1995). Root and branch reform on an avowed scientific or international basis has not been seriously considered.

In the national as well as the international context, it cannot be said that a public or political consensus about meaning and scale exists. For that to happen, social scientists themselves will have to give the lead.

Social exclusion

This is even more true of 'social exclusion'. Analysts such as Hilary Silver, Graham Room and Ruth Levitas, have in their own different ways written about the potentialities of the concept. It is, as Ruth Levitas shows in *The inclusive society* (1998), highly 'contested'. Her approach is helpful in revealing the origins and motivations of three alternative models – redistributive (RED), moral underclass (MUD), and social integration discourses (SID).

Earlier Hilary Silver (1994) had also adopted three paradigms to illustrate the various treatments of the term: solidarity (breaking of social ties), specialisation (differentiation of individual behaviour and exchange), and monopoly (coercive domination – "the excluded are simultaneously outside and dominated"). Each one is grounded in a different political philosophy – republicanism, liberalism and social democracy – and attributes exclusion to a different cause. "Each provides an explanation of multiple forms of social disadvantage – economic, social, political and cultural – and thus encompasses theories of citizenship and racial-ethnic inequality as well as poverty and long-term unemployment" (Silver, 1994, p 539). Ruth Levitas has gone much further than others in showing which policies operate to strengthen which models.

Another procedure is to trace the history, covering at least 25 years, of the treatment of social exclusion in different countries and regions. Apparently the concept was coined in France to explain the problems which were arising because of poor coverage of social insurance (Gore and Figueiredo, 1996, p 9; see also Gaudier, 1995; Rodgers et al, 1995). The implication was that coverage should be improved so that fewer social problems arose.

For observers in the UK this is ironic. At a time when the institution of social insurance is under threat, the government has seized on social exclusion as the governing factor in constructing domestic policy – especially at the neighbourhood level. In France the concept was quickly extended in the 1980s to reflect the increasing concern with long-term unemployment, the worryingly large numbers of unskilled workers, and the problems of integrating immigrants. In formulations of policy Jacques Delors, then president of the European Commission, backed up by a range of organisations such as the European Labour Forum (see for example Coates and Holland, 1995), re-iterated these concerns. The problem has been interpreted even more variously in the republics of the former Soviet Union, and related to multiple forms of deprivation (Tchernina, 1996).

What is needed is scientific precision in the operational definitions of both poverty and social exclusion, so that trends and the extent of national and international problems can be properly measured, causes identified, and priorities for policy put in place. The best illustrations of social exclusion (for example, Walker and Walker, 1997) are built on a variety of imaginative studies on a common theme rather than on a commonly accepted measure. Current examples are Atkinson and Hills (1998), Burchardt et al (1999) and Hills (1999). A research team at the universities of Bristol, York and Loughborough completed a new national survey of both poverty and social exclusion (Bradshaw et al, 1998; Gordon et al, 2000). This proposed an operational measure distinguishing four precise components – impoverishment, labour market exclusion, service exclusion and social exclusion (Gordon et al, 2000).

Building on international agreement

There is scope, therefore, for an analytical ground-clearing operation. However, if we are to adopt practical policies to reduce the two problems of poverty and social exclusion, we need to be clear about how to distinguish them, as well as how they are to be applied cross-nationally, rather than erratically and variously in different cultures. I say 'erratically' because the links between country- or region-specific definition and international definition have neither been investigated thoroughly nor justified – even when we can acknowledge that the research in question is helpful in understanding some internal conditions. 'Erratically' also, because the absence of scientific precision makes for political ambiguity – the great escape for holders of wealth. 'Erratically' too in relation to the international agencies. Here the World Bank's adoption of the crude criterion of $1 per day at 1985 prices for the poorest countries, $2 per day for Latin America, and $4 per day for the transitional economies, without regard to the changing conditions of needs and markets, affronts science as it affronts reasoned development of priorities in international policies[2]. In 1997, UNDP topped this absurdity by suggesting that the US criterion of $14.4 per day might be applied to the Organisation for Economic Co-operation and Development (OECD) countries (UNDP, 1997).

If measurement is arbitrary and irrational, it is impossible either to concoct the right policies for the alleviation or eradication of poverty, or monitor their effects closely. The World Bank persists broadly with the anti-poverty approach of the 1960s, despite continuing evidence of that approach's failure. Thus, following reports in the early 1990s (for example, World Bank, 1990, 1993), there was little sign in the Bank's reports of the mid- and late 1990s of a change in the threefold strategy that continued to be stated time and again:

- broad-based economic growth;
- development of human capital;
- social safety nets for vulnerable groups (World Bank, 1996, 1997a, 1997b, 1997c; Psacharapoulas et al, 1997).

Each of these three requires detailed exposition, documentation and discussion.

The job of social policy analysis is to keep alive alternative strategies and policies that seem to fit the account of global problems and needs. For purposes of illustration, one alternative strategy might consist of:

- equitable tax and income policies;
- an employment creation programme;
- regeneration or creation of collective, or 'universal', social security and public social services;
- accountability and a measure of social control of transnational corporations and international agencies.

There are no signs yet of a debate taking place about the merits of even two alternative strategies, or sets of policies, to establish beyond reasonable doubt which alternative is the most successful – or indeed popular in democratic terms – in reducing poverty and contributing to social development.

We are dealing here with a strategy that has become the conventional wisdom and that wields extraordinary influence throughout the world. We are compelled to elucidate the international social impact of recent models of monetarist theory and neoliberalism.

The discussion of these doctrines cannot be conducted in (over)generalised terms. We have to examine the text and outcomes of international agreements, such as Maastricht and the Multilateral Investment Agreement. We have to review scientific evidence about key issues, such as economic growth. For example, does the empirical evidence that growth is 'trickle-up' oblige us to abandon the blithe assumptions about 'trickle-down' that have been taken for granted for many years (Newman and Thomson, 1989)[3]?

Social polarisation

Whatever the social or political justification for treating poverty and social exclusion ambiguously and overgenerally, it is worth exploring the possibilities of a consensus on precise meaning among social scientists. Despite some obvious problems in adopting exact and perhaps more restricted meanings, measures might be operationalised, trends established by common agreement, and disputes about cause reduced if not eliminated.

Present developments in environmental policies offer a model. There are scientific disagreements about exact thresholds of safety or minimal bad effect, and there are attempts to conceal, or distort, the extent of progress in bringing down levels of pollution, for example. However, scientific measures and accounts of causes have the effect of restricting the range of argument about appropriate policies and measurable effects.

One possible line of attack is to seek clarification, not just of the meanings of poverty and social exclusion, but of other, related ideas, such as deprivation. Another is to get better purchase on structural trends and upheavals.

One virtue ascribed to many interpretations of social exclusion is that it signifies interest in process rather than state, and points to the need to scrutinise actions of governments. But if the problem with the concept of poverty is believed to be its calling attention only to a negative state or condition, then the problem of the concept of social exclusion is to call attention only to a negative process. Both concepts direct attention to only parts of the population. As a direct consequence, scientific investigation becomes distorted and priorities for policy hard to establish. By contrast, the concepts of inequality and social polarisation, which correspond with the ideas of state and process, are all-embracing. These two concepts are necessary, therefore, to the understanding of poverty and social exclusion, the other two concepts discussed so far.

Social polarisation – the third concept in this chapter's title – is therefore the key ingredient. Early in this century it is the correct focus for scientific accounts of development. It is a structural process creating reverberations the length and breadth of global, national and local society. And while there are other concepts and themes that have to be employed to describe and analyse world social problems, social polarisation is indispensable. Poverty and social exclusion are inevitable by-products. I shall try to explain.

A personal history of social polarisation

In the late 1980s, inequality in the UK became fast-growing. In a book entitled *Poverty and Labour in London*, reporting a survey of London households, the authors used the term 'social polarisation' to describe a trend, because it was far from being either small or temporary (Townsend et al, 1987). In its scale and change of direction, this trend was also unprecedented, certainly in the history of recorded measurement during the 18th and 19th centuries. Since the causes had to be unravelled, and because it would be strange if rapid polarisation were to happen in one country and not in another, I began to ask whether the process applied elsewhere.

Although the UK was exceptional, I found that inequality was growing in other European countries – including Belgium and Sweden (Townsend, 1991). During a research and teaching trip to the US in 1992, I found that inequality had widened as dramatically there during the 1980s as in the UK. In one respect the situation there was worse. Average earnings of the poorest 20% in the labour market had decreased significantly in real terms between 1979 and 1992.

An illustration can be given. The 1999 Human Development report from the UNDP shows that the industrialised countries with the greatest inequality (measured by comparing the richest and poorest 20% of each population) are Australia and the UK, with the US third (with a GDP per person ratio of 9.6:1, 9.6:1 and 8.9:1 respectively) (UNDP, 1999). These are also the countries with the largest proportions of the population with less than 50% of the median income (UNDP, 1999, p 149). Although polarisation is well testified for the UK and the US during the 1980s and 1990s, there is some doubt about Australia. In late 1999, I discovered that the international agencies' information about income inequality in Australia was hotly contested by organisations there, who argued it was misleading and outdated. Too little detail is said to be provided in the agencies' reports about methods of standardising comparisons of trends in income distribution across countries.

While there is no doubt of a predominant trend among industrialised countries of growing inequality, there exists wide variation in the extent of that inequality. There are, for example, industrialised countries such as the Czech Republic, Japan, Spain, the Netherlands and Sweden, where the richest 20% have only 3.9, 4.3, 4.4, 4.5 and 4.6 times, respectively, more income than the poorest 20% (UNDP, 1999, p 149).

Turning to developing countries, I have found over the last 15 years a similar growing divide (see, for example, Townsend, 1993a, Chapter 1). There is a problem in a substantial number of countries about civil disorder and war, and the impossibility of giving information about collapse into poverty. For many of the other countries, qualifications have to be entered because of the scarcity of data in some of the poorest countries for different years, or because of doubts about reliability.

After the collapse of the Soviet Union at the end of the 1980s, there was an even bigger growth in inequality in the countries of the Commonwealth of Independent States than elsewhere. The economic transformation had dramatic social effects, including increases in the rates of mortality for different age groups in the 1990s (Nelson et al, 1997; Clarke, 1999; Cornia, 1999; Cornia and Pannicia, 1999; and see Ferge in Gordon and Townsend, 2000). In a visit to the Republic of Georgia in the former Soviet Union, on behalf of UNDP, I found severe impoverishment, especially among poor families, sick and disabled people and pensioners, not only because of the collapse of industry, but also the erosion of unemployment insurance benefits, pensions and other benefits to levels worth a few pence a week (Townsend, 1995, 1996).

A global trend

How can the accumulating evidence of this unprecedented trend now be generalised? Reporting in mid-1999, UNDP found that income inequality had increased "in most OECD countries in the 1980s and early 1990s. Of 19 countries only one showed a slight improvement" (1999, p 37). Data on income inequality in Eastern Europe and the CIS "indicate that these changes were the fastest ever recorded. In less than a decade income inequality, as measured by the Gini coefficient, increased from an average of 0.25-0.28 to 0.35-0.38, surpassing OECD levels" (1999, p 39). In China "disparities are widening between the export-oriented regions of the coast and the interior: the human poverty index is just under 20 per cent in coastal provinces, but more than 50 per cent in inland Guizhou" (1999, p 3). Other East and South East Asian countries that had achieved high growth while improving income distribution and reducing poverty in earlier decades, like Indonesia and Thailand, were similarly experiencing more inequality (UNDP, 1999, p 36).

The gap *between* countries, as well as within them, has also widened. The latest studies show how the trend has accelerated: the average income of the world population's poorest 20% was 30 times as large as the average income of the poorest 20% in 1960, but 74 times as large by 1997 (UNDP, 1999, p 36).

Of course, widening inequality has to be addressed at both ends of the spectrum. Executives' pay, and the disposable income and wealth of the richest people in the world, has been growing at an astonishing rate. For example, the UNDP points out that "the assets of the 200 richest people are more than the combined income of 41% of the world's people" (1999, p 38). The top three have more than the combined GNP of the 43 least developed countries.

A new report for the World Institute for Development Economic Research of the United Nations University confirms the trend. An econometric analysis of 77 countries (accounting for 82% of world population), found rising inequality in 45, slowing inequality in 4, no definite trend in 12, and falling inequality in only 12 (Cornia, 1999a, pp vi and 7). "For most countries, the last two decades have brought about slow growth and rising inequality.... Growing polarisation among countries has been accompanied by a surge in inequality between countries.... Income concentration has risen in many nations of Latin America, Eastern Europe and the former Soviet Union, China, a few African and Southeast Asian economies and, since the early 1980s, almost two-thirds of the OECD countries" (Cornia, 1999a, p 2).

> Since the early 1990s, the international community has made the eradication of poverty its foremost development objective. Yet, the decline of poverty in the years ahead depends also on trends in income inequality, a fact which still attracts little concern by the policymakers. Much of the recent rise in income inequality must thus be viewed with alarm, as it may well prove to be incompatible with poverty reduction objectives. (Cornia, 1999a, p vi)

Explaining polarisation

Defective structural adjustment policies

What are the reasons for this structural change? There is an international analysis that has to be tied in with nationally circumscribed investigation. What has to be accepted is the increasing impact of international developments on national subgroups and local populations. I mean that exposition of familiar problems to do with gender, ageing, disabilities, and families with children, for example, now displays overriding international determinants. I mean also that local problems, such as conflict on inner city housing estates, drugs, closure of local factories, and unsatisfactory privatisation of local services, are generated or enlarged by global market and other international factors.

Among the major policies of the international agencies, national governments and transnational corporations, for which a powerful consensus had been built up during the 1980s and 1990s, are the stabilisation, liberalisation, privatisation and welfare targeting and safety net programmes adopted as a result of the worldwide influence of monetarist theory. For example, the so-called *stabilisation and structural adjustment programmes*, that were advocated and supported by the international agencies, have entailed the reduction of subsidies on food, fuel and other goods, retrenchments in public employment, cuts in public sector wages and other deflationary measures. This not only generates recession, but also distributional outcomes which, as Cornia has argued (1999b, pp 11-12) are adverse in the poorer countries compared with industrialised countries, where wage systems are strongly institutionalised and self protecting, and where long-established social security provides a better cushion for downturns in the economy. Policies to cut public expenditure, and target welfare on the poorest (for example through means testing and the introduction of healthcare charges), have increased inequality and perpetuated poverty, especially in countries where, because of globalised trade and growing influence of transnational corporations, there has been a particularly rapid concentration of wealth.

In recognising what policies have brought about greater inequality within and between countries we have to understand the similarity of the programmes influencing developments throughout the world, at the same time as we recognise that they are calculated to vary in extent and force in different regions. The terminology is not always consistent. Governments as well as international agencies are often eager to adopt new names for conformist (rather than 'convergent') policies, especially when evidence that they are not working begins to accumulate.

In a remarkable shift from its long-standing policies, the World Bank has admitted that poverty has tended to increase during recessions in sub-Saharan Africa, Eastern Europe, and Latin America and not to decrease to the same extent during economic recoveries. Examples were given in a report showing that "crises and recessions may result in irreversible damage to the poor: malnutrition or death from starvation (in extreme cases) and lower schooling levels" (World Bank, 1999, p 109). Higher food prices in the stabilisation programme in Côte d'Ivoire and elsewhere are cited. "Sudden fluctuations in income or food availability can be fatal to already malnourished children". Consequences include lower IQ, retarded physical growth, mental disabilities, lower resistance to infections, and associated problems like dropout from schools (World Bank, 1999, p 103; see also Huther et al, 1997).

Greater sensitivity to the encroachments of poverty also helps to explain the reactions of the international agencies to the financial crisis in East and South East Asia. The magic wand of liberalisation and structural adjustment programmes could no longer be waved, as it had been in Latin America and Africa and then in Eastern Europe and the Commonwealth of Independent States (and in similar strategic form in the industrial countries). The World Bank expected poverty rates, especially in Indonesia, to rise very sharply. Revealingly, the Bank no longer emphasises privatisation and extreme targeting. At one point it even suggests that the possible remedies in a difficult situation "include waiving charges for the poor and extending health care to workers dismissed from their jobs" (World Bank, 1999, p 109).

The concentration of hierarchical power

Due to deregulation and privatisation by governments, often at the behest of international agencies, control of labour markets has veered away from states and towards transnational corporations. Paradoxically, states in which the headquarters of the biggest transnational corporations are located have acquired greater power to influence global economic developments. The G7, or G8, has exerted influence on the development of world trade (for example through the World Trade Organisation and the Multilateral Investment Agreement), and the management of debt.

Therefore, in trade the emphasis on exports from the poorer countries was supposed to favour rural agricultural production and diminish poverty, by removing the imbalance between rural and urban living standards. This has not worked, partly because of the low wages induced by cash cropping, and the corresponding substitution of employed labour and technology for subsistence farming. This has also had a knock-on weakening effect on the vitality of urban markets. In many countries, self-sufficiency in growing a range of crops has given way to a precarious dependence on sales from the export of those crops to finance the purchase of imports at affordable prices. Transnational companies have exceptional power to cut the costs of what they buy and raise the costs of what they sell.

The growth of transnational companies is one of the greatest economic and social changes of the late 20th century. Only 25 countries of the world are now listed as having larger GDP than the annual value of the sales of the biggest transnational corporation – General Motors. The top ten transnational corporations (General Motors, Ford Motor, Mitsui, Mitsubishi, Itochu, Royal Dutch Shell Group, Marubeni Sumitomo, Exxon and Toyota Motor) have bigger sales than the GDP of Malaysia, Venezuela and Colombia, and some of them more than Saudi Arabia, South Africa, Norway, Greece and Thailand. New Zealand's GDP is dwarfed by the sales of each of these corporations, and Australia accounts for only about three times the value of the average sale of all ten (UNDP, 1999, pp 32, 184-7).

The social policies of transnational corporations take at least two forms. On the one hand their internal policies, in relation to their senior staff and permanent and temporary workers scattered through subsidiary companies in many different countries, have to be explained. On the other, the larger role they play in contributing to social change, by influencing developments in world trade, government taxation and redistribution and investment, as well as recommendations for privatisation, also has to be explained (ILO, 1989; Lang and Hines, 1994; Deacon et al, 1997; Hoogvelt, 1997; Kozul-Wright and Rowthorn, 1998).

There are serious shortcomings in both national and international company and social law in relation to transnationals. While capable of contributing positively to social development, one review found that few of them were doing much of consequence. The activities of some were positively harmful (Kolodner, 1994). Recent books on transnational corporations (for example, Korten, 1996) have been assembling a case that governments and international agencies are going to find hard to ignore.

One feature of mergers between companies and the absorption of workforces overseas into the subsidiaries of corporations is not just the extension of the labour force accountable to management, but the elaboration as well as extension of the hierarchy of pay and rights in the corporation. There are many layers in workforces consisting of scores of thousands, sometimes hundreds of thousands, of employees working full-time, part-time, permanently and temporarily in 50, 60 or even more countries. Salaries at the top have been elevated, those at the bottom depressed.

This fast-developing occupational system invades the systems of social class in every country, and alters those systems. In Europe and the US we are aware of the debate about the appearance of an 'underclass', provoked by the work of Charles Murray and others. Critics have fastened on to the stigmatising and inexact reasoning of the proponents (for example, Katz, 1993). But they have also seized on the possible emergence of an *economic* underclass, consisting largely of long-term unemployed and prematurely retired, but also impoverished, people. When considering the debate some years ago there seemed to be grounds for the emergence of an underclass in this sense. Of course, there were also grounds for the emergence of an 'overclass' (Townsend, 1993b). Even if this is a small elite of the super-rich, it is distinctive, not only because of its wealth, but because of its working associations with many different countries and its ephemeral relationships with any social network in the 'host' countries of its members.

This can be characterised as increasing vertical control while diminishing horizontal participation and reciprocation. Some of the social consequences of the new structure of control appear to have been misinterpreted. Therefore, a lot has been made of the so-called 'culture of dependency' as a strategy for enforcing further control instead of questioning the new elite's culture of coercion.

The evolving hierarchy comprises new occupational sets, ranks and classes, involving housing and locality, and not simply workplace. Ideas of supra- and subordination are played out internationally as well as nationally and locally, and are carried over from one context to the other. This evolving hierarchy is also reflected in the development of the interrelationships of states and international agencies – by means of disproportionate representation among senior personnel, origins of finance for research, and responsibility for the publication of statistical and other information to the media. There are different senses in which social stratification is becoming strongly internationalised.

Privatisation

The international financial agencies have been eager to encourage privatisation. They argue that:

• it would enhance global market competition;
• it would weaken the intervening role of the state and reduce government taxation, so that public expenditure in general, and public services in particular, would cost less;
• private companies would have greater freedom to manage their affairs as they wanted.

However, the agencies have thereby adopted a very narrow interpretation of the economic good, and have tended to ignore the fact that economic development is an integral part of social development.

World Bank advocacy of privatisation is explicit or implied in almost every published report of recent years – even in relation to poverty. A key text for the Bank's position was published in 1997. Its author, Pierre Guislain, is a development specialist who has advised many African countries on their privatisation programmes. The book (Guislain, 1997) covers a lot of ground and is testimony to the accelerating scale across the world of privatisation. However, its attempts to be dispassionate are not successful. The arguments especially for public service and cooperative companies are largely absent, and there are no conclusions about the balance that might be struck between the public and private sectors in particular contexts and according to particular objectives. There is a strange indifference to the historical reasons for the growth of public ownership and the welfare state. Certainly there is no dispassionate argument about alternative strategies.

Another Bank report looks at privatisation in different countries and the rapid growth of equity markets in these same countries (Liebermann and Kirkness, 1998). The book interprets the process favourably. Privatisation is said to 'kick-start' newly created capital markets, such as those in Central and Eastern Europe and the Commonwealth of Independent States. It can 'awaken' moribund markets in Egypt and much of Latin America. Examples of well-publicised privatisation programmes in Argentina and Mexico are compared with the less well-known 'achievements' in Egypt, Morocco and Peru. "There are many more privatisations to come in developing and transition economies" (Liebermann and Kirkness, 1998).

In the analysis of many experts, much is made of the necessity of financial deregulation and the privatisation of insurance and the pension funds in order to create the right market conditions. The conflict of public interest in relation to the historical establishment of social insurance (for good reasons) is not discussed.

The rapid growth of privatisation is not, even now, widely appreciated. In 1989 the gross annual revenue from the process was estimated to be $25 billion. In 1994 and 1995 annual revenue reached $80 billion. Over five years $271 billion were generated. By the mid-1990s the developing and 'transition' countries accounted for much of the revenue. Guislain concludes that privatisation is "likely to remain a key policy instrument in many countries for decades to come" (1997, p 3; see also Lieberman and Kirkness, 1998).

Assets have often been sold extraordinarily cheaply, by market standards. Academic reviews, as in the UK, have failed to demonstrate evidence of privatisation being successful in terms of growth and price. There are examples either way (see, for example, Parker and Martin, 1997).

The shortcomings of targeting and safety nets

In developing their structural adjustment programmes, first in Latin America and Africa, and then in the 'transition' countries of Eastern Europe and the former Soviet Union, the IMF and the World Bank tried to balance the unequal social consequences of liberalisation, privatisation and cuts in public expenditure with proposals to target help on the most vulnerable groups in the population. For some years, and still to a large extent today, this has been presented within the principle of means testing. Even if coverage was poor, large sums of money would be saved if the 'almost poor' were no longer subsidised by public funds.

Therefore, a report for the IMF (Chu and Gupta, 1998) seeks to pin responsibility on the transition countries for a failure to transform universal services into targeted and partly privatised services. Unfortunately, this report also reveals serious amnesia about the institutional history of the introduction of legislation establishing public services and social security in particular (see, for example, pp 90-2, 111-12). Ways in which former universal provisions might be modified to allow market competition to grow but not create penury among millions were not seriously considered.

IMF loan conditions demanding lower government expenditures in the poorest countries have led to sharp reductions in general social spending at a time when the poorest fifth of the population in those countries have been receiving only about half their share of education and health expenditures – thus making access worse. This is evidence drawn from the IMF's own studies (IMF, 1997), which shows that "the poorest three-fifths of these nations are being excluded from whatever social 'safety net' exists for education, health, housing and social security and welfare" (Kolko, 1999, p 56).

However, loan conditionalities affect economic security in other ways. There are cuts in the number of government employees and in their salaries, and there are private sector cuts and lay-offs, both of which are designed to raise cost-effectiveness in the world's export markets. Price subsidies for commodities such as bread and cooking oil are cut. Higher value added taxes that are advocated are regressive on income distribution.

In December 1987, the IMF introduced a new stage of its existing structural adjustment programme – the 'Enhanced Structural Adjustment Facility' (ESAF). Of the 79 countries eligible for these ESAF loans – on condition they complied with the IMF in setting "specific, quantifiable plans for financial policies" – 36 had done so. Since World Bank aid also depends on fulfilling IMF criteria there is intense pressure on governments to accede. Critics have now concluded that countries which stayed out of the ESAF programme "began and remained better off by not accepting its advice". Those accepting the programme "have experienced profound economic crises: low or even declining economic growth, much larger foreign debts, and the stagnation that perpetuates systemic poverty". The IMF's own studies provided "a devastating assessment of the social and economic consequences of its guidance of dozens of poor nations" (Kolko, 1999, p 53).

The problem applies sharply to rich and not only poor countries. The biggest struggle of the coming years is going to be between restriction of social security, or 'welfare', largely to means-tested benefits. Those who have assembled evidence for different European countries over many years (for example, van Oorschot, 1999) point out that such policies are poor in coverage, administratively expensive and complex, provoke social divisions, are difficult to square with incentives into work, and tend to discourage forms of saving. What is notable is the recent tempering of World Bank and other agency reactions. It is now conceded that targeting can include 'categorical' policies affecting vulnerable or disadvantaged groups in the population. The prime example of this shift in policies is the social crisis in Eastern Europe and the former Soviet Union (UNDP, 1998).

The World Bank has itself begun to offer grudging concessions. "Safety nets are programmes that protect a person or household against two adverse outcomes: chronic incapacity to work and earn (chronic poverty), and a decline in this capacity from a marginal situation that provides minimal means for survival; with few reserves (transient poverty)." Although social insurance programmes constitute the most dominant form of cash transfer in most countries of Eastern Europe and the former Soviet Union, and provide relief for the poor in the formal sectors, these programmes are not addressed here because issues pertaining to pensions were the focus of a recent World Bank policy study (Fox, 1994 as reported in World Bank, 1997a, pp 2-3).

This is a revealing qualification. When structural adjustment programmes began to be applied in the early 1990s to Eastern Europe and the former Soviet Union, it was clear they would compound the problems of poverty, following liberalisation. Social insurance, and social security generally, were a substantial part of the institutional infrastructures of these states, and the collapse of industry might have led to some external efforts to maintain at least a residual system in order to protect people, especially children, the disabled and the elderly, from the worst forms of destitution and even starvation. Unhappily World Bank and IMF teams lacked expertise in such institutions. They were also influenced by a prevailing ideology of the 'short, sharp shock' following the collapse of communism. An additional factor was that social security systems were weak if not non-existent in the poorest developing countries, and the possibility that structural adjustment as applied to those countries was inappropriate in Eastern Europe.

From an anti-poverty perspective one analyst of events in the former Soviet Union concludes:

> Consideration of social policy has hitherto been dominated by fiscal considerations, which has led to radical proposals for reform of the pension and benefits systems which would have devastating consequences if they did not work as intended. The dependence of many households on age-related pensions and the inability of the majority of wage-earners to support even one dependant make the preservation of the real value of retirement pensions and the restoration of the real value and regular payment of child benefit much the most effective anti-poverty measures in a context in which the introduction of means-tested social assistance is completely unrealistic. (Clarke, 1999, p 240)

A report from UNDP is the most explicit concession yet to the need for change in development policies (UNDP, 1998). In describing the growth of poverty in the early 1990s in Eastern Europe and the former Soviet Union this concedes the strengths of the former institutions of social security.

> Policy-makers attempted to create a relatively egalitarian society free from poverty. Socialist income policy was based upon two main objectives: 1) To ensure a minimum standard of living for all citizens; and 2) To achieve a relatively flat income distribution. (1998, p 90)

> Governments regulated overall salaries and fixed minimum wages high enough to ensure a basic standard of living.... At the core of the social security systems were work-related contributory insurance programmes. The public came to expect that most social benefits would depend upon work-related factors such as years spent on the job and wages earned.... Social insurance schemes were comprehensive. Pensions, like employment, were virtually guaranteed.... Social insurance itself covered numerous exigencies, including accidents, sickness, parental death and child birth.... Overall, means-tested social benefits were almost non-existent, representing on average less than 1% of GDP. This was due largely to the inefficiency and high administrative costs associated with means-testing programmes. (1998, pp 90-2)

The *socially inclusive* advantages of these schemes was recognised. Therefore, pension programmes "became a kind of contract between generations, whereby people invested their efforts in the collective welfare and were rewarded by a guarantee of supplemental income.... Because social assistance allowances are very low in all transition countries, moving pensions towards means-tested social assistance programmes would push practically all pensioners into poverty" (1998, pp 108-9).

All in all, this is the first substantial acknowledgement from any of the international agencies I have read in the last ten years that the 'socialist welfare state' actually had certain strengths (see, in particular, UNDP, 1998, pp 92-3). What is striking is that the authors go on to claim there is a consensus for active labour market policies and work for social benefits as necessary components of the social insurance system. "At the core of welfare policy ... there must also be a comprehensive social insurance scheme that compensates all people in time of need" (UNDP, 1998, p 105). Funding should be both public and private forms of 'Pay-As-You-Go'. "Categorical benefits should be offered to all in need, or at least to all those near or below the poverty line. It is very important to avoid providing support only to the 'poorest of the poor' while neglecting the relatively poor" (UNDP, 1998, p 105). This plea for group or 'categorical' benefits in place of means-tested benefits was qualified by a recognition that some such benefits could be conditional in different ways.

Conclusion: the invention of the international welfare state

Where does this analysis lead? Different contributors to this book develop at length some of the themes that have been raised in this chapter. An alternative international strategy and set of policies concerned with arresting the growth of inequality and radically reducing poverty has been outlined and will be substantiated in later chapters. The 1995 World Summit on Social Development in Copenhagen provides a good precedent of the model of theory, strategy and policy that we are seeking to develop (UN, 1995). However, it will be evident from this book that, despite its strengths, the Copenhagen Agreement and Programme of Action, failed to address, or illustrate, the key explanatory concept of social polarisation discussed earlier in its necessary relationship with concerns about growing poverty and social exclusion.

What elements might the overall international strategy include? First, unless a scientific consensus is achieved in operationally defining, and measuring, international forms of poverty and social exclusion, the fact that the defeat of poverty worldwide has been put at the top of the international agencies' agenda will turn out to be empty rhetoric. Perhaps one hope is to build on the 1995 World Summit agreement to measure, and monitor, agreed definitions across countries of 'absolute' and 'overall' poverty (Gordon et al, 2000; Gordon and Townsend, 2000).

Second, unless, the *policy-related causes* of poverty and social exclusion are properly traced and publicised in relation to structural trends in all societies, we will find it difficult to discriminate effectively between what are the successful, unsuccessful and even counterproductive measures working towards, or against, the agreed objectives.

Third, since poverty and social exclusion can neither be traced nor explained except in the context of the structural changes embodied in social polarisation, it is this phenomenon that has to be explained.

The effect of policies that have been tried has to be clarified. The *stabilisation and structural adjustment programmes* of the 1980s and 1990s are alleged to have contributed to growing inequality. Policies contributing to the *institutionalisation of unequal power* are argued to deepen that process. Far more attention has to be given to the entire hierarchical *system*, and especially rich institutions and rich individuals at the top. The international agencies, regional associations and national governments must begin to analyse the extraordinary growth of transnational corporations, and ask what reasonable limits can be placed upon their powers. All that has happened so far is that agencies such as OECD have issued 'guidelines' exhorting corporations to be socially responsible. The International Labour Organization (ILO) has gone further. In 1977 its governing board put forward a declaration. This sought to exert influence upon governments, concluding that gradual reinforcement could pave the way for "more specific potentially binding international standards", turning codes of conduct into "the seed of customary rules of international law" (ILO, 1989). Policies contributing to the occupational structures or systems of transnational companies seem to deserve special examination.

Agencies have tended to be shy of relating observed impoverishment or unemployment to the policies of transnational corporations. And they have not been keen on self-examination either. Their growing role in shaping social as well as economic development badly needs critical examination. This has sometimes been provided by outside observers (Payer, 1982, 1991; Deacon et al, 1997; Hoogvelt, 1997) but needs to be addressed institutionally by governments and the agencies themselves.

Privatisation policies are a key element. They have been initiated and encouraged by the international agencies, but without much attention being paid to the problems of creating a much weaker public sector. Some of the biggest transnational corporations have adopted a 'Big Brother' relationship with the public sector. This could damage national identity and cohesion and divide society. Research is needed, for example, to systematically compare the performance of the public and private sectors in different fields, and recommend what is the right mix (as well as how the two might be reconstituted).

Policies representing the principles, or ideologies, of *targeting and safety nets* also deserve better assessment. There are grave doubts that they provide the right strategy to compensate for the inequalities and impoverishment induced by liberalisation and the enhanced power of markets. The international agencies are beginning to recognise that, as policy, means testing is neither easy to introduce nor successful. The advantages of modernised social insurance, for developing as well as industrialised countries, are beginning to earn renewed international interest. This is a sign of hope.

There are of course new policies that have to be found as well as existing policies that deserve to be abandoned or corrected if the damaging structural trend of social polarisation is first to be halted, and then turned round. There seem to be two stages. At the first stage the whole critique has to be pulled together and made more forceful. This includes the reformulation of the measurement of poverty, social exclusion and unemployment. It includes insistence on the monitoring and determined fulfilment of international agreements. And it includes the mobilisation of new coalitions or alliances across countries – of parties, unions, campaigning groups and voluntary agencies – to question the conventional wisdom and promote alternative strategies. At the second stage measures for international taxation, regulation of transnational corporations and international agencies, reform of representation at the UN, and new guarantees of human rights, including minimal standards of income, have to be introduced and legally enforced.

Recognition of social insurance as one of the best means of building an 'inclusive' society and preventing the slide into poverty, as well as contributing to social and economic stability, would represent one major step forward.

New legal and political institutions for social good in a global economy have to be built. A start would come with new international company and taxation law, combined with the modernisation and strengthening of social insurance and more imaginative planning and investment in basic services, such as health and education, so that they reflect international and not just national or regional standards.

This amounts to calling for an *international* welfare state (Townsend, with Donkor, 1996). One hundred years ago, different governments, including those of Britain and Germany as well as of smaller countries like New Zealand and Norway, responded to the manifest problems of poverty in those days. There were innovations which led to the establishment of national welfare states and a more civilised form of economic development.

Early in the 21st century the prospect of even greater social self-destruction, experienced as an accompanying feature of social polarisation, looms before us – unless urgent countervailing measures are taken. Collaborative scientific and political action to establish a more democratic and internationalised legal framework to protect human living standards has become the first priority.

Notes

[1] This was the basis of our previous book *Breadline Europe: The measurement of poverty* (Gordon and Townsend 2000). This book is concerned with remedies and policies, rather than definition.

[2] For an extended account, see Chapter Fourteen in this volume.

[3] In 1989, Newman and Thomson provided one of the first elaborate cross-national demonstrations that 'trickle-down' could no longer be, if it ever had been, regarded as a viable assumption.

References

Atkinson, A.B. and Hills, J. (eds) (1998) *Exclusion, employment and opportunity*, CASE Paper no 4, London: CASE, London School of Economics and Political Science.

Bradshaw, J., Gordon, D., Levitas, R., Middleton, S., Pantazis, C., Payne, S. and Townsend, P. (1998) *Perceptions of poverty and social exclusion*, Report on Preparatory Research, Bristol: Centre for International Poverty Research, University of Bristol.

Burchardt, T., Le Grand, J. and Piachaud, D. (1999) 'Social exclusion in Britain 1991-1995', *Social Policy and Administration*, vol 33, no 3, pp 227-44.

Chu, Ke-Y. and Gupta, S. (eds) (1998) *Social safety nets: Issues and recent experiences*, Washington, DC: IMF.

Clarke, S. (1999) *New forms of employment and household survival survival in Russia, Coventry and Moscow*, Coventry/Moscow: Centre for Comparative Labour Studies, University of Warwick/Institute for Comparative Labour Relations Research.

Citro, C.F. and Michael, R.T. (1995) *Measuring poverty: A new approach*, Panel on Poverty, National Research Council, Washington, DC: National Academy Press.

Cornia, G.A. (1999a) *Liberalisation, globalisation and income distribution*, Working Paper no 157, Helsinki: UNU World Institute for Development Economic Research.

Cornia, G.A. (1999b) *Social funds in stabilisation and adjustment programmes*, Research for Action 48, Helsinki: UNU World Institute for Development Economic Research.

Cornia, G.A. and Pannicia, R. (eds) (1999) *The mortality crisis in transitional economies*, Oxford: Oxford University Press.

Deacon, B. with Hulse, M. and Stubbs, P. (1997) *Global social policy: International organisations and the future of welfare*, London: Sage Publications.

Eurostat (1998) *Structure of the taxation systems in the European Union 1970-1996*, Luxembourg: Office for Official Publications of the European Communities.

Gaudier, M. (1995) *Poverty, inequality, exclusion: New approach to theory and practice*, Geneva: International Institute for Labour Studies, ILO.

Gordon, D. and Townsend, P. (eds) (2000) *Breadline Europe: The measurement of poverty*, Bristol: The Policy Press.

Gordon, D., Adelman, A., Ashworth, K., Bradshaw, J., Levitas, R., Middleton, S., Pantazis, C., Patsios, D., Payne, S., Townsend, P. and Williams, J. (2000) *Poverty and social exclusion in Britain*, York: Joseph Rowntree Foundation (www.bris.ac.uk/poverty/pse/).

Gore, C. and Figueiredo, J.B. (1996) *Social exclusion and anti-poverty strategies*, Geneva: International Institute for Labour Studies (in conjunction with UNDP), ILO.

Guidicini, P., Pieretti, G. and Bergamaschi, M. (1996) *Extreme urban poverties in Europe: Contradictions and perverse effects in welfare policies*, Milan: FrancoAngeli.

Guislain, P. (1997) *The privatization challenge: A strategic, legal and institutional analysis of international experience*, Washington, DC: World Bank.

Hills, J. (1999) *Social exclusion, income dynamics and public policy*, Annual Sir Charles Carter Lecture, Northern Ireland Economic Council, Belfast: Development Office.

Hoogvelt, A. (1997) *Globalisation and the postcolonial world: The new political economy of development*, Basingstoke, Hampshire and London: Macmillan.

Huther, J., Roberts, S. and Shah, A. (1997) *Public expenditure reform under adjustment lending: Lessons from the World Bank Experience*, World Bank Discussion Paper no 382, Washington, DC: World Bank.

ILO (International Labour Organization) (1989) *The ILO tripartite declaration of principles concerning multinational enterprises and social policy – Ten years after*, Geneva: ILO.

Katz, M.B. (ed) (1993) *The 'underclass' debate: Views from history*, Princeton, NJ: Princeton University Press (especially pp 440-78).

Kolko, G. (1999) 'Ravaging the poor: the International Monetary Fund indicted by its own data', *International Journal of Health Services*, vol 29, no 1, pp 51-7.

Kolodner, E. (1994) *Transnational corporations: Impediments or catalysts of social development?*, Occasional Paper no 5, Geneva: World Summit for Social Development, UNRISD.

Korten, D.C. (1996) *When corporations rule the world*, London: Earthscan Publications.

Kozul-Wright, R. and Rowthorn, R. (1998) *Transnational corporations and the global economy*, Helsinki: UNU World Institute for Development Economic Research.

Lang, T. and Hines, C. (1994) *The new protectionism: Protecting the future against free trade*, London: Earthscan Publications.

Levitas, R. (1998) *The inclusive society? Social exclusion and New Labour*, London: Macmillan.

Lieberman, I.W. and Kirkness, C.D. (eds) (1998) *Privatisation and emerging equity markets*, Washington, DC: World Bank and Flemings.

McPhail, K. and Davy, A. (1998) *Integrating social concerns into private sector decision making: A review of corporate practices in the mining, oil, and gas sectors*, World Bank Discussion Paper no 384, Washington, DC: World Bank.

Moore, J. (1989) *The end of poverty*, London: Conservative Political Centre.

Nelson, J.M., Tilly, C. and Walker, L. (1997) *Transforming post-communist political economies*, Task Force on Economies in Transition, National Research Council Commission on Behavioural and Social Sciences and Education, Washington, DC: National Academy Press.

Newman, B. and Thomson, R.J. (1989) 'Economic growth and social development: a longitudinal analysis of causal priority', *World Development*.

Oxfam (1995) *Poverty report*, Oxford: Oxfam.

Oyen, E., Miller, S.M. and Samad, S.A. (eds) (1996) *Poverty: A global review: Handbook on international poverty research*, Oslo: Scandinavian University Press.

Parker, D. and Martin, S. (1997) *The impact of privatisation*, London: Routledge.

Payer, C. (1982) *The World Bank: A critical analysis*, New York, NY: Monthly Review Press.

Payer, C. (1991) *Lent and lost: Foreign credit and Third World development*, London and New Jersey: Zed Books.

Psacharapoulos, G., Morley, S., Fiszbein, A., Lee, H. and Wood, B. (1997) *Poverty and income distribution in Latin America: The story of the 1980s*, World Bank Technical Paper no 351, Washington, DC: World Bank.

Rodgers, G., Gore, C. and Figueirido, J.B. (eds) (1995) *Social exclusion: Rhetoric, reality, responses*, Geneva: International Institute for Labour Studies, ILO.

Room, G. (ed) (1995) *Beyond the threshold: The measurement and analysis of social exclusion*, Bristol: The Policy Press.

Silver, H. (1994) 'Social exclusion and social solidarity: three paradigms', *International Labour Review*, vol 133, no 5-6, pp 531-78.

Tchernina, N. (1996) *Economic transition and social exclusion in Russia*, Research Series no 108, Geneva: IILS.

Townsend, P. (1991) 'Poverty and social polarisation', in *Eurocities, cities and social policies in Europe*, Barcelona: Ajuntament de Barcelona.

Townsend, P. (1993a) *The international analysis of poverty*, Hemel Hempstead: Harvester Wheatsheaf.

Townsend, P. (1993b) 'Underclass and overclass: the widening gulf between social classes in Britain in the 1980s', in M. Cross and G. Payne (eds) *Sociology in action*, London: Macmillan.

Townsend, P. (1995) 'Poverty in Eastern Europe: the latest manifestation of global polarisation', in G. Rodgers and R. Van der Hoeven (eds) *The poverty agenda: Trends and policy options: New approaches to poverty analysis and policy – III*, Geneva: International Institute for Labour Studies, ILO.

Townsend, P. (1996) *A poor future: Can we counteract growing poverty in Britain and across the world?*, London: Lemos and Crane.

Townsend, P. (1998a) 'Ending world poverty in the 21st century', *Radical Statistics* vol 68, pp 5-14.

Townsend, P. (1998b) *Will poverty get worse under Labour?*, New Waverley Papers, Department of Social Work, University of Edinburgh, Edinburgh.

Townsend, P. (1999) 'Social exclusion: operational meaning', Paper for Social Policy Research Centre, University of New South Wales, Sydney, 29 July (unpublished).

Townsend, P. with Donkor, K. (1996) *Global restructuring and social policy: An alternative strategy: Establishing an international welfare state*, International Seminar on Economic Restructuring and Social Policy, sponsored by UNRISD and UNDP, United Nations, New York, 1995, Bristol: The Policy Press.

Townsend, P. and Gordon, D. (1989) 'What is enough?', House of Commons Social Services Committee, *Minimum Income, House of Commons 579*, London, HMSO.

Townsend, P. with Corrigan, P. and Kowarzik, U. (1987) *Poverty and labour in London*, London: Low Pay Unit.

UN (United Nations) (1995) *The Copenhagen Declaration and Programme of Action: World Summit for Social Development*, New York, NY: UN.

UN (1999) *Further initiatives for the implementation of the outcome of the World Summit for Social Development*, Report of the Secretary General, Preparatory Committee for the Special Session of the General Assembly, 17-28 May, New York, NY: UN.

UNDP (United Nations Development Programme) (1995) *Poverty eradication: A policy framework for country strategies*, New York, NY: UNDP.

UNDP (1997) *Human development report 1997*, New York and Oxford: Oxford University Press.

UNDP (1998) *Poverty in transition*, Regional Bureau for Europe and the CIS, New York, NY: UNDP.

UNDP (1999) *Human development report 1999*, New York and Oxford: Oxford University Press.

van Oorschot, W. (1999) *Targeting welfare: On the functions and dysfunctions of means-testing in social policy*, Research in Europe Budapest conference on developing poverty measures.

Walker, A. and Walker, C. (eds) (1997) *Britain divided: The growth of social exclusion in the 1980s and 1990s*, London: Child Poverty Action Group.

World Bank (1990) *World development report 1990: Poverty*, Washington, DC: World Bank.

World Bank (1993) *Implementing the World Bank's strategy to reduce poverty: Progress and challenges*, Washington, DC: World Bank.

World Bank (1996) *Poverty reduction and the World Bank: Progress and challenges in the 1990s*, Washington, DC: World Bank.

World Bank (1997a) *Safety net programs and poverty reduction: Lessons from cross-country experience*, Washington, DC: World Bank.

World Bank (1997b) *Poverty reduction and the World Bank: Progress in fiscal 1996 and 1997*, Washington, DC: World Bank.

World Bank (1997c) *World development report 1997: The state in a changing world*, Washington, DC and New York, NY: Oxford University Press.

World Bank (1997d) *India: Achievements and challenges in reducing poverty*, Washington, DC: World Bank.

World Bank (1999) *Global economic prospects and the developing countries 1998/99: Beyond financial crisis*, Washington, DC and New York, NY: Oxford University Press.

TWO

Is rising income inequality inevitable? A critique of the 'Transatlantic Consensus'

Tony Atkinson[1]

Introduction

Is rising income inequality inevitable?

This chapter addresses one of the most important economic issues facing our societies and the world as a whole: rising income inequality. There is a widely held belief that rising inequality is inevitable. Increased inequality is the result of forces, such as technological change, over which we have no control, or the globalisation of world trade, which people believe, despite historical evidence to the contrary, to be irreversible. Kuznets (1955) suggested that income inequality might be expected to follow an inverse U-shape, first rising with industrialisation and then declining. Today, the 'Kuznets curve' is commonly believed to have doubled back on itself: the period of falling inequality has been succeeded by a reversal of the trend. Seen in this way, the third quarter of the 20th century was a 'golden age', not just for growth and employment, but also for its achievement in lowering economic inequality. On this basis, the marked rise in wage and income inequality observed in the US and the UK in recent decades will unavoidably be followed by rises in other countries, and indeed worldwide. Policy can make little difference.

In this chapter, I take issue with the assertion that rising inequality is inevitable. It may in fact turn out that the 21st century sees rising inequality, but this is not inescapable. We do have *some* choice. In challenging the popular position, I focus on the experience of OECD countries, since it is these that I know best. However, what is happening in industrialised economies cannot be divorced from what is happening in developing countries. Indeed, one frequently expressed view is that increased wage dispersion in the OECD countries is due to increased competition from low-wage economies. (I have discussed the rival view, that increased wage dispersion is due to technological change, in Atkinson, 2000.)

The chapter falls into three parts. In the first, I present a critique of the generally accepted explanation of the rise in inequality in OECD countries. Economists are sometimes accused of being slow to react to changing events – that they are always seeking to explain the last generation's economic problems. In my view, economists are in fact quick to respond to changing issues; indeed, they could rather be faulted for being too fashion conscious. In the field of income inequality, there has been a swift response. A 'Transatlantic Consensus' has established itself, one in which increased income inequality in the US and high unemployment in Continental Europe are due to a shift of demand away from unskilled workers towards skilled workers. I refer to it as the 'Transatlantic Consensus' because it provides a unified explanation as to how a single cause has a differential impact on the US and on mainland Europe. It also captures the fact that this view has been widely influential in the policy making of international institutions on both sides of the Atlantic, such as the International Monetary Fund (IMF) and the OECD. This consensus is, however, open to question. The first part of my chapter elaborates the underlying theory of distribution, treating in particular the international trade aspects, and argues that the 'Consensus' view has so far fallen short of providing a complete explanation.

Is there an alternative? The second part of the chapter seeks to describe a different approach to explaining rising earnings inequality. One necessity is to move from a simple 'skilled/unskilled' dichotomy of the labour force to the more realistic assumption of a continuum of earnings capacity. This allows us to focus on the fact that it is not just the unskilled who have lost relative to the median but that the median worker has lost relative to high earners: there has in fact been a 'tilt' in the earnings–skill nexus. The second ingredient in the alternative approach proposed here is the explicit recognition of the role of social conventions or social codes in pay determination. Social conventions may allow the resolution of problems of incomplete contracting, where supply and demand considerations only place limits on the possible wage differentials. Changes in wage differentials may reflect shifts in such social conventions. Social codes, or pay norms, may play an intrinsic, and not just an instrumental, role, where people attach weight to the loss of reputation that follows from breach of the code. The cost of breaking the code depends on the degree of adherence, which is endogenous, and increased pay dispersion may have arisen on account of a shift from a high- to a low-adherence equilibrium.

The first two parts of the chapter, then, concentrate on the determinants of what people receive as wages in the market place. (Capital incomes are also important, but are not discussed in this chapter.) However, market incomes are significantly modified by government policy. Many people in OECD countries, such as those who are retired or unemployed, receive very little in the way of market incomes. They survive because of state transfers (retirement pensions, unemployment insurance, and so on) financed by social security and other taxes.

In the third part of this chapter, I show how the government budget has played a major role in offsetting the rise in inequality in market incomes – a rise that predates the present concerns. The degree of offset differs across countries, as well as across time in any one country. This suggests that national policy may be influential, but also raises the question as to the degree to which national governments can preserve autonomy in their redistributive policy in an increasingly integrated world.

Rising inequality and the 'Transatlantic Consensus'

The phenomenon of rising inequality of income in industrialised countries[2] was first noticed in the US, where inequality as measured by the Gini coefficient began to rise in the 1970s (see Figure 2.1). The Gini coefficient is a summary measure of inequality, varying between 0 when we all have identical incomes and 100% when one person scoops the entire pool. The rise in the US has attracted most attention, but the UK has seen an even larger increase. In the period 1977-90, the Gini coefficient for the distribution by individuals of equivalent household disposable income in the UK rose by some 10 percentage points, from around 23% to around 33% (see Figure 2.1). This increase is 2.5 times the increase in the US over that period[3].

Experience, therefore, is not uniform across OECD countries. Even if it were true that all OECD countries have seen increased income inequality, the extent and timing of the increase has differed. There has been a sharp rise in income inequality in New Zealand, but little apparent increase in Canada, for example. The last of these is striking, as Smeeding (1999) has emphasised. Two North American countries, Canada and the US, share a long frontier, with considerable cross-border economic flows, where the degree of integration has increased with the North American Free Trade Agreement (NAFTA), and yet the time paths of income inequality are noticeably different in each. In the Nordic countries there has too been a variety of experience. In their study of the distributional impact of rising unemployment, Aaberge et al (1997) found that, in the period in question, inequality of disposable income did not respond at all in Finland and relatively little in Denmark, but rose, albeit modestly, in Sweden and Norway (Norway's situation is illustrated by Figure 2.1). In other European countries, there is a similar diversity of experience. In Germany, taking the Western Länder for purposes of comparability over time, the Gini coefficient has increased by some three percentage points since the 1970s, as may be seen by piecing together the two series in Figure 2.1. The increase in the Netherlands in the second half of the 1980s was similar in magnitude. In France, there was no increase in the 1980s.

These figures refer to the inequality of *disposable household incomes*; there is similar diversity in the experience with regard to *gross individual earnings*. Figure 2.2 shows estimates (based largely on data assembled by the OECD) of the changes since 1977 in the ratio of earnings at the top decile to those at the bottom decile (the 'decile ratio')[4]. The picture is again one of diversity. The US, UK and New Zealand are in this case more similar in the extent of the

Figure 2.1: Changes in income inequality

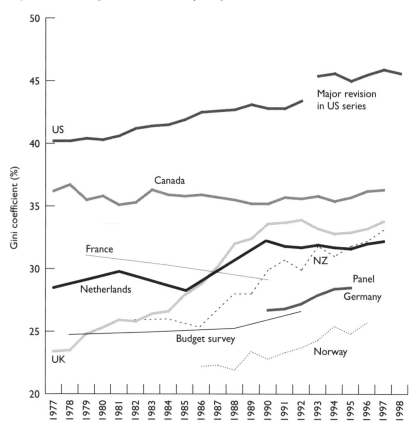

Sources:

Canada: Statistics Canada (1996, text table VI) (1999, appendix table III)

France (1975=100): Atkinson (1997b, table FR2 synthèses series)

(West) Germany (1978 = 100): Becker (1996, tabelle 1); Hauser (1996, tabelle 1, linked at 1993 using Becker [1998, tabelle 4])

Netherlands: data supplied by Central Bureau of Statistics

New Zealand: Statistics New Zealand (1999)

Norway: Epland (1998)

UK: up to 1993 from Atkinson (1997b, table UK3); series constructed by Goodman and Webb (1994); 1994/95-1997/98 from Clark and Taylor (1999, figure 2 and text). Figures prior to 1993 from Family Expenditure Survey; figures from 1994/95 from Family Resources Survey

US: US Department of Commerce (1999, tables B-3, B-6)

increase in dispersion. For other countries, the pattern is mixed, with a rise and then a fall in Canada and Norway, a fall in Germany, a rise in the Netherlands, and variation on a level trend in France. Certainly for the first half of the 1990s there is no dominating pattern. As the OECD has observed, drawing on evidence for a larger number of countries, "No clear tendency emerges of a generalised

Figure 2.2: Changes in earnings inequality

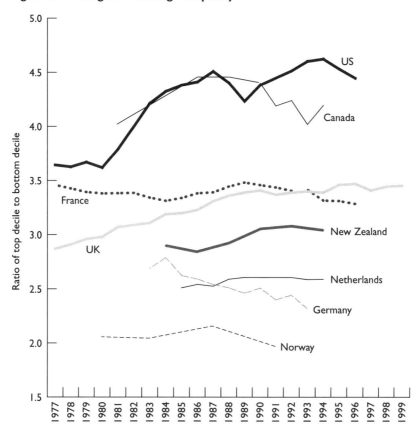

Sources:

Canada (1981=100), (West) Germany (1983=100), Netherlands (1985=100), New Zealand (1984=100) and Norway (1980=100): OECD (1996, table 3.1)

France: Bayet and Julhès (1996, p 48)

UK: Atkinson and Micklewright (1992, table BE1, linked at 1990 to Department of Employment [1999, table A30.2])

US: Karoly (1994, table 2B.2), weekly (consistent) wage and salary income, linked at 1979 and 1987, linked in 1989 to OECD (1996, table 3.1, which refers to male earnings)

increase in earnings inequality over the first half of the 1990s. Of the 16 countries ... dispersion increased in half, and was either broadly unchanged or declined somewhat in the rest" (OECD, 1996, p 63).

The second point to be made about the evidence for incomes and earnings is that, while economists tend to talk glibly about 'trends' in income inequality, this is not necessarily a good way of describing the observed changes over time. As I have argued before (Atkinson, 1997a), it may be more instructive to think in terms of 'episodes' when inequality rose or fell. This is well illustrated in Figure 2.1 by the UK. There has not been a continuous upward trend in the

UK. In the 1980s, inequality increased, and then accelerated. From 1990 to 1997, however, during the John Major led Conservative government, the Gini coefficient appears to have cycled rather than followed an upward trend. Equally, the 1999 report of the US Government (US Department of Commerce, 1999, p *xiii*) commented that there had been no significant annual increase since 1993 (when there was a major revision in the methodology). While there may be cyclical influences in operation disguising the trend, the 1990s do not look like the 1980s in the US and the UK.

The Netherlands provides a third example. Inequality in disposable income clearly increased, but it appears to have been a step increase in the second half of the 1980s, not a continuing trend (the same appears to be true of earnings dispersion in Figure 2.2). To describe recent experience as an inexorable trend is not therefore empirically correct, and it may well put us on the wrong track when seeking to explain the evolution of inequality, which is my main concern here.

The 'Transatlantic Consensus'

As I mentioned earlier, economists seem to have moved rapidly to a consensus view, where increased income inequality is identified with increased inequality of potential earnings (and hence actual earnings or employment), and where increased wage inequality is attributed to a shift in relative demand away from unskilled to skilled workers. There is debate about the causes of the shift in relative demand (see, for example, Burtless, 1995; Dewatripont et al, 1999). It may be liberalisation of international trade and increased trade flows; it may be heightened competition from newly industrialising countries (Wood, 1994). Or, the shift may be the result of technical change biased towards skilled labour, with the introduction of automation and information technology. Or it could be the outcome of technical change biased towards sectors using skilled labour. In this chapter, given its international focus, I concentrate on the international trade version of the story[5], without in any way suggesting that technological change is unimportant.

The trade story is well summarised in a recent bulletin of the Centre for Economic Policy Research (CEPR): "developed countries have become increasingly open to trade with developing countries. The latter are rich in unskilled labour, it is argued: they can supply goods where production is 'unskilled-intensive', such as T-shirts from China, at a fraction of developed country costs. Hence unskilled wages in developed countries must fall" (CEPR, 1999, p 5).

This can be formally demonstrated in a standard trade theory model of the Heckscher-Ohlin type, where there are two blocs of countries (industrialised and newly industrialising, respectively), each with two sectors of production. The sectors produce tradable goods using two different types of labour (skilled and unskilled) in different mixes: one 'high technology' sector uses skilled labour relatively intensively (at all relative wage rates), whereas the other sector is relatively unskilled-intensive (for the sake of simplicity, other factors of production such as capital or land are ignored, as are non-traded goods and services). A reduction in the barriers to trade leads to a new equilibrium, where the industrialised countries expand their output of the high technology sector and contract that of the other good, and the relative wage of skilled labour rises.

All models are abstractions, but that above is an oversimplification in one important respect: the industrialised countries have very different structures. We need to allow for at least two distinct groupings within the OECD: Continental Europe and the US (plus probably the UK and other Anglo-Saxon countries; Japan should perhaps be treated on its own). In what follows, I posit a three-bloc model, referred to as US, Euro Zone (EZ) and Newly Industrialising (NIC). The relevant difference here between the two industrialised blocs (US and EZ) is the existence in the EZ of effective minimum wage protection, or social security benefit levels, preventing wages from falling at the bottom. The demand shift story then predicts increased unemployment – not increased wage dispersion. According to Krugman (1994, p 60), "the upward trend in unemployment [in Europe] is the result of market forces that 'want' to produce greater inequality of earnings. The collision between these market forces and the attempts of the welfare state to limit inequality then lead to higher unemployment".

So we appear to have a unified explanation for what is happening on both sides of the Atlantic: widened wage dispersion in the US and raised unemployment in the EZ. Figure 2.3 shows the position of France and the US as far as earnings are concerned. In the French case, the bottom decile of earnings for male workers was 59% of the median in 1977 and had actually risen slightly to 62% in 1987, whereas the US percentage fell from 50% to 44% over the same period. What happened post-1987 will be discussed later in this chapter.

Moreover, even though the step is not usually taken, we could explain differences *within* the two industrialised blocs in the speed and timing of the rise in earnings inequality by reference to changes in the supply of skilled labour in response to the emerging increased skill premium. Differential performance across countries in the race between technological development and education, as it was described by Tinbergen (1975), does not, in the Heckscher-Ohlin model, cause the unskilled/skilled wage relationship to differ across countries. However, the distribution of earnings *is* potentially affected by changes in the proportions of unskilled workers (and of the unemployed). The unskilled/skilled wage differential is not a complete summary statistic, as is obvious from considering the case of the decile ratio where one group is more than 90% of the total.

Unresolved questions

The relation between wage dispersion and increased international competition is a classic example of the power of economic theorising. A textbook model

Figure 2.3: Earnings distribution in France and the US

Sources: Bernstein and Michel (1997, table 4); Friez and Julhès (1998, p 4)

can be applied directly to explain real world observations. At the end of his survey on growing world trade, Krugman (1995) observes that "the time has come" for general-equilibrium trade theory. By this he meant that one of the most important contributions of trade theory is its general equilibrium perspective, of seeing the world economy as a whole. However, in doing so, we need to go beyond the two-country model which has dominated trade theory, since, as has recently been brought out by Davis (1998a, 1998b), the conclusions can be misleading. In drawing its conclusions, the 'Transatlantic Consensus' in effect carries out parallel analyses of the impact on the US and the impact on Europe of the opening of trade with the NICs. As noted earlier, we require at least a three-bloc model. When we look at the world in this way, we see, extending the analysis of Davis, that the standard Heckscher-Ohlin trade theory falls short of yielding the predictions assumed in the 'Transatlantic Consensus'.

Suppose first that the conditions for factor price equalisation hold. These conditions are strong, requiring that countries differ in their productive capacities only in their factor endowments, having identical (constant returns to scale) production functions. The conditions require that there be equal numbers of goods and factors, and that countries produce all goods. From strong assumptions follow strong implications. In particular, where there are no factor-intensity reversals, free international trade leads to the equalisation of factor prices (see, for example, Bhagwati, 1964; Chipman, 1966; Dixit and Norman, 1980). Put in terms of two factors (skilled and unskilled labour) and two goods, there is a one-to-one relation between the relative goods' prices and the skilled/unskilled wage ratio (the assumption that there are no factor-intensity reversals means that one of the two goods uses skilled labour relatively intensively at all relative wage rates). If we now suppose that one of the two industrialised blocs (the EZ) imposes a minimum relative wage for unskilled labour, then this determines the goods' relative prices and the wage of skilled labour. In the absence of specialisation, the US will adjust to the EZ-determined relative price. The US has a flexible wage, but the wages of the unskilled rise to the EZ level (and those of the skilled fall) as the US expands its exports to the EZ of the goods which use unskilled labour intensively. There will be unemployment of unskilled labour in EZ, but not in the US.

Before questioning the underlying assumptions, we should note the implications of this analysis for the 'Transatlantic Consensus'. If the combined US/EZ trading economy is opened to trade with the NIC, then, providing the EZ continues to produce the good intensive in unskilled labour, the goods' price remains unchanged. The US is unaffected and the impact of the trade is entirely on unemployment in EZ. In neither region is wage inequality affected. We have one part of the 'Transatlantic Consensus' but not the other. As Davis puts it: "So long as Europe maintains a commitment to both free trade and a high-wage policy, America is fully insulated from the NIC shock" (1998, p 485). The factor price equalisation result should not be taken too literally: "[it is] a very ambitious proposition.... One ought to be satisfied with the more plausible Marshallian way of putting things: free trade sets up a tendency to factor price equalisation" (Hahn, 1998, p 18). However, translated to the present context, this means that there is a *tendency* for the low paid in the US to be sheltered by European unemployment.

On this basis, trade theory can explain the widening of wage inequality in the US only to the extent that the conditions of the standard Heckscher-Ohlin model do *not* hold. In order for this to be satisfactorily treated, we need to model the reasons why the factor price equalisation theorem does not apply. One reason is that the EZ, with its minimum wage, may cease to produce the goods in which unskilled labour is used intensively; it becomes specialised in the high-technology goods, importing the other goods from the US, where the wages of the unskilled are no longer tied to those in Europe. In this case, opening of trade with NIC will drive the relative price of the high-technology goods higher, and, reading across from goods' prices to factor prices, hence widen wage differentials in the US. The US side of the story is now in place.

In EZ however, wage inequality will rise, and unemployment will fall (as unskilled labour is substituted for skilled in the production of the high- technology good). The effect will be intensified if there are also non-traded goods and services which use unskilled labour. Therefore, we lose the EZ arm of the consensus.

In brief, the theoretical basis for the 'Transatlantic Consensus' does not appear to be a simple application of standard international trade theory of the Heckscher-Ohlin variety. The model needs to be richer. This enrichment could take the form of more realistic assumptions about the trading economies, such as introducing imperfect competition and product differentiation, or non-traded goods, or allowing for productivity differences, or for transport costs, or incorporating the effect of the Common Agricultural Policy in the EZ. All of these could well lead to an enhanced trade theory which could explain the observed changes in the US and the EZ, but work remains to be done. Alternatively, we could look elsewhere.

An alternative approach to explaining earnings inequality

I want to suggest two ingredients of an alternative approach to explaining earnings dispersion. The first is to abandon the simple unskilled/skilled distinction. A century ago, it might have been relatively easy to apply such a dichotomy. In Aldous Shipyard in Brightlingsea, where my sailing boat was built in 1899, the shipwrights were skilled craftsmen and the men with brooms who kept the slipways free of mud were unskilled. Today's attempts to implement the distinction are less satisfactory. As noted by Cooper (1995, p 366), the practice adopted in many studies of treating all production workers as unskilled and non-production as skilled seems too coarse. In some cases, skill is equated with formal education, and increased wage inequality is associated with the increased return to college-educated workers since the 1970s. But identifying 'skilled' with 'college-educated' shifts the basis for the definition, and makes no allowance for mismatch between the educational qualifications of workers and the requirements of the job they hold.

What I would like to consider instead is a continuum of earnings. One reason for so doing is empirical. Figure 2.3 shows that the most significant widening is not that at the bottom of the US earnings distribution. In fact, the bottom decile, where the unskilled may be expected to be found, has actually been rising, rather than falling, relative to the median in the US over the last 10 years. Between 1987 and 1996 the ratio increased from the 44% mentioned earlier back to 48%. It is true that earnings dispersion has been widening, but this is because of what is happening higher up the scale. From Figure 2.3, it may be seen that, in the US, the top decile's pay rose over the two decades from around 1.8 times the median to around 2.15. In contrast, in France the top decile did not go up significantly relative to the median over the period as a whole. Of course, the ratio in France was initially higher[6], so that one can represent the US widening as 'catching up', but in terms of changes over time

Figure 2.4: Tilt in UK earnings distribution

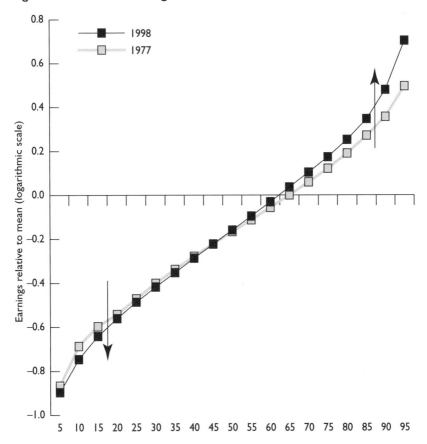

Sources:

1977: earnings data for all workers whose pay was not affected by absence from Atkinson and Micklewright (1992, table BE1)

1998: Department of Employment, New Earnings Survey (1998, table UK 9.1 for all workers whose pay was not affected by absence, paid at adult rates). The former covers Great Britain, the latter UK

the main phenomenon which needs to be explained is the rotation of the wage/rank relationship. Figure 2.4 illustrates this tilt for the UK. It is not just a question of those at the bottom losing out (the downward arrow); indeed, in the second ten-year period from 1989 to 1999 the ratio of the bottom decile to the median in the UK rose slightly. Increased wage dispersion is due more to what has happened in the upper part of the distribution (upward arrow).

In order to understand this, we have to move to a continuum of earnings. This, of course, is not new. A continuum of earnings has been studied in labour economics and in public economics (as in the optimum income tax literature). But it has not been treated explicitly in the present context. Krugman drew just such a tilt in his popular exposition (1994), but did not carry it through to the more formal model (1995). In order to see the implications for international trade, let us suppose that there are two goods, for one of which (the 'high-technology' sector) output is proportional to individual productivity, but in the other (the 'low-technology' sector), all workers are equally productive. Average productivity in the high-technology sector depends on the proportion of the labour force employed. The expansion of international trade, so that the relative price of the low-technology good falls, means that wages fall relatively in that sector, although the proportion employed also falls (the number of less favoured workers is endogenous in this case)[7]. This does not account, however, for the tilt in the upper half of the distribution. Real wages may rise in the high-technology sector, but they rise by the same percentage for the median (assuming the sector accounts for more than half of employment) as they do for the top decile. To understand the tilt, we have, I believe, to investigate the determinants of wage differentials.

Determinants of wage differentials

The 'Transatlantic Consensus' can be described as a triumph of 'supply and demand'. A major economic phenomenon is explained by nothing more than the supply and demand curves which are learned by a first year student. This contrasts markedly with earlier writing on wage differentials, where there has been a creative tension between market force and alternative explanations of wage differentials. Phelps Brown, for instance, opened his *The inequality of pay* (1977) by contrasting the approach to pay determination of the 'economist' with that of the 'sociologist': the economist sees people as engaged in rational, impersonal transactions; the sociologist sees people interacting as members of a society.

How can we move beyond a simple supply and demand representation? From the economist's position, we could suppose that supply and demand only place limits on the possible wage differentials, with other factors such as bargaining or social convention determining where between these limits wages actually lie. Such a 'range theory' of wage differentials was advanced by Lester (1952). The way in which a range of negotiation can arise has been illustrated by models of job matching: "Having come together, the firm and worker have a joint surplus ... there is a wage that makes the worker indifferent between taking this job and waiting for his next job opportunity. There is a wage that makes the firm indifferent between hiring this worker and waiting for the next available worker. The bargaining problem is to agree on a wage between these two limits" (Diamond, 1982, p 219).

The quasi-rents are typically assumed in the job search literature to be shared out as a result of a process of bilateral bargaining, the division reflecting relative bargaining power. On this basis, the tilt in the wage distribution could reflect changes in the relative bargaining power at different points on the wage scale (see, for example, Fortin and Lemieux, 1997). Decline in trade union membership and diminution of union power may have reduced the union wage premium in the lower part of the distribution, whereas individual negotiation higher up the scale may have allowed the better-paid to capture more of the gains from productivity increases. Or, where wage dispersion is negatively correlated with the degree of centralisation of wage bargaining (Rowthorn, 1992), increased dispersion may be due to a decline in centralised bargaining.

Where there is a degree of indeterminacy of the market equilibrium, pay norms may play a role. Introduction of a notion of fairness or equity provides a route to removing the indeterminacy where "individual incentives are not by themselves generally sufficient to determine a unique equilibrium" (MacLeod and Malcomson, 1998, p 400).

In this context, observance of social norms may be consistent with individual rationality, and indeed instrumental in achieving efficient outcomes. Where contracts are not legally enforceable, then general acceptance of a convention may allow firms or workers to make investments which would not be profitable were there a risk that the agreement would later be renegotiated in breach of the convention. This view of social norms attributes no weight to any intrinsic value attached to respecting the convention: "A central assumption of the strategic interpretation of custom is that the rules selected as coordination devices are used *in a purely instrumental manner*. All phenomena of rule obedience, commitment, etc., are assumed to be of only secondary importance" (Schlicht, 1998, p 132).

In this regard, economists can learn from sociology and anthropology, as stressed by Akerlof (1980), who describes a model where individual utility depends not only on income but also on reputation, which is based on conformity with the social code. The loss of reputation – if one departs from the social code – depends on the proportion who believe in the code, which is undermined if people cease to observe it. He shows that there may be a long-run equilibrium with the persistence of a 'fair', rather than market-clearing, wage and involuntary unemployment.

The reputational approach

This reputational approach can be applied to the relation between wages and productivity. Suppose that there is a social code, or pay norm, that limits the extent to which individual earnings increase with earnings potential. Where this code is followed, people are paid a fraction of their productivity plus a uniform amount. Such a policy involves a degree of redistribution and low productivity workers can be expected to subscribe to the pay norm. However, other workers will also accept it, even where they could be paid more if they broke the norm, since – if they believe in the norm – by breaking it they would suffer a loss of reputation[8]. The extent of the loss rises with the proportion of the population who at that time believe in the norm, a proportion which is assumed to adjust over time in a way described below.

Employers are also concerned with their reputations. When they create a job, it is determined in advance whether or not it is paid according to the pay norm. The profitability of the job depends not only on the pay but also on the acceptance of the job by the worker with which it is matched. Matching is assumed to follow a random process, but is only successful where employer and worker either both observe the code or both do not[9]. Employers determine their pay policy (that is, whether or not to observe the social code) on the basis of comparing expected profitability, which depends on the proportion, and characteristics, of workers who accept different pay offers[10]. The expected profitability of breaking the social code has to exceed the consequential loss of reputation, which is assumed to vary between employers, so that some employers may observe the code while others depart from it. There will therefore be a proportion of jobs that accord with the pay norm. If the proportion of the population who believe in the pay norm is less (greater) than this, then the extent of belief grows (falls).

There is therefore a dynamic process of adjustment. As Akerlof (1980) has shown, the process is likely to be of the 'tipping' kind identified by Schelling (1978). Interior equilibria for the proportion believing in the social code may be unstable, and, depending on the initial conditions, a society converges to a high level of conformity with the social code, or to the virtual absence of conformity. In this kind of situation, an exogenous shock may shift the key relationship and switch the society from an equilibrium with conformity to the pay norm, and hence relatively low wage differentials, to an equilibrium where everyone is paid on the basis of their productivity. Such an exogenous shock may have been a fall in the weight attached by employers to reputation. Or, reflecting changes in the capital market, it may be that greater weight is attached to short-run profits. As a result, there are "market forces that have tended to pay everyone more like salespersons – on the basis of what they produce" (Summers, 1999, p 102).

We may therefore observe a discrete change in the wage distribution: an episode of increasing dispersion (not a continuing trend). Such periods of rapid change in differentials have been noted at earlier times. In his account of wage differentials moving in the opposite direction, Reder (1962, p 408) states that, "The long-run decline in the skill margin in advanced countries has not occurred slowly and steadily. Instead, the skill margin appears to have remained constant for relatively long periods of time and then to have declined sharply within a very few years".

One route by which shifts in pay norms may be brought about is government incomes policy. In the UK, it is worth remembering that in 1973 the Conservative government's Stage Two Incomes Policy set a group pay limit of GB£1 plus 4%, with an individual maximum increase of GB£250 a year. Although now distant history, Labour's *Attack on inflation* in 1975 restricted increases to GB£6 a week, with no increase for those earning more than GB£8,500 a year. Alternatively, the wage norm may be enforced through the process of collective bargaining. In Norway, according to Kahn (1998), the agreement negotiated between the trade union federation (LO) and the employers organisation (NHO) allowed in 1989 for a uniform 3 krona per hour increase (with a 1 krona supplement in export industries), and the 1990 contract allowed for a larger absolute increase for the low paid. (Evidence

---

about the role of fairness in collective bargaining at the micro-level in Norway is provided by Strøm, 1995.)

The pay norm model, in addition to helping explain episodes of rising or falling wage dispersion, can also be used to explain differences across countries. The support for pay norms depends, for instance, on the extent of differences in underlying productivity. Where people are relatively homogeneous, then there is more likely to be adherence to an egalitarian pay norm, so that the two elements, one exogenous (productivity differences) and one endogenous (degree of adherence to the code) combine to explain smaller wage dispersion. Moreover, the shifting pay norm explanation can be introduced into the model of trade with a continuum of abilities. A shift from a redistributive pay norm to a payment strictly on the basis of productivity can have the effect of reducing the supply of the high-technology good at any relative price. This arises because the condition for equilibrium in the labour market is based on the marginal worker, who ceases to gain from the redistributive pay norm. Paying wages purely on productivity benefits those higher up the scale. There is a shift in the offer curve. If there is a bloc of countries, say the EZ, where no such shift in the pay norm has happened, then they will see an increased demand for their exports. This is clearly not the whole story, but – just as international trade theory has begun to incorporate considerations of efficiency wages[11] – a model with a richer treatment of the labour market seems well worth exploring.

The view of rising wage dispersion advanced here is certainly not the only way of explaining what has happened in the upper part of the earnings distribution in the US and the UK. At the very top, particularly when one introduces the value of stock options, the 'superstar theory' of Rosen (1981) appears to have considerable relevance. However, the reputational approach to pay norms seems well worth exploring further, and it has a number of implications for policy. In part, the widely advocated policies of skills acquisition remain valid, although the mechanism by which they operate is rather different. The support for a redistributive pay norm depends on the extent of dispersion of productive abilities. Ensuring relatively homogeneous skills in the population may ensure continued support for a redistributive pay norm. In part, the policy implications are different. The role of public sector pay policy is an example. The adoption of performance related pay in the public sector can be expected to influence pay norms elsewhere. Such a shift in the public sector may cause a discrete change in the economy as a whole.

Can redistribution offset market inequality?

This chapter has so far considered what people receive as wages in the market place. However, market incomes are significantly modified by income taxation and by social transfers financed out of the government budget. I now wish to examine how far fiscal redistribution offsets any rise in inequality in market incomes.

Figure 2.5: Redistributive impact of budget

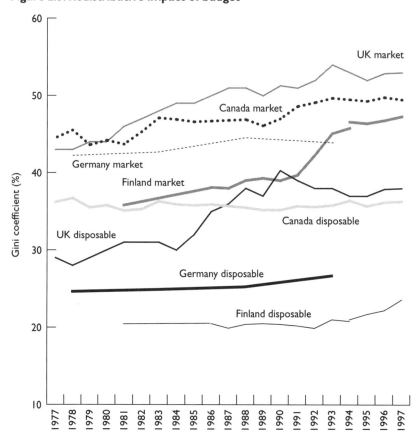

Sources:

UK distribution among households of equivalised original income and post-tax income. There are breaks in the series in 1990, 1992 and 1996/97 (although a figure is given for this year on the previous basis). Office for National Statistics' *Economic Trends* 1998 (April, no 58) for 1977, 1979, 1981, 1983, 1985, 1987, 1989, 1991, 1993/94 to 1996/97; *Economic Trends* 1994 (December, no 65) for 1978, 1980, 1982, 1984, 1986, 1988, 1992; *Economic Trends* 1993 (January 159) for 1990. It should be noted that the definition of the post-tax series differs from the disposable income series in Figure 2.1

Canada: Statistics Canada (1996, text table VI, 1999, appendix table III)

Finland: Statistics Finland (1999, asetelma 3)

Actual redistributive experience

Figure 2.5 illustrates assembled estimates of the overall degree of inequality (measured by the Gini coefficient) before and after redistribution for three OECD countries. The selection of countries is determined by the availability in each country of a long time series of official estimates of the redistributive impact of the government budget[12], but they have in common a rise over the two decades in the inequality of market incomes, represented by dashed lines. In Canada the Gini coefficient for market income increased by some

5 percentage points, in the UK by around 8 points; and in Finland (from 1981) by more than 10 points.

There is again diversity of experience both across countries and across time. Here I focus on the difference between the market and disposable income series. In the case of the UK, inequality of market income increased over the period as a whole, but the Gini coefficient for disposable income showed scarcely any rise over the first part of the period. From 1977 to 1984, the redistributive impact of cash transfers and taxation increased by enough to offset the more unequal market incomes: the Gini coefficient for market income rose by six percentage points but that for disposable income by only one point. After 1984, however, the case of the UK is quite different, reflecting a major reduction in the progressivity of income taxation and cutbacks in benefit levels and coverage. Inequality in market income continued to rise, but between 1984 and 1990 the Gini coefficient for post-tax income increased much more sharply (marked by the upward arrow in Figure 2.5). Measured in terms of the difference between the two coefficients, the redistributive contribution of transfers and taxes fell from 19 percentage points (the difference between the two Gini coefficients in 1984) to 11 percentage points in 1990. The reduction in redistributive impact was attributable to a smaller impact of cash transfers (minus five percentage points), less progressive direct taxes (minus one percentage point) and more regressive indirect taxes (minus two percentage points).

The UK experience contrasts with that of Canada. The coverage of the Canadian data is different, in that disposable income refers to income after direct taxes but before indirect taxes. This may affect the comparison not only of *levels* but also of *trends*. However, the difference in trends from the UK is so striking that this cannot be explained solely by definitions. Over the period 1980-94 as a whole, the Gini coefficient for market income rose by some five percentage points, whereas that for disposable income in 1994 was not significantly higher than 17 years earlier. The picture for Finland in the 1980s and 1990s contains elements of similarity with both Canada and the UK. The 'Canadian' period was that up to 1994. From 1981 to 1994 the Gini coefficient for market income in Finland rose by ten percentage points, particularly post-1990 with the economic difficulties faced at that time. This was however offset by the government budget to the extent that inequality in disposable income did not increase. As is brought out by Uusitalo (1998), the main contributors were transfer payments; the redistributive impact of taxation did not increase in line with the inequality of market income, and actually fell after 1989. Since 1994, however, the situation in Finland has changed as a result of policy measures cutting the redistributive impact of transfers, which have led inequality of disposable income to rise more than that of market income.

The first conclusion I draw is that in all three countries there have been substantial periods of time when the government has succeeded through fiscal policy in offsetting rising inequality of market incomes. The same has been observed in other countries. In the case of France, Piketty (1999, p 842) has summarised the findings of Bourguignon and Martinez (1997) as showing that (from 1979 to 1994) "inequality of primary incomes among working-age households has grown substantially in France since the late 1970s. [The rise in social transfers] is entirely responsible for the relative stability of the distribution of disposable income".

Of course, it is possible that the redistributive policy has itself caused rising inequality of market incomes. The incidence of taxes and transfers is an important issue (see, for example Atkinson, 1999). But to the extent that rising market inequality is due to outside factors, as I have been discussing in this chapter, countries have succeeded in offsetting its effect for significant periods of time. We would indeed expect the government budget to attenuate the impact of rising wage inequality on household disposable incomes. Progressive income taxation should mean that the Gini coefficient of disposable income rises less than that of market incomes. Where a shift in demand away from unskilled workers leads to a rise in unemployment, as posited by the 'Transatlantic Consensus' in the case of Europe, the impact on household disposable incomes is moderated by the existence of other income sources within the household, and by the payment of unemployment benefit. An unskilled man who becomes unemployed may be supported by his skilled partner who keeps her job. Countries differ in the rate of replacement in unemployment insurance, but even the least generous systems in OECD countries offer some financial protection against unemployment.

Fiscal policy would therefore moderate rising market inequality. The same is true where the explanation of rising wage inequality is the alternative one advanced here, based on changes in pay norms. A tilt in the wage/skill nexus would lead to increased revenue from a progressive tax. The distribution of disposable income would again show less increase in inequality. This alternative approach does however raise the issue of *changes* in fiscal policy. There is the possibility that the shift in norms may extend beyond the labour market to influence attitudes to redistribution. The shift from a relatively egalitarian pay norm to one where pay is related more closely to productivity may be accompanied by shifts in the attitudes of voters to redistributive policy, causing governments to become less willing to finance transfers and to levy progressive taxes. The fiscal changes may reinforce, rather than moderate, the tilt in the wage distribution.

As we have seen, there have been periods in two of the three countries when inequality of disposable income has increased as a result of policy choices. The UK and Finnish governments have, to varying degrees, scaled back redistributive transfers. This raises the question as to whether the explanation for these policy shifts is to be found in the national political economy of these countries or whether they too are the product of external forces. Do national governments in fact have room to manoeuvre? Are these fiscal choices, reducing tax progression and cutting the welfare state, in fact ones that all governments will in time be forced to follow?

How much freedom do national governments possess?

The constraints on national policy choices could take several different forms. They may be external economic forces, common to many countries, such as those that arise from increased competitiveness in international trade or increased factor mobility. Where social transfers are financed by payroll taxes on employers, these taxes enter wage costs and raise the prices of the country's goods and services. Firms find it harder, or less profitable, to sell their products abroad. However, in the standard trade model, the exchange rate would adjust, with a depreciation of the currency offsetting the price rise, shifting the burden onto the factors of production (assumed to be in fixed supply). Of course, this assumes that the exchange rate can adjust, and we have to distinguish here between trade between currency unions and trade within currency areas. Within the European Monetary Union this instrument of correction is not available, and this may limit the autonomy of individual member states. On the other hand, the costs of the European Welfare State as a whole can be offset by depreciation of the euro (€) vis-à-vis other currencies, such as the dollar. Autonomy still remains, but at the European level. The constraints on governments could be those of factor mobility. An increased tax burden resulting from social transfers could lead to the out-migration of capital or labour. In the case of labour, there are reasons to doubt whether this will be of sufficient quantitative importance, at least in the foreseeable future. The position with regard to capital is more difficult, and it is possible that this may limit the choice of tax base, but this still leaves open possibilities for the progressive taxation of wage income.

There remains however a further dimension to the argument – and perhaps the more important. Rather than *real* tax competition, based on external economic changes, there may be *virtual* tax competition, based on national threats of the movement of labour or capital. Hirschman (1970) distinguished between 'exit' and 'voice' as reactions to economic change. Workers who perceive that taxes are lower in other member states may not migrate but may seek to exercise political power to achieve lower taxes at home. Comparisons of personal, or corporate, tax rates with those in other member countries may play a role in national election campaigns. I believe that these public choice aspects may be the most important restrictions on the freedom of national governments to carry out social protection. They cannot however be described as purely external, since they arise as a result of interaction with domestic politics. This brings one back to the different explanations of rising wage inequality.

As already noted, if one adopts the alternative approach outlined here, based on shifting pay norms, then one has to recognise that the same norms are likely to influence public as well as private decisions. A society which shifts away from redistributive pay norms is likely to shift away from fiscal redistribution. However, this is not inevitable, and can be influenced, just as the pay distribution can be influenced, by public policy. National governments are not, on this approach, faced with absolute external constraints. There is scope for political leadership.

Conclusions

Carol Shields' novel, *Happenstance* (1991), is to be read from one end for a wife's story, and then turned upside down for her husband's story of the same five days. The husband's story is, in broad terms, one of a person whose five days were at the mercy of outside disturbing events. The wife's story, again loosely interpreted, is influenced and constrained by social custom (the original version of this half was called *A fairly conventional woman*).

Equally, I have presented in this chapter two different perspectives. One, the husband's story, is the 'Transatlantic Consensus', which sees rising inequality as the product of exogenous, inevitable events. Wage inequality in industrialised OECD countries, or unemployment, is increasing on account of technical change biased against unskilled workers, or, the explanation on which I have focused here, on account of the liberalisation of international trade and increased competition from newly industrialising countries. The other, the wife's let us say, sees inequality as at least in part socially generated. There has been a tilt in the wage/productivity relationship, affecting the well paid as well as the low paid. There has been a shift away from a redistributive pay norm to one where market forces dominate. Social conventions in the labour market have changed within individual countries, and this may spill over into other spheres and to other countries.

What do these two stories imply for the inevitability of rising inequality? How do they affect the way in which we see the two key elements on which I have focused: increased inequality of earning power, and redistribution through the government budget? On the first view – the 'Transatlantic Consensus' – there is nothing to be done about rising market inequality. It is pure supply and demand. On the other hand, this does not imply rising inequality of disposable income: there are steps which governments can take to offset rising inequality of market incomes. The experience of a range of countries has shown that tax and transfer systems have been remarkably successful in counteracting the rise in inequality due to unemployment (Atkinson, 1998). The differing experience across OECD countries, described earlier, with regard to inequality in disposable household income is in part a reflection of differences in national redistributive policies.

What about the alternative view which I have put forward because I have doubts about the 'Transatlantic Consensus' on both theoretical and empirical grounds? The Consensus has been advertised as a triumph of trade theory, but in fact the conclusions do not follow directly from standard application of international trade theory of the Heckscher-Ohlin variety. The model needs to be richer. Empirically, the Consensus does not readily explain the tilt in the upper part of the distribution (to understand which a simple unskilled/skilled distinction does not seem adequate). The alternative approach described here argues that the relation between skill and pay reflects social conventions, where adherence to the pay norm is endogenously determined. A view which gives prominence to norms about pay has of course to recognise that the same norms may govern redistribution. If, as I am suggesting, widening wage dispersion in part arises on account of shifting norms, then the same shift may have reduced the willingness of governments to redistribute. Both elements move in the same direction. However, the fact that the driving force is social in origin, rather than trade or technology, means that there is more scope for political leadership. The evolution of social norms is influenceable by policy decisions.

In any two accounts of a marriage, there are undoubtedly elements of truth on both sides, even if one tends to sympathise more with one than the other. However, whether the reader adheres to the 'Transatlantic Consensus', or is persuaded of the need to look at the role of social norms, it remains the case that rising inequality is not inevitable.

Notes

[1] This is a revised version of the 1999 WIDER Annual Lecture, delivered 1 November 1999 at the University of Oslo. I would like to thank the Royal Ministry of Foreign Affairs of Norway, and the Centre for Development and the Environment (SUM) at the University of Oslo, for their generous hospitality. I am grateful to Andrea Cornia and Matti Pohjola for their most helpful comments on a previous draft. Part of the material was presented at a conference marking the 10th anniversary of DELTA in Paris, and a number of useful suggestions made there are reflected in this revised version.

[2] I do not discuss income inequality in developing countries. For general surveys, see Adelman and Robinson (1989) and Kanbur (2000); for discussion of the determinants of income distribution in developing countries, see, among others, Bourguignon and Morrisson (1998), Cornia (1999), and Stewart and Berry (1999).

[3] It should be noted that the series for different countries are based on different definitions. The US figures represent gross income, and are unadjusted for household size, whereas the UK figures relate to disposable income adjusted for household size using an equivalence scale. Not only are the levels incomparable, but also differences in definition may affect the measurement of trends over time.

[4] I have followed the convention of representing cross-country earnings data in the form of decile ratios, rather than Gini coefficients. Again it should be stressed that the data are not comparable across countries; for instance, some relate to all workers, while others to male workers only.

[5] Increased competition from imports from newly industrializing countries is only one aspect of the globalisation of the economy. Among the important dimensions not discussed here is the globalisation of capital markets, allowing the free movement of financial capital, which may well have had a significant effect on income inequality.

[6] There are also issues of comparability of the data, in particular the degree to which remuneration in kind and stock options are omitted.

[7] As a result, the mean earnings may fall in the high-technology sector as well. This aspect of the 'Roy model' of self-selection by workers, applied to international trade, is noted in the survey of assignment models by Sattinger (1993).

[8] They may also accept wage compression as a form of insurance against wage risk, given that this cannot be secured through private insurance. Agell and Lommerud (1992) examine the arguments why unions may on this ground adopt strongly egalitarian wage policies (see also Agell, 1999).

[9] It might be the case that a worker prefers a job paying according to the norm but that the loss of reputation from breaking the code was less than the loss from unemployment. However, it is assumed that employers do not engage workers who take a different view of the social code on the grounds that they will lack motivation.

[10] In the model considered, differences in productivity lead to differences in wages (even if not proportionately). Manning (1994) analyses the case where firms have a company wage policy, paying a rate for the job, but unrelated to productivity.

[11] A different model of fair wages in an open economy is provided by Agell and Lundborg (1995).

[12] Evidence from academic studies exists for other OECD countries: for example, for Germany, see Becker and Hauser (1997) and Hauser (1999).

References

Aaberge, R., Björklund, A., Jäntti, M., Pedersen, P.J., Smith, N. and Wennemo, T. (1997) *Unemployment shocks and income distribution*, Statistics Norway Research Department Discussion Paper no 201, Oslo: Statistics Norway.

Adelman, I. and Robinson, S. (1989) 'Income Distribution and Development', in H. Chenery and T.N. Srinivasan (eds) *Handbook of development economics*, vol 2, Amsterdam: North-Holland, pp 949-1003.

Agell, J. (1999) 'On the benefits from rigid labour markets: norms, market failures, and social insurance', *Economic Journal*, vol 109, pp F143-F164.

Agell, J. and Lommerud, K.E. (1992) 'Union egalitarianism as income insurance', *Economica*, vol 59, pp 295-310.

Agell, J. and Lundborg, P. (1995) 'Fair wages in an open economy', *Economica*, vol 62, pp 335-51.

Akerlof, G.A. (1980) 'A theory of social custom, of which unemployment may be one consequence', *Quarterly Journal of Economics*, vol 95, pp 749-75.

Atkinson, A.B. (1997a) 'Bringing income distribution in from the cold', *Economic Journal*, vol 107, pp 297-321.

Atkinson, A.B. (1997b) 'Measurement of trends in poverty and the income distribution', *Microsimulation Unit Working Paper* MU9701, Cambridge: Department of Applied Economics, University of Cambridge.

Atkinson, A.B. (1998) *Three lectures on poverty in Europe*, Oxford: Basil Blackwell.

Atkinson, A.B. (1999) 'Increased income inequality in OECD countries and the redistributive impact of the government budget', Paper presented at UNU/WIDER conference on Income Inequality and Poverty Reduction, July, Helsinki.

Atkinson, A.B. (2000) 'The changing distribution of income: evidence and explanations', *German Economic Review*, vol 1, pp 3-18.

Atkinson, A.B. and Micklewright, J. (1992) *Economic transformation in Eastern Europe and the distribution of income*, Cambridge: Cambridge University Press.

Becker, I. (1996) 'Die Entwicklung der Einkommensverteilung und der Einkommensarmut in den alten Bundesländern von 1962 bis 1988', in I. Becker and R. Hauser (eds) *Einkommensverteilung und Armut in Deutschland von 1962 bis 1995*, EVS-Projekt, Arbeitspapier no 9, Frankfurt: Universität Frankfurt am Main.

Becker, I. (1998) *Zur personellen Einkommensverteilung in Deutschland*, EVS-Projekt, Arbeitspapier no 13, Frankfurt: Universität Frankfurt am Main.

Becker, I. and Hauser, R. (1997) *Abgaben- und Transfersystem wirkt Polarisierungstendenzen entgegen*, EVS-Projekt, Arbeitspapier no 12, Frankfurt: Universität Frankfurt am Main.

Bernstein, J. and Mishel, L. (1997) 'Has wage inequality stopped growing?', *Monthly Labor Review*, December, pp 3-16.

Bhagwati, J.N. (1964) 'The pure theory of international trade: a survey', *Economic Journal*, vol 74, pp 1-84.

Bourguignon, F. and Martinez, M. (1997) *Decomposition of the changes in the distribution of primary family incomes: A microsimulation approach applied to France, 1979-1994*, Paris: DELTA.

Bourguignon, F. and Morrisson, C. (1998) 'Inequality and development: the role of dualism', *Journal of Development Economics*, vol 57, pp 233-57.

Burtless, G. (1995) 'International trade and the rise in earnings inequality', *Journal of Economic Literature*, vol 33, pp 800-16.

CEPR (1999) 'The Full Monty', *European Economic Perspectives*, no 22, pp 5-6.

Chipman, J.S. (1966) 'A survey of the theory of international trade: part 3, The modern theory', *Econometrica*, vol 34, pp 18-76.

Clark, T. and Taylor, J. (1999) 'Income inequality: a tale of two cycles?', *Fiscal Studies*, vol 20, pp 387-408.

Cooper, R.A. (1995) 'Discussion of Krugman', *Brookings Papers*, vol 1, pp 363-8.

Cornia, G.A. (1999) 'Liberalization, globalization and income distribution', *WIDER Working Papers* no 157, Helsinki: UNU/WIDER.

Davis, D.R. (1998a) 'Does European unemployment prop up American wages? National labor markets and global trade', *American Economic Review*, vol 88, pp 478-94.

Davis, D.R. (1998b) 'Technology, unemployment and relative wages in a global economy', *European Economic Review*, vol 42, pp 1613-33.

Department of Employment (1998) *New earnings survey*, London: The Stationery Office.

Department of Employment (1999) *New earnings survey*, London: The Stationery Office.

Dewatripont, M., Sapir, A. and Sekkat, K. (1999) *Trade and jobs in Europe*, Oxford: Oxford University Press.

Dixit, A.K. and Norman, V. (1980) *Theory of international trade*, Cambridge: Cambridge University Press.

Epland, J. (1998) 'Endringer i fordelingen av husholdningsinntekt 1986-1996', *Statistics Norway Reports* no 98/17, Oslo: Statistics Norway.

Fortin, N.M. and Lemieux, T. (1997) 'Institutional changes and rising wage inequality: is there a linkage?', *Journal of Economic Perspectives*, vol 11, no 2, pp 75-96.

Friez, A. and Julhès, M. (1998) *Séries longues sur les salaires*, Emploi-Revenus No 136, Paris: INSEE.

Goodman, A. and Webb, S. (1994) *For richer, for poorer*, Institute for Fiscal Studies Commentary No 42.

Hahn, F.H. (1998) 'Reconsidering free trade', in G. Cook (ed) *The economics and politics of international trade, freedom and trade*, vol II, London: Routledge.

Hauser, R. (1996) 'Vergleichende Analyse der Einkommensverteilung und der Einkommensarmut in den alten und neuen Bundesländern von 1990 bis 1995', in I. Becker and R. Hauser (eds) *Einkommensverteilung und Armut in Deutschland von 1962 bis 1995*, EVS-Projekt, Arbeitspapier no 9, Frankfurt: Universität Frankfurt am Main.

Hauser, R. (1999) 'Personelle Primär- und Sekundärverteilung der Einkommen under dem Einfluss sich ärnderer wirtschaftlicher und sozialpolitischer Rahmenbedingungen – eine empirische Analyse auf der Basis der Einkommens- und Verbrauchstichproben 1973-1993', *Allgemeines Statistisches Archiv*, vol 83, pp 88-110.

Hirschman, A.O. (1970) *Exit, voice and loyalty*, Cambridge, MA: Harvard University Press.

Kahn, L.M. (1998) 'Against the wind: bargaining recentralization and wage inequality in Norway 1987-91', *Economic Journal*, vol 108, pp 603-45.

Kanbur, R. (2000) 'Income distribution and development', in A.B. Atkinson and F. Bourguignon (eds) *Handbook of income distribution*, Amsterdam: Elsevier, pp 791-841.

Karoly, L.A. (1994) 'The trend in inequality among families, individuals, and workers in the United States: a twenty-five year perspective', in S. Danziger and P. Gottschalk (eds) *Uneven tides*, New York, NY: Russell Sage Foundation, pp 19-97.

Krugman, P. (1994) 'Past and prospective causes of high unemployment', in *Reducing unemployment: Current issues and policy options*, Kansas City: Federal Reserve Bank of Kansas City, pp 49-80.

Krugman, P. (1995) 'Growing world trade: causes and consequences', *Brookings Papers*, vol 1, pp 327-62.

Kuznets, S. (1955) 'Economic growth and income inequality', *American Economic Review*, vol 45, pp 1-28.

Lester, R.A. (1952) 'A range theory of wage differentials', *Industrial and Labor Relations Review*, vol 5, pp 483-500.

MacLeod, W.B. and Malcomson, J.M. (1998) 'Motivation and markets', *American Economic Review*, vol 88, pp 388-411.

Manning, A. (1994) *Labour markets with company wage policies*, Centre for Economic Performance Discussion Paper no 214, London: London School of Economics and Political Science.

OECD (Organisation for Economic Co-operation and Development)(1996) *Employment outlook*, Paris: OECD.

ONS (Office for National Statistics) (various years) 'The effects of taxes and benefits on household income', *Economic Trends*.

Phelps Brown, E.H. (1977) *The inequality of pay*, Oxford: Oxford University Press.

Piketty, T. (1999) 'Can fiscal redistribution undo skill-biased technical change? Evidence from the French experience', *European Economic Review*, vol 43, pp 839-51.

Reder, M.W. (1962) 'WAGES: structure', *International Encyclopaedia of the Social Sciences*, vol 16, New York: Macmillan, pp 403-14.

Rosen, S. (1981) 'The economics of superstars', *American Economic Review*, vol 71, pp 845-58.

Rowthorn, R.E. (1992) 'Corporatism and labour market performance', in J. Pekkarinen, M. Pohjola and R.E. Rowthorn (eds) *Social corporatism: A superior economic system?*, Oxford: Clarendon Press.

Sattinger, M. (1993) 'Assignment models of the distribution of earnings', *Journal of Economic Literature*, vol 31, pp 831-80.

Schelling, T.C. (1978) *Micromotives and macrobehavior*, New York, NY: Norton.

Schlicht, E. (1998) *On custom in the economy*, Oxford: Clarendon Press.

Shields, C. (1991) *Happenstance*, London: Fourth Estate.

Smeeding, T. (1999) 'Income inequality: is Canada different or just behind the times', Invited Plenary Lecture presented to the Canadian Economic Association, Toronto, 30 May.

Statistics Canada (1996) *Income after tax: Distributions by size in Canada, 1994*, Ottawa: Statistics Canada.

Statistics Canada (1999) *Income after tax: Distributions by size in Canada, 1997*, Ottawa: Statistics Canada.

Statistics Finland (1999) *Income distribution statistics, 1997*, Helsinki: Statistics Finland.

Statistics New Zealand (1999) *Incomes*, Wellington: Statistics New Zealand.

Stewart, F. and Berry, A. (1999) 'Globalization, liberalization, and inequality: expectations and experience', in A. Hurrell and N. Woods (eds) *Inequality, globalization, and world politics*, Oxford: Oxford University Press, pp 150-86.

Strøm, B. (1995) 'Envy, fairness and political influence in local government wage determination: evidence from Norway', *Economica*, vol 62, pp 389-409.

Summers, L. (1999) 'Equity in a global economy' in V. Tanzi, K. Chu and S. Gupta (eds) *Economic policy and equity*, Washington, DC: IMF, pp 99-105.

Tinbergen, J. (1975) *Income distribution*, Amsterdam: North-Holland.

US Department of Commerce (1999) *Money income in the United States: 1998*, Washington, DC: US Government Printing Office.

Uusitalo, H. (1998) *Changes in income distribution during a deep recession and after,* Helsinki: STAKES.

Wood, A. (1994) *North–South trade, employment and inequality,* Oxford: Clarendon Press.

THREE

The international measurement of poverty and anti-poverty policies

David Gordon

Introduction

This chapter will describe briefly how international social policy and academic research on poverty has been changing in the past decade and, in particular, how a widening chasm is developing between the anti-poverty policies being advocated by UN agencies and those of the EU. These latter evolving anti-poverty policies have a number of profound implications for the measurement of poverty by international organisations and national statistical offices (NSOs). Without good comparable measures of poverty, it will be impossible to determine if anti-poverty policies are working effectively and efficiently.

International anti-poverty policies

It has long been a dream of humanity to remove poverty from the face of the earth. There have been many fine words and failed attempts to achieve this in the past. However, there is now a strong desire among most of the world's governments to end poverty during the 21st century and a growing international momentum to take concrete action to eradicate poverty on a global scale. If this result is achieved (even partially) then it will have a number of dramatic effects including a significant improvement in the health of the people of the world (WHO, 1995, 1998).

Although there is now widespread agreement on the need to end poverty, there remains considerable international disagreement on the best way this can be achieved. In particular, there is a growing divide between the policies being pursued by the US and the Bretton Woods institutions (such as the World Bank and International Monetary Fund [IMF]) and the EU.

For 40 years, the World Bank, the IMF and other UN agencies have been pursuing what is, basically, the same set of anti-poverty policies (Townsend and Gordon, 2000). These have three elements:

- broad-based economic growth;
- development of human capital, primarily through education;
- minimum social safety nets for the poor.

These policies have been unsuccessful. The number of poor people in the world has continued to increase and, in particular, these same policies have resulted in terrible consequences in many parts of Sub-Saharan Africa, South America and in the countries of the former Soviet Union. In part, they have failed due to a rigid adherence to neo-liberal economic orthodoxy. Joseph Stiglitz – who was chief economist at the World Bank and who has just won the Nobel Prize for Economics for his work on the analyses of markets with asymmetric information – described this orthodoxy as having four stages (Stiglitz, 1998, 2000):

- *privatisation:* this tends to raise prices for the poor;
- *capital market liberalisation:* this allows speculators to destabilise countries' economies, as has happened in Asia and South America;
- *market-based pricing:* this raises the costs of basic foods and fuel for the poor and has often caused rioting, particularly in South America (for example, Bolivia, Ecuador and, more recently, Argentina). Economists should not be provoking riots around the world;
- *free trade:* this is governed by World Trade Organisation (WTO) rules that often severely disadvantage poorer countries. See for example, the Social Watch NGO in Uruguay (www.socialwatch.org) or Oxfam in the UK (www.oxfam.org.uk/wto) and Watkins and Fowler (2002). Despite the advantages of free trade, history has shown that it has often resulted in severe famines and increased poverty (UNDP, 1999; Davis, 2001).

European Union anti-poverty policies

Emerging EU policies on a 'social' Europe are very different to those outlined above. They are based on ideas of social inclusion and social quality. Inter-governmental agreements at Lisbon, Nice and Amsterdam have rejected a 'race to the bottom' for labour conditions and established anti-poverty policy based on:

- active labour market intervention to help create jobs and improve working conditions;
- progressive taxation and redistribution through a comprehensive welfare state.

The 1990s witnessed increasing concern about the high levels of unemployment and poverty in Europe. Widespread unemployment was problematic because European welfare states were founded on the assumption of full employment. They still require high levels of employment to function adequately and also to maintain economic growth in Europe. The EU responded to this challenge by shifting its focus from being virtually exclusively concerned with economic policies (for example, promoting the free movement of commodities, labour, services and capital) towards a more integrated approach of both social and economic policy, particularly in the sphere of employment policy.

In 1992, the governments of OECD countries gave that organisation a mandate to analyse the causes and consequences of high and persistent unemployment and to propose effective solutions (Hvinden et al, 2001). The OECD recommended an urgent shift from passive to active labour market policies (Martin, 1998). These recommendations were rapidly incorporated into EU policy and the *1999 employment guidelines* require member states to increase the percentage of people benefiting from active labour market measures to at least 20% of the unemployed (EC, 1998). Active policies comprise practical efforts to assist people to find paid employment if they are unemployed and to remain in paid employment where they are already working. However, the emphasis of EU labour market policy is on the creation of high quality jobs and not on just 'forcing' people into jobs at any cost, rejecting the 'race to the bottom' in working conditions favoured by some neo-liberal economic commentators. Put simply, high productivity requires good employment relations and good employment relations are dependent on high quality work conditions. EU policy on a social Europe firmly establishes links between economic and social policy and, in particular, between employment and social security policy.

EU member states' policies do not just cover improved education and training for the workforce (social capital interventions) but also such strategies as minimum wages, minimum income guarantees to 'make work pay' and government-backed job creation schemes. European research into social inclusion measures (Gordon and Townsend, 2000) has shown that effective and efficient international anti-poverty policies would ideally include:

- an employment creation programme, designed deliberately to introduce labour-intensive projects to counterbalance patterns of job-cutting in many countries that are often indiscriminate in their social effects. Working conditions of the low paid would also be internationally regulated;
- regeneration or creation of collective, or 'universal' social insurance and public social services – the 'basic needs services' – by introducing internationally sanctioned minimum wages and levels of benefit;
- the introduction of greater accountability and social and democratic control over transnational corporations and international agencies. Growing concern in the 1990s about the 'democratic deficit' invited collaborative international action on a regional – if not wider – basis.

Europe has over 100 years of social policy experience, and this has resulted in a widespread consensus that comprehensive welfare states are the most cost-effective and efficient mechanisms for combating poverty. In the EU, almost everyone pays into the welfare state and everyone gets something back. In 1996, nearly three quarters of EU households, on average, received direct cash payments from the welfare state each month (or week) through state pensions, child support and other benefits (Gordon and Townsend, 2000; Marlier and Cohen-Solal, 2000). On average, EU member states spend 28% of their GDP on social protection benefits (Clotuche, 2001). Their comprehensive welfare states not only provide effective and efficient mechanisms for alleviating poverty, they also protect and improve the welfare of all Europeans. They all redistribute income from 'rich' to 'poor' and from men to women. However, they also equalise income distribution across an individual's lifespan by taxing and reducing income levels in middle age balanced with then paying social benefits to increase income during childhood and old age.

There is considerable debate within Europe on which is the best kind of comprehensive welfare state. Esping-Andersen, for example, uses the principle of the 'commodification' of welfare to identify those countries that characterise a liberal welfare state, a conservative-corporatist welfare state and a social democratic welfare state and argues that social democratic welfare states are the most desirable (Esping-Andersen, 1990, 1996; Goodin et al, 1999). Many European countries (Ireland, for example) do not fit easily into this classification scheme. Nevertheless, it is self evident that – all things being equal – the more comprehensive the redistribution via the welfare state, the lower the rates of poverty will be and international comparative analyses of income poverty lines have clearly demonstrated this fact. Figure 3.1 shows a recent OECD analysis of income poverty (50% median income) in industrialised countries in the mid-1990s.

Figure 3.1: OECD analysis of income poverty rates in the 1990s, pre- and post-transfers

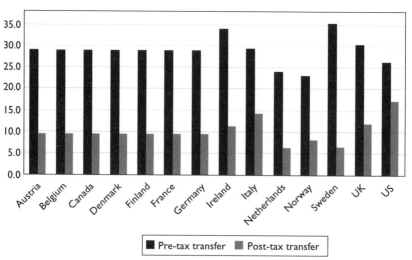

Countries like Sweden, France, Belgium, the UK and Ireland all have much higher rates of low income/poverty than the US – before allowing for taxes and transfers. However, the more comprehensive welfare states in these European countries result in much lower poverty rates than the US after redistribution of national income by taxes and transfers (Förster and Pellizzari, 2000). Similar results have also been reported using other low-income thresholds (Förster, 1994) and by UNICEF researchers with respect to child poverty rates in rich countries (UNICEF, 2000).

There is unanimity within the EU that comprehensive social security provision is a fundamental human right. Article 12 of the revised European Social Charter (Council of Europe, 1996) guarantees the right to social security for "all workers and their dependents". No country can join the EU without having signed and ratified the European Code of Social Security which sets standards for health and welfare benefits and pensions "at a higher level than the minimum standards embodied in International Labour Convention No. 102 concerning Minimum Standards of Social Security". This International Labour Organisation convention)ILO, 1952) provides for minimum standards in nine distinct branches of social security (medical care, sickness, unemployment, old age, employment injury, family, maternity, invalidity, and survivors' benefits) and has been ratified by 40 countries.

Many European social scientists (and policy makers) believe that the World Bank and IMF would have had much greater success at reducing poverty if they had required that countries seeking aid complied with the ILO's convention on Minimum Standards of Social Security rather than pursuing the neo-liberal 'Washington consensus' policies described above. EU countries have flatly rejected the World Bank's ideas about minimum social safety nets for the poor being the best way to combat poverty.

At the Nice Summit (EC, 2001a) in December 2000, EU countries agreed to produce and implement a two-year (July 2001–June 2003) National Action Plan on Social Inclusion (NAPincl) designed to promote social inclusion and combat poverty and social exclusion (see EC, 2001b). These detailed plans are a key component of the member states' commitment to make a decisive impact on the eradication of poverty and social exclusion in Europe by 2010. The EU's aim is to be the most dynamic knowledge-based economy in the world, with full employment and increased levels of social cohesion by 2010. The accurate measurement of poverty and social exclusion is an integral component of this strategy and the recent Laeken European Council concluded that:

> ... the establishment of a set of common indicators constitute important elements in the policy defined at Lisbon for eradicating poverty and promoting social inclusion, taking in health and housing. The European Council stresses the need to reinforce the statistical machinery and calls on the Commission gradually to involve the candidate countries in this process. (EC, 2001c, s 28)

In Europe, during 2001, considerable scientific efforts were made to improve the measurement of poverty and social exclusion (Atkinson et al, 2002[1]) and the proposed new set of statistics and indicators will be a major improvement on previous EU analyses (Eurostat, 1990, 1998, 2000; Hagenaars et al, 1994; Atkinson, 2000; Mejer and Linden, 2000; Mejer and Siermann, 2000).

Implications for poverty measurement

There are a number of serious implications for internationally comparative measures of poverty. Over the past 30 years, there have been a number of international agreements which have clearly defined poverty. In 1975, the Council of Europe defined those in poverty as:

> ... individuals or families whose resources are so small as to exclude them from a minimum acceptable way of life in the Member State in which they live. (EEC, 1981)

The concept of 'resources' was further defined as "goods, cash income, plus services from other private resources".

In 1984, the EC extended the definition as:

> ... the poor shall be taken to mean persons, families and groups of persons whose resources (material, cultural and social) are so limited as to exclude them from the minimum acceptable way of life in the Member State in which they live. (EEC, 1981)

These are *relative* definitions of poverty in that they all refer to poverty not as some 'absolute basket of goods' but in terms of the minimum acceptable standard of living applicable to a certain member state and within a person's own society.

There is now widespread agreement on the scientific definition of poverty as both low income and low standard of living (Gordon and Pantazis, 1997; Gordon et al, 2000). These ideas were enshrined in both the EU's definition of poverty and also in the two definitions of poverty adopted by 117 governments at the World Summit on Social Development in 1995.

These EU definitions are similar to the relative poverty definition devised by Peter Townsend (Townsend, 1979). However, they differ quite substantially from the definitions of poverty that were being used when the welfare state was first established in the UK and other EU countries. In the UK, Beveridge adopted the concept of 'subsistence' which was based on the minimum standards to maintain physical efficiency and was developed from the work of the pioneers of poverty research such as Rowntree. A minimum basket of goods was costed, for emergency use over a short period of time, with 6% extra added for inefficiencies in spending patterns, in order to draw up the welfare assistance rates (National Assistance rates). This was designed to be an emergency level of income and never meant to keep a person out of poverty for any length of time, however, these rates became enshrined into the Social Security legislation.

The current relative poverty definitions used in the EU deliver a much higher poverty line. They are also concerned with participation and membership within a society.

Absolute and overall poverty

There has been much debate about 'absolute' and 'relative' definitions of poverty and the difficulties involved in comparing poverty in industrialised countries with that in the developing world. However, these debates were resolved in 1995 at the UN World Summit on Social Development at which the governments of 117 countries – including all EU governments – agreed on two definitions of poverty – *absolute* and *overall* poverty. They adopted a declaration and programme of action which included commitments to eradicate absolute poverty by 2015 and also reduce overall poverty, by at least half, by the same year (UNDP, 1995).

Absolute poverty was defined by the UN as:

> ... a condition characterised by severe deprivation of basic human needs, including food, safe drinking water, sanitation facilities, health, shelter, education and information. It depends not only on income but also on access to services.

Overall poverty was considered to take various forms, including:

> ... lack of income and productive resources to ensure sustainable livelihoods; hunger and malnutrition; ill health; limited or lack of access to education and other basic services; increased morbidity and mortality from illness; homelessness and inadequate housing; unsafe environments and social discrimination and exclusion. It is also characterised by lack of participation in decision-making and in civil, social and cultural life. It occurs in all countries: as mass poverty in many developing countries, pockets of poverty amid wealth in developed countries, loss of livelihoods as a result of economic recession, sudden poverty as a result of disaster or conflict, the poverty of low-wage workers, and the utter destitution of people who fall outside family support systems, social institutions and safety nets.

The Copenhagen agreements and the EU definitions of poverty are both accepted by all EU countries.

Income is important but access to public goods – safe water supply, roads, healthcare, education – is of equal or greater importance, particularly in developing countries. These are the views of the governments of the world and poverty measurement clearly needs to respond to them.

The need to measure precisely the extent of global poverty is becoming increasingly urgent. At the United Nations Millennium Summit (UN, 2000), an unprecedented 191 countries committed themselves to halving poverty by the year 2015 and to meeting related development targets as described in the Millennium Declaration (see Johnston, 2001). Valid, reliable and comparable measures of poverty are needed in order to monitor the efficiency and effectiveness of anti-poverty policies.

The measurement of poverty by international agencies

There are currently three UN agencies which produce worldwide measurements of poverty[2] – the International Fund for Agricultural Development (IFAD) – which uses administrative statistics on health, education, income and food security; the UN Development Programme (UNDP) – which uses five indicators from administrative statistics on health, education and water supply; and the World Bank – which uses microdata from social surveys to calculate its $1 per day poverty line. This income poverty line is not applied universally and varies from region to region, for example, $2 per day in Latin America and $4 per day in former Soviet states. It is very unclear what standard of living people have who live below these income thresholds in different countries (Gordon and Spicker, 1999). These methods are described in more detail below.

International Fund for Agricultural Development

The IFAD is one of the world's foremost authorities on rural poverty and it has constructed four poverty indices which are designed to measure rural poverty and deprivation (Jazairy et al, 1995):

- The Food Security Index (FSI) attempts to measure the composite food security situation of a country. This index combines relevant food production and consumption variables, including those reflecting growth and variability. The index can take values of zero and above, with 1 being a cut-off point between countries which are relatively food secure and those which are not.
- The Integrated Poverty Index (IPI) is an economic index which is calculated by combining the headcount measure of poverty with the income-gap ratio, income distribution below the poverty line and the annual rate of growth of per capita GNP. According to the IFAD, the headcount index represents the percentage of the rural population below the poverty line. The income-gap ratio is a national measure, the difference between the highest GNP per capita from among the 114 developing countries and the individual country GNP per capita expressed as a percentage of the former. Life expectancy at birth is used as a surrogate measure of income distribution below the poverty line. The IPI follows Amartya Sen's composite poverty index (Sen, 1976) and can take values between zero and 1 with values closer to 1 indicating a relatively worse poverty status.

- The Basic Needs Index (BNI) is designed to measure the social development of rural areas and is composed of an education index and a health index. The education index covers adult literacy and primary school enrolment while the health index includes population per physician, infant mortality rate and access to services such as health, safe water and sanitation. The BNI can take values between zero and 1. The closer the value is to 1, the higher the basic needs status of the population of a country.
- The Relative Welfare Index (RWI) is the arithmetic average of the other three indices (FSI, RWI, BNI). With the FSI normalised to take values between zero and 1, the RWI takes values within the same range.

The IFAD also produces the Women's Status Index (WSI) which is designed to measure the situation of women in order to derive concrete policy recommendations to help improve the status of poor rural women in developing countries.

Having said this, the most recent IFAD (2001) report on rural poverty makes extensive use of the World Bank's $1 per day poverty measure, broken down by area type (for example, urban and rural).

United Nations Development Program

The UNDP has produced a large number of different indices that are designed to measure poverty, inequality and other developmental issues. Since 1990, these have been published in its annual Human Development Reports. The 1997 *Human Development Report* was entirely devoted to poverty as part of the United Nations International Year for the Eradication of Poverty.

The UNDP's concept of poverty is incorporated within the broader concept of human development, which is defined as (UNDP, 1995):

> Human development is a process of enlarging people's choices. In principle, these choices can be infinite and can change overtime. But at all levels of development, the three essential ones are for people to lead a long and healthy life, to acquire knowledge and to have access to the resources needed for a decent standard of living. If these essential choices are not available, many other opportunities remain inaccessible.

> But human development does not end there. Additional choices, highly valued by many people, range from political, economic and social freedom to opportunities for being creative and productive and enjoying personal self-respect and guaranteed human rights.

> Human development thus has two sides. One is the formation of human capabilities – such as improved health, knowledge and skills. The other is the use people make of their acquired capabilities – for productive purposes, for leisure or for being active in cultural, social and political affairs. If the scales of

human development do not finely balance the two sides, much human frustration can result.

According to the concept of human development, income clearly is only one option that people would like to have, though certainly an important one. But it is not the sum-total of their lives. The purpose of development is to enlarge *all* human choices, not just income.

The most influential index produced by the UNDP is the Human Development Index (HDI) which was constructed to reflect the most important dimensions of human development. The HDI is a composite index based on three indicators: longevity – as measured by life expectancy at birth; educational attainment – as measured by a combination of adult literacy (two thirds weight) and combined primary, secondary and tertiary enrolment ratios (one third weight); and standard of living – as measured by real GDP per capita (PPP$). However, there have been a number of changes made to the way the HDI is constructed since it was first produced in 1990 (UNDP, 1990, 1996).

The 1997 *Human Development Report* defined poverty within the human development perspective and introduced the term Human Poverty. This drew heavily on Sen's capability concept and defined poverty as "the denial of choices and opportunities for a tolerable life" (UNDP, 1997) . The *human poverty index* (HPI) attempted to operationalise this concept by focusing on those groups whose choices are heavily constrained in each of the three areas used in the HDI. While the HDI focuses on the average achievements of a country, the HPI focuses on the most deprived. The HPI is made up of five weighted components (UNDP, 1997):

- the percentage of people expected to die before 40 years of age;
- the percentage of adults who are illiterate;
- the percentage of people with access to health services;
- the percentage of people with access to safe water;
- the percentage of children under five years of age who are malnourished.

Aspects of human poverty that are excluded from the index due to lack of data or measurement difficulties are – lack of political freedom, inability to participate in decision making, lack of personal security, inability to participate in the life of the community and threats to sustainability and intergenerational equity. Human Poverty Indices (HPI-2) have also recently been calculated at small area level within the UK to compare local pockets of human poverty (Seymour, 2000).

World Bank

The World Bank has produced the most influential measurement of world poverty and devoted its annual reports in both 1990 and 2000 to poverty eradication issues. The World Bank produces a "universal poverty line [which] is needed to permit cross-country comparison and aggregation" (World Bank, 1990, p 27). Poverty is defined as "the inability to attain a minimal standard of living" (World Bank, 1990, p 26). Despite its acknowledgement of the difficulties in including, in any measure of poverty, the contribution to living standards of public goods and common-property resources, the World Bank settles for a standard which is 'consumption-based' and which comprises:

> ... two elements: the expenditure necessary to buy a minimum standard of nutrition and other basic necessities and a further amount that varies from country to country, reflecting the cost of participating in the everyday life of society. (World Bank, 1990, p 26)

The first of these elements is stated to be "relatively straightforward" because it could be calculated by "looking at the prices of the foods that make up the diets of the poor" (World Bank, 1990, pp 26-27). However, the second element is "far more subjective; in some countries indoor plumbing is a luxury, but in others it is a 'necessity'" (World Bank, 1990, p 27). For operational purposes, the second element was set aside and the first assessed as Purchasing Power Parity (PPP) – $370 per person per year at 1985 prices for all the poorest developing countries. Those with incomes per capita of less than $370 were deemed 'poor' while those with less than $275 per year were 'extremely poor'. This approximate $1 of consumption per person per day poverty line was chosen from a World Bank study of minimum income thresholds used in 8 of the 33 'poorest' countries to assess eligibility for welfare provision (Ravallion et al, 1991)[3].

The *World Development Report on poverty* in 2000 used a similar methodology to revise the poverty line estimate as $1.08 per person per day at 1993 Purchasing Power Parity (Chen and Ravallion, 2000). However, the poverty threshold is now set at the median value of the ten poorest countries with the lowest poverty lines; that is, world poverty rates are set at the level of the country with the fifth lowest welfare benefit eligibility threshold. No explanation has yet been provided for this change.

Equivalent consumption expenditures of $1.08 are calculated for each country using PPP conversions, which are primarily designed for comparing aggregates of national accounts[4] not the consumption of poor people. It is very unclear what the World Bank's poverty line means or even if the new $1.08 at 1993 PPP poverty line is higher or lower than the old $1 a day poverty line at 1985 PPP because the 1985 and 1993 PPP tables are not directly comparable (Reddy and Pogge, 2002).

No allowance was made by the World Bank in either 1990 or 2000 for the second 'participatory' element of its poverty definition. The logic of the Bank's own argument is not followed, the minimum value of the poverty line is underestimated and the number of poor in the World are therefore also underestimated[5].

Table 3.1: Number and percentage of the population living on incomes below half the average in 14 European countries (1994)

Country	Number of people below half average income	% of the population below half average income
UK	11,426,766	20
Germany	11,327,673	14
Italy	9,321,853	17
France	7,949,907	14
Spain	7,196,406	19
Portugal	2,424,533	25
Greece	2,041,923	20
Belgium	1,474,158	15
Netherlands	1,275,048	8
Austria	1,108,082	14
Ireland	837,490	23
Denmark	386,015	7
Finland	192,153	4
Luxembourg	56,734	14

Poverty measurement in the European Union

Although poverty has been clearly defined in Europe as an unacceptably low standard of living caused by low income, the measurement of poverty within Europe has almost exclusively concentrated on measuring only low incomes. The major comparative studies by the European Community Statistical Office (EUROSTAT) have been based on either the European Community Household Panel (ECHP) survey or harmonised national household budget surveys. A range of arbitrary low income thresholds have been used as proxies for poverty, for example, half average expenditure, half average income, less than 60% of median income, less than 50% of median income, and so on.

Table 3.1 shows a recent comparative poverty analysis by EUROSTAT, using the 1994 ECHP data.

These data show that the UK *does* lead Europe in one area – its number of poor households. Despite the fact that Germany has a much bigger population, the UK has more people living on a low income. According to the EU, the total number is nearly 11.5 million and this gives some kind of idea of the scale of the problem the UK government faces if it wants to eliminate poverty *using these definitions*.

However, a look at the comparative circumstances of children shows that the situation is actually far worse. Using the same European data – but for a previous year (1993) – the UK by far and away has the highest percentage of children living in poverty of any EU member state.

By contrast, Finland has the smallest number of households living in poverty of any EU member state, except Luxembourg. Finland also has the lowest poverty rate in Europe, with only 4% of the population living on a low income.

Figure 3.2: UNICEF Child Poverty League Table (% of children living in households with income below 50% of the national median)

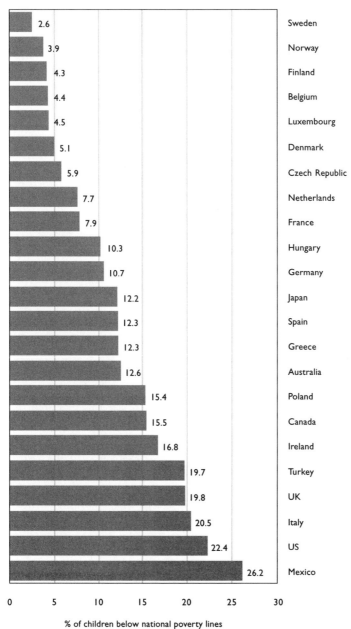

Country	%
Sweden	2.6
Norway	3.9
Finland	4.3
Belgium	4.4
Luxembourg	4.5
Denmark	5.1
Czech Republic	5.9
Netherlands	7.7
France	7.9
Hungary	10.3
Germany	10.7
Japan	12.2
Spain	12.3
Greece	12.3
Australia	12.6
Poland	15.4
Canada	15.5
Ireland	16.8
Turkey	19.7
UK	19.8
Italy	20.5
US	22.4
Mexico	26.2

% of children below national poverty lines

A recent analysis of OECD countries by the UN Children's Organisation (UNICEF) shows that, in a ranking of all the industrialised countries, the UK now ranks below Turkey and just above Mexico and the US in having a higher rate of child poverty (UNICEF, 2000). There are not many social indicators where the UK ranks below Turkey and so this is quite shocking. The UK's position is due to a tripling of poverty or low income in the 1980s as a direct result of neo-liberal socio-economic policies (Thatcherism) pursued by successive Conservative governments. Figure 3.2 shows these UNICEF results on the extent of child poverty in rich countries.

Despite the different definitions of low income poverty used by UNICEF and the EU, a consistent pattern emerges from these analyses. Countries with comprehensive welfare states and social-democratic traditions (such as Finland) usually have low rates of poverty, whereas countries which have in the recent past followed neo-liberal economic policies (such as the UK and US) have very high poverty rates.

Producing meaningful and internationally comparable poverty statistics

The major problem with all the poverty measures produced by IFAD, UNDP, the World Bank and EUROSTAT is that they are of little value for measuring poverty *within* a country or for helping developing or industrialised countries to assess the effectiveness of their own anti-poverty policies. Nor do they correspond to any internationally (or even nationally) agreed definitions of poverty.

The main problem with the World Bank's $1 a day poverty lines is that they are essentially meaningless. It is impossible to tell from the World Bank poverty line whether or not a household with an income below this threshold has sufficient money to live decently or not. It would be much more meaningful to produce low income statistics which show how many households do not have an adequate income to allow them to meet their basic needs (*absolute poverty*) and/or participate in the economic, social, cultural and political life of the country in which they live (*overall poverty*). Low income thresholds and statistics should measure adequacy not arbitrary thresholds and the most widely used method of achieving this goal is to use a 'budget standards' approach.

A budget standard is a specified basket of goods and services which, when priced, can represent a particular standard of living. Budgets can be devised to represent any living standard (Bradshaw, 1993) and, for example, national statistical offices could produce budget standards which corresponded with the *absolute* and *overall* poverty definitions agreed at the World Social Summit (discussed earlier in this chapter). This would produce income poverty thresholds which are both nationally and internationally meaningful.

Budget standards are probably the oldest scientific method of exploring low living standards. Pioneered by Rowntree (1901) in the UK, in his famous studies of poverty in York, they have since been used in many countries to measure income poverty, for example, in the USA, at both national and state level (Orshansky, 1965; Watts, 1980; NYCC, 1982; Renwick, 1993; Citro and Michael, 1995); Canada (Social Planning Council, 1981); the Netherlands (Hagenaars and de Vos, 1988); New Zealand (Stephens, 1995); Hong Kong (MacPherson, 1994); the UK (Piachaud, 1979; Bradshaw, 1993; Parker, 1998, 2000); and in Australia (Saunders, 1998).

Indeed, Mark Malloch Brown, the UN Development Program (UNDP) administrator, recently argued that: "We need a global Rowntree.... A clearer benchmarking of poverty and of its contributing elements, such as child education and healthcare, could provide the political space and focus for action at the community, national and global levels" (Malloch Brown, 2001).

While budget standards-derived income poverty thresholds, using internationally agreed definitions of poverty, would produce meaningful and comparable income poverty statistics for individuals and households, additional (direct) measures of deprivation (low standard of living) are also needed for international poverty comparisons and anti-poverty policy monitoring. This is because poverty is not only dependent on personal/household income but also on the availability of public goods, for example, clean water supplies, hospitals, schools, and so on. One example of how this could be achieved is discussed below.

International measurement of standard of living (deprivation)

During the 1990s, advances in social survey methodology in developing countries have made available a wealth of new data, some of which can be used to measure low standard of living and deprivation. This section outlines some recent work that has been carried out in the UK by the Townsend Centre for International Poverty Research, on behalf of UNICEF, which attempts to operationalise the absolute definition of poverty agreed at the World Summit on Social Development to measure child poverty in the developing world.

There are currently no consistent estimates of the extent or severity of child poverty in developing countries. While many countries do have detailed anti-poverty strategies and statistics on child poverty, these estimates tend to use different methods and definitions of poverty which makes comparison extremely difficult.

The World Bank's method of measuring poverty by low per capita consumption expenditure is singularly unsuitable for measuring child poverty and does not conform with the internationally agreed definitions of poverty adopted at the World Social Summit. For example, the definition of absolute poverty implies that a child is poor if she suffers from severe educational deprivation. In accordance with a number of UN resolutions, this could be operationalised as her lack of receipt of primary education (Gordon et al, 2001). There might be a number of reasons why a child does not receive primary education and low family income is often a very important factor.

However, a lack of government investment in schools and infrastructure can also prevent children from being educated as can prejudice and discriminatory attitudes that consider that certain children are not 'worth' educating. Whichever of these reasons is true, either singularly or in combination, the end result will be the same in that the child will suffer from severe educational deprivation.

Therefore, there is a need to look beyond the World Bank's narrow focus on per capita consumption expenditure and at both the effects of low family income *and* the effects of inadequate service provision for children (Vandemoortele, 2000), as it is a lack of investment in good quality education, health and other public services in many parts of the world that is as significant a cause of child poverty as low family incomes. Nobel Laureate, Amartya Sen, has argued that, in developing countries, poverty is best measured directly using indicators of standard of living rather than indirectly using income or consumption measures.

> In an obvious sense the direct method is superior to the income method ... it could be argued that only in the absence of direct information regarding the satisfaction of the specified needs can there be a case for bringing in the intermediary of income, so that the income method is at most a second best. (Sen, 1981, p 26)

Such direct measures of need or low standard of living are often referred to as *deprivation* measures. Deprivation can be conceptualised as a continuum which ranges from no deprivation, through mild, moderate and severe deprivation to extreme deprivation at the end of the scale. Figure 3.3 illustrates this concept.

In order to measure absolute poverty among children using the World Social Summit definition, it is necessary to define the threshold measures of severe deprivation of basic human need for:

- food;
- safe drinking water;
- sanitation facilities;
- health;
- shelter;
- education;
- information;
- access to services.

Figure 3.3: Continuum of deprivation

Figure 3.4: Distribution of Demographic and Health Surveys

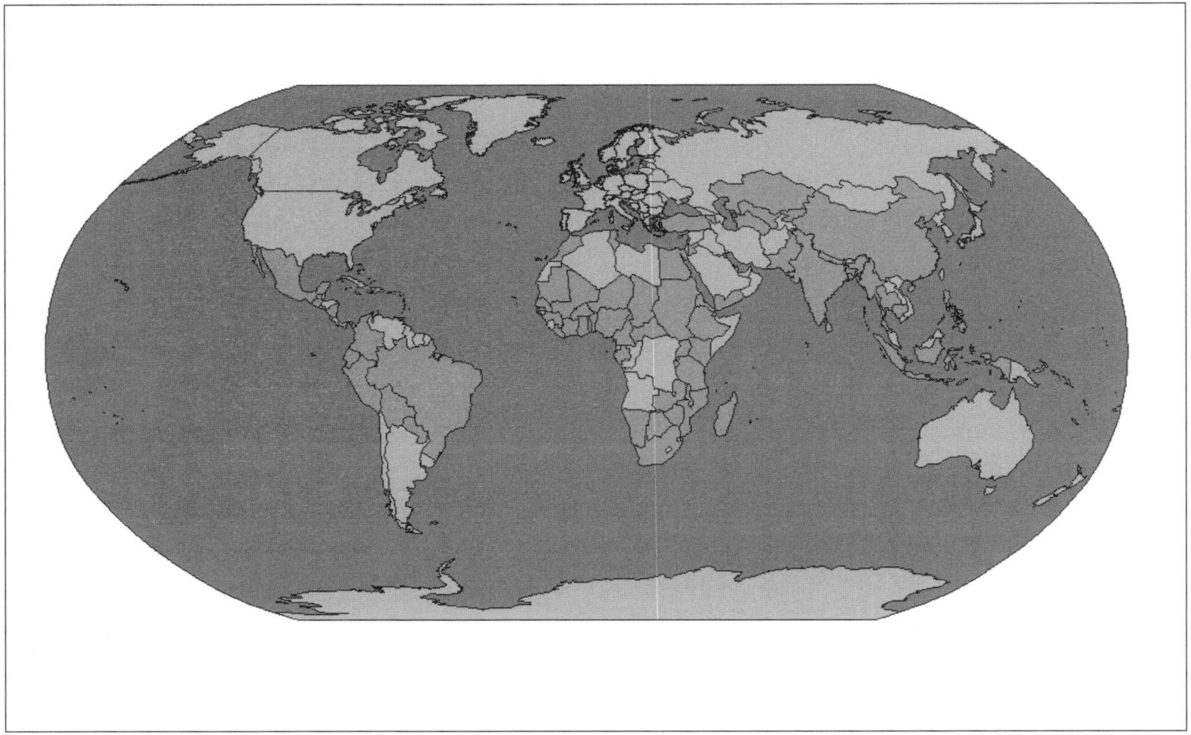

Note: Chinese data is from the China Health and Nutrition Survey (www.cpc.unc.edu/projects/china/)

Table 3.2: Operational definitions of deprivation for children

Deprivation	Mild	Moderate	Severe	Extreme
Food	Bland diet of poor nutritional value	Going hungry on occasion	Malnutrition	Starvation
Safe drinking water	Not having enough water on occasion due to lack of sufficient money	No access to water in dwelling but communal piped water available within 200 meters of dwelling or less than 15 minutes walk away	Long walk to water source (more than 200 meters or longer than 15 minutes). Unsafe drinking water (for example, open water)	No access to water
Sanitation facilities	Having to share facilities with another household	Sanitation facilities outside dwelling	No sanitation facilities in or near dwelling	No access to sanitation facilities
Health	Occasional lack of access to medical care due to insufficient money	Inadequate medical care	No immunisation against diseases. Only limited non-professional medical care available when sick	No medical care
Shelter	Dwelling in poor repair. More than one person per room	Few facilities in dwelling, lack of heating, structural problems. More than three persons per room	No facilities in house, non-permanent structure, no privacy, no flooring, just one or two rooms. More than five persons per room	Roofless – no shelter
Education	Inadequate teaching due to lack of resources	Unable to attend secondary but can attend primary education	Child is seven years of age or older and has received no primary or secondary education	Prevented from learning due to persecution and prejudice
Information	Cannot afford newspapers or books	No television but can afford a radio	No access to radio, television or books or newspapers government, and so on	Prevented from gaining access to information by
Basic social services	Health and education facilities available but occasionally of low standard	Inadequate health and education facilities nearby (for example, less than one hour travel)	Limited health and education facilities more than one hour travel away	No access to health or education facilities

Comparable information on severe deprivation of basic human need among children is available from high quality microdata from the Demographic and Health Surveys (DHS)[11] carried out in 68 countries during the 1990s. The DHS are nationally representative household surveys with sample sizes of about 5,000 households and an estimated cost of $200 per household (Loup and Naudet, 2000). A major advantage of the DHS is their random cluster sampling methodology. On average, 3,000 to 9,000 women of childbearing age were interviewed in each country (average 5,400) and each survey contains between 150-300 clusters, with an average of 200 clusters. Cluster size is around 2-3 km or smaller in urban areas (Gerland, 1996). Figure 3.4 demonstrates the wide coverage of the DHS.

Table 3.2 shows the operational definitions of deprivation for the eight criteria in the World Summit definition of absolute poverty that have been used for the UNICEF study of child poverty using DHS microdata.

Children who suffer from *severe deprivation of basic human need* – as shown in the fourth column of Table 3.2 – are living in absolute poverty as defined at the World Social Summit, that is, "Absolute poverty is a condition characterised by severe deprivation of basic human needs, including food, safe drinking water, sanitation facilities, health, shelter, education and information. It depends not only on income but also on access to social services" (UNDP, 1997).

Cost of ending poverty

The EUROSTAT analysis of poverty (Table 3.1) indicates that almost sixty million people in the EU are 'poor' (have an income of less than half the average). Poverty analyses by the World Bank (2001) have demonstrated that over one billion people in developing countries have to live on the equivalent of less than $1 per day. These are huge numbers of people so a major question remains – is the world's desire to end poverty in the 21st century realistic and affordable?

The costs of ending poverty are much less than the large numbers of poor people would indicate. Table 3.3 overleaf shows how much of the income of the non-poor population would have to be transferred (given) to the poor people in each EU country to eliminate poverty using a 50% and 60% of the median income poverty line in each country (Fouarge, 2001).

In the UK, 1.5% of the income of non-poor households would have to be transferred to poor households in order to raise every person's income above the 50% median income poverty threshold. Similarly, in the UK, 3.0% of income would need to be transferred to poor people to raise their incomes above the 60% median income poverty threshold. The corresponding figures for ending income poverty in Finland are 1% and 1.8% respectively, and, for the EU as a whole, 1.7% and 3%. The cost of ending income poverty in the EU is therefore not unfeasibly large.

UNICEF has carried out a similar analysis on the costs of eradicating *child* poverty in 'rich' countries. Table 3.4 shows how much national income

Table 3.3: Cost of ending poverty in the EU: % of income needed to be transferred from the non-poor to the poor in each country

Country	Cost of ending poverty (50% on median income poverty line)	Cost of ending poverty (60% on median income poverty line)
Luxembourg	0.8	1.5
Denmark	0.8	1.7
Austria	1.0	1.8
Finland	1.0	1.8
France	1.1	2.2
Ireland	1.1	2.2
Belgium	1.5	2.8
Netherlands	2.0	3.0
UK	1.5	3.0
Spain	1.8	3.1
Germany	2.2	3.3
Italy	2.2	3.6
Portugal	2.3	3.8
Greece	2.3	3.9
EU	1.7	3.0

(percentage of GNP) would be needed to close the child poverty gap in 17 OECD countries.

The table shows that relatively little national income needs to be transferred to poor families to eliminate child income poverty – using UNICEF's definition of income poverty (less than 50% of the national median income). In Finland, less than 1% of GNP would need to be spent on helping poor families with children and, even in the UK, which has very high rates of child poverty, less than 0.5% of GNP is needed.

The reason why so much poverty can be ended at comparatively little cost is that welfare states are reasonably good at preventing people from falling into very deep poverty. Most poor households have incomes which are relatively close to the income poverty thresholds that are used in these kinds of analyses. Therefore, relatively small transfers of income will raise a large number of people above these income poverty thresholds.

Lack of good income information has meant that detailed costs of ending poverty analyses, that are available for rich countries, are not available for developing countries. However, the UNDP has estimated (UNDP, 1997) the annual cost over ten years of providing every person in the world with basic social services (Table 3.5).

The UNDP estimated that the additional cost of achieving basic social services for all in developing countries at about $40 billion a year over ten years (1995–2005). This is less than 0.2% of world income and represents about 1% of developing country income. The cost of providing basic health and nutrition

---

Table 3.4: Percentage of GNP required to end child poverty in 17 OECD countries

Country	% of GNP
Sweden	0.07
Finland	0.08
Belgium	0.09
Luxembourg	0.09
Norway	0.12
Denmark	0.12
France	0.14
Hungary	0.24
Germany	0.26
Spain	0.31
Netherlands	0.31
Australia	0.39
Canada	0.46
UK	0.48
Italy	0.50
Poland	0.56
USA	0.66

Source: UNICEF (2000)

for every person in the world was estimated at just $13 billion per year for ten years. This seems a very large figure but, to put it in perspective, in 2000 the US population spent $11.6 billion on dog and cat food (Euromonitor International, 2001). Europe and the US together spend a lot more on pet food than is needed to provide basic health and nutrition for all the world's people.

Ending poverty is largely a matter of lack of political will. It is not a problem of lack of money or scientific knowledge on how to eradicate poverty.

Table 3.5: The cost of achieving universal access to basic social services

Need	Annual cost (US$ billions)
Basic education for all	6
Basic health and nutrition	13
Reproductive health and family planning	12
Low-cost water supply and sanitation	9
Total	40

Conclusions

Poverty is the world's most ruthless killer and the greatest cause of suffering on earth. The 1995 World Health Organisation (WHO) report argued that:

> Poverty is the main reason why babies are not vaccinated, clean water and sanitation are not provided, and curative drugs and other treatments are unavailable and why mothers die in childbirth. Poverty is the main cause of reduced life expectancy, of handicap and disability, and of starvation. Poverty is a major contributor to mental illness, stress, suicide, family disintegration and substance abuse. (WHO, 1995)

Yet the costs of meeting the basic needs of every person in the world are relatively small compared with the vast wealth available. The practical policies and institutional mechanisms needed to end world poverty are well known and widely understood. No scientific breakthroughs are required to provide everybody with a safe water supply, a nutritious diet, adequate housing and basic healthcare. No new knowledge is needed to provide all children with an education. A wide range of comprehensive welfare state models in European countries have been proven to be effective mechanisms for delivering social security and welfare. International agreements are already in place which provide guidance on what the minimum levels of social security benefits should be and the governments of the world have repeatedly made commitments to reduce and eventually end poverty in the 21st century.

The neo-liberal 'Washington Consensus' policies pursued by the World Bank and IMF have failed to even reduce poverty (let alone end poverty) nor are the methods that they (and other international organisations) use to measure poverty adequate. In particular, the World Bank's consumption-based poverty measures ($1.08 per day) are not reliable, valid or particularly meaningful and cannot be used to measure the effectiveness of anti-poverty policies.

New advances in social science *are* needed to produce scientific measurements of poverty which are both internationally comparable and also of use to policy makers within countries – one possible approach has been discussed in this chapter. New research is also needed to identify the best methods of building comprehensive welfare states in countries where currently only residual welfare states exist (see Chapter Seven by van Oorschot).

Notes

[1] See vandenbroucke.fgov.be/Europe%20summary.htm for a summary of the new EU poverty and social exclusion indicators and www.vandenbroucke.fgov.be/T-011017.htm for discussion.

[2] In the past, the Food and Agricultural Organisation (FAO) has also produced estimates of absolute poverty using per capita food expenditure (Engle coefficients): 59% and

over indicated absolute poverty, 50-59% hand to mouth existence, 40-50% a better off life, 30-40% affluence and 30% and below, the richest (Ruizen and Yuan, 1992).

[3] "[A] representative, absolute poverty line for low income countries is $31, which (to the nearest dollar) is shared by six of the countries in our sample, namely Indonesia, Bangladesh, Nepal, Kenya, Tanzania, and Morocco, and two other countries are close to this figure (Philippines and Pakistan)" (Ravallion et al, 1991).

[4] See the OECD FAQ's about PPP at www.oecd.org/oecd/pages/home/displaygeneral/ 0,3380,EN-faq-513-15-no-no-322-513,FF.html.

[5] For a more comprehensive review of the problems with the World Bank's 2000/01 *World Development Report on attacking poverty* see the review by the International Social Science Council's Comparative Research Programme on Poverty (CROP, 2002).

[6] For more information see the Measure *DHS+* website at www.measuredhs.com.

References

Atkinson, T. (2000) 'A European social agenda: poverty benchmarking and social transfers', Unpublished paper (www.nuff.ox.ac.uk/users/atkinson/ CAE2000final.pdf).

Atkinson, T., Cantillon, B., Marlier, E. and Nolan, B. (2002) *Social indicators – the EU and social inclusion*, Oxford: Oxford University Press.

Bradshaw, J. (ed) (1993) *Budget standards for the United Kingdom*, Aldershot: Avebury.

Canberra Group (2001) *The Expert Group on Household Income Statistics: The Canberra Group. final report and recommendations*, Ottawa (lisweb.ceps.lu/links/ canberra/finalreport.pdf).

Chen, S. and Ravallion, M. (2000) *How did the world's poorest fare in the 1990s?*, World Bank Occasional Paper, New York (www.worldbank.org/research/ povmonitor/pdfs/methodology.pdf).

Citro, C.F. and Michael, R.T. (eds) (1995) *Measuring poverty. A new approach*, Washington, DC: National Academy Press.

Clotuche, G. (2001) 'The social protection in the CEEC in the context of the enlargement', *Belgian Review of Social Security*, vol 43, pp 21-8 (socialsecurity.fgov.be/bib/index.htm).

Council of Europe (1996) European Social Charter (revised), conventions.coe.int/Treaty/EN/Treaties/HTML/163.htm

CROP (Comparative Research Programme on Poverty) (2002 'A critical review of the World Bank report: *World Development Report 2000/2007. Attacking poverty*, (www.crop.org/publications/files/report/ Comments_to_WDR2001_2002_ny.pdf).

Davis, M. (2001) *Late Victorian holocausts*, London: Verso.

Drever, F. and Whitehead, M. (eds) (1997) *Health inequalities*, London: The Stationery Office.

EC (European Commission) (1998) *1999 employment guidelines*, Brussels: EC.

EC (2001a) 'Social exclusion: Commission takes first step towards EU poverty strategy', (www.europa.eu.int/comm/employment_social/news/2001/oct/ i01_1395_en.html).

EC (2001b) 'NAPs/incl: National Action Plans on social inclusion', (www.europa.eu.int/comm/employment_social/news/2001/jun/ napsincl2001_en.html).

EC (2001c) 'European Council Laeken: Conclusions of the presidency', (www.europarl.eu.int/summits/pdf/lae_en.pdf).

Esping-Andersen, G. (ed) (1990) *The three worlds of welfare capitalism*, London, Princeton, NJ: Polity Press and Princeton University Press.

Esping-Andersen, G. (ed) (1996) *Welfare states in transition: National adaptations of global economics*, London: Sage Publications.

Euromonitor International (2001) *Pet foods and accessories in the USA 2001*, London (www.majormarketprofiles.com).

Eurostat (1990) *Poverty in figures: Europe in the early 1980s*, Luxembourg: Eurostat.

Eurostat (1998) *Recommendations of the Task Force on Statistics on Social Exclusion and Poverty*, Luxembourg: Eurostat.

Eurostat (2000) *Income, poverty and social exclusion*, Luxembourg: Office for Official Publications of the European Communities.

Fletcher, J. (1849) 'Moral and educational statistics of England and Wales', *Journal of the Royal Statistical Society of London*, vol 12, pp 189-335.

Förster, M.F. (1994) *Measurement of low incomes and poverty in a perspective of international comparisons*, Labour Market and Social Policy Occasional Papers no 14, Paris: OECD (www1.oecd.org/els/health/docs.htm).

Förster, M.F. and Pellizzari, M. (2000) *Trends and driving factors in income distribution and poverty in the OECD area*, Labour Market and Social Policy Occasional Papers no 14, Paris: OECD (www1.oecd.org/els/health/docs.htm).

Fouarge, D. (2001) *Subsidiarity and poverty in the European Union. Fiscal competition or co-ordination?*, Tilburg: Tilburg University (www.sbu.ac.uk/euroinst/EXSPRO/wp3.pdf).

Gerland, P. (1996) 'Socio-economic data and GIS: datasets, databases, indicators and data integration issues', Paper presented to UNEP/CGIAR (Consultative Group on International Agricultural Research), Arendal III Workshop on *Use of GIS in agricultural research management*, Norway, 17-21 June (www.un.org/Depts/unsd/softproj/papers/pg_cgiar.htm).

Goodin, R.E., Headey, B., Muffels, R.J.A. and Dirven, H.J. (1999) *The real worlds of welfare capitalism*, Cambridge: Cambridge University Press.

Gordon, D. and Pantazis, C. (eds) (1997) *Breadline Britain in the 1990s*, Aldershot, Brookfield, Hong Kong, Singapore and Sydney: Ashgate.

Gordon, D. and Spicker, P. (eds) (1999) *The international glossary on poverty*, London: Zed Books.

Gordon, D. and Townsend, P. (eds) (2000) *Breadline Europe: The measurement of poverty*, Bristol: The Policy Press.

Gordon, D., Adelman, A., Ashworth, K., Bradshaw, J., Levitas, R., Middleton, S., Pantazis, C., Patsios, D., Payne, S., Townsend, P. and Williams, J. (2000) *Poverty and social exclusion in Britain*, York: Joseph Rowntree Foundation (www.bris.ac.uk/poverty/pse).

Gordon, D., Pantazis, C. and Townsend, P. (2001) 'Child rights and child poverty in developing countries', Unpublished report for UNICEF, Bristol: Townsend Centre for International Poverty Research.

Hagenaars, A.J.M. and de Vos, K. (1988) 'The definition and measurement of poverty', *Journal of Human Resources*, vol 23, no 2, pp 211-21.

Hagenaars, A.J.M., de Vos, K. and Zaidi, A. (1994), *Poverty statistics in the late 1980s*, Luxembourg: Eurostat.

Hvinden, B., Heikkila, M. and Kankare, I. (2001) 'Towards activation? The changing relationship between social protection and employment in Western Europe', in M. Kautto, J. Fritzell, B. Hvinden, J. Kvist and H. Uusitalo (eds) *Nordic welfare states in the European context*, London: Routledge, pp 168-97.

ILO (International Labour Organisation) (1952) *Social Security (Minimum Standards) Convention, 1952 (No 102)*, Geneva: ILO (ilolex.ilo.ch:1567/scripts/convde.pl?C102)

International Fund for Agricultural Development (2001) *Rural poverty report 2001: The challenge of ending rural poverty*, Oxford: Oxford University Press (www.ifad.org/poverty/index.htm)

Jazairy, I., Alamgir, M. and Panuccio, T. (1995) *The state of world rural poverty*, London: IFAD.

Johnston, R. (2001) *Road map towards the implementation of the United Nations Millennium Declaration: Report of the Secretary-General*, UN General Assembly 56th Session, 6 September, follow-up to the outcome of the Millennium Summit, UN, New York (www.ibge.gov.br/poverty/pdf/millennium_road_map.pdf; see also www.un.org/millennium).

Loup, J. and Naudet, D. (2000) *The state of human development data and statistical capacity building in developing countries*, Human Development Report Office, Occasional Papers no 60 (www.undp.org/hdro/occ.htm#2).

MacPherson, S. (1994) *A measure of dignity. Report on the adequacy of public assistance rates in Hong Kong*, Hong Kong: Department of Public and Social Administration, City Polytechnic of Hong Kong.

Malloch Brown, M. (2001) 'Child poverty and meeting the 2015 targets', statement, London, 26 February, www.undp.org/dpa/statements/administ/2001/february/26feb01.html.

Marlier, E. and Cohen-Sokal, M. (2000) 'Social benefits and their redistributive effect in the EU', *Statistics in Focus*, Population and Social Conditions, Theme 3–9/2000, Luxembourg: Eurostat.

Martin, J.P. (1998) *What works among active labour market policies: Evidence from OECD countries' experience*, OECD Labour Market and Social Policy Occasional Papers no 35, Paris: OECD.

Mejer, L. and Linden, G. (2000) 'Persistent income poverty and social exclusion in the European Union', *Statistics in Focus*, Population and Social Conditions, Theme 3–13/2000, Luxembourg: Eurostat.

Mejer, L. and Siermann, C. (2000) 'Income poverty in the European Union: children, gender and poverty gaps', *Statistics in Focus*, Population and Social Conditions, Theme 3–12/2000, Luxembourg: Eurostat.

NYCC (Community Council for Greater New York) (1982) *A Family Budget Standard*, New York, NY: NYCC.

Orshansky, M. (1965) 'Counting the poor: another look at the poverty profile', *Social Security Bulletin*, June, pp 3-29.

Parker, H. (ed) (1998) *Low cost but acceptable: A minimum income standard for the UK: Families with young children: How much is enough?*, Bristol: The Policy Press (www.bris.ac.uk/Publications/TPP/pages/rp018.html).

Parker, H. (2000) *Low cost but acceptable: Incomes for older people. A minimum income standard for households aged 65-74 years in the UK*, Bristol: The Policy Press (www.bris.ac.uk/Publications/TPP/pages/rp032.html).

Piachaud, D. (1979) *The cost of a child: A modern minimum*, London: Child Poverty Action Group.

Ravallion, M., Datt, G. and Van de Walle, D. (1991) 'Quantifying absolute poverty in the developing world', *Review of Income and Wealth*, vol 37, pp 345-61.

Reddy, S.G. and Pogge, T.W. (2002) 'How not to count the poor', Unpublished paper, Columbia University (www.google.com/search?q=cache:S3mzMaVx31UC:www.ids.ac.uk/ids/pvty/Count.pdf+how+not+to+count+the+poor&hl=en).

Renwick, T.J. (1993) 'Budget-based poverty measurement: 1992 Basic Needs Budgets', *Proceedings of the American Statistical Association*, Social Statistics Section, pp 573-82.

Rowntree, B.S. (1901) *Poverty. A study of town life*, London: Macmillan (republished in 2000 by The Policy Press, Bristol: www.bris.ac.uk/Publications/TPP/pages/at036.htm).

Ruizhen, Y. and Yuan, W. (1992) *Poverty and development: A study of China's poor areas*, Beijing: New World Press.

Saunders, P. (1998) *Using budget standards to assess the well-being of families*, Social Policy Research Centre Discussion paper 93, Sydney, University of New South Wales (www.sprc.unsw.edu.au/dp/dp093.pdf).

Sen, A.K. (1976) 'Poverty: an ordinal approach to measurement', *Econometrica*, vol 44, no 2, pp 219-31.

Sen, A.K. (1981) *Poverty and famines. An essay on entitlement and deprivation*, Oxford: Clarendon Press.

Seymour, J. (ed) (2000) *Poverty in plenty: A human development report for the UK*, London: Earthscan.

Social Planning Council (1981) *The budgets guide methodology study*, Toronto: Social Planning Council of Metropolitan Toronto.

Stephens, R. (1995) 'Measuring poverty in New Zealand, 1984-1993', in P. Saunders and S. Shaver (eds) *Social policy and the challenges of social change*, Volume 1, Reports and Proceedings no 122, Sydney: Social Policy Research Centre, University of New South Wales, pp 229-42.

Stiglitz, J. (1998) *More instruments and broader goals: Moving towards a post-Washington Consensus*, WIDER Annual Lecture 2, UN University World Institute for Development Economics Research (WIDER), Helsinki (www.wider.unu.edu/events/annuel1998.pdf).

Stiglitz, J. (2000) 'What I learned at the World Economic Crisis', *New Republic*, 17 April.

Townsend, P. (1979) *Poverty in the United Kingdom*. Penguin, Harmondsworth.

Townsend, P. and Gordon, D. (2000) 'Introduction: The measurement of poverty in Europe', in D. Gordon and P. Townsend (eds) *Breadline Europe: The measurement of poverty*, Bristol: The Policy Press, pp 1-22.

UN (2000) 'Millennium Assembly', www.un.org/millennium.

UNDP (United Nations Development Programme) (1990) *Human Development Report 1990: Concepts and measurement of human development*, New York, NY: Oxford University Press (hdr.undp.org/reports/global/1990/en/).

UNDP (1995) *The Copenhagen Declaration and Programme of Action: World Summit for Social Development 6-12 March 1995*, UN Department of Publications, sales no E.96.IV.8, New York (www.visionoffice.com/socdev/wssd.htm).

UNDP (1996) *Human Development Report 1996: Sustainability and human development*, New York, NY: Oxford University Press (hdr.undp.org/reports/global/1997/en/).

UNDP (1997) *Human Development Report 1997: Human development to eradicate poverty*, New York, NY: Oxford University Press (hdr.undp.org/reports/global/1999/en/).

UNDP (1999) *Human Development Report 1999: Globalization with a human face*, Oxford: Oxford University Press (www.undp.org/hdro/highlights/past.htm).

UNICEF Innocenti Research Centre (2000) *Innocenti Report Card No. 1. A league table of child poverty in rich nations*, UN Children's Fund, Florence (www.unicef-icdc.org/cgi-bin/unicef/Lunga.sql?ProductID=226).

Vandemoortele, J. (2000) *Absorbing social shocks, protecting children and reducing poverty: The role of basic social services*, UNICEF Working Papers, New York.

Watkins, K. and Fowler, P. (2002) *Rigged rules and double standards: Trade, globalisation, and the fight against poverty*, Oxford: Oxfam.

Watts, H.W. (1980) *New American Budget Standards: Report of the Expert Committee on Family Budget Revisions*, Special Report Series, Institute for Research on Poverty, University of Wisconsin, Madison.

WHO (World Health Organisation) (1995) *The World Health Report 1995: Bridging the gaps*, Geneva: WHO.

WHO (1998) *The World Health Report 1998: Life in the 21st century – A vision for all*, Geneva: WHO.

World Bank (1990) *World Development Report 1990: Poverty*, Washington, DC: World Bank.

World Bank (2001) *World Development Report 2000/2001: Attacking poverty*, New York, NY/Oxford: Oxford University Press.

Part II
Anti-poverty policies in rich countries

FOUR

Social policy in the US: workfare and the American low-wage labour market

S.M. Miller and Jeanette E. Markle

The setting

The US, like many other nations, is reconsidering and repositioning many of its social programmes. The significant change in the income maintenance, or welfare, programme that is discussed in this chapter occurs in the context of efforts to promote the privatisation of public activities (pensions, schools, prisons, social services), and to reduce the federal government's role in social welfare relative to the individual states of the US. These two trends can be observed in recent welfare policy changes. Concurrently, widening inequalities have reawakened concerns that the American poverty line approach inadequately measures what is needed to maintain an above-poverty standard of living.

Administrative trends

Privatisation and reduction in government involvement

The trend towards privatisation and the disputes that ensued are evidenced in recent proposals to change the Social Security system that provides pensions to older Americans[1]. The underlying assumption of privatisation advocates is that, 25 years from now, the system will not be able to cover its outlays due to the increased number of retirees from the 'baby boomer' generation. Their proposal is to privatise the system through investment of the Social Security taxes in stock markets. This move is presumed to offer the likelihood of a much larger return on the investment than does the safer investment in government bonds. One version would give the wage earner complete decision-making control of the investment. An alternative is to create an independent commission to make investment decisions in these private markets.

The outcome of this push to privatise is uncertain. The assumption of future Social Security deficits is questioned by:

- conflicting sets of calculations;
- the recommendation of alternative ways of increasing the size of the fund;
- cooling support for private markets, due to the recent decline in stock markets.

A parallel road to greater privatisation is to increase individual savings for retirement by decreasing income taxes, thereby freeing funds for personal investment. Invested funds and resulting profits would not be taxed. The individual funds would be taxed only when the money is withdrawn for retirement purposes.

Until recently, the public retirement savings system appeared likely to be considerably privatised. The Enron scandal (where employees lost retirement benefits that they invested in their company's stock) is, however, slowing that push, at least for a time.

The general trend towards reducing the role of government and promoting the private and nonprofit sectors is occurring in other policy arenas. An increasing number of cities contract with private companies to run their schools. A school voucher programme, in which parents receive a voucher tagged for a specified amount of money to send their children to for-profit schools, receives a great deal of attention. Feelings on the programme are quite polarised: while it currently maintains considerable political support, strong opposition is braking nationwide implementation of a full-fledged private voucher system. Some worry that such vouchers would injure public schools by withdrawing funds from public education. Others are concerned that the programme blurs the line between church and state since vouchers can be used to subsidise the cost of sending children to religious schools. In 2002 the Supreme Court accepted the principle that vouchers can be used for religious schools. These concerns have caused voucher proponents to undertake a supplementary political effort to provide tax deductions for families sending children to non-public schools. This approach would achieve a similar outcome as would a voucher system while circumventing the political barriers that may prevent passage of legislation that explicitly establishes a true voucher programme.

A privatisation effort is similarly underway in the administration of US prisons. The number of incarcerated individuals grew dramatically over the last few decades, partly because of imprisonment for drug violations, necessitating higher expenditures on prison facilities, services and administration. Some prisons at the local, state and federal level turned to privatisation as a way to minimise costs. The US government's desire to cut costs must be balanced with accountability concerns of the private sector. Whether the private sector can be effective in responding to public complaints and providing adequate services to inmates is inconclusive so far. Negative reports citing the increased level of maltreatment in prisons run by private-sector companies are emerging, however, and may impede privatisation attempts in this area.

Strong political effort aimed at increasing markedly the role of 'faith-based organisations' in the provision of government-funded social programmes has also emerged in recent years. One objective is to reduce the governmental role in social programmes; another is to expand the importance of religious themes and institutions. Opponents, civil libertarians and some religious leaders, question the connection between the state and religion. The likely result is a compromise that would increase the importance of religiously affiliated organisations in social programme implementation while placing some limits on their assistance-providing procedures.

Poverty-related trends

Increasing awareness and the role of the poverty measure in the evaluation of social programmes

Awareness of growing economic inequality in the 1990s has led to increased recognition of the continuing significance of poverty. Economic expansion has not eliminated poverty, as many expected it would. Journalistic accounts report the difficult conditions experienced by the poor. Reducing the number of poor persons, especially poor children, is of growing concern to the US public, politicians, and policy analysts. Consequently, the method for calculating poverty rates is an important policy and political question. US thinking and practice in conceptualising poverty fall well behind developments in Europe. Indeed, American provincialism – or political realism – results in almost no discussion of them.

The 'war on poverty' of the 1960s introduced the 'poverty line' to measure the extent of poverty. It was based on data convenience as well as economic analysis. To calculate the poverty line, the food expenditure in the emergency budget of a low-income family of the late 1950s was multiplied by three (because food spending was a third of total spending). It was adjusted for family size, using controversial estimates of the marginal cost of additional family members, and then indexed to the Consumer Price Index, a commonly used measure of the nation's inflation rate.

From its beginning, this calculation method has been criticised as providing a superficially low poverty-level income (Gordon and Townsend, 2000). Since the calculation's inception, food spending has decreased to one fifth of the average low-income family budget as a result of dramatic housing cost increases (Bergmann, 2000). Many federal and state programmes recognise the inadequacy of the official poverty line and establish eligibility thresholds for means-tested programmes that are as much as twice the poverty measure.

Congress funded the National Academy of Sciences to study the adequacy of the poverty line measurement (Citro and Michael, 1995; Miller and Oyen, 1996). Its 1995 report, *Measuring poverty: A new approach* (Citro and Michael, 1995), carried the brave statement that poverty is a condition relative to the conditions of others in the society, not an absolute state of subsistence. The academy's recommended changes – somewhat timid in our view, far from the social exclusion approach used in the EU – would slightly increase the level of the poverty line calculated annually by the Census Bureau. In a limited experimental programme that does not affect the bureau's continuing report of the official poverty line, data are collected that largely use the calculation method described in the National Academy of Science's recommendations. A political battle is likely to occur if this somewhat revised approach is offered as the substitute for the current poverty line measurement. Any increase in the poverty threshold would effectively lower the 'success' rating of social programmes – a result that makes the revised poverty measurement politically unappealing.

The chapter now turns to US efforts to eliminate, or at least reduce, poverty through welfare – a publicly provided income maintenance programme. The programme has faced considerable political heat in recent years, and by the end of the 20th century was transformed into a workfare programme – a publicly-supported income maintenance programme that makes benefit receipt dependent on participation in employment-related activities for most programme participants[2]. The creation of welfare, its transition to workfare, the problems emerging under the new approach and the proposals for change are discussed below.

Welfare: its beginning and evolution

The New Deal legislation of the 1930s that established the pension and unemployment insurance schemes also created Aid to Dependent Children. This programme, commonly known as 'welfare', was later expanded and renamed Aid to Families with Dependent Children (AFDC). Unlike other programmes of the Social Security Act, it was a means-tested programme. It foreshadowed the second wave of social welfare programmes in the 1960s that were mainly means tested.

At its beginning, AFDC's primary aim was to provide 'relief', or financial aid, to children of low-income widows and single mothers. These children and families were not eligible for the newly formed Social Security programme, and therefore, necessitated the development of a new programme. The programme began as a relatively small, 'worthy' endeavour – a response to the poverty and hardship of the Great Depression of the 1930s.

Welfare was built upon three key assumptions:

- recipients would be allowed to collect benefits in the absence of any work requirement;
- only a small portion of the population would be eligible for such assistance;
- the programme would gradually decrease in size and importance (Bernstein and Garfinkel, 1997).

Save the last assumption, the programme performed as expected. In 1936, its first year of existence, it provided relief to just 534,000 recipients, mostly children of white, female widows (US DHH/ACF, 2000).

Over the years, the programme grew in political importance and drew public criticism, due, in part, to growth in scope and size. In 1950, the programme expanded relief to the caretakers of the needy children (Bernstein and Garfinkel, 1997). Over the next 15 years, the programme shifted to a benefit programme for families with unemployed parents (US DHH/Office of ASPE, 1998).

The size of AFDC also grew at a high rate over its lifetime, partially due to the more inclusive nature of the programme beginning in the 1950s. Bad economic periods increased its rolls, and good periods did not always diminish them. Between 1936 and 1960, the number of welfare recipients increased more than five fold, reaching 3,005,000. In the course of the next ten years, the time of the 'war on poverty', the rolls increased to 8,466,000. Increases slowed in the 1970s and 1980s, reaching just 11,460,382 by 1990. However, rapid caseload growth emerged again in the early 1990s. At its height in 1994, 14,225,591 persons received AFDC payments (US DHHS/AFC, 2000), constituting approximately 5.5% of US citizens[3].

As the caseload grew, national and recipient demographics underwent extraordinary change. The country experienced a surge of women entering the workforce, partly because of a decline in the male-earner 'family wage'. Negative public attitudes towards women working while caring for a family consequently eased. More and more people began to divorce, separate and bear children out of wedlock, leading to a higher proportion of never-married or divorced mothers on welfare. Poverty became 'feminised' as women began to comprise a greater and greater share of the low-income population. The racial composition of the welfare recipient pool also transformed over time as more African American and Hispanic families began to receive welfare assistance, though far less than was popularly believed. Additionally, the number of recipients that were fairly recent immigrants increased.

'Welfare' developed negative connotations. For some US citizens, a moral panic ensued: the traditional family structure was seen as undermined by out of wedlock births, particularly to young minority women. What was once known as 'relief' for a small class of 'deserving' white widows had grown into 'assistance' for a significantly larger (and, as was perceived, undeserving) population that included a great number of minorities and families with absent fathers. The rising number of women in the workforce added to disapproval of the programme; it was seen as not pressuring recipients, predominantly women with children, to work.

The public's false perception of the situation, in part a result of concerted efforts by right-wing think tanks and conservative politicians to promote a negative programme image, combined with racial attitudes to produce a number of myths. The purported easy receipt of welfare, it was charged, promoted conception without marriage – having a child and not having an income made it possible to receive welfare. Many believed that public assistance without a work requirement promoted indolence as well as childbearing.

The public and Congress became increasingly uneasy with the amount of government spending on a programme that many felt promoted socially undesirable behaviour and dependency. Political pressure to pare down the programme grew. Although a substantial amount of money had been poured into social programmes as a result of the 'war on poverty', welfare caseloads had not dropped. The public perceived this spending as high and counterproductive. In the public view, welfare encouraged unacceptable behaviour among the new, demographically 'different' population of recipients, thereby endangering the health of US society. These politically powerful myths about the programme made AFDC an easy target for spending cuts and 'reform'.

The beginning of 'reform'

Largely spurred by political response to public misperceptions, AFDC slowly began to move towards a work-emphasised approach. This occurred as early as the 1960s with the introduction of very limited work requirements for able-bodied adults and the 'earned income disregard'. This income disregard allowed working recipients to keep a portion of increased earnings when they earned more through longer hours or higher wages. Under the previous benefit calculation system, benefits were reduced at a one-to-one rate with increasing earned income – a measure that effectively diminished a recipient's incentive to work (US GAO, 1997b).

Emphasis on improving the employability of AFDC recipients began in 1968 with the creation of the Work Incentive (WIN) programme that established a referral system for unemployed male recipients to improve their work potential. The programme expanded over the years[4] and was eventually replaced with the Job Opportunities and Basic Skills Training (JOBS) programme in 1988 (US DHHS/Office of ASPE, 1998). Not only were more recipients (including women) required to participate in the JOBS version of WIN, but mandatory federal work activity participation rates were introduced. The programme achieved modest increases in labour force participation, but the participation rate in JOBS only reached a low level of 13% of the total adult recipient population by fiscal year[5] 1994 due to a high number of exemptions (US GAO, 1997b).

This low participation level did not meet the political and popular call for reform, causing many states to apply for waivers from federal AFDC and JOBS requirements. These waivers allowed them to experiment with new policy initiatives aimed at increasing the employment rate of welfare recipients. By June 1996, 33 states had secured waivers and were developing stricter work requirements, as well as penalties for non-compliance. States also used the waivers as an opportunity to tinker with the earned income disregard as a way of providing an incentive to work (US GAO, 1997b).

Given the trend towards emphasising work-readiness, the 1996 shift from welfare to workfare – the income maintenance programme that primarily emphasises employment – is not surprising.

The birth of workfare

The modest reform efforts of the late 1980s and early 1990s did not thwart continued discontent among the public. Political pressure to 'do something about welfare' accelerated between 1989 and 1994 as AFDC caseloads experienced an unusually high growth rate. While the debate among social scientists surrounding programme performance was far from conclusive or condemnatory, the political gains of action were too great to stop reform efforts. The political benefits of large-scale change far outweighed the value of exercising caution about changing a programme shrouded in myth and complicated by information gaps. The momentum towards reform continued despite substantial caseload declines from 1994 to 1996. The political climate of the 1990s was ripe for overhauling the old welfare system.

Making good on his 1992 campaign promise to 'end welfare as we know it', President Clinton signed the Personal Responsibility and Work Opportunity Reconciliation Act (PRWORA) into law on August 22, 1996 as the presidential race was in full swing[6]. This legislation changed a wide array of social programmes, including Medicaid[7], the food stamp programme[8], and benefit programmes for disabled and non-disabled children. The legislation also enacted changes aimed at improving compliance with child support laws and promoting family formation (US DHHS/ACF, 1999).

While these components of PRWORA constituted a major change in social policy, the most significant component of the bill was the replacement of AFDC with Temporary Assistance to Needy Families (TANF). Under TANF, states receive block grant funding from the federal government[9], allowing them to adjust the programme to fit their state. States may use the funds to directly or indirectly fulfil any one of four specified federal goals:

- to provide assistance to low-income families;
- to reduce dependency on the government through the promotion of work, training and marriage among welfare recipients;
- to prevent and reduce the number of out of wedlock births;
- to increase the number of stable two-parent families (US DHHS/ACF/OFA, 2001).

None of these stated objectives radically differs from AFDC's. Both programmes aim to help low-income families achieve financial self-sufficiency through employment, family stability and income maintenance. While the federal regulations are not extensive, they changed the provision of social assistance to poor families in a number of truly fundamental ways. The key differences between income maintenance under AFDC and TANF are highlighted here.

Emphasis on work: the emergence of workfare

TANF portrays work as the cornerstone to achieving self-sufficiency[10] – that is, economic self-dependence and stability that put a family above the poverty line. Under AFDC, income maintenance was the most important aspect of welfare, with a modest emphasis on preparing recipients for future work. Under TANF, the focus of public assistance became moving recipients into the workforce and off assistance, rather than supporting them as they raise a family, gain education, prepare for work, or struggle through bouts of unemployment or underemployment.

In keeping with this programme shift, TANF places great emphasis on increasing the percentage of working adult recipients, often called the 'work participation rate'. This emphasis can be seen in four major ways:

- the federal requirement that recipients participate in work or work-related activities within at least two years of receiving assistance[11];
- the stipulation that holds states financially accountable for fulfilling federally established work participation rate requirements[12];
- few federal work exemptions granted in calculating states' work participation rates[13];
- strict definition of a 'work activity' for the federal work participation requirement, with an emphasis on finding a non-subsidised job in the private sector[14].

Retraction of entitlement to benefits

Under the new federal guidelines, no group of persons is entitled to federal assistance. Federal TANF regulations only establish categorical groups that are *barred* from receiving assistance (US DHHS/ACF, 1999). Under AFDC, eligible persons had a right to receive benefits, referred to as one's 'individual entitlement' (Staff of the Committee on Ways and Means, 1996). Now states are responsible for identifying 'needy' families and providing them with benefits, but no person has a right to receive such benefits (US DHHS/ACF, 1999).

Time-limited nature of benefits

In keeping with the elimination of any entitlement to income maintenance, TANF instituted time limits on federally funded benefits, a programme component that has been at the centre of much controversy. In an effort to encourage work and decrease the number of long-term dependants, PRWORA established a five-year limit, or 60-month total lifetime maximum, on the receipt of welfare benefits.

Two key measures may lessen the potential struggle for families that are not able to attain financial security within this time period. First, each state is allowed to exempt up to 20% of its caseload from this requirement. Secondly, since this rule only applies to federally funded assistance, states are free to use their own funds to continue assistance if they wish.

Despite these ways to circumvent the five-year time limit stipulation, few states have exercised this option. This may change as the number of families facing benefit termination increases[15].

Devolution to the states

With the introduction of the block grant funding scheme, states gained considerable freedom and flexibility in designing their welfare programme. The devolution of programme administration and design to the states from the federal government is not surprising given the emergence of the so-called 'new federalism' wave of less national and more state programming. Broad discretion allows a state to create a programme that is tailored to its conditions.

Very few federal requirements are mandatory for inclusion in any state's programme and states are free to further constrain federal programme requirements[16]. Programme aspects that are commonly decided or altered by the state include eligibility requirements, benefit levels, sanction policies, definition of a 'work activity' for purposes of the two-year time limit, the five-year time limit, as well as the kind and breadth of supplemental services and programmes provided to aid welfare recipients in transitioning off welfare (US DHHS/ACF, 2001).

Introduction of rewards for caseload reduction

While the federal government does not order states to reduce their welfare caseload, it provides incentive and an implicit goal for states to do so. The most obvious way in which this principle is asserted in TANF is through the 'caseload reduction credit'. The level required for compliance with the federal work participation rate requirement is reduced one-for-one with the state's reduction in caseload. For example, if a state reduces its caseload by 5%, the federal requirement for work participation is reduced by 5% (Staff of the Committee on Ways and Means, 1996). Since states face serious funding cuts as a result of non-compliance with the work participation requirements, the caseload reduction credit provides ample incentive for states to try to decrease the number of recipients.

Other TANF regulations indirectly contribute to states' motivation to cut welfare rolls, including federal time limits, tougher sanction policies for work-related and non-work offences and the focus on getting recipients into employment.

The success debate: what are TANF's outcomes?

Immediately following enactment of PRWORA, pessimism and fear abounded among some programme administrators, policy analysts and progressive non-profit organisations. States and programme administrators were concerned about meeting the strict work participation standards (US GAO, 1997b) and with the possibility of losing federal funding. Policy analysts questioned the ability of the low-wage labour market and economy to digest the great number of welfare recipients encouraged to enter the labour force as a result of TANF (Bernstein and Greenberg, 2001). Would the low-wage labour market suffer as a result of this increase in its supply side, resulting in job displacement and decreased wages? Would the block grants provide the needed work supports, such as child care, so that the wellbeing of recipient families could be protected? Would the introduction of time limits on benefits and tougher work requirements and sanctions for non-compliance push families off welfare without any help in becoming self-sufficient?

Due to the revolutionary nature of workfare and doubts about its effects, a substantial amount of research and analysis has been generated to address these concerns and provide feedback to programme administrators. A consensus about the performance of TANF has certainly not been reached despite the accumulation of reports on the issue. In large part, analysts disagree because they use different evaluation criteria in their analyses. They also disagree on where credit or blame for programme successes or failures lie. This chapter now discusses areas where the programme has been praised and areas where it has received criticism.

Programme 'successes'

A new model of welfare emerged as a result of the 1996 reforms. The model includes a number of steps to self-sufficiency. Under this model, recipients are provided with incentive to work. Within a short time frame, recipients are expected to secure an unsubsidised position. Through steady employment, recipients gain the training, skills and work experience necessary to advance their career. With the aid of work-supports, such as assistance with childcare, and supplemental social programmes, such as Medicaid and food stamps, recipients become economically self-sufficient and move off welfare. Barring some unforeseen crisis, the recipient should not have to return to welfare in order to sustain her or his family. She (or, less often, he) will continue to maintain economic self-sufficiency and hopefully experience wage increases over time as skills improve and work experience grows.

Two measures commonly cited as evidence that TANF has been successful in carrying out this idealised model are the recipient employment rate and the rate of caseload declines. Indeed, the years following TANF implementation indicate accomplishment in these areas. From 1992 to 1996 (the year TANF was enacted), the employment rate of all adult TANF recipients[17] increased from 7% to 11.3%. In 1997, just one year following the reforms, the employment rate grew to 18.2%. The rate steadily increased since then and as of 1999 had climbed to 27.6% (The Brookings Institution, 2001). The rest of the adult TANF recipients fulfilled their participation requirements in other acceptable ways, such as job searching or participating in education and training programmes (US DHSS/ACF, 1999).

TANF experienced greater success in reducing caseloads. Between 1996 and June 2000, the total welfare caseload dropped by more than half, reaching 5,780,543 – a level not witnessed since 1968 (US DHHS/ACF, 2000). This decrease is especially impressive and surprising given the long history of rising caseload numbers.

Purported successes and the necessity of close examination

Given such persuasive statistics regarding employment rates and caseload declines, it is no wonder that policy makers, programme administrators, politicians, and members of the media and public declare unqualified victory. Not surprisingly, they assign credit to TANF for these areas of success. Statistics, however, never tell the whole truth. It is all too easy to put a 'spin' on the information in order to support one's views. While the programme may have achieved great success in these figures and using the criteria set forth above, there is certainly no consensus about whether TANF is a success, or if workfare really works.

The first question that sceptics pose in the debate over programme success regards the degree of credit due to TANF for these presumably 'successful' outcomes. After all, TANF reforms are not the only factor that could affect employment rates and caseload levels. Of course, disentangling the outcome effects of TANF from the impact of other factors is difficult.

A basic confounding element in the analysis of TANF success is the state of the US economy. Rises in work participation rates and drops in welfare roll numbers are not solely dependent on programme policies, such as work requirements and sanctions. The health of the economy and the ability of the low-wage labour market to absorb more workers are also critical factors. The implementation of TANF fortunately coincided with the emergence of a booming US economy. The economic expansion, no doubt, eased the influx of welfare recipients into the workforce. How much the economy affected the employment rates of welfare recipients and to what extent welfare policy would have created similar outcomes without the presence of an exceptionally strong economy is difficult to estimate.

Numerous reports have analysed the effect of the economy on caseload levels during the pre-TANF waiver period, 1993-96, when the caseload first started declining. Reports estimate that between 25% and 75% of this early stage decline can be explained by the economy rather than by policy-related factors. Unfortunately, analyses of the post-TANF period are far fewer, and less robust. The few that do exist show a much lesser, but still significant, effect of the economy – explaining between 8% and 12% of the dramatic post-TANF decline (Bell, 2001). Regardless of the exact effect of the economy on the outcomes, it is clear that welfare policies do not work independently of the economic environment experienced by welfare recipients (Center for Law and Social Policy, 2001).

Other factors besides the unusually strong economy work to bolster the superficially positive review of TANF outcomes. Proponents often underscore the importance of earning supplements and social programmes. These programmes facilitate TANF recipients in the transition from welfare to gainful employment and are critical to the success of the workfare model.

Both the Earned Income Tax Credit programme[18] and the federally-established minimum wage[19] serve to increase the earnings of low-wage workers. Expansion of Earned Income Tax Credit and increases of the minimum wage level in the 1990s both substantially improved the effectiveness of TANF efforts to move recipients into employment and off assistance[20]. According to a report by the President's Council of Economic Advisors, expansion of Earned Income Tax Credit and the minimum wage increase each explain 10% of the caseload decline from 1996 to 1998 (Staff of the US DHHS, 2000).

Aside from monetary supplemental programmes, numerous social programmes contribute to the ability of families to attain employment and provide a sufficient standard of living. Work-support programmes, particularly childcare subsidies, are vitally important to the ability of single-parent workfare participants to work. PRWORA brought more focus to this concern by consolidating four existing federal programmes into the Child Care and Development Block Grant with considerable state administration and, sometimes, funding.

Families receiving welfare assistance also rely heavily on programmes that provide low-income persons with life necessities. The food stamp programme provides a significant income supplement in the form of food vouchers. Medicaid also makes a substantial difference in welfare families' economic situation. It serves a critical function for those in the low-wage labour market because relatively few employers in this sector provide any level of health benefits. Other important supplemental support areas that boost TANF recipient resources include subsidies for transportation, utilities and one-time emergency payments.

While many TANF proponents cite the use of 'tough love' policies, such as strict work requirements and sanctions, as the primary reason for success in the areas of employment rate and caseload size, this question is still open to debate. Often overlooked, TANF works in coordination with, and to a great extent relies upon, the success of a broad spectrum of other programmes, both economic and social. Little doubt exists, however, that TANF policies deserve some, and perhaps a significant, amount of credit for increasing work participation and shrinking welfare rolls. The Council of Economic Advisors estimates that TANF policies account for one third of the caseload declines from 1996 to 1998 (Staff of the DHHS, 2000). On the other hand, these outcomes certainly cannot be attributed to TANF alone. The effectiveness of TANF's 'tough love' welfare policy in the absence of these other factors is inconclusive at best.

Critiquing TANF's success: faulty criteria and areas for improvement

Critics contend that employment rates and caseload level do not adequately test whether the workfare model is working. While a successful model would certainly result in increases in employment rates and a decrease in recipients, these outcomes do not necessarily signify a successful model. Relying upon these evaluation measures alone may produce very misleading conclusions and even create undesirable incentive mechanisms, as described below.

Problems associated with the employment rate criterion

Unfortunately, securing a job in the current US economy does not necessarily secure an adequate financial position for a family, and therefore does not ensure a safe road from welfare nor from poverty. This is especially true of the low paying and substandard jobs that welfare recipients are sometimes forced to take to remain on welfare. This situation can be easily overlooked when programme proponents rely on employment rate figures to evidence TANF success. Therefore, TANF critics are understandably resistant to using employment rates as one of the two main criteria of programme success.

Problems associated with the caseload reduction criterion

The caseload reduction criterion has the potential for similarly distorting the understanding of programme outcomes. According to the workfare model, caseload reductions should ideally result from a recipient's attainment of stable employment that assures economic self-sufficiency. Other acceptable reasons for declining caseload numbers include termination of benefits to persons who are able but unwilling to work and a drop in the number of new applicants resulting from decreased need.

Evaluating states on the caseload reduction criterion encourages them to reduce caseloads by these acceptable means. Analysing state performance using this evaluation measure, however, also has the potential to reward states for achieving undesirable caseload declines. It induces states to increase recipients' earnings to the eligibility limit and then push them off the rolls even if they are unlikely to remain economically self-sufficient. States may decrease the rolls by increasing the stigma associated with welfare, the administrative hassle of assistance receipt, and the sanctioning of recipients without adequate hearings or good cause. Using caseload decline as a criterion for success has broad potential for rewarding defects in programme administration rather than for excellence in moving recipients into financial security.

Evaluating TANF on broader criteria

What looked like an encouraging picture of welfare reform success under the employment and caseload reduction criteria becomes much bleaker when broader evaluative criteria are used. The results of evaluations based on self-sufficiency, hardship and supplemental support indicators give a new perspective on claims of unqualified success by many politicians and policy analysts. It appears that employment rate and caseload decline indicators present overly encouraging results on the success of the workfare model.

One of the most distressing discoveries of these added criteria is the low level of self-sufficiency among former welfare recipients. A high rate of welfare recipient employment has not led to a similarly high level of economic security among leavers[21]. According to a tri-city study, nearly three quarters of welfare leavers are in poverty (Moffitt and Roff, 2000). Nationally, 58% of *employed* leavers had an earning level below the poverty line (Strawn et al, 2001). The high incidence of poverty among unemployed and employed leavers alike is largely a result of former recipients stuck in dead end, low-quality jobs. According to a national survey, the median hourly wage for leavers was $6.61 (Loprest, 1999). This wage level produces an annual income for a full-time worker that is just below the poverty line for a family of three with two children and one adult using poverty thresholds for 1999.

In addition to low wages and limited hours of work, many welfare leavers experience a high risk of job turnover and a limited earnings growth potential. According to another national survey, one third of leavers who had left welfare as a result of employment or increased earnings were jobless at the point of the study (Strawn et al, 2001). In total, approximately 40% of all leavers are unemployed (Center for Law and Social Policy, 2001). Clearly, many leavers are left without financial security.

The result is not so much increased self-sufficiency as increased financial need. The current welfare programme is simply not meeting the need of those who are eligible for assistance. In 1995, approximately 80% of poor families with children received welfare. This figure declined steadily following the 1996 reforms and reached approximately 50% in 1999[22]. Similarly, in 1994, the percentage of poor children receiving AFDC assistance was 62%, and by 1998, this figure was down to 43% (Loprest, 1999). Therefore, the caseload decline figures partially portray low utilisation rates, not programme success.

The outcomes of TANF are also not encouraging when the focus shifts to hardship indicators. According to a national survey, 38.7% of leavers were not able to make rent, utility or mortgage payments on time and 49.4% of leavers reported difficulties in making food last (Loprest, 1999). Just one year after leaving welfare, approximately one half of leaver adults and one third of leaver children had no medical coverage (Garrett and Holahan, 2000). More than half of even employed leavers experienced difficulty paying for life necessities (Children's Defense Fund, 2000).

Many hardships experienced by welfare leavers result from inadequate coordination of public assistance provision. As discussed above, economic and social programmes must work in conjunction with TANF so that persons receive the necessary work and life supports. Yet almost all of these programmes experience significantly low levels of utilisation. Earned Income Tax Credit is the lone programme that is succeeding in providing substantial assistance to as many as 75% of workfare participants; other programmes cover much smaller percentages (*Wall Street Journal*, 2002). The income tax credit has been shown effective in two important ways: providing single mothers with incentive to work and moving recipients over the poverty threshold. Knowledge and take-up of Earned Income Tax Credit is fairly high, except among Hispanic families (Phillips, 2000).

Other social assistance programmes have not fared as well in providing needed supports for welfare recipients. Even childcare programmes, critical to the employment of single mothers, report low utilisation rates. It is estimated that at least half of low-income children from leaver families are not aided by the childcare subsidy programme, largely due to unawareness (Greenberg and Schumacher, 1999). In one study, difficulty in securing childcare was the major reason why leavers who exited welfare as a result of an increase in earnings were later unemployed. Administrative practices appear to be significantly responsible for this result, as two fifths of leavers reported never being offered assistance in securing childcare by their caseworker (Children's Defense Fund, 2000). Families unable to secure formal childcare make informal childcare arrangements that are often unstable, inadequate and expensive (Greenberg and Schumacher, 1999). Many localities lack organised childcare facilities while the quality of many childcare programmes supported by the Child Care Development Block Grant is frequently indicted.

The sudden drop in utilisation of both food stamps and Medicaid also speaks to the failure of social programmes in providing the necessary TANF supplements. While both programmes are designed so that low-wage workers leaving TANF could still receive assistance, many leavers are not utilising these continued forms of public assistance. Despite these provisions for leavers, approximately half of welfare leaver families do not receive food stamps (Children's Defense Fund, 2000). Lower than expected utilisation rates are also evident in the Medicaid programme. Just over one half of women leavers are covered by Medicaid or a state health insurance plan six months after leaving welfare and one third are entirely without medical coverage. One year following welfare departure, approximately half of these women lack medical insurance. While children fare better than their mothers, one year after leaving welfare, one third of children are not receiving medical coverage of any kind (Garrett and Holahan, 2000).

The low utilisation of supplemental support programmes following welfare termination result from a lack of awareness among leavers that public assistance may continue after exiting TANF, administrative barriers, and complicated eligibility requirements that result in administrative errors (Garrett and Holahan, 2000; Center for Law and Social Policy, 2001).

Clearly the widespread perception that TANF deserves a gold medal for its performance becomes severely tainted once the programme is evaluated on more robust criteria and data. While employment rates are up and caseload numbers are down, self-sufficiency is far out of reach for many TANF leavers. Poverty is still a problem, causing some families to experience substantial hardship after benefit termination. Also, the supplemental support programmes, key factors in enabling families to move above the poverty level, are simply not utilised as they were intended.

Reauthorisation of TANF: an opportunity for reflection on workfare in the US

Reauthorisation of TANF in 2002 will force a reassessment of its outcome – and its goals. The likely issues to emerge in the debate are the future level of funding, dealing with economic recession, the value of current state performance evaluation criteria and the coordination and integration of supplemental social service programmes with TANF.

Congress will, no doubt, express great concern over programme funding levels for the future. Some, particularly right-leaning politicians, will likely propose a reduction in the size of the block grant.

Opposition to this motion to decrease funding levels, however, is likely to be strong. Problems needing to be addressed include: the lack of adequate child care assistance, the number of persons with significant barriers to employment, the need for better job-training services and the great number of persons exiting welfare and remaining in poverty. Opponents of reduced spending will argue that decreases will prevent states from addressing these more difficult concerns, concerns that were largely ignored thus far due to funding constraints. In coordination with discussions about possible funding cuts, opponents will likely highlight the slowing economy and its impact on the workfare programme. The prosperity of the late 1990s cannot be assumed to solve employment and wage issues in the new century.

The promotion of work and economic independence among TANF recipients is also a likely issue for reauthorisation talks. Some consider the current TANF system – stringent sanctions, time limits on benefits, and the WorkFirst approach[23] – to be a proven, effective method for deterring families from living indefinitely off taxpayer money. Politicians in agreement on these issues will likely push for further work-oriented efforts, such as increasing the work participation rates.

Opponents of this view may question whether most states' sanction and time limit policies are unnecessarily harsh, especially given the high rate of administrative error in social service offices. Also of great concern is the continued application of the WorkFirst approach to TANF recipients in many states. Opponents contend that WorkFirst ignores the long-term economic instability that results from placing recipients initially into poor quality jobs as well as the serious barriers to stable employment, such as health problems or low skills, faced by numerous recipients. They will likely push a 'mixed strategy' approach, one that would provide greater job search assistance to employment-ready recipients and allow recipients with significant barriers to employment to receive job preparatory aid, possibly in tandem with part-time work (Strawn et al, 2001).

Criticism of the current criteria for evaluating state performance – criteria based almost entirely on work participation rates and caseload decline – is likely to emerge. Such standards are inadequate for determining if workfare produces more or less self-sufficient families. The hope, no doubt, is that the negative effects associated with the current incentive system would be dramatically reduced if federal funding were to evaluate and reward state performance on more robust criteria. Desirable criteria might include economic security, access to employment support and hardship levels.

The last major issue likely to gain the political spotlight during reauthorisation talks is the issue of wellbeing and the necessary involvement of supplemental social programmes. Faced with data confirming the persistence of poverty and low level of economic stability among welfare leavers, right-wingers sometimes contend that the TANF legislation's main focus was never on improving the wellbeing of low-income US citizens or on decreasing the poverty rate. They assert that TANF was primarily about decreasing dependence on government assistance, with an understanding that this might cause setbacks in wellbeing or poverty rate measures. Now that the rolls have been drastically reduced and employment, not reliance on cash assistance, is widely accepted as the means to attaining an adequate level of subsistence, attention to the issue of wellbeing may emerge, especially if employment rates continue to grow.

Conservatives will likely argue ineffective supplemental social programmes are the cause of many difficulties. Privatisation will likely be pushed as the best means for improving the efficiency of existing social programmes. This strategy is in line with the recent trend among state agencies to contract out services – a trend that is promoted using sometimes unsubstantiated and inconclusive evidence.

While less conservative debaters agree that improvement in supplemental social services is due and that privatisation may be a part of their improvement, they do not see privatisation as a cure-all. The comparative effectiveness of privatisation efforts rests heavily upon the degree of competition in the service procurement, the accountability of the provider to the government in fulfilling acceptable contracts and the quality of monitoring used to ensure adequate delivery of services. All of these components of privatised service provision can be defective. Before further privatisation is legislated and imposed on state social service agencies, the merits of contracting out must be closely scrutinised (US GAO, 1997a).

Sceptics of the privatisation approach will likely argue that these supplemental social programmes simply deserve greater emphasis. States should be held more accountable for their utilisation and outcomes. Requiring performance evaluation criteria that assess the extent to which states effectively implement multidimensional programmes to assist families in gaining a steady foothold above the poverty line could do this. The policy – if not the political – test is whether administrative policy changes or privatisation result in actual, observed improvement, not just assumed improvement as is sometimes the case. What is most important is that these programmes improve and that poor families attain the assistance they need to attain a decent standard of living.

This list of potential debate issues is not exhaustive – it merely highlights some of the key areas that will receive political attention in 2002 and later. As with many policy areas, the issues and proposals that are likely to actually emerge in the debate are not necessarily the ones of foremost concern. In some ways, changes in social welfare policies are insufficient to address effectively the problems that emerge in the recent turn to an employment-focused income maintenance programme. Bringing workfare participants to an income above the poverty line requires improving the low-wage or secondary labour market. What follows is an analysis of the intricate relationship between the future of workfare and the conditions of the low-wage labour market – an issue that is worthy of considerable attention, and one that is unlikely to receive sufficient notice in the coming years.

Changing the low-wage labour market

Workfare participants seek work and income in the low-wage market. That economic context, not only the various regulations governing their employment, will affect outcomes. Government-designed workfare policies alone cannot overcome the special difficulties of workfare participants in the low-wage labour market. The bleak economic situation that low-wage workers face often has an inter-generational effect. It does not encourage high hopes among children of low-wage workers. These children not only suffer from the lack of family economic resources but also from indirect effects of poverty. These may include educational deficiencies as a result of attending low-quality schools in the neglected neighbourhoods that their families can afford, and lower expectation of future achievement.

Macroeconomic solutions are essential to improving the low-wage labour market. We focus, however, on two types of micro-solutions: changing the secondary labour market situation, and improving the mobility of individuals to navigate through it. Improvement in a wide variety of other social programmes must occur in tandem with these low-wage market reforms to support the wellbeing of its workers.

Proposals for changing the low-wage labour sector[24]

Workfare policies alone cannot overcome low-wage labour market problems. The health of the economy, the level of demand for workers, the availability of jobs and the skill level of low-wage workers are not the domain of workfare reforms. In addition to macro and local policies to stimulate the economy, policy makers could improve the employment prospects of low-wage workers in a number of ways. One approach is to change the labour sector itself by increasing the availability of jobs, improving job quality and increasing group mobility. A second approach seeks to improve individual mobility within the low-wage labour market.

Increasing the availability of low-wage jobs

Changing the low-wage job sector involves improving the availability of jobs in this market. A programme of the past that relied on 'government as the employer of last resort' might be revived and expanded, especially in an economic downturn. The intent was to guarantee jobs to all the unemployed, particularly those in the low end of the labour market. In the workfare context, localities that experience particular difficulties in achieving a high rate of job placement for workfare participants should utilise the options provided in the legislation, such as placing recipients into subsidised employment or community service positions.

While the programme experienced a number of problems in its 1960s form, reforms could be implemented to address these issues. Past efforts have been criticised as haphazard, inclined to creaming (offering jobs to the most qualified rather than to the most needy participants), producing meaningless dead end jobs, displacing long-term public employees, creating wastefulness and misusing funds. Sufficient planning and organisation would dramatically reduce these problems and create a well-designed and useful temporary job programme. To do this, each state and locality would need to have a structure in place to design and implement plans to respond to sudden declines in the job situations of its residents. Such plans would need to be updated at least semi-annually. Federal aid could at least partially underwrite the costs. In order to have a political life, the non-displacement of current staff would have to be guaranteed. Revival of this programme should incorporate policies that would improve the participant's chances of advancing her or his employment in the longer-term, such as the inclusion of training at job assignments or assistance with job placement. Finally, in order to avoid the condemnations that reduced its funding in the past, the programme will require much better monitoring of funds.

This programme would be, at best, only palliative if bad economic conditions prevail. It could serve a critical role, especially if workfare supporters do not create plans to deal with adverse economic conditions or if rapid presidential, Congressional and state actions did not occur to improve the situation of workfare and other low-wage workers if bad economic conditions emerge. Since workfare participants are likely to suffer with other members of the low-wage labour force, perhaps a 'trigger' mechanism could be developed to initiate programmes aimed at improving low-wage worker prospects once the unemployment rate reaches a certain level.

Improving low-wage job quality

Another promising way of improving the low-wage labour market situation involves improvement in the quality of jobs offered in the low-wage labour market. The most direct way of improving low-wage jobs is to raise the wage level of these jobs. The introduction of the federal minimum wage in the New Deal legislation of the 1930s did exactly this. It improves the wage prospects for workers in the low-wage economy who have little power in labour market negotiations because they lack desired skills and union organisation.

Unfortunately, the minimum wage's real benefit to low-wage workers waned for many years. Congress set a low initial minimum wage level and, more importantly, did not sufficiently adjust it as inflation and median wages rose. Significant boosts occurred in 1996 and 1997, although they are still inadequate. The minimum wage provides an income at 50% of the median yearly individual income[25] for a full-time, full-year worker – an income that is below the poverty line for a single parent with any number of children.

Further increases in the minimum wage, as well as indexing it to the median worker wage or to the Consumer Price Index, would substantially improve jobs in the low-wage sector. Increases (without indexing) stand a good chance of passage in the near congressional future because of recognition that the minimum wage level has not kept up with rising wages. Ideally, Congress would set the minimum wage at a level that more realistically meets the economic needs of a family, often called a 'Living Wage'.

The living wage campaign, which emerged in several cities and grew to national stature in recent years, is likely to spread to new localities[26]. Whether it will move beyond publicly benefited firms and non-profit organisations to press private businesses to increase minimum wage levels is uncertain. Since some states have minimum wage requirements that are higher than the federal government's, the campaign might move to institute or raise state standards to that of the living wage.

Improving group mobility: unionisation of workers

Another way of improving the opportunity of low-pay jobholders to secure better employment is to address the low-unionisation of workers in the low-wage sector (Bernstein and Garfinkel, 1997). Under present conditions, they have very little bargaining power. Federal regulations concerning union organising have made it difficult for unions to win elections to represent employees in this sector or, for that matter, in better-paid sectors as well. As a result, unions have been reluctant to attempt organising campaigns in low-wage industries. That outlook is beginning to change and several unions are attempting to organise low-wage employees, notably recent immigrant workers. If these campaigns succeed, the conditions of low-wage work and workers would be dramatically improved. Changes in the labour laws, such as not requiring a drawn-out election procedure among employees if 50% of them sign cards that they want a particular union, would make a great difference in low-wage workers gaining a union voice.

Increasing individual mobility: raising workers' skills

Few workfare participants have the possibility of employment in the primary and better-rewarded sectors of the labour market. They lack the educational credentials, which are often unnecessary to perform the job, and work experiences expected by better-paying employers. As a result, the chance that adults entering the low-wage sector will be able to move into good, relatively secure jobs where they are treated with respect and offered opportunities to improve economically is discouraging.

Changing this requires paying greater attention to the availability and quality of training programmes. Upgrading secondary workers' skills and promoting them into better jobs simply is not a concern for private employers. Subsidies to employers for upgrading the skills of the workforce could be an effective way of increasing workers' skills, while simultaneously increasing their chances of moving into better-paying, more secure employment. Additionally, employers could be subsidised to permit employees to use work time to participate in programmes that are not directly related to job possibilities in that firm.

Another, perhaps more effective, way to advance the employability of low-wage workers would be to improve the educational system for low-wage workers. Significant problems face low-wage workers desiring to improve their skills in the 'third tier' education system, that is, programmes located outside of the traditional public and private school and university system. This third tier system contains employer programmes, federal and state supported training programmes, community college courses and degree offerings, and profit-making business and technical schools. While this system is both vast and costly in the US, many programmes and institutions are not of decent quality. In order to improve this third tier system, a comprehensive, integrated network of adult schooling and training, one that connects students to real job possibilities, must be instituted.

In addition to improving the availability and organisation of training programmes, efforts must be made to assist workfare participants with navigating and participating in such programmes. All too often, low-wage workers face serious barriers in taking advantage of educational opportunities and using these opportunities to make real changes in their employment prospects. Problems stem from limited hours of operation that do not complement the work schedules of low-wage workers with families, inconvenient locations and expensive fees for courses. Even if workers are able to take advantage of education programmes, oftentimes these programmes fail to significantly affect a worker's employment opportunities. Many programmes are too general to really increase a potential worker's employment prospects, or alternatively, are too narrow in that they relate only to a specific firm. Finally, follow-up and aid for former students that would facilitate their transition to better jobs are severely lacking.

The problems associated with creating positive outcomes in educational programmes for low-wage workers are surmountable. Hours of operation could be extended, office locations expanded and course fees subsidised or reduced. The non-system of adult education needs to be less vocationalised so that students develop broad talents and understanding that are applicable to a wide range of definitive job possibilities. A civic function to educational and training programmes, which is currently lacking, could be introduced. Finally, these programmes must increase efforts to enhance the job prospects of former students through job search and placement assistance.

Unfortunately, in the US, a panacea-seeking land, education and training have become dominant strategies in approaching employment issues. A Say's Law is assumed: the increased supply of better-educated workers will generate the demand for them – supply creates demand. This overselling of education and training should not compromise the useful upgrading of skills. However, it should not obscure what else has to be done.

Improving other social programmes

The connection between workfare, an employment-promotion programme, and reforming the low-wage labour market appears infrequently on the political screen. A stumbling block is that improving the secondary labour market raises questions about the quality of the primary labour market. For this sector is increasingly moving toward employers' shedding responsibility for their employees by resorting to contracting out, contingent labour practices, periodic downsizing and questionable use of employees' pension contributions. Raising the bottom would question the quality of today's 'good' jobs as well as increase the cost of public social programmes.

Since it is unlikely that Congress will wholeheartedly embrace positive low-wage reform measures, the issue of sustaining the wellbeing of low-wage workers and workfare participants remains at the forefront of concern. As always, an array of economic and social programmes are crucial in raising the resources of low-wage workers and in providing multidimensional support systems.

Supporting the wellbeing of low-wage workers requires improvements to most of the means-tested economic and social programmes discussed earlier (Edelman, 2001). The Earned Income Tax Credits should be raised for low-income earners (Bernstein and Garfinkel, 1997). While knowledge and use of the Earned Income Tax Credits programme is fairly high, room for improvement still exists (Phillips, 2000). Quality, utilisation rates and ease of application for Medicaid and food stamps should be increased. Finally, the availability of childcare programmes must be addressed if mothers with children continue to be forced participants in the labour market. This requires an increase in the number of quality child care facilities, expansion of cost-reducing measures, such as child care subsidies and reduction in parental co-payments, and, as with most programmes, increase in utilisation among eligible persons.

The unemployment insurance programme, which is beginning to receive attention in welfare discussions as unemployment rates increase, has significant potential to act as a very useful supplemental programme (Edelman, 2001). It was also established by the New Deal innovations and has suffered from low payments to the unemployed and the tightening of eligibility rules. It has been of little aid to those in the low-wage sector who frequently do not meet the requirement of a minimum number of weeks in what is defined as 'covered employment'. Changes in the regulations and improvement in benefits could aid those in the secondary labour market.

Another issue that is often lost in the debate over welfare and assisting the poor is that of the dramatic shortage of low-income housing (Edelman, 2001). Since the rise in housing costs is largely responsible for the rise in the budget level necessary to sustain a family and for the superficially low poverty level, the housing crunch deserves forefront attention when debating the future of programmes that aid low-income families. The programmes that currently exist are simply inadequate to provide assistance to all those in need. Low-income families, especially those living in large cities, can be on assistance waiting lists for years before ever receiving aid. The housing shortage necessitates the development of new low-income housing units and the expansion of subsidy programmes.

In combination, changes in these economic and social programmes would bring workfare participants and low-wage workers closer to a level of resources that would bring them above the poverty line of \$13,874 for a family of three with two children and one adult (US DOC Bureau of the Census, 2001a). Optimally, these improvements would be made simultaneously with the low-wage market solutions. Together, these measures would not only create a more effective social welfare floor[27], but also decrease the chances that workers in the secondary market would require emergency aid.

Implications for other nations

Many nations have modified their social welfare system and debated further changes to their social welfare system. Curtailment of benefits both in size and duration, increased means testing for eligibility, privatisation to reduce costs and taxation result from political pressures to pare down expenditure on social programmes, so-called 'retrenchment'. Nations that introduce new programmes or change their efforts to help their more disadvantaged populations face great issues in winning and maintaining approval of such programmes and delivering them effectively.

While recognising that American social programmes and politics differ significantly from the situation of other nations, particularly those in developing nations, some lessons drawn mainly from the emergence of workfare may highlight issues that affect the quite different welfare states. Our concern here is largely with political processes that affect social policies.

1. *Needs are varied and complex, especially among the poorer sections of a society.* No one programme will meet all needs, whether it is about transitions in employment and family situations or sudden emergencies. A slight rise in money income in a poor nation, for example, does not compensate for the absence of available medical help. Comprehensive, well-integrated programmes are needed.

2. *Public and political attitudes and myths play a substantial role in the introduction and promotion of changes in social welfare.* In the US, the great increase in the labour force participation of middle- and working-income mothers reshaped attitudes about the role of women as restricted to the home. Why, then, should not welfare-supported mothers of young children be engaged in paid labour? Racial and ethnic prejudices can play a major role in gaining support for toughening social programmes. The increasing numerical importance of African American and Latina households receiving public assistance in the US strengthened racist calls for a reduction in welfare programmes. Immigration in other nations may have a similar effect.

    Demography can be destiny. It can undercut support for social programmes because of changing expectations and feelings. Ignoring them is not an effective countermeasure.

3. *No news is not necessarily good news.* When there is scepticism or misunderstanding of what is occurring in a programme, negative interpretations are likely to prevail in the absence of reassuring reports (Gornick, 2001; Gornick and Meyers, 2001). A more rounded or balanced picture needs to be available. Nations dependent on outside aid must keep donors aware of successes and difficulties. Suddenly revealed disasters dissolve donor confidence that aid is being used effectively.

    Ignoring criticism or refusing to recognise problems are not effective tactics for defenders of social programmes. No news, late news, catch-up news – all are less effective than positive, realistic, continuing reports and analyses that take the stage in affecting what is known about a social programme. Initiatives are more effective than replies.

4. *Data are weapons in disputes.* It is not only a question of what data are produced and available but how they are presented. The same data can be offered to show, for example, that many people receive welfare for short periods or that a much smaller number of people receive the bulk of welfare expenditures over time. *Data do not talk* – researchers and, much more importantly, journalists and politicians do the talking for the data. Affecting what gets highlighted is a problem for the researcher who does not control what is made of her results as well as for policy makers.

5. *Data alone do not determine policy.* Helping the poor is as much a political issue as who is to pay what taxes or fees. Those concerned about the poor have to think and act so as to win support for a programme, protect it and improve it. Few programmes have full, continuing support. Political backing must be worked for. That is true for internationally funded programmes as well as for domestic ones.

6. *Definitions matter.* How economic wellbeing is conceived and measured is frequently inadequate. In the case of the US, the conception of poverty – that is, poverty defined as an income-based problem alone – is much too limited (Miller and Roby, 1970). In the case of developing nations, international agencies' use of a very low and very limited definition of daily poverty income shapes the amount of aid and how it can be used. If the aspiration is only to barely maintain human life, then changing the situations that produce great hardship and few opportunities and promote exclusion is unlikely to occur. This early definition of poverty in developing nations may be hard to overcome. That has been the experience of critics in the US.

7. *The design and administration of programmes shape outcomes and costs.* Their structure dooms many programmes. Access to programmes can be easy or difficult. Grouping a variety of related programmes under one roof (one-stop services) could greatly simplify the application process for participants. As it currently stands, eligibility often varies for related programmes, burdening the complicated lives of participants. Payment schedules for participants may be haphazard, inflexible or maladapted to changing circumstances. Programmes that should be linked may be uncoordinated or unrelated. Regulations may be complex and onerous to meet. Loose accounting may result in the loss or misuse of funds and to political opprobrium. Overworked staff usually means under-serviced clientele.

    How services are carried out affects the clientele. Administration is not a mere means; often, it is what a programme is about. The political reputation of a programme and its effects on its intended beneficiaries depend on how it is implemented. The administrative predilection to 'cut costs' may compete with 'delivering services'. The 'efficiency' of a programme depends on what and whose criteria are used – politicians', administrators', the public's or the participants'. In turn, the measures used affect how clientele are treated.

    Administration cannot be an afterthought in social programming. How will programmes be carried out under the prevailing conditions? This question is especially important in nations that do not have a strongly developed administrative apparatus at national and local levels.

8. *Monitoring can be a safeguard.* Monitoring and evaluation are crucial if often badly performed activities. It can early detect the inappropriate or

ineffective uses of funds – politically dangerous occurrences. Even inadvertent misuse of funds may result in termination or curtailment of useful programmes by domestic or international aid sources.

Learning about the impact of programmes and regulations through evaluation is important. It can help redirect programmes so that they are more effective. Particularly important in evaluation studies is who and what to study. Which group gains research attention affects what is known about a programme and the political and administrative attention that the group receives.

If evaluation is to be useful and its recommendations implementable, evaluation teams cannot be parachuted into unfamiliar territory. They need contact – which should not mean control – with those involved in the programme to be evaluated. Evaluation is a social and political process, not only an exercise of technical skill.

9. *The economic environment in which a programme is initiated and implemented is fateful.* This is true at the local as well as the national level. Macroeconomic and local conditions, not only programme content, affect employment outcomes. To a major extent, the most important social policy is economic policy for it affects opportunities.

10. *Decentralisation of programmes is not always a good step.* The 50 American states vary enormously in the procedures and effectiveness with which they carry out workfare. These variations are important to participants and politicians.

Decentralisation does not assure that programmes fit well into local conditions and needs nor that democratic procedures are followed. Local and provincial governments may discriminate against certain classes of citizens and immigrants. Corruption can be great at local levels (as well as at national). Political allegiances may affect eligibility: political constituents may be helped more than the most needy.

If not a panacea, decentralisation can be useful – if it is carefully monitored at the national level.

11. *All nations should be ambitious in seeking to reduce and alleviate poverty.* Nations with severely limited resources for improving the conditions of their residents especially need to know the details of the situations of those who are to be helped, even if they are a majority of the population. At the same time, politicians and administrators need to be aware of the limits of what they can accomplish. Declaring victories is not the same as producing them.

12. *Unrelenting attention to poverty is necessary to safeguard useful programmes and improve faltering ones.* Despite strong political efforts to curtail or eliminate social programmes and to increase the role of private enterprise in the conduct of once-public programmes, opposition to these changes has been

able to block or limit many of them. This is true in the US and in some Western European nations (Gornik and Meyers, 2001). In the US, workfare 'success' depends on the continuance and expansion of many social programmes.

What will be done?

Contracting out, privatisation and retrenchment are not inevitable outcomes of this stage in capitalist development. They are political issues. Well-organised and well-directed political activity can make a great difference in how social programmes develop and change. The future of social policy is to be made, not unfolded.

That future will depend on the assigning of responsibility. Is the overriding obligation *individual* – for people to be in paid, preferably private sector, employment and not dependent on public assistance? Then, pressure on poor people to avoid welfare or not to remain long on it will be the order of the day. If the obligation is *societal* – to prevent poverty or to alleviate it – then recognising that many poor people can never or seldom be self-supporting and will need public assistance is crucial (US GAO, 2001). For those capable of self-sufficiency, effective and expensive education, training, and extensive social back-up are necessary if they are to secure jobs that provide more than poverty-level existence (Pear, 2000).

Employment is not the answer for all poor people. Neither is sub-marginal employment – the effective product of some workforce programmes – an adequate response to poverty.

Notes

[1] Social Security is a programme in which employees and employers pay a percentage of wages to a fund that is invested in federal government bonds. On retirement, employees receive monthly cheques out of this fund in a sum that is roughly proportionate to the amount contributed to the programme while working. Since current employees' and employers' contributions pay for current retirees with extra benefits for low-wage workers, demographic changes in the nation's population can upset the programme's balance and operation.

[2] This chapter aims to differentiate between welfare and workfare, using 1996 as the point of transition from one to the next. Workfare, however, is a term that is not often used in the literature to describe the welfare programme after 1996. Most reports still refer to the post-1996 income maintenance programme as 'welfare'. Therefore, any use of the term 'welfare' in this chapter will refer generally to the income maintenance programme, both before and after the 1996 changes. Any use of the term 'workfare', however, specifically refers to the employment-centred income maintenance programme after 1996. Workfare is considered to be the current US programme and policy approach to providing welfare assistance.

[3] The percentage of US citizens on welfare in 1994 is based on population estimates for July 1994 (US DOC Bureau of the Census, 2001).

[4] The WIN programme expanded in 1971 to include unemployed female recipients without children under age six. With the establishment of JOBS, the cut-off decreased to mothers with children under three (DHHS/Office of ASPE, 1998).

[5] 'Fiscal year' refers to the 12-month congressional accounting period that begins on 1 October and ends 30 September of the next year. Fiscal year 1994 refers to the period beginning 1 October 1993 and ending 30 September 1994.

[6] It should be noted that PRWORA represents a compromise between President Clinton's welfare reform proposal and the agenda of the Republican-controlled Congress, and therefore incorporates stricter measures than Clinton envisioned (Mead, 1997).

[7] Created in 1965, the Medicaid programme provides health insurance and access to medical services to many families eligible for welfare and disability benefits, as well as other needy persons, as defined by individual states (DHHS/HCFA, 1995). Medicaid has a mix of federal and state funding that varies considerably between states. One in seven US inhabitants was enrolled in Medicaid in 1997. While members of low-income families constitute approximately 75% of Medicaid recipients, this group only receives 25% of programme spending. The rest of the programme money is spent on the higher-cost care of the elderly and disabled (Kaiser Commission on Medicaid and the Uninsured, 1999).

[8] Established nationwide in 1974, the food stamp programme reduces the cost of food to low-income families (those with income below 130% of the poverty line) by providing vouchers that can be used at authorised retail stores (Food Research and Action Center, 2001). Food stamp eligibility requires that most adults work, seek work or participate in an approved employment and training programme. The average monthly value of these vouchers was $73 per person and the maximum monthly allowance for a family of three was $341 in fiscal year 2000 (US DAFNS, 2001). As family income increases, the value of the voucher decreases.

[9] Block grant funding refers to the scheme established to fund state-administered programmes with federal funds. States receive a sum of federal money that is not tagged for a specific mandated purpose, but rather, marked for use in a general federally-recognised policy area, such as improving children's health. While there are often some federal restrictions on appropriate fund use, states are largely responsible for deciding how to distribute the funds among various state programmes related to the general federal goal.

[10] Some, especially conservative welfare analysts define self-sufficiency by employment and the absence of government-provided income maintenance. This definition, however,

provides an inadequate assessment of family wellbeing. It also ignores the continuing heavy reliance on other public programmes of employed low-income households.

[11] States are responsible for defining 'work' and 'work-related activities' for this federal requirement. In addition to the two-year rule, unemployed recipients are also bound by federal law to participate in community service activities after two months of federal assistance. States are given the option to exempt parents with young children from these requirements (Staff of the Committee on Ways and Means, 1996).

[12] For single-parent families, the federal work participation rate standard required that at least 25% of all adult recipients work at least 20 hours a week in fiscal year 1997. These requirements increase incrementally and will level out at 50% of the entire caseload for 30 hours per week in fiscal year 2002. Two-parent families face a higher percentage rate and working hours requirements compared to single-parent families (US GAO, 1997b). States have significant incentive to abide by these federal work participation rate standards, as the federal grant is reduced with each instance of non-compliance, beginning with a 5% reduction and reaching a maximum of a 21% reduction in the total block grant (US GAO, 1997b).

[13] According to the federal regulations, all adult recipients, excepting single parents with children under age one (an option that states may choose) are included in the work participation rate calculation (Staff of the Committee on Ways and Means, 1996). While many states allow for additional exemptions, such as for disabled persons, pregnant women, victims of domestic violence, and persons of advanced age (State Policy Documentation Project, 2001), these persons are still included in the federal work participation rate calculation. As a result, work is encouraged among a greater population under TANF than under AFDC.

[14] To be included in the work participation rate calculation, a welfare recipient must hold a job that is considered a 'work activity'. A work activity, as federally defined, consists of private or public sector employment positions, with a severely limited allowance for work-related activities, such as participation in educational, training and job search programmes (Staff of the Committee on Ways and Means, 1996).

[15] As of October 2001, a majority of states (26 in total) have at least some families that are denied assistance, either on a permanent or temporary basis. Soon thereafter, the count increased to 35 states. Assuming no change in state policy, by January 2003, all states that impose any sort of time limit (49 in total) will have families that could experience a termination of benefits (State Policy Documentation Project, 2000).

[16] The area in which federal requirements are significant regards the acceptable use of the block grant funding. According to the regulations, the funds must be used to serve the four TANF goals listed above in an amount not to fall below 75% of the 1994 spending level for AFDC (US GAO, 1997b). Also, federal regulations stipulate the states'

right to transfer up to 30% of their block grant funds to other areas of social spending, such as child care and social service provision (US DHHS/ACF, 1999).

[17] The employment rate used here is calculated by the average percentage of all adult TANF recipients who work in an unsubsidised position for any number of hours.

[18] Earned Income Tax Credit is the largest cash transfer programme, in terms of government expenditure, for low-income inhabitants of the US, particularly parents (Phillips, 2000). It serves as a way of returning the social security tax on wages to lower-pay earners and encouraging parents to accept low-wage work. Eligibility depends on having family wage income that is at least (roughly) two thirds of what a full-year minimum wage worker would receive. The Earned Income Tax Credit benefit is graded, declining as income rises. The most that can be received as a wage supplement from Earned Income Tax Credit is about a quarter of the dollar value of the poverty line.

[19] The federal minimum wage, introduced in the 1930s New Deal legislation, establishes a lower limit on hourly wage levels for most workers. It improves the wage prospects for non-unionised, low-skilled workers in the low-wage market.

[20] Earned Income Tax Credit was expanded three times in the latter part of the 1980s and the early 1990s. The largest of these expansions came in 1993, under the Omnibus Budget Reconciliation Act. This legislation greatly increased the subsidy for families at the low end of the income eligible level, raised the maximum credit limit and increased the rate that families receive at higher incomes as the credit is phased out (Eissa and Hoynes, 1999). The minimum wage underwent two increases in the mid-1990s. The first came in October of 1996, increasing the hourly wage from $4.25 to $4.75. Another forty cent increase occurred in September of 1997.

[21] In most welfare studies, a 'leaver' is defined as someone who has received welfare payments within a certain time frame, who has since exited from the programme and who is no longer receiving assistance at the time of the survey. Reasons for leaving are numerous and include increased earnings, a change in family situation that makes a recipient ineligible and sanctions.

[22] These statistics were calculated by dividing the number of welfare families by the number of families with children in poverty. This calculation does not yield a perfect indicator of the amount of unmet need – it is intended to provide a rough indication of the rising level of unmet need since TANF's inception. The calculation uses data obtained from the US DOC Bureau of the Census (2000) and the US DHHS/ACF (2000).

[23] The WorkFirst approach, which most states implemented by 1998, presses for the quick attainment of a job, regardless of its quality, for almost all welfare recipients, regardless of job-readiness.

[24] This section discusses positive means of improving the low-wage labour market. However, other less desirable avenues for improving the market exist and may arise in relevant debates. One such means of reform is reducing the supply of workers in the secondary labour sector. The low-wage labour market is susceptible to reduced wages because of increases in the number of workers willing to accept low wages. Immigration is a major source of the rising supply of low-wage workers. A downturn in Mexico and other parts of the world would increase immigration to the US and the already high number of people seeking jobs in the low-wage sector. As elsewhere, globalisation increases immigration, as people are pushed from rural and urban areas of poorer economies and stream into richer nations. The influx of workfare participants makes job displacement, limited job options and the availability of part-time only positions a distinct threat. Xenophobia, a hardy political perennial, would increase in a deep or long economic downturn. The appeal of limiting immigration and expelling undocumented workers may grow in the US as it has elsewhere.

[25] This statistic was calculated using the national median individual income for 1999, provided by the US DOC Bureau of the Census (2001c).

[26] The living wage campaign was sparked by a large community organisation allied with religious congregations in African American neighbourhoods of Baltimore (MD), and with the Industrial Areas Foundation originated by Saul Alinsky. The campaign's goal was to build effective local coalitions of disadvantaged people. They demanded that firms benefiting from contracts or subsidies from the city pay their employees substantially more than the federal minimum wage. A city law was passed that instituted this requirement. Without coordination, other cities have followed Baltimore, seldom a bell-weather city, in enacting a similar requirement. Students at a number of universities have protested the pay level of its low-pay workers. The most recent of these strikes occurred at Harvard University in 2001, and received great attention. Students took over the administration building for several weeks in an effort to force the university to provide a Living Wage for its low-pay workers.

[27] Social welfare floor, a formerly popular term, is used in lieu of 'social safety net', to describe the myriad of social programmes aimed at assisting persons in need. The latter term, one that is commonly used currently, establishes a misleading connotation regarding such programmes: fail first, then some help may be provided.

References

Bell, S. (2001) 'Why are welfare caseloads falling?', *Assessing the New Federalism Project*, Washington, DC: The Urban Institute, pp 48-59 (newfederalism.urban.org/pdf/discussion01-02.pdf).

Bergmann, B. (2000) 'Deciding who's poor', *Dollars and sense*, issue 228, March-April (www.dollarsandsense.org/2000/0300bergmann.html).

Bernstein, J. and Garfinkel, I. (1997) *Welfare reform: fixing the system inside and out*, Series no 773, Institute for Research on Poverty (IRP) Reprint Series, Madison: IRP University of Wisconsin.

Bernstein, J. and Greenberg, M. (2001) 'Reforming welfare reform', *American Prospect*, vol 12, no 1 (www.prospect.org/print-friendly/print/V12/1/bernstein-j.html).

Bernstein, J. and Hartmann, H. (1999) 'Defining and characterizing the low-wage labor market', in K. Kaye and D. Smith Nightingale (eds) *The low-wage labor market: Challenges and opportunities for economic self-sufficiency*, Prepared for the US DHHS, Assistant Secretary for Planning and Evaluation: The Urban Institute (aspe.hhs.gov/hsp/lwlm99/bernhart.htm).

Center for Law and Social Policy (CLASP) (2001) *Testimony of Mark Greenberg, CLASP*, for the House Committee on Ways and Means, Subcomittee on Human Resources, March 15, Washington, DC: CLASP (www.clasp.org/pubs/TANF/Mark%20Greenberg's%20testimony%20house%203-15.htm).

Children's Defense Fund (2000) *Families struggling to make it in the workforce: a post Welfare report* (www.childrensdefense.org/pdf/CMPreport.pdf).

Citro, C. and Michael, R. (1995) *Measuring poverty: A new approach*, Washington, DC: National Academy Press.

Edelman, P. (2001) 'Many are still stuck in poverty', *The Boston Globe – Sunday Edition*, 19 August, 198D.

Eissa, N. and Hoynes, H. (1999) *The earned income tax credit and the labor supply of married couples*, Discussion Paper No 1194-99, IRP: University of Wisconsin-Madison (www.ssc.wisc.edu/irp/pubs/dp119499.pdf).

Food Research and Action Center (2001) *Federal food programs: Food stamp program* (www.frac.org/html/federal_food_programs/programs/fsp.html).

Garrett, B. and Holahan, J. (2000) 'Welfare leavers, Medicaid coverage, and private health insurance (Series B, No. B-13)', *Assessing the New Federalism Project*, Washington, DC: The Urban Institute, pp 1-5 (newfederalism.urban.org/html/series_b/b13/b13.html).

Gordon, D. and Townsend, P. (2000) 'Introduction: the measurement of poverty in Europe', in D. Gordon and P. Townsend (eds) *Breadline Europe: The measurement of poverty*, Bristol: The Policy Press, pp 1-22.

Gornick, J. (2001) 'Cancel the funeral: reports of the demise of the European welfare state are premature', *Dissent*, Summer, pp 13-18.

Gornick, J. and Meyers, M. (2001) 'Lesson-drawing in family policy: media reports and empirical evidence about European developments', *Journal of Comparative Policy Analysis: Research and Practice*, vol 3, no 1, pp 31-57.

Greenberg, M. and Schumacher, R. (1999) *Child care after leaving welfare: Early evidence from state studies*, Washington, DC: Center for Law and Social Policy (www.clasp.org/pubs/childcareChild%20Care%20after%20Leaving%20 Welfare.htm).

Gullo, K. (2001) 'Bush urges Supreme Court to take up voucher case', *The Detroit News*, 23 June (detnews.com/2001/schools/0106/24/schools-239375.htm).

Kaiser Commission on Medicaid and the Uninsured (1999) *The Medicaid program at a glance*, Washington, DC: Henry J. Kaiser Family foundation (www.kff.org/content/archive/2004/pub2004.pdf).

Loprest, P. (1999) 'How families that left welfare are doing: a national picture (series B, no B-1)', *Assessing the New Federalism Project*, Washington, DC: The Urban Institute, pp 1-5 (newfederalism.urban.org/html/series_b/anf_b1.html).

Mead, L.M. (1997) 'Welfare employment', in L.M. Mead (ed) *The New paternalism: Supervisory approaches to poverty*, Washington, DC: The Brookings Institution Press, pp 39-88 (brookings.nap.edu/books/081575650X/html/index.html).

Miller, S. and Oyen, E. (1996) 'Remeasuring poverty', *Poverty and Race*, vol 5, no 5, pp 1-5.

Miller, S. and Roby, P. (1970) *The future of inequality*, New York, NY: Basic Books.

Moffitt, R. and Roff, J. (2000) 'The diversity of welfare leavers', Welfare, children, and families – a three city study, Policy Brief 00-2, Baltimore, MD: Johns Hopkins University (www.econ.jhu.edu/People/Moffitt/WelfareReform.html).

Pear, R. (2002) 'House Democrats propose making the '96 welfare law an antipoverty weapon', *New York Times*, 24 January, p 22A.

Phillips, K. (2000) 'Who knows about the earned income tax credit (series B, no B 27)?', *Assessing the New Federalism Project*, Washington, DC: The Urban Institute, pp 1-7 (newfederalism.urban.org/html/series_b/b27/b27.html).

Staff of the Committee on Ways and Means (1996) *Summary of welfare reforms made by public law 104-193. The Personal Responsibility and Work Opportunity Reconciliation Act and associated legislation*, US House of Representatives (www.access.gpo.gov/congress/wm015.txt).

Staff of the US DHHS (Department of Health and Human Services) (2000) 'Appendix A: Program Data', *Indicators of welfare dependence: Annual report to Congress – March 2000* (see 'Aid to Families' at aspe.hhs.gov/hsp/indicators00/).

State Policy Documentation Project (2000) *State time limits on TANF cash assistance* (www.spdp.org/tanf/timelimits/tlovervw.pdf).

State Policy Documentation Project (2001) State policies regarding TANF work activities and requirements (www.spdp.org/tanf/work/worksumm.htm).

Strawn, J., Greenberg, M. and Savner, S. (2001) 'Improving employment outcomes under TANF', in *New world welfare conference*, Washington, DC: Brookings Institution Press.

The Brookings Institution (2001) *Welfare reform and beyond – Facts at a glance: Employment Rate of Adult TANF Recipients, 1992-1999* (www.brook.edu/wrb/resources/facts/010404_TANF_employment_rate.htm).

US DAFNS (Department of Agriculture, Food and Nutrition Service) (2001) 'Food stamps: frequently asked questions' (www.fns.usda.gov/fsp/menu/faqs/faqs.htm).

US DOC (Department of Commerce) Bureau of the Census (2000) 'Table 4: Poverty status of families, by type of family, presence of related children, race, and Hispanic origin: 1959 to 1999', *Historical poverty tables*, Poverty and Health Statistics Branch/HHES Division, Current Population Survey (www.census.gov/hhes/poverty/histpov/hstpov4.html).

US DOC Bureau of the Census (2001a) 'Poverty thresholds in 2000, by size of family and number of related children under 18 years', *Poverty 2000*, Poverty and Health Statistics Branch/HHES Division, Current Population Survey (www.census.gov/hhes/poverty/threshld/thresh00.html).

US DOC Bureau of the Census (2001b) *Resident population estimates of the United States by age and sex: April 1, 1990 to July 1, 1999, with short-term projection to November 1, 2000* (eire.census.gov/popest/archives/national/nation2/intfile2-1.txt).

US DOC Bureau of the Census (2001c) 'Table P-7: regions – people (both sexes combined – all races) by median and mean income: 1974 to 1999', *Historical poverty tables*, Income Statistics Branch/HHES Division, Current Population Survey (www.census.gov/hhes/income/histinc/p07.html).

US DHHS (Department of Health and Human Services)/ACF (1996) *Characteristics and financial circumstances of AFDC recipients – FY1996*, Office of Planning, Research and Evaluation – Division of Data Collection and Analysis (www.acf.dhhs.gov/programs/ofa/cfc_fy96.htm).

US DHHS/ACF (Administration for Children and Families) (1999) *President Clinton will announce record numbers of people on welfare are working as businesses hire from the welfare rolls – August 3, 1999* (www.acf.dhhs.gov/news/press/1999/w2w0803.htm).

US DHHS/ACF (2000) *Temporary assistance for needy families (TANF) 1936-1999* (www.acf.dhhs.gov/news/stats/3697.htm).

US DHHS/ACF/OFA (Office of Family Assistance) (2001) *Helping families achieve self-sufficiency: A guide on funding services for children and families through the TANF program* (www.acf.dhhs.gov/programs/ofa/funds2.htm).

US DHHS/ACF/OPA (Office of Public Affairs) (2001) *Fact sheet: welfare: Temporary Assistance for Needy Families* (TANF) (www.acf.dhhs.gov/programs/opa/facts/tanf.htm).

US DHHS/HCFA (Health Care Financing Administration) (1995) *Medicaid eligibility* (www.hcfa.gov/medicaid/meligib.htm).

US DHSS/Office of APSE (Assistant Secretary for Planning and Evaluation) – Human Services Policy (HSP) (1998) 'A brief history of the AFDC programme', in *Aid to families with dependent children: The baseline* (aspe.hhs.gov/hsp/AFDC/afdcbase98.htm).

US Department of Housing and Urban Development (2001) *Housing choice voucher programme fact sheet*, Washington, DC (www.hud.gov/section8.cfm).

US Department of Labor, Bureau of Labor Statistics (2001) 'Average hourly earnings of production workers' in *National employment, hours, and earnings*, Series ID EES00500006 (www.bls.gov/webapps/legacy/cesbtab4.htm?H5).

US GAO (General Accounting Office) (1997a) *Report to the Chairman, Subcommittee on Human Resources, Committee on Government Reform and Oversight, House of Representatives – Social service privatization: Expansion poses challenges in ensuring accountability for programme results* (GAO/HEHS-98-6), Washington, DC: GAO Health, Education, and Human Services Division (www.conginst.org/resultsact/pdf/he98006.pdf).

US GAO (1997b) *Report to the Ranking Minority Member, Committee on Finance, US Senate – Welfare Reform: Three States' approaches show promise of increasing work participation* (GAO/HEHS-97-80), Washington, DC: GAO Health, Education, and Human Services Division.

US GAO/OPA (2001) *Welfare reform: More coordinated federal efforts could help states and localities move TANF recipients with impairments toward employment* (GAO-02-85), summarised in *Month in Review*, November, pp 4-5.

Wall Street Journal (2002) 'What's news', *Wall Street Journal*, 15 January, p 1A.

Zedlewski, S. and Brauner, S. (1999) 'Are the steep declines in food stamp participation linked to falling welfare caseloads (series B, no B-3)?', *Assessing the New Federalism Project*, Washington, DC: The Urban Institute, pp 1-5. (newfederalism.urban.org/html/series_b/b3/anf_b3.html).

FIVE

A European definition of poverty: the fight against poverty and social exclusion in the member states of the European Union

Bernd Schulte

Social exclusion: the new paradigm

Recent years have seen increasing awareness and concern about the growth of poverty and social exclusion within Europe as a whole. In Western Europe this rediscovery of poverty has been associated with the resurgence of high unemployment, while in the 1990s, the problems of the transition to a market economy are now raising similar concerns in Central and Eastern Europe. This growing concern has been evident in debates at the level of the European Community and anti-poverty programmes – sponsored by the European Commission (EC) – have included research studies, efforts at statistical harmonisation, and action project social exclusion was written into the Maastricht Treaty and into the objectives of the structural funds (Room, 1995). The Council of Europe has been commissioning studies of social exclusion as well, focused on the wider range of EC member states, and fuelled by its specific interest in human rights (Duffy, 1995). The term 'social exclusion' has replaced 'poverty' in EC law and policies since then.

These days, it is well accepted that poverty is not simply a matter of inadequate financial resources, and that combating poverty also requires access by individuals and families to decent living conditions and means of integration into the labour market (and society more generally). Accordingly, there is no single legal instrument or social programme which could be put forward as a means of preventing and combating social exclusion, but rather a wide range of such instruments and programmes.

Since the objective of the Treaty of Rome was to construct a European *Economic* Community, little importance was attached to a common social policy. However, a first step towards the development of explicit social policy was taken in the 1970s, by giving practical meaning to the guarantee of equal treatment for men and women in labour law and social security (laid down in

Article 119 of the EEC Treaty). Since then, the EC Council of Ministers has passed five directives referring to this objective. Another important development in the mid-1970s was the recognition of the need to combat poverty as one of the EC's priorities, which evolved in response to debates concerning persistent poverty, which had emerged as a result of changes in family structure and rising unemployment (later termed 'new poverty') in member states. Since then, the EC has set up three poverty programmes to stimulate political debate on poverty and social exclusion in the member states, permit the exchange of experience and the emergence of a network of experts, practitioners and policy makers, and to coordinate activities in the member states for combating poverty and social exclusion.

The first European anti-poverty programme (1975-80) included nine social reports on poverty and anti-poverty policy (EC, 1981). In several member states (for example Germany, Italy) these reports spurred a new national debate and contributed to the rediscovery of poverty, mentioned above (see, for example Hauser et al, 1981).

The second European anti-poverty programme (1986-89) saw action programmes and the beginning of work on the long-term establishment of social indicators (that is, poverty indicators) by Eurostat.

The third programme (1990-94) established the so-called 'observatory' on policies to combat social exclusion, which involved a network of researchers and complemented the other observatories that the EC had already established in the social field, dealing, for example, with family policy and policies in relation to older people and social security. This programme, 'Poverty 3', approved following a Resolution of the European Council in 1989, attempts a multidimensional approach to poverty. It was based on three key principles – multidimensionality of activities, partnership, and participation of the population – and involved 27 model projects and 12 innovative initiatives in Europe. However, the five-year budget of 55 million ECUs (albeit more than twice the budget of the second programme) worked out at less than 1 ECU for each poor person in the European Community.

Within these EC poverty programmes, the poor have been defined as "persons whose resources (material, cultural and social) are so limited as to exclude them from the minimum acceptable way of life in the member states in which they live". This reflects the relative conception of poverty that emerged in the 1950s and 1960s; poverty was to be considered relative to the resources and general standard of living of a particular society at a particular time.

However, poverty refers not only to a shortage of money, but also includes the deprivation of various non-monetary characteristics, such as education, vocational training, work capacity, health and housing, and social participation. According to this definition, poverty is the extreme form of inequality in living standards. Though insufficient income is only one aspect of poverty, it is the common denominator of all poverty situations and can therefore be a useful indicator of the extent of poverty. In the mid-1980s, the proportion of persons with per capita disposable incomes below 50% of the national average was, according to EC statistics:

- *particularly high* (18-32%) in Greece, Ireland, Portugal, Spain and the UK;
- *about average* (15%) in France and Italy;
- *relatively low* (6-11%) in Belgium, Denmark, Germany and the Netherlands.

Newer EC estimates, derived from household surveys, increase the number of persons with low income in 1985 from 44 million to 50 million, corresponding to 15.4% of the total population of the 12 member states. The same calculations for 1980 give a figure of 49 million persons with low income, which means that the number of poor people stabilised between 1980 and 1985, as did the proportion of affected the population. While the absolute level of poverty stabilised between 1975 and 1985, it changed in composition. Poverty among older people decreased at a time when their numbers increased as a proportion of the total population. Instead, poverty began increasingly to afflict the working-age population, particularly families with dependent children. This was linked to the rise in unemployment and the change in family structures, principally the growing number of lone-parent families. *Income poverty* is still, however, the dominant feature, because lack of financial means often leads to the lack of the other components of a decent life.

Compared to poverty, *social exclusion* is characterised by the denial of basic rights. In this sense, social exclusion relates to *social citizenship* (as defined by T.H. Marshall), denoting the whole range of rights, from the right to social security and economic wellbeing, to the right to a full share in the social heritage and to the life of a civilised human being according to the normal standards prevailing in that society. Social citizenship thus includes the right to cash benefits up to a minimum level of subsistence, on the one hand, and access to such benefits and services which are necessary for a minimal degree of participation in the life of the community, on the other.

The growing importance of social exclusion can be seen from some figures. According to EC statistics, in the mid-1990s more than 50 million people in the member states lived below subsistence level (15% of the total population), about 3 million were homeless, and more than 17 million were unemployed. These figures clearly show a rift in European societies.

Of the many factors causing social exclusion, three main causes emerged:

- growing unemployment, which deprives people of their main integration factor;
- the breakdown of family structures, with the result that family cohesion is becoming less and less important;
- economic and social policies of the member states, which have not yet found a satisfactory solution to these urgent social problems (Quintin, 1994).

Those excluded or threatened with exclusion in Europe are, first of all, the young unemployed, the long-term unemployed, the physically, mentally and psychologically disabled, the chronically ill, foreigners, refugees, migrants, women, the homeless, offenders, and, increasingly, children and large families. Social exclusion has increased in recent years, despite the fact that the relatively rich European countries have well-developed social security systems. Special consideration must be given to the risk groups and to the most disadvantaged, including refugees, asylum seekers, Third World migrants and illegal migrants, for whom Europe will continue to be a privileged destination, and who will therefore continue to pose a major challenge.

From a legal point of view, there is a need to define and reappraise basic social rights, while investigating ways in which the socially excluded can be assisted. This involves listing and reviewing the main international legal instruments dealing with civil, political, economic, social and cultural rights with regard to the struggle against poverty and social exclusion (see, for example, Vogel-Polsky, 1993).

Just as the problem of social exclusion has many dimensions, virtually all of the areas of action by member states have an impact on social exclusion, though employment and social protection policies play a particularly vital role while being complemented by broad-based integration actions.

The fight against social exclusion in European Union member states

Policies

Public expenditure by the member states accounts on average for more than half of GDP, and most of this expenditure goes on areas that can help to promote social inclusion. Providing pensions, health care, and other benefits, social protection expenditure amounts to well over a quarter of total GDP across the European Union (EU). This shows both the commitment of the member states to promoting social inclusion and the extent of their means to achieve it.

As employment is a key means of participation for most people of working age, employment policies also contribute to tackling social exclusion. All member states are taking steps to address this problem, especially since the Essen Summit, and above all the Treaty of Amsterdam of 1 May 1999, and within the framework of the European Employment Strategy, which has turned the promotion of employment into a top political priority across the EU. Different member states are taking different steps according to their circumstances, including shaping tax and benefit systems to make it more attractive for people to take up work, and providing training opportunities and 'individual pathways' to social security.

If normalcy goes along with integration into the labour market and, as a consequence, into contributory social security schemes, social assistance should not only aim at providing a minimum of subsistence (that is, income maintenance and insertion into the labour market), but also integration into the systems of social security (for example, by contributing to social insurance schemes on behalf of those who are, for economic reasons, unable to do so). Thus, persons who are unable to pay contributions to social insurance schemes should get access to such schemes by credits financed from general taxation.

Another important policy field is fiscal policy, because the social minimum guaranteed by minimum-income schemes such as social assistance must be taken into account by the tax system, to exempt low earners from family responsibilities to pay taxes and ensure their entitlement to tax-financed social assistance benefits. If minimum-income schemes aim at integrating people into working life then these people must be given an opportunity to make their own living instead of relying on means-tested social assistance. This requires that the tax threshold (that is the break-point of taxation) is set to exempt the guaranteed minimum of subsistence from taxation.

Access to law is another important issue, because people who are income-poor are liable to suffer from deprivation in other areas (for example, health, housing, education and training, employment, leisure and culture, mobility, communication), and in the field of justice.

Despite the fact that economic development and rising unemployment have contributed to an increase in the occurrence of poverty and social exclusion, the perception of these developments, which appear to be more or less the same in all European countries, has not put these problems at the top of the political agenda. Politicians seem more concerned about those social problems that 'middle-class society' and the median voter are confronted with, namely the ageing of society and its consequences, such as the pension problem and the need for long-term care, and the impact of labour market developments on social security systems (that is the financial crisis of the welfare state).

Trends in poverty and social exclusion in the EC member states

Social protection systems play a huge role in promoting solidarity in European societies. Through income distribution and other benefits, nearly 100 million people are lifted out of poverty, reducing relative poverty by more than half, from almost 40% of European citizens to about 18%. Despite this important achievement of the European Social Model, poverty and social exclusion remain a key challenge, threatening the standard of living and quality of life of nearly 60 million people. Moreover, there are signs that social cohesion in European societies may be weakening. The EC's first Cohesion Report presents evidence which suggests that, even though a process of convergence between member states is apparent, economic and social cohesion in most member states experienced a setback during the 1990s. Economic growth is bringing benefits for some citizens and residents, but not for all. Growing social dislocation has become more visible in many cities, in particular through homelessness and the 'ghettoisation' of entire neighbourhoods which have become more and more deprived and cut off from the society around them. Social exclusion weakens participation and integration of people in society. This has many dimensions. It generally combines several types of deprivation, such as poor education, health, environment, housing, culture, access to social services, family support or job opportunities. There is, therefore, no single way to measure social exclusion. Therefore, when looking at trends in social exclusion, we look at a range of relevant indicators and factors, in order to build up an overall picture.

Unemployment, and particularly long-term unemployment, remains high, and hits some groups particularly hard: young people, women, people who are low-skilled or whose skills have become obsolete. For other groups, such as people with disabilities, ex-offenders, immigrants and people belonging to ethnic minorities, it is often difficult to get a job with good terms and conditions. Low pay and precarious forms of employment have led to a significant number of working poor, accounting for about one third of people in relative poverty in the EU.

The increase in long-term unemployment is especially worrying, as it weakens people's chances of employment through deskilling and ever-lower employability. It also has a strong impact on other dimensions of their lives, with people at risk of losing not just income but self-belief. There are also signs of increasing polarisation between 'workless households' and those where everyone of working age is employed. Prevention of long-term unemployment is therefore also the top priority of the European Employment Strategy. In addition to 17 million unemployed, there are another 8-9 million discouraged workers (especially women), people who do not seek a job because they think they cannot get a job. Many people are formally classified as long-term sick, persons with disabilities or early retired, and do not belong to the labour force any more. Their exclusion from the labour market contributes to an average employment rate in the EU of around 60%, which is low by international standards, and their reintegration requires special attention.

There have been widespread efforts in most member states to take active steps to reduce the number of people dependent on social benefits, in particular through a combination of social-protection measures with more active labour-market policies. Such moves toward 'activation' require effective pathways to integration and opportunities for training, retraining and access to employment. Experience with vocational activation, in connection with minimum income and social-assistance schemes, for example, has shown that success depends on improving access to benefits and services, and promoting specific integration measures. As the EC's Social Protection Report for 1997 (EC, 1998) pointed out, 'activation' has not been confined to unemployment benefits, but has been extended to other groups dependent on social transfers, such as people with disabilities, lone parents and those retiring from work early. This has been not just to reduce dependency and expenditure, but to ensure that the people concerned are able to enhance their participation and self-reliance within society.

Access to decent housing proves difficult for many people of low income. European welfare associations estimate that 15 million people across the EU live in substandard or overcrowded accommodation. Homelessness remains a concern, with approximately 3 million people without a fixed home of their own.

In larger cities, poor housing conditions increasingly affect entire neighbourhoods, adding an important spatial dimension to the problem of exclusion. The pattern of homelessness also changed during the 1990s; although adult men remained the largest group, more women, children and young people became homeless.

The physical, social and mental-health situation of people and society is of the utmost importance for inclusion. People are living longer, which contributes to the ageing of populations. Living longer may not necessarily mean living in better health. In general, decreased mortality goes hand-in-hand with more persons having one or more disabilities, and with an increased demand for healthcare services

Health variations continue to persist, both within and between member states. Social inequalities affect people's health, with people in lower socioeconomic positions suffering from higher death rates. Some new health risks have emerged, such as AIDS and drug dependency. Lifestyles detrimental to health, such as smoking and excessive drinking, are having a negative effect on the improvement of health and on the lowering of mortality. Income distribution and poverty figures indicate that disparity and inequality in most member states have not been reduced, in spite of continued economic growth. Roughly one in five European citizens continues to live beneath the relative 'poverty line', measured according to European statistical standards. Inequalities between those on low incomes and those on high incomes are growing. The number of minimum-income recipients in most of the member states has risen since the end of the 1980s.

There is also growing evidence to suggest that vulnerability to poverty is more widespread than 'snapshot' poverty figures indicate. Even in member states where income distribution tends to be relatively equal, between 20% and 40% of the population experience spells of low income over a period of 3-6 years. On the other hand, the number of people in permanent poverty is comparatively low, around 2-6%. Low income also strikes certain groups disproportionately: young and elderly persons, particularly when living alone, families with children, single-parent households and the low-skilled.

Household sizes are declining across Europe, and the number of people living alone is rising. This trend toward changing family structures and more individual lifestyles has both positive and negative impacts. Exclusion of the older people and young people is a particular issue, as the potential for support from within the family shrinks. Single parents and men living alone are over-represented among the recipients of minimum income. The relevance of

Table 5.1: Relative poverty in the EU (1993-94) (measured in terms of proportion of the population below 60% of the national equivalised median income[a])

	First wave (%)	Second wave (%)
Belgium	17.4	18.0
Denmark	9.1	10.7
Germany	17.1	17.1
Greece	22.8	20.7
Spain	19.8	18.9
France	16.3	15.8
Ireland	19.7	21.4
Italy	20.1	18.7
Luxembourg	15.6	14.1
Netherlands	10.7	10.0
Portugal	2.4	23.9
UK	21.3	20.5
Austria (second wave only)		17.0
EU12/EU13	18.6	18.1
Finland[b]	6.2	6.7
Sweden[c]	7.2	7.6

[a] In November 1998, the EU Statistical Programming Committee decided to switch to the median income instead of the mean income to determine the level of poverty, and to use the 60% cut-off as the main reference point (EC, 1999a).

[b] Imputed rent and benefits in kind included in income concept.

[c] The data covers the population aged 20-84, excluding full-time students and young adults of more than 18 years staying with their parents.

Sources: Eurostat-ECIHP, first and second wave 1994-95; Finnish Income Distribution Survey; Swedish Survey of Living Conditions

changing patterns of family structure and support is illustrated by the different risks of poverty among different people.

All these are indications that the risk of social exclusion in our societies may be rising. Reducing that risk raises challenges in the areas outlined above, and beyond, in fields such as culture, education and training, urban and rural development, basic utilities and services. For example, basic literacy and numeracy remains a problem across the EU (often affecting poor and minority communities in particular). In many deprived areas, access to basic facilities and services proves increasingly difficult – from public transport to local shops, from provision of utilities such as electricity and telephones to financial services and culture. Exclusion also results from the denial of social rights and in some cases from discrimination. All of this reflects the multidimensional nature of social exclusion.

These different issues and areas are experienced differently by each person. The effect of the same event (being made unemployed, for example) will then

Table 5.2: Poverty risk – who is vulnerable and to what extent?

I in 2	Unemployed or otherwise economically inactive
I in 3	Single parent with young children
	Young person living alone
I in 4	Retired person particularly when living alone
	Couples with three children or more
I in 5	Single parent with one child
I in 7	Middle-aged person living alone
	Couple without children
	Couple with two children or with one older child
I in 10	Working poor – families whose household reference person is self-employed
	Couple with one young child

Source: Eurostat-ECHP (1994)

clearly be different depending on the situation in other dimensions (such as support from within the family, educational level, the environment where one lives, being a migrant, a refugee or a member of an ethnic minority). Past circumstances are also relevant, as they affect the means and capacity of persons to cope with new challenges and problems. For example, although many of those people on low incomes improve their situations after several months, many of them later fall back into poverty. And as this cycle goes on, it becomes more and more difficult to leave poverty permanently (Leisering and Leibfried, 1999).

Across the dimensions of social exclusion, there are crucial differences between women and men. Women are over-represented among many key risk groups for exclusion, including the unemployed, lone parents, elderly living alone, low-paid and precarious workers, and recipients of social welfare. Studies also suggest that women are particularly affected by exclusion factors such as poor housing, overstretched social services, and poverty, because of their role as the primary managers of household resources. In general, women tend to bear the direct impact of feeding and clothing a family on insufficient income, negotiating for scarce social services, and coping with badly designed, isolated and poorly maintained social housing. And they tend to face specific obstacles, again frequently linked to childcare responsibilities, to participation in decision making even at community level.

While the distinct impact of exclusion on women is very apparent, men are also affected in specific ways. Economic activity rates for men are falling in the EU. Recent studies in some member states point to the overall trend for girls to achieve better than boys throughout schooling, suggesting that in modern employment markets, lower verbal skills are disadvantaging many boys who could once have obtained well-paid jobs as skilled manual labour. At the extreme end, marginalisation and hopelessness appear to be associated with a sharp rise in rates of drug addiction and suicide among young men. The location of exclusion is another key horizontal issue. Social exclusion is not spread evenly; it is frequently concentrated in specific areas of deprivation. As the vast majority of people live in an urban environment, the urban dimension to social exclusion is critical. Social exclusion of course exists in both urban and rural settings, but different issues are involved requiring appropriate responses.

In order to overcome social exclusion it is essential to involve state and society, national, regional and local authorities, the social partners and non-governmental organisations. This means that social exclusion is a task for all political actors. It is for this reason that many countries do not have an explicit policy on social exclusion. However, there are examples of explicit policies: poor as demonstrated by recent research on longitudinal data (Leisering and Leibfried, 1999) and a growing insecurity among the middle classes which are exposed to the risk of unemployment and to the ensuing risk of becoming poor and socially excluded.

The UK has made social exclusion a cross-government priority and established a Social Exclusion Unit (SEU) to coordinate and improve government action to reduce social exclusion by improving understanding of the key characteristics of social exclusion and the impact on it of government policies, and by encouraging cooperation, disseminating best practice, and, where necessary, making recommendations for changes in policies, administrative machinery or delivery mechanisms.

The SEU is intended to focus on issues going beyond individual departments, and has sought to involve a wide range of stakeholders through consultation and involving other non-governmental organisations. The reports of the SEU have also made a series of detailed recommendations for implementation and set specific targets for improvement, particularly on rough sleeping, on truancy and school exclusion, and on deprived neighbourhoods.

Ireland has established 'Sharing in progress: the national anti-poverty strategy', following the UN World Summit in Copenhagen in March 1995. This was drawn up following widespread consultation, especially with people affected by poverty. The strategy has the aim, over the period 1997-2007, of considerably reducing the number of those who are 'consistently poor', from 9-15% to less than 5.1%. This strategy is supported by specific institutional structures at both the political level – a Cabinet Sub-Committee – and administrative level (for example Inter-Departmental Policy Committee and Combat Poverty Agency), using mechanisms including 'poverty and equality proofing' of relevant policies. The strategy is based on a multidimensional understanding of poverty and the principle that addressing poverty involves tackling the deep-seated underlying structural inequalities that create and perpetuate it. It focuses on five key areas:

- educational disadvantages;
- unemployment, particularly long-term unemployment;
- income adequacy;
- disadvantaged urban areas;
- rural poverty.

In Finland, social exclusion as such has not been any special or major issue in politics. Therefore, there is no special or distinct programme for social exclusion. Combating unemployment is the major concern and objective in the programme of the current government. However, poverty and social exclusion have received growing attention. The Ministry of Social Affairs and Health, which is mainly responsible for exclusion-related issues, has set up a working group to collect, maintain and assess the existing data and information about poverty and social exclusion in Finland. This group also prepares annually a short review on the situation (most recent from April 1998). The same group also coordinates and updates a list of various projects that have national importance to combat social exclusion. These projects are presented for different population groups facing the most severe risk of exclusion. The most recent publication is from February 1998. The Finnish state budget for 1999 includes special funding for the renovation of segregated housing areas and socially problematic suburbs. The whole issue of urban poverty and deprivation has gained increasing attention, although it is seen as controversial. Legislation for social assistance was partially reformed, introducing some new conditions for receiving the benefit (for example more sanctions for those refusing work offered, less coverage of housing costs, and so on). The explicit aim of this reform was to stop the growth of the number of recipients, to reduce the costs of the benefit and to shorten the individual dependency spells. According to the Finnish Employment Strategy, which was constructed in line with the Luxembourg Job Summit objectives, every new job seeker is offered a tailored individual plan of increasing employability and of improving their opportunities to find a job. Apart from this, every young unemployed person lacking professional skills is offered an opportunity to participate in vocational training, which also forms a precondition for their labour-market support (flat-rate benefit).

In France, a law of 29 July 1998, relating to the fight against exclusion, grouped together all the main measures involved, aiming to improve coordination and produce more consistency and efficiency. Exclusions are defined in terms of access of all to rights in the fields of employment, housing, health care, justice, education, training, culture, family and child protection. Social inclusion is now a priority for public policies, and all public institutions and other stakeholders should participate in the implementation of the principles settled in the law. Part of the initiative is to inform everyone about their rights and to help them if necessary to be able to use them.

The TRACE 'pathways to jobs' programme, for example, seeks to prevent and fight against social exclusion by providing individual 'pathways' to integration in the labour market, including personalised counselling services for a period of one and a half years, to over 100,000 young people during 1998-2000. Emergency financial aid is available for youth who are in critical situation for lack of resources between the two stages of the TRACE process.

As far as improving access to rights is concerned, the law reinforces representation of vulnerable groups and their corresponding associations in the different social instances where decisions concerning them are taken. It also puts particular emphasis on integration into the labour market (an issue which is emphasised in the Employment National Action Plan and for which part of the European Social Fund appropriations are used), housing for vulnerable groups and health. Provisions are also included for ongoing evaluation of the social exclusion needs and of the impact of the measures.

In Portugal, the national strategy against poverty and social exclusion is given high priority by the government. The 'Programa Nacional de lucha contra la Pobreza' was complemented in 1995 by INTEGRAR, co-financed by the European Social Fund and adapting to the Portuguese realities the principles developed in the previous European poverty programmes: participation, partnership and multidimensionality. With a view to improving the implementation of these two programmes, incentives were given to encourage wider cooperation between all possible stakeholders in the 'Pacto de Cooperaçao para a Solidariedale social'. Also building on the exchanges of experiences at EU level, and the corresponding Council Recommendation, a minimum-income scheme was established in 1997. It combines financial support with measures to foster social and vocational integration. Minimum-income recipients sign integration agreements in which they commit themselves to participate in specific measures relating to education, vocational training, employment, health, social welfare or housing.

Combating social exclusion and preventing the trends towards a two-tier society is also an important concern in Denmark. Government initiatives put emphasis on activation of social policies with a view to employability and social integration and to prevent exclusion from the labour market. Another initiative consists in the promotion of partnership between public authorities and companies in the fight against exclusion. Following the 1995 UN World Summit for Social Development in Copenhagen, the Danish government developed a nationwide campaign for the social responsibility of enterprises, and then created a specific institution, the Copenhagen Centre, to support efforts in this respect, and to cooperate closely with public authorities, companies, trade unions and NGOs (EC, 1999a).

Minimum incomes

Minimum-income schemes operate as a final safety net for those unable to make their living otherwise. As a rule, they make up the shortfall between the guaranteed minimum on the one hand and the income from work, own and family resources or other social benefits on the other hand. All Western European welfare states apply themselves to cover social needs, as a rule in recognition of the basic right of any person to sufficient resources and social assistance to live in a manner compatible with human dignity, mostly as part of a comprehensive and consistent attempt to combat social exclusion. On this basis, such a social minimum is a basic right of a person, as distinguished from the former social-assistance schemes, which developed from traditional discretionary policies of support to the most needy, accessible to everybody and of limited duration.

The levels of the national social minimum incomes are generally defined for the country as a whole, but can take into account regional or even local variations in the standard of living. The amounts taken into account can be indexed to consumer prices, to wages or to social benefits. However, they are usually subject to some sort of political discretion, which takes into account not only the needs of the recipients of minimum incomes, but also the average income, especially of workers, as well as the economic situation and the situation of the labour market. Besides, the levels of payment depend on the composition of the household and are subsidiary to family solidarity. As minimum incomes are always non-contributory, the funding of these schemes is dependent on tax revenues. Minimum incomes are, as a rule, only intended to be a temporary measure to alleviate exceptional situations which the recipient should be expected to escape from, with or without assistance, particularly through remunerative work. Accordingly, recipients are required to be available for work or training, exceptions covering illness, disability, old age or caring for young children or disabled adults. They must be actively looking for work and be, on principle, ready to accept any suitable job. Traditionally, minimum-income schemes concern the most acute situation of lack of financial resources, but are not intended to cover all situations of poverty.

Within the broad range of social transfers provided by social protection systems, minimum incomes are the final safety-net mechanism of income redistribution. They help the poorest people in society by covering basic needs without a requirement for prior contributions. Behind the common principles expressed in the recommendation lie complex and varied national methods of implementation. In fact, minimum incomes do not act in isolation in social protection systems, but form part of a range of benefits and social services, of which the report gives a first overview.

The number of minimum-income beneficiaries has risen since the end of the 1980s. There appear to be two main reasons for this. The first is higher and more persistent unemployment. The second relates to a rise in the numbers who have experienced social disruptions in their lives, such as family breakdown, forced migration, homelessness, over-indebtedness, or prison. Compared to the overall population, single men and single-parent families are over-represented.

Member states, to varying degrees, relate minimum incomes to measures aimed at increasing access to the labour market. The range of action this implies includes: mobilising employment services more strongly for the most disadvantaged people; socially useful activities; job creation in the non-profit sector; financial incentives to employers to hire minimum-income recipients; and helping people to move into employment without loss of income. These measures still have a limited impact and should evolve to improve integration of minimum-income recipients into the labour market. This shift towards more active support for minimum-income recipients of working age is consonant with meeting the commitments of the European Employment Strategy.

In looking for greater effectiveness, several member states are widening their scope of intervention to include measures which aim at improving economic and social integration of minimum-income recipients. This may cover broader social issues such as housing, education, family, health or citizenship. A more individualised approach is also being developed in some member states, which more actively involves minimum-income recipients in designing personal projects with the support of social and employment services, as well as that of local partners.

Minimum-income recipients benefit from general national provisions relating to healthcare, education and family assistance. Table 5.3 only states services and allowances over and above the standard national provisions. Employment and training provisions are treated directly in the text of this report.

The Council Recommendations 92/441/EEC of 24 June 1992 on common criteria concerning sufficient resources and social assistance in social protection systems and 92/442/EEC of 27 July 1992 on the convergence of social protection objectives and policies (EC, 1992) provides scope for action at European Community level that may support and complement the activities of member states in combating social exclusion. For the EC has been entrusted with the task to organise regular exchanges with the member states on the development of their policies both in the field of social assistance and social protection, in general. Furthermore, the EC has to submit regular reports to the council on progress achieved in relation to the objectives laid down in the recommendations. The recommendation on sufficient resources and social assistance, which may be taken as a response of the European Community to the patchy and diverse nature of minimum-income guarantee schemes within member states, aims at combating social exclusion and guaranteeing everyone a level of means and resources which corresponds to human dignity by affirming the need to recognise a general right to a guarantee of sufficient, stable and reliable resources and benefits and by encouraging the member states to adapt their social-protection systems accordingly. This right should also give access to health protection and help in obtaining access to rights, services and benefits needed for economic and social integration.

This approach takes account of the fact that the old discretionary public assessments, which were strongly influenced by the traditional Poor Law, have been converted in the post-war period into a right to social assistance, which includes at least a right to financial assistance up to a minimum level of subsistence and to some degree of participation in the life of the community. At the same time, the traditional distinction between 'social assistance' and 'social security' has been fading away. Social assistance has been considered increasingly as one of the techniques by which the modern Western welfare state provides income security for all its citizens, as an element of social citizenship. The right to a minimum income, which is unconditional, has therefore become a cornerstone of the modern European welfare state.

In accordance with the recommendations the member states are held to recognise the right of a person to sufficient resources and social assistance as a

Table 5.3: National minimum-income schemes, main associated benefits and services

	Basic scheme	Main associated benefits and services
Austria	Sozialhilfe	Housing benefit (suitable accommodation which is not covered by the standard rates of benefit are met by means of additional cash or non-cash benefits). Illness or health insurance.
Belgium	Minimex (minimum de moyens d'existence Minimum inkomen)	In principle, Minimex covers all necessary costs. However, one-off payments may be issued at the discretion of local welfare offices. Main payments are for housing and housing-related costs, medical costs, utilities arrears, and so on.
Denmark	Social Bistand	Housing benefit. Education benefits for students living at or away from home.
Finland	Toimeentnlotuki	Housing benefit. The 'additional part of the living allowance' (for some discretionary expenses) covers especially high healthcare expenses of public health services, children's day-care costs and especially high costs of work-related necessities.
France	Revenu Minimum d'Insertion – RMI	Maximum housing allowance for tenants; exemption from housing tax. Free medical assistance. Within the Integration Contract, various means are put at the disposal of recipients.
Germany	Sozialhilfe	Housing benefit. Health insurance or illness-related expenses. Education allowance; aid for exceptional cases.
Ireland	Supplementary Welfare Allowance – Unemployment Assistance	Housing benefit. Allowance for clothing and footwear for school-age children. Benefits in kind for bedding, fuel and other essential household equipment.
Luxembourg	Revenu Minimum Garantie – RMG	Housing benefit. Free medical insurance.
Netherlands	Algemene Bijstand	Housing benefit. Free medical insurance.
Portugal	Rendimento Minimo Garantido – RMG	Housing benefit. Medical costs (for certain categories), education grants, subsidised public transport.
Spain	Renta Minima	Emergency social aid (housing, appliances, furniture).
Sweden	Socialbidrag	Housing benefit (allowance for single-parent families).
UK	Income Support Income-based Jobseeker's Allowance	Housing benefit; dental treatment, subsidised glasses, fabric supports. Milk and vitamins for children under 5 and pregnant women, school meals. Help with maternity and funeral payments. Cold Weather Payment for pensioners, disabled, those with child under 5; local tax allowance.

Sources: Guibentif and Bouget (1997); EC (1999b)

right based on respect for human dignity. The scope of that right is to be defined vis-à-vis individuals, having regard to legal residents and nationality, in accordance with the relevant provisions on residence, with the aim of progressively covering all exclusion situations in the connection as broadly as possible. Every person *who does not have access* individually or within the household in which he or she lives *to sufficient resources* is to have access to such a right. This right should be *subject to active availability for work or for vocational training* with the view to obtain work in the case of those persons whose age, health and family situation permit such active availability, or, where appropriate, subject to economic and social integration measures in the case of other persons,

Access to such a right is *not to be subject to time limits* assuming compliance with the eligibility conditions and on the understanding that, in practice, the right may be granted for limited but renewable periods.

An effort should be made in parallel to *reintegrate the poorest people into the systems of general rights,* that is, into the other systems of social protection. The right to a social minimum is to be accompanied by policies deemed necessary for the *economic and social integration of* those concerned.

The implementation of this right to a minimum of resources and social assistance is to be organised according to specific practical guidelines: the amount of resources considered sufficient to cover essential needs is to be fixed taking account of living standards and price levels in the countries concerned, for different types and sizes of household. Amounts are to be adjusted or supplemented to meet specific needs. In order to fix the amounts it should be referred to appropriate indicators, such as statistical data on the *average disposable income on household consumption, the legal minimum wage* if this exists or the *level of prices.* Arrangements should be established *for periodic review of these amounts,* based on the indicators mentioned earlier, in order to ensure that needs continue to be covered.

People, whose resources taken at the level of the individual or the household are lower than the amounts thus fixed, should be granted *differential financial aid* to bring them up to the above-mentioned amounts. An *incentive to seek employment* should be safeguarded for persons whose age and conditions render them fit for work. Besides, the necessary measures are to be taken to ensure that, with regard to the extent of the financial support thus granted, the implementation of regulations in the areas of *taxation, civil obligations and social security* takes account of the desirable level of sufficient resources and social assistance.

Every measure should be taken to enable those concerned to receive appropriate *social support,* comprising measures and services such as, in particular, *advice and counselling, information and assistance in obtaining these rights.* Arrangements should be adopted in respect of persons whose age and condition render them fit for work, which will ensure that they receive effective help to *enter or re-enter working life, including vocational training* where appropriate.

The necessary measures should be taken to ensure that the least privileged are *informed of* this right. The administrative procedures and arrangements for examining means and situations involved in claiming the right to sufficient resources and social assistance should be *simplified* as far as possible. Furthermore, the machinery for *appeals to independent third parties,* such as tribunals, to which the person concerned should have easy access should be organised.

However, the main distinguishing feature of minimum–income schemes continues to be the means test, aimed on the one hand at targeting social benefits to the most needy and on the other hand at reducing public expenditure on minimum-income benefits. Both means testing and inherent information, bureaucratic, legal and moral obstacles dissuade people from actually claiming social benefits and services to which they are legally entitled, and reduce the degree to which poverty and social exclusion are successfully, combated, as illustrated by the high degree of non take-up of means-tested benefits. This corresponds to the fact that social benefits can be subdivided into a 'penthouse suite' of measures organised in the form of contributory social benefits (that is, social insurances which are, as a rule, rather well funded), on the one hand, and the 'basement flat' of the tax-financed means-tested benefits aligned towards neediness, on the other. Therefore, special attention should be devoted to the access to social minima.

Another point should be made. Looking at the evolution of social assistance schemes (see Eardley et al, 1996), we can see that issues of costs, targeting of benefits to the most needy, means testing, fraud, selectivity (for example, as regards foreigners, especially immigrants and asylum-seekers), work incentives and work programmes do figure more prominently than in the past in most countries. The steps taken to tackle these issues are quite often contrary to the aforementioned individual right to social assistance, and they are at the same time in some cases contrary to the recommendation on sufficient resources and social assistance.

As regards guaranteed resources, the safety net of social security, there are again practical, administrative, psychological and sociological obstacles to access to these benefits. These include: the administrative complexity of the procedure for granting a minimum income; the ineffectiveness of the information disseminated by the service providers and public institutions; the poor coverage of certain categories of the population, such as the homeless; the appropriateness of the protection systems for the situation of itinerant populations (for example, gypsies, undeclared migrants or asylum seekers); the psychological difficulty for destitute people in admitting the conditions in which they live to social services often perceived as anonymous, indifferent or moralising; the felt impression of dependency; the stigmatising effects of the means test; the prejudices met by assisted people from the active population; the contractualisation of social rights (the tendency to make benefits providing a guaranteed minimum income dependent upon labour-market availability, registration at a local employment exchange, entry into a contract for occupational training or social insertion); the interdependence of social rights (that is, the fact that losing the right to one benefit – on expiry of the maximum duration or as a result of an administrative action – often meaning that the person concerned loses a whole series of other rights concerned with other benefits).

Access to the labour market

There are various measures offering incentives to employers. The most common are grants or a reduction in social-security contributions within a framework of fixed-term contracts. Most member states have made use of such measures without targeting minimum-income recipients specifically. Germany, Luxembourg, Belgium, the Netherlands, France and the UK give incentives to employers to take on minimum-income recipients.

Measures are included to minimise the risk of employers substituting subsidised workers for existing staff. They encourage employers to keep on employees after the subsidised periods ('contracts-types' in Luxembourg, tripartite agreements in Germany, agreements to meet quality criteria of the New Deal options in the UK, 'contrats inititiative emploi' in France). Experience shows that employers are, on the whole, not well disposed to taking on the people who are brought to them in such arrangements. Yet, particularly because of pre-selection by employers before they start, the proportion of those who subsequently find a regular job is higher than with the previously described options. It would be useful in future to evaluate the quality of the jobs offered.

Apart from financial incentives, several member states are trying to draw on the social responsibilities of companies and employees. Denmark organised a national and European conference on this subject in 1997. In France and Portugal, employers and trade unions are brought together in local commissions for integration, designed to help create new employment opportunities at local levels.

In Belgium, the public social welfare centres (CPAS) seek partnerships with employers. A further option has recently been opened to minimum-income recipients in France, Ireland, Spain and Portugal, that of assistance with creating one's own job or setting up a company. Specific subsidies are also given to set up 'enterprises d'insertion', undertakings which welcome and employ people with difficulties who are particularly vulnerable in labour-market terms.

When comparing net minimum-income replacement rates against average wages, the economic incentive to find work is generally preserved in the case of people living alone. They account for almost half of minimum-income recipients in the EU. In the case of couples with two children where only one parent is working, the replacement rates are significantly higher. However, replacement rates are lower in the case of both parents working, which is a very common situation in the Nordic countries and is becoming increasingly commonplace in the rest of the EU. Replacement rates for single-parent families have been somewhat underestimated, as they do not take account of child minding costs, which are a key factor when taking up a job.

The comparison between minimum incomes and minimum wages is a topic of debate in several member states. It would be useful to estimate in future the replacement rates against the statutory minimum wages, as there is a high probability that the wages available to someone leaving minimum-income schemes will be at this level.

As an incentive measure to stimulate job search, member states could, in principle, reduce minimum-income rates. They do not do so because the rates are seen as minimum subsistence levels and decreases would be difficult to justify. Member states have, however, reinforced penalties for people in receipt of benefit who turn down a job or refuse to participate in integration measures. Benefits may be suspended for a few months, and the suspension extended in the event of a further refusal (as in Belgium, Spain, France, Luxembourg and Portugal), or the amount reduced (by 20-25% in Denmark, Germany, and Finland, 15, 20 then 100% in the Netherlands, 40% of the personal allowance in the UK).

To ease transition from minimum income to a paid job, six member states (Belgium, Denmark, France, Germany, Ireland, and the Netherlands) have transitional periods (one to three years) during which minimum income can be used wholly or partly to top-up wages. Ireland and the Netherlands do so with the aim of encouraging part-time work. Luxembourg indefinitely disregards earnings up to a limit of 20% of the overall guaranteed income. Ireland and the UK allow minimum income to be claimed by people working up to 30 and 16 hours per week respectively. Beyond these limits they have opted for a system of in-work benefits applicable only to families with children. Only some autonomous communities in Spain have maintained a strict ban on receiving minimum income and being paid for work. The approach could be extended to associated benefits, as is the case for housing support in Ireland and the UK. Minimum-income recipients would then have stronger positive incentives to take advantage of the possibility of employment. As yet, few member states follow this path, perhaps because the complexity of the process and allocation of responsibilities at different administrative levels tends to slow progress.

The effectiveness of such measures depends on ensuring appropriate connections between labour law, social protection, training and active labour-market measures and tax systems. In line with the EC's White Paper on *Growth, competitiveness and employment* (Guideline Four in the European Employment Guidelines, COM (98) 574 final for 1999), member states have taken steps to lower non-wage labour costs for lower-skilled workers. Furthermore, member states have now agreed upon a specific Employment Guideline aiming at reviewing and refocusing benefit and tax systems and providing incentives for unemployed or inactive people to seek and take up work or training opportunities. Only a minority of recipients are able to leave minimum-income schemes for a paid job. To achieve better results, a new approach is being developed, based on individual contracts by which signatories commit themselves to personal projects.

Member states have begun to investigate other avenues of social integration, to address the complexity of institutional and personal barriers to integration faced by people. For example, minimum-income recipients may have difficulties in relation to family environment, education and housing, which might jeopardise their chances of finding and keeping a job. Tailor-made action plans designed to facilitate a consistent approach over a period of time, taking into account the family and social environment, may include, for example, seeking more social autonomy (language courses, driving lessons, detoxification treatment), improving the family situation (children's education, reducing debts), participating in local self-help schemes, improving housing or training, learning about rights and duties as citizens. Employment remains, in most cases, the final objective.

Member states have made varying amounts of progress in this area. For example:

- Finland: introduced compulsory individual plans in March 1998 for those rejecting a job offer;
- Germany: the 'Gesamtplan' provided for by the Sozialhilfe Act (§ 19 (4));
- Denmark: the 'individual handlingsplan' which the local authorities are obliged to organise for Social Bistand recipients aged over 25;
- The Netherlands: the Dutch 'weg naar de arbeids markt' for the long-term unemployed comprises agreements relating to social integration, education and training;
- UK: Jobseeker's Agreement is a condition of entitlement for Jobseeker's Allowance and is reviewed fortnightly. It sets out the range of jobs which the job seeker is available for and the steps he/she agrees to take to find work.

Other member states have developed the pathway approach as a mutual undertaking, which not only restores to minimum-income recipients responsibility for their future, but also specifies the way the social and employment services should help to achieve his/her objectives. Also, in France and Portugal, these mutual undertakings formally involve local communities represented within specific integration committees, which co-sign the commitments.

These commitments correspond to the 'contrat d'integration' in Belgium, the 'contrat d'insertion' in France, the 'projet d'insertion' in Luxembourg, the 'proyecto de integracion' in Spain, and the 'acordo de inserçao' in Portugal. Employment is one component among others in the overall objective of social integration. For instance, in Portugal, one out of five 'acordo de inserçao' deals with education, health and/or social support and one out of ten covers housing.

Access to social services

In their paper prepared for the 50th meeting of the European Social Security Committee (CDSS) of the Council of Europe under the 'Human Dignity and Social Exclusion' project, Cassiers and Dehon rightly point out that there have been many examinations, research studies and evaluations of European social-security systems since their creation at the end of the Second World War. These have followed mostly either the institutional approach (studying the historical stages in the formation of social-security systems, the political balances that presided over their emergence in Europe and the legal data specific to each national system), or the macroeconomic approach (concerned with the methods of financing social provision and also the demographic trend). Very few studies, however, have been devoted to another nonetheless vital aspect of the development of the crisis of the welfare state, practical accessibility for those entitled to social security benefits (Cassiers and Dehon, 1997). It is increasingly evident that, though it is recognised that everyone has certain rights (for example to health, to social security), there are in practice a whole series of obstacles which prevent or limit the concrete exercise of these rights. Difficulties of an administrative nature (complexity of the procedures, lack of information on the services available, and so on), of a practical nature (for example, low level of social coverage, more and more charges for services), or of a psychological nature (inadequate training of service providers, stigmatising effect of being dependent on benefits, and so on) encountered by people entitled to aid to a large extent explain the relative ineffectiveness of European social-security systems for entire sections of the population.

The report presented to the CDSS aimed at drawing up an exemplary typology of the obstacles encountered by citizens of different European countries, which prevent them from fully benefiting from their national social-security system. The method used consisted of taking account as fully as possible of (i) the experiences of the claimants themselves, through their testimony, and also (ii) the committed standpoint of the associations working with the people in need, without forgetting (iii) the standpoint of the social-service providers.

The main initial result of this approach was the realisation that there was an enormous gap between principles of equity and justice which generally inspire policies to combat social exclusion and the effectiveness of their practical implementation in national social-security systems. The implementation of the principle of equality before the law being one of the characteristics of modern societies, it is a specific task of 'social' law to adapt the granting of social benefits and services to the individual circumstances pertaining in each case, in order to prevent economic and social inequalities from undermining the principle noted above. Against this background, social law is not restricted to compensating 'material' disadvantages by substantive (material) social law, but it also includes compensating 'formal' disadvantages by procedural (formal) social law. In so far as social benefits and services are directed at persons who are at a social disadvantage, the effect of this social disadvantage can also make itself felt in that the individuals concerned are not fully informed of their rights and are largely incapable of enforcing them. Normally, the legal system assumes that the citizen knows his or her rights, and that, if necessary, he or she can obtain expert advice, so as to be in a position to assert those rights, if need be by going to court. Granting a subjective legal entitlement and making access to the courts available might, therefore, appear sufficient to ensure that the guaranteed legal entitlements can be secured. Nevertheless, restrictions to which a citizen is exposed – and people are a good example – can mean that the way of perceiving and securing one's interests in conformity with the law, described above, is not possible.

Information, consultation, advice and effective expert assistance are major additional elements which must be provided alongside to formally guaranteed substantive rights if the gap between the 'legal standard' and 'social reality' is not to make it impossible to enforce one's legal entitlements to benefits and services. The point is that substantive social law remains largely ineffective if there is no appropriate implementation in practice and if those concerned do not benefit from the services to which they are entitled. The consequence of the ineffectiveness of social benefits is that social needs are not met, and that in this respect the benefits do not achieve their objective. Accordingly, knowledge, choice, and participation are criteria for the effectiveness of social benefits and services.

The more differentiated the structure of the overall system of social security and the more it is made subject to rules and regulations, the more complex it usually becomes and the greater the difficulties which citizens have in finding their way within the system of social law. The complexity of social law has even been described as a 'social risk' in its own right (Krasney, 1990). For this reason, one of the most important tasks of legislation and administration in social law is to provide a well designed system of information and consultation in order to guide individuals entitled to social benefits towards the rights due to them.

EC law and policies with regard to social exclusion

The Treaty of Amsterdam contains several new, interlinked provisions, which commit the EU to engage more closely with the promotion of the social wellbeing and employment of European citizens. The treaty marks a new stage in the process of building a Europe for all, with a renewed commitment to social progress and making employment a matter of common concern. The principle of solidarity is also re-emphasised, as shown by the new objectives which have been set by the treaties:

The EU shall set itself the following objectives:

> To promote economic and social progress and a high level of employment and to achieve balanced and sustainable development, in particular ... through the strengthening of economic and social cohesion. (Article 2 TEU, as amended by the Treaty of Amsterdam)

> The Community and the Member States ... shall have as their objectives the promotion of employment, improved living and working conditions ... proper social protection ... and the combating of exclusion. (Article 136 TEC, as amended by the Treaty of Amsterdam)

Improving the prosperity and social wellbeing of European people has always been part of the fundamental purpose of European integration. Solidarity and social justice, too, have been a fundamental principle, the idea that both the burdens and the benefits of growth should be shared across society, and European Community policies have contributed to achieving this. It is a recognition that all people should fully participate in society and be socially integrated. The member states of the EU all have their own means of ensuring that solidarity, but as progress has been made in European economic integration, more stress has been put on accompanying this economic progress with social progress at the European level. To explore how public policies, at EU, national and local level seek to do this is therefore an important first step towards further strengthening of such policies to promote social inclusion. The way to overcome exclusion is through participation, through engaging and involving people. It is essential to involve every part of society in tackling this growing alienation within the EU. This will include national, regional and local authorities in member states, non-governmental organisations and the social partners, professional bodies, private industry and of course excluded people themselves. Only then will European Community action be able to help member states in their effort to clarify their objectives, integrate policies and mobilise all relevant actors to combat social exclusion and promote more inclusive policies in the EU.

Preventing and combating social exclusion is primarily the responsibility of member states. However, the European Community can and must help to this end, and the Treaty of Amsterdam makes it possible for the EU to support member states' efforts and cooperation. Any action by the community must add real value, respecting the principle of subsidiarity by acting only where the objective of combating social exclusion can be better achieved by the community, and not duplicating work done elsewhere.

Previous EU programmes on poverty and social exclusion produced valuable lessons, which have now been largely mainstreamed into wider European Community policies. The need is now for community action to complement and support the existing efforts of the member states. This can best be done by developing and sharing the expertise to integrate social inclusion into the broader actions both of the member states and of the community. There are a range of community policies which are relevant to social inclusion, directly or indirectly.

- The completion of the single market and the introduction of the European Monetary Union and the Euro (€) will bring greater macroeconomic stability and promote competitiveness, thus supporting the economic growth which underpins our social systems and increased prosperity. These two gigantic structural policies, however, will not lead themselves to promoting social inclusion. Aimed at strengthening market forces, they will create winners and losers, and this is why flanking policies are needed to guarantee solidarity with those who are at the margin of the process of economic growth and prosperity. The EC will analyse how these flanking policies could be improved and promoted with a view to supporting the efforts of all those in the member states that are actively working for a more inclusive society.

- The European Employment Strategy makes a major contribution by targeting in particular long-term unemployment and youth unemployment, as well as the lack of equal opportunities for women in the labour market, which are especially damaging to social inclusion. Ensuring that the Employment Guidelines effectively reflect the needs of everyone has been given increased weight in the 1999 Employment Guidelines. There is more emphasis on active measures to reintegrate people. This includes reforms to tax and benefit systems and lifelong learning to enable workers, particularly older workers and people excluded from the labour market (for example disabled, returnees), to improve skills, especially in fast-changing fields such as information and communication technologies.

- The Structural Funds are the main financial means of direct community support for the most disadvantaged regions and people in the EU. Following the current reforms, the funds 2000-06 will do even more to promote social inclusion. Objective 3 aims in particular to reintegrate people excluded from the labour market and to combat long-term unemployment. Current Community Initiatives are also active in promoting social inclusion, especially the INTEGRA strand of the EMPLOYMENT initiative, and URBAN and LEADER on urban and rural integration respectively. The new Community Initiative under the European Social Fund will also support new ways of addressing discrimination and inequalities in employment.

Other Community policies also contribute to promoting social inclusion. Improving knowledge about social exclusion is a major issue in the EC's Framework Programmes for European Research. Promoting social inclusion and equality is an important priority of the EC's *Framework for Action for Sustainable Urban Development*. The promotion of new, more inclusive approaches and policies is also an important dimension of the Education, Training and Youth for Europe programmes. Preventing and combating social exclusion is also a key priority of the efforts undertaken at European Community level to modernise and improve social protection systems. The EC is preparing a series of initiatives to implement the new provisions of the Treaty of Amsterdam on discrimination, including legislative proposals as well as an action programme. The new community strategy on disability contributes to social inclusion of persons with disabilities by mainstreaming the disability perspective into the formulation of EU policies and legislation. The EC has recently proposed a specific action programme for the integration of refugees. Contributing to prevention of urban crime and juvenile delinquency is the aim of the FALCONE programme. More directly, the community programme of distribution of agricultural products to the most deprived provides food aid to around 8 million people in Europe every year.

Together with the member states, the European Community also contributes to cooperation at the international level on combating social exclusion and promoting poverty alleviation. This is taken forward with the Council of Europe, with the UN and its specialised agencies (especially the International Labour Organisation) and with the Organisation for Economic Co-operation and Development.

Specific community support for combating social exclusion should therefore complement these existing actions at both national and community level and add value to them. The European Community can support relevant policies through its capacity to gather and exchange knowledge and good practice, to evaluate individual actions against experiences elsewhere, and by affirming common values. This reflects the mandate given by the Treaty of Amsterdam. Article 137 TEC provides for "measures designed to encourage cooperation between Member States through initiatives aimed at improving knowledge, developing exchanges of information and best practices, promoting innovative approaches and evaluating experiences in order to combat social exclusion".

Cooperation on the integration of people excluded from the labour market is given additional emphasis by the possibility of developing a framework of minimum requirements. The Treaty of Amsterdam therefore sets a clear direction of community support to refine existing efforts combating social exclusion through exchanging experiences and successes, the EC will be expected to bring forward proposals to give effect to this mandate. By soliciting reactions and contributions now to a broad outline of proposals, the aim is to ensure that as the proposals are developed, they reflect the real needs for action at community level to combat social exclusion.

Reflecting the experience of tackling social exclusion within the member states, these preparatory actions will aim to engage the widest possible range of stakeholders in social exclusion action, including in particular non-governmental organisations and associations and the social partners. They are also tightly linked to the specific elements of action described in Article 137 and to how those elements could be implemented. This approach should ensure that the preparatory actions give the best possible insight into how the European Community could most effectively support member states in this area.

These preparatory actions will build on the work already carried out within the framework of various community actions, including those concerning vulnerable groups such as refugees, migrants and older people. The actions will also reflect the multidimensional nature of social exclusion and will cover a range of relevant policy issues, including minimum incomes, housing, education and training, health, urban and rural development, employment, justice, culture and cultural integration, communication, mobility, access to rights, utilities and financial services. It is important that the results of these actions be widely disseminated to gain the maximum benefit from them.

The actions should complement work in related areas, such as under the

European Social Fund and the EC's forthcoming proposals to implement the new Article 13 TEC on anti-discrimination once the Treaty of Amsterdam is ratified.

Better coordination of social exclusion issues at European level would benefit from bringing together all the relevant EC services to look at what contribution is made to combating social exclusion by the full range of European Community policies. Actions and cooperating to promote social inclusion would also need to be linked to the enlargement process and social exclusion issues in the applicant states. Enhancing cooperation with relevant international organisations, such as the Council of Europe, the OECD and the ILO, could contribute to this.

References

Cassiers, W. and Dehon, D. (1997) 'Some practical aspects of non-access to social security in Europe', Strasbourg, 18 November, CDSS (97) 37, Council of Europe, p 1.

Duffy, K. (1995) *Social exclusion and human dignity: The right to self-respect*, Report to the secretariat of the Council of Europe.

Eardley, T., Bradshaw, J., Ditch, J., Gough, I. and Whiteford, P. (eds) (1996) *Social assistance in OECD countries*, vol 1 (Synthesis) and vol 2 (Country Reports), London: HMSO.

EC (1981) Final report on the First European Programme on combating poverty, Brussels: EC.

EC (1998) *Social protection in Europe 1997*, Luxembourg: EC.

EC (1999a) *Towards a Europe for all – How should the Community support member states to promote social inclusion?*, Background document, Brussels: EC.

EC (1999b) *Report from the Commission on the implementation of the Recommendation 92/441/EEC of 24 June 1992 on common criteria concerning sufficient resources and social assistance in social protection systems*, COM (1998) 774 final, Brussels: EC.

Guibentif, P. and Bouget, D. (1999) *Minimum income policies in the European Union*, Lisbon.

Hauser, R., et al (1981) *Armut, Niedrigeinkommen und Unterversorgung in der Bundesrepublik Deutschland*, Bestandsaufnahme und sozialpolitische Perpektiven, Frankfurt am Main.

Krasney, O. (1990) *Richtige Zuordnung der Risiken und Überwindung von Sicherungsdefiziten durch die Rechtsordnung*, Deutscher Sozialrechtsverband, Wiesbaden.

Leisering, L. and Leibfried, S. (1999) *Time and poverty in western welfare states, United Germany in perspective*, Cambridge: Cambridge University Press.

Quintin, O. 'Social exclusion and measures of the European Commission', in *Der Paritätische Wohlfanhrtsverband / Europabüro, Soziale Ausgrenzung, Europäisches Forum in Brüssel*, (Social Exclusion, European Forum in Brussels).

Room, G. (ed) (1995) *Beyond the threshold: The measurement and analysis of social exclusion*, Bristol: The Policy Press.

Vogel-Polsky, E. (1993) *Terms of reference for the paper presenting the work of the Rights / Exclusion Expert Group on asserting the rights of the most underprivileged in the EEC*, Brussels: EC.

SIX

Welfare state solidarity and support: the Czech Republic compared with the Netherlands

Tomáš Sirovátka, Wim van Oorschot and Ladislav Rabušic[1]

Introduction

The problem of reconciling the demands on both the social and economic effectiveness of the social security systems in the transforming post-communist countries has often been pointed out, along with the importance attached to finding a solution (for example, Barr, 1994; Offe, 1996; Standing, 1996; Ferge, 1997; Kramer, 1997). Adequate reduction of poverty and social exclusion is essential for securing long-term public support for – and the legitimacy of – the political and economic changes, as well as for maintaining political stability. However, it is also necessary to reduce non-investment budgetary spending (including spending on social systems), and necessary to accumulate available resources to support investment and economic growth. In addition to these objective factors, political and ideological factors are of specific importance. Departure from collective arrangements commanded broad support, especially at the beginning of the transformation, and neoliberal ideology has had an exceptional influence on the reconstruction of social system strategies in the countries of Central Europe (in the Czech Republic, for example, it was reflected in the requirement of 'teaching citizens self-responsibility', which was also applied to the system of social security).

The tension that exists in this dilemma of conflicting expectations related to the increasing social security system. While the new political elite could take advantage of their strong political credit at the beginning of the transformation, and utilise it as a "political window of opportunity" (Kramer, 1997, p 50) to take radical steps affecting the social security area, for example, they have gradually been forced to pay increasing attention to the social and political costs of transitional measures. However, practical political considerations have often made the Czech government adhere to time serving solutions. With the vision of economic prosperity fading, it might be expected that Czech voters' willingness to accept and tolerate new risks would also fade. However, expectations and demands regarding compensation for such risks seem in fact to be growing among the population (IVVM, 1998). In this context, analyses of the legitimacy of social policy are important.

With regard to such analyses, there are at least two key distinctions that have to be pointed out.

- It is necessary to distinguish between ideology and concrete politics. Ideological views must not be mistaken for expressions of one's opinions on specific social policy. The latter are influenced much more by concrete and factual matters, and are not necessarily consistent with the ideological and political attitudes of the citizens (Ringen, 1987, p 55).
- The balance or possible tension between the two aspects of principle and implementation has an impact on both levels. This point concerns the distinction between a general support for solidarity and the legitimacy of the implemented arrangements which influence public perceptions of the present social security system (Ringen, 1987, p 69).

We discuss both aspects in this article. First, we are interested in what public support exists for solidarity in the present stage of social development. We will look especially at the entitlement criteria that condition this support, and at what this support encompasses. Our second concern is the legitimacy of the present social security system: what general feelings do people have about the system, how do they perceive its effects, and what do they think about the level of benefits? In dealing with these questions, we make use of survey data collected through a national representative sample in the Czech Republic in June 1998, and compare them with the results of a similarly focused public opinion survey carried out in the Netherlands in 1995[2].

The comparative perspective allows us to verify whether certain universal or similar attitudinal structures exist independent of the differences in (Czech and Dutch) social and cultural systems, the level of economic development, and the form of the existing social systems. Also, a comparison provides us with a useful benchmarking control. Since the Czech survey was the first of its kind concentrated on the legitimacy of solidarity and social security, it would be difficult to draw any meaningful conclusions without the opportunity to make cross-cultural comparisons.

Transformation of the social security systems in the Czech Republic and the Netherlands

The Czech Republic and the Netherlands are, of course, very different from one another, yet we have identified a range of similarities. Transformation of the social security systems is not only limited to post-communist countries. Advanced market democracies have been restructuring their social systems with varying intensity since the mid-1980s (cf George and Taylor-Gooby, 1996; Ploug and Kvist, 1996; Daly, 1997). The fact that overall social change in post-communist countries is without doubt more complex and large-scale does not warrant the conclusion that the social security transformation in these countries is more profound. On the contrary, it is necessary to consider the gradual character of this change, and the strong links with the former social system, which have often been pointed out[3]. Also, a strong path dependency should be taken into account in those countries that made use of existing institutions, including social security schemes, and gradually adjusted them[4]. It is also useful to pay attention to certain similarities between the transformation of the Czech and the Dutch social security systems. The general tendency of the contemporary welfare state to "the individualisation of the social" (Ferge, 1997, p 23), the so-called welfare-state crisis, postmodernism, and other factors, such as the demographic ageing of society[5], can be noticed in both countries. This tendency results in a reduction of social security spending, measured by the share of the GDP, accompanied by a simultaneous reduction in the volume of transfers and redistribution by the government. At the same time, the principle of individual responsibility is accentuated, and more importance is attached to the targeting and conditionality of the programmes and social transfers, and to individualised and means-tested and income-tested schemes of social support. Also, universal public and social services are diversified, and their extent reduced, while active labour market participation by the beneficiaries of such services is more strongly demanded and stimulated. With the extent of compensation for liabilities limited to the coverage of basic social insurance, the trend of 'individualisation of the social' also led to an expansion and growing popularity of supplementary non-governmental insurance schemes. The trend gained support, particularly owing to the growing influence of the conservative and neoliberal oriented political elite.

The social consequences of this general tendency probably have had a greater impact on Czech society than on Dutch society, due to its lower overall standard of living. In both cases, however, serious transformations along the lines just sketched have been taking place. We will briefly outline them here.

The Czech Republic

During the initial phase of the transformation, the system was enriched with an unemployment insurance scheme. Replacement rate of unemployment benefit was set at 60% and 50% of net wage (for the first three months of the unemployed period and for the three subsequent months respectively). Meanwhile, the replacement rate of benefit has been reduced from January 1998, from 60 and 50% to 50 and 40%[6]. However, this benefit was designed as a social assistance benefit; the ceiling was set at a mere 1.5 times the subsistence minimum and only in September 1999 was it increased up to 2.5 times the subsistence minimum.

The concepts of the subsistence minimum and of social need became the key instruments of social policy. At the beginning of the transformation they allowed for supplementing social transfers with means-tested social assistance benefits as prevention against falling below the poverty line.

The subsistence minimum also became a chief factor in the construction of a new system which replaced previously universal benefits targeted at families. According to a new law passed in 1995, entitlement and level of income-tested child benefit[7] and other benefits introduced in the 1990s – housing benefits, heating and rent benefits, transportation benefits for families with school-age children – derive from the comparison between the level of household income and the subsistence minimum. The subsistence minimum is indexed by the government, usually with a certain delay, when prices rise by at least 10%. All social benefits which are tied to the subsistence minimum thus gradually fall behind wage increases.

In 1995, retirement age was raised gradually from 60 to 62 years for men and from 53-57 to 57-61 years for women[8]. It will come into full effect in 2007. Pensions are also indexed with relation to increases in the cost of living. With the change of the pension calculation pattern, more weight was attached to the so-called basic flat-rate component. Overall, these changes contributed to a relative decrease in pension value relative to wage growth. Analyses which concentrated on the level of pensions showed that the entire pension system has become more levelled than it was before 1990 (Hiršl, 1997; Rabušic, 1998; Sirovátka, 1998).

In line with the neoliberal strategy of 'contracting out', an optional supplementary pension scheme, based on defined contributions, was introduced in 1994. Beneficiaries qualify for a direct financial contribution made by the government, which is limited, however, to a maximum of approximately 1.5% of the average net wage. The system does not include tax relief for employers, which would be enough to motivate their participation in the system. The scheme is therefore frequently used as a convenient form of short-term savings. However, it is not a powerful enough instrument to compensate for the decline in pensions in relation to wages.

The level of sickness benefits was reduced gradually, mainly due to the fact that the benefit ceiling was not raised between 1993 and 1998[9].

The whole system has thus developed into an elaborate social assistance scheme, with regard to both the definition of entitlement to benefits and to their level. The prime function of benefits directed at families with children (child benefits and others), which are income tested, is above all to prevent low-income groups from falling below the poverty line into the area of substantial deprivation. In the pension system, the function has been reinforced as well, while the general level of pensions in relation to wages has decreased.

During the 1990s, total spending on social security tended to stagnate in relation to GDP, with retirement spending slightly increasing[10]. New expenditure was necessary for the social assistance and employment policy systems. Total social security spending (including healthcare) equals about 20-21% of GDP, and social transfers about 13%. New expenditures were counterbalanced by a reduction in the level of benefits relative to wages – and therefore also to tax

Table 6.1: The Czech Republic: social benefits as % of average net or gross wage

	Net average wage (CZK)	Min wage as % of GW	Min pension individual as % NAW	SM of individual as % NAW	SM of 4-member hsehold as % NAW	Average pension (as % NAW) really paid	Unemployment benefit (six months) as % NAW	Sickness benefit (one month) as % NAW
1990	2,691	x	49.8	x	x	64.3	x	88.0
1991	3,087	52.8	58.3	55.1	181.4	70.5	56.7	88.0
1992	3,715	47.1	53.3	45.8	150.7	65.0	37.8	87.9
1993	4,613	37.7	46.8	42.5	138.7	59.3	35.9	82.9
1994	5,598	31.9	45.6	40.0	130.8	56.7	29.4	85.8
1995	6,341	26.9	42.9	37.9	123.6	56.4	32.4	85.7
1996	7,538	25.8	38.3	38.3	120.9	55.9	30.6	72.1
1997	8,353	24.8	36.4	36.4	114.6	57.9	30.7	65.1

Notes: NAW = net average wage; GW = gross wages; SM = subsistence minimum.

Sources: RILSA bulletin no 11 (1998); authors' own calculations; net average wage according to the Ministry of Labour and Social Affairs, Czech Republic

payments and social insurance contributions (Table 6.1). The social security system was subject to budgetary cuts which made themselves felt, especially in 1997, when the government adopted restrictive measures in consequence of unexpected economic stagnation[11].

The trend demonstrated in Table 6.1 resulted in a decline in the ratio of social income to net financial income for an average working household. It dropped from 13.5% in 1989 to 10.7% in 1996. At the same time, the level of rent and energy prices rose in several successive steps. Since 1996, households with low incomes (up to 1.6 times the subsistence minimum per household member) have been partially compensated for this increase in living costs.

Despite the fact that the goals of social security changes have not been made explicit by the Czech government, reform of the social-policy system, especially after Slovakian separation in 1993, have apparently pursued the following goals:

• to increase the importance of wages and market-generated income in one's overall standard of living, therefore promoting individual self-responsibility;
• to decrease state expenditures within the social-protection system;
• to maintain the preventive function of the system against poverty.

Implementation of these goals has brought about a decrease in social benefit levels and allowances. It has also reduced the number of beneficiaries because of the introduction of means–tested principles.

Generally speaking, the social security system in the Czech Republic has met the objective of preventing broad segments of the population from falling below the poverty threshold. Although income inequalities have increased[12], the number of the poor, whether defined by the official subsistence minimum or by the EC poverty line, has been much lower than the level common in many advanced market economies[13]. However, as a result of the cuts in public spending and price liberalisation, the transformation has had a strong impact not only on the lower classes, but also on the middle classes, whose income in a highly levelled society does not greatly exceed the subsistence minimum. At the same time, the share of the middle classes in the social security system has been on the decline, while their financial contributions have remained basically the same, if not slightly increased. In light of these changes, it is not surprising that the issues of the present system's legitimacy and of the public attitude have become quite topical, as research suggests (Purkrábek, 1996; IVVM, 1998).

The Netherlands

Following the Second World War, a generous and universal system of social security was built up in the Netherlands. It had its heyday between the late 1960s and the early 1980s. Since then it has been under permanent reconstruction.

Of central importance to this has been the steady rise in the number of claims for workers' insurance and for social assistance in the course of the 1970s, followed by an alarmingly steep increase in unemployment and assistance dependency from 1978 to 1982. As Table 6.2 shows, the number of people claiming unemployment benefits doubled from 1970 to 1978, and doubled again between 1978 and 1982, while the number of social-assistance beneficiaries increased between 1970 and 1978 by 100,000, and by more than 250,000 in the next four years. The number of disability claims had a steadier, but by no means less meaningful, growth. Due to a broad definition of disability, based on postwar principles of universality and collective solidarity, the scheme had low access thresholds, and attracted many older workers who otherwise, and with more stringent entitlement criteria, would have been laid off and become unemployed. In other words, the number of beneficiaries of the disability scheme contains a large amount of 'hidden' unemployment. The number rose steadily, from 215,000 in 1970 to 707,000 in 1982.

The lesson from the economic crisis, therefore, was clear: the system could be overloaded, and would eventually collapse. The initial reaction was to try to keep social expenditures under control by lowering the duration and level of benefits. This reaction was known as 'price' policy, because it was mainly directed at keeping the system affordable. However, by 1990, the number of workers' insurance beneficiaries had increased by over 300,000 from 1982,

Table 6.2: Number of benefit recipients in the Netherlands (x 1,000)

	People's insurances			Workers' insurances			Social assistance
	Pension AOW	Survivor's AWW	Child benefit AKW	Unemp- loyment WW	Disability AAW/ WAO	Sickness ZW	ABW RWW
1970	1,061	154	1,614	25	215	223	318
1974	1,171	162	1,734	56	313	261	423
1978	1,280	169	1,763	48	579	289	419
1982	1,376	172	2,185	112	707	261	684
1986	1,898	173	2,113	68	778	263	740
1990	2,043	195	1,812	163	881	348	530
1994	2,152	194	1,812	332	894	175	510

Notes: AOW = National Old Age Pension; AWW = National Survivors Pension; AKW = National Child Benefit; WW = Unemployment Insurance; AAW/WAO = Disability Insurance; ZW = Sickness Insurance; ABW = Social Assistance; RWW = Unemployment Assistance.

Source: CTSV (1995, p 12)

which more than offset the decline in the number of social-assistance beneficiaries during this period. Subsequently, the emphasis was put on 'volume' policies, aimed at reducing the accessibility of schemes and gaining control over the inflow of beneficiaries.

The reconstruction of the people's insurance was not only the result of economic developments. It also reflected changes in Dutch society and culture. Revisions aimed to 'modernise' the schemes by making them consistent with changing roles of men and women, particularly the increased participation of women in the labour force. This modernisation resulted in equal rights for men and women in all schemes. Where the modernisation of schemes implied a broadening of the entitled population, there was a conflict with the general aim of cutting back on social expenditures. The solution was that means tests were introduced to keep total expenditure under control.

The 'price', 'volume' and modernisation measures taken subsequently include:

- a reduction of the earnings replacement ratio from 80% to 70% in unemployment, sickness and disability insurance;
- a sharpening of work-history requirements for entitlement to unemployment insurance benefits;
- a limitation of the duration of earnings related disability and unemployment benefits, depending on age (disability) and work history (unemployment);

- a restriction of the concept of 'disability', which in effect means that entitlement is reduced;
- a re-examination of the disability status of 400,000 disabled workers according to the new concept, resulting in 50% of them losing their benefits (and becoming entitled to unemployment benefit, which has a much shorter duration);
- a 'privatisation' of the first six weeks of sickness, implying that the employer had to pay 70% of the wage during these weeks instead of the national sickness fund, followed by an extension of these six weeks to a full year (which de facto meant the abolition of sickness insurance for almost all workers);
- excluding young people from the right to social assistance (instead, they have to be offered a job by the municipality);
- a lowering of the basic assistance benefit for single people and lone parents by 20% (a top up of 20% is possible if one can testify to not having a partner);
- the introduction of means tests for survivors and old-age pensions;
- a series of reductions in child benefit.

There is no doubt that these measures have contributed to halting the trend towards increasing numbers of beneficiaries and increasing expenditure. The system's collapse was prevented. On the other hand, figures show that, at present, there is no prospect for a substantial decrease in demand and expenditures. Table 6.2, for example, shows that, in 1994, only the number of claimants for sickness benefits and social assistance have dropped significantly since 1986. Table 6.3, showing social security expenditures as a percentage of the net domestic product, confirms that expenditures exploded in the late 1970s and early 1980s. It also shows, however, that the decrease of the percentage since then follows a slow pace.

Due in large part to these figures, the government has realised that its initial 'price' policy and the subsequent 'volume' policy were not enough to substantially reduce social security expenditures, nor to solve the problem of the economic inactivity of a large part of the population. Gradually, therefore, it has developed a new concept of social protection, the core of which seems to

Table 6.3: Social security expenditure in the Netherlands as % of net domestic product

1970	12
1975	16
1980	20
1983	22
1990	18
1994	18

Source: Ministry of Social Affairs (1996)

be a fundamental critique of the model of collective solidarity itself. It is no longer purely for budgetary and economic reasons that changes in the system are proposed and justified; more and more there is a wish to change its entire nature.

The main objection of politicians and policy makers to the model of collective solidarity is its anonymity. The national and collective nature of the system is supposed to undermine individual responsibility and to promote calculative behaviour by all actors involved, be they citizens, workers, employers, unions, or companies. Based on this diagnosis, market elements are introduced, such as freedom of choice (for employers, whether or not to take part in collective insurance) and risk differentiation (industries with higher levels of risk for disability paying higher contributions), which in essence are aimed at reintroducing individual responsibility, by way of confronting all actors more directly with the costs of social protection. The diagnosis is also the starting point for 'activation', which comprises extended policies aimed at the reinsertion of beneficiaries into paid and even unpaid work.

All in all, a shift has taken place, from inclusive solidarity towards exclusive selectivity, from collective responsibility towards individual responsibility. With this shift, the overall level of citizens' social protection has declined. This loss, however, does not affect everybody to the same degree. Those who have lost most of their social protection are people with weaker or no ties to the market for paid labour. These include workers on flexible contracts, young workers, workers with repeated unemployment spells, and beneficiaries who have little chance of returning to the labour market, such as pensioners, disabled workers, the long-term unemployed, and single parents. The total effect of the revisions has been recognised by the central government, and inspired it to declare "work, work, and again work" (a popular slogan often used by the former Prime Minister Kok and his cabinet members) as the central aim of its new socioeconomic policy. Social protection of citizens was believed to be best guaranteed by their participation in the labour market.

Conditionality of solidarity and the legitimacy of the social security system

Both countries share key features of the general trends that dominate the reconstruction of their social security systems. One of the most significant similarities is that social protection is targeted more strongly on 'the truly needy', instead of focusing universally on citizens' rights or on specific categories of citizens. This common trend raises with new urgency the question of entitlement, which addresses people's value orientations towards the rationing of welfare in general: who has the right to what level of collective protection, and why? A second question addressed here deals with the public's opinion on, and support for, more practical aspects of the social security system, its costs and complexity for instance, its effects, and the level of its benefits.

Conditionality of solidarity

In the post-communist countries, the strong political credit of the new political elite, and the strong credit of individualised social arrangements (as opposed to collective arrangements), provided great opportunities for change in the initial stages of transformation. The political elite were able to use this 'window of opportunity' to enforce measures oriented towards establishing a residual model of the welfare state. Despite the fact that this welfare-policy design curtails the rights of a greater part of the population, the middle classes in particular, it may still be acknowledged as legitimate, provided it is grounded on solid principles of conditionality of solidarity, and that such principles are accepted, or at least perceived as just, by a majority of the population. In the Netherlands, strong societal protest against the reconstruction policies has been almost non-existent. This raises the question about the principles of entitlement that are applied by the public at large.

The public's views on entitlement and conditionality of solidarity in relation to social groups are quite similar in the Czech Republic and the Netherlands (see Figure 6.1), suggesting that conditions for solidarity or basic ideas of entitlement are universal elements in the public's approach to the rationing of social support and welfare.

In both countries, certain groups are considered to be highly entitled to benefits (disabled people, pensioners, households with children, single mothers, widows), while other groups clearly are not (persons unwilling to work, immigrants, ethnic minorities, homeless people). The results confirm earlier findings (van Oorschot, 1997) about the type of underlying entitlement criteria that are applied by the public. That is, solidarity with the needy is conditioned by aspects of control, or the degree to which needy people themselves can influence the fulfilment of their needs. Such a pattern explains the high scores of disabled people, pensioners and widows, and the low scores of those who are not willing to work. Solidarity is also influenced by aspects of identity; that is, the degree to which needy people belong to the mainstream culture. This explains the low scores of immigrants, ethnic minorities and asylum seekers. Next to this, reciprocity plays a role; that is, the degree to which needy people have earned support or can do something in return, as well as the level of need, shown by the high scores where households contain children.

Figure 6.1 also reveals two obvious differences between the Czech Republic and the Netherlands. One of them is that the Czech public regards having children as an entitlement criterion more strongly than does the Dutch public. The group 'household with child' scores higher among the Czech public, and the group 'household without children' much lower. This difference can be interpreted by means of the aspect of need. Families with children in the Czech Republic have lost most during the transformation of the social system, and are therefore strongly considered to be needy[14]. In the Netherlands, the groups affected most by the retrenchment measures are single mothers, single female pensioners and the long-term unemployed.

**Figure 6.1: Perceived right to financial support for specified groups
(1-10 scale)**

"If we cut back on benefits, the question of who has a greater or lesser right to financial
support from society will become more important. Would you like to tell to what degree each
group, on a scale from 1 (no right at all) to 10 (absolutely the most right), should have a right to
financial support from society?"

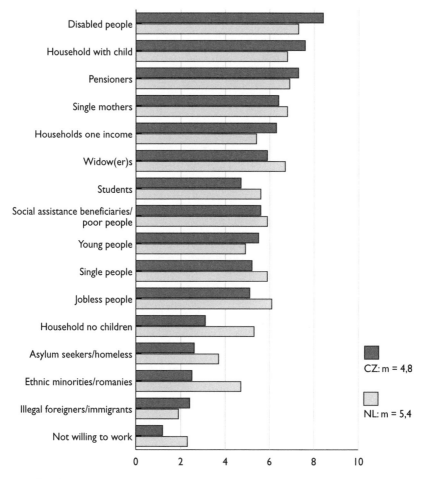

Source: TISSER – *Solidarity study* (1995) (N = 1,405)

The second and more significant difference between the countries is that the
Czech public is more conditional than the Dutch. That is, high-ranking groups
tend to have higher scores among the Czechs, and lower-ranking groups lower
scores. Although the ordering of groups is the same, suggesting that the same
basic value orientations and criteria are at work, the Czech public is more
generous towards highly deserving categories but more reluctant towards less
deserving categories.

Figure 6.2: Perceived and preferred income differences

Perceived: "Do you regard the present differences in income ... ?"
Preferred: "Would you like these differences to be ... ?"

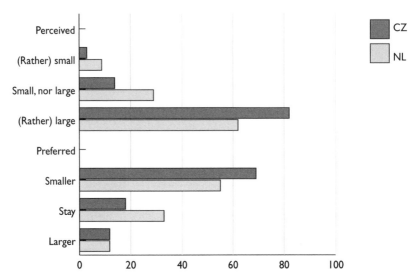

Sources: Czech Republic = *Legitamacy of social security survey* (1998) (N = 1,351); Netherlands = TISSER –
Solidarity study (1995) (N = 1,405)

This cannot be attributed to a smaller preference for egalitarianism among the Czechs. Figure 6.2 shows just the opposite. The Czech public perceives income differences as larger than the Dutch, and more strongly prefers them to be smaller.

Clearly, a strong preference for social equality and high conditionality of solidarity do not contradict each other. We suggest that social-system reconstruction, characterised by limiting universal rights and individualising the social system, combined with the social impact of the transformation, implies a strong need for social security and egalitarian preferences among the public, but at the same time also a stronger requirement for conditioning the solidarity. That is, the Czech public believes that there must be social protection, but that where resources are scarce they must be targeted effectively to the most deserving and needy and not be distributed loosely. In the Netherlands, where there is also a retrenchment of social protection, the situation differs in that resources are still on a relatively high level. The public's conditionality is less restricted there by economic and budgetary scarcity compared to the Czech Republic.

Perception of the present social security system and its legitimacy

Similarities along broad lines, with differences shaped by situational characteristics, also result from the comparison of the Czech and Dutch publics' opinions on practical features and the effects of their respective social security systems.

General feelings about the system of social security

If we look at the public's general beliefs about the social security system presented in Figure 6.3, there are three striking similarities between the Czech Republic and the Netherlands.

First, there is a relatively strong and universal belief about the necessity of the social security system. It is even somewhat stronger in the Czech Republic than in the Netherlands. Further analyses have shown that this belief applies equally to all social groups and categories.

Second, a relatively large portion of both the Czech and the Dutch populations, believe that social security is in their personal interest. This, and the widespread belief about the necessity of the social security system, suggests that the system has become a part of both the population's expectations,

Figure 6.3: Feelings about the system of social security

"What are your feelings about the present system of social security? (indicate your position on a 5-point scale)"

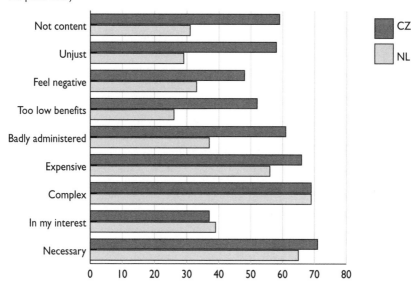

Sources: Czech Republic = *Legitamacy of social security survey* (1998) (N = 1,351); Netherlands = TISSER – *Solidarity study* (1995) (N = 1,405)

irrespective of class, gender, age or dependence on social benefits. This type of support for the social security system might be based on two demands, which are implicit in the concept of social rights, and which have motivated the very genesis of the welfare state – the demand for greater collectively guaranteed safety (security) and the demand for greater equality (see Flora and Heidenheimer, 1984). People appear to be aware of the complex risks inherent in modern market society, and they consider the system of collective protection a suitable form of risk management. This interpretation links up with the finding that a greater part of both the populations believes that present differences in income are too large (over 80% in the Czech Republic) and that they should be smaller (over 70% in the Czech Republic; compare Figure 6.2).

A third resemblance is that both populations regard their present national system of social policy as being very complex. This might not be surprising if we recognise that, because of processes of path dependency and the diverging interests involved in shaping social security, it seems to be impossible to design a system that is genuinely simple and transparent for citizens. In particular the new system of income-tested benefits implemented in the Czech Republic includes very complicated benefit formulas.

With regard to other features of the social security system, the Czech public is evidently much more negative. Many Dutch regard their present system as expensive, but the Czech public do so even more. The Czechs are also more negative about the way in which the present system is administered: they regard benefits as too low more strongly, they are less content with the system, find it more unjust and feel more negatively about it generally. Here again, the differences between the countries might be explained by the fact that the general level of social protection in the Netherlands, despite the retrenchment policies of the last decade, is much higher than in the Czech Republic. The Czech system offers lower protection, and is therefore subjected more to general discontent.

Evidently, the system of social security has a strong legitimacy base, in the sense that it is felt to be a necessary institution in modern society. However, according to the public, social security's main problems are its complexity and expensiveness, while its overall quality has to be improved.

Perceptions of the effects of social security

The way in which the Czech and Dutch populations perceive the effects of social security for the individual, the cultural and social systems, and the economy, differs quite strongly.

Figure 6.4 shows that the Czech public does not believe in the positive effects that social security might have for individuals. Only a very small proportion think that, because of social security, life for people is more pleasant or that people get better chances in life or live a happier life. In the Netherlands, quite large proportions do see such positive effects. With regard to the effects on the cultural system, the Czechs are again more negative than the Dutch.

Figure 6.4: Perceived effects of social security

"The present system of social security could have positive and negative consequences. To your opinion, is the following a consequence of the system?" (3-point scale: yes).

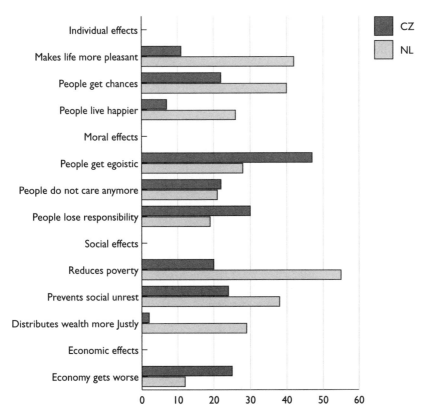

Sources: Czech Republic = *Legitimacy of social security survey* (1998) (N = 1,351); Netherlands = TISSER – *Solidarity study* (1995) (N = 1,405)

About one fifth to one quarter of the Dutch believe that social security makes people more egoistic, less caring for each other, and lacking in responsibility, while among the Czechs these proportions vary between one fifth and about one half. It is striking that the Dutch believe in the positive social effects of social security (that it reduces poverty, prevents social unrest and distributes wealth more justly), in contrast to the Czechs' disbelief in these matters. Almost nobody in the Czech Republic believes that the system of social security distributes wealth more justly. Finally, the Czechs are more pessimistic about the economic effects of social security. About one quarter of them think that the economy suffers from the system of social benefits, while this is the case among only one tenth of the Dutch.

One can conclude that the Dutch population evidently reflects and balances the trade-off between the economic and moral 'costs' of the social system and

Figure 6.5: Perception of how beneficiaries can make ends meet with specified benefit (% difficult/very difficult)

"How do you believe beneficiaries can make ends meet with...?" (5-point-scale: (very) easy, just possible, (very) difficult).

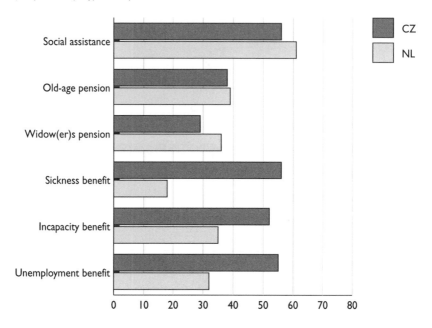

Sources: Czech Republic = *Legitimacy of social security survey* (1998) (N = 1,351); Netherlands = TISSER – *Solidarity study* (1995) (N = 1,405)

the positive effects resulting from these costs. All in all, the Dutch agree more on the positive effects than on the negative ones. Among the Czechs, the negative views are dominant. The negative cultural effects are seen as more significant than the negative economic effects. However, the belief that people get more egoistic because of the system of social security might be influenced by ideas about the 'morality' of the capitalist economy that has entered Czech society. All in all, the Czech population acknowledges limited positive effects of the existing system; it largely admits only its legitimising function (that is prevention of social unrest) and the chance it grants to individuals to do something with their lives. A strongly negative evaluation by the Czech population applies to the functions of the just distribution of wealth and the elimination of poverty. We consider these findings an important message to the politicians and authors of the system, since the decision to target social benefits is governed by the intention to prevent and eliminate poverty and assist 'the needy'. On one hand, Czech society strongly supports redistribution aimed at greater equality, but at the same time it believes the existing social system to be unjust and ineffective regarding the elimination of poverty.

Figure 6.6: Preferred level of specified benefit (% increase/strongly increase)

"If you had the authority, would you decrease the level of benefits mentioned here, let them stay as they are, or would you increase them? Mark that if you increase the level of a benefit the matching contributions or taxes would increase too." (5-point-scale: (strongly) decrease, let them as they are, (strongly) increase)

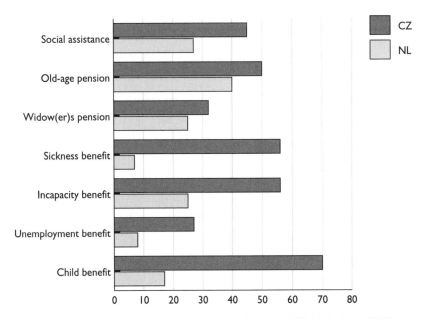

Sources: Czech Republic = *Legitimacy of social security survey* (1998) (N = 1,351); Netherlands = TISSER – *Solidarity study* (1995) (N = 1,405)

Opinions on the level of benefits

The Czechs' negative views on the system of social security and its effects on society, morality, and the economy, as compared to the views of the Dutch, is reflected also in their opinions on the level of benefits (see Figure 6.5).

While social assistance is the only benefit in the Dutch sample which is considered insufficient to live on by more than 50% of the respondents, the majority of Czech respondents regard as insufficient also sickness benefits, disability benefits, and unemployment benefits. The exceptions, however, are old-age pensions and widow(er) pensions, which both are seen as less insufficient by the Czechs than by the Dutch.

The fact that the benefits are mostly thought to be too low is reflected in the respondents' suggestions regarding adjustment of the level of benefits (see Figure 6.6).

The general assertion (for example, Taylor-Gooby, 1985; Cook and Barrett, 1992) that coverage of 'widely shared risks' with benefits, such as old-age and disability pensions and sickness benefits, is universally preferred and supported, while 'marginal' schemes, such as social assistance and unemployment benefits, are supported less by the public, is verified only partially in the Czech Republic as well as in the Netherlands. In both countries, there is only a small preference for increasing unemployment benefits, but a relatively high preference for increasing social assistance. The difference between both countries lies in the fact that, in the Czech Republic, there is a much higher demand for increasing the level of benefits than in the Netherlands. This is especially true for child benefits, disability benefits and sickness benefits. It is likely that this is a result of the fact that, besides general entitlement criteria, the perception of the present social security system and its legitimacy also reflects the current level of benefits and the quality of the system. If there is a strong belief about an entitlement to certain benefits by certain groups of citizens, yet the benefits are not provided to a sufficient extent, the pressure to increase the level of benefits intensifies.

Conclusions

Policies of retrenchment of social security and the trend towards its individualisation adopted both in the Czech Republic and in the Netherlands during the 1990s have halted uncontrolled growth of social security costs. At the same time, it has also managed to protect both populations against the threat of subsistence poverty. However, such policies have also brought about some negative effects. In the Czech Republic, higher taxes and higher contributions to the social security system have been imposed on the middle class, at the same time as its gains from the system have decreased. Also, while the system of social protection has been changed into an elaborate social safety net, the relative living standard of households close to poverty has decreased. Similarly, in the Netherlands, changes in the social security system have negatively affected the groups of people with low ties to the labour market.

The effects of reductions in the generosity of social-policy schemes are tougher in the Czech Republic than in the Netherlands, because Czech GDP per capita in parity of purchasing power is about half of the level of developed countries (the Netherlands included), while at the same time the system of social protection provides poorer coverage.

Comparison of Czech and Dutch public opinion on social security reveals several main patterns. In both countries, the system of social protection has strong public support, in the sense that they are convinced of its necessity. We believe that this attitude is not just an expression of inertia stemming from the social security system having been a strong element in the everyday life of citizens of both the Czech Republic and the Netherlands during the 1970s and 1980s. We believe that public support for social protection reflects current economic developments, with their strong emphasis on market mechanisms, which have brought about higher social inequalities and the danger of social exclusion. These, in turn, have produced more demands for social protection and for decreased levels of inequality.

Trends in current social policy to increase the means-testing mechanisms, thus making social-policy measures more selective, could be seen as contradicting the high public support for the social-policy system so strongly seen as 'necessary'. However, what we also found is that, in many instances, both publics are supportive of the idea that solidarity should be conditional to a certain degree. This pattern is more pronounced in the Czech Republic than in the Netherlands, because of the effects of social transformation. Demand for higher equality goes hand-in-hand with conditional solidarity. Therefore, the entitlement to support of families with children is regarded as high by the Czech public ('families deserve our support') while, for instance, the entitlement of the unemployed is neglected, because in many instances unemployment is reckoned to be 'one's own fault', and also because the unemployed are suspected to earn, or at least to have an option to earn, alternative (often undeclared) income.

We believe that the legitimacy of social-policy schemes consists of several aspects:

- the legitimacy of principles of solidarity and equality that underlie them (which seems to be high in both countries);
- the legitimacy of the criteria of entitlement that are implied by them (which seem to be quite similar in both countries);
- the perceived quality of the system and personal experience with it.

It seems to us that the 'personal experience' aspect is especially important for social policy evaluation. It can help explain the relatively high recorded differences in evaluation of Czech and Dutch social policy. In the Netherlands, the public reflects the trade-off between economic efficiency and social justice. Despite the fact that the Dutch think their system to be very expensive and complicated, they recognise its positive contribution to the quality of life, elimination of poverty, prevention of social tensions and equitable distribution of resources. The Czechs also regard their system as costly and very complex; however, at the same time, they find almost no positive aspects in it. Moreover, they also accentuate – and much more strongly than the Dutch – its negative economic and even moral effects. Such a finding is alarming, and should be taken very seriously by Czech politicians.

Another conclusion is that, while the Czechs ask for less inequality, they do not believe that the existing means-tested system (whose main aim is to eliminate the risk of poverty, and therefore lower inequality), can protect them against poverty, or that it can provide more equitable income distribution. Apparently, reasons for such a strict view of the social-policy system can be found partially in the public's evaluation of its characteristics; the level of most benefits and allowances is regarded as too low and not sufficient to meet the needs of clients, and the administration of the system is assessed as bad. However, we reckon that the main reason for the Czechs' high discontent with the quality of their social-policy system is the general feeling of high subjective poverty. Forty-two per cent of Czechs were under the subjective poverty line (as defined by van Kapteyn) in 1995 (see Mareš and Rabušic, 1997) and about the same proportion of older people (41% and 30% in 1995 and 1996 respectively) were under the subjective poverty lines (Rabušic, 1998)[15].

The present system of social protection and its very legitimacy have been important phenomena in transitional countries of Central and Eastern Europe. Their importance can be expected to increase further in the near future, and they will become, in our understanding, the crucial element of the legitimacy of the whole transformation. Deeper establishment of market mechanisms will necessarily dissolve social homogeneity and egalitarianism, and it will bring new social risks. In the environment of higher economic and social insecurity, new (state) schemes of social protection and their dependency will thus be a logical move. Public expectations of social policy will become high, and it is clear from our analysis that the public expects better-quality provision. If such expectations are not met, they could seriously hamper the process of transformation.

Notes

[1] Our research was supported by the Institute for Human Sciences in Vienna, which is financed by the Austrian Federal Chancellery's Fund for Cooperation with Central and Eastern Europe, and by the Ford Foundation (research project no 97-1-105 'Some consequences and effects of social security transformation in the Czech Republic').

[2] The *Legitimacy of social security* survey included 1,351 respondents, aged 16 years and older. Similarly, in the Dutch TISSER – *Solidarity study*, which was carried out in 1995, 1,405 respondents were polled (see van Oorschot, 1997, 1998). Some of the questions in the Czech questionnaire were inspired by the Dutch survey.

[3] Offe (1993) identifies three stages of a social system reform: emergency measures, institution building and reform, and adjustment within established social-policy institutions.

[4] Due to this link-up with the former systems, which were based on a highly decommodifying welfare state type, János Kórnai labelled the post-communist social policy systems as "pre-mature welfare states" (1992).

[5] The economic crisis was quite persistent in Czechoslovakia during the 1970s and 1980s. However, in the early 1990s it resulted in a transitional decline in production and real incomes. Similarly, the crisis of legitimacy was intrinsic to the entire social and political system prior to 1989. With the democratisation of society, it made itself felt in all societal spheres, including social security. In the Netherlands, as in other parts of Europe, the economic crisis burst out in the first half of the 1980s and again in the early 1990s and was typified by growing unemployment, welfare spending cuts, and reinterpretation of the welfare state's social functions. Demographic ageing, which intensifies economic pressures, is more or less similar in both countries.

[6] The benefit is provided for a short period of time (six months), and the real average benefit is permanently below the level of social assistance benefit (about 30% of the average net wage).

[7] There exist essentially two types of child benefit in the Czech Republic. One of them resembles child benefit common in other countries (pridavek na dite). The other was initially introduced as a state compensatory premium designed to eliminate inflationary effects; since 1996, it has been known as an income-tested benefit called 'the complementary social benefit' (socialni priplatek).

[8] Female retirement age is related to the number of children a woman bears. Childless women will retire at the age of 61 in 2007.

[9] Replacement rate of sickness benefit was changed from 90% to 69% of wage (but, at the same time, the gross wage became a calculation base instead of net wage). This applies to the fourth and the following days of illness; during the first three days it decreased from 70% to 50%.

[10] As a consequence of allowing for early retirement, and of a decrease in the volume of payments resulting from non-payment by employers and lower economic activity (including unemployment).

[11] In the first place, social benefits indexation was associated with a 10% increase in the cost of living (instead of the former increase of 5%) and entitlement to a child allowance was limited to families with income lower than 2.2 times the subsistence minimum per household member and replacement rate of unemployment benefit was decreased.

[12] The Gini coefficient increased from 0.20 in 1992 to 0.26 in 1996 per household consumer unit and from 0.29 to 0.36 in terms of total household income (Vecerník, 1998).

[13] Poverty as defined by the official subsistence minimum concerns 3.7% of the population in 1996, and as defined by the EU poverty line 3.9% according to Vecerník (1998), or 7.8% according to the Czech Statistical Office (ČSÚ, 1998), which used a different equivalence scale. However, this is partly due to the control imposed on the pace of the economic transformation and the low unemployment rate.

[14] While real net incomes of households of employees without children, as well as households of retired people, were basically the same in 1997 as in 1989, these 1997 incomes fell in households of employees with children to 89% of the 1989 level. In the households with lowest incomes they fell even more – to only 69% of the 1989 level.

[15] Despite the fact that the 'objective' poverty rate is not high in the Czech Republic, the middle classes find themselves to be close to the poverty line; for example 16.2% of

the population have income under the level of 60% of average income per capita in the household (ČSÚ, 1998).

References

Barr, N. (1994) *Labour markets and social policy in Central and Eastern Europe: The transition and beyond*, New York, NY: Oxford University Press.

Cook, F.L. and Barrett, E.J. (1992) *Support for the American welfare state: The views of Congress and the public*, New York, NY: Columbia University Press.

ČSÚ (Czech Statistical Office) (1998) *Mikrocensus 1996*, Prague: ČSÚ

CTSV (College van Toezicht Sociale Verzekeringen) (1995) *Kroniek van de sociale verzekeringen 1995*, Zoetermeer: CTSV.

Daly, M. (1997) 'Welfare states under pressure: cash benefits in European welfare states', *Journal of European Social Policy*, vol 7, no 2, pp 129-46.

Esping-Andersen, G. (1990) *The three worlds of welfare capitalism*, Cambridge: Polity Press.

Ferge, Z. (1997) 'The changed welfare paradigm: the individualisation of the social', *Social Policy and Administration*, vol 31, no 1, pp 20-43.

Flora, P. and Heidenheimer, A.J. (1984) *The development of welfare states in Europe and America*, London and New Brunswick: Transaction Publishers.

George, V. and Taylor-Gooby, P. (1996) *European welfare policy: Squaring the welfare circle*, London: Macmillan.

Hiršl, M. (1997) 'Proc je v Ceské republice nutná duchodová reforma',(Why pension reform is inevitable in the Czech Republic), *Pohledy*, vol 5, no 4, pp 6-9.

IVVM (Institute for Public Opinion Research) (1998) *Hodnocení soucasné sociální politiky. Informace z výzkumu*, (Evaluation of contemporary social policy), Prague: IVVM.

Kórnai, J. (1992) 'The postsocialist transition and the state: reflections in the light of Hungarian fiscal problems', *American Economic Review*, vol 82, no 2, pp 1-21.

Kramer, M. (1997) 'Social protection and safety nets in East-Central Europe: dilemmas of the postcommunist transformation', in E.B. Kapstein and M. Mandelbaum (eds) *Sustaining the transition: The social safety net in postcommunist Europe*, New York, NY: Council on Foreign Relations, pp 45-82.

Mareš, P. and Rabušic, L. (1997) 'Subjective poverty and its structure in the Czech Republic', *Slovak Sociological Review*, no 3, pp 279-99.

Ministry of Social Affairs (1996) *Social Nota*, The Hague: Ministry of Social Affairs.

Offe, C. (1993) 'The politics of social policy in East European transitions: antecedents, agents and agenda of the reform', *Social Research*, vol 60, pp 649-84.

Offe, C. (1996) *Modernity and the state: East, West*, Oxford: Polity Press.

Ploug, N. and Kvist, J. (eds) (1997) *Social security in Europe: Development or dismantlement?*, The Hague: Kluwer Law International.

Potucek, M. (1997) 'Spory o povahu Ceské sociální reformy', (Cleavages about the ground of social policy reform), in T. Sirovátka (ed) *Sociální zabezpecení (vybrané texty)*, (Social security (selected papers)), Brno: Masarykova univerzita, pp 172-87.

Purkrábek, M. (1996) *Verejná politika a její aktéri*, (Public policy and its actors), Prague: Fakulta sociálních ved.

Rabušic, L. (1998) 'The poverty of Czech elderly – myth or reality?', *Czech Sociological Review*, vol 6, no 1, pp 5-24.

Ringen, S. (1987) *The possibility of politics*, London: Oxford University Press.

SCP (Sociaal en Cultureel Planbureau) (1996) *Sociaal en cultureel rapport 1996*, Rijswijk: SCP.

Sirovátka, T. (1998) 'Social transfers in the period of transformation and their effects', *Prague Economic Papers*, vol 7, no 4, pp 346-61.

Standing, G. (1996) 'Social protection in Central and Eastern Europe: a tale of slipping anchors and torn safety nets', in G. Esping-Andersen (ed) *Welfare states in transition*, London: Sage Publications, pp 225-55.

Taylor-Gooby, P. (1985) *Public opinion, ideology and state welfare*, London: Routledge and Kegan Paul.

van Oorschot, W. (1997) *Who should get what, and why?*, Working Papers 97/04, Tilburg: Catholic University Brabant, (also presented at the conference of the European Sociological Association, University of Essex, 27-30 August).

van Oorschot, W. (1998) *Dutch public opinion on social security*, Loughborough: Loughborough University, Centre for Research in Social Policy.

Vecerník, J. (1996) *Markets and people*, Aldershot: Avebury.

SEVEN

Targeting welfare: on the functions and dysfunctions of means testing in social policy

Wim van Oorschot

Introduction

The targeting of welfare has regained a central position in the social policy debate in many European countries. In Western Europe, in the prosperous 1960s and 1970s, as well as in Eastern Europe under socialist regimes, the issue of strategic targeting, concerned with the allocation of resources between categories of need or of needy groups, seemed to have been solved definitely. However, with the economic downturn following the 1979 oil crisis, a process of the restructuring of Western welfare states set in, while in the East the political turnovers of the late 1980s and early 1990s were the starting point for the redesign of welfare.

In both parts of Europe 'rethinking welfare' basically means a revival of the debate on the crucial targeting question of who should get what type and degree of social protection, and why. The opinions expressed in the debate vary, and form a mix of economic, political and cultural arguments.

Economic arguments, mostly stemming from budgetary concerns and a wish to protect competitiveness in the global economy, are most often heard. They tend to lead to more selective targeting, so that fewer people are entitled, to lower degrees of social protection.

Political arguments often stress the need for legitimising welfare in the eyes of the 'abused taxpayer' (Rose and Peters, 1978) or the 'individualised middle mass' (Wilensky, 1974). The assumption of these arguments is that the taxpaying middle class dislikes paying for the welfare of others; therefore, welfare should be targeted at the truly and most needy only. Other political arguments relate to basic ideologies. The liberal right, which in the past decades gained a strong position in socioeconomic thinking, on principle argues for individual responsibility, implying a more selective protection. The social democratic left, which traditionally is inclined to solidaristic and collective protection, shifted in practice towards a more 'pragmatic' middle position, or 'third way', in which individual and communal responsibility is stressed also (cf Blair in the UK, Kok in the Netherlands, and Schroeder in Germany). Christian Democrats regularly express their concern over the negative effects of individualisation and the decline of citizenship, which are both seen as a consequence of too liberal and generous a system of welfare provision.

Cultural arguments are often more concealed; moral distinctions between 'the deserving' and 'the undeserving' are central. Aged, sick and incapacitated people, widows or 'the impotent poor', traditionally belong to the first category, while unemployed but capable workers belong to the latter. Modern deservingness-morality is concerned with new needy categories, like single mothers and asylum seekers. Of the criteria applied when distinguishing deserving from undeserving categories, the most important is the degree to which needy people are seen as being responsible, or to blame, for the situation they are in (Will, 1993; van Oorschot, 1998). If regarded as responsible, and therefore undeserving, social support will be more selective and less generous. Therefore, where the ethic of individual responsibility gains significance, in Western as well as Eastern Europe (Kluegel et al, 1995; Halman and Nevitte, 1996; Ferge, 1997), there is also cultural ground for a trend towards more selective targeting.

Comparative studies have shown that the revived debate on who should get what and why has indeed led towards a more selective targeting of welfare all over Europe (George and Taylor-Gooby, 1996; Ploug and Kvist, 1996; Daly, 1997; Ferge, 1997). In many countries, access to universal protection schemes has been limited, solidarity ties in social insurances between good and bad risks and higher and lower incomes have been reduced, welfare to work strategies have been implemented, and not least, means tests are extended and introduced on a wider scale (van Oorschot, 1991; Gough, 1994). With these measures the social protection of citizens in Europe has become less universal and more selective. Needy citizens less readily achieve the status of 'deserving of support', as was the case in the West during the prosperous 1970s or in the East under socialist ideology.

In the Eastern European 'transition' countries, such as Russia, Poland, Romania, Ukraine, the Czech Republic and Hungary, the trend towards selective welfare seems to be particularly strong, and perhaps even unavoidable, given the way in which international organisations like the World Bank and the International Monetary Fund (IMF) tend to link to their financial loans recommendations and even conditions concerning restricted welfare policies and free-market based economic policies (see Townsend in Deacon et al, 1997). Clearly, in these countries, there is tension between the need for economic reconstruction and development on the one hand, and the need for designing a viable and comprehensive welfare system on the other. It has been shown that a certain level of economic development is necessary before an encompassing system of social protection can be established (Wilensky, 1974). However, there are serious risks attached to too strong an emphasis on selectivity. The

Western European experiences with various forms of targeting might help to understand and evaluate these risks.

I do not believe, in this respect, that the present popularity of selective targeting can be evaluated in terms of a simple 'good' or 'bad'. The social and economic context in which it functions in most European countries is too complex. However, it is certainly possible and meaningful to offer a critical discussion of its pros and cons. The basic question put forward here concerns what the functions and dysfunctions of selective targeting might be towards the broader aims of social policy: to do away with poverty, social injustice and dependency, and to integrate all groups and classes into society.

Misunderstandings may easily arise when talking about the targeting of welfare in an international context. In the Scandinavian social policy debate, for instance, targeting tends to be equated with means testing as a way of distinguishing between those people who are entitled to a benefit and those who are not (see, for example, Palme and Wennemo, 1998). A similar view is at the base of Andries' account of recent Belgian social security developments (Andries, 1996). In the British debate, however, means testing is called selectivity (Spicker, 1998), a term used by other authors merely to indicate that benefits do not cover all citizens (as universal benefits do), but only certain categories among them (for example, Ferge, 1997). Given this conceptual confusion, it should be stated here that this chapter follows the idea that targeting in social policy most generally means that policies are directed at someone or something. In this sense all social security benefits are targeted (see also Miller and Tomaskovic-Devey, 1990; Saunders, 1991), be it at categories of citizens (unemployed workers, pensioners or families with children, and so on), at needy groups (sick or disabled people) or at people whose means fall below subsistence level (the 'poor'). Furthermore, I regard policies that are targeted at more narrowly defined target populations as being more selective, and those aimed at more broadly defined groups of people as more universal. From this point of view, the differences between more universal and more selectively targeted policies are mostly gradual, and may not be that large in cases where the targeting variables are confined to neutral and objective demographic and socioeconomic categories. However, when targeting variables concern the neediness of people or households, an important qualitative difference emerges, introducing a number of problems, to be discussed later, that act counter to the broader aims of social policy. Therefore, I would like to narrow down the general question of the (dys)functionality of selective targeting to the (dys)functionality of needs testing in social protection. More specifically, since testing of need in practice is most often carried out as a test of the financial means of clients or claimants, this chapter concerns the functions and dysfunctions of means testing.

Functions and dysfunctions of the means test

Means-tested social protection is used here when entitlement to a benefit or service depends on the financial resources of the claiming unit (persons or households). Therefore, means testing as an administrative method has the function of allocating welfare to claimants on the basis of their financial resources. Alternative methods of administration include allocating benefits on the basis of age (as in pension schemes), physical status (as in disablement schemes), previous earnings and/or individual work history (as in unemployment schemes), marital status (as in widows pension schemes), and family size (as in child benefit schemes). However, means testing is viewed, not only as an administrative method, but also as a social policy instrument for the redistribution of resources in society, then other, social as well as economic, functions become apparent. First, means testing can be used as a way of limiting social expenditure. It is cheaper for society to pay benefits only to those members of a group who have financial resources below a certain level than to all members of a group, irrespective of their resources. Second, means tests have the effect of flattening the distribution of income, contributing to social equality. Third, means tests are used to target income or resources to individuals or households in society who are regarded as 'the truly needy'. The test of means implies that the income or resources to be distributed only reach those people whose own means fall below the income standard set in the welfare scheme. This standard is, in most cases, equal to a level of income that the government regards as a subsistence minimum. Therefore, means testing is an instrument for distributing income or resources to the poor in society.

Deacon and Bradshaw (1983) state that these functions can legitimise the means test for both 'right' and 'left' on the political spectrum, flattening of the income distribution being especially appealing to the left, targeting to the truly needy to the right, while the relative cheapness of the selective means test attracts politicians of both sides. Although, traditionally, means testing in social protection is more strongly related to the ideology of the right, with its emphasis on minimal collective arrangements to be supplemented by private insurances, than to that of the left, with its emphasis on broad and solidaristic collective arrangements, the 'new' left has shown that it is not averse to it under all circumstances (for example, the introduction of the means test in the Dutch survivors' pension under the social democratic presidency of Wim Kok). Clearly, means testing can have a broad political legitimacy. Since means testing is believed to encourage the spirit of responsibility, something that is highly valued in Anglo-Saxon countries (Kluegel and Smith, 1986), but increasingly also in continental European societies (Kluegel et al, 1995; Halman and Nevitte, 1996), means testing also seems to have a broad societal legitimacy among the public at large. Why, then, is it likely to be a controversial instrument? Why should its implementation in social policy be done with great care?

The answer to these questions is that means-tested schemes have a number of inherent problems, schematically presented in Box 7.1.

Some are concerned with the administrative complexity of actually testing means as an indicator of need. Means-tested schemes, for instance, are more costly to administer. In the Netherlands, the administration costs of non-means-tested social insurances are about 4% of total expenditure, while they

Box 7.1: Pros and cons of means testing

Pros

- Limits social expenditure
- Flattens income distribution; promotes social equality at lower end of income scale
- Distributes resources to the truly needy only

Cons

- Administration: higher costs, more errors
- Validity as needs indicator: informal means, new household types
- Conflicts with broader aims of social policy:

poverty trap	↔	end to poverty and dependency
stigmatisation	↔	integration
non-take-up	↔	justice, end to poverty

are 8% in the case of means-tested social assistance (SZW, 1999). Comparable is the situation with regard to the administration of means-tested British Supplementary Benefit (now Income Support) and British non-means-tested schemes (Dilnot et al, 1984, p 45). The administration costs of Dutch means-tested municipal anti-poverty policies often come close to even 50% (van Oorschot, 1994). The complexity of means testing also leads to higher error rates in benefit calculation. In the UK, for instance, 6% of Income Support benefit calculations are erroneous, compared to less than 1% in the case of social insurance (Atkinson, 1992). Other problems are related to the (declining) adequacy of means tests as an indicator of need. First, where the hidden economy is extended and participation in it is high, as is allegedly so in Southern and Eastern European countries (for example, Rose, 1992), informal (and illegal) sources of income seriously invalidate income earned in the formal economy as a measure of a claimant's overall means. Second, means tests often take the family household as the basic unit, on the assumption that people (should) feel responsible for each other and therefore share and care as family members. However, where in the course of the ongoing modernisation and individualisation process the traditional family is replaced with more loose and temporary forms of cohabitation, this assumption will increasingly not hold. As a result, household means testing might either have to become more complex, or be replaced with individualised tests (Gough, 1991).

However, more basic concerns stem from those aspects of means-tested schemes that place them at odds with the broader aims of social policy mentioned earlier. Most important in this respect is that means testing has the general effect of stigmatising beneficiaries, contributing to serious levels of non-take-up of rights and to the 'poverty trap'. Of these, stigmatisation is counterproductive to social integration, non-take-up leads to injustice and contributes to individuals and households being in poverty, and the poverty trap tends to keep individuals and households in poverty and dependent on society.

The rest of this chapter looks at why these effects are inherent to means testing, starting with the poverty trap.

The poverty trap

Since entitlements to a means-tested benefit or service depend on income, a rise in income can have the effect that the benefit is reduced or withdrawn. When this occurs only a part of the gross increase in income remains as an increase in net disposable income. This is partly due to means testing and partly to two other factors that consume part of any gross increase in income: income tax, and social insurance contributions. This difference between gross and net increases in income (that is, a high marginal effective tax rate), can act as a disincentive for people to become better off, either by finding or extending a job or by changing their job or skill-level. People for whom the difference between gross and net increases in income acts as a disincentive are said to be 'trapped in poverty' (using a broad notion of the 'poverty trap' concept[1]).

Examples of serious poverty-trap effects of means testing are numerous. Table 7.1, based on an OECD study on making work pay, shows high marginal effective tax rates (METR), ranging from about 70% to up to 100% or more, that unemployed one-earner couples in different countries face when accepting a job.

Further, in a recent study comparing unemployment insurance and assistance schemes in seven Northern European countries, it was found that the net difference between income from wage and income from benefit in all countries

Table 7.1: Incidence and causes of high marginal effective tax rates (METR) (one-earner couples)

	METR (%)	Tax and benefit combinations causing high METRs
Australia	104	Income tax (34%), Medicare payments (20%), Additional Family Payment (50%)
France	78	RMI disregard (50%), social security (18.7%), CSG (2.3%), housing benefit (16.5% average)
Germany	89	Income tax (51%), social security (18.3%), housing benefit (20%)
Ireland	105.5	Income tax (40%), social security (5.5%), Family Income Supplement (60%)
Sweden	72	Income tax (20%), social security (2%), local tax (31%), housing benefit (20%)
UK	97	Income Tax (20%), social security (10%), Family Credit (70%), Housing Benefit (65%), Council Tax benefit (20%)
US	72	Income tax (15%), social security (7.65%), local tax (5%), food stamps (24%), Earned Income Tax Credit (17%)

Source: OECD (1997, table 16, p 48)

was between 0% and 50% (SZW, 1995). The picture arising from this and the OECD study even underestimates the size of the poverty trap. In practice, marginal rates are often higher, and regularly exceed 100%, implying that people can be financially better off on benefit than working. Petri (1997) presents an example from the US of a low-waged working family earning $12,000 to $14,000 trying to improve itself through higher earnings facing a marginal tax rate of 100%, as a result of income tax, social contributions, loss of food stamps and rent subsidy. In the Netherlands, marginal rates of 100% are commonplace among unemployed and social-assistance beneficiaries accepting a job at 110% of the minimum wage (Dercksen, 1997). Such high rates occur because there may be occupational costs attached to working (for example, travel expenses, day care for children), but especially because entitlements to means-tested benefits and services often cumulate. This is the case in many countries, since unemployed people, social-assistance beneficiaries and low-wage workers are usually entitled to a number of means-tested benefits and services simultaneously, like housing benefit, study allowance for children, day-care subsidy, (local) tax exemptions, public transport reductions, healthcare services and insurance and the like (Eardley et al, 1996).

Various studies have shown that high marginal rates are unevenly distributed among social categories. Usually, social assistance clients are strongly affected (SZW, 1995; OECD, 1997), as well as wives of unemployed men (even after correcting for educational level; Davies et al, 1992; Kersten et al, 1993; Giannarelli and Micklewright, 1995), and families with children, due to higher benefit levels payable for children (SZW, 1995; OECD, 1997). However, the group most affected by the poverty trap seems to be lone parents on social assistance, since in nearly every OECD country they are the category with the highest METRs (OECD, 1997).

Note, however, that the poverty trap is not confined to welfare recipients or low-waged workers only. In practice, it can affect a wide range of incomes, which is why some speak of a 'poverty plateau' (Deacon and Bradshaw, 1983). Giannarelli and Steuerle (1995) show that, in the US, cumulative marginal rates are highest at 150% of the minimum wage, and the European comparative study shows rates as much as 75% for incomes up to 200% of the wage of the average productive worker (SZW, 1995). Governments that try to limit the disincentive effects of high METRs for people on low incomes, by gradually phasing out benefits as earnings rise, create higher METRs higher up the income ladder, thereby reducing work incentives for those already in work.

Whether and to what degree means testing and the resulting high marginal tax rates actually do discourage people from working (more) is not documented very well. In the Netherlands, there is little – but conflicting – empirical evidence of the true disincentive effects of the poverty trap. According to Beenstock (1987), this applies to the UK as well. Atkinson and Micklewright (1991), however, conclude in their review of empirical job search studies that such disincentive effects are significantly present, especially among female partners of male unemployed workers (see also Millar, 1988; Kersten et al,

1994). There are arguments suggesting that the effects, though significant, are not as important as sometimes believed – for example, because some people lack real opportunities to become better off, money is not all that counts, the matter is too complex for people to make rational decisions about whether extra efforts are worthwhile or not, and because people act under administrative control and social pressure. However, data about the 'size' of the poverty trap, and of the number of welfare recipients affected by it, make it quite inconceivable that disincentive effects will not occur. It should be noted in this respect that, in most European countries, the number of people dependent on means-tested social assistance grew substantially from the early 1980s onwards (van Oorschot and Schell, 1991). OECD indexed growth figures on these numbers vary among European countries, from 208 (Sweden) to as much as 967 (Austria) in the period from 1980-92 (OECD, 1997, p 48).

So, through its disincentive effects, means testing tends to be dysfunctional with regard to social policy's broader aims of doing away with poverty and dependency. One might seriously question what fairness there is in the high marginal tax rates that poor or low income households face when they try to better their situation.

Means testing and social division

When trying to describe the ultimate character of social policy, Richard Titmuss (1970, p 212) quoted with assent the way Boulding (1976, p 7) defined social policy as "centred in those institutions that create integration and discourage alienation". This view of social policy implies that its central aim is to integrate all groups and classes into society. That is, to provide for all citizens the prerequisites for participation in society as full members. This may not only require a redistribution of economic wealth from the 'rich' to the 'poor', but also promotion and protection of the self-esteem of the individual citizen (Kaufmann, 1970), ensuring, as Doyal and Gough (1991, p 63) state, "that people have enough confidence to participate in their social form of life". Means testing, as an instrument of social policy, tends to do a poor job with respect both to the economic and the sociocultural prerequisites for integration.

With regard to the economic aspect of integration, means testing creates two problems. First, it contributes to the poverty trap, thereby restricting individuals or households from making full use of their productive capacity, not only for themselves, but also for society as a whole. Second, non-take-up is inherent to means-tested benefits and services and can contribute to being in poverty also.

With regard to the sociocultural aspect of the integration problem, there is a broad consensus among scholars of social policy that means testing is highly intertwined with the problem of stigmatisation of beneficiaries (Titmuss, 1968; Pinker, 1971; Waxman, 1977; Deacon and Bradshaw, 1983; Gough, 1991). The term stigma refers to "an attribute that is deeply discrediting" (Goffman, 1974, p 3). Stigmatisation of individuals means that a negative social identity is attached to them, or as Goffman (1974, p 5) puts it, "we believe the person with a stigma is not quite human". Stigmatisation therefore implies social exclusion, "discrimination, through which we effectively, if often unthinkingly, reduce his [the stigmatised person's] life chances". Since, as symbolic interactionism made clear, much of what we think we are comes from what we believe that others think we are, stigmatisation also implies that stigmatised persons will find it very hard to construct or uphold a sense of self-esteem and self-confidence. No doubt this will have a negative effect on a stigmatised person's own efforts to become integrated in society. From Goffman's notes on stigma it becomes clear why, with its relation to the stigmatisation of beneficiaries, means testing detracts from the integrative aim of social policy. The question remains why means testing and stigmatisation of beneficiaries are related.

At the most general level, it can be argued that, insofar as being in poverty is a discrediting attribute (that is, a stigma), dependence on services or benefits that are specifically targeted at the poor will be stigmatised. That negative views of the poor exist widely can be concluded from the European Values Survey, which in 1990 asked European citizens what they saw as the main reasons for the existence of poor people. The proportions blaming the poor themselves, by giving 'laziness and lack of thrift' as a first or second reason, varied over the countries, but were between one third and one half in the Western European countries. In the Eastern countries, such as the Czech Republic, Hungary, Slovenia, Poland and Bulgaria, negative views of the poor were even stronger in that period (van Oorschot and Halman, 1998).

Further, means testing itself contains several discrediting elements. Claiming a means-tested benefit makes it evident that a person is not able to provide sufficient economic welfare on his or her own. This runs counter to the ethic of self-responsibility, which, as I stated earlier, is highly valued in Western, industrialised and market-oriented societies. Or, as Parker (1975, p 150) puts it "The significance of such an arrangement [means testing] is that rights depend on declaring and establishing some degree of financial poverty, a situation widely viewed in capitalist societies with suspicion, disapproval and hostility". Claiming a means-tested benefit is therefore likely to be seen as deviance from prevailing norms, which in turn can be a basis for stigmatisation and the loss of self-esteem. Second, in the administration of means-tested benefits, discretion and control of potential fraud play a much more important and (to all actors involved) visible role than in the administration of non-means-tested benefits. Being seen as potentially fraudulent is discrediting on its own. Discretion implies that the decision whether or not to grant a claim is in part dependent on the administrators' evaluation of the applicant and the circumstances which led to the claim. This subjective element gives the administrator moral and cognitive power over the applicant, which is likely to invoke a feeling of inferiority on the claimant's part.

Control of potential fraud, discretion and the close enquiry into many aspects of the claimant's personal affairs and relationships, which is inherent to many means-tested schemes, are all elements in administration that are likely to reduce the extent to which a benefit is perceived as being given 'as of right'. Not seeing a benefit as given as of right, but as a form of charity, is believed to invoke feelings of shame and inferiority. As Simmel already noted in 1908, "[T]he humiliation, shame and loss of status ['declassment'] brought about by the acceptance of charity are alleviated for him [the poor man] to the extent that it [the benefit] is not granted out of compassion or a sense of duty or even expediency but rather because he has a valid claim to it," (Simmel, 1908, p 456 author's translation).

In this respect, it is important to note that there seems to be only one abstract principle on which the use of means-tested benefits can be morally justified, which is the principle of citizenship (Parker, 1975). The abstractness of this principle is bound to make it a weak base for the perception of means-tested benefits as being as of right. In fact, the finding of Coughlin (1980) that in eight Western, industrialised nations, expenditure on 'public assistance' (which in all these countries is the main means-tested benefit scheme) received much less support from the public, compared to expenditures for old age, sickness, disablement, family costs and unemployment insurance, indicates that the principle of citizenship has a weak societal legitimacy. Moral justification for receiving a benefit is much easier in the case of non-means-tested benefits, where benefits are 'earned' or 'deserved' because of contributions paid, or where, according to Offe (1988, p 219) "it is much easier to conceive of a broad and inclusive alliance of potential beneficiaries ... (since 'all of us' expect to be old and sick in the future)". In both cases, the moral base can be found in the more concrete principle of reciprocity. Reciprocity is not only one of the strongest mechanisms for social integration and cohesion (see Mauss, 1923; Münch, 1984), but also a prerequisite for the maintenance of self-respect in any system or relation of exchange (Gouldner, 1973). Because of the fact that many recipients of means-tested benefits have no means to 'reciprocate', except through citizenship, they are bound to lose self-respect and to be stigmatised.

The socially divisive character of means-tested benefits and services does not only affect negatively the self-esteem of people in need; it also explains why 'programmes for the poor become poor programmes' (Rainwater, 1979; Ringen, 1987). There is wide evidence that means-tested programmes directed at the poor are generally less supported by the public at large than non-means-tested, more universal programmes (Rainwater, 1979; Coughlin, 1980; Ringen, 1987; Forma, 1997). This lesser societal legitimacy makes them more vulnerable to a less benign and more reserved treatment by policy makers and administrators, leading in practice to lesser quality of services and benefits, and of their delivery.

Due to the lesser societal legitimacy of means-tested schemes, highly selective welfare systems as a whole seem to be subjected to what could be called the 'selectivity trap'. Once such a system is established, as in the US, it might prove to be very difficult to extend welfare coverage beyond the group of the poorest and most deserving citizens, as well as to extend the level of social protection beyond that of mere subsistence. In other words, to the degree that welfare and social protection is exclusively seen and institutionalised as something for the poor only, it will be problematic to motivate the large middle classes for welfare extension.

Non-take-up

Non-take-up, or the phenomenon whereby people who are eligible for a benefit or service do not receive it (fully), is as strongly inherent to means testing as poverty trap effects and stigmatisation. However, it seems that the importance of non-take-up is not self-evident. This despite the fact that, as early as the 1970s, studies in different countries had already showed its existence (see, for example, Lister [1974] for the UK; Bijsterveldt [1975] for the Netherlands; Catrice-Lorey [1976] for France; Geissler [1976] for Germany; Doron and Rotor [1978] for Israel). There may be several reasons for this bias, but I believe that one of the most important factors is the widespread idea that the modern citizen is a rational, calculating individual seeking personal profit from any relationship with the state, not bothered by cultural and personal barriers, such as feelings of shame or insufficient bureaucratic skills. From this perspective, the proper functioning of social policy is seen as being endangered more by over-consumption than by under-consumption of social rights, and as a consequence the existence of under-consumption may easily be underrated. Another widespread idea is that, in the few cases of non-take-up that may exist, people do not want the benefit, either as a result of calculation (they do not think the benefit is worth the effort), or on principle (they do not want to depend on charity). In both such situations, according to the common view, the non-claimants do not really need the benefit to which they are entitled. This leads to the judgement that there is not generally a serious problem of non-take-up, at least not for the non-claimants themselves, and, usually therefore, either for the administration or for policy makers.

Although there will be cases of non-take-up which accord with this common view, results from studies on the topic show that such cases are rare. They show that, in the case of means-tested benefits (and sometimes also for non-means-tested benefits), it is a normal situation for large proportions of eligible populations not to receive the benefits in question. There even seems to be a sort of 'natural ceiling', of about 80-85%, above which take-up rates of means-tested benefits cannot reach (van Oorschot, 1995). Studies also show that many people who are eligible for social security benefits do not behave as well-informed, rational, calculating individuals, and that only in a minority of cases do non-claimants explicitly not want the benefit to which they are entitled. All this implies that non-take-up is to be regarded as a serious problem in means-tested social policy.

Of course, non-take-up of rights manifests an ineffective implementation of a welfare scheme. Where it occurs, the selectivity intended by policy makers fails in practice. But, as Deacon and Bradshaw (1983, p 122) note, "Take-up is not just a technical issue concerned with the effective delivery of welfare". Non-take-up also implies social injustice, because of the difference in the extent to which citizens receive what they are entitled to. Within social security, an institution that is to a large extent based on ideas of justice, this aspect of non-take-up represents a remarkable dysfunction. Moreover, non-take-up can also be the reason for people being in poverty. In the UK (Townsend, 1957; Cole and Utting, 1962), in West Germany (Knechtel, 1960) and in the Netherlands (Oude Engberink, 1984), non-take-up came to be seen as a social problem as a result of the outcomes of empirical research into poverty.

Some authors take a strong standpoint by evaluating the existence of non-take-up as evidence of the failure of the means test (Hartmann, 1985), or even as indicating the failure of the very principle of selectivity (Lynes, 1972, p 505). Lister (1974, p 21) concludes in this respect from her review of early British take-up studies that, "The selectivist solution to poverty has been tried, and it has failed". Others take a more moderate standpoint, arguing that non-take-up generally should be regarded as an important problem in social policy, but not, or to a lesser extent, if only small amounts are forgone (Bendick, 1985), if people genuinely do not want to claim (Beltram, 1984), if non-take-up is only frictional (Adler, 1977), or if people are entitled or non-claiming only for a short period of time (Richardson and Naidoo, 1978; SBC, 1978). Atkinson (1984) would assert that in all such cases non-take-up nevertheless indicates the existence of non-trivial costs associated with claiming. These costs, which claimants will also experience, may justify attention to the problem apart from the amount of unclaimed money or the non-claimants' motives.

Basically, however, it is 'the tragedy of selectivity' that trying to target welfare to the truly needy inherently means that a part of them will not be reached. To understand why means testing and failing take-up are so closely connected, and what type of factors are primarily responsible for the phenomenon, a closer look at the causes of non-take-up is needed.

Causes of non-take-up: clients, administration, scheme structure

Reviews of non-take-up research all show that, traditionally, the causes of non-take-up of social security benefits are studied at the client-level only (Corden, 1981; Falkingham, 1985; van Oorschot and Kolkhuis Tanke, 1989; Craig, 1991). That is, in trying to explain why people do not receive the benefits to which they are entitled, the focus has been on eligible people's knowledge, perceptions, attitudes, motivations, experiences and circumstances. Influencing factors, possibly operating at the levels of scheme structure and administration, have largely been ignored thus far in empirical research (see also Whyley and Huby, 1993; Corden, 1995). Nevertheless, the literature on non-take-up contains much evidence on the importance of influential factors at these two levels.

It is commonly acknowledged that the administration of services and benefits can have a great influence on what citizens actually receive, compared to what is originally intended by policy makers (Blau, 1955; Handler and Hollingsworth, 1971; Leibfried, 1976; Lipsky, 1980; Mashaw, 1983). Administrative influences on non-take-up are direct when administrators decide wrongly to reject a claim, or when they award a smaller amount than a claimant is actually due. Examples of such wrong decisions can be found in Berthoud (1983/84) and Vos (1991). Other studies have shown that administrators of means-tested social security schemes tend to make decisions on the basis of biased and/or insufficient information (Howe, 1985; Knegt, 1986; Vos, 1991), leading to false rejections in at least some cases. Indirect influences arise from practical administrative arrangements and administrators' behaviour that set constraints on clients or lay stumbling blocks in their paths. Clear examples can be found in Briggs and Rees (1980), Corden (1983, 1987), Graham (1984), Richardson and Naidoo (1978), Davies and Ritchie (1988). From these studies, the main factors at the level of administration that enhance the probability of non-take-up can be summarised as follows:

- a way of handling claims and claimants that is experienced by claimants as humiliating or degrading;
- combining a 'service' and a 'fraud control' function;
- poor quality communication with clients, giving insufficient information and advice;
- using complex application forms;
- poor quality decision making (for example, taking decisions on the basis of insufficient information or on the basis of client stereotyping);
- poor quality technical administrative procedures;
- wrong interpretation of scheme rules by administrators.

Recently, Corden (1995) elaborated this list of main factors on the basis of British findings and improved it by offering and applying an alternative, sequential classification of administrative aspects that are influential: aspects of information supply, of service provision, and of application procedure and outcome. Corden presents a wide variety of evidence on the influence of these administrative aspects on non-take-up, and concludes that "every aspect of administration can potentially affect take-up" (Corder, 1995, p 58).

Factors at the level of benefit structure will not lead directly to non-take-up, but indirectly, because they constitute to a large extent the context in which the behaviour of administrators and clients takes place, thereby offering opportunities for and constraints on the behaviour of both sets of actors. From the information available, I have concluded elsewhere (van Oorschot and Kolkhuis Tanke, 1989) that the probability of non-take-up is larger in schemes that:

- are means tested;
- have a large number of rules and guidelines;
- have complicated rules;
- have vague, imprecise, indistinct and/or discretionary entitlement criteria;
- supplement other sources of income;

- are aimed at groups in society which are the subject of negative valuation;
- provide only small amounts of benefit;
- leave the initiative to start the claiming process fully to the applicant;
- provide for a variety of expenses (comprehensive schemes);
- provide for incidental instead of regular expenses;
- offer an unstable entitlement.

Of the structural aspects, the presence of a means test is most widely recognised as a factor inherently associated with non-take-up (Bendick, 1980; Deacon and Bradshaw, 1983; Hartmann, 1985). This is understandable when one realises that, in means-tested schemes, factors from the different levels tend to occur in combination. Means-tested benefits and services often contain complex rules concerning what is to be considered as 'means', what part of available means are to be taken into account, and whose means are to be considered. Most tests are not based on individual means, but on household means. What makes up a 'household' is often vaguely described and can leave room for discretion, and it certainly adds to complexity. On the level of administration, complexity and vagueness are likely to enhance the occurrence of mistakes, false interpretation of rules, insufficient gathering of information on which decisions are to be based, stereotyping of clients to guide the complex decision-making process, the use of complex application forms and so on. On the client level, complexity is likely to induce false perceptions of eligibility or of the amount of benefit to be received, to obscure the claiming process and administrative procedures, and to pose problems in gathering the required information. An important feature of means-tested schemes is that they are in general aimed at 'the poor' (that is, at a social category that is still likely to be stigmatised). Claiming a means-tested benefit is therefore likely to induce a fear of stigmatisation and a feeling of degradation, which can form serious thresholds to claiming (van Bijsterveldt, 1975; Hartmann, 1981). The feeling of degradation is likely to be intensified by the combination of the administrative functions of 'service to the poor' and 'control on potential fraud', a combination so apparent in the administration of means-tested benefits and services (Howe, 1985; Knegt, 1986).

The three different levels – scheme structure, administration and client – can be distinguished analytically quite easily, but the research literature and reviews of it show that, in practice, the factors influencing non-take-up form a complex whole. I propose to see non-take-up as the result of a mix of interrelated factors from different interacting levels, as pictured in Figure 7.1.

Viewing the causes of non-take-up as a mix of multilevel factors leads to recognition that it is not only citizens who are responsible for the problem of non-take-up. Policy makers and administrators also play their role and can be held responsible. Denying this would be a clear case of "blaming the victim" (Townsend, 1979). As for the question of primary responsibility, the answer might be that that is just a matter of the view taken. For example, who is responsible for the non-take-up resulting from lack of sufficient knowledge by eligible people? Is it the clients, as is commonly assumed? Or is it the

Figure 7.1: The multilevel influences on non-take-up: an interactive model

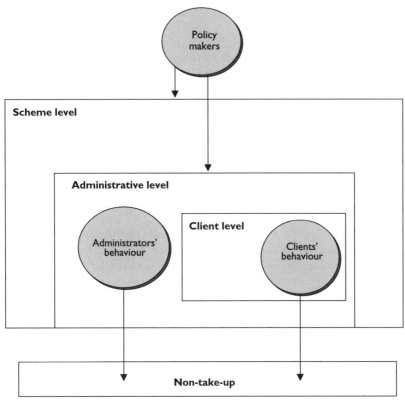

Source: van Oorschot (1995)

administration, for not being active enough in distributing information and giving advice? Or are the policy makers to blame, for designing a large number of complex, vague and therefore incomprehensible rules and guidelines? On the whole, however, based on an extensive review of research and a multi-benefit study among different groups of low-income families in the Netherlands (van Oorschot, 1995), I am inclined to allot the largest part of the responsibility to the level of administration.

Certainly, one might say that the structural level is most important in the process of realising rights, because non-take-up is strongly inherent in means testing. Abolish the means test and by far the largest part of the problem of ineffective delivery of benefits will be solved. However, this is not a realistic option, because means testing is a functional instrument in welfare schemes when considerations of economic efficiency are dominant and solidarity is limited. Given that a scheme is means tested, structural elements are still important. They may facilitate matters at the administrative level, mainly by providing the conditions in which well-targeted information and advice activities can be designed and implemented. And they may facilitate claiming at the client level, by promoting a positive image of a scheme, or by offering a favourable type of benefit.

No doubt the client level is of great importance too, because it is at this level that the decisions whether or not to claim are taken (or not, in which case non-take-up is the result of 'non-decision'). Here, informational factors prove to be the most important, in the sense that usually the largest part of non-take-up is directly caused by simply not being aware of a scheme's existence, followed, among those who are aware, by misperceptions of eligibility.

However, the administrative level is critically important. On one hand, the extent and quality of information and advice activities of administrative bodies have a strong and direct influence on crucial informational factors at the client level, and through these on take-up. On the other hand, favourable structural features are usually only effective when they are put into operation by the administrative bodies. In the Dutch study, exceptionally low rates of non-take-up for housing benefit, and for nearly all schemes among the Nijmegen social assistance clients, could be explained by the well-targeted and intensive information campaigns of the administrative bodies involved, because these led to high levels of basic knowledge. Among the other groups studied, the rates of non-take-up were high. These groups were no different from the Nijmegen social assistance clients on a number of client level characteristics, but they lacked the stimulating administrative context. It was also apparent that, by creating an overall informational context encompassing several benefits (for example, by means of multi-benefit promotions), mutual associations between the take-up of benefits can be stimulated, therefore enhancing the occurrence of full use (that is, of people using all the various benefits and services they were entitled to). An administrative body can stimulate take-up of a range of schemes even more effectively if such an institution has structural relationships with a group of low-income households, and feels responsible for the take-up of the entire programme.

The latter point touches on the more fundamental problem of the ineffectiveness of the implementation of means-tested benefits. It was our experience that administrations usually care relatively little about the problem of non-take-up; their ambitions and feelings of responsibility do not seem to go beyond being there for and helping claimants. Of course, ultimately, the claiming decision is to be taken by clients, but if the approach to non-claimants is one of 'take it or leave it' then high non-take-up is likely to be the result. This is the situation most frequently encountered.

Conclusions

The selective targeting of welfare, and using the means test as an instrument for it, is increasingly popular in both Western and Eastern European countries. This chapter critically discussed the pros and cons of means testing in relation to what I conceive as the broad aims of social policy: to do away with poverty, social injustice and dependency, and to integrate all groups and classes into society. The discussion showed that means testing tends to demotivate poor people from trying to become better off, lays obstacles in their path to full societal participation as respected and self-respecting citizens, and creates an ineffective use of social rights. Although means testing serves purposes of budget control and might have a growing societal legitimacy base, I am nevertheless on the whole inclined to take a reserved position towards the trend.

First, seen from the societal level, because the trend, through its consequences of poverty trap, stigmatisation and non-take-up problems, implies that the institution of social protection is fulfilling its integrating function less adequately. Means-tested protection may be a meaningful and adequate 'safety-net' instrument when its application is necessary in exceptional cases and for short periods between an individual's loss of one 'secure' socioeconomic position and the achievement of another. However, relying on means testing as the major means of guaranteeing a minimum protection for a large group of citizens, who are dependent on it for long periods of time, testifies to a preoccupation with short-term, mainly economic, interests and a related neglect of long-term needs for societal integration and participation.

Second, seen from the level of individual citizens, the trend towards selective targeting implies a loss in the quality of the welfare state for the many citizens whose socioeconomic chances are, or will become in the future, primarily dependent on its benefits and services. Means-tested welfare generally implies lower benefits, stronger and more intrusive controls over personal circumstances and activities, more complex obstacles to the realisation of rights, fewer opportunities to become better off and a greater chance of needy citizens being seen (and treated) as second-rate people.

So, where social policy should balance the economic and social interests of society at large and of the individuals in it, the trend towards the selective targeting of welfare comes down to a one-sided focusing on society's (short-term) economic interests.

The third, and perhaps most important, reason to be critical about the present trend is that it might prove to be irreversible, even in a favourable economic context in which cost-saving arguments would have lost their persuasiveness. It has been my experience that selective and means-tested benefits and services tend to have lesser societal support from the public at large. Introducing stronger selectivity might produce a vicious circle of ever declining support for ever more selective policies. In this way, European welfare states might move themselves into a 'selectivity trap', from which it will be difficult to escape. This danger is particularly present in the Eastern European transitional economies where at present it seems that hardly any alternatives for means-tested safety-net protection are considered as serious options.

Note

[1] It has become custom to differentiate between the 'poverty trap' and the 'unemployment trap' (for example, Deacon and Bradshaw, 1983; OECD, 1997), between the disincentive effects of the working of the tax-benefit system for those in work and for those out of work. Here, where the core problem is that means testing can have disincentive effects for people to become better off than they are, whether they are in or out of work, this distinction is of no relevance. Dilnot et al (1984, p 55) confine the concept of the poverty trap to situations in which households can make themselves even worse off by increasing their income. This confined notion of the concept leads them to the finding that relatively very few British households, in 1982/3, were 'trapped in poverty'.

References

Adler, M. (1977) *Research priorities for improving the take-up of benefits*, Edinburgh: Social Security Research Policy Committee.

Andries, M. (1996) 'The politics of targeting: the Belgian case', *Journal of European Social Policy*, vol 6, no 3, pp 209-33.

Atkinson, A.B. (1984) *Take-up of social security benefits*, International Centre for Economics and Related Disciplines, Discussion Paper 65, London: London School of Economics and Political Science.

Atkinson, A.B. and Micklewright, J. (1991) 'Unemployment compensation and labour market transitions: a critical review', *Journal of Economic Literature*, vol 24, pp 1679-727.

Atkinson, A.B. (1992) *The Western experience with social safety-nets*, Welfare State Programme Discussion Paper WSP/80, London: London School of Economics.

Beenstock, M. (1987) *Work, welfare and taxation: A study of labour supply incentives in the UK*, London: Allen and Unwin.

Bendick, M. (1980) 'Failure to enrol in public assistance programs', *Social Work*, vol 25, no 4, pp 3-14.

Berthoud, R. (1983) *Study of the reformed Supplementary Benefit Scheme: Working paper D: Welfare rights advice experiment*, London: Policy Studies Institute.

Blau, P.M. (1955) *The dynamics of bureaucracy*, Chicago, IL: University of Chicago Press.

Briggs, E. and Rees, A.M. (1980) *Supplementary Benefits and the consumer*, London: Bedford Square Press.

Boulding, K.E. (1967) 'The boundaries of social policy', *Social Work*, vol 12, no 1, p 7.

Catrice-Lorey, A. (1976) 'Inegualités d'accès aux systèmes de protection sociale et pauvreté culturelle', *Revue Française des Affaires Sociales*, no 4, pp 67-98.

Dercksen, C. (1997) *Armoede en armoedeval: de rol van inkomensafhankelijke regelingen*, The Hague: VUGA.

Cole, D. and Utting, J. (1962) *The economic circumstances of old people*, Occasional Papers on Social Administration, Welwyn: Codicode.

Corden, A. (1981) *The process of claiming FIS: Background paper II – review of previous studies on the take-up of means-tested benefits and their relevance to a study of FIS-take-up*, York: University of York, Social Policy Research Unit.

Corden, A. (1983) *Taking up a means-tested benefit: The process of claiming Family Income Supplement*, Department of Health and Social Security, London: HMSO.

Corden, A. (1987) *Disappointed applicants. A study of unsuccessful claims for Family Income Supplement*, Aldershot: Avebury.

Corden, A. (1995) *New perspectives on take-up: A literature review*, London: HMSO.

Coughlin, R.M. (1980) *Ideology, public opinion and welfare policy: Attitudes towards taxes and spending in industrial societies*, Institute of International Studies, Research Series no 42, Berkely, CA: University of California.

Craig, P. (1991) 'Costs and benefits: a review of research on take-up of income-related benefits', *The Journal of Social Policy*, vol 20, no 4, pp 537-65.

Daly, M. (1997) 'Welfare states under pressure: cash benefits in European welfare states', *Journal of European Social Policy*, vol 7 no 2, pp 129-46.

Davies, C. and Ritchie, J. (1988) *Tipping the balance: A study of non-take-up of benefits in an inner city area*, DHSS Research Report no 16, London: HMSO.

Davies, R., Elias, P. and Penn, R. (1992) 'The relationship between a husband's unemployment and his wife's participation in the labour force', *Oxford Bulletin of Economics and Statistics*, vol 54, no 2, pp 145-71.

Deacon, A. and Bradshaw, J. (1983) *Reserved for the poor: The means-test in British social policy*, Oxford: Blackwell.

Deacon, B., Hulse, M. and Stubbs, P. (1997) *Global social policy: International organisations and the future of welfare*, London: Sage.

Dilnot, A., Kay, J. and Morris, C. (1984) *The reform of social security*, Oxford: Clarendon Press.

Doron, A. and Roter, R. (1978) *Low wage earners and low wage subsidies*, Jerusalem: National Insurance Institute.

Doyal, L. and Gough, I. (1991) *A theory of human need*, London: Macmillan.

Eardly,T., Bradshaw, J., Ditch, J., Gough, I. and Whiteford, P. (1996) *Social assistance in the OECD countries*, London: HMSO.

Falkingham, F. (1985) *Take-up of benefits: A literature review*, Benefits Research Unit Review Paper 1:85, Nottingham: University of Nottingham, Department of Social Administration.

Ferge, S. (1997) 'A central European perspective on the social quality of Europe', in W. Beck, L. van der Maesen and A. Walker (eds) *The social quality of Europe*, The Hague: Kluwer Law International.

Forma, P. (1997) 'The rational legitimacy of the welfare state', *Policy & Politics*, vol 25, no 3, pp 235-49.

Geissler, H. (1976) *Die neue Soziale Frage*, Freiburg: Herder Verlag.

George, V. and Taylor-Gooby, P. (1996) *European welfare policy: Squaring the welfare circle*, London: Macmillan.

Giannarelli, L. and Steuerle, C. (1995) *The twice poverty trap*, Washington, DC: Urban Institute.

Giannarelli, L. and Micklewright, J. (1995) 'Why do women married to unemployed men have low participation rates?', *Oxford Bulletin of Economics and Statistics*, vol 57, no 4, pp 471-86.

Goffman, E. (1974) *Stigma: Notes on the management of spoiled identity*, New York, NY: Aronson.

Gough, I. (1994) *Means-tested benefits in a comparative perspective*, The Richard Titmuss Memorial Lecture, Hebrew University of Jerusalem, 31 May.

Gouldner, A. (1973) 'The norm of reciprocity', in A. Gouldner (ed) *For sociology: Renewal and critique in sociological theory*, London: Allen Lane.

Graham, J. (1984) *Take-up of FIS: Knowledge, attitudes and experience, claimants and non-claimants*, Stormont: Social Research Division, PPRU, Department of Finance and Personnel.

Halman, L. and Nevitte, N. (eds) (1996) *Political value change in Western democracies*, Tilburg: Tilburg University Press.

Handler, J. and Hollingsworth, E.J. (1971) *The deserving poor: A study of welfare administration*, Chicago: Markham.

Hartmann, H. (1985) 'Armut trotz Sozialhilfe. Zur nichtinanspruchnahme von Sozialhilfe in der Bundesrepublik', in S. Leibfried and F. Tennstedt (eds) *Politik der Armut und die Spaltung des Sozialstaats*, Frankfurt am Main, pp 169-189.

Howe, L.E.A. (1985) 'The "Deserving" and the "Undeserving": practice in an urban local security office', *Journal of Social Policy*, vol 14, no 1, pp 49-72.

Kaufmann, F.X. (1970) *Sicherheit als soziologisches und sozialpolitisches Problem: von Untersuchungen zur einer Wertidee hochdifferenzierter Gesellschaften*, Stuttgart: Enke.

Kersten, A., Jehoel-Gijsbers, G., Smit, L. and van Oorschot, W. (1994) *Samen zonder werk?*, SVR Report 93/7, Zoetermeer: Sociale Verzekeringsraad.

Kluegel, J. and Smith, E. (1986) *Beliefs about inequality: Americans' views of what is and what ought to be*, New York, NY: de Gruyter.

Kluegel, J., Mason, D. and Wegener, B. (eds) (1995) *Social justice and political change: Public opinion in capitalist and post-communist states*, New York, NY: de Gruyter.

Knechtel, E. (1960) 'Die Zahl der einkommensschwachen kinderreichen Familien in der Bundesrepublik', *Soziale Welt*, vol 3, no 2, pp 330-9.

Knegt, R. (1986) *Regels en redelijkheid in de bijstandsverlening: participerende observatie bij een Sociale Dienst*, Proefschrift, Amsterdam: Universiteit van Amsterdam.

Leibfried, S. (1976) 'Armutspotential und Sozialhilfe in der Bundesrepublik: zum Prozess des Filterns von Anspruchen auf Sozialhilfe', *Kritische Justiz*, vol 17, pp 376-93.

Lister, R. (1974) *Take-up of means-tested benefits*, Poverty Research Series 18, London: Child Poverty Action Group.

Lipsky, M. (1980) *Street level bureaucracy: Dilemmas of the individual in public services*, New York, NY: Russell Sage Foundation.

Lynes, T. (1972) 'Welfare men', *New Society*, September.

Mashaw, J.L. (1983) *Bureaucratic justice: Managing social security disability claims*, New Haven, CT: Yale University Press.

Mauss, M. (1923) *The Gift*, London: Routledge.

Millar, J. (1988) 'Barriers to equal treatment and equal outcome: means-testing and unemployment', in ISSA (ed) *Equal treatment in social security*, Studies and Research No 27, Geneva: International Social Security Association.

Miller, S. and Tomaskovic-Devey, D. (1990) 'Targeting processes', *Research in Social Policy*, vol 2, pp 91-117.

Münch, R. (1984) *Die Struktur der Moderne (II: Gemeinschaft)*, Frankfurt.

OECD (Organisation for Economic Co-operation and Development) (1997) *Making work pay: Taxation, benefits, employment and unemployment*, Paris: OECD.

Offe, C. (1988) 'Democracy against the welfare state? Structural foundations of neoconservative political opportunities', in J.D. Moon (ed) *Responsibility, rights and welfare: The theory of the Welfare State*, London: Westview Press, pp 189-228.

Oude Engberink, G. (1984) *Minima zonder marge*, Rotterdam: Gemeentelijke Sociale Dienst Rotterdam.

Palme, J. and Wennemo, I. (1998) *Swedish social security in the 1990s: Reform and retrenchment*, Stockholm: Stockholm University, SOFI.

Parker, J. (1975) *Social policy and citizenship*, London: Macmillan Press.

Petri, T. (1997) 'The real problem of low income families', www.house.gov/petri.

Pinker, R. (1971) *Social theory and social policy*, London: Heinemann.

Ploug, N. and Kvist, J. (eds) (1997) *Social security in Europe: Development or dismantlement?*, The Hague: Kluwer Law International.

Rainwater, L. (1982) 'Stigma in income tested programs', in I. Garfinkel (ed) *Income tested transfer programs: The case for and against*, New York, NY: Academic Press.

Richardson, A. and Naidoo, J. (1978) *The take-up of supplementary benefits: A report on a survey of claimants*, London: University of London, Chelsea College.

Ringen, S. (1987) *The possibility of politics*, Oxford: Clarendon Press.

Rose, R. and Peters, G. (1978) *Can government go bankrupt?*, London: Macmillan.

Rose, R. (1992) *Who needs social protection in Eastern Europe?*, Paper for the International Workshop on Poverty and Social Protection in Central and Eastern Europe, Budapest.

Saunders, P. (1991) 'Selectivity and targeting in income support: the Australian experience', *Journal of Social Policy*, vol 20, no 3, pp 299-326.

SBC (Supplementary Benefits Commission) (1978) *Take-up of supplementary benefits*, Supplementary Benefits Administration Papers No 7, London: HMSO.

Simmel, G. (1908) *Soziologie: Untersuchungen über die Formen der Vergesellschaftung*, (Siebentes Kapitel: Der Arme), Leipzig: Duncker und Humblot.

Spicker, P. (1998) *Targeting and strategic intervention*, paper presented at the Second Research Conference of the International Social Security Association, Jerusalem, 25-27 January.

SZW (Ministry for Social Affairs and Employment) (1995). *Unemployment benefits and social assistance in seven European countries*, The Hague: Ministry of Social Affairs and Employment.

SWZ (1999) *Sociale nota 1999*, The Hague: Ministry of Social Affairs and Employment.

Titmuss, R.M. (1968) *Commitment to welfare*, London: Allen and Unwin.

Titmuss, R.M. (1970) *The gift relationship: From human blood to social policy*, London: Allen and Unwin.

Townsend, P. (1957) *The family life of old people: An inquiry in East-London*, London: Routledge.

Townsend, P. (1979) *Poverty in the United Kingdom: A survey of household resources and standards of living*, Harmondsworth: Penguin.

Van Bijsterveldt, Q.M. (1975) *Een sociale voorziening en haar cliënten: een onderzoek naar de bijstandsverlening aan vrouwelijke gezinshoofden*, Proefschrift, Tilburg: Katholieke Hogeschool Tilburg.

van Oorschot, W. (1994) 'Las administraciones locales y la proteccion financiera de las familias de escasos recursos', *Quaderns de Serveis Socials*, no 8, Diputacio de Barcelona, p 49-64.

van Oorschot, W. (1995) *Realizing rights: A multilevel approach to non-take-up of means-tested benefits*, Aldershot: Avebury.

van Oorschot, W. (1998) 'Deservingness and conditionality of solidarity', *Sociale Wetenschappen*, vol 41, no 3, pp 54-78.

van Oorschot, W. and Halman, L. (1998) *Blame or fate, individual or social? An international comparison of popular explanations of poverty*, Utrecht: AWSB.

van Oorschot, W. and Kolkhuis Tancke, P. (1989) *Niet-gebruik van sociale zekerheid: feiten, theorieën, onderzoeksmethoden*, COSZ series, 16, The Hague: Ministry of Social Affairs.

van Oorschot, W. and Schell, J. (1991) 'Means-testing in Europe: a growing concern', in M. Adler, C. Bell, J. Clasen and A. Sinfield (eds) *The sociology of social security*, Edinburgh: Edinburgh University Press.

Vos, J.G. (1991) *Recht hebben en recht krijgen: een studie over beleidsvrijheid, niet-gebruik van rechten en verantwoord ambtelijk handelen*, Lelystad: Vermande.

Waxman, C. (1977) *The stigma of poverty: A critique of poverty theories and policies*, Oxford: Pergamon Press.

Wilensky, H. (1974) *The welfare state and equality: structural and ideological roots of public expenditures*, Berkeley, CA: University of California Press.

Will, J. (1993) 'The dimensions of poverty: public perceptions of the deserving poor', *Social Science Research*, no 22, pp 312-32.

Whyley, C. and Huby, M. (1993) *Take-up and the Social Fund: Applying the concept of take-up to a discretionary benefit*, York: University of York, Social Policy Research.

Part III
Anti-poverty policies in poor countries

EIGHT

Structural adjustment and mass poverty in Ghana

Kwabena Donkor

Introduction[1]

The 1980s witnessed the phenomenon of Structural Adjustment Programmes (SAPs) imposed on the African continent with widespread repercussions. By 1993, at least 40 of the 56 countries of Africa were involved in one or another of these programmes. Structural Adjustment Programmes of the World Bank and the International Monetary Fund (IMF) have transformed the realism, if not the interpretation, of African political and social economy. This transformation – from devaluation, privatisation to cost recovery and deregulation – has been effected not only in the economic and social spheres, but also the political. The hitherto near sacrosanct certainty of the centrality of the state and the seeming inevitability of development have been overtaken by the weakening of the state and the concentration on growth (as opposed to development), which in any case has been most erratic.

In examining the contemporary African economy, therefore, scholars and practitioners alike must abandon the paradigmatic state–centrism of one-party, military or 'one man' rule that characterised African states in the 1960s and 1970s. The spectacular responses and outcomes of droughts, food riots, widespread informal sectors, gender development and adjustment conditions have critical long-term implications that cannot be ignored. Adjustment has transformed not only the terms of trade (internal and external), but also the social relationships which underpin the terms of trade. As Shaw argues (1992), the very political economy of Africa – that is, definitions and relations of state, class, society and community – has changed. But has this change affected the deprivation of the mass of the Ghanaian and indeed, African poor?

The historical setting

Africa, and Sub-Saharan Africa in particular, has recorded the weakest economic growth rates, let alone development, of all developing regions of the world in recent decades. Between 1965 and 1985, GDP per capita (even forgetting one's reservations about accuracy and meaning), increased by less than 1% a year on average. Arising from this negligible GDP growth rate, a large number of African states had lower per capita levels in 1985 than they did at independence. For most Africans, real income in the 1980s was lower than in 1970!

The SAPs of the World Bank and the IMF in the late 1970s and early 1980s came in for much criticism (for example, Helleiner, 1990; Herbst, 1993). A major element of this antipathy was the role of conditionality in the scheme of adjustment. While the use of conditionality was not new in World Bank and IMF financing prior to SAPs, its use became highly excessive and shifted from project specific to sectoral and cross-sectoral conditions.

A theory of adjustment

A major problem for students of adjustment is the absence of a cohesive body of knowledge that can safely pass as a theory of adjustment. This problem emanates, among other things, from the conflicting ideological and idiosyncratic philosophies of the two key players – the IMF and the World Bank. Adjustment programmes are, at their roots, intended to improve economic management and thereby raise the standard of living of the population in the medium term (Nashashibi, 1992, p v). Therefore the overriding consideration has been economic management. Exacting maximum economic efficiency from the macro economy has been the implicit goal of adjustment programmes in Africa. This is where the structural conflict between social provision (which in itself can be a stimulus to increased productivity) and short-term economic goals is manifested. In the short term, per capita increases as well as GDP/GNP growth rates are the dominant factors, whereas educational investment and innovation, health delivery and job training have a longer gestation period but are equally crucial to long-term development.

A key problem of adjustment, therefore, has been deciding the mix between stabilisation and structural reform instruments. While a greater dependence on structural reform instruments is preferable from the point of view of growth, the extent of the stabilisation instrument would be dictated by the urgency of reducing the imbalance of the macro economy to a sustainable level. And even in the case of identifying which adjustment instruments to use, policy makers would still have to contend with the problem of deciding which instruments have the effect of reducing the imbalance, preserving or promoting growth and protecting the poor. Accepting that the probability of a particular instrument achieving the three objectives is minimal, I still deem it important that the overall package achieves these objectives.

The critical conditions prevailing in a country must be paramount in the determination of which instruments – or combination of instruments – and mechanism to adopt in the adjustment process. It must not be overtly ideological, although the adjustment process in Africa has been bedevilled with ideological definitions, as opposed to empirical ones. Adjustment is supply driven, on the lines of right-wing economic conservatism of dominant Western economic powers. Unfortunately, the weight of the stabilisation instruments in particular has become dependent on external circumstances that determine the magnitude and sequencing of adjustment.

The sectoral lending approach prior to 1983 was considered weak in leverage and the more omnibus Structural Adjustment Loan (SAL) gave the Bank entry to the top policy making levels in developing countries. This was to facilitate loans large enough to enable the Bank to pressurise decision makers to switch to more orthodox economic models. The conditionality had to be economy-wide to both justify the large loans and also to be effective, considering the large loss of trade terms most African countries encountered. Conditionality has been variously described as 'leverage' and 'policy dialogue'. It illustrates the need 'to increase the effectiveness, or productivity of capital resources supplied' by the twin institutions. It is also a set of changes in economic policy that the recipient must implement in return for a loan or grant.

Composition of adjustment

Adjustment programmes have a number of components both from an institutional point of view and from the point of inputs such as facilities and design elements. From a design perspective, SAPs have two major components: stabilisation and structural reform.

Stabilisation

The IMF singularly has the role (with borrower country) of designing and supervising stabilisation policies of indebted countries seeking assistance. Stabilisation aims at reducing macro-economic deficits, inflation and crunching out domestic credit expansion.

In pursuing these objectives, the IMF's posture, if not philosophy, has been that external disequilibrium is always the outcome of excessive credit expansion (Bacha, 1987, p 1457). From this position therefore, the IMF sees a purging of excessive demand as the cure. This approach to stabilisation has often been a major cause for strained relations with its twin institution – the World Bank, which the IMF has consistently regarded and treated as the junior institution.

Stabilisation programmes often include three sets of policies (see Cornia, 1987):

- expenditure reducing policies;
- expenditure switching policies;
- switching productive resources (labour and capital) from non-tradable to tradable sector.

It is important to recognise that stabilisation is short term in nature, averaging about eighteen months in most cases.

Structural reform

This is the second stage of SAPs, although this stage can run in tandem with stabilisation – and is increasingly doing so. Unlike stabilisation, structural reforms are medium to long term and aim at tackling the underlying disequilibrium of the macro economy as a whole – and not just the balance of payments.

Structural reforms have come to involve the price incentive, the role of the state in production and productivity, public sector policy capacity, the banking system, internal terms of trade and so on. Elements also include desubsidisation, privatisation, public sector reform, redundancies, export promotion, liberalisation of the macro economy, among others.

Whereas the IMF has hegemony in stabilisation policies, the same cannot be said of the World Bank in structural reforms. Until the mid-1980s, all medium and long-term reforms were assumed to fall under only Bank competence, but with the establishment of the Structural Adjustment Fund and the Extended Structural Adjustment Fund by the IMF, this balance of power changed. Both the World Bank and IMF are now involved, therefore, in structural reforms.

Facilities of adjustment

The key to understanding the complexity of SAPs rests within the confines of a number of specific financial facilities provided by both the IMF and the World Bank. These facilities or loans provide the means of imposing adjustment leverage on adjusting countries. The facilities are:

• Structural Adjustment Loan (SAL);
• Sectoral Adjustment Loan (SECAL);
• Structural Adjustment Fund;
• Enhanced Structural Adjustment Fund.

In both the design and implementation of SAP in Africa, the historical conflicts between the World Bank and the IMF have been constant. While it is tempting to assume that conflicts between the two institutions are new, they are not. Conflicts between the World Bank and the IMF have been legendary and are as old as the institutions themselves. Such conflicts have reared their heads almost from the very beginning but by the 1960s, with most former colonies having attained nationhood, the need to resolve these perennial conflicts had become unavoidable. A Concordat was therefore reached in December 1966 between the two institutions that attempted to delineate the spheres of competencies of the institutions. The agreement gave the IMF responsibility and lead in "exchange rates and restrictive (trade) systems ... adjustment for temporary balance of payment disequilibria ... and stabilisation programmes" (Feinberg, 1986, p 5). The Bank was to lead on "development programmes and project evaluation, including development priorities" (p 5). However, the big grey area of financial institutions, capital markets, domestic savings, domestic and foreign debt remained an overlapping responsibility (see Mosley et al, 1991, p 36). In addition to the specific areas of joint competencies, there have always existed the more subjective options, routes and responsibility for the development process. Whereas the World Bank seems to have a broader remit, the remit is also largely 'unquantifiable', leading to greater reliance on subjectivity.

The Concordat of 1966 did not bring to an end the World Bank and IMF's disagreements. The 1970s and 1980s witnessed the widening of these conflicts as many economies of developing countries took a battering. The Bank found the IMF very restrictive in its handling of its exchange rate remit. The IMF's overenthusiastic wielding of the axe regarding public expenditure cuts also drew World Bank displeasure. However the IMF's concerns were mostly in line with its own institutional priorities and ideology, particularly on balance of payments, deficit reduction and so on. The problem was worsened with the introduction of the IMF's Extended Fund Facility in 1974. For the first time, a medium-term element was introduced to the IMF's lending, pushing the IMF into areas of development hitherto monopolised by the World Bank, thereby threatening the Bank with loss of institutional identity[2] (see Mosley et al, 1991, pp 51-54).

The limitations placed on the Bank by its Articles of Agreement restricting it from advancing programme loans except in 'exceptional' cases also strengthened the hands of the IMF. To get around the limitations on the introduction of SALs, the Bank this time imposed another conditionality, but this time on itself! It made the disbursement of SALs dependent on the existence of a Stabilisation Programme between the borrowing country and the IMF.

Structural Adjustment Loans further complicated World Bank/IMF relations. The SALs moved the Bank into conditional programme lending as stated above and added conditionality to areas or situations where IMF conditionality was already in operation, creating the problem of cross-conditionality between the two institutions. These are essentially of two kinds:

- problems arising from the different nature of the two conditionalities;
- problems arising from the need to harmonise the content of the two kinds of conditionality.

The Ghanaian situation

Stages in the management of the macro economy

Ghana's SAP is best examined in the context of the pre-1983 state of the economy. The state of the economy gives the programme its defining character. The country's relationship with the World Bank commenced in 1961 when the Akosombo hydroelectric project was being built (World Bank, 2002, p 6). By the end of December 2001, the Bank had approved 134 loans worth $4.3

billion. Thus, Ghana's programme is often cited as the best and most comprehensively implemented in Africa (World Bank, 1994).

A clear account of the Ghanaian situation is not only desirable as a means of understanding how a specific country develops, but as portent for the rest of Africa and indeed the low income developing Third World. Ghana's SAP experience also mirrors in a major way, the current state of North–South cooperation in the development arena, with the key Northern roles played by international financial institutions and other international development agencies such as the UNDP, UNICEF, UNFP (UN Fund for Population Activities) and UNEP (UN Environment Programme).

For a country whose declared aim on achieving independence in 1957 was the achievement of sustained economic development, it is extremely difficult to comprehend the set of policies pursued thereafter. A crystal ball was not required to foresee that the policies run counter to the declared objective. The gulf between declared intention and actual results aroused the classic conundrum: "Why should responsible men adopt public policies that have harmful consequences for societies they govern?" (Bates, 1981, p 3).

External shocks

In 1982, a number of exogenous shocks – over which the Ghanaian State had no control – added to the problems of the polity. They influenced not only the move to macro policy reform, but also quickened the reform process itself. The worst drought in the country's history occurred in 1982-83, leading to unprecedented food shortages. The same drought reduced the generation capacity of the Akosombo hydroelectric dam resulting in power rationing both to industries and domestic use. The effect of the loss of generating capacity was a further erosion of industrial capacity to a meagre 20-25% of installed capacity (see Toye, 1990, p 47).

The drought caused horrific bush fires, which, although affecting the whole country, seemed to have reserved the worst for the food producing middle belt of the country. The bush fires destroyed about one third of all farms, both food and export crops including cocoa. Food imports on a commercial basis had to be undertaken at a time when national coffers were literally empty. The overall effect on agriculture was devastating, recognising that agriculture provides about 65% of total employment in the country and is the largest contributor to the GNP. No other sector, facing a similar adversity, could have induced the same level of mass impoverishment. The 1979 oil price shock further debilitated the economy by imposing huge import bills on the country while inducing a lowering of the price of primary commodities on the world market through the global recession that it created.

Economic developments

The perilous economic position of the country was instrumental in determining the internal politics of the country. By 1982, real per capita income was lower by 30%, real export earnings by 52% and import volumes by 30% than in 1970. Depressed real wages had caused a large-scale emigration of skilled workers (Heller, 1983, p 36). One major source of the fall in real GDP per capita had been the persistent large government deficits financed essentially from Central Bank drawing and inflation. Conflated by exchange rates fixed over long periods, inflation generated one of the most critical reductions in real exchange rates ever recorded. Government deficits exploded from less than half a billion cedis (¢) in 1970 to nearly five billion cedis by 1982. The real exchange rate in 1982 was less than 10% of its 1957 value, indicating a grossly overvalued currency. By 1976, the cedi – still officially pegged at ¢1.15 = US$1 – was 60% overvalued, compared to parallel market trends. In 1982, the market rate was 250% above the official rate of ¢2.75 = US$1, that is, ¢61.6 to the same dollar (Wood, 1988, p 122).

Social developments

The deterioration of the Ghanaian polity was not limited to the economic sphere. The social consequences and implications were just as important, if not more in the Ghanaian case. By April 1983, the real purchasing power of formal wages was already very low, not only in terms of imported goods, but also foodstuffs and other necessities (Ewusi, 1987, pp 56-57, table 26).

The educational and health services had also ceased to deliver to the majority of the population due to shortages of inputs and breakdown of service infrastructure. By 1981, government expenditure on education amounted to less than 1.9%, and on health than 0.7% of GDP. These contrast to the average for all Sub-Saharan Africa of 4.6% and 1.6% respectively (UNDP/World Bank, 1989). Although the figures should be taken with utmost caution (as indeed all statistics on Africa), it is still an accurate representation of the extent of the decline. Simply put, health and education had ceased to deliver (down from its trailblazing days of the 1960s). For the working class, survival became more dependent on emigration, accounting for the massive emigration to the new booming economies of countries like Nigeria and Gabon.

Political

The adoption of the April 1983 reform programme, dubbed the Economic Reform Programme (ERP) was influenced by developments in the political arena, thus partly creating an enabling environment for reform. The specific occurrences were not always related, but collectively, served the same purpose. The initial option of the Provisional National Defence Council (PNDC)[4] government was not for a 'market forces' led structural adjustment programme, but for a collectivist, national democratic and independent development. To this end, between January and June 1982 the government energetically courted financial assistance from the then USSR, Eastern Europe and Libya. Other than Libya, which made an initial token gesture of some food shipment and 500,000 barrels of oil, nothing was forthcoming from this option. Indeed, the rapprochement with Libya had a major negative consequence, since Nigeria[3], the traditional source of Ghanaian oil imports, withdrew credit facilities to Ghana and insisted on down payments.

The leading advocates of an independent and anti-imperialist development path were from the left wing of the PNDC. This faction held the dominant position in government during the early days of the regime. The failure of the radical left to secure external assistance from fraternal sources was a big blow to the national democratic development approach and was possibly, the single most important factor that threw Ghana into the laps of the IMF and the World Bank. The left was further lumbered with the creeping acceptance by the general populace that the statism of the past had not worked (or more correctly, had not been effectively and efficiently applied). By the end of 1982, therefore, social chaos, the failure of the regime's foreign policy initiatives, the severity of the country's decline and the antipathy of the populace towards messianic solutions, had compelled influential members of the government to acknowledge that the regime's preferred populist approach to national resuscitation was not going to be viable. Even the most committed leftists in government had written off the possibility of getting assistance from the then Eastern Bloc or Libya. The preparedness of the Bretton Woods institutions to work with the Ghanaian state at reform was not surprising. These institutions traditionally have had a disposition to favour what they refer to as 'strong' leadership; which in the developing world invariably means authoritarian regimes. The IMF had indicated in April 1981 that any new external assistance for the intended stabilisation programme of the previous government (which many saw as long overdue) could only be provided if certain policy conditions were met or included in the programme. The conditions included devaluation, increased producer prices for cocoa, increased interest rates, increased repayments of debts (including by 1982 $580m arrears) and reduction in government expenditure, especially its payroll (Ray, 1986, p 123). The World Bank, approached at about the same time for an Export Rehabilitation Credit, also insisted on a major overhaul of the Cocoa Board in addition to some of the issues already raised by the IMF. However, the then administration, held hostage by the experiences of the Armed Forces Revolutionary Council (AFRC) era and the vehement ideological opposition to any talk of devaluation[5], procrastinated until the 31 December 1981 coup ushered in the PNDC. Ironically, an IMF mission was still in Accra on the day of the coup.

Character of adjustment

The character of Ghana's SAP has often defied standard categorisation. A number of commentators such as Frimpong-Ansah, Leith, Toye, Herbst, Mosley, and Abbey have been unable to agree on whether it was an indigenous grown programme or a World Bank/IMF diktat. There is very little doubt that the initial decision to restructure the Ghanaian economy was taken by the Ghanaian authorities. The deliberations of both the Committee of Secretaries and the Interim National Coordinating Committee of People's and Workers' Defence Committees point to this[6]. The constitution of a small group of economists and other senior bureaucrats[7] to come up with a blueprint in 1982 was the first major move in this direction.

The April 1983 Programme aimed at a fundamental break with not only the PNDC's policies of the previous 15 months, but also from the thrust of economic practice since independence with the possible exception of the short-lived Busia period. In the finance minister's[8] words, this required "a complete overhaul of policy in areas of incomes and pricing, including pricing of foreign exchange" (*People's Daily Graphic*, 25 April 1983, p 4). The head of state further justified the government's position in a major broadcast. He stated:

> We have reached a critical stage in our history and we need to ask ourselves serious questions: Why has it become so profitable in this country simply to engage in trade instead of production? Why are the most productive and industrious people usually the poorest? Why do we make it less profitable for a person to produce maize here than for him to get an import licence to import it from abroad? Idleness and parasitism have become more rewarded in this country than production work…. This is the time to reverse the process. (Rawlings, 1983, pp 4-5)

The same budget statement also raised the issue of a new relationship between the state and the economy. The finance secretary noted that "the rigid enforcement of prices unrelated to costs of production is (not) a satisfactory basis for action", but affirmed that "pricing … be based on production costs together with appropriate incentive margins". Dr Obed Asamoah (the foreign secretary) also reflected that there was the "realisation that some adjustment has to be made in the exchange rate of the cedi, but at the same time, there was some feeling in the country that success stories based on IMF devaluation prescriptions are hard to come by" (*People's Daily Graphic*, 6 October 1982).

The SAP was staggered over a number of years with different components. Some of these components overlapped between periods and/or sections thus making distinct divisions unworkable and unhelpful. The first critical stage was dubbed the Economic Recovery Programme, which was implemented in two stages.

Economic Recovery Programme – Stage One

Economic Recovery Programme One (ERP I) was formally launched in 1984, although its implementation started earlier with the announcement of the April 1983 budget. This has created unnecessary confusion and most publications seem unable to make this distinction. The goals of ERP were many and varied, but ERP I was essentially a stabilisation package and should be recognised as such.

Being a stabilisation bundle, its thrust was predominantly 'fire fighting'. Its goals included:

- shifting relative prices in favour of production, particularly exports;
- restoring fiscal and monetary discipline;
- initiating rehabilitation of the country's productive base and its economic and social infrastructure, and restoring incentives for private savings and investment.

The programme concerned itself with what was to be done immediately to tackle the proximate cause of Ghana's economic atrophy by changing the exchange rate to a level, which would both restore an incentive to export, and remove rents from foreign exchange and tackling the government budget deficit.

The IMF played the lead role in providing additional resources during ERP I, providing about 60% of the $1 billion channelled to Ghana with the World Bank providing 13% and the rest coming from bilateral sources (Loxley, 1988, p 24). This division of financial responsibility reflected the IMF's lead role in macro-economic stabilisation, narrowing the gap between official and parallel rates of the cedi, curbing inflation by cutting government aggregate demand, removing price controls and providing foreign exchange to ease import strangulation (see Government of Ghana, 1984; Toye, 1990, p 52).

Economic Recovery Programme – Stage Two

Economic Recovery Programme Two (ERP II) was launched in 1987 for a three-year period as a sequel to the ERP I and was a hybrid between stabilisation and structural reform. Reform was intended for both medium- and long-term duration. The second-stage programme was to ensure economic growth of around 5% per annum in real terms, stimulating significant increases in savings and investment, improving public sector management and placing the external sector on a sound footing (Government of Ghana, 1987b).

Structural reform as opposed to ERP I, which as indicated earlier, was a stabilisation programme. ERP II (or SAPI) was:

- To establish an incentive framework that would stimulate growth at around 5% per annum;
- To encourage substantial savings and investment;

- To strengthen the balance of payments;
- To improve resource use particularly in the public sector, while ensuring fiscal and monetary stability;
- To implement the Programme of Action to Mitigate the Social Cost of Adjustment (PAMSCAD).

It was to increase public investment to 25% and domestic savings to 15% of GDP. Social expenditure was also to be increased considerably via the instrumentality of PAMSCAD (Government of Ghana, 1987b, p 10).

Segments of reform

Within the general character of adjustment, reform was conducted in the context of 'segments'. The state of decay, and therefore the task of restructuring at hand was such that appropriate policy initiatives were worked out and implemented via a series of correlated segmentations. These segments included public sector and enterprise reform that aimed at privatising the majority of state-owned enterprises and improving the efficiency of the remaining enterprises to be retained. Another segment was the civil service reform that was seen as critical to both the success of the public sector/enterprise reform programme and to the government machinery itself. The civil service reform in particular drew a lot of attention from the IMF and this became its pet reform project through its Structural Adjustment Fund (SAF) and enhanced SAF facilities. The divestiture of state-owned enterprises was another segment of the reform package. More than a hundred state-owned enterprises were sold off in rolling back the state.

At the heart of the Ghanaian SAP was fiscal policy reform. The tax base in Ghana, prior to adjustment, like in many other developing countries tended to be very narrow. It excluded relatively important sectors of the economy that may not be fully monetarised or encapsulated into the formal economy, such as large segments of agriculture and services (see Tanzi, 1987). Tax avoidance was and still is rampant in the body politic with the most powerful classes avoiding the most. Ghana's fiscal policy since 1983 is said to have been "aimed at correcting the fiscal imbalances, reforming the tax system to augment revenue collection and to enhance economic incentives, increasing public and private savings, and rehabilitating the economic and social infrastructure" (Kapur et al, 1991, p 29).

Complementing fiscal reform during the stabilisation phase was a heavy reduction in public expenditure on areas the IMF considered non-core. Invariably, this was the social sector. Education, health, mass transport among others suffered deep expenditure cuts.

Monetary policy reform also received a lot of attention as a segment of reform. The general objectives of monetary policies in developing countries are usually related to money and credit control, price stabilisation and economic growth. It is argued that price stability is the most important task of monetary policy for developing countries. This is said to be because developing countries, particularly the least developed countries (LDCs) generally suffer higher rates of inflation than developed countries (see Ghatak, 1995, for a detailed discussion). However, the particular peculiarities of the Ghanaian problem required radical measures that did not necessarily conform to the ordinary prescriptions of monetary policy. Monetary policy reform also took in the reform of the banking and allied institutions, a financial sector reform programme and the establishment of a stock exchange and other intermediation services.

A new interest rate regime was introduced with the aim of ensuring positive rates as well as to provide incentive returns for development. Interest rates became flexible and depending on the level of inflation, rates were allowed to move up or down in tandem with other instruments of monetary and fiscal policies.

Another of the instruments used effectively was devaluation. The devaluation route becomes more dramatic when juxtaposed with the background of historical antipathy. Refusal to devalue had become a political sticking point, treating the cedi exchange rate as a matter of national pride (Richards, 1989, p 79). Rather than reform exchange rates in the face of balance of payments problems, Ghanaian governments – as is historically the case with most African governments – have found it easier to administratively control imports. Unfortunately, administrative controls in practice have often led to an overvaluation of the local currency. Dependence on administrative instruments minimises the need to adjust exchange rates to reflect the differences between domestic inflation and inflation rates of major partners. In a perverse way, this encourages the ever increasing overvaluation of the exchange rate because the more overvalued the currency, the more largesse the government is able to bestow on its selected few who gain access to official foreign exchange.

On previous fears and links between devaluation and coups, for example, Acheampong overthrowing Busia and the Limann administration's overtures to the IMF/World Bank partly responsible for the overthrow of that regime by the PNDC, Dr Abbey, the leading technocrat of the reform programme noted:

> Procrastination of successive governments over a prolonged period in refusing to adopt appropriate stabilisation policies destroyed the country's economy, giving the widespread belief that a stabilisation policy, especially devaluation of the exchange rate inevitably conjured up threats of a coup in Ghana. Consequently, a succession of governments had held on until the bitter end before attempting any sort of stabilisation policy so that economic conditions were particularly bad when they finally did make policy changes. (Abbey, 1987, p 4).

Rather than announce formal devaluation, the government in April 1983 introduced a system of bonuses for exports and surcharges for imports, creating a de facto weighted average exchange rate of about ₵25 to the US dollar. This compared to the standing ₵2.75 to the dollar and which had been static since

August 1978, notwithstanding annual inflation rates averaging 60% in between. The system of bonuses and surcharges was to persuade recipients of foreign exchange to turn over their proceeds and provide finance for the bonuses/ surcharges regime[9]. Although this approach did not please the IMF, who argued that the strategy was tantamount to the introduction of multiple exchange rates, which in the eyes of the IMF was an unacceptable transgression of its fastidious code, while equally claiming that the system was going to be difficult to administer, the Ghanaian government stuck to its strategy.

The government's position was that this was an essential first step, mindful of the psychological effect of the word devaluation on the populace. The strategy was, therefore, pursued for six months until October 1983 when the government felt embolden enough to formally float the currency at ¢30 to the dollar.

Poverty in Ghana

The elimination or minimisation of poverty is and must be the aim of any genuine interpretation of development, at least in the developing world. It is also a worthy national goal for countries of the industrialised North, although the degree of urgency may not necessarily be the same, even if that is getting less true in recent years[10]. This objective for the developing world is probably one of the few areas of agreement between students of development and allied professionals and activists. Beyond this, there is hardly any consensus on other aspects of the 'old enemy' called poverty. This inability stems largely, but not exclusively from the failure to formulate and agree on a single concept of poverty.

There are presently three major concepts or approaches to poverty in mainstream thought. These are the subsistence approach, basic needs and relative deprivation. It has been argued that these three definitions or concepts are not sensitive to the experiences of the developing world. Vic George argues that "definitions of poverty used in advanced industrial societies are not sensitive enough to cope with the breadth and depth of deprivation in the third world countries" (1988, p 27). The Ghana Poverty Reduction Strategy sees poverty as a multidimensional concept which encompasses levels of income, nutrition, health, literacy and insecurity (Ghana Living Standards Survey, 1998/99, p 10).

Mass poverty

While the foregoing refers essentially to individual or case poverty, the incidence of mass poverty is of particular importance in Ghana and other developing countries. Mass poverty differs from case poverty where a relative few are poor in a generally affluent society. The term helps to direct attention to 'structural causes'. Mass poverty is the norm: not to be poor is the exception. In the former, poverty is often attributed (even if wrongly) to various characteristics – moral, genetic, familial, environmental, educational, racial, social and so on, while in case of the latter, explanations have to be sought elsewhere (see Galbraith, 1979).

> Mass poverty is largely the function of acute, often contrived socio-economic inequality, which in turn is engendered and reinforced by acuminate, often deliberately organised, social stratification. It is not a static, fortuitous, ahistorical and purely economic phenomenon, but a dynamic, structured, historically conditioned, and multi-dimensional experience of the peoples of the South. (Bandyopadhyaya, 1988, p 263)

In Ghana, where 40% of the population were said to be below the poverty line in 1998/99 with 27% in extreme poverty (Ghana Poverty Reduction Strategy, 2002-04, p 10), a conclusion of mass poverty becomes indisputable. The low level of per capita national income, $490 in 2000, also signifies the mass nature of national poverty. Even at the relatively more accurate purchasing power per capita calculation, per capita income is still less than $1,000.

Causes of poverty

The causes of poverty, and thus underdevelopment, are many. Arguments about the causes have throughout modern history, travelled the whole distance from the absurd to the scientific. The 'old' establishment saw poverty as resulting largely from the inherent weaknesses of the poor. People were poor because they were either lazy or did not have it in them to do otherwise. To this class the causes of poverty "rest overwhelmingly in individual and sub-cultural defects and disposition" (Townsend, 1993, p 6). Structural factors and the like are totally absolved from blame. This position is of course, false or at best inadequate in explaining individual or mass poverty. Explanations need to be found elsewhere.

Global politico-economic structures

So significant is the role of global economic and political arrangements in the impoverishment of individuals, communities and nations, that some writers have tended to see such arrangements as the fundamental cause of world poverty (see Bandyopodhyaya, 1988). Notwithstanding this, the poverty of the developing world is treated as if it has no bearings on the accumulated wealth of the developed world.

In the 20th century, social stratification, and by extrapolation poverty, is global in character. It is the by-product of colonialism and neo-colonialism of economic, political and social arrangements that in turn originated from capitalism and imperialism. It is therefore impractical, if not unethical, to attempt to separate national and individual poverty from world poverty since the two are intrinsically linked. Within the theatre of global economic relations, a country and its people, manoeuvred into economic disenfranchisement by powerful global forces would be relatively poor on the global scale, no matter how egalitarian its internal distribution of resources are. A good internal distribution would at best, only lessen the extent of individual poverty but would do nothing for national poverty.

The post-colonial period still witnesses unequal terms of trade, the use of official trade and aid policies of Northern governments and international financial institutions to entrench Northern interests, the perversion of the developing world by multinational corporations as well as the dominance of international political and economic space by the industrialised North. This, side by side with the freedom and status of the Ghanaian bourgeoisie and civil-bureaucracy, allowed economic, political and social doctrine to be formulated in a way that siphons off a disproportionate percentage of the fruits of a slow growing GNP for themselves. By so doing, the mass of society is sentenced to poverty.

Unlike the umbilical cord between a mother and a baby, the link between the developed metropolis and the peripheral country paradoxically transfers nourishment from the weaker to the stronger! While Ghana and other developing countries are 'encouraged' to be primary commodity producers[11], developed countries are continually moving up to even higher technology led production sophistication. Tragically, the prices of primary commodities have consistently fallen in real terms since the mid-1970s while manufactured products have done the very opposite. The effect of this has been to reduce earnings of developing countries while increasing developed world earnings. If the price of cocoa, for example, had stayed at even its 1975 levels, instead of its historical slump, at least a multiplier effect of 5-10% of GDP could have been achieved, expanding GDP to levels far higher than the 1980-90 period witnessed.

In the specific case of Ghana, the foreign domination of the economy allows the transfer abroad of potential surplus in the form of visible export profit or concealed profits inherent in unequal exchange. Amin, looking at this occurrence in the early 1970s, argued that while private transfers, income from investment and a large part of current services (which conceal transfer of profits), totalled about ¢100 million or 6% of GDP in 1968, on the hypothesis that labour in Ghana's export sector should be rewarded half the rate of labour in a developed country, the real drain from the country to the international system is ¢350 million or 17% of GDP (Amin, 1972, p 250).

The effect of globalisation in the post-cold war period has further marginalised the developing world with international capital on the loose without any national or international checks. The world system is now so dominated by international capital that the relevance of governments particularly in economically weaker states must be questioned. Even in the only remaining superpower, the Enron debacle raises fundamental questions about the ability and willingness of governments to regulate and police its economic space.

National policies/structures

The causes for both individual and mass poverty can also be located within individual countries and their structures or pursuit of policies. While the global environment marginalises a country, thereby denying such a country the resources to fight poverty, the ability of the privileged to protect and extend their privileges equally creates havoc on poverty levels (see Elliot, 1975, p 2).

The introduction of a small dependent capitalist sector to the traditionally agricultural and communal economy in Ghana, largely in the form of cocoa, timber, mining, import and export and general recorded trade, aggravated the traditional stratification of society, leading to class domination and exploitation of the mass of the people by the few that had been co-opted into the 'modern' sector. In the post-colonial state the co-opted is isomorphic to the ruling capitalist class in the various metropolises of global economic and political power. Symbiotic linkages between the ruling political and commercial classes in both the global metropolises and the Ghanaian periphery has relegated the mass of the people, who are outside these structures of linkage, to irrelevance in the distribution and ownership of resources.

The end result of the above distortions is the rise of poverty. Poverty arises because the poor do not have the assets needed to generate an adequate level of income. Secondly, they are prevented from using these assets by unemployment or lack of demand for what they produce; or the economic conditions are such that the rate of return on their productive assets does not generate enough income[12].

Specific to mass poverty, the following explanations have been advanced at one time or the other as responsible for mass poverty:

- 'Naturally poor'. Here, countries are said to be naturally poor in terms of physical or natural resource endowment. However, the experiences of Japan, Taiwan, Hong Kong, Singapore and Israel do not support this contention.
- The political system of administration has often been advanced as an explanation for the poverty of nations. The political 'right' stresses the absence of free 'enterprise' as being the cause of mass poverty while the 'left' argues that the appropriation of the gains of production by the land and capital owners leaves no incentive for peasants to increase productivity. Empirical evidence does not, however, seem to support to any credible extent either of these absolutes. China and India, endowed almost equally, have attained different levels of mass prosperity, with China obviously the better off (see World Resources Institute/UNEP/UNDP, 1994).

Features of poverty in Ghana

Ghanaian poverty, in consonance with most developing countries of Africa and South Asia, is quite widespread and on the mass scale. An analysis of the national household surveys of 1974 by Ewusi (Ewusi, 1976) indicated that about 75% of the Ghanaian population at that time had incomes, which placed them below the poverty line of $100. UNICEF (1986) estimated that 30-35% of urban households and 60-65% of rural households were below their respective poverty line of $307 and $130 (1978 prices).

Ghana also generally exhibits a relative inequality between the various decile groups with the poorest 10% of the population only earning 6.45% of the ₵280,764 attributed to the wealthiest 10% of the population as the 1987-88 survey showed (see Table 8.1).

It is worth mentioning that the average Ghanaian household devoted 50.6% of its expenditure on food in 1991-92 (see Table 8.2) with the rural household spending a higher 52.2%.

Urban/rural

Poverty is predominantly concentrated in rural Ghana, irrespective of how it is defined; whether in monetary terms or in terms of basic needs provision (amenities as well as food and other items like fuel and clothing for household consumption). This is also true of both case/individual poverty or mass poverty (see Ewusi, 1976; Boateng et al, 1990). In analysing a survey undertaken in 1974/75, Ewusi found that while 75.4% of the population fell below the poverty line[13], the rural component was 85.08% while the urban sector accounted for 53.48% (see Ewusi, 1976; Boateng et al, 1990)[14].

Expenditure

Another exercise conducted in 1987/88 concluded that 83.3% of the poorest 20% of the population were to be found in the rural part of the country while

Table 8.1: Characteristics of the distribution of public expenditure of individuals of per capita household expenditure

Decile	Expenditure cut-off (constant ₵)
I	18,119.0
2	23,897.0
3	29,300.0
4	35,272.0
5	40,897.0
6	47,583.0
7	56,239.0
8	68,684.0
9	91,420.0
10	280,764.0
Mean PCHHE	49,471.0

Source: Boateng et al (1990, p 13)

54.5% of the wealthiest 20% are found in urban areas. While the average resident of Accra had an average expenditure of ₵149,542 in 1987/88, the average non-Accra resident had an adjusted expenditure of ₵63,940 (Glewwe and Twum-Baah, 1991, pp 25-26).

The dichotomy between urban and rural dwellers becomes even more striking in relation to expenditure on food. The poor, as stated earlier, are predominantly engaged in agriculture and are thus rural based. Yet rural dwellers spend 52.2% of all expenditure on food, while the urban average is 48.65% (see Table 8.2).

The poverty gulf between urban and rural extends more significantly to the provision and uptake of basic economic and social rights such as the right to education. While 65% of all Ghanaian adults surveyed in 1991/92 were literate, the equivalent for rural Ghana was 48.8% (see Table 8.3). The effect of this is seen more in agriculture where farmers, predominantly rural, find themselves unable to adopt agricultural practices being encouraged by the Ministry of Agriculture because they are unable to read accompanying instructions.

Table 8.2: Mean annual household cash expenditure by locality and expenditure group

	Locality				Locality			
	Accra	Other urban	Rural	Country	Accra	Other urban	Rural	Country
	₵	₵	₵	₵	%	%	%	%
Expenditure group								
Food and beverages	367,575	348,198	234,925	276,511	48.5	48.8	52.2	50.6
Food and tobacco	102,89	15,313	21,688	18,948	1.4	2.1	4.8	3.5
Clothing and footwear	82,921	56,948	43,903	51,107	10.9	8	9.7	9.3
Housing and utilities	82,189	70,161	35,201	48,652	10.8	9.8	7.8	8.9
Household goods, operation and services	57,815	43,900	34,071	38,924	7.6	6.2	7.6	7.1
Medical care and expenses	18,664	26,032	22,046	22,691	2.5	3.7	4.9	4.2
Transport and communications	58,472	43,288	27,399	34,501	7.7	6.1	6.1	6.3
Recreation and education	37,657	42,392	18,012	26,057	5	5.9	4	4.8
Miscellaneous goods and services	42,356	66,818	13,097	29,397	5.6	9.4	2.9	5.4
All groups	757,938	713,050	450,342	546,788	100	100	100	100

Source: GLSS (1995, p 147)

Table 8.3: Adult literacy rates, by sex and locality (%)

	Urban			Rural	All
	Accra	Other urban	All		
Male	84.7	71.2	74.8	53.5	60.8
Female	73.1	51.1	57.0	28.3	38.5
All	78.3	60.3	65.0	40.0	48.8

Note: 'Adult' refers to anyone aged 15 years and over. Anyone who could write a letter in English or any Ghanaian language was counted as being literate.

Source: Ghana Living Standards Survey (1995, p 16)

Treated pipe-borne water was only available to 13.8% of rural dwellers, compared to 100% in Accra and 67.5% for all other urban areas. The prevalence of water-borne diseases in Ghana is, therefore, not surprising considering the inadequate provision of safe drinking water for the majority of the population living in rural Ghana.

Geographical

The northern Regions (Northern, Upper East and Upper West) constitute 40% of the landmass of Ghana but with 20% of the population. Together the three account for 14% of agricultural output (Roe and Schneider, 1992, p 35), have one main crop cycle, and the least rainfall in the country. Ewusi in 1976 found that the then Northern and Upper Regions scored 13 and 13.9 for Physical Quality of Life Index (PQLI[15]) compared to between 36 and 52 in all other Regions (Roe and Schneider, 1992, p 35). In the 1998/99 Living Standards Survey, the three regions were the only ones that experienced an increase in the levels of poverty.

Occupational

Surveys have reported a correlation between employment status and poverty in Ghana. The First Ghana Living Standards Survey (GLSS) (1987/88) found that 85% and 87% of the 'very poor' and 'poor' respectively were self-employed but only 4% and 6% respectively were in government employment. This finding confirmed the view that a government job was a relative way out of poverty. Poverty was also greatest among non-cocoa farmers[16] with only 6% and 18% respectively of the 'very poor' and 'poor' engaged in cocoa farming (Roe and Schneider, 1992, p 34). The link between public sector work and poverty is extremely important in the context of the downsizing of the public sector under structural adjustment.

The correlation between poverty and agriculture is shown in various studies. In 1970, 43.3% of the farming population or 80.3% of all smallholders or 1.95 million rural people were below the poverty line. This shot up to 67.3% of the total farming population in 1984 (1984 has to be interpreted in the context of the 1983 famine) and settled at 54% of the total farming population being below the poverty line in 1986 (Sarris and Shaw, 1991, p 66). The GLSS survey of 1987/88 concluded as per Table 8.4; that is, 65.10% of the income of the poor came directly from agriculture. In the 1998/99 survey, about 58% of all food crop farmers were classified as poor. Even for export crop farmers, over 35% fell below the poverty line. Therefore the link between agriculture and poverty is further confirmed. The agricultural poor were also the least likely to receive educational scholarships in a country where education still provides a workable route out of poverty (see Table 8.4).

The nature of occupation is a more important correlation with poverty than whether the head of the household is employed or not. Indeed the household with an unemployed head was better off than where the head was a farmer. The unemployed was only slightly worse off than the average Ghanaian (Glewwe and Twum-Baah GLSMS, 1991, p 33). Glewwe and Twum-Baah argued that individual unemployment is neither concentrated among the poor nor is it a major cause of poverty. Twum-Baah (1983) explained this as resulting from extended family mode of living, with its network of social relationships and economic security. As long as such unemployment remains minuscule, transfers would make up for any loss of income, but where unemployment becomes en masse, this traditional insurance would be unable to cope as is increasingly evident.

Basic needs

The most useful avenue for analysing poverty in low- and middle-income developing countries is the use of Basic Needs Indicators. This is particularly helpful in the case of Ghana where as a result of the preponderance of the informal sector, the compilation of national accounts is at best a thankless exercise and at worst, a piece of enlightened guesswork. The traditional social cohesion, as indicated by the extended family system, also softens the unequal distribution of individual wealth and accumulations as an adequate means of assessing or analysing poverty.

Table 8.4: Sources of income by poverty groups

	All	Non-poor	Poor
Employment income	7.30 (100)	8.10 (86.6)	4.40 (13.4)
Agricultural income	55.60 (100)	52.90 (74.0)	65.10 (26.0)
Non-farming self-employment	28.20 (100)	29.70 (82.0)	22.80 (18.0)
Actual and implied rent	1.70 (100)	1.60 (72.9)	2.10 (27.1)
Educational scholarship	0.08 (100)	0.10 (89.4)	0.04 (10.6)
Remittances received	4.10 (100)	4.10 (77.4)	4.20 (22.6)
Other income	3.00 (100)	3.50 (89.7)	1.40 (10.3)
All	100 (100)	100 (77.8)	100 (22.2)

Source: Boateng et al (1990, p 21)

The adoption of basic needs does not, however, infer that such a route is smooth. The difficulty of reducing publicly supplied services like subsidised public transport and others such as clean drinking water, an alternative sewerage system or public provision of education (quality as well as quantity) ad infinitum to a single numeraire is often sidestepped by separating private consumption from basic indicators (Boateng et al, 1990, p 4). However, any meaningful poverty analysis in Ghana must take on board, both private consumption and public consumption of not just goods and services provided by the 'market', but also of basic needs provision and facilities.

Health provision

The uniqueness of poverty and its perception vis-à-vis health provision in developing countries is reflected in the 1988 Ghana Living Standards Survey (GLSS 1). The survey based on self-reporting found that the incidence of illness increases as people move from very poor categorisation to poor and average Ghanaian. This trend was also present in a similar Living Standards Survey in Ghana's western neighbour, the Ivory Coast (Boateng et al, 1990, p 24). The credible explanation for this occurrence is the greater propensity for the rich or well off to classify themselves as ill. What constitutes illness in the minds of the rich and poor are different. In my own Ghanaian experience, while the middle and well-off classes will often report to clinics and hospitals when they contract malaria, or a common cold (and therefore stay away from work), the poor will normally treat such a minor irritation, self-medicate and report to work. The poor cannot in this scenario afford to be ill and would not self-report such minor problems as illness. This is therefore reflected in the answers of the various categorisations in Tables 8.5 and 8.6.

Table 8.5: Percentage of individuals ill during the past 28 days, by locality and poverty group

	Very poor	Poor	All
Rural	24.3	29.6	35.2
Urban (excluding Accra)	24.3	33.9	38.4
Accra	*	33.3	38.9

Note: 'Very poor' relates to the lower poverty line of one third of mean per capita consumption. There are no individuals classified as 'very poor' in Accra.

Source: Boateng et al (1990, p 24)

Table 8.6: Percentage of sick individuals who consulted health personnel, by locality and poverty group

	Very poor	Poor	All
Rural	29.5	37.5	44.4
Urban (excluding Accra)	41.5	41.9	50.8
Accra	*	57.1	59.1

Source: Boateng et al (1990, p 24)

The variance in Table 8.5 even within the categorisation reflects the depth or otherwise of health provision in rural, general urban and the capital. Also significant is the difference between the poor rural population (37.5%) who consulted health workers and the same for the Accra 57.1%, a 50%+ of the rural consultation rate (Table 8.6).

A significant element of health provision and uptake is the type of consultation experienced. Among 460 people in Accra who reported ill during the survey sample period of GLSS 1 (1990), 188 (40.9%) did not see a health worker (see Tables 8.7a and 8.7b). However, of those who did, 91.9% (272) consulted a doctor. The corresponding figures for rural Ghana is 55.6% not consulting a health worker. But of the 1,454 who did (44.4% of the rural sample), 38.9% (566) consulted a doctor, with 31.3% consulting a medical assistant.

The comparison reflects the predominance of doctors in Accra. There are very few doctors in rural Ghana. Equally important is the use of medical assistants in rural areas. Therefore from a policy perspective, Table 8.6 reflects the success of the medical assistantship project as making the case for more medical assistants to be trained. The disparity of medical provision between rural Ghana where the bulk of the country's wealth is produced and Accra, the parasitic seat of government and influence, must remain a concern[17].

Table 8.7b presents an interesting picture of the health provision and intake landscape. For the very poor (recognising that poverty is largely rural), clinics are the most important sources of treatment. The preponderance of hospital

Table 8.7a: Type of consultation by ill people in sample, by locality

	Rural	Urban (excluding Accra)	Accra
Doctor	566	518	250
Nurse	182	52	9
Medical assistant	455	117	2
Other	251	60	11
None	1,819	724	188
All	3,273	1,471	460

Source: Boateng et al (1990, p 25)

Table 8.7b: Where consultation took place for those who were ill and consulted someone by poverty group

	Very poor	Poor	All
Hospital	23	192	1,020
Dispensary	0	10	46
Clinic	38	281	1,046
Other	18	117	361
All	79	600	2,473

Source: Boateng et al (1990, p 25)

visits by the rich is also established by the fact that although the very poor and poor record 29.1% and 32% intake respectively, the national average is pushed up to 41.2% because of the relatively high intake by the rich.

It is estimated that 61% of all Ghanaians have access to health services, although hundreds of thousands in the rural areas depend on herbalists and other forms of unorthodox healthcare (Assenso-Okyere, 1993, p 3). So important is the role of herbal medicine in particular that a number of well managed herbal clinics and hospitals are being set up by both the government and the private sector to improve healthcare delivery. The government-owned Centre for Research into Plant Medicine at Mampong-Akuapem has attracted a lot of interest both from within and outside of the country from practitioners of orthodox medicine. Indeed some aspects of herbal medicine such as herbal first aid and traditional birth delivery methods have been incorporated into the country's Primary Health Scheme.

While health delivery, especially immunisation has improved considerably over the years, such as the proportion of one year olds immunised increasing from 34% in 1981 to 67% in 1989, and with 40% of all births now attended by trained professional health personnel (Assenso-Okyere, 1993), the same cannot be said for general public health. Diseases such as yaws and yellow fever, which had virtually been eliminated by the campaigns of the early 1960s and early 1970s, have reappeared in the 1980s and 1990s as health provision degenerated (see Sarrisand Shams, 1991, p 79; Loewenson Reve, 1993). It is estimated that the under-five mortality rate, which had come down from 215 per 1,000 in 1960 to 157 in 1980 had risen to 170 by 1991 (World Resources Institute, 1994, p 272, Table 16.3). However, between 1993 and 1998, under-five mortality rates decreased from 119 per 1,000 to 108 per 1,000 as the effects of the government's Cuban style primary healthcare became noticeable.

Expenditure on healthcare in 1982/83 was only 23% of its 1974 value on a per capita basis, (World Resources Institute, 1994, p 272, Table 16.3). For the rural population, the consequence of decreased provision is even more acute, recognising the traditional urban bias of medical allocation and delivery. In a typical year, 79% of the total health budget goes to medical care, of which Korle-Bu Teaching Hospital, the biggest in the country, alone appropriates 22%, with Public Health Delivery only 12% and training 6%. Eighty per cent of total health expenditure is typically recurrent (World Resources Institute, 1994, p 272, Table 16.3). In the 1995 budget provision for example, 88.58% (₵65,448,995.00) of the total provision was earmarked for recurrent expenditure with only 11.42% being 'development' expenditure on health (Budget Statement, 1995). The total health budget itself was only 8.11% of the total expenditure, compared to the allocation of 10.47% to Roads and Highways.

Education

Education is another recognised category of basic needs that calls for examination in the context of poverty analysis in Ghana. Education does not only enhance empowerment and therefore expanding opportunity to move out of poverty, but its provision also increases productivity and employability. Published in 1990 the GLSS 1 saw lack of education as a causal contributory factor to poverty. As a result of poverty (in lack of education), individuals only have the opportunity to work in lowly paid jobs. I had indicated that people in government jobs are the least likely to fall below the poverty line and since education is often a precondition of obtaining a government job, it is by implication recognised by many people to be a major route out of poverty (Boateng et al, 1990, p 27).

Significantly, educational provision also mirrors the various strata of inequality by location, gender, income group and so on established by the preceding pages. Table 8.8, for example, captures the inequality of literacy achievement between the sexes, both for adults and children. While the gap has somewhat closed between male and female literacy rates between 1970 and 1990, there are still unacceptable differences among both adults and infants by gender.

Table 8.8 establishes the link between education and poverty. The educational attainment of the head of household plays a major role in determining the household's access to resources through the employment market. The lack of access to formal education is established as a concomitant to poverty in the Ghanaian situation. The Ghana Poverty Reduction Strategy (2002-04) paper admits that gross primary school enrolment has not increased significantly since 1992 and that the drop-out rate is gender biased in favour of males.

Water and sanitation

The degree and severity of mass poverty in Ghana can also be gauged by examining the provision of safe drinking water, sanitation and housing for the population. Rural households are once again, worse off than their urban

Table 8.8: Education and the poor (%)

	Poorest 10%	Poorest 30%	All Ghana
Education of household head:			
None	80.3	71.7	53.9
Primary	3.5	6.9	8.1
Middle	15.7	20.6	31.3
Secondary:'O' levels	0.0	0.0	3.0
Secondary:'A' levels	0.0	0.0	0.3
Teacher training	0.0	0.5	1.8
Other post-secondary	0.0	0.3	0.4
University	0.0	0.0	1.2
School attendance by household members (by age group):			
6-10	43.2	57.2	66.8
11-15	46.0	60.5	70.8

Source: Rothchild (1991, p 103)

counterparts in the provision of toilet facilities with 28.6% having no access to any kind of toilet infrastructure and having to use the bush (free range) for such purposes. For the country as a whole, three quarters of a million households have no toilet facilities, with 40,000 of these in Accra, 110,000 in other urban areas and a colossal 620,000 in rural areas (GLSS, 1995, p 53). For sanitation services in general, only 63% and 60% respectively of urban and rural dwellers had access to safe sanitation infrastructure in 1990 (World Resources Institute, 1994). The urgency of improving sanitation services in Ghana is self-apparent if public health, particularly cholera and other wind- and water-borne communicable diseases are to be brought under control. Good sanitation goes a long way in fighting diseases and enhancing good health of the population.

The 1995 Ghana Living Standards Survey paints a worse picture of safe drinking water provision. Only 36% of the population have access to treated pipe-borne water, with only 13.8% of all rural dwellers enjoying the facilities of treated pipe-borne water. This highlights the widespread nature of mass poverty in Ghana. The country definitely qualifies for membership of the poor category of nations since 34.2% of the population still depend on untreated spring or river water to meet their daily requirements.

Adjustment effects on poverty

The complex task of examining the impact of the SAP on Ghanaian poverty has to be carried out at the levels of the national, mass and case poverty. In each of these segments, the effect of policy might not be such as to bring out a clear-cut message or picture. While a particular policy might pull poverty along a progressive direction, a second policy within the same package might do just the opposite, thus blurring the overall effect.

A number of policy instruments are used in the Ghanaian adjustment. The instruments encompass the whole gamut of money and credit policy, fiscal policy, pricing, labour markets, trade and trade liberalisation and so on. They have impacted and indeed will continue to impact on various poverty groups in Ghana by influencing aggregate demand, supply, overall price levels, including the composition of demand and supply and therefore relative prices of goods and services.

There is also to consider the struggle between the short-term and the long-term developments in assessing the effects of structural adjustment on poverty. Although labour restraint, for example, might negatively affect poverty in the short term, should such restraint enable the economy to turn around and start increasing output, more jobs would be created in the long term. Potentially this can then lead to improved wage rates in the long term if distribution of the gains of increased production is equitable. But the long term includes so many variables that one cannot take the outlook for granted.

Another complication in assessing the impact of adjustment on poverty is the tendency to see the growth rate of GNP as the ultimate test of success in the developing world. However, more important than mere growth rates is the removal of illiteracy, ill health, malnutrition and social and cultural deprivation. These should be seen as valuable goals in their own right and not just as enhancing the 'economic growth' process.

Incomes

It is difficult to generalise the effects of adjustment on the various income groups in the economy. Yet it is still a worthwhile exercise as income levels have bearings on the state of poverty in any given country. However, one is conscious of the time frame within which wages and incomes may swing from the positive axis of the pendulum to the negative. For example, while real wages in the informal sector doubled from ₡23.58 in 1983 to ₡67.74 in 1986 largely as a result of improved monetary policy, by 1990, the levels had fallen again to ₡52.58 (see Donkor, 1997, p 230). Additionally, what statistics do not often reveal is the increased cost of essential services, which were hitherto subsidised by the state. These subsidies should be included in the calculation of real wages to make comparisons in pre-adjustment and adjustment periods meaningful. The Trades Union Congress (TUC) took up the position when it argued that:

> although the various statistical indicators are moving in the programme, the going is still hard for the working people. ... The effect of the World Bank and IMF sponsored economic policies are the cheapening of the local currency ... the high rate of unemployment and a rising cost of living brought about by the decontrolling of prices, removal of subsidies on essential goods and services, and the partial freeze on wages and salaries of the working people. (TUC, 1988, p 32)

The boast of adjustment raising real income is inconclusive. For example, cocoa farmers, traditionally among the well-off in Ghanaian agriculture, and hailed by the World Bank as beneficiaries of adjustment, were not found to be better off than the average Ghanaian, analysing the Ghana Living Standards Survey 1987/88 (Glewwe and Twum-Baah, 1991, p 33). The lower employment levels in the formal sector under adjustment generally raises the supply of labour to the informal sector, thereby reducing the real earnings of the poor engaged in the informal sector. Unemployment reduces not only the incomes of the poor in the short term, but also lowers their longer-term potential for employment (see Blanchard and Summers, 1986). To attract foreign capital, Ghana has been encouraged to keep wages low, and this has been reflected in low purchasing power among the working population.

Distributional effects

Extensive price control under the previous regime of controls had shifted the supply of goods and services to the parallel market where the poor were victimised by their inability to access these goods and services from official sources. Decontrolling prices did not necessarily make the poor worse off (the only exemption being public provision of basic needs) vis-à-vis the powerful in society and their social and political acolytes at the point of purchase (see Heller, 1988, p 17). It only confirmed price levels existent in their 'real world'. The problem of the poor at this stage was, and still is, income. Agriculture, the predominant occupation still suffers an internal terms of trade disadvantage and therefore, the incomes of agricultural workers have not kept pace with other sectors of the economy. The critical mass of inequality for the poor can and should, therefore, be located here. Ghana traditionally had one of the lowest inequality thresholds in the developing world with a Gini coefficient of only 0.3471 in 1988 (see Table 8.9).

Labour

The upheavals that characterised industrial relations, remuneration relationships and labour market employment generation and so on affected the poverty profile of the country. The huge number of workers retrenched was bound to have serious effects on the numbers in poverty. By the end of 1991, 15% of the core civil service for example had been laid off, excluding the thousands who suffered the same fate at Ghana Education Service. At the Ghana Cocoa Board, about 57,000 names were removed from the payroll between 1983 and mid-1989. Indeed Yeebo (1991, p 205) estimates that over 100,000 jobs were lost in the public sector (excluding the civil service) between 1982 and 1989.

The implications of the job losses are obvious. With the public sector providing the surest employment route out of poverty, the loss of such large job numbers reduced from the Ghanaian economy, in the short to medium term at least, the opportunity of a commensurate number either staying out of poverty or climbing out of the poverty trap. It must not be forgotten that these were not just any jobs but public sector jobs, the plum jobs in the body politic.

The closing down of a number of productive state enterprises, such as the African Timber and the Plywood Factory at Samreboi in Western Region

Table 8.9: Inequality in consumption expenditure in five countries

	Gini coefficient	Thiel T	Thiel L	Log variance
African				
Ghana	0.3471	0.2141	0.2046	0.3998
Ivory Coast	0.4350	0.3530	0.3254	0.6079
Mauritania	0.4144	0.3074	0.3062	0.6297
Non-African				
Jamaica	–	0.3487	0.3203	0.6044
Peru	0.4299	0.3534	0.3194	0.5967

Source: Glewwe and Twum-Baah (1991, p 57)

further reduced paid industrial employment availability in one of the most depressed rural districts in the country where the only alternative employment available was smallholder farming.

At first sight it would appear that no jobs were created during the adjustment period with the potential of making a mark on poverty. However, this impression would be misleading, as data about the increasing growth of the service sector (hotels, insurance, financial services, private medicine and so on) testifies (see 1995 budget statement). The nature of services job creation is such that apart from those at the apex of the sector, the majority of the jobs created are low paying hotel and other clerical jobs compared with the manufacturing and industrial jobs that had been lost.

Public provision

If one is to put a finger on a single factor that has had the most adverse effect on poverty in Ghana, it is the curtailment of public provision of services. The state regarded the provision of public services as critically important to national development up to the introduction of the structural adjustment programme. Such provision had given Ghana a human development capacity consistently above the sub-Saharan African average. For example, Kenya had a gross educational enrolment ratio of 13% 15 to 20 years ago while Ghana was already enjoying a 37% enrolment ratio (World Bank, 1993, pp 127, 175). While Ghana had a population per physician ratio of 12,900 during this same time frame, oil rich Nigeria had a ratio of 20,200 (World Bank, 1993, pp 127, 249).

The lower level of public provision, a component of the cost recovery regime, led to hospital fees being introduced in 1983. The fees were increased in 1985 and have now been fine-tuned and labelled 'cash and carry' dispensed like any other commodity at the point of need. The increasing cost of hospital attendance (hospital fees) is, therefore, felt most by the poorest of the society who are the least capable of paying. While the legal minimum wage is ¢7,150 per day, admission to any state hospital, let alone private ones, currently costs the individual not less than ¢10,000 per day[18]. The introduction of 'cost recovery' in health went hand-in-hand with a decrease in public investment in health provision. Per capita health expenditure decreased from $4.93 constant dollars (ie with the same purchasing power) in 1972 to $1.63 in 1987 (Carrin, 1992, p 31, Table 3.4).

Increased inequality

One of the far-reaching consequences of the broader SAP on equity, and therefore poverty in rural Ghana, has been the increasing social and economic inequality and diversity in recent years. A major cause of the increasing inequality has essentially rested on the enhanced price differential between export crops such as cocoa, coffee, cotton and so on, and non-export food crops. Producer price reform altered the internal rural terms of trade making exports the most lucrative. Another is a increased salary differential between the enclave multinational and multilateral sector and the rest of the public and formal sector.

National food security/agriculture

The credit policy pursued as part of banking and monetary reform impacts negatively on agriculture. Agricultural workers, as already established, form the biggest poverty group in the economy. Largely because of this and also conceding to the fact that agriculture credit has not been the most profitable form of banking in Ghana, previous regimes had moved to ring-fence a proportion of available credit to agriculture. Interest on such credit was also mandated to be lower than for other sectors and small-scale farmers became a priority for agricultural credit. The Financial Sector Adjustment Programme (FINSAP) deregulated credit. Sectoral fencing was deemed incompatible with the new market ethos of credit supply and management in the economy, hence losing its place in the scheme of things. The lower interest rate extended to agriculture was also abolished by FINSAP. With banks no longer required by regulation to advance credit to agriculture and smallholders on favourable terms, rural farmers, among the least able to provide the type of collateral security ordinarily demanded by banks, have become increasingly unable to access credit from regular sources, thus suffering productivity and income losses. And with the deterioration of the terms of trade between export crops and food crops, the little available credit is channelled to export crops. This not only leaves most farmers (the majority of Ghanaian farmers cultivate food crops) poorer, but critically compromising national food security. The relative decline in the production of food crops coinciding with FINSAP is not unconnected and since agriculture provides the highest percentage of income for the poor, their fate is thus worsened.

The above further pushes farmers and thus most rural dwellers into increased poverty (see Heller et al, 1988, p 3). The liberalisation of food imports, above and beyond making up for local shortfalls, adds to the downward spiral of agricultural prices in real terms and lower incomes for the already poor Ghanaian farmers. The inability of the country to establish a creditable national food security has other disastrous outcomes for poverty. Lower incomes have resulted in Ghanaians spending over 55% of their income on food in 1998. This was a higher proportion than in the 1970s.

National debt

A lasting consequence of adjustment is the increased national debt. External debt had increased from slightly over one billion dollars in 1982 to six billion by 2000. Internal debt had also reached six trillion cedis during the same period (Budget Statement 2001). This was the result of a dependency culture where over 70% of government expenditure was externally funded (GPRS,

2002-04, p 18). By 1998, about 40% of the country's total export earnings went into external debt servicing thus requiring more donor inflows to balance the budget. External inflows became far more important than domestic mobilisation leading to a debt overhang. It is therefore not surprising that Ghana was encouraged by the same multilateral institutions to go for debt relief by subscribing to the Highly Indebted Poor Country Initiative (HIPC). The country formally subscribed to the initiative in 2001. Under HIPC conditionalities, Ghana would be entitled to $250 million of debt relief if it reaches the decision point. A possible $3.7 billion could accrue to the country over the next 20 years if Ghana stayed the course (Ghana and World Bank, 2002).

Ghana joining the HIPC initiative after decades of being the star pupil of SAP in Africa is an indictment on the efficacy of that programme to address the general African and Ghanaian development challenges.

Poverty alleviation under adjustment

The first instrument of poverty alleviation under adjustment has been the Programme of Action to Mitigate the Social Cost of Adjustment (PAMSCAD). Proposals for the establishment of PAMSCAD were presented to the Paris Donors Conference on Ghana in 1987 and accepted by implementation beginning in 1988. The drawing up of PAMSCAD saw UNICEF playing a leading role. PAMSCAD was a series of projects undertaken largely by community groups and part or wholly funded by foreign pledges administered by the government. The aim was to generate works (and incomes) through the construction of basic needs facilities and provide both work and training for retrenched workers in rural and urban deprived areas. The programme was transitional in nature, at least in terms of design and was to have a quick-time implementing regime.

PAMSCAD was an admission by both the government of Ghana and the multilateral and bilateral donors[19] that the social consequences of reform were massive and needed corrective action. The social disenchantment and the increasing impoverishment of the people could no longer be overlooked if the programme was to stay on course; neither could the increasingly militant stance of the TUC nor the barrage of criticism emanating from the universities and other progressive[20] circles be ignored.

PAMSCAD was, therefore, both a recognition and an attempt to lessen the worse effects of a market led adjustment in the Ghanaian situation. The social consequences of adjustment had been ignored in both the drawing up and pursuance of adjustment because of the fixation of lead players (the government, the IMF and the World Bank) with aggressive economic growth theories. Social consequences only came in for belated attention in the form of PAMSCAD when the consequences threatened to derail the pursuit of the 'golden fleece'. No wonder PAMSCAD was designed as an interim scheme to effectively buy time for economic growth.

The programme was in its initial and 'exciting' phase funded to the tune of $84 million with a foreign exchange component of $37.6 million over a three-year period by external donors. It was also expected to create 40,000 mostly unskilled jobs during its 'initial' phase. Feeder road construction using labour intensive methods, non-formal education and basic level health projects were some of the other activities targeted for PAMSCAD assistance (PAMSCAD, 1987, p 1).

With the prevailing levels of social deprivation, the selection of projects had to be critical in the success or otherwise of PAMSCAD. The government in recognising this, established that:

> [T]he criteria for the selection of projects under the programme was that they should have a strong poverty focus, high economic and social rates of return, modest institutional requirements permitting speedy implementation; and in sensitive areas, a *high profile to enhance the sustainability of adjustment*. (PAMSCAD, 1987, p 21; my emphasis)

Conclusion: poverty reduction strategy in Ghana

Attempting to assess the effectiveness of the Programme of Action to Mitigate the Social Cost of Adjustment to poverty alleviation leads one into the uncharted territories conjured up by such programmes. The dilemma here, as is often the case, is where to draw the line in interpreting the objectives of the programme. If one were to go by the volume of literature and official publications and mutual back slapping of agencies such as UNICEF, in its description of PAMSCAD as "a good example of what is meant, in practice, by 'adjustment with a human face'" (UNICEF, 1990, p 10), then one is tempted to assess the programme positively. A number of small-scale community initiated projects were completed with funding from PAMSCAD. By the end of the first and euphoric stage, the World Bank reckoned that over 200 projects were either completed or initiated. On the other hand, a careful study of the text of the programme and its practical outcomes can lead only to the conclusion that PAMSCAD was a gargantuan political fraud perpetrated on the poor of Ghana by the government and its international backers. PAMSCAD was underfunded and lacked clear direction. It was not surprising that by 1995, the only funding available was a $288,000 equivalent provided by the Ghanaian government (Budget Statement 1995). It neither mitigated poverty nor did it indeed have the capacity to do so.

The Ghana Poverty Reduction Strategy is yet another conditionality imposed by the World Bank and the IMF for accessing the reliefs under the Highly Indebted Poor Country Initiative. In 1996 the country had developed a Vision 2020[21] as the long-term development blueprint for the country. This widely published plan missed almost all of its targets in its first five years. Instead of the plan target of 7.8% needed to make Ghana a middle income developing country by 2020, GDP growth actually averaged 4.3%. The biggest single drawback had been the debt overhang, hence the truncation of the Vision 2020 Plan to be replaced by the Ghana Poverty Reduction Strategy.

This strategy aims at developing "new and comprehensive policies in support of poverty reduction and growth and to strengthen extant policies and activities" (GPRS, p 1). Would this be another fad in the passing? Whether this turns out to be a fad or not, the death throes of structural adjustment policies are there for all to see.

Notes

[1] I have drawn quite extensively from my 1997 book *Structural adjustment and mass poverty in Ghana* (Donkor, 1997).

[2] The seemingly insurmountable differences between the two institutions have led to the call since the late 1960s, for a merger. This was picked up again in the 1990s with John Smith, the late Labour Party Leader (Britain) returning to the theme of merging the two institutions in 1993. The call has been echoed in 1995 (the 50th anniversary year of the institutions) by both governmental and non-governmental institutions with the US Congress being the most vocal, even if for a different set of reasons.

[3] Nigeria's antipathy to anything Libyan was the consequence of the belief at that time that Libya was destabilising the West African sub-region.

[4] The Provisional National Defence Council (PNDC) itself being a coalition of various interests in the Ghanaian polity.

[5] The youth wing of the party was the most vocal in its opposition to any downward revaluation of the cedi.

[6] Minutes of the joint meetings of these two bodies during the period, and which I have had the privilege of reading.

[7] This group came to be known as the Akuse Group after the hydro town of Akuse, where a secluded government guest house was put at their disposal for their deliberations.

[8] Cabinet ministers were formally titled PNDC Secretaries of State.

[9] This semantic wizardry enabled an influential member of the PNDC, Mrs Aana Enin, to tell market women that the cedi had not been devalued, since the official rate was still pegged at ¢2.75 to the dollar at that time.

[10] The Ghana Living Standards Survey 1998/99, concluded that 39.5% of Ghanaians fell below the World Bank's poverty line of $1 a day.

[11] The 'doctrine' of division of labour is invoked by multilateral institutions and agencies to support this.

[12] David Woodward (1992) views the lack of access and or resources as the most critical causes of poverty in the developing world.

[13] Defined in the survey as $100 per capita household income.

[14] It is useful to note here that the poverty line at the historical standard of 1975 for $100 was higher than the line drawn by the GLSS of the late 1980s and early 1990s, reflecting the relative decline of Ghanaian living standards.

[15] A composite measure which combines infant mortality, life expectancy and literacy.

[16] Explaining in part the poverty of the Savannah North.

[17] Ghana presently has one of the worst population/physician ratios in the developing world. The World Bank's Social Development Indicators (1993) put the ratio as one physician to 22,970 as against 1:12,900 15-20 years ago. Togo, has a ratio of 1:11,954, Kenya 1:10,133, Malaysia 1:2,701, South Korea 1:1,366, and so on.

[18] This excludes the government-approved charges for every medical attention from consultation to major surgery.

[19] These bodies included 14 donor governments and 12 multilateral organisations some of which were the IMF, World Bank, UNICEF, UNDP, WFP, IFAD, ILP, CIDA, USAID and ODA (UK) (Zaya Yeebo, 1991, p 215).

[20] The National Union of Ghana Students (NUGS) and some of the other left leaning pressure groups which initially supported the PNDC in 1982 are worthy of mention.

[21] This was originally entitled, the 'National Development Framework'.

References

Abbey, J.L. (1987) *Ghana's experience with structural adjustment*, Accra, mimeo.

Amin, S. (1972) *Neo-colonialism in West Africa*, New York, NY: Monthly Review Press.

Assenso-Okyere, W.K. (1993) *Policies and strategies for rural poverty alleviation in Ghana*, Technical Publication No 57, Legon: Institute of Statistical, Social and Economic Research, University of Ghana.

Bachar, E.L. (1987) 'IMF conditionality: conceptual problems and policy initiatives', *World Development*, vol 15, p 12.

Bandyopadhaya, J. (1988) *The poverty of nations*, New Delhi: Allied Publishers.

Bates, R. (1981) *Markets and states in tropical Africa: The political bias of agricultural policies*, Berkeley, CA: University of California.

Blanchard, O.J. and Summers, L.H (1986) 'Hysteresis and the European unemployment problem', Havard Institute of Economic Research Discussion Paper Series no 1240, Cambridge, MA: Harvard University Press.

Boateng, O., Ewusi, K., Kanbur, R. and McKay, A. (1990) *A poverty profile of Ghana*, Ghana GLSS 1, Accra: Ghana Statistical Service/World Bank.

Carrin, G. (1992) *Strategies for healthcare finance in developing countries*, Basingstoke: MacMillan.

Cordova, J. (1986) 'El Programa Mexicano de Re ordenacion Economica, 1983-1984', in Sela, *el FMI, el Banco Mundial y la Crisis Latinoamericana*, Mexico: Siglo xxi Editores.

Cornia, G., Richard, J. and Steward, F. (eds) (1987) *Adjustment with a human face*, vol 1, New York, NY: Oxford University Press.

Donkor, K. (1997) *Structural adjustment and mass poverty in Ghana*, Aldershot: Ashgate.

Elliot, C. (1975) *Patterns of poverty in the third world*, New York, NY: Praeger.

Ewusi, K. (1976) 'Measures of levels of development among regions and localities in Ghana', Paper presented at the seminar on urbanisation and rural development, Legon: ISSER.

Ewusi, K. (1988) *Trends in the economy of Ghana*, Legon: ISSER.

Feinberg, R. (1986) 'The changing relationships between World Bank and International Monetary Fund', Unpublished, Washington, DC: Overseas Development Council.

George, V. (1988) *Wealth, poverty and starvation. An international perspective*, Hemel Hempstead: Harvester Wheatsheaf.

Gilbraith, J.K. (1979) *The nature of mass poverty*, Cambridge, MA: Harvard University Press.

Glewwe, P. and Twum-Baah, K. (1991) *The distribution of welfare in Ghana*, LSMS Working Paper No 91, Accra: World Bank.

Government of Ghana (1983) *J.J. Rawlings: Ghana's moment of truth*, Accra: Information Services Department.

Government of Ghana (1984) *Economic Recovery Programme, 1984-86: Review of progress in 1984 and goals for 1985 and 86*, Second meeting of Consultative Group for Ghana (Paris), Accra: Ministry of Finance.

Government of Ghana (1987) *National programme for economic development*, Accra: Government Printer.

Government of Ghana (2002) *Ghana poverty reduction strategy 2002-04*, Accra: Government Printer.

Heller, P.S. and Tait, A.A. (1983) *Government employment and pay: Some comparisons*, Occasional Paper No 24, Washington, DC: IMF.

Heller, P.S. and Tait, A.A. (1988) *The implications of food supported adjustment programmes for poverty*, Washington, DC: IMF.

Heller, P.S., Bovenberg, A.L., Catsambas, T. and Chu, K.Y. (1988) *The implications of fund supported adjustment programmes for poverty: Experience of selected countries*, Washington, DC: IMF.

Herbst, J. (1993) *The politics of reform in Ghana, 1982-91*, Berkeley, CA: University of California Press.

Kapur, I., Hadjimichael, M.T. and Hilbers, P. (1991) *Ghana: Adjustment and growth 1983-91*, Washington, DC: IMF.

Loxley, J. (1988) *Ghana: Economic crisis and the long road to recovery*, Ottawa: North-South Institute.

Mosley, P., Harrigan, J. and Toye. J. (1991) *Aid and power: The World Bank and policy-based lending*, vol 1, London: Routledge.

Nashashibi, K., Gupta, S. and Liuksila, C. (1992) *The fiscal dimensions of adjustment of low income countries*, Washington, DC: IMF.

Ray, D.I. (1986) *Ghana: Politics, economics and society*, London: Pinter.

Richards, J. (1989) 'Ghana: The political economy of self rule', in D. O'Brien and R. Rathbone (eds) *Contemporary West African states*, Cambridge: Cambridge University Press.

Rothchild, D. (1991) *Ghana: The political economy of recovery*, London: Lyne Reinner.

Sarris, A. and Sham, H. (1991) *Ghana under structural adjustment. The impact on agriculture and the rural poor*, New York, NY: IFAD New York University.

Shaw, T.M. (1992) 'Africa after the crisis of the 1980s: The dialectics of adjustment', in M. Hawkesworth and M. Kogan (eds) *Routledge Encyclopaedia of government and politics*, London: Routledge.

Tanzi, V. (1987) 'Quantitative characteristics of the tax systems of developing countries', in D. Newberry and N. Stern (eds) *The theory of taxation for developing countries*, New York, NY: Oxford University Press.

Toye, J. (1990) 'Ghana's economic reform 1983-1987: origins, achievements and limitations', in J. Pickett and H. Singer (eds) *Towards economic recovery in sub-Saharan Africa*, London: Routledge.

Townsend, P. (1993) *International analysis of poverty*, Hemel Hempstead: Harvester Wheatsheaf.

TUC (Trades Union Congress) (1988) 'Economic survey of Ghana 1980-1987', Accra, mimeo.

UNICEF (1986) *Ghana: Adjustment policies and programmes to protect children and other vulnerable groups*, Accra: UNICEF.

UNICEF (1990) *The state of the world's children*, New York: UNICEF.

Walter, D. (1963) *Report and economic survey, 1962*, Accra: Government Printer.

Wood, A. (1988) *Global trends in real exchange rates, 1960-84*, Washington, DC: World Bank.

World Bank (1993) *Social indicators of development papers*, Washington, DC: World Bank.

World Bank (1995) *World debt table*, Washington, DC: World Bank.

World Bank (1994) *Adjustment in Africa*, Washington, DC: World Bank.

World Bank (1994) *Adjustment in Africa: Reforms, results and the road ahead*, Washington, DC: World Bank.

World Bank (1994) *Trends in developing economies*, Washington, DC: World Bank.

World Bank (2002) *Ghana and the World Bank*, Washington, DC: World Bank.

World Bank/UNDP (1989) *African economic and financial data*, Washington, DC: World Bank.

World Resources Institute/UNEP/UNDP (1994) *World resources 1994-1995*, New York, NY: Oxford University Press.

NINE

Social funds in sub-Saharan Africa: how effective for poverty reduction?

Nazneen Kanji

Social funds in the context of structural adjustment

Since the mid-1980s, the International Monetary Fund (IMF) and World Bank have promoted and supported Structural Adjustment Policies in sub-Saharan Africa (SSA). Aid from international financial institutions and a range of bilateral agencies is conditional to the implementation of these policies. The first generation of adjustment programmes were focused exclusively on macroeconomic issues, exchange rates and budget deficits, and the issue of debt repayments. Underpinned by a renewed commitment to neoliberal ideology, the World Bank explicitly argued that poverty reduction belonged to the future. In any case they argued that the 'market' would be more effective than state interventions and social programmes – structural adjustments of African economies would impact positively on poverty through 'trickle down' effects. Economic liberalisation – especially supply-side reforms such as trade liberalisation and sectoral reforms – would provide enhanced opportunities for expanding investment and employment. Beyond employment creation, liberalisation would also, according to the Bank, benefit the poor by reducing inflation following the increased volume of goods and services available in the market.

These adjustment operations and the deepening economic crisis in Africa led to a widespread critique of the World Bank's prescriptions for economic reform. Calls for a rethink and revision of policies came not only from African organisations and governments, but also from a range of non-governmental organisations (NGOs), UN organisations and a 'likeminded group' of Western donor countries. A major focus of the criticism was the perceived negative impact of the Bank's economic policies on poverty and insufficient attention to social issues, well captured in the landmark UNICEF report which called for "adjustment with a human face" (Cornia et al, 1987).

The first response to this criticism was the *Social Dimension of Adjustment* (SDA), a joint programme between the World Bank, the African Development Bank, UN Development Programme, and bilateral donors. The short-term goal was to alleviate poverty, while the long-term goal was to strengthen a government's capacity to do so. SDA emphasised social safety net programmes, but also provided funding for the collection and analysis of data on poverty in individual African countries. In a sense, the pendulum swung from direct poverty orientation with the basic needs approach to development in the 1970s, to a focus on economic growth and trickle down in the 1980s, and back to a position of renewed attention to social issues and poverty reduction. However, the perceived role of the state has varied enormously. The 1990 *World Development Report* outlined the Bank's strategy for poverty reduction, based on three pillars: broad based growth, human development, and safety nets (with the last formally incorporated at a later stage). The first pillar focused on the need for a more labour intensive growth pattern, while the other two were intended to assist poor groups through investments in social sectors and safety net programmes.

Social funds have become an increasingly popular instrument for donors, particularly the World Bank, to deliver safety nets. Over time, the emphasis has shifted from emergency relief towards more general 'developmental' programmes and projects, and objectives have shifted from the short to the long term, focusing on facilitating 'community-driven development'. Social funds have grown and evolved rapidly since the first experiments in the late 1980s, and almost US$9 billion is expected to be spent by various agencies in the first half of this decade.

At present, social funds exist in over 50 countries, mostly in Latin America and SSA, and increasingly in other regions. They continue to receive attention and support from many quarters and are likely to remain a feature of the development landscape for the foreseeable future. Social funds are extremely diverse, and have been set up in the poorest countries, as well as former communist countries marked by a crisis of social security systems. Apart from differences in objectives resulting from varying contexts, there is a great variation in the kinds of activities that they can undertake or facilitate, organisational set-up, the extent to which they target the poor, or even whether targeting is a central approach.

Given this diversity, it is important to specify what the focus is here: social funds for community activities aimed at poverty reduction. There has been a shift from seeing them as specific instruments for social protection, to "quasi-financial intermediaries that channel resources, according to pre-determined eligibility criteria, to small-scale projects for poor and vulnerable groups, and implemented by public or private agencies" (World Bank Quality Assurance Group, 1998).

There is an ever-expanding literature on social funds, much of it positive. However, when examined more closely, it appears that there are grounds for caution regarding their effectiveness. The purpose of this chapter is to identify the strengths and weaknesses of social funds and to argue that expectations, particularly in the SSA context, have to be more realistic of what such funds can achieve in terms of poverty reduction.

It is worth highlighting some conventional development indicators for the region. The proportion of population living below US$1 per day poverty line (at 1993 prices) remained approximately the same in 1998 as in 1987 (46%). SSA has the highest proportion of population in this category for any region in the world. Population growth has meant that, from 1987 to 1998, the number of poor people increased from 217 million to 291 million, leaving almost half the population poor. Social indicators for SSA also show high levels of social deprivation relative to other developing countries, with low life expectancy, high infant mortality and high levels of illiteracy (UNDP, 2000; World Bank, 2001).

This chapter is based on a review of social funds carried out for the Department for International Development, UK (DfID) (Fumo et al, 2000)[1], but draws particularly on the material relating to funds in SSA. Donors have had a major role in the planning and implementation of funds in the region. It also draws on the author's own work on poverty and livelihoods in sub-Saharan Africa, including a review of the World Bank's poverty reduction strategies in Zambia, Zimbabwe and Malawi at the end of the 1990s (Tjonneland et al, 1998)[2]. Section Two of this chapter summarises the evolution of social funds, and highlights some of their common features. Section Three addresses key organisational concerns of social funds, including the strengths and weaknesses of the demand-driven approach. Section Four examines the issue of targeting and poverty reduction in the sub-Saharan African context. The conclusions are drawn in Section Five.

Overview of social funds

Social funds have been in existence for nearly 15 years. The first funds emerged in the late 1980s and early 1990s as emergency measures, to alleviate the impacts of structural adjustment programmes and economic shocks. In Ghana, the Programme to Mitigate the Social Costs of Adjustment (PAMSCAD) was initiated in 1987 by the government, with the help of the World Bank and the specialised agencies of the UN. It was a short-term action programme to address the immediate needs of the poor and vulnerable groups whose situation had deteriorated during economic decline and adjustment (Gayi, 1995). Target groups were:

• the 'new poor': the retrenched workers from the private and public sectors;
• the 'chronic poor': rural poor, small farmers especially in the Northern and Upper regions of Ghana, and low-income unemployed or underemployed urban households (ISSER, 1993).

Other programmes, such as the Programme to Alleviate Poverty and Social Costs of Adjustment (PAPSCA) in Uganda, were set up later in a similar vein.

Presently, social funds exist in over 50 countries (and counting): in Latin America and the Caribbean, in at least 24 countries in sub-Saharan Africa (including in the form of 'AGETIPs' which are discussed later in this chapter), several in the Middle East and North Africa – of which the Egypt Social Fund is the world's largest – and about a dozen in Eastern Europe and Central Asia. Social funds have been relatively rare in Asia, but agencies exist in India and Indonesia that share many operational characteristics with social funds. In Thailand a relatively new social fund has focussed on establishing a new economy following the 1997 crisis, and funds exist in Cambodia, Laos and the Philippines. In some cases (for example, Bolivia, Malawi, Ethiopia) more than one fund or several generations of social funds have been implemented. The World Bank and the Inter-American Development Bank (IDB) are the largest funding bodies.

The variety of existing and partly overlapping forms of social funds is illustrated as follows (based on Reddy, 1998):

- Emergency Social Funds (ESF): intermediary institutions intended to disburse funds to NGOs for social protection objectives;
- Social Investment Funds (SIF): like ESFs, disbursing funds to intermediary institutions, but tending to be oriented towards longer-term goals of poverty alleviation;
- Social Action Programmes (SAPs): multi-sectoral funding programmes established to meet social protection and other objectives. PAMSCAD in Ghana was the first of this sort, followed by Madagascar's Economic Management and Social Action Programme (EMSAP). These are sometimes seen as regular investment projects, and not always considered as social funds (Marc et al, 1995);
- AGETIPs (*Agence d'Execution de Travaux d'Intéret Public* [Public Works and Employment Agency]) was set up in Senegal in 1989, and the model has been replicated in a large number of countries. AGETIPs have a strong focus on public works, but have adopted more recently more general characteristics of social funds.

Many of these institutions have evolved over time. They continue to balance multiple objectives, all of which fall broadly under the umbrella of efforts to improve the living conditions of the poor. The objectives include:

- improvement in social and economic infrastructure;
- creation of employment (often short-term or temporary);
- community development, specifically to build community capacity to demand and manage development resources;
- improvement of social service delivery; and support for decentralisation and municipal strengthening.

Keeping in mind the great diversity among social funds, the main operational characteristics shared by social funds can be summarised as follows:

- with the exception of AGETIPs (which have delegated execution authority) they appraise, finance and supervise the implementation of small social projects but do not identify, implement and maintain or operate the projects;
- they establish menus, procedures and targeting criteria to support investments benefiting the poor;
- they respond to demand from local groups (community groups, NGOs, local governments or local representatives of regional or national governments). At the same time, most also have a set menu of eligible and ineligible projects (thereby limiting community choice);
- almost all insist on co-financing from the beneficiaries, ostensibly to ensure that projects are responding to demand;
- even though most are part of the public sector, they often have operational autonomy and enjoy exceptions from public sector rules, such as civil service rules or procurement and disbursement rules;
- most have a small staff employed on the basis of performance contracts, higher salaries and higher performance standards than in the civil service;
- most social funds are heavily dependent on external financing.

Key organisational concerns of social funds

Social funds usually are institutionally and organisationally distinct from government sectoral policies and services. A central administrative entity, often a semi-autonomous unit set up for the purpose, disburses funds to intermediary organisations including local government, private firms and NGOs. However, the organisational set-up varies enormously. At one end of the scale, there are social funds administered by units within one government ministry. At the other, autonomous structures operate outside government bureaucracies. Social funds raise important and interesting issues precisely because their design departs from that of standard public programmes, and is meant to overcome some of the problems associated with the public sector.

Social funds are intended to take quick, effective and targeted actions to reach poor and vulnerable groups. They aim to stimulate participatory development initiatives by providing small-scale financing to local NGOs, community groups, small firms and entrepreneurs. A number of reports have praised social funds for their rapid disbursement, flexibility and ability to respond to demand from poor communities, while commenting on the need for improvement (Marc et al, 1995; Narayan and Ebbe, 1997; Subarrao et al, 1997; Bigio, 1998). However, some independent researchers have been more critical about these claims, particularly in relation to service delivery (Stewart and van der Geest, 1995; Tjonneland et al, 1998; Tendler, 1999). The focus here is on the structures and partnerships that have been created, and their sustainability, from national through to local levels.

Location and degree of autonomy

The location of social funds varies enormously – from entirely autonomous agencies outside regular government bureaucracies to location within a ministry, or office of the president – but where the fund has a substantial degree of independence. Senegal's AGETIP was established as an autonomous agency with nonprofit legal status, subject only to ex post monitoring by the government. Some social funds can deal directly with donors, enabling them to mobilise external resources, and donors to deal with a single, relatively small and transparent agency. At the other end, the Zambia Microprojects Unit is located within the Ministry of Finance, but with a protected budget and full control over approval and monitoring of subprojects.

Egypt's social fund, the world's largest, is a special agency outside the bureaucracy, reporting directly to the Prime Minister. The fund's board of directors has representation from various ministries as well as the private sector. It is charged with defining strategy, approving development plans and implementation programmes and monitoring the selection of subprojects. This arrangement has contributed to conflicts in the board over funding to NGOs, related to government views as to the appropriate roles and powers of NGOs vis-à-vis government. Such partnerships are particularly difficult in countries where government tends to view NGOs as havens for political opposition (Marc et al, 1995, p 54) and where there is a climate of mistrust.

Personnel, procurement and budgetary implementation

Many social funds have set up procedures which aim to overcome the problems of the public sector's poorly administered, time-consuming bureaucracy. The first measure is to recruit staff at much higher rates than civil service standards. The rationale is that civil service pay scales are too low to attract the most competent and talented professionals who will show high levels of commitment and motivation and produce results in a relatively short period of time. This was done by Bolivia's ESF, one of the first social funds, and repeated in many others, including most funds in Africa.

The second measure is to avoid complex disbursement and procurement procedures. Small-scale contractors often find it difficult to work under government contracts, because of the payment delays and administrative procedures. To avoid these problems, social funds are given great control over their budgetary procedures. Approval, release and auditing of expenditures are handled internally, without submission to central government. Small-scale contractors are able to participate, either by direct contracting or simplified local bidding systems. However, governments do share the costs of the social funds, and degrees of autonomy vary. Cumbersome government disbursement procedures have resulted in implementation delays. This was the case in the Uganda PAPSCA where Action Aid, the NGO that was executing a small-scale infrastructure component, had to interrupt implementation for months because of the government's inefficient disbursement procedures.

Social funds have experimented with a range of community contracting models: project funds managed entirely by communities (for example, Malawi), an elected community committee works with an intermediary organisation which manages the contract on behalf of the community (Ethiopia), or a combination of these approaches (Eritrea). Research by de Silva (2000) emphasises that political will in favour of community management, as well as community cohesion and previous experience, are important conditions for success.

Central-level organisational concerns

Not all funds create parallel structures. In Zimbabwe, the Community Action Programme operates through a sectoral ministry, albeit the weakest one (Labour and Social Work), in terms of skills, capacity and size of budget. In most cases, however, social funds do create new structures, rather than work to reform existing government institutions.

This raises a number of problematic issues. The first is whether policy and programming lessons from social funds are integrated into sectoral programmes. Are social funds moving in the same direction as national policies and strategies? The evidence is patchy but does indicate that this aspect of lesson learning receives much less attention than it deserves. In Zambia in 1997, for example, no mechanisms were in place to provide the health sector reform programme or the Ministry of Education with lessons from the Social Recovery Programme (SRP) and yet the SRP directed most of its funds to micro-projects in these two sectors. The phasing out or integration of social funds into existing structures did not seem to be a focus at the planning stages (Tjonneland et al, 1998, p 72).

Another aspect of autonomy relates to the higher salaries paid to social fund staff. What are the longer-term implications of this? Recruiting high quality professionals at ministerial salaries is no doubt problematic but the high salaries are likely to have an impact on reform processes in the civil service, and reinforce the movement of staff to the private sector and donor agencies.

A third question relates to fungibility: do ministries reduce their allocations to areas which are targeted by social funds? Egypt's central government allocations to local government were explicitly cut back because of expected donor inflows for the social fund.

Decentralisation and partnerships at the local level

An institutional feature shared by many social funds is the devolution of planning and executive responsibility away from capital cities to regional, district and local levels, in order to be more responsive to local needs, and build administrative capacity at the district and municipal levels. In Zambia, for example, subproject proposals received from local NGOs and community groups are first submitted to the local district council which determines if the proposal is consistent with district plans. It is then passed to the Provincial Planning Unit which determines if it is in line with provincial priorities and arranges to meet any recurrent costs entailed by the subprojects. Only then is it passed on to the Microprojects Unit in the capital. This model is designed to increase both policy coherence and sustainability. Longer-term costs for project maintenance are considered, which has not been done in many cases. Other social funds, for example those that focus on employment creation through labour intensive public works (as in Senegal), tend to work directly with local government. Yet others (for example, Egypt) work with government and private groups. In general, interventions through line ministries tended to lack participatory practices, and lack resources to supervise interventions and work closely with beneficiaries.

Social funds which used to concentrate on subproject appraisal and promotion at central level have moved towards more decentralised models[3]. A recent study of social funds and decentralisation indicates that as an increasing number of countries move to decentralise, social funds are finding ways to increase the involvement of local governments, including the transfer of project cycle responsibilities to them, for example, in Zimbabwe (Parker and Serrano, 2000).

Narayan and Ebbe (1997) provide a comprehensive overview of the organisational features which are designed to increase demand orientation, community participation and local organisational capacity. Some 40% of the 51 projects they reviewed had community development objectives and most projects included community groups in initial project planning. However, while half the projects included assessment of community participation in the appraisal process, few described whether participation had occurred. Similarly, 42% required the creation of operation and maintenance committees prior to implementation, but in most cases neither the commitment nor the capacity to carry out maintenance was verified, nor was there verification of the willingness and capacity of intermediary agencies to follow through commitments to support community groups in the long run. Concern about the sustainability of benefits over time was also raised by Owen and Van Domelen (1998): arrangements for operations and maintenance revealed many weaknesses, particularly the lack of training given to communities.

Effective demand orientation exists when people are offered a range of options and impartial information to assist in making choices – in conditions usually of asymmetrical information and power – and when evidence of commitment is required through cash or in-kind contributions and labour. Of 50 reviewed projects, 24% did not use any design features that enable demand orientation, 68% scored low or average and only 8% were highly demand-oriented (Narayan and Ebbe, 1997, p 31). Similarly, Owen and Van Domelen (1998, p 26) found "a significant and fairly universal problem with the lack of information and/or misunderstandings on the part of beneficiaries about the roles and rules of the game of the social funds". Tendler (2000) emphasises that contractors, politicians and fund staff may have an interest in *limiting* information, while on the other hand experience with the social fund in Mali indicated that many people understood how the fund worked (Marcus, 2000). More recently approved projects do include innovative approaches, such as information and outreach activities in the Eritrea Social Fund. Therefore, there may be a growing number of exceptions.

Poor groups rarely have strong organisations to make their voices heard. Therefore, social fund projects must invest in the building capacity of local groups. A positive evolution was noted by Narayan and Ebbe (1997): the number of projects investing resources in capacity building of community groups rose from 17% in 1987 to 67% of projects in 1996. However, even in the more well-designed projects, this tended to be 'technical' rather than 'organisational' training (for example, the handling of funds, subproject implementation including operation and maintenance), and task managers reported that even that is often not conducted. Few beneficiary assessments (Owens and Van Domelen, 1998, p 30) probed the strengthening of local capacity, and the longer-term effect of social fund projects on communities is little understood. Investment in organisational capacity to achieve ownership and sustainability is the least developed element of social funds.

Key local level organisational concerns

For a demand-driven process to function effectively and inclusively, social funds must devote time and resources to reach disadvantaged groups and build local organisational capacity to represent diverse interests at community level. The extent to which efforts have been made to reach and involve women and other disadvantaged groups is unclear and variable. Women have been under-represented in formal participation in projects, particularly in management and decision making around projects. Where project committees are formed, women make up relatively small percentages. Funds that do pay adequate attention to issues of exclusion at the local level seem to be the exception rather than the rule.

While there have been attempts to employ geographical targeting of communities on the basis of existing poverty data, there is little evidence that particularly vulnerable groups and individuals *within communities* are included or supported to formulate projects, although this is beginning to happen in some social funds. This highlights a disadvantage of demand-driven approaches, when organised and materially better off groups within communities are able to reap greater benefits, particularly when significant local contributions in cash, labour and time are required. Problems are likely to be greater in contexts where communities are heterogeneous and where there are marked inequalities in income, power and access to information.

An extensive review of cross-country experience with safety nets showed that demand-driven approaches have not ensured that the poorest regions and groups receive resources (Subarrao et al, 1997). People within communities are not necessarily or automatically more accountable, or representative of community interests, than outsiders (including bureaucrats). Safety nets for particularly vulnerable groups cannot be left to largely demand-driven initiatives but have to be based on more active attempts at inclusion based on an analysis of poverty and vulnerability in particular contexts.

Questions have been raised about how demand-driven social funds are in reality, in terms of the outcomes of community consultations. In Malawi and Zambia, communities often prioritised micro-enterprise development; yet they accepted social service infrastructure projects because social fund staff asserted that they did not have the organisational resources to support micro-enterprise projects (Tjonneland et al, 1998). In most African social funds, requests for infrastructure rehabilitation subprojects have been faster to identify, screen and implement than other types. In part this is because it may be easier to reach consensus over and obtain results out of local public goods and services which can be 'shared' by communities, than more private benefits such as credit or employment (Marc et al, 1995, p 50).

According to beneficiary assessments, social fund projects overwhelmingly reflect felt needs of poor communities. However, the methodology used to query community needs is not always convincing. Few assessments explore beneficiary perceptions as to what should be included in the project menu (Owen and Van Domelen, 1998).

A second area of concern relates to partnerships between local government, local private firms and communities. Social funds have sometimes provided support to local private construction firms. On the other hand, there are potential conflicts between the efficiency goals of firms and the need for time-consuming and costly processes to promote community ownership and decision making, particularly if previously excluded groups are to be included. The profit and efficiency orientation of local firms demands standardised design in social infrastructure. It discourages time-intensive deliberations by community groups, replicating some of the problems of government interventions. Information is seen as a key tool to involve communities, but the volume of current demand encourages a restriction of information on the part of governments and social fund staff since workload and pressure to disburse funds quickly is very high. Pressure to disburse funds in the social fund in Zambia restricted the targeting of resources to poorer groups.

The third area of concern relates to the role of NGOs and their links with donors and government. NGOs have varied technical, administrative and participatory capacities, and in many cases require capacity building work. Assumptions that NGOs have the ability to reach poor groups, mobilise local resources and stimulate participation and to generate innovative solutions to local problems need to be verified and monitored regularly. NGOs, like local government, may relate mainly to community leaders in the identification and implementation of projects, and assume that the targeting of benefits will be equitable. Expansion of NGOs may be an opportunistic response of downsized bureaucrats, and is not necessarily driven by goals of local capacity building and empowerment. On the other hand, NGOs may view social funds as part of government structures, managed by institutions that are close to a president or prime minister (Bigio, 1998, p 32). Experienced NGOs with a good record of participatory development projects may not accept the time and disbursement pressures of social funds.

In summary, contextual factors are paramount in assessing the effectiveness and sustainability, both at central and local levels, of organisational partnerships created by social funds. Partnerships probably work best where governmental and non-governmental structures and organisations function in accountable ways. Yet these may be the very contexts in which it would seem *less* worthwhile to set up separate social fund structures, but rather to work through central and local levels of government, encouraging partnerships with NGOs, local groups and the private sector. Social funds with independent structures reporting to the highest level of central government will undermine decentralisation processes. Certainly, there should be critical appraisal of existing institutional capacity in government and NGOs in relation to the types of interventions to be funded, before setting up independent social fund structures.

Social funds, targeting and poverty reduction

The origins of the social fund as a policy instrument lie in the perceived need to transfer resources quickly, efficiently and accurately in order to mitigate temporary states of deprivation caused by economic crisis and adjustment. This genesis as an instrument of support to the poorest and most vulnerable has created a strong rhetorical commitment to poverty targeting. Subbarao et al (1997, p 161) distinguish three types of social fund target groups and related programme objectives:

- *those able to work but whose incomes are low and irregular.* Programme objectives for this group should be income and consumption smoothing in slack seasons, or regular livelihood creation;
- *those unable to provide for themselves through work (such as disabled people).* The programme objective for this group should be long-term assistance;
- *those capable of earning adequate incomes, but who cannot earn temporarily because of shocks (such as economic reform or transition).* Programme objectives for this group should include short-term assistance, public works, and income-generation programmes.

From a World Bank perspective, targeting fulfils a key function in allocating project budgets. The most recent, ongoing World Bank evaluation, for instance, includes a criterion relating directly to poverty targeting under "efficacy" (World Bank, 2000). In practice, however, many social funds do not adopt a clear poverty targeting methodology, often because they are driven by objectives, such as participation and decentralisation, that are seen to supersede a crude targeting procedure.

Geographical targeting is quite widespread in Latin American social funds. It has also been used in the Middle East and North Africa, but in SSA it tends to be less widespread, due, it is said, to a lack of detailed, disaggregated poverty data (Khadiagala, 1995; World Bank, 1998, p 17). Criticism of geographical targeting often stems from a concern that communities are not homogeneous but conceal high levels of inequality and exclusion. A sole reliance on geographical targeting, whatever the level of spatial disaggregation, may be inadequate. It can be a blunt and ineffective tool, or even create a scenario – particularly when compounded by weak communication and outreach by social fund staff – in which benefits are captured by more powerful or articulate groups within 'poor' communities.

In most instances, however, subproject targeting relies additionally on targeting against eligibility criteria for either groups or individuals. Many funds, in addition to geographical or beneficiary targeting, have prioritised certain types of subproject, such as primary education or basic health care facilities, that are likely to have a strong positive impact on the poor. Some funds use 'negative' subproject menus to effectively exclude certain types of projects. Finally, social funds can employ self-targeting by designing services in such a way as to discourage the non-poor from using them. Examples include requiring people to stand in line, and paying workers at below-market wages (Marc et al, 1995, p 57). The latter is used particularly in public works programmes where low wages ensure that only very poor groups have the incentive to take up project employment.

The World Bank's Portfolio Review concludes that "social funds have often succeeded in targeting the poor" (1997, p viii). However, social funds are far from universally successful in reaching the poorest regions or poorest groups. A review of budget allocation in four social fund projects (Subbaro et al, 1997) found that there was either a negative correlation between geographic poverty levels and per capita social fund expenditure, or that actual expenditures lagged behind allocation in higher income-poverty regions while they far exceeded allocations in lower income-poverty regions.

The requirement of community contributions also influences targeting. Beneficiary assessments indicated that the requirement can lead to favouring projects where contributions can be more easily quantified and therefore projects approved (such as school-building projects), but also the possible regressive effect on poorer and rural communities, and the opportunity costs for individuals of in-kind contributions (Owen and Van Domelen, 1998, pp 22-23).

A recent World Bank impact assessment of funds in six countries provides the most comprehensive overview of poverty targeting so far (World Bank, 2001). Although the draft report is generally very positive about reaching poor areas and households, only one country (Zambia) in sub-Saharan Africa is included in the study. The specific results of this country study illustrate clearly the difficulties of targeting in the region. In Zambia, more than 65% of the population in 75% of the districts live below the national poverty line. As the report points out, given this distribution of poverty, geographical targeting does not make sense and was not employed by the fund. In addition, the share of poor households benefiting from the fund, which focuses on social

Table 9.1: Poverty targeting in the Social Fund in Zambia

Social Fund beneficiaries:	
Poor	71%
Of which extreme poor	57%
Non-poor	29%
National population:	
Poor	72%
Of which extreme poor	56%
Non-poor	28%

Source: Extract from World Bank (2001)

infrastructure investment, is about the same as the share of such households nationwide (see Table 9.1).

Jorgensen and Van Domelen (1999) point out that certain types of programmes, such as those providing broad public health services or physical infrastructure, are less easily targeted by their nature. This is the focus which social funds in Africa have taken – the AGETIP agencies of West Africa concentrate on small-scale infrastructure and public works while the social funds of Eastern and Southern Africa tend to concentrate on human resources development in health and education.

Although the lack of targeting in SSA is said to be due to a lack of detailed, disaggregated poverty data (Khadiagala, 1995; World Bank, 1998, p 17), the focus that these funds have taken is perhaps due to the difficulties in targeting per se, in a situation where poverty levels are so high (see Section One of this chapter). It raises questions about the relevance of some forms of poverty targeting in SSA, especially given the weakening of institutional and administrative capacity in many countries through the structural adjustment period.

The broader economic situation is relevant here. Countries in SSA continue to be dependent on primary commodity exports that are subject to price volatility as well as declining terms of trade. The terms of trade for SSA at the end of the 1990s were 21% below those attained in the 1970s. Although the region's dependence on trade, measured as a share of GDP, increased from 38% to 43% between 1988-89 and 1999-2000 (UNCTAD, 2001, p 26), it has become increasingly marginalised through a declining share of total world trade (G8 Genoa Summit, 2001; Killick, 2001; UNCTAD, 2001). The region's dependency on primary commodity exports is an important factor in its marginalisation in world trade since approximately 80% of SSA's exports are composed of oil and non-oil commodities. UNCTAD estimates that if non-oil exports had not suffered this decline in the terms of trade over the previous two decades, per capita GDP would have been 50% higher (US$478 instead of $323) as a result.

This broader context translates into a reality where the livelihoods of the majority are still largely dependent on small-scale agriculture and the natural resource base, investment is low, markets are weak and segmented and institutions are fragile but are increasingly exposed to international market forces through trade liberalisation (in both rural and urban areas). Areas of smallholder agriculture are where the majority of the population, usually estimated at between 60% and 90%, are poor or very poor (Whitehead and Kabeer, 2001). There is consensus that small-scale agriculture and rural development, particularly in sub-Saharan Africa, is in a troubled state, as evidenced by high levels of poverty in rural areas and declining flows of investment (private and public) to this sector, with the situation worsened by environmental degradation (Oxfam, 2000; Killick, 2001). Detailed case studies have shown recent increases in the extent of livelihood diversification. Rural livelihoods are ever more dependent on a variety of sources: small-scale farming, agricultural labouring, petty trading and service provision, migration and remittances (Bryceson, 1999; Francis, 2000)[4].

A range of agencies and researchers (Bryceson, 2000; Oxfam, 2000; Ellis and Seeley, 2001; Rahman and Westley, 2001) argue that, since it is inconceivable in the foreseeable future that cities or commercial agriculture can offer employment to vast numbers of poor people in the countryside, attention to and support for small-scale agriculture is essential for progress on poverty reduction, including policies favouring small farms and related rural industries (the non-farm economy). In the context of SSA, the groups which are generally targeted by social funds tend to represent the majority of the population in many, particularly rural, areas. This raises questions of how effective social funds can be for poverty reduction, if due attention is not paid to other relevant policy interventions.

Conclusions

Many social funds have evolved from a context in which social transfers were seen as temporary and ameliorative, and are increasingly conceived of as longer-term and more development oriented in their ambition and impact. The emergence of social funds with long-term objectives has important implications for poverty analysis, yet the analytical and methodological adaptations required to respond to this transition do not seem to have taken place on the same scale, reflecting a tendency for social funds to change their time horizons without changing their development perspective (Covey and Abbott, 1998, p 175).

The questions raised in this chapter relate to two sets of issues. The first is about the negative and positive effects social funds can have on wider national policies and public sector performance, particularly when it comes to the focus on infrastructure and social service delivery in sub-Saharan Africa. The setting up of a parallel system, particularly when conditions for fund staff are much better than in mainstream public institutions, may harm the morale and efficiency in fields outside the social fund. Establishing funds may displace other sources of funding. It may sidetrack from tackling tough issues regarding transparent and accountable government structures: donors may pay less attention to those than they should, and social funds may deflect the attention of the users of public services. Bypassing existing structures of governance may be an important temporary solution, but cannot be sufficient in the long term. Decisions to implement social funds should be based on a consideration of alternatives, of opportunities to reform line ministries to incorporate and implement effective community-based initiatives. Social funds should certainly be designed to minimise negative effects on mainstream services.

There is a need to address more directly if and how social funds can enhance positive effects on the broader policy agenda. Key questions include:

- Can social funds encourage pro-poor government budgeting, policy making and implementation?
- Links to decentralisation, or strengthening local governance structures: do social funds coordinate with, or strengthen the representative institutions of local government?
- Enhancing accountability: what effects do the funds have on governance outside the social funds? Do they set standards for accountability, transparency and quality, or strengthen citizens' voices that contribute to greater accountability? What effects do political struggles over autonomy have on both funds and government institutions?
- Do innovative mechanisms of partnership with local groups or mechanisms of community participation feed into the practices of mainstream institutions? Do they help to mainstream principles of participation, of voices of poor people being heard, in local level government and service delivery?

The second issue that this chapter raises is the need to situate social fund interventions much more firmly in a wider analysis of poverty which examines the causes of poverty in particular contexts. Development agencies should be clear about the relative contributions that these funds can make in sub-Saharan Africa. A focus on public works employment, paying low wages, enables survival but not security nor accumulation to escape from poverty. The focus on infrastructure for social services, as discussed earlier, may not be best tackled through social funds, nor is it clear that the poorest regions and communities will gain access. Social funds can be improved and particularly those which set in motion processes of local organisation and capacity building may make positive contributions to a broader poverty reduction policy agenda. However, they are no substitute for wider economic and social policies which address the distribution of material and social assets in highly unequal societies and which do not rely on market-based mechanisms alone to reduce the unacceptable levels of poverty and deprivation which exist in SSA.

Notes

[1] The perspective taken in this chapter is entirely my responsibility, and not that of the co-authors of that volume.

[2] That volume's sections on social funds were written by the author.

[3] Tendler (2000) questions the extent to which funds are decentralised. Decision-making power often remains at the central level. This implies that funds would work at cross-purposes to decentralisation reforms.

[4] Income diversification has also taken place in urban poor populations with income deriving from a variety of sources including trade, services, manufacturing and agriculture. For an overview, see Beall and Kanji (1998) and Tacoli and Satterthwaite (1999).

References

Beall, J. and Kanji, N. (1998) 'Households, livelihoods and urban poverty', Background Paper for the ESCOR Commissioned Research on Urban Development.

Bigio, A.G. (ed) (1998) *Social funds and reaching the poor. Experiences and future directions*, Proceedings from an international workshop, EDI Learning Resources Series, Washington, DC: World Bank.

Bryceson, D. (1999) *Sub-Saharan Africa betwixt and between: Rural livelihood practices and policies*, Leiden: Africa Studies Centre.

Bryceson, D. (2000) *Rural Africa at the crossroads: Livelihood practices and policies*, London: ODI.

Cornia, G.A. (1999) *Social funds in stabilization and adjustment programmes*, Research for Action 48, Helsinki: UNU/WIDER.

Cornia, G.A., Jolly, R. and Stewart, F. (eds) (1987) *Adjustment with a human face*, vol 1, Oxford: Oxford University Press.

Covey, J. and Abbott, T. (1998) 'Social funds: an expanded NGO critique', in A.G. Bigio (ed) *Social funds and reaching the poor. Experiences and future directions*, Proceedings from an international workshop, EDI Learning Resources Series, Washington, DC: The World Bank, pp 167-78.

De Silva, S. (2000) *Community-based contracting: A Review of stakeholder experience*, Washington, DC: The World Bank, HDNSP.

Ellis, F. and Seeley, J. (2001) 'Globalisation and sustainable livelihoods: an initial note', University of East Anglia, DEV/ODG, prepared for DfID.

Francis, E. (2000) *Making a living: Changing livelihoods in rural Africa*, London: DESTIN, LSE; Routledge.

Fumo, C., de Haan, A. Holland, J. and Kanji, N. (2000) *Social fund: An effective instrument to support local action for poverty reduction?*, Social Development Department Working Paper no 5, November, DfID.

Gayi, S. (1995) 'Adjusting to the social costs of adjustment in Ghana: problems and prospects', *European Journal of Development Research*, vol 7, June, pp 77-100.

G8 Genoa Summit (2001) *A globalised market – Opportunities and risks for the poor*, African Development Bank, Asian Development Bank, EBRD, IADB, IMF, World Bank.

ISSER (Institute of Statistical, Social and Economic Research) (1993) *Policies and strategies for rural poverty alleviation in Ghana*, Technical Publication no 57, Legon: University of Ghana.

Jorgensen, S.L., and Van Domelen, J. (1999) 'Helping the poor manage risk better: the role of social funds', Paper presented at the IADB Conference on Social Protection and Poverty, February.

Khadiagala, L. (1995) *Social funds: Strengths, weaknesses and conditions for success*, ESP Discussion Paper Series, Washington DC: Education and Social Policy Department, Human Resources Development and Operations Policy, World Bank.

Killick, T. (2001) 'Globalisation and the rural poor', *Development Policy Review*, vol 19, no 2, pp 155-80.

Levine, A. (ed) *Social funds: Accomplishments and aspirations*, Proceedings from the Second International Conference on Social Funds, 5-7 June, Washington, DC: World Bank (www.worldbank.org/sp).

Marc, A., Graham, C., Schacter, M. and Schmidt, M. (1995) *Social Action Programs and social funds. A review of design and implementation in sub-Saharan Africa*, World Bank Discussion Papers, no 274, Washington, DC: World Bank.

Marcus, R. (2000) 'PAIB – a social fund in Mali. A rapid assessment of lessons from Save the Children's work with the Projet d'Appui Aux Initiatives de Base dans la Lutte contre la Faim et la Pauvreté', Mimeo, London: Save the Children.

Narayan, D. and Ebbe, K. (1997) *Design of social funds. Participation, demand orientation, and local organizational capacity*, World Bank Discussion Paper no 375, Washington, DC: World Bank.

Owen, D. and Van Domelen, J. (1998) *Getting an earful: A review of beneficiary assessments of social funds*, Social Protection Discussion Paper 9816, Washington, DC: World Bank.

Parker, A. and Serrano, R. (2000) 'Promoting good local governance through social funds and decentralization', Paper presented at the Second International Conference on Social Funds, Washington, DC: World Bank.

Rahman, A. and Westley, J. (2001) 'The challenge of ending rural poverty', *Development Review*, vol 19, no 4, pp 553-62.

Reddy, S. (1998) *Social funds in developing countries: Recent experiences and lessons*, UNICEF Staff Working Papers, EPP-EVL-98-002, New York, NY: UNICEF.

Stewart, F. and Van der Geest, W. (1995) *Adjustment and social funds: Political panacea or effective poverty reduction?*, Employment Papers no 2, Geneva: ILO.

Subbarao, K., Bonnerjee, A., Braithwaite, J., Carvalho, S., Ezemenari, K., Graham, C. and Thompson, A. (1997) *Safety net programs and poverty reduction: Lessons from cross-country experience*, Directions in Development, Washington, DC: The World Bank.

Tacoli, C. and Satterthwaite, D. (1999) *Sustainable urban livelihoods: Lessons from the experience of some urban poverty reduction programmes*, DfID Sustainable Urban Livelihoods Workshop, London: IIED.

Tendler, J. (1999) 'The rise of social funds: what are they a model of?', Mimeo, Cambridge: MIT, for UNDP.

Tendler, J. (2000) 'Why are social funds so popular?', in S. Yusuf, W. Wu and S. Evenett (eds) *Local dynamics in the era of globalization*, Oxford: Oxford University Press, for the World Bank.

Tjonneland, E.N., Harboe, H., Jerve, A.M. and Kanji, N. (1998) *The World Bank and poverty in Africa: A critical assessment of the Bank's operational strategies for poverty reduction*, Evaluation Report 7.98, Oslo: Royal Ministry of Foreign Affairs.

UNCTAD (United Nations Conference on Trade and Development) (2001) *Economic development in Africa: Performances, prospects, and policy issues*, Geneva: UNCTAD.

UNDP (United Nations Development Programme) (2000) *Human Development Report 2000*, New York, NY: UNDP.

Whitehead, A. and Kabeer, N. (2001) *Living with uncertainty: Gender, livelihoods and pro-poor growth in Sub-Saharan Africa*, Brighton: Institute of Development Studies.

World Bank (2001) *World Development Report 2000/1: Attacking poverty*, Washington, DC: World Bank.

World Bank Operations Evaluation Department (2001) *Letting communities take the lead: A cross-country evaluation of social funds*, Mimeo Draft, September, Washington, DC: World Bank.

World Bank Quality Assurance Group (1998) *Portfolio improvement program: Review of the Social Funds Portfolio*, I. Working Group for Social Funds Portfolio Review, Mimeo, September, Washington, DC: World Bank.

World Bank Social Protection Sector (2000) *Social protection strategy: From safety net to spring board*, Draft Final Report, August, Washington, DC: World Bank.

TEN

Urban water supply, sanitation and social policy: lessons from Johannesburg, South Africa

Jo Beall, Owen Crankshaw and Susan Parnell

Introduction

Although the inextricable relationship between ecology and society has long been understood (Yearly, 1991; Martell, 1994; Bruntland, 1997), the link between social policy and the environment in the industrialised countries, referred to here as 'the North', has only been drawn quite recently (Hill, 1993; Huby, 1998). That the environment is increasingly understood as a social policy issue derives in part from growing concern with the global commons (Yearly, 1996; Goldman, 1998[1]), and in part from changes in social policy itself, related to the valuing of integrated approaches and the promotion of intersectoral partnerships. It is in this context and alongside a convergence of paradigmatic approaches to social development internationally, that greater attention is being paid to lessons from late developing countries. This chapter engages with these issues through a discussion of the urban environment and, more specifically, urban water supply and sanitation in cities of the developing world, referred to here as 'the South'. We argue that social wellbeing is inextricably linked to secure access to an adequate and safe water supply, along with appropriate and affordable sanitation. As such, basic urban services constitute a critical area of concern for social policy in late developing countries. Through a case study of Johannesburg we consider the enormous challenges for urban governance that are presented by the dual requirement of addressing the pressing service needs of burgeoning numbers of historically disadvantaged urban dwellers, without compromising the standards of services and supply to better-off rate paying citizens. This chapter concludes by suggesting that while a policy focus on *basic* services might address urban poverty and indeed be environmentally sound, issues of inequality are not addressed.

Environmental health and the 'brown agenda'

While the North has for a long time been urbanised, this is a more recent phenomenon for the South. Nevertheless, it will soon be the case that more than half the world's population will be living in urban centres. In absolute terms, by 2000 the urban population of late developing countries was more than twice the urban population of industrialised countries, and by 2025 the global urban population is expected to be five billion, almost equal to the entire world population at present (Buckley, 1996). Moreover, it is from cities and towns that the majority of people already derive their livelihoods, either directly or indirectly. However, urban economic growth comes at a price, being closely associated with increased resource consumption. As urban populations grow, so do environmental problems such as pollution, congestion and hazards deriving from unsafe water, poor sanitation and inadequate waste management. One corollary of the scale and pace of urbanisation is increasing demand on urban services as well as deterioration in urban living standards and environmental quality.

International environmental activists have tended to see their task as protecting greenbelt environments from the inexorable encroachment of urban developers rather than one of preserving or developing cities. Globally the campaign for environmental justice has been firmly directed at the 'green agenda' (global warming, biodiversity, resource depletion and deforestation) and international agreements on these issues. The report of the World Commission on Environment and Development (Brundtland, 1987) dedicated only one chapter to the urban environment, and the United Nations Conference on Environment and Development (UNCED) (at the Rio Summit in 1992) was guilty of similar neglect, even though two thirds of recommendations in its *Agenda 21* document, the UNCED action plan, were to be taken at the local level (Atkinson, 1994). That single chapter on the urban environment identifies overcrowding, inadequate housing, inadequate access to clean water and sanitation, growing amounts of uncollected waste, and deteriorating air quality as key issues for cities and towns. Together these issues constitute what has become collectively known as the 'brown agenda'. This in turn has been defined as the most immediate and critical environmental problem facing cities in the South and "closely linked to the poverty-environment nexus" (Bartone et al, 1994). Ismail Serageldin of the World Bank has said that the "short-term urgency of this [brown] agenda adds to the moral urgency of reducing poverty and developing the world's poorest communities" (Serageldin et al, 1994, p 17).

The connection between environmental risk and ill health has been well known for a long time and, together with the well-known adage that 'germs don't carry passports', was the foundation upon which the impressive and resilient Victorian public health infrastructure of 19th century Britain was built. In cities of the South environmentalists have also made the link between poverty and ill health on the one hand and poor environmental conditions on the other (Bradley et al, 1991).

Poor living conditions are often characterised by contaminated water, inadequate or absent sanitation, the threat of floods, landslides or industrial pollution, often in circumstances of appalling overcrowding. For people living in cities today, the most threatening environmental problems are usually those close to home (McGranahan, 1993). As such, the urban environment in terms of the 'brown agenda' and its relationship to poverty and public health, is a critically pressing urban social policy issue.

The social dimensions of urban water supply and sanitation

Although hygienic conditions and safe water and sanitation are recognised as fundamental human rights (WSSCC, 2000a), 1.1 billion people in the world lack safe water and 2.4 billion do not have access to adequate sanitation, with over 90% living in Asia and Africa (WSSCC, 2000b). While people living in urban areas are more likely to have access to safe water and sanitation than rural dwellers, 173 million urban dwellers lack safe water and 403 million do not have adequate sanitation and live in conditions where the health risks are greater because of high population density (Harpham et al, 1988; Cairncross et al, 1990; Esrey, 1996a). Urban water supply and sanitation systems include the supply of fresh water, rainwater drainage, solid waste (refuse) collection and disposal, grey water (sullage) disposal and excreta (sewage) disposal. Most important for poverty reduction is access to a safe and affordable supply of drinking water. This is a basic human need and right for the present generation and a precondition for the development and care of the next. However, providing adequate quantities of safe drinking water is inextricably linked to the other elements of the system such as sanitation, drainage and solid waste management[2].

Water shortage, poor quality water or unreliable supply can have profound effects on people's wellbeing. At any one time, about half of all people in developing countries are suffering from one or more of the six main diseases associated with water supply and sanitation (diarrhoea, ascaris, dracunculiasis, hookworm, schistosomiasis and trachoma) (DFID, 1998, p 4) and, although improvements to water supply and sanitation are important for everybody, children are the most vulnerable to avoidable diseases resulting from lack of water, dirty water, lack of sanitation and poor hygiene education. In developing countries each child has an average of ten attacks of diarrhoea before the age of five, and one in ten children die of diarrhoea and dehydration (Institute of Child Health, cited in Black, 1994, p 1). Improved health status is a frequently cited goal of water and sanitation projects, although in practice the relationship between improved water supply and improved health is difficult to establish in the short term. Nevertheless, a reduction in health risk and environmental hazard can be demonstrated, and over the long-term significant health-associated benefits from improvements in water supply and sanitation provision have been demonstrated, measured by significant reductions in morbidity rates and higher child survival rates (WASH, 1990).

The benefits of safe water supply and sanitation provision go beyond improvements to health and wellbeing. Water is also a fundamental economic resource upon which people's livelihoods often depend, whether we are talking about cattle herders in rural Tanzania, washermen in Calcutta, batik makers in Accra or cooked food sellers in Buenos Aires.

Access to convenient and affordable water can save people time and energy, and enhance their livelihood opportunities. Beyond health impacts, improvements in sanitation also address issues of privacy and human dignity, which are significant and legitimate social development concerns, and can add value to properties and status to low income areas. These often less quantifiable benefits are usually among the advantages of water supply and sanitation reported by people in low-income communities themselves. It is often a surprise to engineers and urban development planners how people on very low incomes are prepared to pay quite a large proportion of their incomes for convenience and privacy in water supply and sanitation. Demand for water and sanitation or for particular levels of technology and delivery is commonly understood and measured through 'willingness to pay' rather than just need. However, this tends to obscure the issue of affordability. Since water is vital for life, poor people will go without almost everything else before they go without water. Consequently, they pay inordinately high proportions of their income for water, whether they access water from small-scale private water vendors or from formal sources.

There are also equity issues at work. Reticulated water supply and waterborne sewerage connections usually apply to better-off urban areas rather than to those occupied by poor urban dwellers. As such, resources for ongoing maintenance are channelled at existing rather than new services, which in turn attract service subsidies. This perpetuates a skewed distribution of infrastructure and services in cities. In terms of water quality, this is often threatened when people living in slums and informal settlements use local water bodies for ablutions. However, degradation of water quality is more likely to be a result of industrial effluents being discharged into streams, rivers and lakes. Many city authorities are themselves responsible for serious water pollution; for example, when untreated sewage and storm water drainage is fed into local water sources.

Technical and managerial issues in urban water supply and sanitation

It is ironic that while many of the urban poor may be located, quite close to existing service lines, the informal and unplanned nature of their settlements frequently precludes access to services. For example, informal settlements may be constructed on rocky terrain or steep hillsides. Settlement layout may bear little resemblance to the grid patterns of formal developments, and roads may be too narrow to accommodate trunk sewer lines, piped water and adequate drainage. A wide range of technical and management options for planning and providing urban infrastructure exists in these circumstances, including on-site technologies which can offer both affordable and sustainable long-term solutions. For example, pit latrines can be affordable, environmentally friendly and nowadays can be constructed in such a way that they are hygienic and inoffensive. Hence low-tech solutions need not necessarily be regarded as short-term or second best solutions and can often be the best in environmental terms. That said, there are many less tangible reasons why people prefer indoor flush toilets and piped water, such as convenience and the value it adds to their properties. It is for this reason that even for low-income households and areas, urban policy makers increasingly favour demand-driven approaches.

Historically, responsibility for rural water and sanitation in late developing countries has rested with ministries of health, while urban water supply and sanitation was usually divided between city administrations and central ministries of water affairs. Over the recent past there has been a trend towards turning water utilities into semi-autonomous public bodies, as a means of increasing private sector participation in urban water supply (World Bank, 1996). There has been a tendency, in relation to sanitation, to 'unbundle' responsibilities for different parts of the system (Wright, 1997), implying subsidiarity or management at the lowest appropriate level. However, if applied as a blanket or blueprint rule, this can lead to piecemeal approaches and a lack of agreement over norms and standards. Additionally, the two major UN international conferences related to the urban environment, The United Nations Conference on Environment and Development held in Rio de Janeiro in 1992 and the Habitat II Conference (or City Summit) held in Istanbul in 1996, emphasised the role of community involvement and management in water supply and sanitation. Both conferences placed emphasis not only on formal development partnerships, but also on effective urban service delivery on grassroots organisations and individual citizens.

The rationale behind intersectoral approaches has been to increase effectiveness and efficiency. Unfortunately, however much contracting out or privatising parts of the system might potentially relieve local authorities of onerous financial and administrative tasks, it can also lead to problems of coordination. While allowing local governments to shed responsibility for delivery and operational and maintenance responsibilities, these new approaches require that they take on a more strategic role. This involves more complex managerial tasks and the coordination of multiple organisations, something that is often beyond the competence of local authority structures in cities of the South. Although Johannesburg is better off in terms of financial and human resources than many cities of the South, it has faced many of these dilemmas and policy choices in the post-apartheid period and it is to this experience that we now turn.

Urban water supply and sanitation in post-apartheid Johannesburg

Greater Johannesburg is a city of about three million people but is part of an urban conurbation comprising a population closer to eight million. The city has recently emerged from a past dominated by apartheid policies and institutions where wealth, largely in the hands of white South Africans, was highly visible. Poverty by contrast, was mainly the fate of black South Africans and was discreetly hidden from view, either in distant rural reserves or townships and informal settlements on the far-flung peripheries of urban centres. The city and its environs constitute the industrial and commercial heartland of South Africa and, as home to the majority of the country's rich and well-educated population, average urban wages and overall levels of urban infrastructure in Johannesburg are relatively high by local and international standards. However, this obscures the extent of urban poverty and intra-urban patterns of inequality in Johannesburg. Many of the problems that are manifest in the city can be traced back to the very specific legacy of apartheid. However, the challenges facing the new post-apartheid Greater Johannesburg Metropolitan Council (GJMC) are not unique to South Africa and reflect those of highly unequal urban centres elsewhere in the South (Beall et al, 2002). As such, Johannesburg's successes and failures in addressing social disadvantage and disparity through the provision of infrastructure and services are lessons in urban social development elsewhere.

If access to water supply and sanitation is used as an indicator of urban poverty, then Johannesburg's poor are better off than many others living in cities in sub-Saharan Africa (see Chapter Nine of this volume), where 36% of the urban population are thought to be without a safe, regular or proximate water supply, and 45% are not covered by sanitation (WHO/UNICEF, cited in Nunan and Satterthwaite, 1999, p 7). In other words, nearly half of urban dwellers in sub-Saharan Africa do not have access to individual or communal toilets or latrines in their houses, compounds or settlements. It should also be pointed out that the situation of Johannesburg's poor also compares well with national figures. For example, it has been estimated that in the same period for South Africa as a whole, only 21% of households had access to piped water and only 28% to sanitation facilities. Over 80% of poor rural households had access to neither (May, 1998). Nevertheless, South Africa's urban centres are home to over half the total national population of around 38 million people (CCS, 1996). Ongoing urbanisation means that cities are expected to increase their proportional share of total population, so the state of urban infrastructure and services will constitute a pressing issue for some time to come.

According to surveys conducted at the time of the first democratic elections in South Africa in the mid-1990s, 18% of the total urban population, or about five million people, have only a minimal level of water supply. An additional 16% has access to only a basic water supply (PDG, 1994a). In the Johannesburg metropolitan area alone, about one million people had only a basic or minimal

Table 10.1: Soweto (Johannesburg) housing types

	Population by housing type
Formal public or council housing	613,565
Private sector housing	93,108
Backyard structures including additional outside rooms and informal shacks	391,749
Informal shack settlements	78,713
Hostels that formerly housed migrant workers	102,224
Site and service schemes[a]	46,676

[a] Where informal settlements are upgraded to formal housing through the council providing serviced plots on which residents or developers construct basic core (often single room) houses.

Source: Morris (1999)

level of water supply (PDG, 1994b), understood as access to a shared standpipe, a stream or river, or water delivered by municipal water trucks. Key among the many challenges facing Johannesburg at the time of the political transition from apartheid, therefore, was that of providing water to a divided and expanding urban population. Moreover, this had to occur in a context where there were water resource constraints nationally and an explicit commitment on the part of the post-apartheid national government to give priority to rural development.

The issues confronting the delivery of urban water supply and sanitation in contemporary Johannesburg cannot be investigated without understanding apartheid's legacy of social injustice in the city, seen no more starkly than through the vast and legendary disparities in the built environment. These are most visible in relation to the city's housing stock. Although most of Johannesburg's citizens (including black South Africans) live in formal housing, there is a rapidly expanding proportion of the urban poor who are housed in informal accommodation. This in turn is a complex category, comprising many different forms of accommodation. For example, while 46% of Soweto's population, which comprises apartheid's former African townships that lie to the south west of Johannesburg, live in ex-council houses (usually of four rooms), as many as 30% live in tiny backyard rooms. Moreover, only half of these are permanent structures; the rest are shacks (Table 10.1).

Differences and inequalities are more difficult to observe in the case of urban services, which are buried underground. Nevertheless there are a number of respects in which the apartheid legacy has impacted very directly on current service levels in Johannesburg. The most crude was the policy of providing inferior quality services for black people. While water was piped to all white homes under apartheid, most of which were also connected to the city's waterborne sewerage system, standards of social and physical infrastructure were intentionally set lower for black South Africans, and from 1968 investment in urban 'African areas' practically ceased altogether. As such, racially defined standards of construction and service gave tangible expression to the political

Table 10.2: Main source of domestic water by race (%) (authors' analysis of the 1995 October Household Survey)

	African	Coloured	Indian	White	All races
Tap in house/flat	67	100	100	97	80
Tap on the stand	29	0	0	3	18
Public tap/kiosk/borehole	4	0	0	0	2
Total	**100**	**100**	**100**	**100**	**100**

Source: Beall et al (2000)

Table 10.3: Main source of domestic water by type of housing (%) (authors' analysis of the 1995 October Household Survey)

	Formal dwelling		Informal dwelling				All housing types
	House or flat	In backyard	In backyard	Not in backyard	Hostel	Other	
Tap in house/flat	90	65	0	4	100	40	80
Tap on the stand	10	34	55	78	0	60	18
Public tap/kiosk/ borehole	0	2	45	18	0	0	2
Total	**100**	**100**	**100**	**100**	**100**	**100**	**100**

Source: Beall et al (2000)

and economic hierarchy on which white supremacy was based (Beall et al, 2000).

Therefore, although when compared to other African contexts, urban living standards in Johannesburg for all population groups and all housing types are relatively high, considerable inequalities remain. Indeed, it is the intra-urban inequalities in infrastructure and services that are most startling in Johannesburg. While these inequalities were premised almost entirely on race and segregationist policies under apartheid (see Table 10.2), there is now increasing evidence in the post-apartheid era of differentiation within the African population, with housing type being a reliable predictor of access to water (see Table 10.3). The worst off in terms of water supply are those living in informal settlements that piped water networks have yet to reach. A small fraction of the city's population depends on water from rivers and streams and there are limited cases where water is trucked into informal settlements. They are the most vulnerable as the supply is often irregular and unreliable and it is also a very expensive and unsustainable way for the municipality to deliver water to its residents.

While the figures from large-scale surveys – such as those used to compile

Table 10.4: Type of sanitation by housing type (%) (Johannesburg, Randburg, Roodepoort and Soweto only) (authors' analysis of the 1995 October Household Survey)

	Formal dwelling	Informal dwelling					All housing types
	House or flat	In backyard	In backyard	Not in backyard	Hostel	Other	
Flush toilet in dwelling	79	54	0	0	98	0	70
Flush toilet on site	20	43	55	13	2	100	23
Toilet off site (all types)	0	3	40	19	0	0	3
Other toilet on site (chemical and bucket)	0	0	0	50	0	0	3
Pit latrine on site	0	1	4	18	0	0	1
Total	**100**	**100**	**100**	**100**	**100**	**100**	**100**

Source: Beall et al (2000)

these tables – are revealing they do not always present the whole picture, and need to be supplemented by local level studies. A recent survey of informal settlements in greater Johannesburg demonstrated that as many as 12% of residents in clusters of poorly serviced land depend on non-piped water (CASE, 1998a). There is also a range of informal institutional arrangements that determine people's access to water. Compared with other cities of the South, purchase of water from private vendors is relatively uncommon in Johannesburg. However, rental arrangements mean that poor landlords charge even poorer tenants and subtenants for water, while in some informal settlements 'shacklords' control access to water sources such as communal standpipes. This means that many people in Johannesburg are paying for water, but are paying an intermediary rather than the service provider. Intermediaries in turn may well oppose overall improvements in water supply if they are making profits from existing sources of water.

With regard to sanitation, statistics reveal coverage in Johannesburg to be fairly extensive and the standard of formal sanitary services comparatively high, with flush toilets being the norm. Waterborne sewerage and wastewater treatments dominate over on-plot sanitation such as septic tanks and pit latrines, covering almost 80% of the metropolitan population. As Table 10.4 illustrates, 70% have flush toilets in their houses and 93% in their dwelling or on site. Historically, areas without waterborne sewerage used a bucket system, with local authorities being responsible for disposal of 'night soil'. However, today chemical toilets constitute the main form of on-plot sanitation, used most commonly in informal settlements, where they have to be shared among a large number of households.

Formal townships such as Soweto have bulk sewerage connections but even here there are still important differences in standards of sanitation. Results from the Soweto survey (Morris, 1999) show very clearly that it is only in the elite new private sector developments in Soweto that indoor flush toilets are the norm. Levels of service differ dramatically across different housing types and there are important variations within settlements and the issue of service standards has as much to do with the number of people per toilet as with the technical quality of the service. Moreover it cannot be disentangled from the social relations governing access. The micro-politics of access to sanitation have emerged from contextual studies rather than from large-scale surveys. For example, in Alexandra, a densely settled former township to the north of Johannesburg, it was found that 87% of households shared toilets. Many tenants complained that toilets did not always work and that landlords locked them at night to prevent unauthorised use, barring all but key holders from evening access. Many tenants living in backyard rooms or shacks, therefore, continue to use buckets inside their shacks or rooms, which they empty into the communal toilet once or twice a day. They are often required to clean ablution areas and toilets as part of their obligation as tenants, something many resented. Indeed, difficulties over sanitation were cited by interviewed squatters as one of the reasons for moving away from more centrally located townships to peripheral informal settlements. However, it would be wrong to suggest that sanitation is less contested in informal settlements, where tensions also exist in relation to access, cleaning and maintenance of toilets and sanitation areas. To reinforce the point that macro-level statistics of coverage do not tell all about access, the example of Soweto's hostels is worth citing. The hostels used to comprise single-sex barrack style accommodation for male migrant workers. Today many hostels have been refurbished and divided up into individual rooms or family accommodation. As such they are reported in the statistics as being low density and having flush toilets.

The hostels are desperately overcrowded and the bathrooms and toilets lacking in maintenance. The limited ablution facilities, which are used by women and children as well as men, are associated with the worst humiliations of abject living conditions such as lack of privacy, hygiene and basic dignity (Crankshaw, 1996; CASE, 1998b; Morris, 1999; Beall et al, 2000, 2002).

The politics of urban services in Johannesburg

The history of racial inequality and conflict in Johannesburg has meant that the political dimensions of urban service delivery have been ever present. Having denied African people political representation throughout the apartheid era, during the 1980s and in accordance with its policy of 'separate development', the nationalist government created elected Black Local Authorities (BLAs) which were charged with the task of taking over urban government in South Africa's former black South African townships. They commanded few resources and lacked credibility and legitimacy, and therefore received a lukewarm response that quickly turned into hostility when they were given the responsibility of introducing service charges. In the townships around Johannesburg their loss of legitimacy reached crisis proportions during the mid-1980s, when residents used the non-payment of rents and service charges as a political vehicle. The boycott of urban service charges resulted in increasingly widespread political mobilisation, first in Greater Soweto, then in other townships around Johannesburg and Pretoria and later across the entire country.

While protest against the undemocratic BLAs and the apartheid government was an important part of this urban movement, it had much to do with dissatisfaction with the services themselves. In response to a survey which asked why Sowetans supported the boycott, over half the respondents said it was because people thought housing and services were inadequate; around a third said it was because they were unaffordable (Swilling and Shubane, 1991) and it has been convincingly argued that the urban services issue only fuelled urban-based political action towards fundamental social change in South Africa (Mayekiso, 1996). It is also the case that once the political battle was won in 1994, protests over services continued. Despite the coming of democracy in South Africa, inadequate urban services persisted and so did Johannesburg's rent and services boycott, which has become so entrenched that it has proved difficult to stop. As Goldblatt has argued:

> The attraction to urban residents of not paying for services is obvious, particularly in the light of the slow delivery of improved urban services.... Uncontrolled rent and service boycotts are a powerful example of the role that external political forces can play in hampering sound financial performance of utilities. Although successful as a political strategy against inadequate services to black townships, the South African rent boycotts have had the perverse effect of limiting the ability of local government to improve services through the generation of what has been called a 'culture of non-payment' among urban residents. (1997, p 14)

The transitional local authority in Johannesburg tried to address its fiscal crisis by introducing a 150% increase in the rate bill of high-income areas. However, the wealthy property owners in one of the most affluent areas to the north of Greater Johannesburg, adopted boycott tactics too and demonstrated their objection by withholding payment. The notorious Sandton Rates Boycott, as it became known, was resolved by a constitutional court ruling that stated the municipal council was within its legal rights to levy the charges and the Sandton ratepayers settled their accounts. The incident was safely confined to history but this well-publicised boycott on the part of some of the city's more influential residents, served as a trenchant reminder to the local authorities that they had to be mindful of the priorities of powerful vested interests in the city. The challenge for the new metropolitan city council, then, was to address the high expectations of the city's historically disadvantaged and mainly black population, while at the same time being mindful of the resistance of better-off and mainly white residents, to financing the extension of services to others (Beall et al, 2000).

Policies for water supply and sanitation

In the immediate post-apartheid period, Johannesburg's municipal councils and the transitional metropolitan authority were acutely aware that the city's extensive network of water supply and sanitation coverage was not universal and standards varied enormously. As a result, extending the provision of services and the construction of infrastructure became a widely accepted priority for the Greater Johannesburg Metropolitan Council (GJMC) and infrastructure and services constituted critical areas of fiscal commitment in Johannesburg. In doing so the GJMC took its steer from national policy. The issue of water as a basic human right was dealt with by the 1996 Constitution, which stated that everyone had the right of access to sufficient water. In 1994 the Department of Water Affairs and Forestry (DWAF) produced a White Paper, which recognised that water was a basic human right but that its supply incurred costs that somehow had to be recovered. In policy terms, this DWAF translated into what it referred to as a 'lifeline' or 'social tariff', which meant that everyone was supposed to get a basic amount of free water, defined by the department as 25 litres of good quality water per person per day, provided at a maximum distance of 200 metres from the home and on a regular and reliable basis[3]. This benchmark, together with a policy of rising block tariffs[4] (where water is priced at a low initial rate up to a specified volume or block, and then at higher rates for successive specified volumes) received widespread acceptance in South Africa and Johannesburg (Beall et al, 2000)[5].

Within this framework, water supply and sanitation became the constitutional responsibility of local government, which had an obligation to ensure basic needs provision[6]. The position adopted by DWAF was that, where poor communities had no water supply and sanitation and were not able to afford basic provision, then the government could subsidise installation costs. However, DWAF was absolutely unswerving in their assertion that operating and maintenance costs had to be funded and entirely recoverable at a local level. As DWAF was not the only line ministry to devolve responsibility without resources to the local level, a key problem facing post-apartheid local government in South Africa was the issue of unfunded mandates. As Steven Friedman has argued:

> The term 'unfunded mandate' has become the buzzword of the day as lower tiers of government struggle to perform their tasks without being given the funds to do so.... Half a loaf, says the cliché, is better than no bread. But half-decentralisation in government can be worse than none. (1998, p 2)

In effect, the GJMC only controlled the operating budget for infrastructure and services, generated from rates and tariffs, but it also became involved in funding and managing capital expenditure, in order to provide new services to all those who were deprived under apartheid. Equally exercising the GJMC has been the fact that, under apartheid, the overall management of most of

Johannesburg's townships was funded by central government, but under the new political dispensation they became the responsibility of local government. For Johannesburg this meant that around half of the current population now needs to be funded out of the single metropolitan tax base (Beall and Lawson, 1999).

Against this background the GJMC opted for a commercial response to meeting its social responsibility. In an interview at the time that the council's medium-term policy document *iGoli 2002* was launched the then Chief Executive Officer of the GJMC made the following points:

> "Sixty five percent of Johannesburg's income is actual revenue from the sale of services and only thirty five percent of its income is a tax of some sort, either property or commercial. And I think the plan is basically suggesting that we become more commercially minded without undermining the need for political control, accountability and a focus on our social responsibility to provide services particularly to the poor.... This is a plan that tries simultaneously to address two very diverging constituencies. One is providing that basic level of service to the poor while upgrading systematically the services to the rich northern suburbs. I live in the northern suburbs and I would like the city to take basic responsibility for keeping the place clean and tidy and ensure that I get water and electricity and the lights work, and traffic lights operate and other basic things. The northern suburbs' residents are paying a huge premium for a very poor quality of service at the moment, and I think we owe them value for money. So that's the story of Johannesburg. That's the story of South Africa." (Beall and Lawson, 1999)

Ironically, the imperative of committing resources to the extension of services to the poor also raised awareness of the deteriorating condition of the ageing infrastructure in the rest of the city. Not all of the infrastructure and service challenges in Johannesburg can be ascribed to racist policies. The city is over 100 years old and, as it continues to grow, some of the contradictions of past planning and servicing are beginning to emerge (Parnell and Pirie, 1991). The most important technical demands on infrastructure and services are the increasing density of neighbourhoods in and near the city centre, and the dramatic expansion of low-income informal areas at its periphery. Approximately 10% of the area of the council has some spare bulk infrastructure capacity, and a further 60% would be able to cope with limited densification (GJMC, 1997). However, shortages in capacity are already apparent. There are also uncoordinated patterns of infrastructure provision across the city and, for example, sewerage and water supplies are not necessarily strong in the same locations and are showing signs of strain[7].

As a cash-strapped city government facing historical backlogs and competing constituencies, the GJMC saw increased revenue raising and enhanced financial stability as the only way of solving the tension that existed between maintaining established service levels in better-off and historically white areas, and extending services to poorer, under-serviced historically black areas. With these contradictions firmly at the forefront and in line with international thinking, Johannesburg produced *iGoli 2002* (GJMC, 1999), which made clear that the council was determined to establish the commercial viability of urban service delivery. The justification was improved efficiency and cost effectiveness, and the need to provide a solid fiscal foundation upon which to facilitate cross-subsidisation and the maintenance of service standards across the city. Within this framework, water supply, sanitation and solid waste management are considered 'trading services' that are meant to pay for themselves, and even make a profit. The utilities that deliver them operate as independent companies but with the council as the major shareholder and customer, as well as playing a regulatory role. There are strong neoliberal overtones to *iGoli 2002* and subsequent policy documents of the GJMC, which have been strongly influenced by international agencies such as the World Health Organisation (WHO) and the World Bank, with cost recovery becoming the mantra governing public provision and performance in South Africa (Goldblatt, 1997, p 6).

However, it was also evident to the council that the introduction of rates and service charges, no matter how minimal, would represent a significant increase in living costs for the poor (Beall et al, 2000). Nor could they ignore the popularly held view that under apartheid, Johannesburg's strong black-supported tax base allowed the city to subsidise white ratepayers. For reasons of social justice, therefore, it was recognised that some form of cross-subsidisation was warranted, in order to redress the past and to address the issue of substandard services in Johannesburg's townships and informal settlements (Bond, 2000). For example, those supporting a 'uni-city', or single city, model, under the slogan "One city, one tax base – one city, one future", recognised that inequities would persist if places such as Soweto only benefited from the wealth generated in the poorer southern part of the city. However, others – such as the Sandton Ratepayers – had a vested interest in confining redistribution to a more contained municipal area and one that was closer to home. They argued that the rates and services boycotts in Johannesburg's black African townships since the 1980s had meant that the state, supported by the contribution of white ratepayers, had effectively subsidised the consumption of water, sewerage and electricity in black residential areas for the past decade and more.

Another key post-apartheid debate relates to the issue of service standards and technology choice. A basic services approach has been adopted, largely under the advice of World Bank urban policy advisers, with shared communal standpipes being provided instead of house water connections and with on-plot sanitation or communal chemical toilets being the technology of choice over the extension of bulk waterborne sewerage connections. These are expeditious solutions, and therefore more politically responsive and more affordable. Indeed, one could also argue they are more environmentally sound than waterborne sewerage in a water scarce regional context. However, as high standard options were the norm for historically white areas and even some of apartheid's former black African townships, residents of informal settlements believe there are equity issues at stake and that the same standard of services should be extended to them. Opponents argue that excessively low standards – for example communal standpipes and pit latrines over on-plot or house connections and water-borne sewerage – are inappropriate for a country that the World Bank classifies as "upper middle-income" (Bond, 2000, p 54).

Johannesburg has pleaded clemency, arguing that it has faced a financial crisis that has compelled it towards fiscal austerity. Despite being cash-strapped and clearly without reserves, we have argued elsewhere that the financial 'crisis' in Johannesburg has been deliberately talked up in order to push through neoliberal policy reforms under difficult political conditions (Beall et al, 2002). A more valid defence might be that post-apartheid policy towards decentralisation has seen more and more responsibilities quietly devolving to the local level in a process we have elsewhere called 'decentralisation by stealth' (Beall et al, 2002). Consequently, urban infrastructure and services, which were traditionally the local government competencies, are now being crowded out by numerous other competing domains; for example, the implementation of health and education policies by local authorities. Without an adequate resource base and with increasing numbers of unfunded mandates, there are limits to how far the GJMC and other metropolitan and municipal governments in South Africa can tackle issues of poverty reduction and redistribution on their own. To take on the powerful elites of the city through redistributive rates and taxes has already proved to be a gargantuan task, and certainly one that will be impossible if they go against national policy trends, which in South Africa are increasingly neoliberal. For Johannesburg to make sustainable choices that consistently integrate social development goals and that address both poverty and inequality, the challenges it faces need to be supported within a national policy and institutional context.

Conclusions

Social inequalities in urban water supply and sanitation are bound up with institutional arrangements that are all too often biased towards addressing the interests of better-off residents and citizens rather than the needs of the urban poor. In this respect Johannesburg has done a good job in extending water supply and sanitation to low-income residential areas, particularly as competing interests in the city have chosen to exercise themselves along the fault line of urban services. Nevertheless, the consultative and participatory processes that permeated the first flush of post-apartheid democracy and which might assist Johannesburg in making and articulating difficult choices have not been sustained. Moreover, in Johannesburg and elsewhere, they are important but have proved to be no panacea. There is also the issue of service standards. Johannesburg has been relatively successful in delivering urban infrastructure and services to the poor through 'basic services' provision and in tackling the 'brown agenda'. However, the GJMC has been less brave in grasping the nettles of inequality and redistribution.

Manuel Castells (2002, pp ix-x) has recently argued that "Our blue planet is fast becoming a predominantly urban world and that in this context, *sustainable development* is the code word for the most important social debate of our time". And yet in environmental policy as with social policy, immediate interests and matters often take precedence over more sustainable, longer-sighted approaches. In the case of Johannesburg, the imperative for a 'quick-fix' is understandable and well-motivated – to extend service provision in a timely way to the most needy areas and to address the insecurities and anxieties of poor people. However, as with social policy everywhere, there are invariably other considerations at work. In the case of Johannesburg, these included not upsetting powerful 'apple carts' and keeping an eye on political futures and, some might argue, back pockets. If short-term concerns always take precedence over forward-looking strategies, even in the relatively progressive political and policy context of post-apartheid Johannesburg, then one has to wonder more generally at the prospects for policy that seeks simultaneously to sustain natural resources, create liveable urban environments and guarantee social wellbeing for future generations. Similar policy challenges were debated in Rio de Janeiro in 1992 and Johannesburg at the second Earth Summit in September 2002, with resolution still a distant goal. Although prospects are as yet limited, progress has been made internationally. At least at the Earth Summit in Johannesburg, urban issues were firmly on the agenda, particularly in relation to the 'brown agenda'. It remains for social policy makers, working internationally and transnationally, also to regard urban water supply and sanitation provision as a critical social policy issue.

Notes

[1] The term 'global commons' usually refers to the air, the atmosphere, the ozone shield, the seas, the forests and other depletable resources, as well as the communal natural resources, such as rivers and grazing land, on which many people depend for their livelihoods and survival.

[2] Providing an adequate supply of water alone is not enough, as water can quickly become unsafe. If people do not have appropriate sanitation, diseases can be spread through contamination of water. In many poorer parts of the developing world this is a cause of continuing concern. Many cities face a shortage of fresh water, which adds greatly to the problem of disposal of liquid wastes. In some contexts, however, an improved water supply alone can actually create public health problems by increasing sullage and exacerbating waste water disposal problems, if the drainage infrastructure does not exist. By the same token, poor solid waste management, being the collection and disposal of refuse, in addition to being a health hazard in itself, can block drains and sewers, preventing disposal of sullage and excreta, with all their attendant problems.

[3] The DWAF White Paper tries to balance its obligations to South Africa's historically neglected majority population, within the context of a water policy that does not endorse

free universal access to state supplied water. Indeed, Hardoy and Satterthwaite (1989) would see this as an outrageous underestimate of people's needs, and DWAF does recognise that this amount of water constitutes a bare minimum for health.

[4] This is a system where cross-subsidisation takes place within the water supply system itself (Cairncross, 1990, p 118).

[5] Targeting of any sort is costly and administratively complex, yet the GJMC has committed itself to what it calls "lifeline services" rather than lifeline tariffs, and believes that a universal approach is possible. However, this depends on having the technology and administrative capacity in place, and that is still not guaranteed. Moreover, the problems of monitoring consumption in the context of fluid populations and rapidly changing occupancy are notorious in cities of the South.

[6] A regional 'parastatal', or part-state-owned company, sells water to the GJMC, which is then responsible for water reticulation and the actual delivery of water and sanitation services within the metropolitan area.

[7] Personal communication with W. Ovens, Independent Planning and Local Government Consultant, Johannesburg, 1998.

References

Atkinson, A.B. (1994) 'Introduction: the contribution of cities to sustainability', *Third World Planning Review*, vol 16, no 2, May, pp 97-101.

Bartone, C.J., Bernstein, J., Leitmann, J. and Eigen, J. (1994) 'Toward environmental strategies for cities, policy considerations for urban environmental management in developing countries', *Urban Management Programme Policy Paper no 18*, Washington, DC: The World Bank.

Beall, J. and Lawson, S. (1999) *Smart Johannesburg: Leading the African renaissance?*, Milton Keynes: Open University audio-cassette.

Beall, J., Crankshaw, O. and Parnell, S. (2000) 'Victims, villains and fixers: the urban environment and Johannesburg's poor', *Journal of Southern African Studies*, vol 26, no 4, December, pp 833-55.

Beall, J., Crankshaw, O. and Parnell, S. (2002) *Uniting a divided city: Governance and social exclusion in Johannesburg*, London: Earthscan.

Black, M. (1994) *Mega-slums: The coming sanitary crisis*, London: Water Aid.

Bond, P. (2000) *Cities of gold, townships of coal: Essays on South Africa's new urban crisis*, Trenton, NJ: Africa World Press.

Bradley, C., Stephens, C., Harpham, T. and Cairncross, S. (1991) *A review of environmental health impacts in developing countries*, Washington, DC: The World Bank.

Brundtland, G. (1987) *Our common future*, The World Commission on Environment and Development, Oxford: Oxford University Press.

Buckley, R. (1996) 'Healthy cities: improving urban life', *Understanding Global Issues*, no 4.

Cairncross, S. (1990) 'Water supply and the urban poor', in J. Hardoy, S. Cairncross and D. Satterthwaite (eds) *The poor die young: Housing and health in Third World cities*, London: Earthscan, pp 109-26.

CASE (Community Agency for Social Enquiry) (1998a) *Investigating water and sanitation in informal settlements*, Johannesburg: CASE.

CASE (1998b) *Determining our own development: A community-based socio-economic profile of Alexandra*, Johannesburg: CASE.

Castells, M. (2002) 'Preface. Sustainable cities: structure and agency', in P. Evans (ed) *Livable cities? Urban struggles for livelihood and sustainability*, Berkeley. CA: University of California Press.

Central Statistical Services (1996) *Census 1996 – Preliminary estimates of the size of the population of South Africa*, Pretoria: Central Statistical Service.

Crankshaw, O. (1996) 'Social differentiation, conflict and development in a South African township', *Urban Forum*, no 7, pp 53-68.

DfID (Department for International Development) (1998) *Guidance manual on water supply and sanitation*, London: DfID.

Esrey, S. (1994) 'Water and sanitation service levels important for diarrhoea and nutritional status', *International Resources Centre Newsletter*, no 227.

Friedman, S. (1998) 'National government must stop passing the buck', *Synopsis*, vol 2, no 1, January, p 2.

GJMC (Greater Johannesburg Metropolitan Council) (1997) *Composite land development objectives*, Johannesburg: GJMC.

GJMC (1999) *iGoli 2002*, Johannesburg: GJMC.

Goldman, M. (ed) (1998) *Privatizing nature: Political struggles for the global commons*, London: Pluto Press.

Goldblatt, M. (1997) 'The provision, pricing and procurement of water: a willingness to pay survey in two informal settlements in Greater Johannesburg', MSc Dissertation, Faculty of Science, University of the Witwatersrand, Johannesburg.

Hardoy, J., Cairncross, S. and Satterthwaite, D. (eds) (1990) *The poor die young: Housing and health in Third World cities*, London: Earthscan.

Hardoy, J. and Satterthwaite, D. (1989) *Squatter citizen*, London: Earthscan.

Harpham, T., Tanner, M. and Tanner, T. (eds) (1995) *Urban health in developing countries: Progress and prospects*, London: Macmillan.

Harpham, T., Lusty, T. and Vaughan, P. (eds) (1988) *In the shadow of the city*, Oxford: Oxford University Press.

Hill, M. (1993) *Understanding social policy*, Oxford: Blackwell.

Huby, M. (1998) *Social policy and the environment*, Buckingham: Open University Press.

Martell, L. (1994) *Ecology and society*, Cambridge: Polity Press.

May, J. (ed) (1998) *Poverty and inequality in South Africa: Meeting the challenge*, Cape Town: David Philip Publishers.

Mayekiso, M. (1996) *Township politics, civic struggles for a new South Africa*, New York, NY: Monthly Review Press.

McGranahan, G. (1993) 'Household environmental problems in low-income cities: an overview of problems and prospects for improvement', *Habitat International*, vol 17, no 2, pp 105-21.

Morris, A. (ed) with Bozzoli, B., Cock, J., Crankshaw, O., Gilbert, L., Lehutso-Phooko, L., Posel, D., Tshandu, Z. and van Huysteen, E. (1999) *Change and continuity: Soweto in the late 1990s*, Johannesburg: Department of Sociology, University of the Witwatersrand.

Nunan, F. and Satterthwaite, D. (1999) *The urban environment*, Theme Paper 6, ESCOR Commissioned Research on Urban Development, University of Birmingham, International Institute for Environment and Development, London School of Economics, and University of Wales.

PDG (Palmer Development Group) (1994a) *Water and sanitation in urban areas: Financial and institutional review – An investment-tariff model for urban water supply*, Working Paper 15, Pretoria: Water Research Commission.

PDG (1994b) *Water and sanitation in urban areas: Financial and institutional review. Report Two: Overview of the demand for and costs of water supply and sanitation services in South Africa*, Water Research Commission Report no 571/2/94, Pretoria: Water Research Commission.

Parnell, S. and Pirie, G. (1991) 'Johannesburg' in A. Lemon (ed) *Homes apart, South Africa's segregated cities*, Cape Town: David Philip Publishers, pp 129-45.

Rees, W. (1992) 'Ecological footprints and appropriated carrying capacity: what urban economics leaves out', *Environment and Urbanization*, vol 4, no 2, October, pp 121-30.

Serageldin, I., Cohen, M. and Sivaramakrishnan, K.C. (eds) (1994) *The human face of the urban environment*, Environmentally Sustainable Development Proceedings Series no 6, Washington, DC: World Bank.

Swilling, M. and Shubane, K. (1991) 'Negotiating the urban transition: the Soweto experience', in R. Lee and L. Schlemmer (eds) *Transition to democracy: Policy perspectives*, Oxford and Cape Town: Oxford University Press, pp 223-58.

United Nations Centre for Human Settlements (Habitat) (1996) *An urbanizing world: Global report on human settlements, 1996*, Oxford: Oxford University Press.

WASH (Water and Sanitation for Health) (1990) *Principles of tariff design for water and wastewater services*, Field Report no 348, Washington, DC: USAID.

World Bank (1996) *World development report on infrastructure*, Oxford: Oxford University Press.

WSSCC (Water Supply and Sanitation Collaborative Council) (2000a) *Vision 21: A shared vision for hygiene, sanitation and water supply*, Switzerland: WSSCC.

WSSCC (2000b) *Global water supply and sanitation assessment*, Switzerland: WSSCC.

Wright, A.M. (1997) *Towards a strategic sanitation approach, UNDP/World Bank Water and Sanitation Programme*, Washington, DC: World Bank.

Yearly, S. (1991) *The green case: A sociology of environmental issues, arguments and politics*, London: Routledge.

Yearly, S. (1996) *Sociology, environmentalism, globalization*, London: Sage Publications.

ELEVEN

Round pegs and square holes: mismatches between poverty and housing policy in urban India

Sunil Kumar

Introduction

There is growing acknowledgement that poverty, especially in urban areas of poorer countries, is much more than just income poverty captured through poverty lines[1]. There is increasing consensus that poverty analyses should also take into account vulnerability, deprivation and wellbeing (Moser, 1995). These features of urban poverty are a set of relationships and a process, rather than a state (Rakodi, 1995).

Several manifestations of poverty arise from this wider definition, one of the most visible ones being the appalling housing conditions of the urban poor in low-income countries[2]. It is estimated that:

> at least 600 million urban dwellers in Africa, Asia and Latin America live in 'life- and health-threatening' homes and neighbourhoods because of the very poor housing and living conditions and the lack of adequate provision for safe sufficient water supplies and provision for sanitation, drainage, the removal of garbage, and health care. (UNCHS, 1996b, p 114)

More recently, the *State of the worlds cities 2001* report notes that:

> worldwide, 18 percent of all urban housing units (some 125 million units) are non-permanent structures, and 25 percent (175 million) units do not conform to building regulations. Most deficient housing units are found in the cities of developing countries, with more than half of all less-than-adequate housing units located in the Asia and Pacific region. (UNCHS, 2001b, p 30)

Official statistics would lead us to believe that 92% of the urban population in developing countries have access to water, and 80% to sanitation. However, independent analyses (for example, UNCHS, 2001a) provide damning condemnation of the reliability of these figures. Moreover, it also casts grave doubt over the appropriateness of the definitions of what is 'safe' and 'adequate' (UNCHS, 2001a, pp 122-6).

Housing is both a cause and an outcome of poverty, as it comprises differential access to resources and control over them. It is also an important component of urban social policy, since it intersects with a number of social concerns, such as livelihoods, health, gender, age, identity and citizenship.

Therefore, if deprivation underlies or extends to income poverty, what strategies should policy makers and planners adopt in addressing housing poverty? A large part of the problem concerns either a lack of understanding of the nature of the problem or an unwillingness to deal with the complexities of the living reality of the poor.

Despite a sea change in housing policy from the 1970s – when the conventional role of governments as providers of completed housing units began to give way to a non-conventional 'enabling' role involving the provision of serviced land sites (sites and services), or the environmental improvement of squatter settlements (upgrading) – most national housing policies continue to address housing problems through a mixture of formal planning processes and technical fixes. Ownership remains the primary means of conferring housing access and rights. This is evident, for example, in the recent Government of India's Draft Slum Policy (Government of India, 2001a). Contrast this with the fact that the inability of public authorities to meet the housing needs of the urban poor has created spaces that have been usurped by economic and political agents. Most housing is therefore produced outside of formal planning processes and is underpinned by complex informal social, political and economic relationships. These informal housing markets and submarkets are predicated on a combination of credit and tenure arrangements.

In this chapter I argue that contemporary housing policies are myopic to the living reality of the poor. The housing and tenure choices currently available to the poor are decisive to the urban livelihoods they pursue. The conundrum for policy makers and planners is how to retain this vitality while at the same time ensure that quality of shelter and services are improved. Tenure choice should be a key ingredient in any such attempt as it provides opportunities for tenants and landlords alike.

This chapter draws upon recent research entitled *Social relations, rental housing markets, and the poor in urban India* (Kumar, 2001b; henceforth referred to as the Indian Rental Study), conducted in two Indian cities – Bangalore, capital of the south Indian state of Karnataka, and Surat, the second largest city in the western state of Gujarat. Although these cities vary in population, the nature of their employment opportunities, the role of public housing and urban development institutions, and the extent and nature of kinship and ethnic networks, they illustrate the fact that rental housing is a thriving housing submarket, and that it plays a key role in housing the poor and providing opportunities for economic and social mobility.

Two contemporary developments – first, the changing global locus of urban–

rural population distribution, and second, widening perspectives on the nature of poverty, especially urban poverty – will be discussed briefly. Thereafter issues relating to tenure choice are examined in more detail.

Living in an urbanising world

In 2000, just under half of the world's population (47%) lived in urban areas. It is predicted that the majority will do so by the year 2007 (UN, 1999). These averages mask huge inter- and intra-regional variations. For example, it is estimated that three out of four people in Latin America and the Caribbean live in urban areas; just over one in two in Africa and Asia (UN, 1999)[3].

More importantly, the sheer number of urban dwellers in developing countries – 1.94 billion (68%) out of a total world urban population of 2.85 billion in 2000 – pose a serious challenge to city governments.

> Many urban managers are either 'unwilling' or 'unable' to deal with these pressures. 'Unable' because the scale of the problem is so enormous. In the course of the last decade for instance, developing countries have had to accommodate an astonishing 150,000 new urban dwellers every day. During this decade, the figure is likely to rise to 180,000 daily, or more than one million a week. This places huge pressures on access to land and shelter in already overcrowded settlements, on the capacity of infrastructure and service industries to meet rising demands, and on regulatory systems to protect workers from discriminatory and exploitative practices in formal and informal sector employment. It also places increased pressure on the ability of existing urban inhabitants to secure their livelihoods, where competition for land is intense and access to a regular flow of income is critical. The potential for corruption is high under these circumstances.... 'Unwilling' because many urban governance systems discriminate against the rights of particular groups of people and their governments manage their urban problems by dividing the poor between the legitimate (those entitled to services and citizenship rights), and the illegal. (DfID, 2001, pp 13-14)

As will be seen later, the 'unwillingness' as well as the 'inability' of policy makers at all levels permeates the formulation and implementation of a rental housing policy.

With one sixth of the world's population (1.03 billion), India is not as urbanised as other countries, such as those in Latin America for instance. India's urban population is currently estimated at 28% (Census of India, 2001) a modest increase of 2.1% since 1991. In absolute terms, however, this is an addition of just under 70 million people in ten years, roughly equivalent to five and a half times the current population of Mumbai or fifteen times that of Kolkata (the two largest cities).

There are competing views on where the emphasis of anti-poverty strategies should be. For example, the International Fund for Agricultural Development

Table 11.1: Urban and rural poverty in India

Year	Rural (%)	Urban (%)	Combined (%)	Rupees per person per month	
				Rural	Urban
1973-74	56.4	49.0	54.9	49.6	56.8
1977-78	53.1	45.2	51.3	56.8	70.3
1983-84	45.6	40.8	44.5	89.5	115.7
1987-88	39.1	38.2	38.9	115.2	162.1
1993-94	37.3	32.4	36.0	205.8	288.3
1993-94[a]					
Poverty gap	8.4	7.4	8.1		
Squared poverty gap[a]	2.8	2.4	2.7		

[a] World Bank (1997)

Source: Government of India (2001b)

argues that "the majority of the world's poor are rural, and will remain so for several decades. Poverty reduction programmes must therefore be *refocused* on rural people if they are to succeed" (IFAD, 2001, p 15, emphasis added). On the other hand, there are others who point to the lack of attention that urban poverty has received in the World Development Report 2000-01 (Amis, 2001). The issue is not a 'pro-rural' versus a 'pro-urban' one because strict demarcation between the two is fast diminishing (see the 'Introduction' in this volume and the special issue of *Environment and Urbanisation*, 1998). The issue is not just recognition of the difference between urban and rural poverty, but also the heterogeneity of poverty and the need to design anti-poverty strategies accordingly.

The majority of India's population live in rural areas – therefore, this is where the majority of the poor live. This should not however distract from taking urban poverty into consideration. Official Indian poverty line statistics indicate that the proportion of the urban and rural poor almost coincided in 1983-84 but widened slightly in 1993-94. More importantly, there are indications that there was little difference in the depth (poverty gap) and severity of poverty (squared poverty gap) between urban and rural areas in 1993-94 (World Bank, 1997).

Second, the ability to gain access to housing and services is more difficult in urban areas. The ninth five-year plan (1997-2002) estimates that the "new housing stock required is about 9.0 million units in urban areas and 7.7 million units in rural areas during 1997-2002 and about 77.0 million and 63.0 million units in the longer term perspective, extending up to 2021" (Government of India, 1997, para 3.7.11).

Changing perspectives on poverty

Issues relating to the measurement of poverty and the need to include wider indicators of deprivation and exclusion have been discussed at some length in an earlier companion volume to this book (Gordon and Townsend, 2000). Many of these concerns are applicable to poorer countries. However, there is a growing body of literature that has considerably widened and enhanced the nature and therefore the understanding of poverty in low-income countries (particularly in urban areas) that needs to be highlighted.

Since the 1990s, a renewed interest in poverty in middle- and low-income countries has been accompanied by a growing conceptual debate on the meaning and measurement of poverty. Proponents range from those who adopt conventional approaches (income or consumption) to those who believe that subjective, non-conventional and participatory stances better portray the diverse and local realities of the lives of the poor (Moser, 1998, p 2). This debate is important in so far as it emphasises the relevance of local contexts in poverty analyses as well as the policy and programme mismatches that are likely to arise if there is a lack of understanding of how the poor perceive poverty. Caution must therefore be exercised in relation to externally imposed poverty definitions.

A number of commentators have noted the inadequacy of either income- or consumption-based poverty lines for poorer countries, particularly for urban areas (see, for instance, Amis and Rakodi, 1995; Rakodi, 1995; Moser, 1996; Jonsson and Satterthwaite, 2000). Rakodi (2002) notes that, although consumption is generally considered to provide a better indicator than income, it is difficult to estimate in economies that are only partially monetised. Furthermore, she notes that levels of publicly supplied goods vary between households and may not always be included in consumption estimates. In short,

> poverty line analysis has neglected the dynamics of poverty and has failed to distinguish between transient and persistent poverty, and between different household trajectories: impoverishment, stability or improved well-being.... A further problem with poverty line analysis is that indicators based on household consumption do not capture all the dimensions of poverty, especially from the viewpoint of poor people themselves. (Rakodi, 2002)

This is not to say that previous accounts of 'income' and/or 'consumption' poverty line analyses have not stressed the importance of income in-kind, or the income that is equivalent to assets, or the value (in income) of access to free or subsidised public services, as necessary improvements in the determination of the poverty line (see Chapter Twelve, for example). Neither is it to say that multiple forms of material and social deprivation have not been used to compose the independent criteria for selecting an 'income' or 'consumption' poverty line (see for example Townsend, 1993; Appasamy et al, 1996; ; Nolan and Whelan, 1996; Gordon et al, 2000). The point is that such attempts to correct poverty lines have not permeated the measurement of urban poverty in developing countries, mainly due to the quality of the data sets.

However, there are signs that the gap between quantitative and qualitative measurements are narrowing, albeit slowly. For example, the production of the World Development Report 2000-01 was preceded by a series of consultations with the poor entitled *Voices of the poor*.

> As the new millennium begins, the World Bank has collected the voices of more than 60,000 poor women and men from 60 countries, in an unprecedented effort to understand poverty from the perspective of the poor themselves. *Voices of the Poor*, as this participatory research initiative is called, chronicles the struggles and aspirations of poor people for a life of dignity. Poor people are the true poverty experts. Poor men and women reveal, in particular, that poverty is multidimensional and complex – raising new challenges to local, national and global decision-makers. Poverty is voicelessness. It's powerlessness. It's insecurity and humiliation, say the poor across five continents. (World Bank, 1999)

The World Development Report 2000-01 recognises that the traditional view of material poverty (measured by income and consumption) should now also encompass non-material dimensions such as low levels of education and health. Moreover, the Report accepts that it "also broadens the notion of poverty to include vulnerability and exposure to risk – and voicelessness and powerlessness" (World Bank, 2001a, p 15). It argues that a broader characterisation of poverty not only enables its causes to be better understood but also emphasises the need for a broader range of policies since the "different aspects of poverty interact and reinforce one another in important ways" (World Bank, 2001a, p 15).

Widening perspectives on urban poverty

As noted earlier in this chapter, information about the incidence of urban poverty depends on estimates from nationally defined poverty lines. Rakodi (1995) has noted the numerous methodological difficulties associated with the use of poverty line measurements in urban areas. For example, it has been shown that poverty estimates vary widely for urban India depending on whether prices are used countrywide or are state specific, and when they are further differentiated by rural and urban prices at the state level (Minhas et al, 1992).

Apart from methodological difficulties, there are concerns as to whether poverty line analyses (especially in urban areas) capture all forms of deprivation. Satterthwaite argues that the scale of urban poverty is underestimated because income-based poverty lines do not account for other forms of deprivation and that they are set "unrealistically low in relation to living costs in urban areas, especially in large or prosperous cities" (2000, p 2). In a more recent paper he notes that "here we confront one of the mysteries of most poverty statistics –

they purport to measure the proportion of people 'living in poverty,' but exclude any criteria related to housing conditions, including access to water and sanitation" (Satterthwaite, 2002, p 4). Therefore:

> According to these definitions, a household with no secure home, no provision for water, sanitation and electricity, no access to health care, and no children in school would be considered as suffering the same deprivations as a household with the same income but with all these. This helps explain why estimates of the scale of urban poverty world-wide are so much lower than the estimates for the number of people living in very poor quality housing that lacks basic services. (Satterthwaite, 2002, p 4)

Moser et al (1996) identify three key aspects of urban poverty that distinguish it from rural poverty:

- commoditisation (reliance on the cash economy);
- environmental hazard (the density and location of the housing of the poor);
- social fragmentation (lack of community and inter-household mechanisms for social security).

In addition, the cost of living (particularly in large cities) is more expensive in terms of food, land, shelter and transport. Furthermore, although the urban poor are technically in closer proximity to public services they are often excluded both economically and politically (Satterthwaite, 2002).

Satterthwaite (2000), adopts the rural poverty pyramid proposed by Baulch (1996) to enhance an understanding of the nature of urban poverty. The pyramid here takes the form of inadequate income at the top and goes through a series of iterations resulting in a range of indicators at the bottom that include:

- inadequate income (and therefore inadequate consumption);
- limited asset base (non-material and material including housing) for individuals, households or communities;
- inadequate provision of 'public infrastructure' (piped water, sanitation, drainage, health care, schools, emergency services, etc) and therefore no 'safety net';
- inadequate protection from the law (for instance civil and political rights, health and safety in the workplace, environmental legislation, protection from violence and so on);
- voicelessness and powerlessness within the political system (and therefore no right or possibility to make demands and get a fair response);
- exploitation and discrimination (for example by gender, caste, age, and so on).

Cynics may argue that these broader deprivation indicators of urban poverty are equally applicable to rural areas. This may be the case but for the poor in urban areas, these aspects of poverty can be particularly acute (Rakodi, 1995; Beall, 1997).

Unfortunately, there is little sign of a narrowing of the gap between an improved understanding of poverty and institutional responses.

> Institutional responses ... tend to focus on income generation without considering the social, political and psychological factors which constitute the indivisible character of poverty. Public sector responses to poverty are also usually based on a simplified view of the poor as a homogeneous group. In reality, since the poor are very diverse in their difficulties, needs and capacities, they require a differentiated – but coordinated – assessment and response. (UNCHS, 1996a)

Such concerns are also echoed in relation to policies directed at the alleviation or eradication of urban poverty. The Recife Declaration on Urban Poverty, resulting from a meeting hosted by the UN Centre for Human Settlements (UNCHS, now UN Habitat) prior to the second UN Conference on Human Settlements in Istanbul in 1996, notes:

> Urban poverty presents a paradox for assessment and policy. For the poor, it is an indivisible whole, an ongoing, day-to-day reality. Yet for institutions established to eradicate it, poverty is a condition to be responded to with a diverse array of programmes, often compartmentalised, disparate and at best partially effective. There is a manifest discord between the unity of experience and the diversity of institutional responses. (UNCHS, 1996a)

It is clear that adopting a definition of urban poverty that includes vulnerability, deprivation, risks and shocks requires not only changes to poverty indicators, but also a framework that provides the basis for relational analysis.

As Rakodi notes:

> [T]his more sophisticated understanding of poverty and deprivation[4], as a set of relationships and a process rather than a 'state', implies that the poor are not passive.... The implications of improved understanding of the changing extent and nature of urban poverty are that a number of policy approaches are needed: safety nets for the most vulnerable; opportunities for households to increase their assets; assistance to enable people to take advantage of income earning opportunities; provision of basic utilities and services; and the creation of a policy framework, as well as legal and physical context which is favourable to the activities of the urban poor. (1995, p 407)

Livelihoods: recognising the multidimensional nature of urban poverty

A framework that is increasingly being adopted by a range of institutions for a multidimensional approach to an analysis and implementation of pro-poor poverty strategies is the 'sustainable livelihoods framework' (see, for instance, Ashley and Carney, 1999). The most widely used definition of a livelihood, drawing on Chambers and Conway (1992), is "the capabilities, assets (including both material and social resources) and activities required for a means of living" (Carney, 1998, p 4). The framework builds on five assets – natural, physical, human, financial and social – which the poor use to meet basic needs and buffer them from shocks and stresses. Access to and control over these assets are determined by policies, institutions and processes and thus set the wider vulnerability context within which the poor live[5].

Although the sustainable livelihoods framework originates from analyses of rural poverty, it is progressively being adapted to urban settings (Rakodi, 2002). In a study of household responses to poverty and vulnerability in four poor urban communities, Moser has elaborated an "asset vulnerability framework" that comprises five tangible and intangible assets[6]:

- labour;
- human capital;
- productive assets (such as land and housing);
- household relations;
- social capital (1996, p 24).

The basic premise of this framework is that the poor are "managers of complex asset portfolios [and] in highlighting both obstacles and opportunities in asset accumulation [it is possible to assess] how asset management affects household vulnerability" (Moser, 1998, p 1).

Moser defines vulnerability "as the well-being of individuals, households or communities in the face of a changing environment" (1996, p 24). She goes on to note that:

> Environmental changes that threaten well-being can be ecological, economic, social or political, and they can take the form of sudden shocks, long-term trends, or seasonal cycles. With these changes often come increasing risk and uncertainty and declining self-respect. Analysing vulnerability involves identifying not only the threat, but also the 'resilience' in exploiting opportunities and in resisting or recovering from the negative effects of the changing environment. The means of resistance are the *assets* that individuals, households or communities can mobilise in the face of hardship. Vulnerability is therefore closely linked to asset *ownership*. The more assets people have, the less vulnerable they are, and the greater the erosion of people's assets, the greater their insecurity. (Moser, 1996, p 24, emphasis added)

A brief overview of changes to urban housing policy follows before the relationship between tenure and the two key features of a livelihood perspective – 'assets' and the issue of 'ownership' – are explored.

International housing policy iterations

The principal thrust of housing policies in Asia and Africa in the mid-20th century was based on the notion of housing as a consumption good. The conventional wisdom at that time was that national governments would be responsible for housing their poor. This, within the then dominant paradigm of modernisation, took the form of the construction and delivery of completed housing units. Urbanisation was seen as being the domain of the better off, with the poor not only being viewed as parasites on city resources but their settlements and informal employment activities as matters that conflicted with the ideology of modernisation. Drastic measures were taken to prevent the migration of people from rural to urban areas and the expulsion of the poor back to their rural origins (Hardoy and Satterthwaite, 1989). Although this is a potted history of public authority attitudes to housing, it dominated housing policy until the early 1970s in Africa, Asia and Latin America (for Latin America, see for example, Rojas, 1995).

There are huge variations in the quantity and standards of publicly provided housing. These range, for example, from the Mark I to the Mark IV versions of public housing in Hong Kong (where services such as toilets and bathrooms were initially communal for the occupants of each floor of high rise housing blocks and were gradually brought in to the dwelling), to the one room and kitchen units (25-30 square metres) in four-storied walk-up tenements of Chennai (formerly Madras) India[7]. Indicators from selected cities in the developing world demonstrate that the construction of conventional housing units (public and private) rarely exceeds 10% of the total (UNCHS, 1996b).

Since then, however, there has been a sea change in housing policies. The role of governments as providers of housing gradually began to be replaced by an 'enabling role' under the broad rubric of aided-self-help housing policies. The main premise underlying this shift was that the poor are better managers of housing processes; governments need to facilitate this by the provision of serviced land, access to credit and a regulatory framework that was pro-poor (see, for instance, Turner, 1968, 1976; Skinner and Rodell, 1983; World Bank, 1983, 1993; Hardoy and Satterthwaite, 1989; Pugh, 1995). The two main urban housing strategies adopted in poor countries were upgrading (the in situ provision of infrastructure and the granting of land title) and sites-and-services (the provision of new serviced sites on which the poor could take control over house construction). Since the mid-1980s, however, upgrading has become the key housing policy. For example, between 1994 and 2000 the Inter-American Development Bank has lent US$4 million for neighbourhood upgrading projects in nine Latin American countries (see, IADB, 2000, p 8). In a similar vein are initiatives such as 'Cities without slums' (World Bank, 2001b).

Housing policy in India is illustrative of many of these iterations (Pugh, 1990). Although housing is a state subject (Ramachandran, 1989), national five-year plans[8] set out central and state expenditure within the wider framework of the National Housing and Habitat Policy (Government of India, 1998). Low priority has been accorded to housing (rural and urban) and urban development as evidenced from the budget allocations in the five-year plans (Table 11.2).

While 'enabling housing strategies' have become the cornerstone of housing policy in India, there seems to be little change in official attitudes to housing. Even within an enabling framework, housing that does not conform to conventional norms (brick walls and reinforced concrete roofs – house construction that in India is called 'pucca') is not really counted as housing. It is important to recognise housing as a process (Turner, 1972) and its wider links with employment and poverty alleviation (Mitlin, 2000). Despite the futility of estimating housing shortages using conventional norms (Hardoy and Satterthwaite, 1989), the housing problem in India is still expressed in terms of a shortfall in the number of dwelling units. For example, the ninth five-year plan (1997-2002) estimates that:

[The] new housing stock required is about 9.0 million units in urban areas and 7.7 million units in rural areas during 1997-2002 and about 77.0 million and 63.0 million units in the longer term perspective, extending up to 2021. Housing upgradation has to cover about 7.5 million units and 20.0 million units in urban and rural areas, respectively, during the Ninth Plan period. As regards drinking water, the aim is to cover the total urban and rural population with existing norm and then take up qualitative and quantitative upgradation. Total conversion of dry latrines into low-cost wet latrines is the immediate task in urban areas. (Government of India, 1997, para 3.7.11)

Table 11.2: Percentage allocation of budget for housing and urban development by five-year plan

Plan period	Housing and urban development (%)
I (1951-56)	2.1
II (1956-61)	2.5
III (1961-66)	1.5
IV (1969-74)	1.7
V (1974-79)	2.9
VI (1980-85)	2.6
VII (1985-90)	2.3
VIII (1992-97)	2.4

Source: Government of India (2002)

Tenants, landlords and housing tenure

The link between tenure and the lifecycle of households is not new: attention was drawn to it in the late 1960s. In the initial or 'bridge-header' stage, proximity to employment was the key priority with ownership figuring only in the 'status-seeker' stage (Turner, 1968). Turner makes this explicit when he notes that:

> [A] young, unskilled migrant to the transitional city will be primarily concerned with getting himself a job and, through it, an urban skill and income that will enable him and his (present or future) family to live tolerably well. A very cheap bedspace or, if he has a family, a rented room in a run-down tenement would be far more appropriate than a modern standard dwelling that would absorb an impossibly high proportion of his income ... unlike the mortgaged house, the rented room can be given up with very short notice, and the occupier is free to move quickly to another location.... Overcrowding, discomfort, and even the usually avoidable filth of the slum might be a price the aspirant to better living standards is quite willing to pay for improved opportunities. (Turner, 1968, p 355)

However, an emphasis on the provision of title deeds in sites-and-service projects and upgrading programmes has tended to result in tenure security and ownership being treated synonymously. Tenure security does not necessarily mean ownership but protection from arbitrary and illegal evictions either from land that is squatted upon or from accommodation that is rented. It is the illegality of the process in the former and the informality of the process in the latter that are the key elements that make policing and enforcing secure tenure problematic.

An interest in tenants in cities in poor countries began emerging only from the 1980s (see, for instance, Edwards, 1982; Gilbert, 1983, 1987, 1991; Gilbert and Varley, 1990). The main thesis forwarded was that tenants chose to rent but rented as a result of constraints on access to ownership (Gilbert, 1983). The 1990s saw the beginnings of research into the role of landlords (Gilbert and Varley, 1989; Aina, 1990; Edwards, 1990; Pennant, 1990; Hoffman et al, 1991; Datta, 1995; Kumar, 1996a; Crankshaw et al, 2000). These and other studies show that 'landlordism' in cities in poor countries is normally a small-scale activity (Edwards, 1982; Gilbert, 1983, 1987; Gilbert and Varley, 1989; Aina, 1990; Pennant, 1990) and in many instances landlords are as poor or even poorer than their tenants (Gilbert, 1983; World Bank, 1988; Lee-Smith, 1990; Gilbert et al, 1993)[9]. Much of this research, however, attempts to categorise landlords by the number of rooms rented – an empirical categorisation that does not help much as it does not provide the basis of cross-city comparison and was thus in need of theorising (Kumar, 1996b).

Tenure concerns have also been slow to appear on the international agenda. The first World Bank housing policy paper, entitled *Housing: Sector policy paper* (World Bank, 1975), made no reference to rental housing at all. However, in its second paper in 1983, there were a few paragraphs devoted to it (World Bank,

1983). And, in its third and latest housing policy paper in 1993, entitled *Housing: Enabling markets to work*, a couple of pages were devoted to the topic (World Bank, 1993). Similarly, it was not until the mid-1980s that the UNCHS produced a series of documents calling for more attention to be given to the rental housing option (UNCHS, 1989, 1990, 1993). Despite this body of research, landlordism in relation to the poor is often tainted with notions of 'exploitation':

> Much of the rest [of unauthorised dwellings] are built by 'slum-lords' for rent to low income people. (UNCHS, 2001b, p 30)

> A house provides a location for access to employment, collateral for securing credit, and is a potential source of income through renting out rooms and home-based or small scale enterprise. However, with high population growth rates and inappropriate government controls on land, housing and house construction, the cost of conventional housing is frequently beyond the reach of the majority of the poor. Rooms are therefore commonly rented from someone else, sometimes at exploitative rates. (DFID, 2001, p 18)

There are two interrelated contradictions in relation to rental housing that need to be resolved. First, that landlordism is an exploitative activity that needs to be discouraged. Monopolistic forms of landlordism (resulting in exploitative rents) are rare (Amis, 1988). Second, the activity of renting a room is often used to illustrate the asset value of housing. Thus, promoting home ownership for all inherently reduces such an asset value. In sum, if the renting out of rooms is an activity that reduces the vulnerability of the poor and enhances their livelihood opportunities, all landlordism cannot be bad.

Similarly, the poor can only let rooms if there is demand from tenants. This is another area where there is a serious mismatch between housing policy and the role of housing as an asset. Therefore, although India's national housing policy recognises the need for taking tenure into consideration, particularly rental housing (Government of India, 1998), the issue of rental housing does not figure in the recent *Draft national slum policy* (Government of India, 2001a). There is a need for a more balanced and tenure neutral approach to housing policy.

Social relations and rental housing markets

In relation to housing tenure, there are three key features that underpin mismatches between official policy and the lived reality of the poor. These are the need to recognise, (1) access as an asset; and (2) opportunity as an asset. Both of these are inextricably linked to livelihoods. The third mismatch relates to the embedded nature and complexity of social, economic and political relationships that characterise the usurped spaces within which the agents of informal housing markets operate. Each of these can be illustrated from the Indian Rental Housing study.

Access as an asset

Emphasising the physical components of housing (for example, land, finance, construction, and infrastructure) and housing markets as the World Bank (1993) housing policy paper – *Housing: Enabling markets to work* – does, detracts from the opportunities that housing creates for a range of tenure groups. The Indian Rental Housing Study argues that in Bangalore as well as Surat, tenure choice provides opportunity for both landlords and tenants, albeit differently.

In 1991, Bangalore had 2.7 million people living within its municipal boundary, the majority of whom were second or third generation residents. Access to land is particularly critical partly because of its extensive acquisition by the state for the setting up of national defence, telecommunications and electronics industries (Heitzman, 1999) and the involvement of a number of urban development authorities. This has led to a clustering of livelihood opportunities for the poor in certain geographical areas of the city (Benjamin, 2000). Access to many of these opportunities are predicated on recommendations or social guarantees to be able to obtain credit (for example in the case of iterant traders or waste recycling) or hire a vehicle (as in the autorickshaw trade). The chances of being recommended is improved with residing locally. Therefore, for those unable to own property, access to rental accommodation becomes an important part of securing an urban livelihood (Kumar, 2001b).

The picture in Surat is somewhat different. Sixty per cent of the city's 1991 population of 1.5 million is estimated to be first generation migrants (Shah, 1997), while the figure in squatter settlements is estimated to be as high as 80% (Das, 1994). Two main industries – textiles and diamonds – dominated employment in the mid-1990s, providing work for a third of the workforce, estimated at 1 million (Breman, 1996). The predominantly migrant nature of Surat's population enhances the importance of rental accommodation and provides a 'waiting-room function' for those seeking to settle in the city. For those without such intentions, such as the migrants from the states of Orissa and Andhra Pradesh (the former employed in the powerloom sector, and the latter in the dyeing and printing industry) rental housing provides the much needed space to ensure that remittances home are maximised. Cheap rental accommodation and the social practice of a number of single men being able to share accommodation are common strategies (Kumar, 2001b).

Common to both cities, is the fact that the rental housing that is produced is diverse in its location, quality and levels of services. This not only enlarges choice but, more importantly, reduces the extent to which the poor are excluded from getting housing at all.

Opportunity as an asset

For landlords, the opportunity to generate rents by letting out rooms is an asset. As the income from rent in Bangalore and Surat is not the landlords' main source of income, the letting of rooms adds to a diversification of their livelihood portfolio. This therefore reduces vulnerability. The low-income rental housing market is a continuum of responses for landlords – for most it is a subsistence activity, for others it provides the chance to improve material wellbeing and for some is a primary livelihood (Kumar, 1996b, 1996c). It is important to note that there were only a few instances of large-scale renting, especially in Surat. This helps to dispel the myth that rental housing markets are monopolistic and thus exploitative.

Similar to many other cities in poorer countries, renting was found to be a common stage in the trajectory of household residential mobility in both Bangalore and Surat for two reasons – land and credit. Access to land in Bangalore is primarily mediated through market exchange and to some extent political patronage. In contrast, access to land in Surat is predominantly secured through kinship or caste networks rooted in employment niches in the diamond and powerloom industries. Formal institutional credit is rarely available to the poor in either city. In Bangalore, where an upfront payment for land is the norm, savings and credit groups are the main forms of raising finance. Residential mobility by those living in squatter settlements takes place by investment in privately developed quasi-legal residential settlements.

In Surat the predominant channels of credit are predicated on dyadic ethnic or caste relationships between private land developers and their clients. Those seeking to settle in the city, accessed land through contact with their supervisors (both in the powerloom and diamond industries) who had now assumed the role of land developers. Ethnic relationships developed in the workplace have been transferred to land markets to provide the credit and security for the purchaser and seller alike. The renting of rooms is also closely linked to the nature of employment. Work in both the diamond and powerloom industries is short lived mainly as a result of the nature of the work involved as well as working conditions. Workers in both industries seek to find alternative livelihoods – in petty trading or services – with the renting out of rooms providing a safety net during this transition. Migrants in the powerloom industry repeatedly stressed the importance of being able to find low-quality rental accommodation, and the ability of being able to reduce the rent burden by sharing with other people. This served two purposes: it reduced monthly rent, and increased remittances. This helps highlight another mismatch between official policy and lived reality – that of standards appropriate to the priorities of individuals and households.

In Bangalore, another innovative mechanism – the lease – was found to be in extensive use. This involved tenants making lump sum payments to landlords for a fixed period (normally three years) in return for rent-free accommodation and the return of the deposit (without interest as this is replaced by rent-free accommodation) after the lease period is over. Tenants benefit from this practice in a number of ways: they are ensured of tenure security for that period, the pressure to find monthly rent disappears, and the lump sum payment acts as a form of savings. Landlords also benefit: they are able to use the lump sum for business investment, invest in upgrading their dwelling or to meet consumption expenditure. This lease system was found to be less common in Surat, primarily due to the way in which the city's population is constituted and the predominance of kinship and ethnic ties.

There is a certain vibrancy in the operation of rental housing markets in both cities. Rarely were rooms found to be vacant – as compared to the middle-income rental market with high void rates. This is not because the poor are risk averse, but that they are not able to afford the luxury of holding on to vacant rooms.

Explanations of the variations in the operation of low-income rental housing markets in the two cities are complex. They derive from a mixture of the nature and level of government intervention, the changing nature and significance of social networks and the demand and supply dynamics related to local employment structure and practices (Kumar, 2001a). In all, these complexities are intricately linked to production as well as the consumption of rental accommodation in particular and residential mobility in general. The relationship between rental housing markets and the livelihoods of the poor is thus more than just housing as it is conventionally viewed. The tenure on which accommodation is made available is adapted to bridge the needs of both owners and prospective occupants. Much of this mismatch is the result of a top-down approach that focuses on conferring ownership rights without recognising that the difference and diversity of urban residents, within and between cities, requires a more flexible policy that increases the housing options of the poor. When the need is huge, and resources relatively scarce, more improvisation in the provision of housing is required: more temporary accommodation of a short-term nature, incentives for owners to build rooms for rent and opportunities intending occupants to be able to save towards ownership in the future.

Usurped spaces and informal relations

A combination of the inability and the unwillingness of governments to cater to the housing needs of poorer individuals has not only resulted in the poor having to find their own solutions but has unwittingly created opportunities that economic and political power brokers have capitalised upon. Therefore, the vast majority of the poor access housing through mechanisms that are not legally recognised or approved. In other words, there is a mismatch between the formulation of housing policy and the way in which the urban poor access housing in urban India.

In both Bangalore and Surat, the majority of the poor live in squatter settlements. The housing mobility of the better off among the poor is in the form of access to private developer led settlements where the sale of land is legal but the use of land for housing contravenes land-use regulations. Access to both is political and belonging to the right networks is crucial in terms of information sharing and the provision of 'social' guarantees for credit. The vertical dyadic relationships that underpin access to these housing submarkets is the primary channel for housing transactions and the resolution of disputes. The Global Report on Human Settlements recognises the nature of these relationships:

> [I]n many countries, for low-income families, rental – which is the most used form of tenure – is seldom formal or regulated. Agreements are arrived at informally, with little or no recourse to legal advice, and the agreements are enforced in a non-legal manner.... Indeed, a major part of the Campaign [for secure tenure] will have to address the urban poor segment of the rental sector, and the tension that exists between secure tenure for tenants and sub-tenants and the property rights of the owners. Both in percentage and in policy terms, addressing the informal rental sector will be one of the most significant challenges for the Campaign, and the one which will have the most impact for the urban poor.
>
> Secure tenure is but the first component of the progressive realisation of the right to housing; a necessary but insufficient condition for a successful shelter strategy that will lead to further economic and social benefits. Within the context of tenure, an overall strategy must necessarily be concerned not only with strengthening security of tenure, but also with developing and supporting appropriate forms of tenure.... For economic and political reasons, housing policies typically are not 'tenure neutral', but seek to promote home ownership through a variety of means.... Housing policies must recognise the range of relevant tenure alternatives and provide each with alternative support. (UNCHS, 2001a, p 207)

Recognising the existence of these relationships is the first step. In addition there is the need to also recognise that it is these relationships that mediate access as well as resolve disputes. Pro-poor poverty interventions that are piecemeal and ignore the significance of dyadic relationships for the poor increase the vulnerability of the latter as it gives rise to a breakdown of trust between dyadic actors.

Conclusion: the starting point *matters* in determining tenure choice

This chapter has argued that there is a wide gap between institutional positions on housing policy and the needs and priorities of the poor in urban India. Little attention has been given to the juxtaposition of livelihood opportunities with housing processes[10]. Tenure security is the only discussion relating to housing tenure, with the granting of legal title being the principal means by which tenure security is to be ensured (Banerjee, 2002). *In sum, the emphasis is on ownership.* There is little recognition of the poor's diverse needs and the way in which informal markets, especially rental housing markets, cater to this diversity. There is also little sign of attempting to incorporate lessons from studies of informal processes of land supply and or credit arrangements –

especially the extent to which they are able to quickly respond and adapt to the needs of poorer individuals and households. The politics of housing the poor is ignored.

One of the most critical determinants of a move from a preoccupation with ownership to more diverse tenure arrangements and opportunities is the need to reconcile the long-term intentions of housing policy with the short- to medium-term needs and priorities of the poor. Therefore, *the premise is important*. Almost all low-income households are known to prefer ownership to renting. However, when questioned about their ability to pay for ownership and considering the weak institutional capacity of governments to make ownership accessible to all, local realities soon become evident. It must not be forgotten that ownership has a cost that is often more than renting. The starting point therefore should not be what tenure is politically astute but what forms of tenure are most appropriate given current realities and the role of such forms of tenure in creating opportunities for reducing the more intangible effects of urban poverty. The unfavourable treatment of rental housing pushes this important housing market underground. Neither landlords nor tenants benefit.

There needs to be more open debate on how the production of rental accommodation can be supported and encouraged. The politics of ownership invite careful scrutiny. Tenure neutral policies by their nature necessarily involve a range of actors and strategies. The involvement of not-for-profit organisations as providers and managers of rental housing should be considered. Lessons from Bangalore, where tenants are able to raise lump sums to pay short-term leases, could provide capital for rotation if non-governmental organisations were to be involved in the provision of rental housing. The formalisation of such relationships would help guarantee the safe return of lease deposits. There are also lessons from the experience of 'housing associations' in the UK, for example. Poor households could be encouraged to produce and manage rental accommodation with the help of formal institutional support. Means could be found of providing credit to poorer households to build rooms for rent and ensure that part of the rental income could be used to repay the loans. This is how the informal process works in Surat. In some ways, this would serve to redistribute income between poorer and better-off households. Finally, given that private land developers currently play a significant role, their involvement should also be explored. Government agencies on their own are unlikely to replicate the wide ranging provision of informal providers. Therefore, housing policies need to be devised so that the activities of informal providers could be incorporated within formal processes. A mixture of policies and programmes that better reflect the reality on the ground are likely to be more successful than one-dimensional responses to the multidimensional needs of the poor. It is time to rethink round solutions to square needs.

Notes

[1] See, for instance, Amis and Rakodi, 1995; Rakodi, 1995; Baulch, 1996; Moser, 1996; Moser et al, 1996; UNCHS, 1996b; Satterthwaite, 2000; World Bank, 2001a.

[2] The term housing is used in the broad sense of the word to include physical dwelling and the associated physical (water, sanitation, electricity, and so on) and social infrastructure (schools, clinics, and so forth).

[3] It is important to note that the definition of an urban area varies widely. It would only take, for example, a change in the Indian or Chinese definitions to alter this figure radically (UNCHS, 1996b).

[4] Although the two concepts of poverty and deprivation are joined together here, they are not synonymous. It is important to keep them distinct and to treat deprivation as the independent criterion for choosing the level of income that represents the core meaning of poverty.

[5] The importance of assets is also recognised by the *World Development Report 2000-01: Attacking poverty*:

> Lacking assets is both a cause and an outcome of poverty. Poor health, deficient skills, scant access to basic services, and the humiliation of social exclusion reflect deprivations in personal, public and social assets. Human, physical and natural assets also lie at the core of whether an individual, household or group lives in poverty – or escapes it. These assets interact with market and social opportunities to generate income, a better quality of life, and a sense of psychological well-being. Assets are also central to coping with shocks and reducing the vulnerability that is a constant feature of poverty. (World Bank, 2001a)

[6] Income does not figure in the asset framework as a combination of assets can give rise to livelihood strategies and supports that are income, as well as non-income, based. Social networks that provide moral support or access to credit are some examples of non-income based livelihood support structures.

[7] Most housing construction statistics provide data on the number of conventional housing units constructed. These are rarely disaggregated into public and private sector contributions. In addition, there is little data on the space or quality standards of public housing.

[8] Gaps in the five-year plans are replaced by national plans.

[9] An exception to this are the rental housing markets in Nairobi (see, for instance, Amis, 1984, 1988, 1996; Syagga et al, 2002).

[10] For example, the Tamil Nadu Slum Clearance Board has been awarded a third prize in the all-Indian Low Cost Housing Competition on Squatter Settlements for the resettlement of 10,000 families in a site situated about 15km south of the city. These families were displaced as a result of the construction of a mass rapid transport project. Although located in different parts of the city no mention is made of what impact this has had on their livelihoods. The managing director of the Housing and Urban Development Corporation (HUDCO), a national level housing agency, is reported to have stressed the architectural and engineering challenges that the project has faced (Ahmed, 2002).

References

Ahmed, F. (2002) 'TNSCB Thoraipakkam model bags low-cost housing prize', *The Hindu*, 26 April (www.hinduonnet.com/stories/).

Aina, T.A. (1990) 'Petty landlords and poor tenants in a low-income settlement in metropolitan Lagos, Nigeria', in P. Amis and P. Lloyd (eds) *Housing Africa's urban poor*, Manchester: Manchester University Press, pp 87-101.

Amis, P. (1984) 'Squatters or tenants – the commercialization of unauthorized housing in Nairobi', *World Development*, vol 12, no 1, pp 87-96.

Amis, P. (1988) 'Commercialised rental housing in Nairobi, Kenya', in C.V. Patton (ed) *Shelter: International perspectives and prospects*, Philadelphia: Temple University Press, pp 235-57.

Amis, P. (1996) 'Long run trends in Nairobi's informal housing market', *Third World Planning Review*, vol 18, no 3, pp 271-85.

Amis, P. (2001) 'Attacking poverty: But what happened to urban poverty and development?', *Journal of International Development*, vol 13, no 3, pp 353-60.

Amis, P. and Rakodi, C. (1995) 'Urban poverty: concepts, characteristics and policies', *Habitat International*, vol 19, no 4, pp 403-05.

Appasamy, P., Guhan, R., Hema, R., Majumdar, M. and Vaidyanathan, A. (1996) *Social exclusion from a welfare rights perspective in India*, Geneva: International Institute for Labour Studies

Ashley, C. and Carney, D. (1999) *Sustainable livelihoods: Lessons from early Experience*, London: DfID.

Banerjee, B. (2002) 'Security of tenure in Indian cities', in A. Durand-Lasserve and L. Royston (eds) *Holding their ground: Secure land tenure for the urban poor in developing countries*, London: Earthscan, pp 37-58.

Baulch, B. (1996) 'Neglected trade-offs in poverty measurement', *IDS Bulletin*, vol 27, no 1, pp 36-42.

Beall, J. (1997) 'Assessing and responding to urban poverty: lessons from Pakistan', *IDS Bulletin*, vol 28, no 2, pp 58-67.

Benjamin, S. (2000) 'Governance, economic settings and poverty in Bangalore', *Environment and Urbanisation*, vol 11, no 2, pp 35-56.

Breman, J. (1996) *Footloose labour*, Cambridge: Cambridge University Press.

Carney, D. (1998) 'Implementing the sustainable rural livelihoods approach', in D. Carney (ed) *Sustainable rural livelihoods: What contribution can we make*, London: DfID, pp 5-23.

Census of India (2001) *Population, population in the age group 0-6 and literates by residence and sex – India and States/Union territories: 2001*, New Delhi: Office of the Registrar General (www.censusindia.net/results/).

Chambers, R. and Conway, G. (1992) *Sustainable rural livelihoods: Practical concepts for the 21st century*, Brighton: Institute for Development Studies, University of Sussex.

Crankshaw, O., Gilbert, A. and Morris, A. (2000) 'Backyard Soweto', *International Journal of Urban and Regional Research*, vol 24, no 4, pp 841-57.

Das, B. (1994) *Socio-economic study of slums in Surat City*, Surat: Centre for Social Studies, South Gujarat University Campus.

Datta, K. (1995) 'Strategies for urban survival? Women landlords in Gaborone, Botswana', *Habitat International*, vol 19, no 1, pp 1-12.

DfID (Department for International Development) (2001) *Meeting the challenge of urban poverty*, London: DfID.

Edwards, M. (1982) 'Cities of tenants: renting among the urban poor in Latin America', in A. Gilbert, J.E. Hardoy and R. Ramirez (eds) *Urbanisation in Contemporary Latin America*, London: John Wiley & Sons, pp 129-58.

Edwards, M. (1990) 'Rental housing and the urban poor: Africa and Latin America compared', in P. Amis and P. Lloyd (eds) *Housing Africa's urban poor*, Manchester: Manchester University Press, pp 253-72.

Environment and Urbanisation (1998) 'Beyond the rural–urban divide', Special Issue.

Gilbert, A. (1983) 'The tenants of self-help housing: choice and constraint in the housing markets of less developed countries', *Development and Change*, vol 14, no 3, pp 449-77.

Gilbert, A. (1987) 'Latin America's urban poor: shanty dwellers or renters of rooms?', *Cities*, vol 4, no 1, pp 43-51.

Gilbert, A. (1991) 'Renting and the transition to owner occupation in Latin American cities', *Habitat International*, vol 15, no 1/2, pp 87-99.

Gilbert, A., Camacho, O.O., Cohlomb, R. and Necochea, A. (1993) *In search of a home: Rental and shared housing in Latin America*, London: UCL Press.

Gilbert, A. and Varley, A. (1989) *The Mexican landlord: Rental housing in Guadalajara and Puebla*, London: Institute of Latin American Studies.

Gilbert, A. and Varley, A. (1990) 'Renting a home in a third world city: choice or constraint?', *International Journal of Urban and Regional Research*, vol 14, no 1, pp 89-108.

Gordon, D. and Townsend, P. (eds) (2000) *Breadline Europe: The measurement of poverty*, Bristol: The Policy Press.

Gordon, D., Adelman, L., Ashworth, K., Bradshaw, J., Levitas, R., Middleton, S., Pantazis, C., Patsios, D., Townsend, P. and Willaims, J. (2000) *Poverty and social exclusion in Britain*, Kork: Joseph Rowntree Foundation.

Government of India (1997) *Ninth Five-Year Plan*, Planning Commission (www.planningcommission.nic.in/fiveyr/).

Government of India (1998) *National housing and habitat policy*, New Delhi: Ministry of Urban Affairs and Employment.

Government of India (2001a) *Draft national slum policy*, New Delhi: Department of Urban Employment and Poverty Alleviation, Ministry of Urban Development and Poverty Alleviation (urbanindia.nic.in/slumpol.htm).

Government of India (2001b) *Indian planning experience: A statistical profile*, New Delhi: Planning Commission.

Government of India (2002) *Urban India*, New Delhi: Ministry of Urban Affairs and Employment Policies (urbanindia.nic.in/policy.htm).

Hardoy, J.E. and Satterthwaite, D. (1989) *Squatter citizen: Life in the urban third world*, London: Earthscan.

Heitzman, J. (1999) 'Corporate strategy and planning in the science city – Bangalore as "Silicon Valley"', *Economic and Political Weekly*, vol 35, no 5, pp PE2-PE11

Hoffman, M.L., Walker, C., Struyk, R.J. and Nelson, K. (1991) 'Rental housing in urban Indonesia', *Habitat International*, vol 12, no 1/2, pp 181-206.

IADB (Inter-American Development Bank) (2000) *Social development, sustainable development*, Department, Social Development Division (www.iadb.org/sds/doc/SOC-Nov2000E.pdf).

IFAD (International Fund for Agricultural Development) (2001) *Rural poverty report 2001: The challenge of ending rural poverty*, Oxford: Oxford University Press.

Jonsson, A. and Satterthwaite, D. (2000) *Income based poverty lines: How well do the levels set internationally and within each country reflect (a) the cost of living in larger/more prosperous/more expensive cities; and (b) the cost that the poor have to pay of non-food items*, Mimeo, London: International Institute for Environment and Development.

Kumar, S. (1996a) 'Landlordism in Third World urban low-income settlements: a case for further research', *Urban Studies*, vol 33, no 4/5, pp 753-82.

Kumar, S. (1996b) 'Subsistence and petty capitalist landlords: a theoretical framework for the analysis of landlordism in Third World low income settlements', *International Journal of Urban and Regional Research*, vol 20, no 2, pp 317-29.

Kumar, S. (1996c) *Subsistence and petty-capitalist landlords: An inquiry into the petty commodity production of rental housing in low-income settlements in Madras*, unpublished PhD dissertation, London: Development Planning Unit, UCL.

Kumar, S. (2001a) 'Embedded tenures: private renting and housing policy in India', *Housing Studies*, vol 16, no 4, pp 425-42.

Kumar, S. (2001b) *Social relations, rental housing markets and the poor in urban India*, London: Department of Social Policy, London School of Economics and Political Science.

Lee-Smith, D. (1990) 'Squatter landlords in Nairobi: a case study of Korgocho', in P. Amis and P. Lloyd (eds) *Housing Africa's urban poor*, Manchester: Manchester University Press, pp 175-87.

Minhas, B.S., Kansal, S.M. and Jain, L.R. (1992) 'The incidence of urban poverty in states (1970-1 to 1983)', in B. Harriss, S. Guhan, and R.H. Cassen (eds) *Poverty in India: Research and policy*, Bombay: Oxford University Press.

Mitlin, D. (2000) 'Addressing urban poverty: increasing incomes, reducing costs, and securing representation', *Development in Practice*, vol 10, no 2, pp 204-15.

Moser, C.O.N. (1995) 'Urban social policy and poverty reduction', *Environment and Urbanisation*, vol 7, no 1, pp 159-71.

Moser, C.O.N. (1996) *Confronting crisis: A comparative study of household responses to poverty and vulnerability in four poor urban communities*, Washington, DC: World Bank.

Moser, C.O.N. (1998) 'The asset vulnerability framework: reassessing urban poverty reduction strategies', *World Development*, vol 26, no 1, pp 1-19.

Moser, C.O.N., Gatehouse, M. and Garcia, H. (1996) *Urban poverty research sourcebook module II: Indicators of urban poverty*, Washington, DC: UNDP/UNCHS (Habitat)/World Bank.

Nolan, B. and Whelan, C.T. (1996) *Resources, deprivation and poverty*, Oxford: Clarendon Press.

Pennant, T. (1990) 'The growth of small-scale renting in low-income urban housing in Malawi', in P. Amis and P. Lloyd (eds) *Housing Africa's urban poor*, Manchester: Manchester University Press, pp 189-201.

Pugh, C. (1990) *Housing and urbanisation: A study of India*, New Delhi: Sage Publications.

Pugh, C. (1995) 'The role of the World Bank in housing', in B.C. Aldrich and R.S. Sandhu (eds) *Housing the urban poor: Policy and practice in developing countries*, London: Zed Books.

Rakodi, C. (1995) 'Poverty lines or household strategies: a review of conceptual issues in the study of urban poverty', *Habitat International*, vol 19, no 4, pp 407-26.

Rakodi, C. (2002) 'A livelihoods approach: conceptual issues and definitions', in C. Rakodi (ed) with T Lloyd-Jones *Urban livelihoods: A people centred approach to reducing urban poverty*, London: Earthscan, pp 3-22.

Ramachandran, R. (1989) *Urbanisation and urban systems in India*, New Delhi: Oxford University Press.

Rojas, E. (1995) *The IDB in low-cost housing: The first three decades*, Washington, DC: IADB.

Satterthwaite, D. (2000) 'Urban poverty: what do recent insights into its nature and causes imply for reducing it', Paper prepared for the Swiss Agency for Development and Cooporation (mimeo), London: IIED.

Satterthwaite, D. (2002) 'Poverty and exclusion among urban children', Paper prepared for UNICEF (mimeo), London: IIED.

Shah, G. (1997) *Public health and urban development: The plague in Surat*, New Delhi: Sage Publications.

Skinner, R.J. and Rodell, M.J. (eds) (1983) *People, poverty and shelter: Problems of self-help housing in the Third World*, London: Methuen.

Syagga, P.M., Mitulla, W. and Karirah-Gitau, S. (2002) *Nairobi situation analysis supplementary study: A rapid economic appraisal of rents in slums and informal settlements*, Nairobi: UNCHS (Habitat).

Townsend, P. (1993) *The international analysis of poverty*, Hemel Hempstead: Harvester Wheatsheaf.

Turner, J.F.C. (1968) 'Housing priorities, settlement patterns and urban development in modernising countries', *Journal of the American Institute of Planners*, vol 34, no 5, pp 354-63.

Turner, J.F.C. (1976) *Housing by people*, London: Marion Boyars.

Turner, J.F.C. (1972) 'Housing as a verb', in J.F.C. Turner and R. Fitcher (eds) *Freedom to build*, New York, NY: Macmillan, pp 148-75.

UN (1999) *World urbanisation prospect: The 1999 revision* (www.un.org/esa/population/publications/wup1999/urbanization.pdf).

UNCHS (United Nations Centre for Human Settlements) (1989) *Strategies for low-income shelter and services development: The rental housing option*, Nairobi: UNCHS (Habitat).

UNCHS (1990) *Rental housing*, Proceedings of an expert group meeting to review rental systems and rental stability, jointly organised by the UNCHS (Habitat) and the Institute for Housing Studies, Nairobi: UNCHS (Habitat).

UNCHS (1993) *Support measures to promote rental housing for low-income groups*, Nairobi: UNCHS (Habitat).

UNCHS (1996a) *Urban poverty: A world challenge*, The Recife Declaration, Recife: UNCHS (Habitat).

UNCHS (1996b) *An urbanising world: Global report on human settlements*, Oxford: Oxford University Press.

UNCHS (2001a) *Cities in a globalising world: Global report on human settlements 2001*, Nairobi: UNCHS.

UNCHS (2001b) *The state of the world's cities 2001*, Nairobi: UNCHS (Habitat).

World Bank (1975) *Housing: Sector policy paper*, Washington, DC: World Bank.

World Bank (1983) *Learning by doing: World Bank lending for urban development: 1972-82*, Washington, DC: World Bank.

World Bank (1988) 'Weighing the benefits of rent control', *Urban Edge*, vol 12, no 7, pp 1-6.

World Bank (1993) *Housing: Enabling markets to work*, Washington, DC: World Bank.

World Bank (1997) *India: Achievements and challenges in reducing poverty*, Washington, DC: World Bank.

World Bank (1999) *Voices of the poor*, Washington, DC: World Bank (www.worldbank.org/poverty/voices/).

World Bank (2001a) *World development report 2000-2001: Attacking poverty*, Oxford: Oxford University Press.

World Bank (2001b) *Upgrading urban communities: Cities without slums*, Washington, DC: World Bank (www.worldbank.org/urban/urb_pov/up_body.html).

TWELVE

Urban poverty in China: incidence and policy responses[1]

Athar Hussain

Introduction

Poverty in China used to be regarded as a largely rural phenomenon. The urban poor were assumed to consist of a small group characterised by the three 'no's – no ability to work; no savings or other income source; no relatives to depend on. The able-bodied were expected to work, and the government was under obligation to provide them with a job, albeit at very low pay. Since the mid-1990s, however, urban poverty has come to be seen as a problem that potentially threatens a substantial percentage of the urban population.

There are three differences between the 'old' and the 'new' urban poor:

- the new urban poor outnumber the old urban poor;
- the emergence of new urban poverty is in tandem with rising inequality in urban areas. The contrast between the 'haves' and the 'have nots' is starker now more than ever in the Republic of China's (PRC) history;
- unlike the old urban poor, a large percentage of the new urban poor are able and willing to work but have no jobs.

The first two differences are related. The rise in urban poverty is due partly to a changing perception of poverty. Urban poverty, which in the past was barely distinguishable from the then prevalent living standard, now stands out against the background of a comparatively high and rising average living standard. The third difference is the distinguishing feature of new urban poverty, and one that reflects a fundamental change in the urban economic environment, especially from 1994. The public sector[2], traditionally the main source of employment for the urban labour force, has been losing jobs. In the period 1995-2000 the sector lost 48 million jobs, 33.4% of the total in 1995. The non-public sector has been creating new jobs but not in sufficient numbers to offset job losses.

This chapter sets out to answer two sets of questions. Firstly, how many urban poor are there in China, and what percentage of the urban population do they represent? Secondly, what social safety nets are there to rescue the urban population from poverty? In order to answer the first set, I draw upon urban household data collected by the Chinese National Bureau of Statistics, using 'best practice' described in the Appendix to this chapter. The second set of questions is answered in terms of an assessment of the two income maintenance schemes that serve as supports of the social safety net for the urban population.

Incidence and patterns of urban poverty

The poverty lines that underlie the estimates of urban poverty in this chapter (Table 12.1) represent the expenditure per person in Chinese currency (yuan ¥) on basic food and non-food items. (The determination of this 'basic' expenditure is explained in the Appendix.) In the first instance, the poverty lines are determined separately for each of the 31 Chinese provinces using the urban household data for 1998. It is these poverty lines which are used to estimate the number of poor. The national poverty line, which is not used for estimation, is calculated by taking the arithmetic mean of provincial poverty lines weighted by respective provincial shares of the total urban population. For 1998, this comes to ¥2,310 per person per year, which requires only a minor adjustment to be valid for 2002 because of very low inflation subsequently. How does this compare with the $1 per person per day line ($1.08 per person per day in 2001) promoted by the World Bank, and widely used as the indicator of the minimum acceptable living standard in developing economies? A reasoned answer to this question is premised on answers to the following two related questions:

- What does $1 per person per day actually represent in terms of living standard?
- What exchange rate should be used to convert $1 per person per day into domestic currency?

It is not clear what $1 per person per day exactly represents in terms of living standard – just adequate food or a bare minimum of non-food necessities as well[3]. Turning to the dollar/yuan ($/¥) exchange rate, the current market rate of $1= ¥8.27 is not appropriate because it is not a Purchasing Power Parity (PPP) rate. That is, $1 buys far less in the US than ¥8.27 does in China. The implication is that in terms of PPP $1 is worth less than ¥8.27. However, it is not known how many yuans one dollar is actually worth. The $/¥ PPP rate used by the World Bank is the inflation adjusted rate[4] computed in 1994 on the basis of available price data for 1992 and 1993. The computed rate was based on a number of strong assumptions and was one of the several and widely divergent rates that were computed[5]. Even if one assumes that the calculated PPP rate provided a reasonable approximation to the actual PPP rate in the first half of the 1990s, the same is far from the case in 2002. Relative prices have undergone a major change since then. A price index can adjust for inflation but not substantial changes in relative prices. Despite its wide currency and the air of authority that surrounds it, $1 per person per day is more of a hindrance than a help in the analysis of world poverty (see Deaton, 2001; Srinivasan, 2001).

Given a poverty line (see the Appendix for a description of this chapter's derivations), a household is poor if it falls below the line. However, it can do so in two different ways: either its *income* per capita or its *expenditure* per capita is lower than the poverty line. As the time patterns of income and expenditure diverge, the headcount of the poor can differ significantly depending on whether income or expenditure per capita is used as the poverty indicator. In contrast to the usual pattern, as we shall see below, the headcount of the poor in China in terms of expenditure per capita is much higher than that in terms of income per capita. The implication is that among households above but near the poverty line savers outnumber non-savers, which is the reverse of the usual situation. Leaving aside why this may be so, there are arguments both for and against using either income or expenditure per capita. Neither side is decisive enough to rule out the alternative. The argument in favour of using income per capita is that it indicates whether the household is financially capable of financing the expenditure indicated by the poverty line without resorting to borrowing, an option that may not be available. This fits in with means testing which is concerned with resources at the disposal of households not with how they actually use their resources. However, one has to be clear that a household classified as non-poor in terms of income per capita may actually be spending less than the poverty line and thus going short on basic needs. It may be doing so for one of various reasons, such as saving to purchase durable goods or to cater for a future contingency, or repaying a loan. The conclusion is that there is a strong argument in favour of measuring the incidence of urban poverty in terms of both income per capita and expenditure per capita to get an idea of the difference the choice of the identifier of poverty makes.

The estimate of the number of poor presented here contributes to a better understanding of the topical issue of urban poverty in China. However, it is subject to three limitations arising from the method of measurement. First, the basic needs that serve to define a poverty line are blurred at the edges. Focusing on the cost of satisfying basic needs, poverty is separated from its converse by a range rather than a line, which may convey a mistaken impression of clarity (Deaton, 1997). A practical way of addressing this deficiency is to present the headcount and the poverty rate for a number of poverty lines, which are defined here by shifting the reference line (Table 12.2). Second, assuming agreement on basic needs, the cost of meeting them – rather than being the same for all – may vary with individuals or households. To take two examples that have a particular resonance in urban China, the cost of medical care for individuals suffering from a chronic illness is of a different order of magnitude from that for healthy individuals. Similarly the cost of schooling is a substantial expenditure for households with children, but not for those without. By its very nature, a poverty line glosses over differences in the cost of meeting basic needs across individuals or households, which can be very large. Third, the translation of 'basic needs' into a sum of money is fraught with omissions and distortions. Some of the goods and services that satisfy basic needs in a particular social context may have prices or conditions of access that differ with individuals. In urban China, housing, schooling and medical care are examples of such goods and services. House rents and prices can vary widely in the same city because housing is still far from being fully commercialised. Similarly medical care cost depends crucially on whether or not the individual is covered by health insurance. Migrants generally have to pay more for housing, schooling and medical care than permanent residents. Both the second and third limitations described here deal with the problems of differential incidence of poverty across individuals or households because of variation in attributes or socioeconomic status (for a discussion see Townsend, 1993). The appropriate way of dealing with such problems is to supplement the perception of poverty in terms of a poverty line complete with indices of deprivation in specific dimensions such as under-nutrition, inadequate housing and insufficient medical care. This is not done here due to a lack of appropriate data.

Turning to a profile of urban poverty, Table 12.1 presents the provincial headcount and headcount rate using income per capita and expenditure per capita respectively as the indicator of poverty. The figures refer to 1998 and are presented separately for each of the 31 Chinese provinces. Individual provinces are used as the basic units of analysis rather than China as a whole because of their large populations and heterogeneity. The largest, Henan, has a population of 92.6 million, and 14 provinces have a population of over 40 million each (figures apply to 2000). They also differ widely in the levels of development and economic structure. The national headcount of the poor (the last row) is the sum of the provincial total, and the national poverty rate is the weighted average of the provincial rates, with provincial population shares as weights. Here, income refers to income net of taxes (disposable income) and, in turn, expenditure is net of expenditure on consumer durables. The immediately striking feature of Table 12.1 is the huge difference a switch from *income* to *expenditure* per capita makes. The national headcount and the poverty rate shoot up by over 250%, from 14.7 million to 37.1 million, or from a rate of 4.7% to 11.9%, when the poor are identified in terms of expenditure per capita instead of income per capita. This huge increase, which is also obtained for rural areas, emphasises the importance of reporting the poverty headcount and rate in terms of both indicators, rather than just one. Further, the increase caused by the switch varies widely across provinces; it is dramatically high (more than 400%) in five provinces and comparatively modest (between 100% and 200%) in eight.

The higher headcount in terms of expenditure per capita than that in terms of income per capita suggests that low-income households tend to have positive savings. Further, for a large number of such households savings are sizeable enough such that they have a higher income per capita but a lower expenditure per capita than the relevant poverty line. For this to be the case, it is not necessary that households have large savings relative to their income, but simply that their incomes per capita are only slightly higher than the poverty line. Our preferred explanation of the huge

Table 12.1: Urban poverty patterns (1998)

	Headcount of the poor			Poverty rate	
	Income p/h (1)	Expenditure p/h (2)	% ratio (1)/(2) (3)	Income p/h (4)	Expenditure p/h (5)
Beijing	54,000	422,000	7.73	0.7	5.6
Tianjin	360,000	969,000	2.69	6.8	18.2
Hebei	651,000	2,010,000	3.08	5.2	16.0
Shanxi	596,000	1,637,000	2.75	7.2	19.7
Inner Mongolia	510,000	1,778,000	3.48	6.4	22.3
Liaoning	1,150,000	2,383,000	2.07	6.1	12.7
Jilin	853,000	1,295,000	1.52	7.5	11.4
Heilongjiang	1,154,000	2,743,000	2.38	6.9	16.5
Shanghai	314,000	584,000	1.86	3.2	6.0
Jiangsu	244,000	1,298,000	5.33	1.2	6.4
Zhejiang	153,000	463,000	3.02	1.6	4.9
Anhui	348,000	1,060,000	3.04	2.9	8.8
Fujian	145,000	319,000	2.19	2.2	4.8
Jiangxi	310,000	1,261,000	4.07	3.4	13.9
Shandong	1,172,000	4,689,000	4.00	5.0	20.2
Henan	1,410,000	3,088,000	2.19	8.4	18.4
Hubei	934,000	1,763,000	1.89	5.7	10.7
Hunan	462,000	1,336,000	2.89	3.6	10.4
Guangdong	154,000	244,000	1.57	0.7	1.1
Guangxi	246,000	620,000	2.52	3.0	7.6
Hainan	150,000	418,000	2.78	7.9	22.1
Sichuan	711,000	1,102,000	1.55	4.7	7.3
Guizhou	260,000	864,000	3.33	5.0	16.6
Yunnan	225,000	595,000	2.64	3.7	9.7
Tibet	39,000	65,000	1.68	11.3	19.1
Chongqing	260,000	548,000	2.11	4.1	8.6
Shaanxi	932,000	1,567,000	1.68	11.9	20.1
Gansu	304,000	792,000	2.60	6.4	16.8
Qinghai	76,000	131,000	1.73	5.6	9.8
Ningxia	210,000	403,000	1.92	13.5	25.9
Xinjiang	383,000	625,000	1.63	6.2	10.1
Total	**14,770,000**	**37,072,000**	**2.51**	**4.7**	**11.9**

difference that the switch in the indicator makes to the poverty headcount is that, ranked according to income per capita, households are densely clustered around the poverty line. This is confirmed by an examination of how the poverty rate changes when the poverty line is shifted, while keeping income per capita as the poverty indicator. Table 12.2 presents the national poverty rates with respect to a schedule of hypothetical poverty lines, expressed as multiples of the national poverty line.

The notable feature of Table 12.2 is the very large change in response to comparatively small shifts in the poverty line. An increase in the national poverty line by 15% (denoted by 1.15*PL in Table 12.2) raises the national poverty rate by as much as 72.7% – from 4.7% to 8.2% of the urban population. Raising the poverty line by another 10% (denoted by 1.25*PL) raises the national poverty rate by 43.2% – from 8.2% to 11.1% of the urban population. The latter rate is close to the poverty rate when expenditure instead of income per capita is used as the indicator. This indicates that, in terms of impact on the national poverty rate, the change in the poverty indicator from income to expenditure per capita is equivalent to raising the poverty line by just over 25%, while keeping income per capita as the indicator.

What implications follow from the high sensitivity of the poverty rate to a comparatively small shift in the poverty line? One straightforward implication is the importance of checking the robustness of the poverty rate (or the headcount) estimates to shifts in the poverty line. The second implication that is relevant to policy is that a significant percentage of the non-poor urban population remains highly susceptible to a fall into poverty. Such a fall may be the result of a relatively small reduction in income or, for example, a rise in irregular expenditure such as that due to a serious illness. The latter is equivalent to a reduction in income in the sense that the affected households are forced to cut expenditure either on food or on non-food items. This suggests that the focus of poverty alleviation measures should not be confined to those who fall below the poverty line, it should also extend to the population with a high risk of falling into poverty. The appropriate policy response with respect to the latter group is not social assistance but increasing the capability of low-income households to cope with risks, by, for example, provision of health insurance against serious illness. The vulnerability of a substantial percentage of the urban population falling into poverty as a result of a comparatively small decrease in household income per capita also emphasises the importance of a social safety net that covers all urban populations rather than – as occurred in the past and often continues to do so – a small section of the population with no ability to work, no savings and no relatives to depend on.

Table 12.2: Sensitivity of the poverty rate

Poverty line as multiple of the poverty line (PL)	National poverty rate
0.75*PL	1.9
0.85*PL	3.4
PL	4.7
1.15*PL	8.2
1.25*PL	11.1
1.35*PL	14.4
1.5*PL	20.1

Note: Poverty rates are measured with respect to income per capita.

Table 12.3: Regional variation in urban poverty rates

Regions	1995 poverty rate (1)	1998 poverty rate (2)
Total average	6.6	4.7
Eastern	5.0	3.3
Central	8.9	5.9
Western	5.8	6.2

Another notable feature of Table 12.1 is the wide variation in the provincial poverty rates. The provinces with very low rates are, with the exception of Beijing, all coastal and among the richest provinces. Beijing, being the capital, is very similar to a coastal province. The ones with high rates are all interior and mostly in the west. However, the pattern in between the two extremes is mixed. Table 12.3 presents a summary picture of interprovincial variation in poverty in terms of the three-part grouping of provinces into 'Eastern', 'Central' and 'Western' for 1995 as well as for 1998[6].

In both 1995 and 1998, the eastern provinces have a below average and the central ones an above average poverty rate. Whereas these two groups of provinces experienced a substantial fall in the poverty rate between 1995 and 1998, the western region saw its poverty rate rise over the period. On a comparable basis the rural poverty rate is between two to three times higher than the urban rate (see also Ruizhen and Yuan, 1992, 1996; Khan, 1998; Gustafsson and Zhong, 2000). Maintaining the geographical focus, the regional distribution of the urban poor is very different from that of the rural poor (Table 12.4).

The western region with close to half of the rural poor (47%) has less than a quarter of the urban poor (23%). In contrast, the eastern region, which has slightly higher than 10% of the rural poor (11%), has close to one third of the urban poor (31%). The major reason for the contrasting pattern of rural and urban poverty is that the proportion of the urban population in the total is much higher in the eastern than in the western provinces. As a result, the eastern provinces end up with almost a third of the urban poor, despite their below average poverty rate (Table 12.3). A policy implication is that a narrow geographical targeting of poverty alleviation policies may miss out a majority of the poor. For example, a policy targeted at the western region, which is currently covered by a preferential development plan, would reach almost half of the rural poor, but would miss out over three quarters (77%) of the urban poor. Second, the urban poor are more evenly dispersed across all three regions,

Table 12.4: Regional distribution of the rural and urban poor (1998)

Regions	Rural poor (%)	Urban poor (%)
Eastern provinces	11.3	30.8
Central provinces	42.1	46.2
Western provinces	46.6	23.0

whereas close to 90% of the rural poor are in the western and central regions. The suggestion is that the coverage of urban poverty alleviation has to be far wider than that of rural poverty alleviation policies.

Box 12.1: Household registration disadvantage

Each Chinese citizen is officially registered and classified as either 'urban' or 'rural'. Migration from a rural to an urban locality does not automatically lead to a reclassification from rural to urban. This can result in cruel anomalies for the urban poor as the following cases from Xining, the capital of the north-western province of Qinghai, exemplify. These cases are based on the fieldwork conducted in October 2000.

- Zhao is 34 years old and originally from Henan province in the centre. His household consists of his wife, aged 29 and also from Henan, and their four-year-old daughter. His wife moved to Xining following their marriage in 1996. She had an agricultural registration and had to pay ¥4,000 (equivalent to just over 18 months of pay at the local minimum wage of ¥220 per month) to obtain Xining city registration. Zhao was laid off in April 2000 and receives ¥200 per month as living allowance. His wife does not work because of poor health. The family does not receive Minimum Living Standard Insurances (MLSI) and manages to survive thanks only to help from Zhao's retired parents.
- Ma is a widow, 42 years old and of *Hui* nationality. Her husband died of cancer in 1996. She lives with her father (aged 76 and disabled) and mother-in-law (aged 65 and suffering from cancer). She also has two sons living with her. The older son, 18 years old, stays home to take care of his grandparents. The family receives only ¥300 per month in MLSI, which disregards Ma's elderly parents-in-law because of their registration as 'rural', even though they have been residents in Xining's urban district for many years.
- Bian Shuqing, divorcee and 43 years old, lives with her 16 year old daughter and 3 year old adopted daughter, Miao. She found Miao as a baby, only a few months old and abandoned outside her husband's shop. She took the baby home, initially with the intention of handing Miao to another family or to the authorities but decided to keep the baby. Miao has no registration and is therefore a non-person in law. The family lives below the poverty line and is applying for MLSI, which, if granted, would disregard Miao because she has no legal existence.

To convey individual circumstances in China, three instances are described in Box 12.1 above. The problems that have necessarily arisen in the recent modernisation of China can also be illustrated from conditions in particular localities. In the national and even provincial administration of a huge country problems can arise when localities experience dramatic change. Two forgotten localities are described in Box 12.2.

Box 12.2: Anping and Yaying, two forgotten localities

Anping and Yaying are two settlements on the outskirts of Bengbu in the eastern province of Anhui, called villages or *cun*. They stand out because an overwhelming majority of their inhabitants are desperately poor. Anping has 300 families and Yaying 90 families. The causes of poverty differ between the two villages. Anping inhabitants are predominantly ex-urban youths who were dispatched to the countryside during the Cultural Revolution. They were finally allowed to return in the 1980s, but for various reasons remained on the margins of the urban life. The Yaying village is made up of ex-farmers who once grew vegetables on the outskirts of Bengbu. They stopped being farmers when their land was taken over by the government for non-farm use. They received compensation including non-rural registration. They do not have regular jobs and earn their living through casual employment, collecting garbage or petty trading. Housing in the two villages is very poor and public facilities and infrastructure almost non-existent.

When interpreting the urban poverty figures presented above, the connotation of 'urban' has to be kept in view. The official designation 'urban' in China does not denote usual place of residence and work, such as urban districts of cities, but the label 'non-rural' (*fei nongye*) on the personal register (*hu kou*), which is inherited from one's mother. Migration does not automatically lead to a change in one's inherited label, even after a long period of time. As a result, millions of rural-to-urban migrants resident and working on a long-term basis in an urban locality continue to be regarded as 'rural' and therefore excluded by design from the sample frame of the urban household data that are used to calculate the urban poverty rate presented above. There is no doubt that for the purposes of poverty analysis, long-term immigrants (that is, according to the Chinese classification those resident for at least six months) should be regarded as part of the urban population. In the case of short-term migrants, however, it is far from obvious whether they should be regarded as part of the urban or rural population. This decision takes on a special importance in the Chinese context because the urban poverty line exceeds the rural poverty line by a very wide margin. The inclusion of long-term rural immigrants in the urban population would raise the urban poverty rate. The magnitude will depend on two factors:

1. the number of long-term migrants relative to the population of permanent urban residents;
2. the poverty rate among long-term residents compared with that among permanent residents.

Unfortunately it is impossible at present to provide precise answers to these questions. It will be possible to answer the first factor when the data from the population census conducted at the end of 2000 are released. Concerning the second, an analysis of a cross-section survey conducted in 1999 yields poverty rates among immigrants that are on average around 50% higher than among permanent residents. This estimate appears plausible but is subject to two major qualifications. First, the survey reports income and expenditure over one month only (August 1999), which is too short. Second, the data set does not distinguish between immigrants according to the length of their stay. Therefore, the general conclusion is that the poverty rate among immigrants is in many cities higher than that among permanent residents and their inclusion will raise the urban poverty rate.

Safety nets for the urban population

Currently, the urban population benefits from three lines of defence against poverty:

- Minimum Living Standard Insurance (MLSI);
- Unemployment Insurance (UI);
- Living Allowance for laid-off employees.

MLSI is a recent addition to the social security package for the urban population that includes social insurance[7]. The scheme, which is non-contributory and means tested, is intended to provide the last line of defence against urban poverty. The third, which is a type of unemployment compensation scheme, is rapidly being phased out, leaving the first and second as the supports of the social safety net for the urban population. To these two one can also add the old-age pension scheme that covers a part of the urban labour force, but this chapter concentrates on the two schemes only. Unemployment Insurance dates back to 1986 when it was introduced to facilitate, not the then urban unemployed, but the replacement of employment for life with employment for a limited period as part of the transition from the planned to a market economy. It remained a small scheme until the latter half of the 1990s, and has grown rapidly since, and turned into an income maintenance scheme for the whole of the urban labour force in the event of unemployment. The interesting feature of the MLSI is that, instead of being instituted from the top by the central government as UI was, it began as a local initiative in 1993 when Shanghai introduced MLSI for its urban population. Since then the scheme has gone through a development process very similar to that of numerous Chinese reforms since 1979. That is, to begin with experimentation in selected localities followed by extension and finally universalisation across the country and formalisation through laws and regulation. However, in contrast to many of the reforms, the universalisation of the MLSI has turned out to be far more rapid than initially envisaged or thought feasible, driven by two interrelated developments in the latter half of the 1990s:

- a steep rise in labour lay-offs in the state sector and urban unemployment;

- rapid erosion of the employment-unit based social welfare system that has traditionally been the mainstay of urban social security.

Three examples of individuals receiving MLSI are provided in Box 12.3.

Box 12.3: Functioning of MLSI

In many cities, the MLSI operates on the assumption that other income–maintenance schemes operate as they should regardless of whether they do so or not and that those in employment receive at least the local minimum wage. The procedure insulates MLSI against malfunctions of Social Insurance schemes and is aimed at saving expenditure. Besides, the procedure also provides an incentive to the able-bodied to engage in remunerated work. However, as evidenced by interviews with poor households in Shenyang in the north-eastern province of Liaoning conducted in September 2000, this leads to an exaggeration of household per capita income and consequently an under-payment of MLSI assistance.

- Li Liwen, a widow aged 34, has a seven year old son. She earns around ¥200 per month from casual cleaning jobs. She receives MLSI. However, her income is presumed to be ¥234 per month and, as a result, she receives ¥156 in assistance instead of ¥190, the amount needed to bring the family's income up to the local poverty line of ¥195 per person per month.
- Wang Yinghan, divorced, aged 43, lives with his mother and 16 year old daughter. He suffers from pleurisy and has been laid off. However, he has never received the unemployed employees living allowance to which he is entitled. He receives MLSI of ¥141 based on the presumption that he receives ¥234 in the laid-off employees living allowance.
- Liu Guilian, a widow aged 72, lives with her granddaughter aged 13. She receives ¥150 in old-age pension. The family receives MLSI of ¥105 per month on the assumption that Liu Guilian receives the minimum old-age pension of ¥204 per month – which she does not.

There are now operational MLSI schemes in all cities, covering all the bona fide urban population, excluding migrants. An overview of MLSI and UI is presented in Table 12.5.

In principle, the combination of a contributory scheme, such as UI, and a non-contributory scheme, such as MLSI, provides a social safety net without any gaping holes. The net, although narrow compared to those in Western welfare states, is more comprehensive than in any other large developing economies. However, it is marred by some problems due in part to the systemic characteristics of the Chinese social security system and in part to particular design features of the two schemes and implementation problems.

Taking the systemic characteristics first, there are two that run through the current Chinese social security system:

- segmentation;
- highly decentralised financing and management.

The rural–urban segmentation runs wide and deep through the Chinese social security schemes and the labour market. In keeping with this general characteristic, both UI and MLSI apply only to the bona fide urban population and exclude the rural population including migrants in cities. This is, however, changing in a few coastal provinces, such as Zhejiang, Guangdong and Shanghai.

The social safety net for the rural population is meagre, in contrast to the

Table 12.5: Components of social safety net for the urban population

	UI	MLSI
Potential beneficiaries	Employees contributing to scheme	Permanent urban residents excluding migrants
	104 million contributors in December 2000	458 million (end 2001)
Condition for receiving benefit	Adequate contribution record	Household per capita income less than the poverty line
	Not in paid employment	
Numbers assisted	7 million (end 2001)[a]	12 million (end 2001)
Cash benefit	Monthly living allowance, ranging between 60-80% of the local minimum wage	Monthly living allowance equal to the difference between the local poverty line and the household per capita income
	No account taken of the family circumstances	No health insurance
Non-cash benefit	Contribution towards health insurance	
	Subsidised participation in retraining and job search schemes run by Labour Bureaux	
Benefit duration	Three months of benefits per 12 months' contribution with a maximum of 24 months	Unlimited, subject to the eligibility condition
Administering agency	City Labour and Social Security Bureaux	City Labour and Social Security and Civil Affairs Bureaux
Sources of finance	Payroll based contributions: 1% employee and 2% employer, with residual financing from the city government	Government budget, with cost sharing between the central and territorial governments
Status	In principle, participation is mandatory for the whole urban labour force	Some provinces are extending the scheme to rural inhabitants

[a]Provisional figure.

urban population, and is aimed at relieving severe poverty. A pronounced urban bias in social security provision is not particular to China but a common feature in developing economies. Although inequitable, the bias is unavoidable to a degree, given serious problems in designing contributory social security schemes (social insurance) for the informally- or self-employed even in developed economies (Atkinson, 1995). Rather, the main problem in China lies with the anachronistic administrative distinction between the urban and the rural population, which implicitly regards the rural labour force as self-employed. This distinction has been rendered obsolete with the rapid growth of wage employment in rural village and township enterprises (TVEs) and of rural migrants working in urban areas.

Both urban and rural schemes are highly decentralised. In the case of urban areas, many of the details are left to the discretion of the provincial or municipal governments, despite social insurance – which includes UI and MLSI – being underpinned by regulations issued by the central government. More consequential, the financing and management of social security schemes is decentralised to municipal government. As a result, the operation and benefit levels can vary widely even within cities of the same province. The decentralisation has been associated with both advantages and disadvantages. It has allowed flexibility to adapt in line with local circumstances and given local governments freedom to take initiatives. In some cases, local government initiatives have later been adopted as a national policy. For example, the MLSI, now a nationwide scheme, was first pioneered by a few coastal cities. In a vast and diverse country such as China, a certain degree of decentralisation is both necessary and desirable. On the disadvantage side, the budgetary units for UI and MLSI comprise about 226 cities, which, with few exceptions, are too small a population unit to provide sufficient risk pooling for sustainability. This highly decentralised budgeting weakens the financial foundation of UI and other social insurance schemes because the balance between contributions and expenditure varies widely across cities and normally deficits have to be covered from municipal budgets. Cities with high poverty and unemployment rates tend also to have strained public finances.

Assessment of UI and MLSI

An assessment of UI and MLSI as income maintenance schemes raises the following questions:

- Who qualifies for assistance, and who is excluded?
- How many are actually assisted and what percentage of those eligible for assistance do they constitute? How significant is the abuse of the system?
- What benefits are provided and in what form? Are these adequate to ensure freedom from deprivation?
- How is the scheme financed? And is the system of financing equitable and adequate for achieving the aims of the scheme?

Coverage

Formally, the MLSI extends to the bona fide urban population, which numbers 458 million or 36.2% of the total. In turn, UI covers the 212 million strong urban labour force (2000 figures; NBS, 2001b). There are two sets of issues that can be raised here: first, those concerning the formal coverage of the schemes and, second, the percentage of the eligible group actually covered. On both counts there are problems with each scheme. There is no justification for confining a means-tested social security scheme such as MLSI to one section of the population other than it would be difficult to remove the urban–rural distinction immediately. Besides, the way 'urban' is defined in China, it does not coincide with the category of 'long-term residents of urban localities' as it should. The cause of the divergence is that rural-to-urban migration does not automatically lead to a change of classification from 'rural' to 'urban' in the household register. With the large-scale rural-to-urban migration from the mid-1980s, this has created the glaring anomaly where tens of millions of long-term urban residents continue to be classified as 'rural'. Chinese cities offer numerous instances where some household members may be classified as 'urban', thus covered by the MLSI, while the rest being classified as rural are treated as if they do not exist. As for UI, by design the scheme has to be restricted to wage employees. However, the problem with UI is that it excludes 128 million wage employees (around 26% of the rural force) from UI on the grounds not of their employment status but simply their classification as 'rural'.

Turning to the actual coverage, the MLSI also excludes bona fide urban inhabitants resident and working in a city other than the one in which they are registered. This is due to the decentralisation whereby the scheme is managed at the level of cities with no settled framework for the portability of social security entitlements across municipal boundaries. As for UI, in principle it covers the whole of the urban labour force of 212 million. Only 134 million of these, however, nominally participated in the scheme and 103 million actually paid contributions (NBS, 2001b, p 445). Therefore the percentage of the urban labour force actually covered by UI in 2000 was less than half (48.5%). The 78 million who are completely outside the umbrella of UI are mostly employees of small enterprises, casual workers or self-employed, groups that are difficult to enrol in contributory social security schemes. The 31 million or so who failed to pay contributions are mostly employees of loss-making enterprises. Notwithstanding the fact that over half of the urban labour force is left uncovered, the coverage of UI in China is comparatively high by the standards of developing economies. Although there is scope for extending coverage in the urban labour force, the problem with UI is that its coverage is unnecessarily restricted by the rural–urban segmentation. Except in a few provinces migrants, even in formal wage employment, are excluded by design, as are wage employees of rural enterprises. The experience of Guangdong province, next to Hong Kong, in extending social insurance to migrants shows the practical feasibility of widening the coverage of UI.

Numbers assisted

Since its introduction countrywide in 1999, the number of MLSI recipients has almost quadrupled in three years (Table 12.6).

Table 12.6: Number of MLSI recipients

Year	Number of recipients
1999	2,810,000
2000	4,316,000
2001	11,200,000

The sharp increase is due to three factors:

1. a steep rise in unemployment;
2. insufficient old-age pension;
3. a rise in the proportion of individuals below the poverty line receiving assistance, especially between 2000 and 2001.

Here it is instructive to point to the difference between MLSI recipients and the recipients of the superseded urban poverty relief that was narrowly targeted at individuals with three 'no's (see page 297). Table 12.7 shows MLSI recipients by type in 2000.

Excluding those in the 'Miscellaneous' category, less than one quarter (23%) would in the past have qualified for poverty relief. The remaining 77% of the recipients, however, were largely made up of the 'new' urban poor, including the following groups:

• laid-off employees; that is, those still formally attached to their employment units;
• unemployed workers not receiving UI;
• pensioners and the working poor.

Table 12.7 raises the question: what percentage of the identified poor receives MLSI assistance? Given the available data, it is possible to provide only a partial answer. In 2000, while the MLSI recipients totalled 4.3 million (Table 12.6), a survey conducted by the Ministry of Civil Affairs (MOCA) in August 2000 estimated the number of urban residents with incomes below the local poverty line at 14 million. Other estimates put the number even higher. According to the MOCA figure, only 31% of the bona fide urban poor actually received assistance. Fieldwork in three cities conducted in 2000 yielded estimates of the take-up rate ranging from 25% to 29% (Table 12.8).

Local officials in charge of MLSI recognise the low coverage rate as a serious problem, which they attribute to a severe shortage of funds. A common response

Table 12.7: Composition of MLSI recipients (2000)

Categories	Total recipients (%)
No work, income or relatives to depend on	20.1
Employed, laid-off employees and pensioners	41.7
Unemployed and out of the labour market	25.9
Miscellaneous	12.3

Table 12.8: Percentage of identified poor receiving assistance (2000)

	Number identified as poor	Number receiving assistance (%)
Shenyang	130,000	38,000 (29.2%)
Xining	75,000	19,000 (25.3%)
Bengbu	40,000	10,000 (25.0%)

to the shortage of funds is to reduce the numbers of potential beneficiaries by tightening the qualification for receiving the MLSI assistance. A widely used method is to assume that all those capable of working earn a certain wage regardless of what they claim. However, the almost threefold increase in the number of MLSI recipients from 4.3 million in 2000 to 12.1 million in 2001 suggests a sharp rise in the coverage rate because there is no circumstantial evidence to suggest that the headcount of the urban poor in 2001 was significantly higher than that in 2000.

What percentage of the urban unemployed actually receives UI benefit? By design, UI benefit is only available to the 'registered unemployed' with a requisite contribution record, which rules out new entrants to the labour force and those who have exhausted their entitlement. Moreover, the 'registered unemployed' includes only a percentage of the unemployed because those outside the umbrella of UI have little or no incentive to register. As pointed out above, more than half of the urban labour force is not covered by UI, and migrants are excluded from registering as unemployed. Table 12.9 shows the percentage of registered unemployed receiving unemployment benefit for 1998, 1999 and 2000.

The percentage of registered unemployed receiving UI benefit has been rising both in absolute numbers and relative to the registered unemployed.

Table 12.9: Registered unemployed receiving unemployment benefit

	1998	1999	2000
Registered unemployed (millions)	5.7	5.7	5.9
UI benefit recipients (millions)	1.6	2.7	3.3
Receiving UI benefit (%)	28.0	47.1	55.5

Source: NBS (1999b, 2000b, 2001b)

The numbers receiving UI benefit is reported to have more than doubled in 2001 with the phasing out of a separate allowance for 'laid-off employees' and their transfer to UI with a benefit entitlement of up to two years.

Magnitude and form of assistance

The predominant form of assistance under the MLSI is just a cash allowance equal to the difference between the current household per capita income and the local poverty line that, in principle, is sufficient to cover basic needs. Two aspects of the assistance are worth noting:

• unit of calculation;
• adjustment for the size and age composition of the household.

For the purposes of the MLSI, poverty is measured with reference to the combined income of the household on the assumption that income is shared equally. In contrast, unemployment insurance benefit is paid to individuals without a job regardless of their family income, as long as they have the requisite contribution record. As a result, the section of the population that qualifies for MLSI assistance does not fully coincide with the section that is entitled to the unemployment benefit. In particular, MLSI assistance may also be payable to a household of which none of the members qualifies for unemployment insurance. In such cases, which are increasingly common, MLSI caters for the section of the population that is bypassed by UI. Moreover, a household with all its working age members receiving the UI benefit may be eligible for MLSI assistance because of its dependent members. In such cases MLSI serves as the supplement to social security schemes that do not take into account recipients' households. In the Chinese context this holds for all income maintenance schemes under social insurance, including old-age pension and disability compensation as well as unemployment benefit.

MLSI assistance is calculated with reference to household income per capita only and is not affected by the number of household members or their ages. The underlying assumption is that the poverty line for a couple, let us say, is twice that for a single individual. Although there are good theoretical reasons for taking into account the number of household members, its neglect in China can be justified on the grounds of not having a widely accepted schedule of adjustment for household size and also keeping the administration of the MLSI simple. The MLSI simply makes up the difference between the poverty line and the household per capita income. The actual MLSI benefit per recipient is quite low. Over the nine months from January to September 2001, the average cash benefit amounted to ¥66 per person per month, less than half (45%) of the average of local poverty lines, ¥148 per person per month. The procedure for calculating the MLSI benefit targets assistance perfectly, and, given the limited funds for poverty relief, helps to raise the number of assisted households. However, a salient feature of the procedure is that for every extra yuan assisted households earn through additional work, for example, they lose one yuan in assistance. In effect, assisted households face a marginal tax rate of 100% and extra earning up to the difference between the actual income and the poverty line does not make them better off. The procedure sets a poverty trap whereby assisted households have neither the incentive nor the possibility to improve their economic situation unless the improvement is substantial enough to lift them above the poverty line and thus disqualify them from receiving assistance.

As argued above, poverty is a multidimensional state and the income or expenditure based poverty indicator may weed out some households as not poor even when they are deprived in some crucial respects. There are strong arguments in favour of a national framework for the provision of targeted assistance in three areas:

1. medical care;
2. schooling and training;
3. housing.

Currently housing is not a major issue in relation to registered urban residents, but it is in the case of migrants. Housing for low-income urban households looks likely to become a major issue in the near future. However, the high cost of schooling is already a serious problem for low-income urban households. In principle, the poverty line takes into account schooling cost, but households do not receive earmarked assistance to cover the cost of schooling, which has risen sharply in recent years. In principle, poor households receive part or full remission from school fees. However, there is no formal provision to ensure this. A survey of poor urban households in Shanghai conducted at the end of 1998 by the Centre for Research into Social Policy of the Chinese Academy of Social Sciences and the Ministry of Civil Affairs revealed a number of disturbing findings about the heavy burden of schooling cost. Of the surveyed families receiving MLSI benefit, 83% received no assistance towards schooling cost. Around 55% reported severe difficulty in paying the tuition fee and ancillary education costs of their children. Some of these were seriously considering withdrawing children from school and putting them to work. The findings of the survey are corroborated by interviews with poor households conducted in several cities.

A yawning gap in the MLSI is that assistance recipients are not provided with any healthcare insurance. There is a notional healthcare allowance included in the poverty line but the allowance is the same for everyone regardless of the state of health and has not kept pace with the rise in healthcare costs. As indicated by field studies in Shenyang (north-east), Xining (north-west), Bengbu (east) and Guiyang, the dread of illness hangs over the urban poor. MLSI beneficiaries, many of whom suffer from chronic illnesses, forego necessary medical care and avoid visits to doctors and hospitals. They also run the risk of severe economic hardship in the case of a serious illness.

Poverty lines (benefit lines)

The government regulations governing the MLSI stipulate that the minimum living standard (or the benefit line) should be determined on the basis of the cost of food, clothing and housing necessary for basic subsistence. They also recommend that due consideration should be given to the cost of schooling for children and public utility charges: water, electricity and fuel. However, the determination of benefit lines is left to local governments for two reasons. First, prices and the pattern of consumption and average income per capita vary widely across localities. Second, the benefit line determines assistance under the MLSI, which is financed principally by city governments. In principle, cities set the benefit line by the direct method of costing the goods and services for basic subsistence (the so-called 'basic needs' approach). Such an approach raises the question of what particular items should be included in the living necessities for the residents. There is as yet no detailed national framework to guide local governments in setting the poverty line. Methods vary across cities. Some have set up a special group to set the poverty line. These groups compile a detailed list of goods and services, including their quantities, and survey their prices. Some cities rely on no more than an informed guess in setting the benefit line.

Besides 'goods and services necessary for basic subsistence', two other considerations enter into the determination of local benefit lines. One is the public finance of the city and the other is the relation between the poverty line and other social security benefits. The city governments that set the benefit lines are also responsible for financing the MLSI. As a result, fiscal considerations enter into the determination of local benefit lines. Generally poor cities use a narrow definition of poverty and richer cities a broad definition. Moreover, given a close relationship between the benefit line and benefit levels under other income maintenance schemes and wages, the local benefit lines adhere to the following order:

Minimum wage > Allowance for laid-off employees > UI benefit > Poverty line

The Labour Law mandates local government to set a minimum wage for the locality taking account of the local labour market, the living standard and prices. Therefore the minimum wage is similar to a poverty line that sets an upper boundary to various social security benefits. This ordering preserves the incentive to take up employment at the minimum wage. However, it leaves open the possibility that the local benefit line may be too low to prevent severe hardship, especially in cities with high rates of unemployment. In addition to local governments, a number of national organisations also calculate poverty lines for the purposes of estimating the headcount of the urban poor. There are strong arguments in favour of the determination of poverty lines purely for diagnostic purposes that is not influenced by the immediate problem of financing poverty alleviation and these can provide a valuable benchmark for assessing the poverty lines set by city governments.

Notwithstanding a wide variation, the local attempts in setting benefit lines represent considerable progress in the diagnosis and alleviation of poverty. Associated with these attempts there is a change in the perception of urban poverty from a problem confined to particular groups, such as widows, orphans and older people without close relatives, to a risk that potentially threatens a large section of the population. The compilation of benefit lines widens the list of goods and services beyond just food and clothing, which it tended to be in the past. Arguably, the low incidence of urban poverty in the past compared to that now was in large measure due to the equation of poverty with extreme deprivation, such as not having enough to eat or wear.

Financing

A crucial criterion for assessing schemes such as MLSI is whether or not the method of financing matches the obligations. Formally, each city is responsible for financing the MLSI within its jurisdiction. This financing arrangement is too decentralised to ensure the sustainability of the MLSI. In particular, it implies an onerous burden on cities caught between the scissors of a strained budget due to a deterioration in the financial condition of local enterprises, on the one hand, and a high unemployment rate on the other. There is a sharing of the cost of MLSI between government tiers, not only between the central and sub-central but also between all tiers of the latter, from provinces down to urban districts. The pattern of cost sharing varies. Currently only 21 out of 31 provinces contribute towards the cost of the MLSI with the aim of relieving the financial pressure on cities with a high burden. There are still ten provinces that do not contribute towards the cost of the MLSI. Correlative to that between cities and provinces, the cost-sharing formula between cities and their urban districts varies as shown by the following examples of the division of cost that is not covered by higher government tiers (Table 12.10).

Despite cost sharing by higher government tiers, urban districts (the last but one government tier) still end up bearing a high share of the cost of the MLSI. The rationale for this is weak, if not entirely missing. City districts are too small a unit to spread the cost. As evidenced by the case studies of seven cities conducted in 2000/01, the percentage of the poor is not evenly distributed but

Table 12.10: Cost sharing between city and urban district governments

	City share	District share
Dalian	30%	70%
Qingdao	70%	30%
Shenyang, Wuhan and Chongqing	50%	50%

varies widely across districts of a city. Added to this, districts with a higher percentage of the poor also tend to have more strained public finances. Shifting a substantial part of the cost to urban districts accentuates inequality between different parts of the city and introduces unwarranted variation in the standards of provision. In general, the arrangement for financing the MLSI is makeshift. As it currently stands, it is neither equitable nor does it yield sufficient funds relative to obligations.

Turning to UI, it is financed by a payroll tax split between employers and employees. The current recommended rate by the central government is 3% of earnings, split 2:1 between employers and employees. However, the actual contribution rate varies across cities depending upon the pressure of demand on the UI fund, as shown in the following examples:

- Beijing: 0.5% employees;   1.5% employers;
- Xian: 1% employees;   2.5% employers;
- Some cities in Guangdong still have a contribution rate of 1%.

Until a few years ago, the UI fund tended to run to a substantial surplus and was used for a variety of purposes, some with no relation to unemployment. In response to reports of mismanagement and misuse, the Ministry of Finance has tightened control over the use of UI funds. Starting from 1999, city governments have been forbidden to charge any administration cost to social security funds. This prohibition deals with a serious problem of the misuse of social security funds but at the cost of creating a problem of under-investment in administrative capacity, especially in cities with strained finances. The rise in the recommended UI contribution rate from 1% to 3% in 1998 was prompted by a sharp increase in registered unemployment and lay offs, and reports of widespread default on UI benefits and on living allowances to 'laid-off' employees. As well as raising funds, this rise introduced two important principles that have implications for the financial sustainability of the system. First, a relation between total cost and the contribution rate and, second, of shifting a part of the cost to employees without compensation. The second has become a norm for social insurance schemes, and, in the Chinese context, is equivalent to a personal income tax because it is not shifted back to employers.

The financial integrity of UI is far from secure because the budgeting units are 226 cities and the deficit on UI and its ratio to the municipal budget varies from city to city. Residual financing from the municipal budget is in keeping with the government policy of splitting the social security costs among employers, employees and the government. The current financing system is under severe stress in cities caught between rising unemployment, on the one hand, and an eroded tax base due to the parlous financial situation of local enterprises on the other. The financial sustainability of UI as a national scheme over the medium to long term would depend crucially on raising the level of the territorial government at which the social insurance account is balanced and a deficit is financed. There is as yet no regular framework for spreading the financial burden of UI and other social security schemes across cities, although provincial governments and the central government provide subsidies to cities with high unemployment rates. The need for such a framework will grow in importance as the number of claimants relative to contributors rises with the transfer of 'laid-off' employees from enterprises to UI over the coming years.

Improving the social safety net

Policy measures to enhance the effectiveness of social assistance and social insurance in dealing with urban poverty are divided as follows:

- improvements in measuring and monitoring poverty;
- strengthening the administrative infrastructure;
- reforming the financing system;
- rectifying the design problems of social insurance and social assistance schemes.

Starting from a situation of a non-existent statistics system in 1978, China has come a long way towards establishing a modern statistical service. Household surveys that provide much of the data for poverty monitoring are conducted annually (see, for example, Bramall, 2001). In addition to regular surveys there are also special surveys conducted by the national and territorial statistics bureaux. However, currently available household survey data suffer from a number of gaps and defects that limit its usefulness in diagnosing poverty incidence and assessing the impact of poverty alleviation schemes. The most serious of these problems is that the urban and rural household surveys are conducted separately and, more consequential, use different questionnaires. As a result, the rural and urban household data are not fully compatible, which makes it impossible to estimate the incidence of urban and rural poverty on a comparable basis. An integrated analysis of urban and rural poverty is assuming increasing importance with rising urbanisation caused by rural-to-urban migration, on the one hand, and a shift in the economic structure of rural localities away from farming on the other.

For effective poverty alleviation and mitigation China needs to take the following three steps:

- standardised statistical surveys aimed at the estimation of poverty;
- a national framework for the calculation of poverty lines by territorial governments;
- longitudinal poverty surveys of selected sections of population and localities.

The purpose of the first will be to ensure that data yielded by various surveys are compatible in terms of the sampling frame and the definition of variables such as income and expenditure, which currently they are not. This would help to improve the value of the multitude of statistical surveys currently conducted by organisations and territorial governments. The second is based on the problem that poverty and benefit lines differ across localities. As with the first step, the aim would be to ensure comparability. The third is already done in selected rural localities in the north-west and south-west under a World Bank project. With the growing importance of urban poverty as a major social issue, there are strong arguments in favour of instituting longitudinal sample surveys of poverty black spots in urban localities. Benefits from an improvement in poverty diagnosis and monitoring would be long-term or permanent, and would include the following:

- a more accurate targeting of poverty alleviation schemes through a reduction in the number of false negatives (misclassification of the poor as non-poor) and false positives (misclassification of the non-poor as poor).
- a finer assessment of changes in the pattern of poverty and of the relative effectiveness of various poverty alleviation schemes.
- improvements in the design and implementation of schemes to alleviate and mitigate poverty.

The present arrangement for financing social insurance and the MLSI are neither equitable nor sufficient to ensure financial sustainability. With a few exceptions, cities are too small for a budgetary unit to provide sufficient risk pooling for social insurance schemes. The balance between contributions and expenditure varies widely across cities, as does the state of their finances. The need for upgrading the level of budgeting is fully recognised by the Chinese government. A pooling of social insurance contributions and expenditures at the provincial level is the policy aim, and would seem to be an urgent priority in the case of old-age pensions, which is by far the largest scheme in terms of expenditure. In most cases, this would be sufficient to put the urban social security system on a sound financial footing and to begin to provide coverage for whole populations. Many of the Chinese provinces are as populous as sizeable countries. As with social insurance, cities are too narrow a base to provide the MLSI with a sound financial footing, the lower government tiers of 'districts', and 'streets' even less. The percentage of poor in the urban population varies widely across cities and their districts. In many cases, cities and districts with a higher percentage of the poor also tend to have more strained public finances. The solution to the problem does not lie in a unitary social security covering the whole country. Given China's diversity, that is neither feasible nor desirable. A province-level social security system would in most cases provide sufficient risk pooling for financial viability and also allow flexibility to adapt to regional differences. However, to ensure compliance with a common core of minimum standards and social security entitlements that are portable, the provincial social security schemes have to be embedded in a national framework. This already exists to a degree in that urban social security schemes are underpinned by a corpus of national regulations.

Appendix: Derivation of poverty lines for measuring urban poverty

This chapter distinguishes between the two types of poverty lines on the basis of their uses:

- diagnostic poverty lines;
- poverty lines used for poverty relief work (referred to as the benefit line).

Although related, the two are in principle distinct and can be very different. The diagnostic poverty line is purely for the purpose of identifying the poor. While sensitive to the prevalent living standard, it is not constrained by how to provide assistance to those below the poverty line. Such a line can also serve as a benchmark for assessing the adequacy of the existing benefit lines and setting a horizon for poverty alleviation. The poverty lines used in this chapter for measuring the poverty rates are 'diagnostic poverty lines' (see Table 12.1).

The following two sets of poverty lines are computed for each of the 31 Chinese provinces in Chinese currency, yuan, using the urban household data for 1998 collected by the Chinese National Bureau of Statistics (NBS). For the whole of China, the two lines are averages of the corresponding provincial lines with the provincial share of the total urban population as weights:

- food poverty line;
- general poverty line.

The general poverty line (hereafter the poverty line) is regarded as the sum of two components: basic food expenditure, as given by the food poverty line, and basic non-food expenditure, which is determined by means of regression.

The food poverty line is a popular method of setting poverty lines in developing economies where adequate nutrition is the first priority of poverty alleviation.

The contents of the food basket that underpins the provincial food poverty lines are chosen with reference to the average per capita consumption of various food items by the first quintile (the bottom 20%) of the sampled households in the province in question ranked by expenditure per capita, excluding expenditure on consumer durables. The choice of the bottom 20% as the reference percentile is based on two considerations. Firstly, it should include all poor households as well as those on the margin. Secondly, it should have enough households to smooth out variations across households that are not directly related to income/expenditure. The reason for excluding durables is that they are purchased at irregular intervals, and therefore introduce white noise in the relation between current consumption and current living standard. The basket thus chosen obviously represents the local (in this case provincial) dietary pattern and is also cost effective. The latter because the bottom 20% represents low income/expenditure households and such households use cheaper food to acquire necessary calories. The calorie content of the basket is calculated by multiplying physical quantities of food items, which are provided by the NBS urban survey data, with their respective calorie content from the physical quantity-nutrients table compiled by the Nutrition Society of China[8]. To meet the requirement of 2,100 per day, the basket is scaled up or down depending upon the case. In effect the calorie requirement functions as a scaling factor that can be varied depending on the purpose. The cost of the chosen food basket is obtained automatically because the urban household data provides for a long list of food items both the physical amount purchased (where applicable) and the total expenditure on each item. The advantage of calculating costs in this way is that the cost is automatically adjusted for the prices actually paid by the household and the quality of purchased items. Aside from serving as the 'food poverty line', the cost of the minimum calories requirement can also serve as the provincial price index[9] that is a more accurate index of the cost of living than the urban price index reported in published statistics. It is important to emphasise that although the food poverty line, which for the whole of China comes to ¥1,392 per person per year, can be used to estimate severe poverty, it is on its own insufficient. The line only covers the cost of purchasing uncooked food and excludes all non-food expenditure including that incurred in cooking food.

The cost of 'basic non-food expenditure' is determined by answering the following question by means of a regression exercise on the urban household data classified by provinces:

• What is the non-food expenditure per capita when expenditure per capita is just equal to the non-food poverty line?

In order to answer this, the following regression equation is applied to household data separately for each province:

$$S_i = \alpha + \beta (X_i/Z) + \gamma N_i + \varepsilon \qquad (1)$$

Subscript i ($_i$) denotes household. Therefore, S_i denotes the share of total expenditure in household i devoted to food. X_i is the total expenditure in household i. Z is the food poverty line for the province in which the household is located. N_i denotes the number in household i. Having obtained the parameters, the poverty line is calculated by setting food expenditure per capita equal to the food poverty line and setting N_i equal to the average household size.

$$S_i*(X_i/Z) = \alpha*(X_i/Z) + \beta (X_i/Z)^2 + \gamma*N_i*(X_i/Z)$$

S_i*X_i is expenditure per capita on food, when this is equal to the food poverty line the term on the left $S_i*(X_i/Z) = 1$. The equation can be written as:

$$(\alpha + \gamma^*N_i)^*(X_i/Z) + \beta(X_i/Z)^2 - I = 0$$

The above is a straightforward quadratic equation. Of the two possible solutions, the higher of the real solutions is chosen as the poverty line for the province in question. For a discussion of the procedure see Ravallion (1994). The poverty line for the whole of China for 1998, which is the average of provincial poverty lines, comes to ¥2,310 per person per year.

Notes

[1] This chapter draws on a project on urban poverty in China funded by the Asian Development Bank (TAR: PRC 33448). The project team was led by Athar Hussain (author of this chapter) and included Rong Mo (Ministry of Labour and Social Security, PRC), Jun Tang (Chinese Academy of Social Sciences), Youjuan Wang (National Bureau of Statistics, PRC), Zhikun Wang (Ministry of Civil Affairs, PRC) and Shujie Yao (University of Middlesex, UK). Shantong Li of the Development Research Center of the State Council served as adviser to the project team.

[2] The 'public sector' covers the government and the diverse range of public institutions and state and collective enterprises.

[3] According to the World Development Report 2000/01 (World Bank, 2000) the $1 per person per day is the median ten lowest poverty lines calculated by the World Bank and converted at the 1993 PPP rate (see p 17).

[4] Adjusted on the basis of the difference in the US and the Chinese inflation rate since 1994.

[5] A detailed account of the methods of estimation of various $/¥ PPP rates for China is provided in World Bank (1994).

[6] The 'eastern' region comprises: Beijing, Tianjin, Shanghai, Liaoning, Hebei, Shandong, Jiangsu, Zhejiang, Fujian, Guangdong and Hainan. The remaining 20 provinces divide along the lines of ten each into the 'central' and 'western' regions.

[7] Social insurance covers old-age pension, disability compensation, healthcare insurance, maternity benefit and unemployment insurance (also see Shangkuan and Fulin, 1996).

[8] This involves excluding those food items for which no physical quantities are reported. These usually consist of meals outside home.

[9] Strictly speaking, not a price index but a unit-value index.

References

Atkinson, A.B. (1995) *Incomes and the welfare state: Essays on Britain and Europe*, Cambridge: Cambridge University Press.

Atkinson, A.B. (1998) *Poverty in Europe*, Oxford: Oxford University Press.

Bramall, C. (2001) 'The quality of China's Household Income Surveys', *China Quarterly*, vol 167, pp 689-705.

Deaton, A. (1997) *The analysis of Household Surveys: A microeconometric approach to development policy*, London: Johns Hopkins University Press for the World Bank.

Deaton, A. (2001) 'Counting the world's poor: problems and possible solutions', *The World Bank Research Observer*, vol 16, no 2, pp 125-47.

Gustafsson, B. and Li (1998) 'The structure of Chinese poverty', *Development Economics*, vol 36, no 4, p 387.

Gustafsson, B. and Zhong, W. (2000) 'How and why has poverty in China changed?: a study based on microdata for 1988 and 1995', *China Quarterly*, vol 164, pp 983-1006.

Khan, A. R. (1988) *Poverty in China in the period of globalisation*, ILO Issues in Development Discussion Paper No 22, Geneva: ILO.

NBS (National Bureau of Statistics) (2001a) *Statistical yearbook of China 2001*, Beijing: NBS.

NBS (2001b) *Labour and wage statistics yearbook of China 2001*, Beijing: NBS.

Ravallion, M. (1994) *Poverty comparisons*, London: Harwood Publishers.

Ruizhen, Y. and Yuan, W. (1992) *Poverty and development: A study of China's poor areas*, Beijing: New World Press.

Ruizhen, Y. and Yuan, W. (1996) 'China: poverty in a socialist market economy', in E. Øyen, S.M. Miller and S.A. Samad (eds) *Poverty: A global review*, Scandinavian University Press.

Shangkuan, G and Fulin, C. (eds) (1996) *China's social security system*, Beijing: Foreign Language Press.

Srinivasan, T.N. (2001) 'Comment on "Counting the world's poor"', *The World Bank Research Observer*, vol 16, no 2, pp 157-68.

Townsend, P. (1993) *The international analysis of poverty*, London: Harvester Wheatsheaf.

World Bank (1994) *China: GDP per capita*, Report No 13580-CHA, Washington, DC: World Bank.

World Bank (2000) *World development report 2000-2001: Attacking poverty*, Oxford: Oxford University Press.

THIRTEEN

'A new branch can be strengthened by an old branch'[1]: livelihoods and challenges to inter-generational solidarity in South Africa

Jo Beall

Introduction

The rapid growth in the numbers of older people is at the heart of the current global demographic transition. In the year 2000 there were about 550 million people over 60 years of age, a figure expected to reach 1.2 billion by 2025. The *Ageing and development report* (HelpAge International, 1999, p xii) dispels the assumption that older populations do not exist in the developing world as a myth – ageing populations everywhere are testimony to the fact that the development decades have seen some success. Improvements in hygiene, water supply and control of infectious diseases have greatly reduced the risk of premature death, so that older people no longer constitute a social policy issue associated primarily with the industrialised countries, referred to here as 'the North'. Even in sub-Saharan Africa, a continent ravaged by complex emergencies and the devastating effects of HIV/AIDS, the proportion of people over 65 years is expected to increase by over 90% between 2000 and 2020 (Apt, 1997, p 4).

Nevertheless, the growth in life expectancy when accompanied by poverty is a mixed blessing, and the African experience of ageing is one associated with poor diet, ill health, inadequate housing, few material assets, and minimal incomes for the majority. As the HelpAge International Report goes on to point out:

> Older people are often isolated, living on the margins of families and communities and deeply vulnerable. The extent to which they are reached by services and support is a litmus test of the development process.... Ageing is often perceived as a burden for countries and communities. But channelling resources to enable older people is an investment in society. (HelpAge International, 1999, pp xii-xiii)

The United Nations International Year of Older Persons (IYOP) in 1999 had as its theme, 'Towards a society for all ages', and its recipe for successful ageing was good health, work skills and self-knowledge. Importantly it acknowledged older people's contribution to development, and called for the creation of multi-generational social policies. The IYOP also pushed for a life course perspective, understanding older people within their wider communities (UNFPA, 1998). At one level this sat comfortably with the growing salience of a 'sustainable livelihoods' perspective (Chambers and Conway, 1992; Francis, 2000; Beall, 2002) which held prominence at the time in international development discourse (Carney, 1998, Carney et al, 1999; Rakodi and Lloyd-Jones, 2002). The 'livelihoods' perspective recognises that poor rural and urban households in middle- and low-income countries do not generally rely on a single income source (for example, farming or waged employment) to support themselves. It seeks to understand the complex ways in which households make a living, balance multiple tasks and engage in trade-offs between income earning and alternative supporting activities. The release of younger household members for paid work is often only possible because of the domestic work, childcare and community reproduction undertaken by older members, particularly women (Cross and Baker, 1991; Bunchandranon et al, 1997; Cattell, 1997; Heslop, 1999; Beall, 2002).

Studies published to coincide with the IYOP highlighted the need to support family welfare systems with social assistance, social security and support for family caring structures (ILO, 1997). The Human Development Report of the same year (UNDP, 1999) situated older people at the receiving end of care within an invisible part of the global economy – unpaid caring work – that in turn was seen as worthy of support. As welcome as this emphasis was, older people were still largely stereotyped as frail and dependent. As such, the contribution made by older people themselves was often ignored, contributions not only in terms of their own welfare but that of their families, as well as contributions to the broader development process (Gorman, 1996; HelpAge International, 1999).

This chapter takes as its starting point this position, which is informed by a livelihoods perspective and emphasises the agency of the poor, and in this case, older people among the poor. In addition, however, it makes the case that as well as making important contributions to households, communities and local and national economies, older people have rights. The analytical starting point is that the notion of 'the inter-generational bargain', which is very much a Western concept, while serving to highlight the role of older people as agents and contributors, can obscure their needs and rights, often denied through relationships and institutions embedded in social structure. In preference and for reasons both of equity and efficiency, the concept of 'inter-generational solidarity' is used, to encourage a social policy discourse that is not directed exclusively or primarily at the young and those of working age, at the expense of older people. This is particularly salient in contexts where multiple household livelihood strategies are necessary for survival and security. It is within this framework that the present chapter seeks to explore inter-generational relationships in South Africa, and by so doing to contribute to the emerging discourse on older people and development.

Kinsella and Ferreira (1997) have estimated that South Africa has the greatest number of older inhabitants in Africa, with more than one in eight persons (5.6 million) being over 50 years of age, and nearly 7% (2.9 million) being aged 60 and above. It is projected that by 2030, 71% of the elderly population (60 years and above) in South Africa will be African and many will be poor[2]. Given these figures and the extent of rural and urban poverty in contemporary South Africa, and the complex and multifaceted ways in which people are required to construct and maintain household livelihood strategies, the old age pension provides a major source of income for South Africa's poorest families. Although a number of African countries have policies that relate to older people, South Africa is almost unique in sub-Saharan Africa and indeed stands out among late developing countries, in having made pension provision universal and the implications of this for inter-generational solidarity are explored.

This chapter draws on research undertaken in South Africa in 1999, which examined the contribution of older people to development in South Africa as understood and explained by older people themselves[3]. The study was conducted with HelpAge International and adopted a participatory action research and analysis approach[4]. A key aim of the research was to 'give voice' to poorer older people by drawing directly on their views and experiences. An additional aim was to understand how younger people and policy makers and social development practitioners perceived elders.

Inter-generational relations and the mechanisms of redistribution

Much of the social policy literature on industrialised countries places social security, health services and caring for older people in the context of an inter-generational contract or bargain. This is not a directly negotiated relationship but one that is imposed and mediated by the state. As concern grows over ageing populations, and as the social identity of older people is increasingly constructed in negative terms, so this is reinforced by neoliberal principles that shift economic and caring responsibilities away from the state and on to families. If, at the micro-level of the household, the inter-generational contract is seen to be based on reciprocal resource transfers and caring over time, at the macro-level this contract is seen to be based on "inter-cohort transfers of resources through mediums of taxation and social expenditure" (Walker, 1996, p 13).

According to Walker (1996), the interaction between macro- and micro-level inter-generational relations can be both positive and negative. For example, pensions are shown to enhance the acceptance and status of older people, whereas the duty of care for older people with little or no support, makes the value of an inter-generational bargain suspect. In the European context, for example, Dagmar Lorenz-Meyer (1996) provides empirical evidence of the gender inequalities involved in both the public and private sides of the inter-generational contract. In the public domain of social security policies, women are disadvantaged because they are low paid and are seen as secondary earners. In the private domain for related reasons, women take on the greatest burden of interpersonal support. She argues that the hidden economy of inter-generational support based on obligation, duty and unequal power, remains "hidden, unnamed and devalued" (Lorenz-Meyer, 1996, p 30). In her view too, therefore, the public and private spheres sustain each other as part of a single system.

In the African context it has been argued that inter-generational linkages are important for the care economy. Writing in relation to Ghana, Nana Apt (1996) has argued that inter-generational relations comprise a three-way reciprocity between generations of kin (child-adult-older person) in terms of financial support, personal care and services. She makes the point that the existence of this tripartite relationship serves to reduce the level of state intervention in care for older people and in turn, formal welfare costs. Apt (1992) has also argued that in Africa, inter-generational solidarity is breaking down due to a process of modernisation, which entails a shift from the extended to nuclear family, the erosion of older people's power and influence in the home and in society, as well as increasing impatience on the part of younger people with customs and traditional authority structures. She cites the example of Sierra Leone's 'short-changed generation', which paid its dues when young but whose payoff is now begrudged due to the complex emergencies faced by that country (Apt, 1992). These ideas and arguments would be familiar to social policy audiences in the North and as the war grinds on in Sierra Leone, her words echo those of Longman, writing on the problems of the baby boomers in America:

> Even if the more affluent members of the next generation decide not to subsidise the working poor, we have every reason to believe that they will nonetheless be forced to commit more resources to pay for police, jails, private security guards, and other measures to protect themselves against the expanding underclass. (Longman, 1987, p 23)

While the 'perils of modernisation' argument might be overdone (Gorman, 1999), it is also clear that, as in the US and in Europe, inter-generational solidarity in Africa can no longer be taken for granted. In this context, introducing the concept of 'inter-generational bargains' into policy discourse, imbued as it is with overtones of Western economic individualism, risks importing uncritically or reinforcing, market rules into reciprocal and cooperative relationships across the continent, without thinking about the consequences[5].

The South African context

South Africa is classified by the World Bank as an upper-middle-income country, and by the United Nations Development Programme (UNDP) as having a medium level of human development. There are, however, huge differentials in the quality of life of the different population groups, due not least of all to the legacy of apartheid, which served to severely disadvantage the black population of South Africa, most particularly the African population[6]. Here the so-called 'inter-generational bargain' is overlaid by centuries of racial inequality and apartheid policies that saw a hierarchy of welfare benefits extended first to whites, then mixed race or so-called 'Coloureds' and Indian South Africans, and finally to the African population. As a result, the non-racial governments that have been in power since the first democratic elections in 1994 have had to address the challenges of poverty and inequality against a background of extreme structural inequality. Among these challenges are an ageing population and one that is increasingly entrusted with the burden of social care.

According to the United Nations Population Fund (UNFPA, 1997), South Africa has one of the most skewed income distribution profiles in the world. In 1997 some 27% of African households earned less than R500 compared with around 3% of households in the other population groups[7]. About 23% of White and Indian households earn more than R9000 per month, an amount earned by less than 1% of African households (South African Survey, 1998, p 226). Chief among the problems inherited by the new government is unemployment, with an estimated 41.1% of Africans being unemployed, compared to 6.4%, 17.1% and 23.3% for Whites, Asians and 'Coloureds' respectively. Poverty is most prevalent among Africans living in rural areas or urban squatter settlements, and May (1998) estimates that the rural areas while containing 45% of the population, are home to over 70% of the total poor population.

Furthermore, poverty is identified as being gender differentiated in South Africa. Women-headed households constituted 35% of all households in 1997, and the largest proportion of women-headed households (26%) were in the lowest income group. This is significant given that globally ageing is an increasingly female experience, with women outliving men in nearly all countries, both rich and poor (HelpAge International, 1999, p xiii).

Older people in South Africa play a critical caring and parenting role that extends over a long period of time, not only to their own children but also to grandchildren and extended families. This role will undoubtedly continue to increase as the HIV/AIDS epidemic in South Africa escalates. Through pensions older people make critical and, in the context of high unemployment, sometimes the only contributions to the incomes of poorer households and extended family networks. Nevertheless, older people in South Africa are vulnerable in a range of ways. Problems of poverty and frail health are exacerbated by difficulties in accessing pensions and health services. They are also subject to abuse in homes and communities and due to these and other factors it is important that older people are recognised as a 'vulnerable group' and accorded social protection and, according to a 1995 discussion document on ageing in South Africa (cited in HelpAge International, 1999, p 170), "[T]he protection of the rights of older persons requires special attention in view of the prevalence of age discrimination and abuse".

Lastly, and of particular import in relation to the dynamics of inter-generational solidarity in South Africa, is that older people constitute a significant and growing proportion of those citizens who were historically disadvantaged under apartheid and who contributed in various ways to the struggle for equality. Many older people lost property during forced removals and times of political violence, were subjected to the disintegration of family life as a result of migratory labour and influx control laws and were denied the advantages of education and the right to skilled employment. As such, the legacy of apartheid has meant poor preparation for old age and a lack of access to resources and opportunities. For reasons of social justice, therefore, it is important that they are recognised not only as lifelong contributors but also as having rights. The case was eloquently put by Beauty Zuane Mthethwa in an open letter to the newly elected President Thabo Mbeki from a pensioner, who said, "We have shown you how much we trust you and now the ball is in your hands" (*Star*, 19 June 1999). What follows is a brief review of the state of social policy and social sector reform as South Africa enters the 21st century and the extent to which democratic government has taken up Beauty Mthethwa's challenge.

Health

As with other social sectors there are serious health inequalities, with some South Africans having good health and decent access to health services and others experiencing poor health and with poor access to healthcare facilities (Barron, 1998). Significant health care reforms are underway, claiming 10% of the national budget and being the second largest sector to benefit from international development assistance. In this context, the White Paper on the Transformation of the South African Health System (Government of RSA, 1997) set out a plan for a decentralised health care delivery system with a primary health care focus based on public, private and non-governmental organisation (NGO) provision. Problems inherent in the health care system that particularly affect older people are physical distances from health facilities and transportation costs, especially in the rural areas, hours of opening and the high cost of treatment. May (1998) points to the high usage of costly private care by poor households due to the absence or poor access and low quality of public sector clinics. Moreover, some of the new reforms have had negative effects for older people who previously came under the care of district geriatric nurses but with restructuring have been left housebound and often bedridden without any medicine or proper nursing care (*Saturday Star*, 21 November 1998).

There is growing evidence that South Africa is experiencing the fastest growing

HIV/AIDs epidemic in Africa, with KwaZulu-Natal displaying prevalence in 1997 of 27% of pregnant women attending public sector clinics. National estimates for all pregnant women attending antenatal clinics are that 14.07% are HIV positive, giving a total estimate of 2.4 million HIV positive people at the end of 1996. The rate of infection is highest in women aged 20-24 years, with levels highest among African women (Barron, 1998). The implications for older people are that HIV/AIDS will likely account for ever-mounting proportions of health expenditure, while older people and particularly women, take on the role of caring and parenting 'AIDS orphans'.

Welfare policy reform

Mkhabela and Thapelo (1999) state that while South Africa has witnessed far-reaching political and socio-economic changes since the elections in 1994, the skewed social security budget remains an issue of grave concern. Discriminatory aspects of the welfare system which continue to disadvantage Africans and to a lesser extent Coloureds and Indians are gradually being addressed. In this regard the following reform initiatives are significant:

- There is a new formula for the subsidisation of residential care that aims to ensure that only older people in need of 24-hour care are accommodated in frail care facilities. Government policy otherwise emphasises community-based rather than institutional care for older people.
- Parity in old-age grants may help ensure equal opportunities for older people who cannot provide for themselves but individuals are encouraged to make adequate provision for their own retirement.
- The repeal of the Fundraising Act of 1978 and the passing of the Non-Profit Organisations Act (Act 71 of 1997) is designed to encourage and support the role of non-profit organisations in meeting the diverse needs of the people of South Africa including older people.

The overall tenet of policy, therefore, is to increase the focus on community-based care and support, rather than the emphasis on residential care which characterised the apartheid era.

About 88% of the total welfare budget is currently allocated to social assistance of various types, constituting 7.5% of total government spending. The Department of Health and Social Welfare administers the following social grants, administered directly by the Welfare Section of the Department: social pensions, child support, care dependency, war veterans, foster care and disability grants as well as grants in aid. Grants for older persons form the largest proportion of this budget with an estimated 61% of the national welfare budget being spent on social security and welfare services for the elderly. In all, in 1998 3 million beneficiaries received various social grants of which the majority were pensions.

There are problems with current policy regarding welfare in general and services for the elderly more particularly, in that it does not take into consideration that the population is ageing within a context of structural inequality. Moreover, although policy is premised on older people remaining in their communities for as long as possible, community services are not sufficiently developed to permit older people to become and remain independent members of their communities. Within the new Department of Health and Social Welfare there is a commitment to addressing the needs of older people but resources do not even begin to address the current need, let alone that of the future (van den Heever, 1999). Moreover, recent media 'scandals' on the department's consistent tendency to underspend its budgets point to a severe lack of institutional capacity within a low-status ministry.

Social grants and the old-age pension

With the exception of a few countries (Namibia and, to some extent, Tanzania), South Africa stands out as the only country in sub-Saharan Africa with formal economic support for older citizens in the form of an old-age pension (OAP)[8]. Research highlights the critical role played by pensions in the alleviation of poverty in South Africa (Lund, 1993; Ardington and Lund, 1995; Lund et al, 1996) and this was confirmed by the research presented in this chapter.

The Department of Welfare (later Welfare and Pensions) was established in 1937 to serve all races, but by the time of high apartheid in the 1950s under the Nationalist Party government, it had been divided into separate departments to serve different races. This fragmentation was extended with the establishment of 'self-governing areas' and the 'independent states' or so-called *Bantustans*. Therefore the post-apartheid government elected in 1994 inherited 17 state departments of welfare, coordinated by three others (Lund, 1992). As a result, organisational restructuring of the Department of Health and Social Welfare has proved a challenge.

The state pension is a statutory right for all qualifying South Africans. It was established in 1928 primarily for Whites and was extended to all racial groups in 1944, but with disparate gains in favour of Whites, and with Africans being the least favoured. During the twilight years of apartheid (1991-94), the welfare budget grew rapidly as the government attempted racial parity in social pensions. This was achieved for the first time in 1993. Taken up by the new Government of National Unity, African pensions were raised and by 1999 the maximum monthly pension was around R500 (about GB£50). The OAP is non-contributory, with monies coming out of general taxes and benefits being means tested. It is payable to women at 60 and men at 65 years of age. According to Kinsella and Ferreira (1997), in 1993 61% and 68% of age-qualified men and women respectively received the state OAP.

The distribution of OAPs across racial groups and rural and urban areas is shown in Table 13.1. According to Kinsella and Ferreira (1997) nearly 80% among the African population of those who qualify have been reported to receive a pension. They also argue that 85% of all pensioners live in three-generation households, suggesting a high incidence of this household structure

Table 13.1: The distribution of OAPs in 1996

	Total	African	Coloured	Indian	White
Households (%)	100	71.4	7.7	2.7	18.2
OAP HH[a] (%)	100	89.2	5.3	1.5	4.0
HHs in group with OAP (%)		23.7	13.6	10.8	4.5
OAPs rural (%)	66.4	73.9	5.5	0.0	10.3
OAPs urban (%)	19.1	15.5	57.4	56.8	32.4
OAPs metro (%)	14.6	10.6	37.1	43.2	57.4
Take-up rate: women/men[b]	62/69	77/80	61/66	64/67	5/14

[a] Of all households receiving OAP, the proportion received by different population groups.

[b] Calculations by Deaton and Case based on the 1993 Living Standards and Development Survey.

Source: Lund et al (1996, p 101)

among the African population. Viewed over time the number of white pensioners is declining as more people make private provision for their retirement. The number of African people receiving pensions is increasing as the system becomes better known, as mobile pay points extend further into the rural areas and as the life expectancy of black South Africans increases (Lund, 1992).

Nevertheless, many organisations have expressed fear that already older people face destitution unless the government channels more resources into community-based care. Coupled with this is the fact that in some areas, community-level social support systems, which provided care for older people have disintegrated due to violence and displacement. Moreover, there is constant pressure and some firm proposals encouraging government to reduce state assistance to older people (South African Race Survey, 1998). It is against this background that the research sought to provide first-hand information and perceptions on the situation of older people in South Africa and the various livelihood strategies they are adopting.

The contribution of older persons

While older people are still respected as guardians and custodians of tradition and custom in South Africa and see this role as important themselves, the reality of their experience is often exhausting tedium and grinding poverty alongside declining health and growing dependency. All too often they find themselves left as head of a family, separated from their sons and daughters and looking after their grandchildren, providing their food and other material needs from their pensions. Health and welfare practitioners interviewed emphasised older peoples' need for security in advancing age, emphasising the importance of the presence of a family, providing food, shelter and emotional support. It was pointed out that the reality for many older people, especially women, was one of being continuously overburdened by the responsibility of rearing grandchildren and often maintaining both these children and their adult parents as well. Most young people interviewed during the research confirmed that they themselves had been raised by older people.

The meaning of old age

In all four study areas, older people saw ageing as a natural and inevitable process which brought with it the benefits of experience but also declining health and the emotional and physical stress associated with forgetfulness and unexplained emotional outbursts. Interestingly, older people identified different categories of old age associated with the chronology of the ageing process. For example, in the rural search site in Limpopo Province a distinction was drawn between *mkhegulu* (one who is old but still able to care for himself/herself) and *xikoxa* (one who is frail and helpless and dependent on care from others). In KwaZulu-Natal older people were described as *insizwa e qinile* (meaning young-old), *indoda e ndala* (meaning old-old) and *ikhehla* (meaning very old). In the urban study area in Gauteng Province, older people, whether relatives or not, were identified in terms of fictitious kin, for example *gogo* (meaning grandmother) and *umkhulu* (meaning grandfather), and then the terms for great-grandmother, great-great-grandfather and so on. What became clear in the context of the research is that such chronological definitions of old age became particularly important inasmuch as they related to people's physical, financial, emotional and mental health needs.

Everywhere young adults were preoccupied with older people's declining physical capacity and growing dependency on others. In rural Limpopo Province, young people spoke quite harshly of very old people as behaving like children or infants, constantly demanding attention especially when feeling neglected or forgotten. They bemoaned their lack of personal hygiene due to their inability to perform basic tasks, such as bathing and feeding themselves. In the urban study sites, young adults talked of older people less in terms of reverting to childlike behaviour and more in relation to continuous nagging and complaining about everything, especially the lifestyle and consumption patterns of younger people. Despite these overwhelming perceptions of older people as being difficult and burdensome, it was also recognised that they continued to play a very significant role in society. The positive attributes of older people are expounded in traditional folktales, which emphasise their experience and knowledge but more particularly in relation to the research, many of the younger people interviewed were highly dependent on the caring capacity of the older people in their households and communities. However, service providers and practitioners working in health and welfare emphasised that this was only one side of the story and that older people were also very neglected, exploited and vulnerable. They regarded the present OAP as inadequate to meet the growing needs of increasing numbers of grandchildren and other dependants living off pensions alongside older people themselves.

Organisational activities

Although the contribution of older people is most significant within family and household structures, through providing caring and 'parenting' roles and financial support for their immediate next of kin and extended family members, they also contributed at a wider community level. Men retained their traditional status as household heads, irrespective of whether they were employed or productive. However, all too often they did so without the financial capacity to carry out the providing responsibilities associated with this role. They complained of a loss of purpose in relationships with their families and felt an acute lack of status. In rural areas older men were involved in traditional leadership structures like the *kgoro* or tribal council in Limpopo Province where as elders, they acted as advisers to the chiefs and community. They also played a ceremonial role in traditional festivities and engaged in dispute settlement. In urban areas they were more likely to come into conflict with younger political leaders in this role. Older women in all the study sites were regular churchgoers and often ranked the church as the most important social institution in their lives, above all for the personal satisfaction and community it provided. They also played an important role in communities, as child-minders, advisors and peace brokers, as well as organisers of burial societies and by performing nursing and midwifery roles where health facilities were inadequate.

A number of social development programmes have been initiated since 1994 that are targeted at or embrace older people, including income-generating activities and support schemes to micro-enterprises, skills development and cooperative activities in rural areas. Voluntary sector and community-based organisations also have independent programmes similar to government schemes and depend largely on funding from international development agencies for these activities. Many of these programmes encourage participation by older people with the intention of improving their wellbeing. Older men were fairly sceptical of such development initiatives, while older women were far more engaged in activities designed to enhance incomes, such as craft and sewing programmes or chicken rearing. Those involved were emphatic that this had improved their wellbeing, perceived in terms of an improved diet and the ability to afford decent clothing and other basic commodities. Women were also more active in organisations catering for older people, such as through literacy projects, health promotion and support to victims of crime and violence. They talked of how participating in these activities relieved their tedium. Men, by contrast, saw organised social activities and small-scale income-generating projects as feminine activities. An exception appeared to be the Community Policing Forums set up by the Ministry of Safety and Security in which they participated. They saw this as an extension of their customary roles as disciplinarians and as custodians of tribal laws and practices, as well as an important contribution to the fight against crime in South Africa. In two of the research sites they claimed to regularly meet with police officers, providing information and identifying victims of crime.

Lastly in relation to different forms of organisation, older people spoke passionately about their role in the political history of the country and were conscious of how this had affected them in their youth. Many talked with pride of their participation in the first democratic elections in 1994 and their active political affiliation was highlighted during the registration process for the country's second democratic elections in June 1999. Focus group discussions revealed that in a context where voter registration declined overall, the majority of older people had registered. Nevertheless, older people felt largely forgotten by the current political leadership with its emphasis on the youth and saw their contribution as being ignored at a time when they were still keen to play a political role in the democratic processes of the country.

Livelihood activities

The overwhelming contribution of older people in South Africa relates to the way they directly facilitate the livelihood strategies of poorer households. Despite the widespread emphasis placed on the caring and child-rearing role of older people, they are also vitally important to the livelihood strategies of low-income households and families. Their pensions are especially important here but so are their on-going economic activities. In rural areas the main opportunities available were found to be in subsistence agriculture. The research suggested that a typical day for older rural women included spending some time working on a garden plot and looking after livestock, with inordinate amounts of time being spent searching for firewood and collecting water. Participation in income-generating projects was minimal because of the demands on their time and the absence of easily accessible and viable markets for their products. As such, older rural dwellers were found to rely more heavily on pensions and other grants for their subsistence than urban and peri-urban dwellers[9].

In urban and peri-urban areas there were more opportunities for income earning on the part of older people but at a high cost. Women reported that their typical day started at 5am as they did household chores, took care of grandchildren and engaged in income-earning activities. Older people were able to augment their pensions in a number of ways. For example, the shortage of housing and overcrowding in low-income urban areas enabled some older people who have secure tenure to sublet rooms or backyard shacks. Older people were also likely to participate in *stokvels* (revolving savings and credit clubs) and informal trading and service activities such as *spaza* shops[10] and the sale of marketable produce and second-hand clothing. Some older men in urban areas were able to draw on their former work experience and operate as tradesmen or sell skills in the informal economy to secure an income.

For most of the frailer people interviewed, however, their pension was the main source of income for themselves and often the only source of income for their households. A participatory research exercise conducted with a group of older people in rural Limpopo Province involved allocating 50 beans to different items of expenditure. The results are very revealing (Table 13.2). They show

Table 13.2: Expenditure patterns of older people in rural Limpopo Province[a]

Women		Men	
School expenses	16	School fees	19
Food	12	Food	15
Clothing	6	Clothing	10
Electricity	5	Beer	2
Church and clubs	4	Cigarettes	2
Annual cost of Title Deed	2	Building materials	1
Debts to shops	2	Funeral benefits	1
Transport	1		
Seeds and fertilisers	1		
Building materials	1		
Total	50	Total	50

[a] Proportional expenditure represented by 50 beans.

Source: Mohatle and Agyarko (1999)

the tiny proportion of an already tiny sum, which older people spend on themselves. When asked to show what proportion of their pensions older people spent on their families and on themselves they took 20 beans. They allocated five beans to the pensioner and 15 beans to children and grandchildren. It was acknowledged that women in general contributed more than men towards the livelihoods of their families. When asked to demonstrate the relative proportions they used 10 beans. Of these they used seven to represent older women's contribution and three to represent that of older men. They reasoned that this was because men had always been absent leaving women to raise the children and take responsibility for household livelihoods and women just continued to spend their income on household bills and food and on their children and on educating their grandchildren.

Livelihood strategies and opportunities differed between rural and urban environments but pensions constitute the major source of income for South Africa's older people everywhere. In urban and peri-urban areas there were a few further options available such as domestic work and trading and service activities in the informal economy but older people engaged in income-earning activities often at great personal cost to themselves. Moreover, expenditure was greater in urban areas where a larger proportion of the pension was consumed by food and school fees and where municipal rates and service charges such as for electricity became major expenditure items.

Poverty and vulnerability

Generally, older people associated poverty with the inability to meet basic needs like shelter and food, having no pension and poor purchasing power.

Material wealth was measured by the possession of a house, a car and educated children. In rural and peri-urban areas men associated wellbeing with having livestock, land, a number of wives, and large families. In urban contexts, having business ventures and luxury goods were seen as evidence of wellbeing. Apart from material wealth, wellbeing was seen to be associated with being healthy and able to participate in leisure activities. Above all importance was attached to having a close-knit family that could support you and having siblings as guarantors of security and comfort.

Older people invariably explained their poverty in terms of their inability to recover economically from apartheid policies such as the migrant labour system and most importantly, the 1913 Native Land Act that reserved most of the land for whites and forced Africans to move from their original land to unproductive reserves. Care providers and professionals cited factors causing poverty among older people as urbanisation and cross-cultural marriages, which eroded practices guaranteeing security in old age. Also mentioned was the continued practice of customary law in some contexts, which treated women as perpetual minors[11]. Ethnic differences and political conflict reached civil-war proportions in some parts of the country during the transition from apartheid, notably in KwaZulu-Natal. As different groups battled for control of the post-apartheid political dispensation, older people were caught in the crossfire between rival groups, losing the homes, possessions, even their children and this has had a profound impact on their current socio-economic status. One informant in KwaZulu Natal emphatically maintained that a key factor contributing to his state of poverty was the political violence that had erupted around him. It had claimed the life of his son who was stabbed to death before his eyes. It had forced him to give up his employment and to move repeatedly. He had ended up in a two-roomed mud house in an informal settlement with 22 unemployed children and grandchildren, all of them depending on his pension.

There was a marked difference in the way that poverty was seen to manifest itself in rural and urban settings. In urban areas, high-levels of crime and political violence, along with racial discrimination and low self-esteem, were identified by older people as important elements of their experience of poverty. They spoke of their experience of unemployment and the historical legacy of apartheid education policies that left them with very low levels of literacy, as well as problems with the living environment such as poor sanitation and vulnerability to related diseases. In rural areas older people measured poverty in terms of the absence of land and livestock for agriculture and the inability to build a *kraal* or homestead for the family. In peri-urban areas of KwaZulu-Natal three categories of wellbeing emerged from the research process:

- *Poverty stricken:* being the majority of older people who are solely dependent on their pensions and who are depended on by large unemployed families and their children and grandchildren;
- *Better state of being:* referring to those who have other income-generating strategies such as subletting their backyard rooms for rental by tenants;

- *Wellbeing:* those older persons who are properly prepared for death and burial.

Factors increasing their vulnerability were seen by older people to be their frailty and poor health. This they saw as the reason for their exposure to abuse and as victims of crime or violence. Although in South Africa as elsewhere, the fear of crime and violence is greater than experience of it, older people and children are still those most likely to be victims of rape and robbery with assault. As such, the escalation of crime was an important issue for older people.

In looking back to identify factors contributing to their vulnerability, older women talked of how in the past African girls were discouraged from attending school or pursuing their education beyond primary level, thereby restricting their earning opportunities. Older women in KwaZulu-Natal also blamed their poverty on failed marriages. They believed these to have been a curse from the ancestors because people no longer conformed to customary practices such as paying *lobola* (bride price) and *ukwaba* (the presentation of marital gifts). They argued that neglect of these rituals led to serious consequences for families at later stages in their lives. In the rural areas women raised the issue of husbands who migrated to the cities in search of work and were absent for long periods of time, some times as long as twenty years. The women were left to become the sole breadwinners for their families, only occasionally receiving remittances. As one older woman in Limpopo Province put it:

"Men go to Johannesburg 'forever' then they come back when they are sick or almost dead. The woman is left back in the village to take care of the family and to bury him when he comes back to die."

Abuse of older persons

Evidence of elder abuse emerged across all the research sites, with abuse being physical, emotional, financial and psychological. Service providers said that the worst form of abuse facing older people was domestic abuse, including physical and emotional assault. Older people experienced deep pain when their own children or grandchildren became their worst abusers. According to a focus group with older people in KwaZulu-Natal, an important factor contributing to their poverty and vulnerability was the treatment they had received from their families. Some felt their families had only pretended to love them when they received their pensions but kicked them out as soon as the money was spent. As an older person in the largely urbanised province of Gauteng said with resignation, "We are important to our families when we get our pensions".

Older women live under the threat of being accused of practising witchcraft, especially in rural areas. According to police officers interviewed in Limpopo Province, witchcraft accusations are mostly levelled at older women once they are frail and living alone. Commonly they are banished from the community and in rarer cases murdered. Younger interviewees described how older people, and particularly women, were often viewed suspiciously when they displayed changes in appearance and behaviour. Ewing has described the threat of witchcraft accusations to older women's rights in Africa more generally:

> The bloodshot eyes, hunched posture, gnarled skin and solitary air of an older woman in a rural village may be easily attributed to her living conditions. Decades of cooking over smoky fires in confined spaces, of carrying children, wood and water, of labouring in the fields – only to be abandoned or neglected in your final years – takes a heavy toll on health and appearance. However, these and other characteristics are often seen not as the harsher signs of ageing but as the marks of a witch. The belief in witchcraft is strong in many parts of Africa.... If a child falls suddenly ill and there is no prospect of treatment, if the crops fail and there is no food to fall back on, if a family suffers recurrent misfortune and there is no explanation, sometimes a scapegoat must be found. Older women will often provide the scapegoat, being blamed as witches for all manner of death and disaster. (Ewing, 1999, p 40)

Nor is witchcraft an issue confined to rural areas. In an informal settlement in a peri-urban area of KwaZulu-Natal, the research team was told of one older woman who used to place her rubbish in a certain spot near to her home. When another family moved in and erected a house on that spot, she continued taking her rubbish there. Her new neighbours deemed this an evil act and accused her of being a witch. One issue that becomes clear from the prevalence of witchcraft accusations in South Africa is that they cause already poor and marginalised old women to be ostracised and further impoverished and as such, they can be viewed as an African example of inter-generational solidarity breaking down.

However, atrocities against older people are committed more often by family members than the wider public. Reports of abuse ranged from the taking of pensions by force, to physical assault, sometimes stemming from family members wanting to evict older people and take over their house. Women were more likely to be affected by violence, with examples being given in focus group discussions of sole providers being stabbed and raped by grandchildren.

Members of one of the women's organisations interviewed said that beyond physical and mental abuse, they saw the persistent 'parenting' role of older women a form of abuse in itself. They argued that older people were being denied the opportunity to 'age gracefully' because they were under continual pressure to support and raise their grandchildren. A lack of financial and material support during this protracted process of caring threatened their long-term physical and emotional wellbeing. Other people described the imposition of grandchildren on elderly women by their children and others close to them as similar to treating older people as 'refuse bins' or 'dumping places'. Interviews conducted in old-age homes revealed that some older people had been placed in residential care to avoid family abuse.

Older people are vulnerable for many reasons associated with contemporary poverty, facing abuse from their immediate families and victimisation within their communities, unaware or intolerant of the natural processes associated with ageing. They live in a society where lack of public safety is a grave problem for everyone and where they are more vulnerable because of their frailty. This compounds the poverty they already face as a result of the historical effects of and the protracted struggle against apartheid. Ironically, although the social pension was important for older people in meeting their basic needs and raising their status and self-esteem as family providers, in some cases it also exposed them to abuse by unscrupulous and uncaring family members.

Access to support and services

Despite efforts by the post-apartheid dispensation to maintain the universal old-age pension and the introduction or extension of a range of welfare policies to improve conditions of the poorest South Africans, there have been problems of access, not least of all associated with the difficulties of restructuring welfare services and the dismantling of the racially fragmented system of delivery under apartheid. This has been accompanied by a move to computerisation and a re-registration programme, which includes among its objectives, addressing leakage, and malfeasance by weeding out payments to 'ghost' pensioners. The result for genuine pensioners has often meant delays and loss of income. One pensioner who had been waiting over a year said, "I rely on part-time jobs and cannot ask for support from my neighbours because I know I cannot pay back". Another told how his pension was stopped without any notification and he did not know how to reapply so he had resorted to begging for food and money on the street. Compounding the problem is that older people do not always have the necessary documentation for re-registration.

Welfare officials in KwaZulu-Natal said they had evidence that some older people did not re-register for their pensions in order to avoid the abuse they endured on pension day. Many older people reported being forcefully marched off to collect their pensions by relatives who then claimed it, and of being ambushed by criminals on the way home from the pay point. They are also daunted by the long queues at the pension pay points and one nearby clinic reported routinely treating cases of fainting, exhaustion and sometimes serious illness and death on pension days. Even though pensions can be deposited into bank accounts, this is not a popular option with many older African people, who are illiterate or unfamiliar with a traditionally hostile or unwelcoming banking system. The Department of Welfare is trying to establish mechanisms for providing better and safer access to pensions and a task team is currently working on this issue[12].

While it is important to highlight the contribution of older people themselves and to point out the harsh nature of elder abuse in South Africa, it is equally important to remember that the family plays a critical role in offering support for older people and extended families are common. Older people themselves saw the family as the main provider of security even when they themselves were the main financial providers. They saw 'support' as the benefit of living in the company of people who provided them with care and love. They also derived a great sense of emotional comfort and a sense of belonging from the presence of siblings and other close family members and this in turn allayed fears of isolation. On the part of professional carers, regular contact with children and family closeness was seen as crucial to their sense of emotional health. For many African families, therefore, inter-generational solidarity is alive and well at the micro-level.

Moreover, African culture prides itself on *ubuntu*, a term understood as the extension of family values to the broader community[13]. In many communities, despite rising levels of unemployment, crime and associated challenges, the spirit of *ubuntu* was seen and reported to prevail and as such, older people continue to receive social respect and support, with inter-generational solidarity being rooted in relations of reciprocity that are widely understood. The challenge for the ruling African National Congress and successive governments in South Africa is to find policies that support rather than undermine reciprocal relationships and solidaristic practices of its poorest citizens. As is the case elsewhere, there is a danger that a policy focus on family support and care in the community is entirely residual, relying on and depleting the assets of South Africa's urban poor rather than conserving and restoring them, thereby penalising them for their very resilience and resourcefulness.

Conclusion

Older people play a vital role in South Africa's social and economic life. Socially, the care provided in households and communities by older people, especially women is indispensable to younger adults seeking and engaging in work. They are single-handedly responsible for the rearing and socialisation of thousands of children and they are crucial to the maintenance of social networks and the fostering of *ubuntu* or the spirit of community. Financially the income of older people and notably the social pension is crucial for the survival of many low-income households and extended families. The perspectives of older people, their families and the front-line workers most familiar with the situation of older people in South Africa, support the argument for universal pensions, perhaps supported by a minimum income so that the livelihoods of the poorest families are not so reliant on transfers meant to relieve the financial stress of older people.

Politically, older people in South Africa have paid a high price during the struggle against apartheid and have proved consistent supporters of the new post-apartheid order. In terms of inter-generational solidarity, therefore, they have more than paid their dues. Their efforts have given rise to a constitution espousing equality and social justice, the advantages of which younger generations will reap. They have been rewarded by parity in social pensions and the introduction of a number of social development initiatives aimed at alleviating their poverty. However, in the context of continued poverty and rising unemployment they are continuing to contribute to household, community and national development, often in a context where younger adults are not keeping to their side of the inter-generational contract.

Contemporary policy in South Africa has had to address itself to high expectations from historically disadvantaged populations under apartheid. In addition to the ageing veterans of the anti-apartheid struggle and the many long-suffering victims of racially discriminatory policy, it also has to meet the equally high expectations of its youth, both those who were the 'young lions' of the national democratic movement and those for whom apartheid is something they now read about in history books. For reasons of economic growth as well as social stability, the government sees as urgent the need for policies that prioritise the youth and those of working age. While understandable, the findings of this chapter's present research suggest it would be both shortsighted and unjust to ignore as a result, the contribution of the country's senior citizens. The multiple and inter-generational livelihood strategies of South Africa's poorest households reflect the understanding inherent in the African proverb cited in the title of this chapter:

A new branch can be strengthened by an old branch.

Policies that give value to and support inter-generational solidarity hold the prospect of ensuring that the mutual support encouraged within families and communities is nurtured. This means extending inter-generational solidarity to the level of national and indeed international social investment. In the words of another proverb from Limpopo Province, *Xiwandi xi ta ku wundla* – "look after it as much as it looked after you".

However, internationally the needs and contributions of older people are severely neglected and "the implications of ageing are all but invisible in international policy" (HelpAge International, 2002, p 3). This implies, not only a focus on national policies, but policies on ageing within the context of international development. The International Plan of Action on Ageing, adopted by member states in 1982, held low status within the menu of imperatives and demands on the UN system, and the Year of Older People in 1999 had very limited impact. Although ageing is seen as a critical issue for OECD countries, it remains fearfully neglected in countries of the developing world. Even international agencies and initiatives concerned with social development tend to include older people as an afterthought – a vulnerable group in need of residual welfare or relief. The argument in this chapter is that older people also need to be included in existing policies and interventions, not only as a matter of equity and human rights, but also because the impact of ageing on development policy cannot be ignored. As argued in *State of the world's older people 2002*:

Many development policy makers have not taken account of the extent or character of demographic change in low-income countries and have assumed that policies for older people and ageing are not necessary. In fact, the speed and extent of population ageing and the size of older populations, even in the poorest countries and those worst affected by HIV/AIDS, makes policy on ageing and older people essential. The contribution of millions of economically active older people cannot be ignored in the fight against poverty, and the changing roles of older people and nature of intergenerational links need to underpin social policy. (HelpAge International, 2002, p 77)

The much heralded 'livelihoods perspective' that informs much of the analysis and practice of social development, could do much to demonstrate the reality of how older people contribute to their own welfare and that of their households and wider networks. It remains a matter of political will to translate such insights into policy nationally and internationally.

Notes

[1] Rihlamfu leva khale vi fiysiwa hi lerintshwana, a Shangaan proverb from Bungeni, Northern Province, South Africa.

[2] It is predicted that the percentage of older persons in South Africa will increase from the current 4.4% of the population to 7.7% by the year 2025 (South African Survey, 1998).

[3] The research was undertaken while I was academic adviser to an ESCOR funded project 'The contributions of older people to development in Africa', undertaken by HelpAge International, with Amanda Heslop as project leader and Robert deGraft Agyarko as principal researcher. This chapter could not have been written without their efforts and insight and an early version was presented at the Development Studies Association Conference, held at the University of Bath in September 1999, and was written with the helpful collaboration of Amanda Heslop. The work was carried out in partnership with HelpAge International members and partners in South Africa between June 1998 and September 1999.

[4] Both participatory research methods and mainstream qualitative research techniques were used. Policy makers and service providers concerned with older people were involved as part of the research team in order that the research fed into policy and practice. To this end, findings were also presented and discussed at a consultative workshop held in August 1999 in South Africa. Four areas in three provinces of South Africa were selected as sites for the research to reflect the diverse nature of older people's conditions. The major criteria for selection were rural-urban differences, socio-cultural groupings and settlement and housing conditions. They included a low-income township and peri-urban informal settlement in KwaZulu-Natal, a typical urban settlement and squatter camp in Gauteng and a rural community under traditional leadership in Northern Province.

[5] My thanks to Gail Wilson for her help in developing these ideas.

[6] The term 'black' is used here to refer to all those population groups classified as 'non-white' under apartheid: the majority black African population (comprising nine linguistic groups), Asians (the majority of whom are of Indian origin), and the so-called 'Coloureds' (the mixed-race population of South Africa).

[7] The current exchange rate between the South African rand and the British pound is R9-10 = GB£1.

[8] It is beyond the scope of this chapter to make reference to the extensive system of private pensions in South Africa or the civil pensions system for state employees. In any case these rarely apply to the poorest pensioners.

[9] Peri-urban areas are those on the perimeter of cities of developing countries or 'the South', where rural pursuits often persist amidst high density living conditions and labour commuting to urban workplaces.

[10] *Spaza* shops are tiny enterprises operating out of kitchen windows or backdoors. They sell bread, milk and a range of consumer items in very small quantities.

[11] Although the South African Constitution accords women equal rights with men, in practice customary law, which sees women as minors, is often upheld by traditional leaders.

[12] According to officials in the Department of Welfare in all three provinces, there have been recent efforts to improve the dissemination of information on the availability of different grants and warning pensioners of fraudulent schemes directed at them, such as bogus funeral policies.

[13] Within a livelihoods perspective, concepts used to evoke the same sentiments and practices include social capital and social assets.

References

Apt, N. 'Trends and prospects in Africa', *Community Development Journal*, vol 27, no 2, pp 130-39.

Apt, N. (1996) *Coping with old age in a changing Africa: Social change and the elderly Ghanaian*, Hants: Avebury.

Apt, N. (1997) *Ageing in Africa*, Geneva: WHO.

Ardington, E. and Lund, F. (1995) 'Pensions and development: social security as complementary to programmes of reconstruction and development', *Development Southern Africa*, vol 12, no 4, pp 557-77.

Beall, J. (ed) (1997) *A city for all: Valuing difference and working with diversity*, London: Zed Books.

Bozzoli, B. (1991) *Women of Phokeng: Consciousness, life strategy, and migrancy in South Africa*, Portsmouth, NH: Heinemann.

Brown, M. (1999) 'The plight of rural elderly in South Africa: a case for a community development cadre?', *Community Development Journal*, vol 34, no 2, pp 143-50.

Bunchandranon, C., Howe, G. and Payumo, A.S. (1997) 'Ageing as an urban experience', in J. Beall (ed) *A city for all: Valuing difference and working with diversity*, London: Zed Books, pp 141-58.

Carter, M.R. and May, J. (1999) 'Poverty livelihood and class in rural South Africa', *World Development*, vol 27, no 1, pp 1-20.

Cattell, M. (1997) 'Ubuntu, African elderly and the African family crisis', *Southern African Journal of Gerontology*, vol 38, no 6, pp 37-39.

Chadha, N.K. and Mongia, R. (1997) 'Intergenerational solidarity', *Indian Journal of Medical Research*, vol 106, pp 370-75.

Charlton, K. (1998) 'Health, healthcare and ageing in Africa: challenges and opportunities', *Southern African Journal of Gerontology*, vol 7, no 2, pp 23-6.

Crehan, K. (1992) 'Rural households: making a living', in H. Berstein, B. Crow and H. Johnson (eds) *Rural livelihoods: Crises and responses*, Oxford: Oxford University Press for The Open University, pp 87-112.

Cross, N. and Barker, R. (1991) *At the desert's edge: Oral histories from the Sahel*, London: Panos Publications Ltd.

Darkwa, O. (1997) 'Reforming the Ghanaian social security system: prospects and challenges, *Journal of Cross-Cultural Gerontology*, vol 12, no 2, pp 175-87.

DfID (Department for International Development) (1999) *Social development*, Dissemination Note no 2, London: DfID, Social Development Department.

Ewing, D. (1999) 'Gender and ageing', in HelpAge International *The ageing and development report. Poverty, independence and the world's older people*, London: Earthscan, pp 33-45.

Francis, E. (2000) *Making a living*, London: Routledge.

Gorman, M. (1999) 'Development and the rights of older people', in HelpAge International *The ageing and development report. Poverty, independence and the world's older people*, London: earthscan, pp 3-21.

Government of the RSA (1999) 'Department of Welfare financial policy notice 463 of 1999', *Government Gazette*, vol 405, no 19888.

Government of the Republic of South Africa (RSA) (1997) 'Ministry for Welfare and Population development notice 1108 of 1997', *Government Gazette*, vol 405, no 19888.

Grimard, F. and Barton, H. (1999) 'Estimating the elderly's returns on the farm: evidence from Cote d'Ivoire', *Journal of Development Economics*, vol 58, no 2, pp 513-31.

Grown, C. and Sebstad, J. (1989) 'Introduction: toward a wider perspective on women's employment', *World Development*, vol 17, no 7, pp 937-52.

HelpAge International (1997) 'The older women as a change agent: a new workshop from ATCOA', *AGEWAYS*, vol 43, pp 25-8.

HelpAge International (1999) *The ageing and development report. Poverty, independence and the world's older people*, London: Earthscan.

HelpAge International (2002) *State of the world's older people 2002*, London: HelpAge International

Heslop, A. (1996) *Report of participatory needs assessment with Muthande Society for the Aged in Clermont township, Durban, South Africa*, London: HelpAge International.

Heslop, A. (1999) 'Poverty and livelihoods in an ageing world', in HelpAge International *The ageing and development report. Poverty, independence and the world's older people*, London: Earthscan, pp 22-31.

Howe, N. (1997) 'Why the graying of the welfare state threatens to flatten the American Dream – or worse', in R.B. Hudson (ed) *The future of age-based public policy*, Baltimore: The Johns Hopkins University Press, pp 36-45.

ILO (International Labour Organisation) (1997) *Ageing in Asia: The growing need for social protection*, Bangkok: ILO Regional Office for Asia and the Pacific.

Ingstad, B., Brunn, F. and Tlou, S. (1997) 'AIDS and the elderly in Tswana', *Journal of Cross-Cultural Gerontology*, vol 12, no 4, pp 357-72.

Kinsella, K. and Feirreira, M. (1997) *International brief, ageing trends: South Africa*, IB/97-2, August, Washington, DC: United States Department of Commerce, Bureau of the Census.

Lloyd-Sherlock, P. (1997) *Old age and urban poverty in the developing world*, Basingstoke: Macmillan Press.

Lloyd-Sherlock, P. (1998) 'Old age, migration, and poverty in the shanty towns of Sao Paulo, Brazil', *The Journal of Developing Areas*, vol 32, no 4, pp 491-514.

Longman, P. (1987) *Born to pay the new politics of aging in America*, Boston: Houghton Mifflin Company.

Lorenz-Meyer, D. (1996) 'The other side of the intergenerational contract', London School of Economics (LSE) Gender Institute Discussion Paper, London: LSE.

Lund, F. (1992) 'Social security and social assistance in "The New South Africa"', Paper presented to the International Conference on Social Security: 50 years after Beveridge, University of York.

Lund, F. (1993) 'Social security in South Africa', *International Social Security Review*, vol 46, no 1, pp 32-41.

Lund, F. with Ardington, S. and Harber, M. (1996) 'Welfare' in D. Budlender (ed) *The women's budget*, Cape Town: Institute for Democracy in South Africa (IDASA), pp 97-120.

May, J. (ed) (1998) *Poverty and inequality in South Africa*, Durban: Praxis Publishing.

McKendrick, B. and Shingwenyana, B.Z. (1995) 'Are old age pensions for urban Africans family allowances? Implications for the reconstruction and development programme', *Social work*, vol 31, no 3, pp 228-35.

Mkhabela, I. and Thapelo, M. (1999) *HelpAge International evaluation report*, Johannesburg: HelpAge International.

Mohatle, T. and Agyarko, R.D. (1999) *Contributions of older persons to development: The South African study*, Draft report, Johannesburg: HelpAge International, April.

Moller, V. (1998) 'The South African pension scheme', *Ageing and Society*, vol 18, no 6, pp 715-19.

Mupedziswa, R. (1999) 'Bruised and battered: the struggles of older female informal traders in urban areas of Zimbabwe since the economic reforms', *Southern African Journal of Gerontology*, vol 8, no 1, pp 9-13.

Prescott, N. (1997) *Choices in financing health care and old age security*, World Bank Discussion Paper no 392, Washington, DC: World Bank.

Sagner, A. (1997) 'Urbanisation, ageing and migration: some evidence from African settlements', *Southern African Journal of Gerontology*, vol 6, no 2, pp 13-19.

South African Institute of Race Relations (SAIRR) (1998) *South African survey*, Johannesburg: SAIRR.

SAIRR (1999) *South African survey*, Johannesburg: SAIRR.

Tamang, D. (1996) 'Working with older people in urban areas', in N. Hall, R. Hart and D. Mitlin (eds) *The urban opportunity: The work of NGOs in cities of the south*, London: Intermediate Technology Publications, pp 39-47.

Tlou, S. (1998) 'HIV/AIDS education programmes for rural old women in Botswana', *Southern African Journal of Gerontology*, vol 7, no 2, pp 23-26.

UNDP (United Nations Development Program) (1999) *Human development report*, New York, NY: UNDP.

UNFPA (United Nations Population Fund) (1998) *Population ageing: Improving the lives of older people*, Report of the ICPD+5 Technical Meeting on Population Ageing, Brussels, 6-9 October 1998, UNFPA.

van den Heever, C. (1999) Keynote Address by the Director of Social Services, Department for Social Welfare, South Africa to *The contribution of older people to development*, a Research Dissemination Workshop of HelpAge International, mimeo.

Van Onselen, C. (1996) *The seed is mine: The life of Kas Maine, a South African sharecropper, 1894-1985*, Cape Town: David Philips.

Van Rensberg, T.R. (1997) Draft Policy Paper for the Department of Welfare, Aged, Pretoria: Republic of South Africa.

Walker, A. (ed) (1996) *The new generational contract: Intergenerational relations, old age and welfare*, London: UCL Press.

Part IV
Future anti-poverty policies:
national and international

.

FOURTEEN

Human rights, transnational corporations and the World Bank

Peter Townsend

This book finds that the UN's aim to free the world of poverty sits uneasily with the current reality of unremitting social polarisation and persisting mass poverty. This is not just one of those familiar ironies about the difference in the relationship between government and governed, over tub-thumping promises and delivery of those promises. It is a paradox consistently revealed in countless shapes and sizes. Therefore, the abasement of many millions of people in the world's increasingly unequal hierarchical social structure stands in sharp contrast to the plans agreed by the overwhelming majority of countries to establish universal human rights. If the violation of those rights is to be understood, and acted upon, the scale and severity of the violation of different kinds of rights – especially economic and social rights – has to be explained in relation to policies being applied at different levels.

In Parts I to III of this book the principal thrust of current international anti-poverty policies has been described, and the anti-poverty policies as well as trends in poverty of rich and poor countries laid out for comparison and appraisal. The case for an alternative approach to policy has been made. How can some of the lessons that may be drawn be put into international and national practice? In this part of the book some of those specific as well as general lessons are explained.

Theoretical context

This chapter picks up three elements of an alternative strategy for particular scrutiny:

1. the theoretical basis of social and economic development, including human rights;
2. the future role and functions of the major transnational corporations in relation to social as well as economic objectives;
3. the necessary recasting of the role and social and economic actions of the international financial agencies, particularly the World Bank.

Inevitably a theory has to be put forward to explain the extremes of human conditions and experiences, not as if these conditions and experiences were fixed but as a rapidly evolving, and deepening, reality. Providing such a multidimensional theory is not the purpose of this chapter. However, one reminder is relevant. The evolution of global capitalism must necessarily be a key theme of theory.

Samir Amin, a major theoretician of the 'Third World', or 'the South', insists on treating capitalism as a concrete historical reality that does not lead to 'development' in the meaning currently given to that word. He argues that the expansion of capital is not to be confused with human development. For example, capitalism, he writes,

> does not imply full employment, or a pre-determined degree of equality in the distribution of income ... [or by those who control such possibilities and are] endowed, for this purpose, with the monopoly represented by private property.... Actually existing capitalism does not work as a system of competition.... [To work] it requires the intervention of a collective authority representing capitalism as a whole. Therefore, the state cannot be separated from capitalism. [The expansion and contraction of employment] are not the expression of abstract 'market laws', but requirements of the profitability of capital under certain historical conditions. (Amin, 1997, pp 14-15)

Expansion is guided by the search for profit by companies.

The powers behind the scene

Historically, therefore, the state was the principal agent in setting the scene, and any conditions, within which companies had to operate. That situation has rapidly changed. Since the late 20th century increasing numbers of writers have pounced on the 'disjuncture' between the formal authority of the state and "the spatial reach of contemporary systems of production, distribution and exchange which often function to limit the competence and effectiveness of national political authorities" (Held, 1995, p 127). Transnational corporations (TNCs) have helped to organise the globalisation of production and of financial transactions. Investment and production decisions do not invariably reflect local or national conditions. Information technology has transformed the mobility of economic units like currencies, stocks, shares and 'futures'. Companies locate, produce and manage manufactured goods and services in different countries with an eye to deriving benefit from different production and marketing conditions across the world. The most powerful companies can determine and change those conditions directly.

TNCs have become major institutional players, along with states, in organising production, employment and trade in large constellations of countries, and therefore necessarily influencing the collective as well as individual living standards and social conditions of the great majority of people making up national populations. This has of course seized the interest of social scientists and commentators; accounts of their growth and functions are to be found in an increasing number of books (for example, Scott et al, 1985; Lang and Hines, 1993; Kolodner, 1994; Korten, 1996; Stichele and Pennartz, 1996; Kozul-Wright and Rowthorn, 1998; Madeley, 1999; Monbiot, 2000; Sklair, 2001; George and Wilding, 2002). The growth of TNCs has been spectacular by any standards in the last three decades. According to one analyst "Corporations have become behemoths, huge global giants that wield immense political power" (Hertz, 2001, p 6). One hundred of the largest corporations now control about 20% of foreign assets. Fifty-one of the world's largest economies are now corporations and the rest nation states. The scale of financial power was described in Chapter One.

The pace of their growth is testified by the continuing phenomenon of 'mega-mergers'. In 2000 Vodaphone, the communications corporation, merged with Mannesmann; SmithKline Beecham, the pharmaceutical conglomerate, merged with Glaxo Wellcome; the internet service provider AOL merged with the media corporation Time Warner. Mergers between huge companies are frequently reported on the business pages of the press.

In absorbing the full significance of the development a number of the features of corporate action have to be explained. One is the creation of mergers and subsidiaries in 20, 30 and many more countries. Such a system or network overpowers competitors. It has a snowball effect. It reduces costs and increases profits. Another feature is the location of production and services. Transfer of working capacity and labour to a new country can attract subsidies from the government of that country to boost jobs and economic viability, just as the threat to withdraw activity from another country can cause a government to reduce its taxes and offer other deals to reduce corporation costs and persuade the TNC to reconsider its plans for relocation.

A third feature is taxation. Operating in scores of different countries TNCs find it convenient to invest off-shore or arrange accounts of production and distribution to avoid or greatly reduce taxable profits, income and expenditure. One method of handling taxation is 'transfer pricing'. TNCs have subsidiaries in different countries. The parent corporation sells materials to one of its subsidiaries in another country at an artificially high price. When these materials are turned into final products profits are thereby reduced and less tax has to be paid. The price has been transferred to the overseas country and the untaxed 'excess' profit pocketed in the headquarters country. Transfer pricing is a form of tax avoidance. In Columbia local subsidiaries reported a 6% profit when the real profit was estimated to be more than ten times higher (Madeley, 1999, p 12). The extent of transfer pricing is not known and evidence is hard to assemble.

Another feature is access to the law. Corporations have the resources to command the highest paid counsel. This provides a huge advantage in dealing with smaller competitors but also in dealing with governments. Most important of all is the ramifying issue of political power. Scale of operations can mean that local councils and governments try to please incumbent plants and labour forces, and attract others. Sponsorships can deliver good names for companies. Rough justice can be passed off as unavoidable adjustment.

The reassessment of the power of transnational corporations

The corporations are closely linked with the international financial agencies and with states. Samir Amin has cast the Bretton Woods international financial agencies – the World Bank and the International Monetary Fund (IMF) – as "managerial mechanisms protecting the profitability of capital" (Amin, 1997, p 17). A big problem is that different UN agencies – IMF, World Bank, WTO, UNCTAD, and the UN itself – offer little or no information either about their own links with the biggest corporations or about the economic, labour and social policies followed by the corporations – whether these are internal policies for their own employees working in many different countries, or are policies affecting consumers and the general populations of particular countries in which they operate.

Secretary General Boutros Boutros-Ghali presided over the UN's demolition of three modest-sized monitoring units of TNCs at the beginning of the 1990s. A small stream of information at the time (represented in, for example, UN, 1988) virtually dried up. The corporations were scarcely even mentioned in the proceedings of successive World Summits. Examples are the Copenhagen World Summit on Social Development in 1995 and the 2002 summit at Monterrey. As a consequence, there is all too little standard public information from public sources about the activities and developments of huge corporations.

Some information can of course be extracted from the publicity that has been given to the flow of court cases and protest campaigns involving the TNCs. Damaging revelations surface frequently in relation to McDonalds, Nestle, Nike, Gap, Exxon, Shell, Unilever and Enron, for example. At the time of the collapse of Enron in 2001 caustic testimony was given by Arundhati Roy, among others, about the 1993 agreement of Maharashtra state to let Enron build India's biggest, and first private, power plant. After considerable opposition the state government was defeated in elections in 1995 and the contract was scrapped – only to be revived when intervening political pressure was exerted (for example by the US ambassador, who was subsequently appointed a director of Enron). A minority government in office for only 13 days in 1996 took the step on its last day to approve the contract that had provoked prolonged opposition. The contract for 695 megawatts in the first stage involved payments to Enron of $210 million annually. In the second stage (2015 megawatts) the state electricity board was legally bound to pay back a total of $30 billion. It was estimated that $210 million per year would be needed for the next 40 years, constituting "the largest contract ever signed in the history of India" (Roy, 2001, p 3). "Experts ... have called it the biggest fraud in the country's history. The project's gross profits work out at between $12b and $14b" (Roy,

2001, p 3). The Maharashtra State Electricity Board had to set aside 70% of its revenue to pay Enron. The fixed charges were destroying the board – which was trying to crack down on local companies providing electricity far cheaper. Their prices were being forced up to the Enron level and this was putting them out of business.

Extreme practices have been vilified but information about standard practices is difficult to find. The general merits of the loans made to poor countries by the international financial agencies are widely debated but the general merits of contracts awarded to TNCs are given small attention. By 2001 the World Bank was awarding some 40,000 contracts annually to private firms. The US Treasury department calculations also show that for every $1 contributed by the US to the international development banks, US corporations receive double that amount in bank-financed procurement contracts (www.corpwatch.org; and see also Karliner, 1997).

There is no global code of conduct for TNCs. There have indeed been attempts to introduce binding codes of conduct, without success (see van der Pijl, in Overbeek, 1993). There is the ILO code to regulate labour issues (ILO, 1998) and OECD Guidelines for Multinational Enterprises (OECD, 2001), but these are general statements and contain injunctions rather than powers or even universally agreed norms of conduct. While the courts certainly have powers over law breaking, they tend only to be used as measures of last resort, as they are extremely expensive. Activities short of law breaking can be shown to have serious consequences for society and are not in any serious sense 'accountable' (for example, see Korten, 1995; Madeley, 1999; Sklair, 2001). Many of the biggest TNCs have established codes and collaborative institutions under the concept of 'global corporate governance'. In the US a movement for 'caring capitalism' was led by Business for Social Responsibility (BSR), operating from Washington in 1992. By the mid-1990s, BSR had a national membership and affiliations of 800 (Sklair, 2001, p 159). Sometimes such corporate initiatives are good attempts to face up to new problems; but they can also be cynical attempts to sidestep costly issues by constructing images on the cheap.

International financial agencies

The international financial agencies have played an increasing role in developing social policies favourable to TNCs – and other UN agencies have lamely followed suit. World Bank conditional loans have given the impetus to social security reforms that have privileged private company business – especially for pensions. "The privatisation of social security has benefited international corporations that become partners with local business elites" (Armada et al, 2001, p 729). Analysts have also shown that by endorsing the privatisation of health services, for example in Latin America, the WHO has converged with these policies (Armada et al, 2001, p 729). Other international agencies than the World Bank and the IMF are supporting their interpretations of current social policies. The alliance between transnational corporations, international financial agencies and the richest states is posing the major problem for the satisfaction of human rights and objectives like the elimination of poverty.

Privatisation of the kind promoted by the agencies seems to be impelling an increase in inequality and making much more difficult the reduction of poverty. Certainly this seems to be the view of no less an authority than Ravi Kanbur, director of the World Bank's World Development Report on Poverty, until his resignation in May 2000. Later in 2000 he revealed that poverty was often greater than the figures given in the Bank's handbooks of statistics. Among the reasons "it is quite possible for public services to worsen considerably and yet for this effect to not show up in the income-expenditure based measures of poverty incidence" (Kanbur, 2000, p 10). Technically this means that if the measure of income were to include the value to families of goods and services received in kind, many more people in countries that were privatising public services would be found to be below the poverty line. Effectively, Kanbur's explanation is also an admission that structural adjustment policies, giving priority to privatisation and cuts in expenditure on public services, had counteracted some if not all of any benefits from economic growth that had accrued to many poor countries. Kanbur's post-resignation account of the ideological and technical context of the work of the World Bank shows the central importance he attaches to the definition and statistical measurement of the extent of poverty. Unwittingly, his retrospective analysis justifies renewed concern about the construction of a poverty line and the value of fresh investigation of its scientific basis.

In 1990 the problem of poverty was given top billing on the world's agenda for action. Since then, however, as in the previous three decades, its reduction and eradication has proved to be elusive. This was due partly to economic and social policies that were shown to move trends in poverty in the wrong direction. However, it was also due partly to explicit and implicit explanations of the causes of the problem adopted alike by governments and international agencies that have been shown to be misplaced. The overhaul and substitution of previous entrenched conceptions will be a long and bitterly resisted process.

The World Bank

The difference between what the governing structures of the IMF and the World Bank are, and what they might be, can be illustrated from their history. Keynes was a central figure in the creation of the Bretton Woods institutions in 1944 but the result was not what he wanted. He had advocated the creation of an international credit-creating institution and in the early years of war he called attention to the serious financial liquidity problems that would arise at its end, that needed concerted action if dangerous forms of instability were to be avoided. The industrialised countries of Western Europe had been devastated. They were obliged to restrict imports, devalue currencies, maintain tight price controls and cut public expenditure because they had insufficient resources combined with inevitably high levels of debt. In addition, their recovery would be long-delayed and economic growth kept low. This would worsen economic prospects of growth, and indeed restrict the US economy itself. On top of the need of these countries for post-war reconstruction was the problem of ensuring enough liquidity to finance the growth of world trade. The governments should not be forced by fluctuating balance of payments problems into cycles of deflation and competitive devaluation. That would depress employment and living standards in economically strong and not only weak countries.

Keynes therefore argued for a kind of world central bank or 'Clearing Union' that created a deposit of new currency for every country in the world which it could count on at times of difficulty to pay creditor governments. The big countries would create a giant fund from which countries in demonstrable financial adversity could draw – up to a sizeable minimum level – without strings. Up to that minimum level they would not have to justify their policies. The total amount of currency deposited would rise steadily in rough proportion to world trade. In fact what materialised was a pale shadow of Keynes' intentions. Total resources were less than a third of what he advised. Countries were not awarded an allocation. They had to contribute to the total fund to be eligible for membership and hence the opportunity to apply for loans – to which stringent conditions could be attached. Membership was conditional rather than universal; debtors had less independence, aid had strings, and the US remained predominantly in charge of those strings. And a system intended to promote the post-war recovery of the industrialised countries was soon converted into an instrument providing loans to the poorest countries.

Created at the Bretton Woods Conference in 1944 as an adjunct of the IMF – and broadly taking on the programme for long-term development while the IMF dealt with short-term financial stability – the World Bank Group is made up of five agencies making loans or guaranteeing credit to the 180 member countries. The five are:

- the International Bank for Reconstruction and Development (accounting for more than half the Bank's lending and $10.5 billion in 2001);
- the International Development Association (accounting for about a quarter, and $6.8 billion in 2001);
- the International Finance Corporation ($3.9 billion in 2001);
- the Multilateral Investment Guarantee Agency ($2 billion guarantees in 2001);
- the International Settlement of Investment Disputes.

Total Bank lending in each year has to be set against loan repayments – but also the value of contracts arranged with corporations. In 1993 net disbursements by the World Bank, that is, gross disbursements minus repayments to the Bank, totalled just over $7 billion – a miniscule amount by comparison with World GDP and less even than the expenditure of most *single* departments of state in the OECD countries. However, the borrowing countries paid out nearly as much in that year – $6.8 billion – to corporations from the OECD countries, leaving only a marginal positive cash flow into the treasuries of the recipient countries (Karliner, www.corpwatch.org, 1 December 1997).

The redefinition and re-measurement of poverty is a necessary part of the process of justifying, and constructing, international loans, and cannot be separated from the choice of theory required to explain the problem and specify the action required to resolve it.

The World Bank's measure of poverty

The World Bank has been under increasing pressure about the persistence of mass poverty. In the early 1990s the Bank conceded a "loss of momentum during the 1980s" in reducing poverty (World Bank, 1993a). Yet 10 years later the research development group conceded the same for the 1990s (Chen and Ravallion, 2001). A succession of World Bank reports trace the story (World Bank, 1990, 1993a, 1993b, 1995a, 1995b, 1996, 1997a, 1997b, 2000, 2001). On 28 April 1993, Lewis T. Preston, the president of the World Bank at the time, had stated "Poverty reduction is the benchmark against which our performance as a development institution must be judged".

That 'benchmark' has to be explained. It was a 'global' standard – a "universal poverty line [which] is needed to permit cross-country comparison and aggregation" (World Bank, 1990, p 27). Poverty was defined as "the inability to attain a minimal standard of living" (World Bank, 1990, p 26). Despite acknowledgement of the difficulties of capturing the contribution to standards of living of public goods and common-property resources in any measure of poverty the World Bank settled for a standard which is 'consumption-based'. This standard comprises "two elements: the expenditure necessary to buy a minimum standard of nutrition and other basic necessities and a further amount that varies from country to country, reflecting the cost of participating in the everyday life of society" (World Bank, 1990, p 26).

For operational purposes the second of the two elements said to be necessary in the definition of poverty was set aside. Twelve years later it has still to be systematically examined in relation both to the distribution of income and the results of applying only the first element in the definition to the incidence and depth of poverty worldwide. This serious omission is highlighted in the discussion below. It is argued that data from surveys of material and social deprivation could be used constructively to restore the original scope of the Bank's definition.

Technical limitations of the World Bank's 'partial' poverty line

How well was the first element of the Bank's definition in fact operationalised? This element of the definition was assessed as Purchasing Power Parity (PPP) $370 per year per person at 1985 prices for all the poorest developing countries

(World Bank, 1993a, p 4; and see also World Bank, 1990, especially pp 25-29). For 1990 this produced an estimate of 1,133 million of poor in the developing world. The fact that this was a rough and ready measure adopted – by implication temporarily – for the purposes of simplicity and convenience can be illustrated best by a further statement made at the time. "An extra $0.70 per day added to the poverty line implies a doubling of the number of people counted as being poor" (World Bank, 1993a, p 4). This alternative statistic suggests that research needed to be undertaken to find whether people with incomes higher than the threshold adopted were also exposed to unacceptably high levels of deprivation, poor health and lack of access to basic services. While a measure that is rough and ready can be accepted for a time pending further investigation, it cannot be accepted indefinitely. The circumstances of those just above the threshold have to be compared with those on, or just below, the threshold to justify and confirm its adoption.

In 1990 the World Bank had argued "the case for basing international comparisons" on this threshold (World Bank, 1990). However, its argument was inconsistent. First, later measures differ from earlier measures put forward by the Bank and, second, separate references are made confusingly to definitions of 'absolute poverty' and the 'poverty line' in the same report. Therefore in a 1993 report absolute poverty was defined as "the position of an individual or household in relation to a poverty line the real value of which is fixed over time"; and the poverty line was "the standard of living (usually measured in terms of income or consumption) below which people are deemed to be poor" (World Bank, 1993a, p vii).

The Bank began to be challenged on technical grounds. The 'primary conclusion' of the World Development Report for 2000 that the world was on the right track to reduce poverty was challenged, because the Bank's estimates "should not be accepted" (Reddy and Pogge, 2001, p 2). There was a "lack of a well-defined poverty line that permits of meaningful and reliable inter-temporal and inter-spatial comparisons, and relatedly, the use of a misleading and inaccurate measure of purchasing power 'equivalence', that may systematically distort estimates of the level and trend of global poverty" (Reddy and Pogge, 2001, p 1). For example the 1985 Summers and Heston PPP conversion factors were varied in the 2000 exercise, without precise specification of what had now been done and why (Reddy and Pogge, 2001, pp 3-7). These criticisms did not extend to challenging the Bank's overall conception of a poverty line, or why the 'second element' of the Bank's definition could not be included operationally, but they are nonetheless damaging.

The World Bank has continued to argue for a fixed poverty line. The standard below which people are deemed to be poor is supposed not to change. This seems to have been applied inter-temporally but not inter-spatially. For Latin America and the Caribbean the World Bank actually adopted a different poverty line of $2 per day (World Bank, 1993a, p 6). Subsequently a standard of $4 a day was adopted for Eastern Europe and the republics of the former Soviet Union. It would be hard to claim that these figures are not arbitrary and that relativity can stand the test of time. Different countries and regions have experienced different trajectories of growth and distribution and such variation is likely to persist.

Nonetheless, the Bank had given an impression in its 1990 report that its conceptualisation of poverty could be extended to all countries including the industrial countries. As emphasised above poverty had been defined as "the inability to attain a minimal standard of living" (World Bank, 1990, p 25). This could have been a good starting point for consistent scientific and international definition. What exactly was this standard of living? "Household incomes and expenditures per capita are adequate yardsticks" (World Bank, 1990, p 25). The Bank admitted that there were drawbacks because income and expenditure measures did not capture dimensions of welfare like access to public goods and services, clean drinking water and other 'common property' resources. However, historically, wider definitions of income have included monetary equivalents to free or subsidised goods and services. The World Bank's definition, accordingly, could have included the same, and thereby could have solved the problem of comparing countries, and rural versus urban regions in those countries – with different mixes of cash and goods in kind.

So the World Bank's admission that 'common property' was not included in its measures of income does not seem to have prompted scientific enquiry to produce a more consistent or 'objective' poverty line. The procedure developed at the time was not clear. The drawbacks specified had only to be examined in relation to 'some norm' – namely a 'consumption-based' poverty line (World Bank, 1990, p 26). At the time, as noted above, the Bank made a case for measuring two elements, the expenditure necessary to buy a minimum standard of nutrition and other basic necessities, and an additional amount reflecting the cost of participating in the everyday life of society (World Bank, 1990, p 26).

The first was believed to be unproblematic. The cost of calorific intakes and other necessities could be calculated by "looking at the prices of the foods that make up the diets of the poor". The second "is far more subjective; in some countries indoor plumbing is a luxury, but in others it is a 'necessity'" (World Bank, 1990, pp 26-27). This is a very odd statement. In what sense is the need for indoor plumbing, as distinct from the need for food, 'subjective'? And when is it a 'luxury' and when a 'necessity'? Does not the cost of food, as much as the cost of plumbing, reflect participation in the everyday life of society? If plumbing is a 'luxury' in some societies does that mean that food never is in any society?

This chapter does not provide an exhaustive account of the World Bank's procedures. We have sought only to provide some of the steps that have to be questioned, in order to call attention to the unexplained, and un-researched elements in the specification. Otherwise the World Bank is left to fulfil a false prospectus on false premises. There are illustrations in different Bank reports for the period. For example, at one point the text explains that country-specific poverty lines are plotted against per capita consumption "for thirty-four developing and industrial countries", but the figure on the same page shows only the plotted figures for the poorest 12 countries among them. For the 22 richer countries country-specific poverty lines are not plotted. The need to move towards clearly formulated international standards of poverty, that provide the right basis for cross-national comparison, analysis and formulation of more effective policy, has now existed for much longer than a decade.

The Bank's definition of poverty assessed

In reaching this severe conclusion it is only fair to acknowledge the particular strengths in what the World Bank did initially. In the early years the Bank's standard was simple to comprehend and apply. It did not depend on the arduous and continuous collection and compilation of data about types as well as amounts of resources, changing patterns of necessities and changing construction of standards of living.

At the same time there were, and are, major weaknesses in the Bank's approach. It is fixed in time. It ducks any acceptance that 'need' is fundamentally a social construct as well as having specifically social elements. As a social construct it is international in scope and therefore has to be open to scientific investigation and accreditation – as well as challenge. It turns out to be not in fact a 'global' poverty line at all. It is not assumed to be applicable to countries other than the poorest. On the Bank's own admission an international poverty line that is more than 'consumption-based' should, ideally, be constructed. No cost is in fact estimated for the second 'participatory' element of the definition. So the logic of the Bank's own argument is not followed: the minimum value of the poverty line is therefore underestimated and the number of poor in the world also underestimated. These criticisms gain force if it is accepted that, as time goes on, social polarisation in many countries is making the construction of an international poverty line ever more necessary, because the poorest conditions in the world now apply conspicuously to some sections of the population in middle income and even high income countries.

As noted above, the second element of the World Bank's 1990 definition of the poverty line was set aside. Surprisingly, the first was not much investigated or defended. The type, number and amounts of necessities other than food, for example, are not tracked down and discussed. And questions of diet – and especially thresholds of under-nutrition, in relation to income – are not rigorously investigated. Variations in the sheer quantity of the diet required among populations with widely varying work and other activity obligations and customs, as well as in the types of diet socially preferred or indeed available in local markets, and at what cost, are left unexplored. These points apply in particular to children.

In the World Bank's huge programme of research, one recurring problem has been the lack of quantitative illustration of the poverty problems of different types of family or household. Information was collected about average consumption of calories or protein by males and females of different age, including children, but the distribution by income or occupational status, or by reference to other features of standard of living, such as housing, conditions of work, environmental and sanitary facilities and access to health and education, has not comprised an essential part of the investigative strategy.

There have been certain exceptions. More varied information for particular countries is to be found in the Bank's Living Standards Measurement Study surveys. The survey is a multi-topic instrument in which information is collected from all members of households. It covers a wide range of subjects, including, for example, housing, family demography, education, health, migration, economic activity, expenditure and time use.

The surveys can be illustrated from recent reports. One is entitled *Dominican Republic: Managing risks* (2000c). The report states "As a consequence of both growth and reduction in the employment rate, the percentages of poor households have declined from about 22% in 1992 to about 15% in 1998". However, "entrenched 'hard core' poverty is ... widespread in marginal urban areas and especially in rural areas and appears to have been little affected by economic growth". The poor of the Dominican Republic shared "many of the characteristics identified in many Latin American countries". They had larger families, disproportionately large numbers lived in rural areas, were self-employed and had agricultural jobs. Sixty-five per cent use outdoor latrines, 44% were without access to in-house running water and 15% still had mud floors.

The report examined separately conditions affecting different age groups. Young children aged 0-4 had the highest risk of intellectual impairment, "low human capital formation", chronic poverty and being in households with "permanent losses in productivity". Other children had problems of access to primary and secondary schooling, and those in their teens of deficient skills. Those who were unemployed were of course exposed to the 'risk' of low income, and yet "the key risk prevention strategy for the working age poor is a sound macroeconomic framework that promotes labour-intensive growth, employment creation ... [and] labour market flexibility".

The distributional structure of poverty is implied, or illustrated, rather than precisely stated, with data showing that more of those aged 0-4 and 65 and over "belong to the poorest deciles" than other age groups. The data are elaborate and informative. They are still placed in the approved framework of definition, analysis and policy formulation advocated by the Bank. However, by virtue of giving some exposition of the experiences of different groups in the population, concessions are made to strategies other than the trio of economic growth, human capital formation and safety nets. Therefore in the case of the elderly "only about 4% belonging to the poorest 30% of the population are covered by any pension.... The best risk prevention strategy ... is to implement a social security reform, which increases coverage to all population in the future".

The high point in the attempts to justify the World Bank's technical approach to the definition and measurement of poverty perhaps arrived with a report on

Table 14.1: Population living below $1.08 per day, at 1993 PPP

Region	Population in households consuming less than the poverty line (%)		Number of poor (millions)	
	1987	1998	1987	1998
East Asia (including China)	26.6	15.3	418	278
East Asia (excluding China)	23.9	11.3	114	65
Eastern Europe and Central Asia	0.2	5.1	1	24
Latin America and Caribbean	15.3	15.6	64	78
Middle East and North Africa	4.3	1.9	9	6
South Asia	44.9	40.0	474	522
Sub-Saharan Africa	46.6	46.3	217	291
Total (including China)	**28.3**	**24.0**	**1,183**	**1,199**
Total (excluding China)	**28.5**	**26.2**	**880**	**986**

Source: Chen and Ravallion (2001, Table 2)

trends in poverty during the 1990s (Chen and Ravallion, 2001). The report came from its Development Research Group. Table 14.1 shows that despite a percentage fall in poverty as measured by the Bank it was found that the numbers in poverty were slightly higher in 1998 than in 1987, even when the doubtful estimates for China were included.

At face value these results offered little demonstration of the success of World Bank policies. The research group said they drew on 265 national sample surveys in 83 countries to conclude that there was a "disappointing rate of poverty reduction" (Chen and Ravallion, 2001, p 1). The 1990s "did not see much progress against consumption poverty in the developing world" (Chen and Ravallion, 2001, p 18). Yet the overall rate of growth in real consumption per person for low- and middle-income countries during the first eight years of the 1990s was 2.6% per year. "Even assuming no growth from 1987 to 1990, an annual rate of growth in mean consumption of 2.6% over 1990-97 alone would have virtually halved the aggregate poverty gap, as long as overall inequality did not worsen" (Chen and Revallion, 2001, p 18). What went wrong? They admit that "There is now evidence of quite sharply rising inter-personal income inequality in the world during this period" (Chen and Revallion, 2001, p 18). They referred to work by Milanovic (1999) that showed that, on average, inequality in the world as measured by the Gini coefficient had increased by 5% between 1988 and 1993. "This could easily wipe out the gains to the world's poor from global economic growth" (Chen and Ravallion, 2001, p 18). There was no reference to the responsibility of World Bank growth and structural adjustment policies for increasing inequality. The furthest that the authors were prepared to go was to admit that "there is evidence that initial inequality is too high in some countries to assure poverty-reducing growth even when the fundamentals are conducive to growth" (Chen and Revallion, 2001, p 19, referring to Ravallion, 1997, and Ravallion and Datt, 1999).

There is one chink of light in this account of recent developments. The representatives of the Development Research Group at the World Bank showed from their use of the survey data that an opportunity to rebuild a measure of poverty had emerged, but had not yet been acted on.

The work of compiling reliable general statements about conditions and trends in different groups of countries remains to be done. The potentiality for that certainly exists, and a new start can in principle be made. What remains at issue in reviewing the various country reports is the need to develop a consistent threshold measure of poverty across countries. This would allow better identification of severe conditions, determination of priorities and a better focus for future research and development – combining to make major inroads into an appalling world problem.

Approaches by other agencies

Although other international agencies adopt their own programmes they compound the problem. The poverty line is defined by UNDP as "that income level below which a minimum nutritionally adequate diet plus essential non-food requirements are not affordable" (UNDP, 1993, p 225). The steps by which a minimum nutritionally adequate diet, and 'essential non-food requirements' can be defined as appropriate for different countries, and the criteria according to which these can be said to be 'affordable', are not investigated.

The specialised work of the International Fund for Agricultural Development has resulted in reports that resemble the World Bank's approach but introduce some flexibility into a 'fixed' poverty line by taking note of measures which originate nationally, and which depend on more sophisticated investigation of changes in consumption as well as consumption prices. The poverty line is defined as "a commodity bundle tied to the minimum requirement (calories and protein for food, and some notional minimum for non-food items), and the determination of an appropriate set of prices to be applied to individual commodities to calculate the poverty expenditure and income" (Jazairy et al, 1992, p 461).

The ILO has contributed over the years to a more 'structural' interpretation of poverty and its causes (International Institute for Labour Studies, 1993; but also see, for example, Franklin, 1967). In particular, its work on the structure of the labour market and questions of access to that market help to balance the monetarist perspectives of the IMF and World Bank. The ILO began in the 1970s to show the part to be played in explaining poverty by lack of community utilities or infrastructure – water, sanitation, health centres, primary schools, and transport. The development of measures of collective or community need, as distinct from individual need, as a contribution to understanding poverty, and its alleviation, deserves renewed attention. Therefore, some commentators have pointed out that the World Bank's 1990 report on poverty:

> ... represents a step away from neoliberalism and back toward the Bank's attitude of the 1960s: that the continuing existence of the poor in poor nations is the development problem. Indeed, the insistence [in the Bank's annual development reports] on remedying water and air pollution resembles nothing more strongly than 20-year-old strategies aimed at satisfying developing countries' basic needs. (Taylor, 1992, p 57)

The ILO preoccupations of the 1970s are back in fashion (Townsend, 1993a, Chapter 2).

When many governments agreed the report on the World Summit for Social Development at Copenhagen the international agencies were slow to follow up the recommendation, among others, to measure 'absolute' and 'overall' poverty separately – as a means of making comparisons between countries, and especially between rich and poor countries, more feasible. Prior to the five-year review of the programme of action in July 2000 UNDP was the first to collect reports from countries. The reports covered work to establish definitions and estimates of poverty, set targets for poverty reduction or eradication and formulate national plans (UNDP, 1998, pp 28-30). Estimates were given for some countries of the extent of 'extreme' and 'overall' poverty. In the case of India, therefore, the two figures were 6% and 36% respectively; for the Republic of Moldova 21% and 43%; for the Central African Republic 36% and 63%; for Malaysia 2% and 9% and for Panama 22% and 37%. Results on both measures were available only for 11 countries although 75 of a total of 130 countries had officially endorsed operational definitions of extreme poverty and 69 of overall poverty (UNDP, 1998, pp 22, 30).

In 2000 UNDP reported that 64 countries now provided information about the extent of both forms of poverty. Other countries provided information on one or the other (UNDP, 2000, pp 24-29). But UNDP offered no prescriptions for standardisation internationally. Its position is admittedly difficult. In successive reports on poverty it has simply reproduced data at $1, $2, $4 or even $14.40 per person per day as measures of convenience for countries in different regions (see, for example, its Human Development Report devoted to the eradication of poverty, 1997, pp 32-33).

The World Bank's measures have also become more diffuse. The Bank accepts measures of a 'national' poverty line put forward by individual governments, and also gives two alternative measures of an 'international' poverty line – $1 and $2 per person per day (World Bank, 2000, 2001). During these years the problem of ambiguity in international debate has multiplied because little guidance about a 'core' international or scientific measure has been offered, and a puzzling general distinction between 'income' poverty and poverty has been introduced.

Developing an alternative poverty line

The general shortcomings of the World Bank's approach to measurement would have been evident sooner if the question 'Who is poor?' had been systematically investigated in relation to the dollar-a-day information produced, and efforts made to make strict comparisons between countries and examine trends over a number of years.

Once the distributional structure of poverty is correctly identified in different countries then both causes and anti-poverty strategies become easier to discern. Therefore in countries as diverse as India, Kyrgyz, Tanzania, Kenya and the Yemen it can be shown that poverty is above average among women, the elderly and disabled – especially women, the unemployed, lone parents, households with children, particularly households with lone parents, and households with several rather than one or two children. Poverty is also above average in rural areas and among most ethnic minority groups and most groups with low occupational status, including, for example, day labourers (see, for example, Hashem, 1996). This structural 'bias' cannot be remedied by economic growth governed only by market considerations but by 'redistribution with growth'. High priority in anti-poverty policies, according to such evidence, plainly has to be given to children, elderly and disabled people who cannot gain paid employment, and those in the labour market whose earnings are insufficient to ensure a household income adequate for health, wellbeing and social viability.

A strategy of 'redistribution with growth' to eradicate absolute poverty is not something new. It has been put forward for many years, for example in the Indian government's national five-year plans from 1961-66 onwards. Therefore an influential Planning Commission report of 1962 stated that "the time has now come when we should sharply focus our efforts on providing an assured minimum income to every citizen of the country within a reasonable time. Progressively this minimum would itself be raised as development goes apace" (Appasamy et al, 1996, p 10).

Two improvements to measurement can be made. First, existing data about incomes of households with and without children can be reviewed and an account given of the extent and severity of material and social deprivation among adults and children, with information about access to necessary services and the kind of policies that had improved conditions of people in other countries or in the previous history of particular countries. This would be an exercise in which existing information would be reassembled for the purpose of reviewing policies as prime causes of consequential conditions. The second would be to devise improvements to the national surveys introduced as a result of the 1995 World Summit and the country studies issued by the international agencies and collect information directly about poverty. This could pave the way for a renewed determination to restore the two-part treatment of the poverty measure originally put forward in 1990.

The World Bank constructed graphs which were supposed to show the rising real per capita value of 'country-specific' poverty lines in relation to average per capita consumption the graph did not in fact fulfil this intention: it merely showed an upper and a lower poverty line fixed by the Bank in dollars at 1985 prices for a small number of poor countries in relation to the average per capita consumption in those countries.

Conclusion

World anti-poverty policies have been shown to be ineffective, and need to be recast. This chapter has sought to show that a plan of action is best constructed by linking the growing international consensus in favour of the fulfilment of human rights to the analysis of the activities of powerful TNCs and the related policies of the international financial agencies, especially the World Bank.

Human rights

First, there has been a gathering momentum in favour of the specification, and delivery, of human rights. However, policies designed to confer equal rights are neither policies to bring about greater inequality in the distribution of resources, including income, nor are they selective or discriminatory conditional policies for just some of the poor. Energies on the part of governments and campaigning groups during the decades of the 1980s and 1990s have been put into statements about rights, rather than into the close monitoring of trends in access to rights and the exact contribution of the principal policies to those trends. Good examples are Articles 22 and 25 of the Universal Declaration of Human Rights. They are set out in the boxes below:

Article 22
Everyone, as a member of society, has the right to social security and is entitled to realisation, through national effort and international cooperation and in accordance with the organisation and resources of each State, of the economic, social and cultural rights indispensable for his dignity and the free development of his personality.

Article 25
Everyone has the right to a standard of living adequate for the health and well-being of himself and of his family, including food, clothing, housing and medical care and necessary social services, and the right to security in the event of unemployment, sickness, disability, old age or other lack of livelihood in circumstances beyond his control.

These fundamental rights have to be related to existing national and international policies. Following the argument presented, therefore, four human rights policies might be proposed to mark a change in direction of world strategy to eradicate poverty:

1. Construction of an index of human rights

International and national agreement needs to be reached both on what are the specific indicators of the non-fulfilment of adult and, independently, child rights that will allow trends in different countries to be measured, and on what are the policies, negative and positive, that are contributing substantially, and to what degree, to those trends (an example is the EU set of commonly agreed and defined social indicators to be found in Atkinson et al, 2002). Direct policies to reduce poverty would be a minimum national wage, and state unemployment benefits, pensions and disablement pensions for the elderly and disabled who cannot work at a properly substantiated level of adequacy.

2. International and national specification of what is an adequate income and what are the new policies to achieve that income.

The Universal Declaration of Human Rights includes, in Article 25 set out above, the right to 'an adequate income'. The fulfilment of this fundamental right can be interpreted as requiring a defined income-poverty line to be brought into being, as measurement of level of income required from earnings and/or state benefit. This is not to deny the need for supporting policies to fine-tune taxes or conditions for the receipt of benefit.

3. The introduction of child benefit

Article 27 of the Convention on the Rights of the Child – which has attracted more signatures from countries than any other treaty or convention on human rights – includes, like the Universal Declaration, the right to social security. Many countries have already introduced schemes for child cash allowances. Some countries have only introduced these in part. Others could start by introducing a mixture of cash allowances and benefits in kind – through rights to quantities of food or to free or subsidised school meals.

4. The introduction of a financial transactions tax

Article 22 quoted above includes a clear reference to "international cooperation and in accordance with the organization and resources of each State" and a universal tax to provide resources would properly reflect the spirit of the entire Universal Declaration of Human Rights. The principle of an international financial transactions tax to finance development and not only the post-war reconstruction of the industrial countries was implicit in Keynes' approach to Bretton Woods. The economist James Tobin resurrected the idea in 1972, and it was revived again in the 1990s. Prior to the 2002 conference at Monterrey a preparatory report by the UN Zedillo panel repeated the possibility of such a tax, but gave it no serious discussion (for historical and contemporary discussion see Raffer, 1998; and Townsend, 2001). But support was voiced from a number of nations during the Monterrey conference. For example, a tiny automatic tax on all financial exchanges, say 0.1% could raise up to $400 billion annually for support for the poorest countries, including support for the establishment of social insurance and social security of different forms. In particular, the tax could be designed to provide the revenue for an international child benefit scheme of the kind described above.

Many other human rights policies deserve consideration. However, these are examples of policies most likely to contribute to the reduction of poverty. They are put forward because, unlike the indirect policies of overseas development aid or for economic growth, they are direct, and could have an immediate and not indeterminate effect on the scale of poverty.

Transnational corporations

The discussion above shows the need for socially sensitive policies on the part of the TNCs themselves to be developed, for better regulation by democratically elected governments and groups of governments, and for a better framework of international company law.

1. The social policies of TNCs need to be transparent

Codes of conduct have sometimes been drawn up by transnational corporations, or by agencies such as the ILO and OECD. While often sincerely motivated they are seriously short on detailed prescription and have no teeth. The biggest TNCs and the international agencies must lead the way. A model international code should be developed by the UN and approved at one of the early World Summits – rather like the initiatives that have been taken by groups of countries over the years on behalf of the extension of universal human rights. Additionally governments must commit themselves to annual reports that are intended to monitor developments and social policies of TNCs registered in their domain, who will be expected to submit annual reports on their policies for employees in different countries and their wider activities.

2. Better government frameworks for TNCs

Codes of behaviour for TNCs registered with, and/or operating within, nation states must be developed and, where necessary, must involve the review and amendment of national, particularly company, law.

3. Urgent development of international company law

In present circumstances the case for international company law has become stronger. Voluntary codes of conduct are weakly expressed and hold little prospect of wide adoption. Although national models of the kind suggested by the ILO and OECD would represent an improvement there is small likelihood of major change until a framework of international law also exists for TNCs. There are valuable precedents on which to build new law in the histories of national company law and recent discussions and developments of European law. The awkward question is whether national laws can be satisfactorily harmonised in an era when TNCs naturally take advantage of loopholes and shortcomings across countries or whether regional and international law is the only realistic vehicle by which common standards of behaviour or performance can be tracked and controlled.

One route is by finding how a new framework of codes of conduct might complement international law. Therefore, in 1977 the Governing Board of the ILO put forward a declaration. This sought to exert influence on governments, concluding that gradual reinforcement could pave the way for "more specific potentially binding international standards", turning codes of conduct into "the seed of customary rules of international law" (ILO, 1998).

The World Bank

The World Bank's operational definition of a poverty line needs urgent reappraisal. It is not suitable for international comparison. It is therefore an unreliable basis for analysis of the nature and causes of trends and the construction of effective anti-poverty policies.

1. The need for a genuinely international poverty line

Instead, the resources, including income, required in countries across the world by individuals and families to surmount absolute and overall poverty have to be specified, on the basis of empirical information about the extent of material and social deprivation experienced by people at different quantified levels of resources, including income. This lies at the core of the development of anti-poverty strategies and of course the measurement of trends.

2. A scientific grounding for anti-poverty policies

The World Bank's theory or account of the existence and growth of poverty is not grounded adequately in the history or empirical analysis of social development. Implicitly and explicitly the Bank's explanation concentrates on lack of modernisation and growth instead of control and management of the distribution of resources. A more scientific and less ideological form of explanation would lead more readily to the identification of the structural components of an anti-poverty policy. For example, modernisation tends to be defined as emulation of the values as well as practices of Western powers; and growth tends to be defined without reference to the value of unpaid work or the countervailing environmental and social costs of production. Instead, the developing hierarchy of political and social power has to be explained in relation to international agencies, regional associations, governments, regional and local markets, corporate, especially transnational, non-government and community organisations, and populations, and especially in relation to the availability and changing flow of resources to individuals and families. The need to trace outcomes of different policies for children and vulnerable groups such as disabled persons and lone-parent households is urgent.

3. Policies for the many, not the few

The World Bank's liberalisation, structural adjustment and 'safety-net' policies have tended to deepen, or confirm, the already weak situation of the poorest 20% of the world's population, rather than lay a basis for changes in the unequal distribution of growing world resources. There is strong support for the proposition that for several decades growth has not had much 'trickle-down' effect, often the reverse (for example, Newman and Thomson, 1989). Again, there is strong evidence for the proposition that high investment in public social services has not had a deleterious effect on growth – in fact, quite often the reverse (Goodin et al, 1999). As one research team concludes, "greater distributional equality provides a favourable 'initial condition' for rapid and sustainable growth;... redistribution of current income and assets, or redistribution of an economy's growth increment, is the most effective form of poverty reduction for most countries; and ... mechanisms to achieve the redistributions are feasible for most countries" (Dagdeviren et al, 2001, p 23).

In short, human rights and democratic values have to be more universally, and securely, established, redistribution restored to priority status in action programmes on poverty, and preventive steps taken to strengthen collective principles of public service, planning and social insurance.

References

Amin, S. (1997) *Capitalism in the age of globalization*, London and New York, NY: Earthscan.

Appasamy P., Guhan S., Hema R., Majumdar M. and Vaidyanathan A. (1996) *Social exclusion from a welfare rights perspective in India*, Research Series no 106, Geneva: International Institute for Labour Studies.

Armada, F., Muntaner, C. and Navarro, V. (2001) 'Health and social security reform in Latin America: the convergence of the World Health Organisation, the World Bank and the transnational corporations', *International Journal of Health Services*, vol 31, no 4, pp 729-68.

Atkinson, T., Cantillon, B., Marlier, E. and Nolan, B. (2002) *Social indicators: The EU and social inclusion*, Oxford: Oxford University Press.

Carvalho, S. and White, H. (1997) *Combining the quantitative and qualitative approaches to poverty measurement and analysis: The practice and the potential*, World Bank Technical Paper no 366, Washington, DC: World Bank.

Chen, S. and Ravallion, M. (2000) 'How did the world's poorest fare in the 1990s?', Development Research Group, World Bank, *Review of Income and Wealth*, pp 1-33.

Chossudovsky, M. (1998) *The globalisation of poverty: Impacts of World Bank reforms*, London and New Jersey: Zed Books.

Dagdeviren, H., van der Hoeven, R. and Weeks, J. (2001) *Redistribution matters: Growth for poverty reduction*, Employment Paper 2001/2010, Geneva: ILO.

George, S. (1999) *The Lugano Report: On preserving capitalism in the twenty-first century*, London: Pluto Press.

George, V. and Wilding, P. (2002) *Globalisation and human welfare*, Basingstoke and New York, NY: Palgrave Macmillan.

Goodin, R.E, Headey, B., Muffels, R. and Dirvan, H.-J. (1999) *The real worlds of welfare capitalism*, Cambridge: Cambridge University Press.

Held, D. (1995) *Democracy and the global order: From the modern state to cosmopolitan governance*, London: Polity Press.

Hertz, N. (2001) *The silent takeover: Global capitalism and the death of bureaucracy*, London: William Heinemann.

Hines, C. (2001) *Localization: A global manifesto*, London: Earthscan.

Hudson, E. (ed) (1996) *Merchants of misery: How corporate America profits from poverty*, Maine, MA: Courage.

Huther, J., Roberts, S. and Shah, A. (1997) *Public expenditure reform under adjustment lending: Lessons from the World Bank experience*, World Bank Discussion Paper no 382, Washington, DC: World Bank.

ILO (International Labour Organisation) (1998) *The ILO tripartite declaration of principles concerning multinational enterprises and social policy – ten years after*, Geneva: ILO.

Jazairy, I., Algamir, M. and Panuccio, T. (1995) *The state of world rural poverty*, London: IFDA.

Kanbur, R. (2000) 'Economic policy, distribution and poverty: the nature of disagreements', Paper presented to the Swedish Parliamentary Commission on Global Development, 22 September.

Karliner, J. (1997) *The corporate planet: Ecology and politics in the age of globalisation*, San Francisco, CA: Sierra Club Books.

Kolko, G. (1999) 'Ravaging the poor: the International Monetary Fund indicted by its own data', *International Journal of Health Services*, vol 29, no 1, pp 51-57.

Kolodner, E. (1994) *Transnational corporations: Impediments or catalysts of social development?*, Occasional Paper no 5, World Summit for Social Development, Geneva: UNRISD.

Korten, D.C. (1996) *When corporations rule the world*, London: Earthscan.

Kozul-Wright, R. and Rowthorn, R. (1998) *Transnational corporations and the global economy*, Helsinki: UNU World Institute for Development Economic Research.

Lang, T. and Hines, C. (1993) *The new protectionism*, London: Earthscan.

Madeley, J. (1999) *Big business, poor peoples: The impact of transnational corporations on the world's poor*, London and New York, NY: Zed Books.

Martin, H.-P. and Schumann, H. (1997) *The global trap: Globalisation and the assault on democracy and prosperity*, London: Zed Books.

Monbiot, G. (2000) *Captive state: The corporate takeover of Britain*, London: Pan Books.

Narayan, D. (1997) *Voices of the poor: Poverty and social capital in Tanzania*, Washington, DC: World Bank.

Newman, B. and Thomson, R.J. (1989) 'Economic growth and social development: a longitudinal analysis of causal priority', *World Development*, vol 17, no 4, pp 461-71.

OECD (Organisation for Economic Co-operation and Development) (2001) *The OECD guidelines for multinational enterprises 2001: Focus: global instruments for corporate responsibility*, Paris: OECD.

Oxfam (1995) *Poverty report*, Oxford: Oxfam.

Oyen, E., Miller, S.M. and Samad, S.A. (eds) (1996) *Poverty: A global review: Handbook on international poverty research*, Oslo: Scandinavian University Press.

Payer, C. (1982) *The World Bank: A critical analysis*, New York, NY: Monthly Review Press.

Payer, C. (1991) *Lent and lost: Foreign credit and third world development*, London and New Jersey: Zed Books.

Psacharapoulos, G., Morley, S., Fiszbein, A., Lee, H. and Wood, B. (1997) *Poverty and income distribution in Latin America: The story of the 1980s*, World Bank Technical Paper no 351, Washington, DC: World Bank.

Raffer, K. (1998) 'The Tobin Tax:reviving a discussion', *World Development*, vol 26, no 3, pp 529-38.

Ravallion, M. (1997) 'Can high inequality developing countries escape absolute poverty?', *Economics Letters*, vol 56, pp 51-7.

Ravallion, M. (1998) *Poverty lines in theory and practice*, LSMS Working Paper no 133, Washington, DC: World Bank.

Ravallion, M. and Datt, G. (1999) *When is growth pro-poor? Evidence from the diverse experience of India's states*, Policy Research Working Paper WPS 2263, Washington, DC: World Bank.

Reddy, S.G. and Pogge, T.W. (2001) 'How not to count the poor', Unpublished paper, Departments of Economics and Philosophy, University of Columbia.

Roy, A. (2001) 'The biggest fraud in India's history', *The Guardian*, G2, 30 November, extracted from A. Roy (2002) *Power politics*, London: South End Press.

Scott, J. (1986) *Capitalist property and financial power: A comparative study of Britain, the United States and Japan*, Brighton: Wheatsheaf Books.

Scott, J., Stokman, F.N. and Ziegler, R. (1985) *Networks of corporate power*, London: Polity Press.

Sklair, L. (2001) *The transnational capitalist Class*, Oxford: Blackwell.

Stichele, M.V. and Pennartz, P. (1996) *Making it our business – European NGO campaigns on transnational corporations*, London: CIIR.

Subbarao, K. et al (1997) *Safety net programs and poverty reduction: Lessons from cross-country experience*, Washington, DC: World Bank.

Townsend, P. (2001) 'The role of the UN: directing global resources to the rural poor', Paper for Expert Group meeting on *Globalisation and poverty reduction: Can the rural poor benefit from globalisation?*, UN Division for Social Policy and Development, 8-11 November, New York, NY: UN.

UN (United Nations) (1988) *Transnational corporations in world development*, New York, NY: UN.

UN (1994a) *World Summit for Social Development: An overview*, Preparatory Committee for the World Summit for Social Development, Report of the Secretary-General for the first substantive session, New York, 31 January-11 February.

UN (1994b) *Outcome of the World Summit for Social Development: Draft declaration and draft programme of action*, Preparatory Committee for the World Summit for Social Development, Report of the Secretary-General for the second substantive session, New York, 22 August-2 September.

UN (1995) *The Copenhagen Declaration and Programme for Action: The World Summit for Social Development 6-12 March 1995*, New York, NY: UN Department of Publications.

UN (1996) 'Special Issue on the Social Summit', *Social Policy and Social Progress*, A review published by the UN, vol 1, no 1, New York, NY: UN Department of Publications.

UNCTAD (UN Conference on Trade and Development) (1996) *Globalisation and liberalisation*, New York, NY and Geneva: UNCTAD.

UNCTAD *Transnational corporations, services and the Uruguay round*, New York, NY: UNCTAD.

UNDP (United Nations Development Programme) (1992) *Human Development Report, 1992*, New York, NY: Oxford University Press.

UNDP (1993) *Human Development Report, 1993*, New York, NY and Oxford: Oxford University Press.

UNDP (1995) *Human Development Report 1994*, New York, NY and Oxford: Oxford University Press.

UNDP (1996) *Poverty eradication: A policy framework for country strategies*, Policy Paper, New York, NY: UNDP.

UNDP (1997) *Human Development Report 1997*, New York, NY and Oxford: Oxford University Press.

UNDP (1998) *Overcoming human poverty, UNDP Poverty Report 1998*, New York, NY: UNDP.

UNDP (1998) *Human Development Report 1998*, New York, NY and Oxford: Oxford University Press.

UNDP (1999) *Human Development Report 1999*, New York, NY and Oxford: Oxford University Press.

UNDP (2000) *Overcoming human poverty: UNDP Poverty Report 2000*, New York, NY: UNDP.

UNDP (2000) *Human Development Report 2000*, New York, NY and Oxford: Oxford University Press.

UNRISD (UN Research Institute for Social Development) (1995a) *States of disarray: The social effects of globalisation*, UNRISD Report for the World Summit for Social Development, Geneva: UNRISD.

UNRISD (1995b) *Adjustment, globalisation and social development*, Report of the UNRISD/UNDP International Seminar on Economic Restructuring and Social Policy, New York, January, Geneva: UNRISD.

US Department of Commerce (1992) *Income, poverty and wealth in the United States: A chart book* (by L. Lamison-White) Current Population Reports, Consumer Income, series P-60, no 179.

Van der Pjil, K. (1993) 'The sovereignty of capital impaired: social forces and codes of conduct for multinational corporations', in H. Overbeek (ed) *Restructuring hegemony in the global political economy: The rise of transnational neo-liberalism in the 1980s*, London: Routledge.

World Bank (1990) *World Development Report 1990: Poverty*, Washington, DC: World Bank.

World Bank (1993a) *Implementing the World Bank's strategy to reduce poverty: Progress and challenges*, Washington, DC: World Bank.

World Bank (1993b) *World Development Report 1993: Investing in health*, Washington, DC: Oxford University Press for the World Bank.

World Bank (1995a) *Advancing social development: A World Bank contribution to the Social Summit*, Washington, DC: World Bank.

World Bank (1995b) *Investing in people: The World Bank in action*, Washington, DC: World Bank.

World Bank (1996) *Poverty reduction and the World Bank: Progress and challenges in the 1990s*, Washington, DC: World Bank.

World Bank (1997a) *Poverty reduction and the World Bank: Progress in fiscal year 1996 and 1997*, Washington, DC: World Bank.

World Bank (1997b) *The state in a changing world: World Development Report 1997*, Washington, DC: World Bank.

World Bank (2000a) *World development indicators*, Washington, DC: World Bank.

World Bank (2000b) 'Emerging directions for a social protection sector strategy: from safety net to spring board', Social Protection Sector, Washington, DC: World Bank.

World Bank (2000c) *Dominican Republic: Managing risks*, Washington, DC: World Bank.

World Bank (2001) *World Development Report 2000/2001: Attacking poverty*, Washington, DC: World Bank.

FIFTEEN

Are we really reducing global poverty?

Jan Vandemoortele

The association of poverty with progress is the great enigma of our times.
(Henry George, 1882, p 6)

Introduction[1]

Poverty reduction has become a top priority for international development; new norms, facts and findings on global poverty are gradually becoming part of the established economic wisdom. But contrary to popular belief, poverty is not easy to define and quantify. Some of that wisdom needs to be challenged, based on the premise that knowledge and learning are best served by questioning established tenets rather than by readily believing them; by doubting theories rather than being blindsided by them. Indeed, arguments about global poverty are often presented in a one-sided and over-simplified way. J.K. Galbraith (1958) argued "the articulation of the conventional wisdom … is an act of affirmation like reading from the Scriptures or going to church" (p 10). However, conventional wisdom is frequently mistaken.

Five questions are raised in this chapter:

- Is $1 per day a valid poverty gauge?
- Are statistics for China unduly biasing global poverty trends?
- Is much of the global poverty debate about 'misplaced concreteness'?
- Is equity good for the poor?
- Is a social shock absorber feasible and affordable?

Each of these questions is addressed below; a final section points to two incorrect conclusions the international community is drawing regarding global poverty trends and anti-poverty strategies. Before addressing the first question, a brief review of global poverty trends since 1990 is in order.

Global poverty trends

The average proportion of people in developing countries living on less than $1 per day fell from 32% to 25% between 1990 and 1999, according to the latest estimates (World Bank, 2002)[2]. The simple extrapolation of this trend to the year 2015 results in a headcount index of about 16%, indicating that the world is on track for reaching the global goal of halving poverty between 1990 and 2015. Unfortunately, the reality is more complex and progress less satisfactory. The number of people below the international poverty line declined by a mere 1% per year between 1990 and 1999; decreasing from 1.3 billion people to 1.1 billion respectively. Furthermore, poverty trends for most regions showed little or no progress (see Figure 15.1). The incidence of income poverty remained largely unchanged in sub-Saharan Africa (SSA), Latin America and the Caribbean (LAC) and in the Middle East and North Africa (MENA). Actually, the number of income-poor in these three regions combined increased by about seven million people each year between 1990 and 1999.

Regional trends show that the decline in global poverty was driven by East Asia(EA) in 1993-96 and by South Asia (SA) in 1996-99. China and India in particular are responsible for the apparent decline in global poverty. When East Asiais excluded from the calculations, the average proportion of income-poor in developing countries declined less dramatically – to 33% in 1998, down from 35% in 1990. At this rate, poverty will not be halved by 2015; it will only be one quarter below its level in 1990.

Progress towards other goals has also been painfully slow. In 1990, the global target was set to reach universal basic education by the year 2000. The good news is that the gender gap was halved, although it remains a concern in many

Figure 15.1: Most regions failed to reduce poverty in the 1990s (% of people below $1 per day)

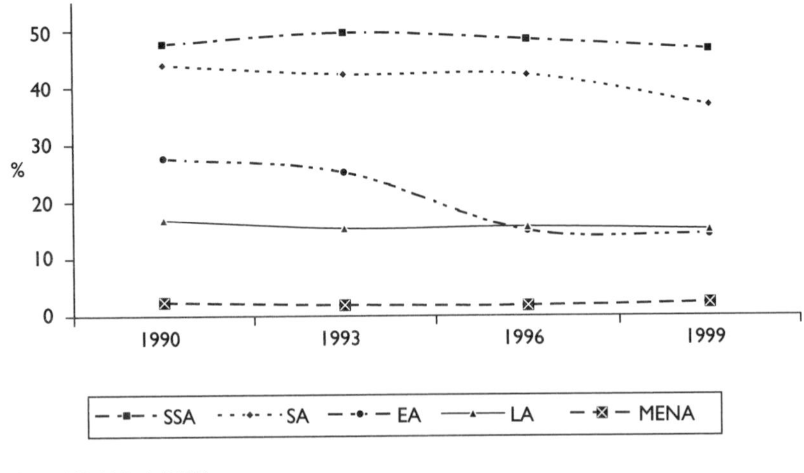

Source: World Bank (2002)

countries in SSA, South Asia and MENA. The sad truth is that global progress during the 1990s was only one fifth of what was needed to achieve universal primary education. It is not surprising that the goal was moved to 2015; but at the current rate of progress, that promise will not be kept either if progress does not accelerate twofold. In 2000, nearly 120 million school-age children were not enrolled in primary education – about the same as a decade earlier. They will join the ranks of the nearly one billion adults who cannot read or write, and who are increasingly concentrated among women. Widespread illiteracy is a source of deepening poverty, rising inequality and slowing growth. Countries cannot expect to integrate into the global economy without equipping their people with basic capabilities.

Failure to meet the education goal also impacts negatively on the chances of reaching the other goals and targets for human development[3]. Progress on under-five mortality, maternal mortality, child malnutrition, access to safe drinking water and adequate sanitation was too slow to reach agreed targets. Progress actually slowed down compared with earlier decades. Figure 15.2 displays global trends for primary education and child mortality, spanning the past four decades. It is clear that progress levelled off in the 1990s.

There are no obvious reasons that can readily explain the slowdown. Average economic growth in the 1990s was higher than in the 1970s and 1980s, often fuelled by rapid expansion in trade and financial flows, yet social progress

Figure 15.2: Average under-five mortality rate and primary enrolment ratio in developing countries

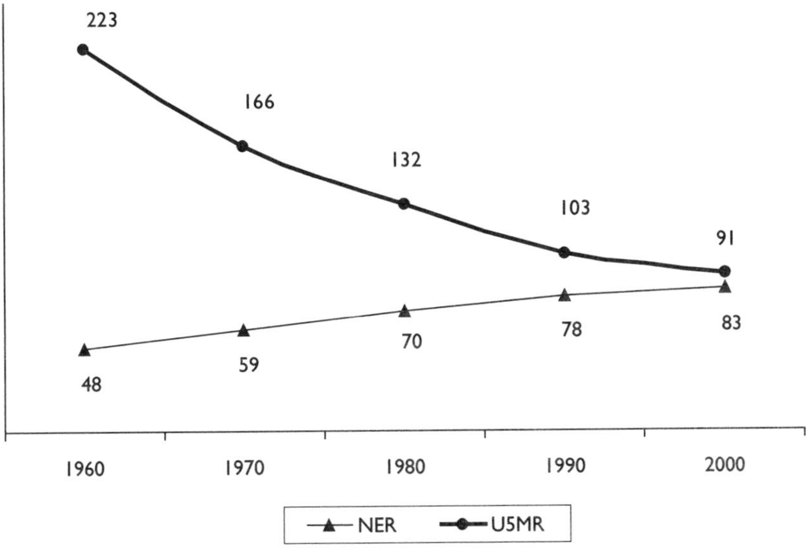

Source: Based on UNICEF (2001) and UNESCO data

slowed down. The reasons for slowdown are likey to be country-specific; but often relate to insufficient and inefficient public spending, crippling debt burdens, falling commodity prices, inadequate access to markets in developed countries, declining official development assistance and widening gaps between rich and poor. If the 1980s are remembered as the 'lost decade for development', the 1990s may go down in history as the 'decade of broken promises'.

In the early 1990s, the late James Grant (then Executive Director of UNICEF) argued "the problem is not that we have tried to eradicate global poverty and failed; the problem is that no serious and concerted attempt has ever been made". Indeed, without concerted and intensified efforts, 2015 will meet few of the Millennium Development Goals at the global level. The HIV/AIDS pandemic poses a formidable threat to accelerating progress in the future.

Is $1-per-day a valid poverty gauge?

Poverty is now broadly interpreted as multidimensional, yet its principal measure remains one-dimensional. Indeed, $1 per day per person has become the international benchmark for measuring the extent of poverty in developing countries. It is based on studies conducted in the 1980s in some 33 countries. Eight countries – Bangladesh, Indonesia, Morocco, Nepal, Kenya, Pakistan, the Phillipines and Tanzania – turned out to have a national poverty line of about $1 per day per person, expressed in purchasing power parity (PPP) of 1985 (Ravallion et al, 1991). The international poverty line has been updated, using an expanded set of PPP values at 1993 prices. The new poverty line of $1.08 is the median value of the lowest 10 poverty lines among the same 33 countries (World Bank, 2000).

It should be pointed out that the international poverty line is not based on a global common basket of basic goods and services; but on the average or median of some 8-10 national poverty lines – each based on a different basket but converted into the same numerator, using PPP values.

Technical issues relating to PPP values affect the reliability of global poverty trends. Information is not readily available to appreciate whether the updated poverty line is based on the same 8-10 countries. In addition, the updated line is based on the median value, whereas the original one is based on the average, raising some questions about their comparability. PPP conversion rates for different years are also not comparable, so that the claim that they measure similar purchasing power in terms of the command over domestic goods (Chen and Ravallion, 2001) is ultimately unverifiable[4].

The international poverty norm presents another difficulty, apart from the technical issue of PPP values. The fundamental question is whether the $1 per day norm is valid for tracking change over time or for comparing poverty levels among countries. The main problem with the norm is that it violates the standard definition of income poverty, that is, a person is considered poor when he/she does not reach a minimum level of economic wellbeing set *by society*.

Absolute poverty inevitably has a relative dimension. For the purpose of measuring income poverty over time or for comparing poverty levels across countries, the norm cannot be kept static and applied uniformly to all societies. As societies reach higher levels of development, the conceptual relevance of $1 per day gradually erodes as a measure of income poverty.

At the beginning of the 20th century, for instance, Rowntree (1901) estimated a poverty line of 26 shillings per week for a family of six in the city of York. It would be inappropriate to use the same poverty line – adjusted for inflation and family size – to estimate current levels of poverty in the UK. Keeping the poverty line unchanged at Rowntree's level would mean that some basic goods and services would never have a place in the basket of basic necessities, such as piped water, electricity, urban transport and essential drugs[5].

The poverty line must be sensitive to the average level of economic wellbeing of the group or society for which poverty is monitored. Oster et al (1978), for example, show that the poverty line in the US rose by more than 40% in real terms between 1935 and 1960. Based on 60 family budgets in the US between 1905 and 1960, Fisher (1997) reports that the minimum subsistence budget rose by about 0.75% for every 1% increase in disposable per capita income of the general population. He adds that more recent evidence from other high-income countries indicates that the income elasticity of the poverty line ranges between 0.6 and 1.0[6]. It could be that the poverty line is less elastic at lower levels of per capita income, but the elasticity is unlikely to be zero – as global poverty estimates assume.

Hanmer et al (1999) find a clear tendency for more affluent countries to set higher poverty lines, based on 26 poverty assessments in sub-Saharan Africa. The international poverty line for Latin America is often fixed at $2 per day, while that for countries in Eastern Europe and the former Soviet Union is sometimes set at $4 per day – an implicit admission that the income elasticity of the poverty line is not equal to zero.

A recent report on rural poverty in China calculates that the official poverty line is equivalent to $0.66 per day (in constant 1985 PPP values). It states that such an austere standard was useful when the incidence of extreme poverty was high, but argues that government should "consider whether the international standard [of $1 per day] may now be a more appropriate measure to gauge the extent of poverty" (World Bank, 2001a). If the income elasticity of China's official poverty line is seen to be greater than zero, that of the international poverty line can no longer be assumed to be zero.

Therefore, the poverty line cannot be frozen by disassociating it from the average standard of living of society. Ravallion and Bidani (1994), for instance, note that Indonesia and the US reported a similar level of income poverty for 1990. Obviously, their poverty lines were very different, based on the respective average standard of living in the two countries. As countries become wealthier, societies gradually adopt a higher level of minimum economic wellbeing.

A change in the proportion of people struggling to survive on less than $1 per day does not necessarily mean a similar change in the incidence of poverty[7].

The fact that the proportion of the population below the $1 per day norm decreased from 30% to 10% (as was the case, for instance, in Indonesia between 1980 and 1995) cannot be equated with the interpretation that poverty fell by two thirds. The minimum poverty norm set by that society is likely to have risen over the period, due to increased national prosperity.

In short, the use of the $1 per day poverty norm underestimates the extent of global poverty; at the same time it overestimates progress in reducing income poverty. These distortions could be avoided by using national poverty lines that are regularly adjusted. Updating the poverty line is not without controversy, but it does not justify the use of a frozen poverty line by assuming an income elasticity of zero[8]. Adjustments must be made to the poverty norm to take account of the changes in national prosperity.

Monitoring progress toward the global poverty target does not require an international poverty line. The use of national poverty lines – without accurate PPP conversion rates – may not readily yield a quantitative estimate of global poverty, or produce internationally comparable poverty data. However, global poverty estimates based on $1 per day are not robust either, and the quest for comparable poverty data is elusive. When poverty estimates are subject to very large margins of error, they cease to be useful for tracking progress over time or comparisons across countries.

Given the inherent weaknesses associated with the fixed and static international poverty line of $1 per day and the inaccurate PPP conversion rates, global poverty estimates are not a reliable source of information for the international community[9]. Instead, trends based on national poverty lines are likely to provide more meaningful information on whether the world is on track for achieving the global target of halving income-poverty between 1990 and 2015[10]. The advent of the Poverty Reduction Strategy Paper (PRSP) – if prepared in a participatory way – offers a timely opportunity for using an appropriate and adjustable national poverty norm to track progress over time.

Are statistics for China unduly biasing global poverty trends?

Poverty estimates for China influence global poverty levels in a substantial way. Getting them right is important for an accurate assessment of global poverty trends. However, different sources give very different poverty trends for that country. The latest estimates – based on the international poverty line of $1 per day in PPP values – show little change in poverty between 1987 and 1993, a steep decline between 1993-96, followed by stability in 1996-98 (Figure 15.3)[11].

This implies that the number of people who struggled to survive on less than $1 per day dropped by a staggering 138 million between 1993 and 1996 – an average of 125,000 people per day for three years running[12]. An annual decrease of four percentage points in the poverty headcount index for three consecutive years is unprecedented, indeed.

It is not clear why poverty nosedived between 1993 and 1996. Economic

Figure 15.3: Poverty incidence in China

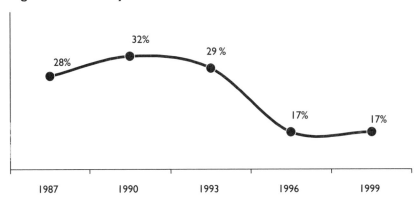

Source: World Bank (2002)

growth was high throughout the 1980s and 1990s, and no major pro-poor policy reforms took effect before or around the 1993-96 interval that could explain the sudden drop.

National poverty estimates, on the other hand, show a more gradual decline in poverty without a significant acceleration in 1993-96. The poverty estimates reported by the Ministry of Agriculture show that the incidence of income poverty fell by about one percentage point per year between 1993 and 1996, compared with the four percentage points suggested by the World Bank estimates[13]. Similarly, Gustafsson and Zhong (2000) estimate that income poverty fell by three percentage points between 1988 and 1995; considerably less than the 11 percentage points drop shown by the $1 per day estimates for the period 1987-96. Based on survey data, researchers at the Economics Institute of the Chinese Academy of Social Sciences found that the rate of rural poverty reduction slowed down significantly between 1988 and 1995, and that urban poverty showed signs of increase (Khan and Riskin, 2000).

In short, the reported reduction in global poverty during the 1990s cannot be taken at face value[14]. The discrepancies in poverty trends for China are too large to be dismissed as unimportant. Further analysis and debate are needed before firm assertions can be made about global poverty trends.

Finally, China is often quoted as an example of dazzling economic growth dramatically reducing income poverty. However, Gustafsson and Zhong (2000) question the main cause of the poverty reduction. Not only do they point out that the decline in income poverty was surprisingly small considering the country's impressive growth record, they also show that growth was not the principal force behind the fall in income poverty. Instead, their data indicate that demographic change was the key factor; that is, households became smaller in size. Large households represented a much larger proportion of the income-poor in 1995 than in 1988. Pal (2000) draws a similar conclusion from other data sources.

Is much of the global poverty debate about 'misplaced concreteness'?

In its search for general laws and rules to explain complex realities, macro-economics tends to analyse poverty's causes at the aggregate level. However, averages can be misleading, and excessive reliance on aggregate indicators and averages can unduly bias policy making. An average is nothing more than an abstract concept created to help us understand complex realities more easily. Yet averages do not exist in reality; they exist only in the human mind. The moment one ceases to realise that 'the average' is an abstract concept, one can fall victim to the fallacy of 'misplaced concreteness'[15]. The fallacy can lead to unwarranted conclusions about concrete realities – based on deduction from abstractions, not on real observations[16]. Policy analysis, therefore, must go beyond averages to avoid this fallacy. Kanbur (2001) argues that disagreement on economic policies can be explained, in part, by differences in the level of disaggregation of economic analysis.

Poverty estimates based on the frozen $1 per day norm not only tend to overestimate the number of people who escape from poverty over time, they are also likely to reinforce the belief that aggregate growth is the best – and often the sole – strategy for reducing poverty. Indeed, the assumption that the income elasticity of the poverty line is zero can lead to a tautological interpretation of the link between growth and poverty. Figure 15.4 shows that the incidence of income poverty and per capita GDP are indeed correlated.

Although the evidence may look compelling, correlation is beside the point. Poverty and growth are endogenous variables; the close correlation between

Figure 15.4: Poverty incidence by average income level

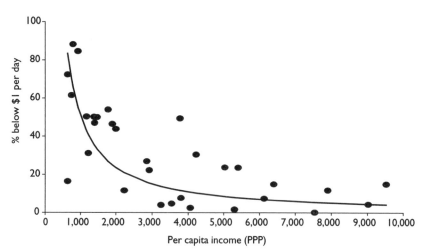

Source: Based on World Bank data

income poverty and economic development is, to a large extent, due to circular reasoning based on the use of a frozen poverty line.

A logarithmic regression fitted on the 31 country observations in Figure 15.4 yields a slope coefficient of −1.1. This implies that for every 1% increase in per capita income, poverty declines by 1.1%. Statistically speaking, the coefficient is not significantly different from 1. Recent analyses have used similar cross-country data to examine the relationship between growth and poverty (for example, Roemer and Gugarty, 1997; Gallup et al, 1999; Dollar and Kraay, 2000). They generally find a coefficient that is not significantly different from 1. Dollar and Kraay (2000), for instance, use 370 observations from 125 countries and conclude that the average income of the poor increases by the same proportion as overall income. They argue that the finding holds true for both poor and rich countries, as well as for countries that experienced positive or negative growth. Is it possible that simple hydraulic systems exist in the real economy? No! Such findings merely illustrate the danger of 'misplaced concreteness'.

The fact that the income of the poor rises one-for-one with overall per capita income may be statistically valid, but it is not necessarily true. The application of the same method to random numbers yields similar results[17]. The argument that a one-for-one relationship exists between the income of the poor and average per capita income is more the result of the methodology and definitions used rather than of actual behavioural relationships − more theory than reality; nothing other more an example of the fallacy of 'misplaced concreteness'.

Based on available evidence, it is safe to conclude that there is no solid empirical ground or intuitive reasoning to argue that a systematic relationship exists between average aggregate growth and the income of the poor[18]. More growth does not necessarily mean less poverty. It is striking that the results of a simple regression can exert so much influence on so many people − policy makers, researchers and journalists alike. Scientific evidence, especially in the social sciences, is usually gradual and cumulative; findings are often more persuasive than clinching. Admittedly, different people need different levels of persuasion but the totality of available data is insufficient to be swayed by simple cross-country regression analyses[19].

Is equity good for the poor?

The money-metric poverty gauge invariably leads to the conclusion that lack of growth is the main cause of poverty. Concerns about equity are often ignored; based on either belief in the Kuznets curve, or the argument that growth is distribution-neutral, or the conviction that inequality is a necessary incentive for growth. The fact remains that a money-metric measure of poverty leads to the conclusion that poverty reduction is best served by stepping up the rate of economic growth.

However, two stylised facts emerge from recent analyses: high inequality limits the impact of aggregate growth on poverty; and it slows economic growth. Persson and Tabellini (1994) state that "inequality is harmful for growth" (p 600). After reviewing the growth literature, Temple (1999) concludes, "it has become extremely difficult to build a case that inequality is good for growth" (p 146). Dagdeviren et al (2000) find that "greater distributional equality provides a favourable initial condition for rapid and sustainable growth" (p 23). Ravallion (2000) writes, "On balance, the existing evidence ... appears to offer more support for the view that inequality is harmful to growth than the opposite view, which was the prevailing view in development economics for decades" (p 15).

Economic growth has an obvious role to play in poverty reduction, but if inequality inhibits growth then equity must be good for the poor because it will help sustain growth. This is not a matter of being against growth but about identifying relevant and specific policy measures that will improve the economic wellbeing of the poor in particular[20]. If inequality slows economic growth then the conventional argument that a policy of redistribution will merely share poverty, not wealth, is not valid. Empirical evidence shows a very close link between asset inequality (in particular, land and education) and slow growth.

A growing body of data suggests that income disparities are widening, both between and within countries (see UNCTAD, 1997; Galbraith et al, 1998; UNDP, 1998; Cornia, 1999). No matter how it is measured, it is increasingly difficult to dismiss as anecdotal the evidence that inequality is on the rise in most countries, as well as at the global level. Milanovic (1999) derives a world income distribution by combining the results of household budget surveys covering 85% of the world's population into one grand distribution – using PPP values. The results indicate that the richest 10% of the world population control about half of global income, while the bottom half earn less than 10% of global income. He also shows that income distribution worsened markedly between 1988 and 1993.

More seriously, however, is that the poor not only lost in relative terms but also in absolute terms. Milanovic arrives at the stunning conclusion that three quarters of the world population saw their real income fall between 1988 and 1993 – with the largest drop occurring among the poorest (Figure 15.5)[21].

That inequality is harmful to the poor is further confirmed by data provided by Demery and Squire (1996). They show that disparities are not only increasing between rich and poor, but also among the poor. Nigeria, for instance, saw the poverty headcount index decline by nine percentage points between 1985 and 1992; but the incidence of extreme poverty increased by three percentage points[22]. This led to the paradoxical situation in which the number of poor declined, yet the number of destitute people increased[23].

Anti-poverty strategies often overlook equity concerns. The three conventional prongs are labour-intensive growth, investment in education and health, and social safety nets (World Bank, 1990). Equity is seldom mentioned as an explicit goal. From an operational point of view, however, an anti-

Figure 15.5: Disaggregated change in real income (1988-93), by income quartile, based on world income distribution estimates

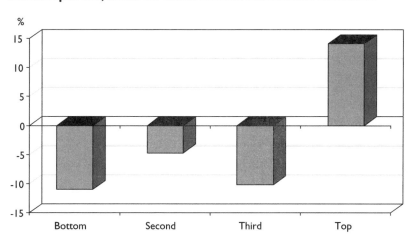

Source: Milanovic (1999)

poverty strategy that includes equity as an explicit objective can be translated into specific policy instruments, such as progressive taxation, income transfers, subsidies, elimination of user fees for basic social services, public work programmes and land reform[24]. An anti-poverty strategy that is growth-led is much shorter on specific policy instruments.

Aggregate growth is not a choice variable, but the outcome of many factors and interactions – including inequality. Not only does the concept of 'pro-poor growth' lack credibility in a world where income gaps are widening and where the poor see their income fall, it also remains fuzzy in terms of choosing and sequencing appropriate policy reforms. It is not clear whether pro-poor growth is pro-jobs or pro-wages, pro-agriculture or pro-industry, pro-government or pro-business.

Economists have to admit that there is no simple answer to the question of what causes rapid economic growth; let alone what makes it pro-poor. Trickle down seldom reaches far beyond the middle class. Aggregate growth and more jobs do not guarantee a ticket out of poverty because they seldom address its structural causes. Most of the poor are either unaffected by aggregate growth[25] or have a job but belong to the 'working poor'. Among the testimonial evidence presented in *Voices of the poor* (Narayan et al, 2000), a poor woman in Cambodia says, "Poverty means working for more than 18 hours a day, but still not earning enough to feed myself, my husband, and my two children" (p 39).

Is a social shock absorber feasible and affordable?

The 1990s saw strong economic recovery in Latin America. Stiglitz (then chief economist of the World Bank), noted that "the region followed our advice and carried out some of the most successful macroeconomic stabilization programs the world has ever seen" (1998, p 1). However, the single-minded determination to implement the Washington Consensus did not prevent unemployment and poverty from rising and inequality from worsening (Birdsall and de la Torre, 2001). A decade of sustained reforms and economic liberalisation resulted in a meagre harvest in terms of social progress and equitable development. And Latin America was not alone; faster growth in South Asia did not prevent the number of income-poor from rising. Clearly, social equity has been the missing link between economic growth and poverty reduction.

If robust economic growth in places as far apart as South Asia and Latin America does not significantly reduce income poverty, there is a strong case for social policy to ensure that growth is translated into poverty reduction. At some point, people are likely to oppose inequitable market outcomes; no one knows where the breaking point is, but it would be unwise for any government or for the international community to experiment to locate it.

If inequality between and within countries continues to rise, it could affect the sustainability of the globalisation process. At a time when the world was experiencing an earlier spell of globalisation, Henry George put it succinctly:

> So long as all the increased wealth which modern progress brings goes but to make sharper the contrast between the House of Have and the House of Want, progress is not real and cannot be permanent. (1882, p 7)

Economic history of the first half of the 20th century shows that the sustainability of globalisation should not be taken for granted.

It is the disregard of the fate of those who bear the costs associated with globalisation that fuels popular discontent – even fear[26]. Inadequate cushions to protect them – both at the global and local levels – drives the movement against 'globalisation as we know it'. It is no coincidence that small open OECD economies, such as the Benelux and Nordic countries, have one of the largest public sectors to cushion some of the negative effects of openness on the vulnerable groups (Rodrik, 1998).

It would be a great tragedy were the wheels of progress to be slowed down by the inability of national governments and the international community to assist those who are bearing a disproportionate share of the cost of globalisation. The powerful forces of technological progress cannot be arrested, just as the benefits from market principles cannot be ignored. But the distribution of the costs and benefits of globalisation among socio-economic groups must be made more equitable, mainly through public action and social policy – both locally and globally. Markets can be made to deliver more equitable outcomes, which will ultimately prove efficient and effective in reducing poverty.

The onus of good social policy should not be placed on national policies alone, but should also have a bearing on the formulation of global rules and regulations – for fairer trade and more aid, limited protection of intellectual property rights[27], more effective commodity price stabilisation schemes, and other measures. This is in line with the call made by the ministers and heads of aid agencies in donor countries for greater consistency in industrialised countries between agricultural, trade and investment policies on the one hand, and development cooperation on the other (OECD/DAC, 1996).

Proponents of rapid globalisation and liberalisation often use the metaphor of the bicycle to argue that the economy needs constant reforms and liberalisation to maintain momentum. The same metaphor can be used to emphasise comfort instead of speed. Until recently, bicycles came without shock absorbers; the idea of installing them came after potholes appeared on the road to globalisation, especially in the wake of the East Asian crisis in 1997. As the road to globalisation will be bumpy, an economic shock absorber is being installed on the front wheel to help control the handlebars. It includes Chile-styled cooling mechanisms of so-called 'hot-money'; flexible exchange rate regimes, better banking supervision, greater transparency in financial reporting, and adequate bankruptcy legislation.

However, a social shock absorber is needed too. The countries that were hardest hit by the financial crisis in East Asia lacked a good social shock absorber. Indonesia's and Thailand's under-investment in basic social services contributed to their vulnerability to the financial crisis[28]. Therefore, the next step is to install a shock absorber on the rear wheel for a smooth and uninterrupted journey into the global economy. Universal coverage of basic social services plays this role. It is financially affordable and technically feasible.

As a concrete example of partnership between developing and industrialised countries, the UN launched the 20/20 initiative in the early 1990s. The initiative calls for the allocation of an indicative 20% of the national budget in developing countries and 20% of donor aid to basic social services[29]. The initiative's aim is universal access to an integrated package of basic social services of good quality – by spending more and by spending better. Studies in over 30 countries show that the share of the national budget allocated to basic social services ranges between 12% and 14% (UNICEF and UNDP, 1998). Few countries spend close to 20%; fewer still spend less than 10% on these services. The share of official developmental assistance (ODA) directed to basic social services varies greatly between countries, as well as over time. Overall, about 10-12% of total ODA is allocated to basic social services (OECD/DAC, 2001).

The financial cost of achieving universal coverage is modest, whereas the benefits that beckon are enormous. The global shortfall in public spending to ensure universal coverage of a minimum package of basic social services is equivalent to about one third of current spending – or about $80 billion per year (at 1995 prices) (UNDP et al, 1998). The full implementation of the 20/20 initiative would generate enough resources to bridge the gap. Although large in absolute terms, $80 billion represents about 0.25% of global annual income.

But social policies recommended by the international financial institutions during the 1990s were not driven by the objective of installing such a social shock absorber. Although IDA lending[30] to the social sectors doubled in importance during the 1990s (from about 20% to 40%) an independent evaluation by the Operations Evaluation Department of the World Bank makes sobering reading (World Bank, 2001c). After reviewing IDA's anti-poverty work between 1994 and 2000, it concludes, "the development outcomes of IDA programs have been partially satisfactory" (p 91)[33]. IDA countries had a mixed record in sustaining growth. While macro-economic stability improved and many economic distortions were removed, no strong evidence emerged as to whether the poor saw their income and employment opportunities increase. It proved difficult to come up with practical policies to achieve not just growth but equitable growth; concrete measures were usually missing to transmit the benefits of policy reforms to the poor. Access to and quality of service delivery to the poor hardly improved.

User fees, narrow targeting and safety nets were central to social policy recommendation based on the Washington Consensus. A review of the theoretical arguments and empirical evidence regarding user financing of basic social services leads to the following conclusions (Reddy and Vandemoortele, 1996):

- user fees reduce demand for services, particularly among the poor;
- protecting the poor is difficult; exemption schemes are costly to administer and are seldom effective;
- user fees tend to aggravate gender biases, seasonal variations and regional disparities;
- user fees collect very modest amounts of money compared with the budgetary resources allocated to basic social services;
- basic social services are subject to principal–agent interactions and asymmetrical information so that price signals will not automatically lead to optimal demand;
- user fees do not guarantee greater efficiency and effectiveness because basic social services are public goods that have strong synergies and positive externalities.

Inadequate social budgets often lead to targeted interventions on narrowly defined groups or areas. Narrowly targeted programmes are increasingly prescribed for reasons of efficiency and cost savings, for they minimise leakage to the non-poor. Obviously, the merits of narrow targeting depend on the nature of the goods and services that are being targeted. Targeting fertiliser subsidies to smallholders or micro-credit to poor women, for instance, is very different from targeting vouchers for primary education. Therefore, generalisations about targeting are of limited use. With respect to basic social services, narrow targeting has important hidden costs (Vandemoortele, 2000):

- mis-targeting, due to the difficulty of identifying the poor;
- failing to reach the poor, since the non-poor seldom let subsidies pass by;

- administering narrowly targeted programmes; control of mismanagement and petty corruption;
- out-of-pocket expenses to document eligibility (such as bus fares);
- non-sustainability.

Once the non-poor cease to have a stake in narrowly targeted programmes, the political commitment to sustain their scope and quality is at risk. The voice of women and the poor alone is usually too weak to maintain strong public support and this is why programmes for the poor frequently end up as poor programmes.

Although social safety nets promote rapid responses to crises, they are not sufficient as social shock absorbers. They claim to be efficient but they are not necessarily effective. Indeed, ex post safety nets are usually underfunded, slow to take off, and seldom reach the poorest. There is no doubt that public spending on basic social services includes wastage; but those who argue that existing budgets have to be used more efficiently before investing more public money miss the important point that insufficiencies often create inefficiencies. The dichotomy between more money versus more efficiency is a false one. Most policy makers do not face a choice between either improving efficiency or increasing budget allocations; both have to be addressed simultaneously. Indeed, inefficiencies and insufficiencies are not independent, but very much *inter*dependent.

In short, a social shock absorber should not be dismissed on the basis of non-affordability. User fees, narrow targeting and safety nets cannot be the mainstay for ensuring universal coverage of basic social services. They are likely to yield savings that are 'penny-wise but pound-foolish'. High-achieving countries such as Costa Rica, the state of Kerala (India), the Republic of Korea, Mauritius, Sri Lanka and others all applied broad targeting; none of them relied on shortcuts.

Conclusion

Poverty has many dimensions that cannot be adequately captured by one single indicator. Global poverty estimates based on the $1-a-day norm are inaccurate and misleading. They understimate global poverty and overestimate poverty reduction, giving a false sense of progress and unwarranted complacency. Therefore, they cannot be taken at face value. The norm has led the world community to internalise two incorrect conclusions: that good progress is being made toward the global target of halving poverty by 2015; and that aggregate growth is the best means of further reducing poverty.

The following statement is emblematic of the first point:

> If current growth trends and policies persist, it turns out that the world has a pretty good chance of meeting the international targets even if we do nothing. (Collier and Dollar, 2000, p 7)

Given the inherent limitations of global poverty estimates and the danger of 'misplaced concreteness', it seems inappropriate to draw such optimistic inference about the feasibility of the 2015 poverty target[32]. The poor themselves are unlikely to be as upbeat about progress as global trends suggest.

Even if all conceptual and measurement issues could be resolved, it must be kept in mind that most of the progress has been due to a few large countries – particularly China, India and Indonesia. When China is excluded, global progress during the 1990s was less than half the rate needed for halving income poverty by 2015. In addition, the causes for the rapid decline in China's poverty level remain unclear. If demographic change has been a key factor – as some analysts have documented – then it would be unwise to assume that income poverty will continue its rapid decline. Therefore, a simple extrapolation of global trends to 2015 is invalid because large countries will gradually become less able to pull global poverty down as they reach lower levels of poverty. Global poverty projections will only be meaningful if they are based on country-specific projections.

The following quote is illustrative of the second incorrect conclusion:

> Poverty rates will continue to fall if growth continues. (World Bank, 2001d, p 21)

Aggregate growth undoubtedly has its place in an anti-poverty strategy; the problem is usually to keep it in its place. The poverty debate cannot be reduced to a series of unhelpful generalisations about aggregate growth and averages indicators. They merely add to the fallacy of 'misplaced concreteness' and risk overlooking the many human faces behind economic realities. This is not about downplaying the importance of growth, but it must be questioned whether aggregate growth is a priori good for the poor – irrespective of what happens to equity. If growth is good for the poor and if inequality inhibits growth, then equity must be good for the poor.

Equity does matter for poverty reduction. It would be incorrect to assume that more growth will automatically translate into less poverty. Equity concerns are not about charity, but about laying the foundation for a strong economy and a just society. The fact that the poor do not gain from economic stagnation and recession does not prove, regrettably, that the opposite will be true. The fact that macro-economic instability hurts the poor does not necessarily mean that they will benefit from macro-economic stability. Much will depend on how stability is achieved. More nuanced positions and conclusions are warranted given the many complexities that govern the relationship between growth and poverty.

Global inequality and global warming share similar characteristics (Wade, 2001). Despite the fact that both are less shrouded in scientific uncertainty, they continue to be pushed off the political agenda by other pressing issues. This is partly due to their diffuse and long-term impact, and partly because nobody appears to be responsible or able to do something about them.

By questioning some of the accepted norms, facts and findings on global poverty and by arguing that equity is good for the poor, one runs the risk of being accused of clinging to outmoded values and defunct policy instruments. However, one can draw strength from the words of J.K. Galbraith: "There are times when the enunciation of the most elementary common sense has an aspect of eccentricity, irrationality, even mild insanity".

Notes

[1] The views expressed in this chapter do not necessarily reflect those of the United Nations Development Programme. I am grateful to Jacques Loup, Selim Jahan and Jafar Javan of UNDP; Gisele Kamanou of the UN Statistical Division; and Enrique Delamonica of UNICEF for helpful comments and suggestions. The usual disclaimers apply.

[2] This represents a sharper decline than that reported on page 363 for 1987-1998. Global poverty estimates fluctuate from year to year, regional estimates change as new information becomes available, and changes are sometimes introduced into technical calculations, as pointed out elsewhere (pp 358-60 and pp 378-85). All these can lead to apparent inconsistencies in global poverty estimates.

[3] The Millennium Declaration distils the major development goals and targets that were agreed at global conferences and world summits during the 1990s (UN, 2000).

[4] Reddy and Pogge (2002) give a thorough discussion on the important technical aspects of the international poverty line.

[5] Another weakness of the $1 per day poverty norm is that it does not measure access to basic goods and services that are publicly provided. Access to such services is often critically important for the poor; but an income above or below $1 per day says nothing about access to and quality of public services.

[6] An income elasticity of 1 turns the absolute poverty line into a relative one, defining the poor as those with an income below one third, for instance, or one half of the average national income level. Poverty reduction is then made entirely dependent on improvements in the distribution of income.

[7] 'Struggling to survive on less than $1 per day' is a more accurate than the expression 'living below $1 per day' to describe the daily reality faced by millions of poor people.

[8] Fisher (1997) documents that analysts were aware of the importance of the income elasticity of the poverty line before the first official poverty line was set in the US in 1969. He ascribes the assumption about zero-elasticity to the growing involvement of macro-economists in poverty studies during the 1960s, replacing social workers and advocates of disadvantaged groups as primary actors.

[9] Morrisson (2002) correlates malnutrition with income poverty, using national and international poverty lines. He concludes: "The results of the econometric tests are clear: the number of malnourished children is correlated to the number of poor individuals if we use the national poverty line (values of R2 reach 0.70). The results are less satisfactory, however, when we use the measure of $1 or $2 per day" (p 13).

[10] In 1997, a group of experts from the UN, World Bank and OECD discussed relevant indicators for monitoring progress towards the international development targets. Some made the case for using national poverty lines, but that view did not prevail and current practice favours the norm of $1 per day.

[11] Global poverty estimates are often presented with a decimal point, which may give a false sense of sophistication and accuracy. Given their approximate nature, rounded figures are more appropriate.

[12] Implicitly, virtually all poverty reduction in developing countries between 1993 and 1996 occurred in China, while the number of income poor in sub-Saharan Africa, South Asia and Latin America combined, reportedly increased by about 15 million per year.

[13] The data of the Ministry of Agriculture relate to rural poverty, whereas World Bank data refer to total poverty. Since poverty in China is overwhelmingly rural, the discrepancy cannot be explained by the difference in geographical coverage.

[14] Footnote 5 on page 6 of a mimeographed World Bank paper (2001b) refers to some reliability problems with poverty data for China. But such data problems are not limited to China; they are inherent in the use of the $1 per day in PPP values poverty guage.

[15] Daly and Cobb (1994) explain this term in detail, which was coined by Alfred North Whitehead who wrote in 1925 that economics "fixes attention on a definite group of abstractions, neglects everything else, and elicits every scrap of information and theory which is relevant to what it has retained" (quoted in Daly and Cobb, 1994, p 36).

[16] Abstractions that commonly lead to the fallacy of 'misplaced concreteness' include assumptions of perfect information, perfect competition, neutral institutions, Homo Economicus and independent utility functions. A concrete example of 'misplaced concreteness' is when average per capita GDP is used as a proxy for economic wellbeing, thereby forgetting that it measures only a limited range of welfare dimensions that involve market transactions. The use of computers – which make number crunching easier and cheaper – certainly augments the danger of 'misplaced concreteness' in economic analyses.

[17] A series of 370 random numbers between 100 and 20,000 (a plausible range for average per capita income levels) is multiplied by another series of 370 random numbers between 10% and 50% (a plausible range for the income of the bottom quintile as a proportion

of the average per capita income level). This yields a random series for the average income of the poor. Next, the logarithmic value of series 1 and 3 are regressed. The resulting R^2 is 0.84, only slightly less than 0.87 obtained by Dollar and Kraay (2000); the slope coefficient is 1.03 compared with 1.07. Statistically speaking, both are not significantly different from 1.

[18] This is shown by several studies, including Ravallion and Chen (1997) and Deininger and Squire (1998).

[19] Given the conceptual and measurement problems associated with global poverty data, a code of conduct for running cross-country regressions may be warranted, if not an outright moratorium.

[20] The experts who met in 1997 to select appropriate indicators for monitoring the poverty target agreed to include the share of the bottom quintile in national consumption. However, current practice largely ignores the equity measure, and relies almost exclusively on the headcount index based on the international poverty line.

[21] A recent study by the US Congressional Budget Office depicts a similar trend. It shows that the average after-tax income of the wealthiest 1% of households in the US swelled by more than 150% between 1979 and 1997, dwarfing the income growth of households making less money. The bottom quintile actually saw their average after-tax income drop. The ratio of the average income of the top 20% compared with that of the bottom 20% jumped from 9 to 15 respectively.

[22] A similar story emerges for rural Kenya (1981-91) and rural Tanzania (1983-91).

[23] Therefore, the threshold at which the poverty line is fixed very much influences the resulting poverty trend. Pyatt (1999) notes "the conclusion that 40% of the population in country X is poor should be read as saying that the poverty line has been drawn for country X in such a way that 40% of the population is poor" (p 13).

[24] Hanmer et al (1999) find that most poverty assessments in sub-Saharan Africa during the 1990s were silent on land reform, as they were on other forms of asset redistribution. So far, most PRSPs are also silent on equity-enhancing policy reforms.

[25] It must be pointed out that the rate of economic growth for a country is an average indicator that hides enormous differences among groups of households and individual families, including changes in opposite directions. It is likely that the distribution of growth within the country will be strongly influenced by the distribution of human, physical and financial capital. Hence, an average growth rate of 5% is no guarantee that the poor will see their income rise by a similar rate, if at all.

[26] Recent polls show a deep divide regarding the perception on free trade. Only one-third of American families with less than $50,000 in annual income hold a positive view

of free trade, while nearly two thirds of those with an annual income above $75,000 hold such a positive view; and that percentage increases as income rises.

[27] Including the expansion of mechanisms such as compulsory licensing and parallel imports of products that are subject to trade-related intellectual property rights (TRIPS).

[28] Their female secondary enrolment ratio was considerably lower than in Malaysia and the Philippines – two countries that weathered the crisis better (40 versus 70 respectively). One third of Indonesia's children under the age of five were underweight in 1995 – a proportion that was higher than the average for sub-Saharan Africa. These indicators are uncharacteristic for a so-called 'miracle economy' that reduced poverty in a spectacular way.

[29] Basic social services comprise basic education, primary health, reproductive health, water and sanitation, and nutrition.

[30] The International Development Association (IDA) was established in 1960. Funds come from donor contributions, augmented by transfers from net earnings of the International Bank for Reconstruction and Development (IBRD). IDA credits have to be repaid over a period of 35-40 years, after an initial grace period of 10 years. They carry no interest, but have an annual service charge of 0.75%. No specific figures are available, but a 70% grant element of IDA loans is often quoted. Since 1960, IDA has lent over $100 billion. Repayments are turning IDA into a quasi-endowment fund – expected to be self-financing by 2015.

[31] A footnote makes it clear that "Management [at the World Bank] does not agree with OED's [Operations Evaluation Department] assessment" (World Bank, 2001c, p 109).

[32] The impact on future poverty trends of HIV/AIDS, environmental degradation, gender discrimination, debt overhang and widening income gaps appears to be absent from the analysis. Vandemoortele and Delamonica (2000), for instance, show that the social epidemiology of HIV/AIDS increasingly discriminates against illiterate and poor people, especially young women.

References

Birdsall, N. and de la Torre, A. with Menezes, R. (2001) *Washington contentious: Economic policies for social equity in Latin America*, Washington, DC: Carnegie Endowment for International Peace and Inter-American Dialogue.

Chen, S. and Ravallion, M. (2001) 'How did the world's poorest fare in the 1990s?', *Review of Income and Wealth*, vol 47.

Collier, P. and Dollar, D. (2000) *Can the world cut poverty in half? How policy reform and effective aid can meet the international development goals*, Washington, DC: Development Research Group, World Bank.

Cornia, A. (1999) *Liberalization, globalization and income distribution*, Working Paper No 157, Helsinki: WIDER.

Dagdeviren, H., van der Hoeven, R. and Weeks, J. (2000) *Redistribution matters: Growth for poverty reduction*, Employment Paper No 2000/10, Geneva: ILO.

Daly, H. and Cobb, J. Jr (1994) *For the common good: Redirecting the economy towards community, the environment and a sustainable future*, Boston, MA: Beacon Press.

Deininger, K. and Squire, L. (1998) 'New ways of looking at old issues', *Journal of Development Economics*, vol 57, no 2, pp 259-87.

Demery, L. and Squire, L. (1996) 'Macroeconomic adjustment in Africa: an emerging picture', *World Bank Research Observer*, vol 11, pp 39-59.

Dollar, D. and Kraay, A. (2000) *Growth is good for the poor*, Washington, DC: Development Research Group, World Bank.

Fisher, G. (1997) 'Poverty lines and measures of income inadequacy in the United States since 1870: collecting and using a little-known body of historical material', Paper presented at the 22nd meeting of the Social Science History Association, Washington, DC.

Galbraith, J. (1958) *The affluent society*, (40th anniversary edition, 1998) Wilmington, MA: Houghton Mifflin.

Galbraith, J., Darity, W. and Jiaqing, L. (1998) *Measuring the evolution of inequality in the global economy*, Austin, TX: University of Texas at Austin.

Gallup, J., Radelet, S. and Warner, A. (1999) *Economic growth and the income of the poor*, CAER Discussion Paper No 32, Cambridge, MA: Harvard Institute for International Development.

George, H. (1882) *Progress and poverty*, New York, NY: Appleton and Co.

Gustafsson, B. and Zhong, W. (2000) 'How and why has poverty in China changed? A study based on microdata for 1988 and 1995', *The China Quarterly*, vol 164, no 1, pp 983-1006.

Hanmer, L., Pyatt, G. and White, H. (1999) 'What do the World Bank's poverty assessments teach us about poverty in sub-Saharan Africa?', *Development and Change*, vol 30, pp 795-823.

Kanbur, R. (2001) *Economic policy, distribution and poverty: The nature of disagreements*, Ithaca, NY: Cornell University (www.people.cornell.edu/pages/sk145/).

Khan, A. and Riskin, C. (2000) *Inequality and poverty in China in the age of globalisation*, New York, NY: Oxford University Press.

Milanovic, B. (1999) *True world income distribution, 1988 and 1993: First calculation based on household surveys alone*, Washington, DC: Development Research Group, World Bank.

Narayan, D. with Patel, R., Schafft, K., Rademacher, A. and Koch-Schulte, S. (2000) *Voices of the poor: Can anyone hear us?*, Washington, DC: Oxford University Press for the World Bank.

OECD/DAC (Organisation for Economic Co-operation and Development/ Development Assistance Committee) (1996) *Shaping the 21st century: The contribution of development cooperation*, Paris: OECD/DAC.

OECD/DAC (2001) *Development co-operation report 2000*, Paris: OECD/DAC.

Oster, S., Lake, E. and Oksman, C. (1978) *The definition and measurement of poverty*, Boulder, CO: Westview Press.

Pal, S. (2000) 'Economic reform and household welfare in rural China: evidence from household survey data', *Journal of International Development*, vol 12, pp 187-206.

Persson, T. and Tabellini, G. (1994) 'Is inequality harmful for growth?', *The American Economic Review*, vol 84, no 3, pp 600-21.

Pyatt, G. (1999) 'Poverty versus the poor', in G. Pyatt and M. Ward (eds) *Identifying the poor: Papers on measuring poverty to celebrate the bicentenary of the publication in 1797 of the State of the Poor by Sir Frederick Morton Eden*, Amsterdam: IOS Press.

Ravallion, M. (2000) *Growth, inequality and poverty: Looking beyond averages*, Washington DC, Development Research Group: World Bank.

Ravallion, M. and Bidani, B. (1994) 'How robust is a poverty profile?', *World Bank Economic Review*, vol 8, no 1, pp 75-102.

Ravallion, M. and Chen, S. (1997) 'What can new survey data tell us about recent changes in distribution and poverty?', *World Bank Economic Review*, vol 11, no 2, pp 357-82.

Ravallion, M., Datt, G. and van de Walle, D. (1991) 'Quantifying absolute poverty in the developing world', *Review of Income and Wealth*, vol 37, no 4, pp 345-61.

Reddy, S. and Pogge, T. (2002) *How not to count the poor*, New York, NY: Columbia University.

Reddy, S. and Vandemoortele, J. (1996) *User financing of basic social services: A review of theoretical arguments and empirical evidence*, Evaluation Policy and Planning Division, Working Paper No 6, New York, NY: UNICEF.

Rodrik, D. (1998) *Has globalisation gone too far?*, Washington, DC: Institute for International Economics.

Roemer, M. and Gugerty, M. (1997) *Does economic growth reduce poverty?*, CAER Discussion Paper No 5, Cambridge, MA: Harvard Institute for International Development.

Rowntree, B. (1901) *Poverty: A study of town life*, London: Macmillan, reissued by The Policy Press, 2000.

Stiglitz, J. (1998) 'The Asian crisis and the future of the international architecture', Washington, DC: World Bank (www.worldbank.org/knowledge/chiefecon/articles/wea21/).

Temple, J. (1999) 'The new growth evidence', *Journal of Economic Literature*, vol 37, pp 112-56.

UN (United Nations) (2000) *Millennium declaration*, New York, NY: UN.

UNCTAD (United Nations Conference on Trade and Development) (1997) *Trade and development report, 1997: Globalization, distribution and growth*, Geneva: UNCTAD.

UNDP (United Nations Development Programme) (1999) *Human development report 1999: Globalisation with a human face*, New York, NY: Oxford University Press for UNDP.

UNDP, UNESCO, UNFPA (United Nations Population Fund), UNICEF, WHO and the World Bank (1998) *Implementing the 20/20 initiative: Achieving universal access to basic social services*, New York, NY: UNICEF.

UNICEF (2001) *Progress since the world summit for children: A statistical review*, New York, NY: UNICEF.

UNICEF and UNDP, with contributions from the World Bank and UNFPA (1998) *Country experiences in assessing the adequacy, equity and efficiency of public spending on basic social services*, Document prepared for the Hanoi meeting on the 20/20 Initiative, New York, NY: UNICEF.

Vandemoortele, J. (2000) *Absorbing social shocks, protecting children and reducing poverty: The role of basic social services*, Working Paper No 1, New York, NY: UNICEF, Evaluation Policy and Planning Division.

Vandemoortele, J. and Delamonica, E. (2000) 'The "education vaccine" against HIV', *Current Issues in Comparative Education*, vol 3, no 1 (www.tc.columbia.edu/cice).

Wade, R. (2001) 'Winners and losers', *The Economist*, 26 April.

World Bank (1990) *World development report: Poverty*, Washington, DC: Oxford University Press for the World Bank.

World Bank (2000) *World development report: Attacking poverty,* Washington, DC: Oxford University Press for the World Bank.

World Bank (2001a) *China: Overcoming rural poverty. A country study,* Washington, DC: World Bank.

World Bank (2001b) *The international development goals: Strengthening commitments and measuring progress,* mimeo, Washington, DC: World Bank.

World Bank (2001c) *IDA's partnership for poverty reduction (TY94-TY00): An independent evaluation,* Washington, DC: Operations Evaluation Department, World Bank.

World Bank (2001d) *World Bank atlas 2001,* Washington, DC: World Bank.

World Bank (2002) *World development indicators,* Washington, DC: World Bank.

SIXTEEN

1% of €10,000 billion[1]

Tony Atkinson

December 2001/January 2002 saw two highly significant developments in the EU – the adoption of a common set of indicators for social inclusion, and the introduction of the euro (€). The conjunction of these two mean that it is now important and opportune for the EU to take yet another major step: the adoption of the target of providing official development assistance equal to 1% of GNP. The purpose of this chapter is to make the case for such an *EU aid target*, which is more ambitious than that advocated by the UN (0.7% of GNP), and considerably more ambitious than the 0.39% committed by the EU in its (very welcome) statement before the Monterrey Conference on Financing for Development in March 2002. It would more than double the world total of aid and bring within the realm of feasibility the aspiration that developing countries should not be prevented by lack of resources from reaching the Millennium Development Goals agreed at the Millennium Summit of September 2000.

The background to this proposal is that in December 2001, the EU adopted for the first time a set of commonly agreed and defined indicators for social inclusion. These indicators, which cover financial poverty and its persistence, income inequality, regional cohesion, long-term unemployment and joblessness, low educational attainment, life expectancy and poor health, are to be used to judge progress towards Social Europe. They embody the social objectives of the EU. The indicators are to be used to assess current performance, construct league tables of member states, and to monitor the National Action Plans for Social Inclusion.

On 1 January 2002, the euro came into circulation, which means that 300 million people share a common currency as part of a monetary union. A further 75 million people live in the EU, but do not use the euro. If we add the accession countries, due to join in the next few years, then the total population becomes some 450 million and the total gross national product will then be around €10,000 billion (using the American definition of a billion as a thousand million).

The case for an EU aid target: important and opportune

The adoption of an ambitious aid target is important because it underlines that the EU is an outward-looking, and not purely inward-looking, community, and because it recognises that the domestic economic policies of the EU, taken on their own, threaten to have negative effects on developing countries.

Fears that the establishment of a customs union will divert trade, at the expense of third parties, have been expressed since the founding of the EEC. James Meade (1962), for example, argued that the key test for the UK in deciding whether or not to join should be the treatment of Commonwealth countries. Very important is the Common Agricultural Policy, but the impact on manufacturers is also significant, with quantitative restrictions limiting the opportunities for the Newly Industrialising Countries (NIC). To this has been added concerns about the impact of domestic policy, such as subsidies, regional assistance and public procurement. In its enthusiasm to drive forward the European project, the EU has often emphasised the advantages to Europe's citizens and downplayed the external impact. According to Sheila Page (1991), the European Commission (EC) in its 14-volume study of the Single European Market made only passing references to the rest of the world.

The ambition set out at the Lisbon Council of March 2000 of making the EU perform as a highly dynamic and flexible economy may have both positive and negative effects on developing countries. To the extent that productivity rises in the high technology sectors, this may turn the terms of trade in favour of developing countries, and faster growth in Europe will stimulate demand for their exports. If, however, the aim of greater flexibility is to reduce wage costs, and make Europe more competitive in low technology sectors, then this policy reduces the demand for the products of the NIC. The exemption of the first tranche of earnings from social security taxes, for example, may generate increased (or maintain) employment for low-skilled workers, but it does so by reducing the relative price of the import-competing sector. It means that textile production remains profitable in the face of competition from lower-wage countries. There may still be a positive effect of faster European growth, but the policy of making Europe 'more competitive' has potentially damaging implications for the rest of the world that should not be overlooked.

A policy of domestic labour market reform has distributional implications within, as well as outside, Europe. The adoption in 2001 of the common set of social indicators for social inclusion means that any adverse effects of labour market flexibility on the extent and persistence of poverty will be regularly monitored. The member states are committed to implementing National Action Plans on Social Inclusion, taking these, and other social objectives, as the criteria for judging the level of social development. Under the principle of subsidiarity, member states are free to determine their own methods of achieving the objectives. Some countries may favour universal benefits, such as child benefit; others may favour income-tested in-work benefits. However, the objective of protecting the least advantaged is held in common, and embodied in the agreed social indicators.

This conjunction of economic progress towards integration, with adoption of a social agenda to protect its own citizens, means that it is highly opportune for the EU to make a more ambitious statement of its concerns for those less

Figure 16.1: Net official development assistance flows (2000)

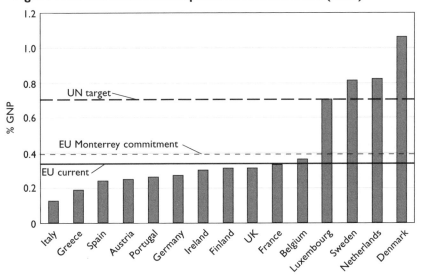

Source: Development Assistance Committee Annual report at www.oecd.org

fortunate who live outside its boundaries. Since the Treaty of Rome, Europe has seen a role for common action in the field of development assistance, notably via the association of certain countries, and the successive Yaoundé (1963 and 1969) and Lomé (1975) conventions. Since the Maastricht Treaty, development cooperation has had a specific legal basis (articles 177-181 of the Treaty on European Union). Together, the EU and its member states provide around half of all official international development aid.

However, the scale of assistance needs to be considerably increased. The EU member states, like all other members of the UN, have adopted the Millennium Development Goals agreed at the Millennium Summit of September 2000. The 'road map' towards their implementation, recently published by the UN (2001), makes clear that achievement of the growth of poverty eradication requires more generous development assistance, noting that the net flow of official development assistance to developing countries has in fact been declining (United Nations, 2001, p 26). Few countries reach the UN target of 0.7% of GNP for official assistance (see Figure 16.1 for the position of EU countries in 2000). In the EU, only Denmark, Luxembourg, the Netherlands and Sweden attained this level. Overall, the EU only reached 0.33%. The March 2002 European Council statement affirmed that all member states would strive to reach 0.33% as a minimum, but the collective average promised at the Monterrey Conference would only reach 0.39% by 2006 (European Council, 2002).

Finally, the declaration of an EU development aid target would be opportune in the light of the forthcoming accession of a number of new members. This will involve a substantive degree of redistribution within the enlarged EU. It is important to underline that redistribution is not confined within the boundaries of the EU, and that external development assistance to the poor worldwide is an essential part of the *acquis communautaire*.

An EU target

I am here proposing a more ambitious target than that of the UN, proposing that the EU as a whole seek to provide development assistance at the level of 1% of GNP; in other words, 1% of €10,000 billion. There are two reasons for this choice. The first is that it harks back to the 1% target advocated by President Kennedy's advisers when he came into office in 1961. It is not clear that they were in fact being more ambitious, since the 1% may have included private as well as official flows, and was related to national income rather than GNP (see Singer, 1969). More importantly, a total of €100 billion of aid from the EU would more than double existing total development aid. On a global scale, this would really make a difference. Finally, some member states already exceed the UN target, and we should be seeking to match best practice.

The target cannot of course be attained immediately. The EU governments would have to readjust their public finances, and the increases expected for Germany, France, Italy and the UK are very large in absolute terms. Overall, the size of the proposed increase means that its effectiveness depends on there being the appropriate machinery for administration, which will undoubtedly have to be expanded in scale. Obviously, this cannot be achieved overnight. However, the EU should aim to move progressively towards the target over the course of the next decade[2].

In proposing the target, I do not have in mind that member states should necessarily each contribute 1% of GNP, particularly when the accession countries join the EU. Devising a progressive formula taking account of differences in per capita income, purchasing power adjusted, would take the EU into territory not explored as part of the social indicators exercise. Measures of poverty adopted by the EU relate to incomes below 60% (or another percentage) of the median *in* the member state. Union-wide measures, with a common EU poverty line, have however been calculated by Eurostat (2000, p 20). If we take as a yardstick such a figure of 60% of the median income for the EU as a whole (adjusted for family size and for differences in purchasing power), then a progressive aid contribution can be calculated as a percentage of all incomes in excess of this amount (referred to as 'the European poverty line'). The resulting total excess income would then be that country's 'tax base'. The size of the tax base relative to total income in a country would then depend on its income per head relative to the EU mean, and on its distribution of income. Put another way, the amount that a country can deduct from its total income to arrive at its tax base would be equal to the European poverty line times the total population *if no one had income below the European poverty line*. To the extent that people *do* fall below the European poverty line, then *less* can be deducted to arrive at the tax base. If some people fall €X below, with this money going to people above the poverty line, then the tax base is increased by this amount. The consequence

Figure 16.2: Contributions with a progressive formula

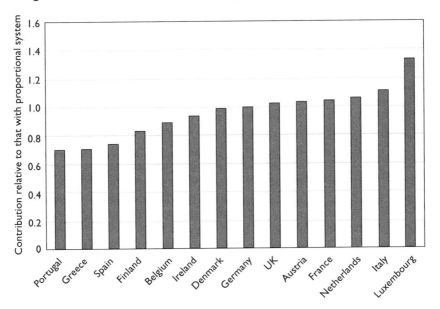

is that countries with higher proportions below the European poverty line (or, more accurately, larger poverty deficits) would, other things being equal, find their contribution higher than those of countries with a smaller proportion in poverty. (At the extreme if all income goes to one person, then essentially all national income is in the tax base.)

In order to calculate the country-distribution of aid according to the progressive formula, we can make use of EUROMOD, a tax-benefit model for the EU as a whole[3]. Figure 16.2 shows the contribution by member states (excluding Sweden, not yet incorporated in the model) with the progressive formula, compared with that from a proportional tax on total income. (It should be noted that the calculations refer to household disposable income, which differs from GNP.) As is to be expected, the contribution from Portugal, Greece and Spain is lower: around 0.7 times that with a proportional system.

It should be emphasised that I am here advocating an EU role in setting the overall target, and leaving open the question as to how far the aid programmes are to be administered at EU level. There is at present a mix, with national programmes predominating. It seems likely that this will continue, and it is not here proposed that the increase in aid should be run as part of an EU programme. There may be advantages from multilateral cooperation, and the EU may be better able to reform the conditionality of aid (see Kanbur, 2000), but this is not part of the proposal. In the same way, I am not proposing that the aid need be channelled via recipient country governments; there is clearly an important role for non-governmental organisations (NGOs).

Arguments against an EU aid target

Attitudes towards development aid today exhibit a degree of ambiguity that was not found 40 years ago when aid targets were first proposed. Peter Townsend, in his *International analysis of poverty* (1993), criticises the rich countries for having reduced their aid as a percentage of GNP, but goes on to say that aid is "increasingly recognised across the world to be an unhappy euphemism" (1993, p 23). Critics from the left see aid as serving donor interests and retarding genuine development; critics from the right see aid as having been misappropriated, and as a disincentive to domestic development effort by recipient countries. Here I consider three main objections to the proposed EU aid target:

• aid is not effective;
• aid is a matter for member states, not the EU;
• targets should be set in terms of outputs, not inputs.

These arguments have to be taken seriously, but in my judgement they do not outweigh the case of setting the EU aid target.

Effectiveness of aid

The effectiveness of aid in stimulating the growth of recipient countries has long been investigated by economists (see, for example, Little and Clifford, 1965; Cassen, 1986). In part the analysis has been concerned with ex ante calculations of absorptive capacity. There is undoubtedly a limit to the amount of aid that can be productively invested and to the speed with which aid programmes can be increased in scale. The implications of the large increase in aid proposed here certainly need fuller examination, but for the present I note the conclusion of Robin Marris that "it is very difficult to suppose [that] if the current total of world aid were doubled ... there would be any significant difficulty of 'absorption'" (1999, p 63). In part the analysis has been based on an ex post evaluation of growth performance. A number of studies, from Griffin and Enos (1970) to Boone (1996), have concluded that aid has no (or negative) effects on growth. The recent review by Hansen and Tarp (2000) concludes, however, that, while the relation is intricate, the weight of evidence is that there is a positive relationship, with the marginal benefit higher when there is a favourable policy context. Overall, it seems fairly clear that one cannot reach a categorical conclusion. To quote Drèze and Sen, "like all other policies and institutions, aid too has to be assessed by balancing its positive and negative consequences in the respective contexts" (1989, p 274).

Here I proceed on the assumption that the EU aid programme is so designed that the positive outweighs the negative. Moreover, one must remember that aid can play a role in raising not only future growth, but also current living standards. Even were aid to go to finance current consumption, this can have a positive impact. Of course, how we assess this impact depends on who benefits. Much effort has been devoted in recent years to ensuring that aid is targeted towards poverty reduction (see, for example, Healey and Killick, 2000). It would be possible to make the increased aid explicitly conditional, as in the proposal of Marris that the cost of eliminating unsafe water be shared equally between the richest 20% of the populations of the First and Third Worlds (1999, p 64). However, there are limits to such conditionality, and aid may simply displace other transfers from the better off in poor countries[4]. There may remain some truth in the old gibe that "aid is a transfer from poor people in rich countries to rich people in poor countries". However, the fact that there is some leakage from a transfer programme does not mean that it should be abandoned. The typical social insurance or universal benefit scheme in an OECD country involves some spillover of benefits to the upper income groups. The correct response is surely to try and improve the design of the transfer programme, not to reject it out of hand. Moreover, in the present context, the coupling of the EU aid target with the recently adopted indicators of social inclusion means that we have some guarantee that the cost of additional foreign aid is not going to fall on those below the EU poverty line. European Union monitoring will make clear when achievement of the overseas assistance target has been at the expense of increased domestic poverty.

The role of the EU

That there should be a role for the EU in development assistance follows directly from the recognition that it is EU-wide actions, such as the Single European Market, that impact upon the rest of the world. This was taken into account from the outset, with measures to protect the ex-colonial territories that lost favoured access to markets. The legal basis has now been embodied in the Treaty on European Union.

The more specific issue remains however as to the appropriateness of the EU setting an overall target for development assistance The standard argument is that such collective action will avoid a situation where individual states free ride, leading to under-provision. If there are positive spillovers to other donors, then joint coordination, which the EU can achieve, can secure a superior outcome[5]. Little and Clifford (1965, p 252) note that one reason for establishing the OECD Development Assistance Committee was to put pressure to increase the contributions of some European countries. The same may be true today. Just as with domestic social indicators, the attainment of targets depends on political will, and peer pressure from other countries can play a powerful role. Ministers of Development can use the EU target in their budget negotiations with their ministries of finance.

Externally, the adoption of the EU-wide aid target means that the EU as a whole would be able to exercise more influence on the world's aid giving. Even today the combined population of the EU is bigger than all countries in the world, apart from China and India. It has a larger GNP than all countries other than the US. As already noted, achievement of the 1% target by the EU would more than double the current aid total for OECD donors as a whole. The EU would, if there were no change in the levels of aid from other countries, account for three quarters of the total. It seems unimaginable that the US will allow itself to be permanently sidelined in this way, and the EU would be well-placed to bring pressure to bear.

Moreover, while the EU has made limited progress in its attempt to negotiate agreements with developing countries, as the enlargement process reaches the geographic limits of Europe, attention will naturally turn more closely to intermediate forms of association, such as the partnership agreements with Mediterranean countries inaugurated at Barcelona in 1995 (Aoudia and Tubiana, 2000). These already involve negotiations at an EU level, and this will be even more significant if developing countries themselves operate more extensively through regional groupings.

Inputs and outputs

In the construction of EU indicators for social inclusion, considerable emphasis was placed on outcomes rather than the means by which they were achieved (EC, 2001, p 4). Concern is with the level of poverty reduction achieved, not with the increase in benefit expenditure. The reasons why, for the purpose of the EU Social Agenda, targets should be defined in terms of outputs not inputs are set out in the background report by Atkinson et al (2002). The rationale for emphasising outputs lies in the principle of subsidiarity. Since member states are free to determine the form of the social policy, it is on the objects of policy that there is common agreement, not on the policies to be pursued.

In the case of development assistance, I am advocating the reverse approach. The aid target is defined in terms of net spending: that is, the inputs. The reasoning is the inverse of that for domestic social policy. The common objective is that the EU should make a significant contribution to helping low-income countries. Views are likely to differ among member states about the output from that contribution. Some countries see their development aid as 'purchasing' improved life expectancy or higher school enrolment rates. Others see development aid as a means of ensuring sustained development, an investment in future economic growth. Still others see aid as a form of global income redistribution. It is therefore quite possible that there would be disagreement among member states as to indicators of outcome, but agreement about the scale of resources that can be allocated to development assistance, and this is the basis for the present proposal.

This does not mean that I believe that outcomes are unimportant. Processes for monitoring the effectiveness of aid, at member state and at EU level, are clearly highly important. The adoption of specific outputs, such as safe water, may well help build the political coalition necessary for the target to be adopted, but the bottom line is our willingness, as rich nations, to forego a (small) fraction of our national income.

Envoi

A great deal needs to be refined in the present proposal, but the conjunction of events in Europe, together with current concerns about global justice, mean that, in my view, now is the time for it to be seriously discussed. The EU should seek to dispel the mood of 'aid weariness'. Aid is not on its own sufficient to ensure world development, but a sizeable increase would have a major impact on poor countries. In this way, the EU can make concrete the ambition of becoming "a power seeking to set globalisation within a moral framework ... to anchor it in solidarity and sustainable development" (Laeken Declaration, 15 December 2001). The Laeken Declaration rightly highlights both *solidarity* and *development*. Worldwide, and not just domestically, solidarity means redistribution of current consumption as well as investment in development. Aid is directed at achieving global justice today as well as growth for the future.

Notes

[1] I am most grateful to Holly Sutherland for her help with the calculations using EUROMOD of a progressive distribution of the aid cost within the EU, and for her comments, although she is not responsible for the views expressed in the paper. Thanks are also due to Andrea Brandolini, Eric Marlier, and Peter Townsend for their most helpful suggestions. The same disclaimer applies.

[2] One issue not discussed here is the definition of development assistance; here I simply assume that it would follow the practice of the OECD Development Assistance Committee.

[3] For details of EUROMOD, see Immervoll et al (1999), where full information is provided about the data sources. The EUROMOD project has been financed by the Targeted Socio-Economic Research programme of the EC (CT97-3060) and is currently part of the MICRESA project financed by the Improving Human Potential Programme HPSE CT-2001-00099. None of the data suppliers bears any responsibility for the analysis or interpretation of the data reported here.

[4] Another possible impact is on contributions to international public goods, such as environmental protection. It is possible that the redistribution may have offsetting effects on the contributions of aid donors and recipients (see Jayaraman and Kanbur, 1999, who caution against treating international public goods as an argument for aid).

[5] Although it should be noted that some studies, such as Dudley (1979), have found a positive interaction between national aid spending, and hence a higher total level of aid when decisions are made in isolation.

References

Aoudia, J.O. and Tubiana, L. (2000) 'Euro-méditerranée: recentrer le partenariat', *Questions européennes*, Paris: Conseil d'Analyse Economique, La Documentation Française, pp 207-42.

Atkinson, A.B., Cantillon, B., Marlier, E. and Nolan, B. (2002) *Social indicators: The EU and social inclusion*, Oxford: Oxford University Press.

Boone, P. (1996) 'Politics and the effectiveness of foreign aid', *European Economic Review*, vol 40, no 2, pp 289-329.

Cassen, R. et al (1986) *Does aid work?*, Oxford: Oxford University Press.

Drèze, J. and Sen, A.K. (1989) *Hunger and public action*, Oxford: Clarendon Press.

Dudley, L. (1979) 'Foreign aid and the theory of alliances', *Review of Economics and Statistics*, vol 61, no 4, pp 564-71.

EC (European Commission) (2001) *Indicators' sub-group: Report from the chairman*, Brussels: EC, Social Protection Committee.

European Council (2002) 'Conclusions on the International Conference on Financing for Development', Press Statement, 15 March.

Eurostat (2000) *Income, poverty and social exclusion in member states of the European Union*, Luxembourg: Office for Official Publications of the European Communities.

Healey, J. and Killick, T. (2000) 'Using aid to reduce poverty', in F. Tarp (ed) *Foreign aid and development*, London: Routledge, pp 223-46.

Griffin, K.B. and Enos, J.L. (1970) 'Foreign assistance: objectives and consequences', *Economic Development and Cultural Change*, vol 18, no 3, pp 313-27.

Hansen, H. and Tarp, F. (2000) 'Aid effectiveness disputed', in F. Tarp (ed) *Foreign aid and development*, London: Routledge, pp 103-28.

Immervoll, H., O'Donoghue, C. and Sutherland, H. (1999) 'An introduction to EUROMOD', EUROMOD Working paper EM0/99, Cambridge: Microsimulation Unit, Department of Applied Economics, University of Cambridge.

Jayaraman, R. and Kanbur, R. (1999) 'International public goods and the case for foreign aid', in I. Kaul, I. Grunberg and M.A. Stern (eds) *Global public goods: International cooperation in the 21st century*, Oxford: Oxford University Press, pp 418-35.

Kanbur, R. (2000) 'Aid, conditionality and debt in Africa', in F. Tarp (ed) *Foreign aid and development*, London: Routledge, pp 409-22.

Little, I.M.D. and Clifford, J.M. (1965) *International aid*, London: Allen and Unwin.

Marris, R. (1999) *Ending poverty*, London: Thames and Hudson.

Meade, J.E. (1962) *UK, Commonwealth and Common Market*, Hobart Paper no 17, London: Institute of Economic Affairs.

Page, S. (1991) 'Europe 1992: views of developing countries', *Economic Journal*, vol 101, pp 1553-66.

Singer, H.W. (1969) 'That 1 per cent aid target (some reflections on the arithmetic of international targetry)', *IDS Bulletin*, vol 2, no 2, reprinted in H.W. Singer (ed) (1988) *Growth, Development and Trade*, Cheltenham: Edward Elgar, pp 262-7.

Townsend, P.B. (1993) *The international analysis of poverty*, New York, NY: Harvester Wheatsheaf.

United Nations (2001) *Road map towards the implementation of the United Nations Millennium Declaration*, Report of the Secretary-General, New York, NY: United Nations.

SEVENTEEN

Conclusion: constructing an anti-poverty strategy

Peter Townsend and David Gordon

The analysis in these chapters of trends in world living standards has led to a disturbing conclusion: mass poverty is set to persist and, worse still, to increase. This conclusion can be based narrowly on the harsh conventional standard of the numbers of people found to be below the World Bank's 1985 inflation-proofed poverty line, as reported by the Bank's own research staff (see Chapter Fourteen [Table 1] and Chapter Fifteen of this volume; and Milanovic, 2000). Or, more correctly, it can be based on the realistic or dynamic standard of the numbers found to be below a poverty line adjusted according to the institutional conditions and structural demands on individual members of society, and their needs, of today, not yesterday. However, while estimates of an indirect or partial kind can be constructed on this basis, the standard remains to be put firmly in place by the social scientific community[1].

As in any other era, people's needs are governed by the societies and the institutions in which they live and work, and the kind of conditions they experience themselves – not what prevailed in the societies of a previous generation. Today's necessities may be yesterday's luxuries. Or today's shortages may be yesterday's universals. Inequalities in living standards continue to grow – between groups of countries and within most countries.

Therefore an alternative standard of measuring poverty must be developed[2]. The normative practices, customs and market relationships of ongoing societies change constantly. There are new organisations, goods and services. Modern forms of technology, including transport and communications, alter the priorities of work and life. Wage and pensions systems falter and are replaced. There are corresponding changes taking place in forms of material, social and income deprivation, corresponding with the *annually developing* distributional norms and policies of the international community and of national governments.

And yet the level of world resources is huge and still growing. In 1985, average world GDP *per person* per day was $13.6, and, at 1985 prices, approximately $16 in 2002[3]. These figures take account of population growth. They show that considerable scope exists for policies of redistribution to raise everyone above the World Bank's $1 per person per day poverty standard. The difference between 'developed' and 'developing' countries makes an even stronger case. Through the 1980s and 1990s GDP at 1995 prices *per person* per day grew from $3.0 to $3.8 in 'developing' countries but from $55.7 to $81.1 in 'developed' countries (UN, 2000, p 245). Of course, some developing countries had smaller, and some, negative, growth compared with the average for those countries.

These data show inequality *between* countries. When growing inequality *within* the majority of countries is brought into the analysis the situation of the poor is more serious. Nonetheless, the institutional capabilities of rich governments, corporations and agencies – despite individual setbacks – are burgeoning. There is good reason to believe, then, that the problem of mass poverty can be cracked.

And what of the solution? Certainly, better definition and measurement are part of it. There has been little significant progress according to the historical – and arbitrarily drawn – baseline of $1 per day per person. Like any conclusion that applies to a fifth or a quarter of the world's population – substantially more than a billion of the 6 billion – there are situations far worse or far better for some groups among them than this unsophisticated generalisation implies. However, given the expectations of the Bretton Woods institutions in the 1960s, and the repeated testimony from governments and international agencies about the need to eliminate poverty, this is an uncomfortable and challenging conclusion. Our first recommendation (also to be found in the full list in the 'manifesto' in Appendix A) is therefore that:

• An international poverty line defining a threshold of income (including the value of income in kind), ordinarily required in different countries to surmount material and social deprivation, should be agreed. As a first step the 1995 Copenhagen Agreement (UN, 1995) to introduce (and monitor) measures of 'absolute' and 'overall' poverty in every country must be fulfilled. This would allow the gap that currently exists between rich and poor countries in their methodologies of addressing poverty to be bridged.

While the categories of material and social deprivation are universal, the *precise form* and *content* depend on local and national systems of employment, industry, services, communications and relationships. Some variation in the wording and scope of standard questions are necessary to pin down the extent and severity of multiple deprivation, as shown in pilot research in poor as well as rich countries[4]. Illustrations of survey questions that can be developed in the two groups of countries are set out in Appendix B of this volume. Like 'malnutrition' and 'homelessness', *poverty* has to be operationally specified if it is to be monitored, explained and remedied. There can be objective alternative specifications of meaning which make good sense (and good science) but, like alternative specifications of 'family', one or more operational meanings have to be agreed for the purpose of making scientific and policy-related progress.

This opens up the need for a second crucial strategy. We require a detailed, sophisticated and convincing explanation for, say, the last 10 years, of the persistence (and growth) of mass poverty. This will be carried out through investigation of the negative as well as positive role played by different international and national policies. This is a necessary baseline for knowledge and action. It is only upon such a baseline that an effective anti-poverty strategy can be developed. It will allow governments and agencies to assess prospects for the next 10 years, and to determine what kind of support, if any, might be given to existing policies and the development of new policies. Our second recommendation, therefore, is that:

• Anti-poverty policies must be monitored and evaluated regularly. Further steps have to be taken to fulfil the 1995 Copenhagen Agreement on poverty at the World Summit for Social Development and to regularise the publication of annual anti-poverty reports by governments, in addition to the corresponding reports by the UN and other principal financial agencies. Inevitably this also means routine evaluation of the quantitative contribution of different national and cross-national policies to reduce poverty.

Mass poverty

The nature of mass poverty was diagnosed a quarter of a century ago by John Kenneth Galbraith. As ambassador to India in the 1960s, Galbraith, an internationally renowned economist, wanted to better understand the persistence and causes of poverty in that sub-continent. He distinguished between the poverty that afflicted the few, or at least the minority, in many (usually industrialised) countries; and the poverty that afflicted all but the few in other countries. While he described fascinating variations in both groups of countries, which invited speculation and explanation, Galbraith said:

> My concern is with the causes of poverty in those communities, rural in practice, where almost everyone is poor – where, if there is wealth or affluence, it is the exceptional fortune of the few. (Galbraith, 1979, p 2)

Causes were not much investigated, he found. Relative success and failure could be traced in communist as well as capitalist countries, although the former could be said to have an impressive record by historical standards. Hard work, skill, climate, population growth, natural resources – such as minerals, culture, ethnic identity – all had only a limited explanatory power. Building on a much earlier book (Galbraith, 1956) he pounced on inequalities in market structure between fragmented and weak agricultural procedures and "the oligopolistic strength inherent in the positions of General Motors, Shell, DuPont, Nestlé, and the other characteristically powerful oligopolists of the industrial countries. This disparity in power explains and perpetuates the poverty of the poor countries – of the Third World" (Galbraith, 1979, p 19).

As a result of its contemporary impact, Galbraith's analysis of 25 years ago leaps into the present day. He identified corporate power as a major cause of mass poverty. Of course mass poverty has to be characterised differently from what it was in 1975. Poverty declined substantially in some OECD countries, partly because of the rise of middle-class jobs and jobs generally, and also redistributive social insurance programmes put in place in the 1950s and 1960s. 'Mass' poverty, however, has remained or become larger in other countries – for example, in Sub-Saharan Africa and parts of Latin America – especially in countries which were formerly colonies that have been exposed to civil war and, in some such instances, genocide. Mass poverty has arrived in many countries of the former Soviet Union, as testified in a stream of new reports (UNDP, 1998; Atal, 1999; Braithwaite et al, 2000; UNICEF, 2001). As one research team put it, "incomes tumbled, poverty 'exploded' and the safety net organised around enterprise-provided protection 'evaporated'" (Braithwaite et al, 2000, p 164). Underlying this account of principal changes since 1975 are the deepening social divisions or stratification representing the growing inequality reported in several chapters of this book. Inevitably this threatens the return of mass poverty to countries where everyone believed it had been eliminated.

This disjunction is the principal theme that emerges from this book. Allegiances between the big national powers; the structural terms, if not barriers, of world trade; the hierarchical power exerted by the largest transnational corporations (TNCs); the obdurate economic strategy pursued by the international financial agencies; and the restraints imposed on the UN – each of these have to be investigated far more deeply today if the failures of anti-poverty policies are to be properly explained.

The problems of the Washington Consensus

Persisting or growing poverty and its insufficiently traced causes has been a primary preoccupation of the authors of this book. Dissatisfaction with current policies has prompted exploration of alternative policies. Plainly these take a variety of forms, and a comprehensive strategy needs to be laid out. Accordingly, we have presented a manifesto of international action that must be taken to defeat poverty in Appendix A.

A key feature is identifying the new international hierarchy of power, so that more realistic anti-poverty policies can be devised. The problem can be expressed as that of the 'Transatlantic Consensus' (see Chapter Two of this volume) or, more widely, the Washington Consensus (see Gore, 2000). This involves "not simply a swing from state-led to market-oriented policies, but also a shift in the ways in which development problems [are] framed and in the types of explanation through which policies [are] justified" (Gore, 2000, p 789). The focus of attention is the promotion of GDP growth, implemented by means of a top-down, donor conditionality-driven and outside expert-led approach, combined with privatisation of public services, cuts in public expenditure, removal of state and labour powers to redistribute resources, and the substitution of more costly public social security and services by smaller-scale 'safety-nets'.

These World Bank and IMF anti-poverty policies are based on the over-simplistic assumption that, since industrialised countries have lower levels of poverty than developing countries, broad-based GDP growth on its own will alleviate poverty. Recent World Bank analyses by Dollar and Kraay (2000) purport to show that "*income of the poor rise one-for-one with overall growth*", that is, for every 1% increase in GDP the incomes of the poorest 20% also increase by 1%. They concluded from these analyses that public spending on education and health is of little benefit to the poor. However, their findings are a statistical artefact resulting from a flawed methodology. If their method is applied to random numbers (instead of real data) then the same relationship between the incomes of the poorest 20% and general growth is found. Dollar and Kraay's results are no different from random results and therefore no conclusions can be drawn from their analyses (as set out above by Jan Vandemoortele in Chapter Fifteen). And scientific analysis of the same data used by Dollar and Kraay by other researchers has unsurprisingly shown that there is no simple relationship between GDP growth and the incomes of poor people (Foster and Székely, 2001). Indeed, 'trickle-down' due to growth has become difficult to demonstrate (Newman and Thomson, 1989).

This shift from state-led to market-oriented policies can be explained historically by the end of the Cold War, the ascendancy of the US, the control exercised by the G8, as well as the institutional links between the US government, the UN, the international financial agencies, and many of the biggest TNCs (see Chapter Fourteen above). It can also be explained by the neoliberal tradition of economic theory, represented in earlier years by Hayek and Friedman. This connected hierarchy of power has not attracted sustained examination from those concerned with world development. Therefore, alternative perspectives to that of the Washington Consensus – such as a 'latent Southern Consensus', loosely related to 'East Asian developmentalism and Latin American neostructuralism' – have been described, but have not been given much prospect of making dramatic headway (Gore, 2000). However, the structural changes of the kind illustrated in this book – for example, the rise of TNCs, but also of the UN and other international agencies and regional governance and alliances – which all contribute to the global problem – have not yet been given comprehensive attention. That is why the problem has become so difficult, some would say intractable. The close links between the complex of institutions are only now beginning to be questioned. Will Hutton has graphically described US corporate power (Hutton, 2002) and Kevin Watkins its unashamed control of world trade (Watkins, 2002). Campaigning groups point out the growing resistance of poor countries to World Bank and IMF policies (World Development Movement, 2002). And independent expert organisations are deeply concerned about better integration of the institutions primarily involved in globalisation (Grunberg and Khan, 2000). A telling example is provided by Joseph Stiglitz, who has argued that the conflicts of interest driving US financial scandals are being replicated on a global scale. He writes of the 'intertwining' of public and private incentives:

There are private incentives to distort public policy in ways which in turn distort private incentives, and sometimes to prevent public policy from correcting market failures. (Stiglitz, 2002a; see also Stiglitz, 2002b)

He comments at length on the international financial agencies.

The IMF is a public international institution, but critics claim it is not democratically accountable – and that as the central bank governors to whom it reports increasingly become more independent, it is becoming even less so. (Stiglitz, 2002a; and see Kolko, 1999).

The problem is also illustrated in calls for a global 'new deal', whereby a modern Marshall Plan for the developing world might be drawn up – a proposal put forward by the UK government (HM Treasury, 2002, and see Cm 3789, 1997). Without changes in the hierarchy of power, such calls fall on deaf ears, however impassioned they may be.

Steps to moderate the international hierarchy of power

Action to democratise government is as important as action to introduce new policies. Among the measures that have to be distinguished (see also the full list in Appendix A) are the following:

- The structure of the international financial agencies has to be recast with more representative membership and greater protection of the independence of the agencies from the whims of the most powerful states and corporations. Membership should be automatically open to all countries, funded by an agreed percentage of national GDP (say, 0.3%), with equal regional representation on governing councils and committees, and a five-year circulation of chairmanship. Terms of reference are to be subject every five years to majority vote at the UN.
- The UN itself must also be further democratised. Representation of populous countries, and especially of the poorest 100 countries, must be increased on UN committees, especially the powerful economic and social committees. The objective would be to progress by stages to equal representation of regions by population size.
- Regional policy alliances are becoming more important with globalisation, and since developments are uneven, some must be further strengthened and all require better coordination through multi-regional initiatives and global accountability. Collaborative working relationships between regional or global non-government organisations (NGOs) and governments must be introduced or strengthened, as part of improved democratisation. The UN can play a leading role, and the provision of a legal framework is one option.

Perhaps the hardest step to visualise is more public-spirited action by the TNCs. The OECD and the ILO have published codes of social responsibility that corporations are encouraged to adhere to (ILO, 1998; OECD, 2001). However, events between 2000 and 2002, including the crash of Enron and WorldCom, teach us the necessity of collective action by governments and of the need for new international company law.

- The priority must be the introduction of new international company law requiring TNCs to curb anti-social activities and curb excessively high profits from poor countries.
- Each TNC will be required to draw up a policy 'prospectus'; that is, a policy statement both for employees (including employees in subsidiary companies), and for countries in which the corporation has operations of significant scale. The latter policy statement should be subject to approval by a consultative body representing the corporation, the national electorate in the 'headquarter' country and the governments of the countries from which overseas profits are derived (one third representation each).

World trade and employment

Trade is a source of unprecedented wealth. Yet, as an Oxfam report puts it, "millions of the world's poorest people are being left behind. Increased prosperity has gone hand in hand with mass poverty and the widening of already obscene inequalities between rich and poor" (Watkins, 2002, p 3). The terms of trade between rich and poor countries cannot be justified on scientific, including economic, grounds. Developing countries who export to markets in the richest countries face tariff barriers that are four times greater than the tariff barriers in the reverse direction. This costs them $100 billion per year – twice as much as they receive in aid. Part of the problem is the World Trade Organisation (WTO). "Many of its rules on intellectual property, investment, and services protect the interests of rich countries and powerful TNC's, while imposing huge costs on developing countries. The WTO's bias in favour of the self-interest of the rich countries and big corporations raises fundamental questions about its legitimacy" (Watkins, 2002, p 4)[5]. As Amartya Sen writes in the foreword to this report, "Institutional change and policy reform can radically alter the prevailing levels of inequality and poverty, without wrecking the global economy" (Watkins, 2002, p 17). Among the range of measures that need to be taken, international agreement to set the appropriate framework for even-handed trade is clearly the priority. This means:

- Agreeing a new operational specification of fair trade. Representatives of each world region should agree the terms of a framework plan, to be endorsed by a majority of the UN and agreed in stages over 10 years. This will necessarily involve removal of protective agricultural subsidies in rich countries to allow fair trade and the subsequent removal of tariffs and other barriers to trade on the part of poor countries. Agreements should also be reached about kinds and levels of desirable domestic food production, combined with a fair price standard for food commodities produced in developing and developed countries. This would be administered by a democratised WTO.

Effective backing to fairer trade would also have to be given in new agreements to promote higher levels of employment and stability in employment. This contradicts current policy. Zygmunt Bauman, arguing that the poor are no longer the 'reserve army' of labour, graphically describes the new situation:

> Today, there is no labour-greedy industry waiting for more people to be employed. Technological progress means fewer working places; good accounting means less money spent in hiring labour; better productivity means slimming and 'downsizing'; good management means selling or phasing out the branches which do not bring enough profit. Nowadays wealth grows through investment in high technology, scientific research and information, and higher employment may only impair its chances. Stock exchanges ... lavishly reward companies shedding labour. (Bauman, 1999, p 21)

While downsizing and job loss have been significant factors in many countries, more complex patterns of labour market change have also occurred. The UK and many European countries have witnessed a net increase in part-time jobs (particularly for women) and a net decrease in full-time male manual jobs. Sassen (1998a, 1998b) has noted that a two-tiered economy is emerging in many 'global' cities, as well as within and between entire countries. The financial industry has flourished, resulting in an increase in the number of high-wage jobs and also in an increase in low-waged service jobs (cleaners, servants, and so on) which are often filled by low-wage, immigrant labour. In these circumstances it is 'traditional' middle-class jobs that are often being lost (such as bank tellers)

Human rights *in work*, and not only for work, must be supported. We recommend the following:

• Extend measures for full employment and set up an International Full Employment Agency (Article 23 Universal Declaration of Human Rights). Where unemployment and under-employment is most severe and extensive, the UN must devise, in agreement with governments, plans to curb the scale of job losses and promote alternative employment. This will be funded, along with child benefit, by the new international financial transactions tax discussed below. Action against specific violations of human rights, like the eradication of child labour and of the abuse of street children, would be a key part of the new agency's role.

Redistribution and human rights

A multiple strategy is required to make major inroads in world poverty. The case for institutional – as well as definitional and procedural – change has been summarised. What remains is perhaps that part of the problem which will be the most difficult to agree – to bring about extensive redistribution of resources between and within countries to eradicate poverty and establish decent human rights, and to get this accepted at all levels. Fortunately this objective is now more plausible to world opinion than it was even five years ago. There are three new factors. The recent failure of many privatisation schemes and corporations, and large parts of the financial services industry, have provoked calls for radical new policies. Reported instances of corporate corruption and greed have grown in number and significance. These have captured attention from unexpected sources. For example, Joseph Stiglitz, the former chief economist at the World Bank, has written revealingly about corporate greed (Stiglitz, 2002a; 2000b, see also Hutton, 2002). Again, in the wake of the $4 billion WorldCom scandal in June 2002, Digby Jones, Director-General of the Confederation of British Industry, said:

> It is high time the US understood there's a difference between power and leadership. Look at US attitudes to world trade, the protectionism in steel and airlines, and now the lack of corporate governance and accountancy standards. (*Observer*, Business and Media Supplement, 30 June, pp 1, 4-5)

A second factor in preparing world opinion for a new strategy in attacking poverty is that public and collective values are being expressed more forcefully in reaction to the stream of weak, negative or otherwise gloomy reports from successive world summits – including those of Monterrey and New York (for children; UN, 2002). The number and frequency of muted international agreements are now treated more sceptically in relation to the exaggerated and often euphoric language used in the reports that are issued immediately after such meetings. Public expectations raised by successive summits have become almost negative in character. By contrast, trust in the charters and conventions expressing human rights has continued to grow.

This book has sought to call attention to the close links between 'universalism' or what is represented historically and contemporaneously by the provision of comprehensive public social services or social insurance, and human rights (see Chapter Fourteen of this volume). As a principle and as a strategy for economic and social development this is very different from the 'selectivism' preferred by the IMF and the World Bank in their structural adjustment and subsequent policies (see especially Part III of this volume)[6]. There are as many obstacles in trying to accommodate human rights to targeted or means-tested services in the developing countries as in the developed countries (see, for example, Part II of this volume).

This is concerned with gradual recognition of the failure of 'targeting' by means testing and selectivity. In relation to the anti-poverty policies in both the rich and poor countries intended to restrict public expenditure by targeting resources, success has turned out to be elusive. The strategies of the last two decades have become unconvincing to the public and to economists and other social scientists alike. Targeting by means of universal benefits and services (for example, pensions, child benefit, student grants) is a very effective mechanism of eradicating poverty. By contrast, 'targeting' by means testing is an expensive, inefficient and ineffective method of combating poverty. Richard Titmuss argued in the 1950's that welfare services should not be perceived as a stigmatizing 'benefit' the use of which involves a loss of status, dignity and/or self-respect. They should be universal, available and accessible to the whole populations through channels that would not involve a shame, stigma or a sense of inferiority, preferably as social or welfare *rights* of all citizens (Titmuss, 2001). In this book different authors have provided evidence about slow progress in reducing mass poverty (especially Chapters One, Fourteen and Fifteen); counter-productive political and economic control (this chapter, and Chapter Two); the long-term value to economic growth as well as social stability of strong public social services or the welfare state (Chapters Two, Five, Eight and Fifteen)[7]. Governments can, in the words of Tony Atkinson, play a major role "in offsetting the rise in inequality of market incomes" by influencing the wages dispersion itself, and by following redistributive policies. Progressive income taxation and social transfers can substantially reduce the income inequalities that may arise in the market place (see Chapter Two of this volume).

There are policies that redistribute resources between and within countries. We recommend the following (see also Appendix A).

- All developed countries should adopt a legally binding minimum level of 1% GNP overseas development assistance. The EU must take the lead, implemented immediately by some member countries and in stages by the poorer member countries. (The case is a powerful one and is set out by Tony Atkinson in Chapter Sixteen of this volume.) Agreement at an early stage by all OECD countries, and not only the EU member countries, can then be achieved.

What is necessary for investment in public social services and the expansion of social security is a strong revenue base:

- A priority for each country must be to rebuild and/or strengthen tax administration. Taxation systems must be introduced and strengthened where necessary, and be answerable to representatives of national electorates, with independent powers to monitor policies and outcomes. Monitoring by an independent international inspectorate will also be necessary.

Given that many of the poorest countries pay more annually in debt repayments than they can afford to invest in basic social services, substantial internal revenue must be found from external, international sources:

- An international financial transactions tax to be administered by the UN must be introduced. In the first instance a tax at a rate of 0.2% would be payable on all currency exchanges at banks and currency exchange offices. Half the gross revenue would be administered by the UN to subsidise the establishment of child benefit in developing countries. This makes the proposal somewhat different from that of James Tobin (see Chapter Fourteen of this volume; also discussion in Ul Haq et al, 1996; Raffer, 1998).

The key role in an anti-poverty strategy for social security, linked to human rights

How might social security systems evolve to add to this argument for more substantial redistribution? Human rights now play a central part in discussions of social policy. This applies to civil and political rights, less so to social and economic rights. Articles 22 and 25 in the Declaration of Human Rights, which deal with the rights to an 'adequate' standard of living and social security (see p 399 above) have been overlooked in the general assembly and other reports from the UN. The fundamental right to social security is also spelt out in Article 26 of the Convention on the Rights of the Child and to the related rights to an adequate standard of living in Article 27.

These rights have not been invoked during the last two decades when high rates of poverty have continued to persist. For example, they were not believed to be a necessary element in the discussions about structural adjustment policies and then the Social Fund, especially in the particularly fraught regions of Sub-Saharan Africa, Latin America, South Asia and Eastern Europe (see Chapter Nine of this volume). The discussion in the 1980s and 1990s consequently focussed on targeting and short-term means-tested benefits rather than on long-term minimal living standards for all. In reports in the late 1990s and early 2000s the international agencies have begun to recognise the strengths of comprehensive or universal public services and benefits. However, that has not yet led to the wholesale reformulation of development policies to reduce poverty.

One analyst points out that social security in industrialised countries "reached its apogee in the 1970s" (Ghai, 2001). He believes a broad consensus was reached among countries about comprehensive welfare and social security policies. This had developed after the Second World War due to the inclusion of social security as a fundamental human right in the 1948 Declaration on Human Rights and later in the 1967 Covenant on Economic, Cultural and Social Rights. A major factor was the US Social Security Act, passed in 1935 (Committee on Economic Security, 1937).

In the 1980s globalisation and economic doctrines in favour of cutbacks in taxation and public expenditure and support for the privatisation of public services brought changes to the welfare state to a different degree in many countries. Some programmes were unscrambled. In others the level and range of benefits were diluted – partly because of alleged welfare abuses and the harmful effects on savings and investment of high rates of taxation.

Wholesale abandonment of programmes became a feature of the breaking up of the Soviet Union in 1989. Some of the republics are only now discovering the virtues of previous social security programmes and are putting into place new, although smaller, public programmes.

The social security systems of developing countries present a more diverse picture. The relevant colonial authorities had introduced the bones of a system in most of Asia, Africa and the Caribbean. They were extended in the first instance to civil servants and employees of large enterprises. There were benefits for relatively small groups that included health care, maternity leave, disability allowances and pensions (Midgley, 1984; Ahmad et al, 1991). In India there are differences among major states as well as a range of schemes for smallish categories of population (Ghai, 2001, p 6; Prabhu, 2001). In Latin America some countries introduced schemes before the outbreak of war in 1939, and others followed suit after the war. Benefits tended to be limited in range and coverage. There were different systems for particular occupations and categories of workers, and a multiplicity of institutions. Between 20% and 60% of the workforce were covered, compared with 5-10% for most of Sub-Saharan Africa and 10-30% for most of Asia.

> The greatest challenge facing the developing countries is to extend the benefits of social security to the excluded majority to enable them to cope with indigence and social contingencies. (Huber in Esping-Andersen, 1996, pp 180-1)

In Chapter Thirteen of this volume, Jo Beall discusses the acute problems in South Africa of providing pensions for older people.

Developments in social security in Latin America have been extensively reviewed in the 1990s and early 2000s. One authority points out that, as a proportion of GDP, social security is of variable significance across the region but remains substantial in most countries. Huber concludes that in addressing:

> ... the problem of poverty in old age and sickness for the entire population, non-contributory schemes, or schemes with minimal contribution requirements, for those in the informal sector are needed. A system of basic flat rate pensions, financed out of general revenue and with entitlement based on citizenship, would meet these needs. This system should be complemented by a public system of contributory, non-subsidised, capitalised pensions. (Huber in Esping-Andersen, 1996, pp 180-1)

The privatisation of social security has benefited international corporations that become partners with local business elites. Thus the WHO, international financial institutions and TNCs have converged in the neo-liberal reforms of social security in Latin America. (Armada et al, 2001, p 729 and see Laurell, 1999)

Social security systems can be extended in developing countries, to fulfil the fundamental right to social security laid down by the UN after the Second World War and serve the objective of eradicating poverty. Bodies such as the ILO and ISSA have provided much of the detailed evidence (see Dagdeviren et al, 2001; Reynaud, 2001). The component parts of strategy can be listed as follows:

• Operational plans must be prepared internationally and by nation states, in conjunction with the agreement at the 1995 Copenhagen World Summit for Social Development, to fulfil the fundamental right to *social security* (Article 22 of the Universal Declaration of Human Rights). Schemes to implement this fundamental right by introducing or extending social security and especially public provision of social insurance and/or basic income for all citizens by stages must be introduced. This step will make the current flow of anti-poverty reports more realistic and their recommendations more practical.

• A related step must be to make possible the legal enforcement of the right to an *adequate standard of living* (Article 25). This can be implemented by adoption of state-defined minimum earnings in conjunction with state-defined minimum cash benefits for those not in paid work, including the equivalent value of benefits (goods and services) in kind. What countries decide must conform with an internationally acceptable framework promulgated by the UN and scrutinised regularly by UN monitors.

What are the priorities to be followed in this development? The needs of children in severe deprivation, especially in refugee camps, urban ghettos, and conditions provoked by civil unrest, war and famine as well as severe unemployment have attracted continuing concern. As the single most important step to reduce child poverty we recommend that:

• A legal right to *child benefit* (Articles 25 and 27 of the Convention on the Rights of the Child) must be introduced or strengthened. Each country must specify in its annual anti-poverty report what practicable measures are being introduced, giving corresponding information about progress in reducing child poverty. Provision will be made for every child of a universally adequate monthly cash benefit or the equivalent in value included of goods and services to surmount material and social deprivation. This can be financed internationally and nationally by such measures as the proposal made in this volume for the introduction of an international financial transactions tax.

People with incomes that fall below an internationally agreed poverty line depend not only on any direct entitlement to benefit or compensation that they receive, but also indirectly on free – or subsidised – basic health, education, housing, water, sanitation and other public services. Therefore, we recommend that:

- The universal right of access locally to publicly provided basic health care and education services (with reference to Articles 21, 25 and 26 of the Universal Declaration of Human Rights, but also such agreed objectives as stated in the Copenhagen World Summit for Social Development, 1995), must be strengthened and spelt out in annual anti-poverty plans. The purpose here is to clarify and give tangible support for the provision in all countries of a network of geographically accessible institutions and services and check annually about introduction and coverage. Again, the plans need to be jointly underwritten by national governments and the UN. Easy access to safe drinking water and sanitation must be included in the provision within a defined number of years in accordance with Article 21 concerning 'equal access to public service'.

Inadequate housing is a deprivation multiplier, and often shortens life. It is found in every country. In developing anti-poverty policy it is clearly a key issue. The balance between public and private housing projects is difficult to get right for any government, but is clearly related to the extent, and severity of the effects of poverty. As an asset, housing is of tangible household value in relation to income. No successful, long-term anti-poverty strategy can be complete without substantial, or at least some, new public investment in housing. It is recommended that:

- Annually revised anti-poverty schemes must therefore provide temporary and permanent public housing units for homeless people and people living in seriously substandard accommodation. The aim must be to prioritise the housing needs of the poorest 10% of the population by means of national and local ownership and administration of minimally adequate standard accommodation. The needs of immigrant, refugee, asylum-seeking and resident families must be balanced fairly in such programmes.

Finally, there has to be a declared over-arching resolution from the UN to recast incomes more equitably. Such a resolution may threaten many interests and will have to be justified stage by stage. However, it is an inescapable, if nonetheless daunting, condition for the success of anti-poverty policies put forward by international agencies, governments and NGOs alike. Individual proposals have to be pulled into place. Specific measures are unlikely to succeed unless they are conceived and implemented within a measured, and carefully expressed, international framework. The expression of this resolution has to be reasonably exact. How can this be achieved?

• The UN and other international agencies and national governments must agree an action plan for staged greater equalisation of resources within and between countries (with particular reference to Commitment 2 of the 1995 World Summit for Social Development). Just as the 1945 target of 0.7% GDP for overseas development assistance on the part of the developed countries will be replaced by a 1.0% target (see Chapter Sixteen of this volume), every government will adopt an upper limit of income inequality, say a standard of 0.4 on the Gini coefficient.

The programme of work discussed in this chapter is presented in Appendix A as a manifesto to defeat poverty. Not all the parts of this anti-poverty strategy have been – or could be – fully explained within these pages. Nor does every author agree with every recommendation. But in the range and depth of the analysis of this book a case has been made, and we believe with authority, for thoroughgoing and immediate change in the international policies directed at reducing world poverty.

Notes

[1] This has been a prime motivation of much recent European research. See, in particular, Chapter Three of this volume; also Nolan and Whelan (1996); Hallerod (1998); Gordon et al (2000, especially appendices 1 and 2); Gordon and Townsend (2000, Chapters Four, Five and Ten).

[2] See note 1.

[3] Calculated and updated from UN (2000) World Economic and Social Survey, 2000, p 245).

[4] Gore and Figueiredo (1996, p 18); Hashem (1996); Kaijage and Tibaijuka (1996); Tchernina (1996).

[5] Watkins (2002, p 4): "It is the advanced industrialised countries and the larger industrial developing countries that make use of the WTO's services". See also George and Wilding (2002, p 85).

[6] Among the vast number of supporting reports are Loewenson (1993, Africa); Banerjee (1994, India); Laurell and Wences (1994, Mexico). See also Brand (1994) and Chossudovsky (1997).

[7] The most telling comparative research investigations include those that conclude that economic growth, paradoxically, is correlated better with high than with low investment in public social services, and that when social distribution is ignored economic growth trickles up, not down (see, for example, Newman and Thomson, 1989; Goodin, et al, 1999).

References

Ahmad, E. Dreze, J., Hills, J. and Sen, A. (1991) *Social security in developing countries*, Oxford: Clarendon Press.

Armada, F., Muntaner, C. and Navarro, V. (2001) 'Health and social security reforms in Latin America: the convergence of the World Health Organisation, the World Bank and the transnational corporations', *International Journal of Health Services*, vol 31, no 4, pp 729-68.

Atal, Y. (ed) (1999) *Poverty in transition and transition in poverty: Recent developments in Hungary, Bulgaria, Romania, Georgia, Russia, Mongolia*, Paris and New York, NY: UNESCO and Berghahn Books.

Banerjee, D. (1994) 'A simplistic approach to health policy analysis: the World Bank Team on the Indian health sector', *International Journal of Health Services*, vol 24, no 1, pp 151-9.

Bauman, Z. (1999) 'The burning of popular fear', *New Internationalist*, March, pp 20-3.

Braithwaite, J., Grootaert, C. and Milanovic, B. (2000) *Poverty and social assistance in transition countries*, Basingstoke: Macmillan.

Bramall, C. (2001) 'The quality of China's Household Income Surveys', *The China Quarterly*, vol 167, September, pp 689-705.

Brand, H. (1994) 'The World Bank, the Monetary Fund, and poverty', *International Journal of Health Services*, vol 24, no 3, pp 567-78.

Chossudovsky, M. (1997) *The globalisation of poverty: Impacts of IMF and World Bank reforms*, London: Zed Books.

Committee on Economic Security (1937) *Social security in America: The factual background of the Social Security Act as summarised from staff reports to the Committee on Social Security*, Washington, DC: Government Printing Office.

Cm 3789 (1997) *Eliminating world poverty: A challenge for the 21st century*, White Paper on International Development, London: The Stationery Office.

Dagdeviren, H., van der Hoeven, R. and Weeks, J. (2001) *Redistribution matters: Growth for poverty reduction*, Employment Paper 2001/10, Geneva: International Labour Office.

Dollar, D. and Kraay, A. (2000) *Growth is good for the poor*, World Bank Policy Research Working Paper, Washington, DC: World Bank (http:// www.worldbank.org/research/growth/pdfiles/growthgoodforpoor.pdf)

Esping-Andersen, G. (1996) *Welfare states in transition*, Geneva and London: UNRISD and Sage Publications.

Foster, J. and Székely, M. (2001) 'Is economic growth good for the poor?' Paper presented at the *WIDER Development Conference on Growth and Poverty*, 25-26 May, Helsinki, Finland (http://www.wider.unu.edu/conference/conference-2001-1/foster%20and%20szekely.pdf)

Galbraith, J.K. (1956) *American capitalism: The concept of countervailing power*, Boston, MA: Houghton Mifflin.

Galbraith, J.K. (1979) *The nature of mass poverty*, Cambridge, MA: Harvard University Press.

George, V. and Wilding, P. (2002) *Globalisation and human welfare*, Basingstoke: Palgrave.

Ghai, D. (2001) 'Social security for all', *Technical commissions*, Leo Wildmann Symposium, Stockholm, September, Geneva: International Social Security Association.

Goodin, R.E., Headey, B., Muffels, R. and Dirvan, H.-J. (1999) *The real worlds of welfare capitalism*, Cambridge: Cambridge University Press.

Gordon, D., Adelman, A., Ashworth, K., Bradshaw, J., Levitas, R., Middleton, S., Pantazis, C., Patsios, D., Payne, S., Townsend, P. and Williams, J. (2000) *Poverty and social exclusion in Britain*, York: Joseph Rowntree Foundation.

Gordon, D. and Townsend, P. (eds) (2000) *Breadline Europe: The measurement of poverty*, Bristol: The Policy Press.

Gore, C. (2000) 'The rise and fall of the Washington Consensus as a paradigm for developing countries', *World Development*, vol 28, no 5, pp 789-804.

Gore, C. and Figueiredo, J.B. (1996) *Social exclusion and anti-poverty strategies*, Geneva: IILS.

Grunberg, I. and Khan, S. (eds) (2000) *Globalisation: The United Nations development dialogue: Finance, trade, poverty, peace building*, Tokyo, New York and Paris: UN University Press.

Halleröd, B. (1998) 'Poor Swedes, poor Britons: a comparative analysis of relative deprivation', in H.J. Andreß (ed) *Empirical poverty research in a comparative perspective*, Aldershot: Ashgate.

Hashem, M.H. (1996) *Goals for social integration and realities of social exclusion in the Republic of Yemen*, Research Series no 5, Geneva: IILS.

HM Treasury (2002) *Tackling poverty: A global New Deal. A modern Marshall Plan for the developing world*, London: HM Treasury.

Huber, E. (1996) 'Options for social policy in Latin America: neoliberal versus democratic models', in G. Esping-Andersen (ed) *Welfare states in transition*, Geneva and London: UNRISD and Sage Publications.

Hutton, W. (2002) *The world we're in,* London: Little, Brown.

ILO (International Labour Organization) (1998) *The ILO tripartite declaration of principles concerning multinational enterprises and social policy – Ten years after*, Geneva: ILO.

Kaijage, F. and Tibaijuka, A. (1996) *Poverty and social exclusion in Tanzania*, Research Series no 109, Geneva: IILS.

Kolko, G. (1999) 'Ravaging the poor: the International Monetary Fund indicted by its own data', *International Journal of Health Services*, vol 29, no 1, pp 51-7.

Laurell, A.C. (1999) 'The Mexican social security counter reform: pensions for profit', *International Journal of Health Services*, vol 29, no 2, pp 371-91.

Laurell, A.C. and Wences, M.I. (1994) 'Do poverty programmes alleviate poverty? The case of the Mexican National Solidarity Programme', *International Journal of Health Services*, vol 24, no 3, pp 381-401.

Loewenson, R. (1993) 'Structural adjustment and health policy in Africa', *International Journal of Health Services*, vol 23, no 4, pp 717-30.

Midgley, J. (1984) *Social security, inequality and the Third World*, New York, NY: Wiley.

Milanovic, B. (2000) 'True world income distribution, 1988 and 1993: first calculation based on household surveys alone', *World Bank, Development Research Group*, Washington, DC: World Bank.

Newman, B. and Thomson, R.J. (1989) 'Economic growth and social development: a longitudinal analysis of causal priority', *World Development*, pp 461-71.

Nolan, B. and Whelan, C.T. (1996) *Resources, deprivation and poverty*, Oxford: Clarendon Press.

OECD (Organisation for Economic Co-operation and Development) (2001) *The OECD guidelines for multinational enterprises 2001: Focus: global instruments for corporate responsibility*, Paris: OECD.

Prabhu, K.S. (2001) *Socio-economic security in the context of pervasive poverty: A case study of India*, SES Papers, Geneva: ILO.

Raffer, K. (1998) 'The Tobin Tax: reviving a discussion', *World Development*, vol 26, no 3, pp 529-38.

Reynaud, E. (2001) 'The extension of social security coverage: the approach of the International Labour Office', *Technical commissions*, Leo Wildmann Symposium, Stockholm September, ISSA Review, Geneva: ISSA.

Sassen, S. (1998a) *The mobility of labor and capital*, Cambridge: Cambridge University Press.

Sassen, S. (1998b) *Globalization and its discontents: Selected essays 1984-1998*, New York, NY: New Press.

Stiglitz, J. (2002a) 'Corporate corruption', *The Guardian*, 4 July.

Stiglitz, J. (2002b) *Globalisation and its discontents*, London: Allen Lane.

Tchernina, N. (1996) *Economic transition and social exclusion in Russia*, Research Series no 108, Geneva: IILS.

Titmuss, R. (2001) 'Welfare state and welfare society', in P. Alcock, H. Glennerster, A. Oakley and A. Sinfield (eds) *Welfare and wellbeing: Richard Titmuss's contribution to social policy*, Bristol: The Policy Press, pp 113-23.

Ul Haq, M., Kaul, I. and Grunberg, I. (1996) *The Tobin Tax: Coping with financial volatility*, New York, NY: Oxford University Press.

UN (United Nations) (1995) *The Copenhagen Declaration and programme of action: World summit for social development*, New York, NY: UN.

UN (2000) *World Economic and Social Survey 2000*, New York, NY: UN.

UN (2002) *A world fit for children. Report of the special session of the General Assembly on Children*, New York, NY: UN.

UNDP (United Nations Development Programme) (1998) *Poverty in transition? Regional bureau for Europe and the CIS*, New York, NY: UNDP.

UNICEF (United Nations Children's Fund) Innocenti Research Centre (2001) *A decade of transition. The Monee Project: CEE/CIS/Baltics*, Regional Monitoring Report no 8, Florence: UNICEF.

Watkins, K. (2002) *Rigged rules and double standards: Trade, globalisation and the fight against poverty*, Oxford: Oxfam.

World Development Movement (2002) *States of unrest II: Resistance to IMF and World Bank policies in poor countries*, London: World Development Movement.

Manifesto: international action to defeat poverty

1. **Introduce and develop schemes to fulfil fundamental right to social security** (Article 22 of the Universal Declaration of Human Rights). To be implemented by introducing or extending social security and especially public provision of social insurance and/or basic income for all citizens.

2. **Legally enforce right to adequate standard of living** (Article 25 of the Universal Declaration of Human Rights). To be implemented by adoption of state-defined minimum earnings in conjunction with state-defined minimum cash benefits for those not in paid work, including the equivalent value of benefits (goods and services) in kind.

3. **Introduce or strengthen legal right to child benefit** (Articles 25 and 27 of the Convention on the Rights of the Child). Provision to be made for every child of a monthly cash benefit, or the equivalent in value included of goods and services, which is universally adequate, to surmount material and social deprivation.

4. **All developed countries to adopt legally binding minimum level of 1% GNP overseas development assistance.** To be introduced first by the EU, immediately in the case of some member states, and in stages by the poorer member states, and extended to all OECD countries.

5. **Establish universal right of access locally to publicly provided basic health care and education services** (with reference to Articles 21, 25 and 26 of the Universal Declaration of Human Rights, but also such objectives as agreed by governments at the Copenhagen World Summit for Social Development). The purpose here is to clarify and give tangible support for the provision in all countries of a network of geographically accessible institutions and services, and check annually about introduction and coverage. National plans to be underwritten jointly by governments and the UN. Easy access to safe drinking water and sanitation must be included in the provision within a defined number of years of "equal access to public service" (Article 21).

6. **Provide temporary and permanent public housing units for homeless people and people living in seriously substandard accommodation.** The aim must be to prioritise the housing needs of the poorest 10% of the population by means of national and local ownership and administration of minimally adequate standard accommodation. The needs of immigrant, asylum-seeking and resident families must be balanced fairly in the programme.

7. **The UN with other international agencies and national governments to agree action plan for staged greater equalisation of resources within and between countries** (with particular reference to Commitment 2 of the Copenhagen World Summit for Social Development). Just as the 1945 target of 0.7% GNP for overseas development assistance on the part of the developed countries will be replaced by a 1.0% target (see Manifesto 4), every government will adopt an upper limit of income inequality; for example, a standard of 0.4 on the Gini coefficient.

8. **Extend measures for full employment and set up an International Full Employment Agency** (Article 23 of the Universal Declaration of Human Rights). Where unemployment and under-employment is most severe and extensive, the UN – in agreement with governments – must devise plans to curb the scale of job losses and promote alternative employment. This will be funded, along with child benefit (see Manifesto 3) by the new international financial transactions tax (see Manifesto 12). Action against specific violations of human rights, like the eradication of child labour and of the abuse of street children, will be a key part of the new agency's role.

9. **Agree a new operational specification of fair trade.** Representatives of each world region to agree the terms of a framework plan, to be endorsed by a majority of the UN and agreed in stages over 10 years. This will necessarily involve removal of protective agricultural subsidies in rich countries to allow fair trade and the subsequent removal of tariffs and other barriers to trade on the part of poor countries. Domestic food production and a fair price standard for food commodities produced in the developing countries to become rules operated by the World Trade Organisation.

10. **Introduce new international company law.** The priority must be the introduction of a new international law requiring transnational corporations (TNCs) to curb anti-social activities and curb excessively high profits from poor countries.

11. **Rebuild and/or strengthen tax administration.** Taxation systems to be introduced and strengthened where necessary, and to be answerable to representatives of national electorates, who should have independent powers to monitor policies and outcomes. Monitoring by an independent international inspectorate will also become necessary.

12. **Introduce an international financial transactions tax to be administered by the UN.** In the first instance a tax at a rate of 0.2% would be payable on all currency exchanges at banks and currency exchange offices. Half of the gross revenue would be administered by the UN to subsidise the establishment of child benefit in developing countries.

13. **Reconstitute international financial agencies.** Membership to be automatically open to all countries, funded by an agreed percentage of national GDP, for example 0.3%, with equal regional representation on governing councils and committees, and five-year circulation of chairmanship. Terms of reference to be subject every five years to majority vote at the UN.

14. **Transnational prospectus to be agreed.** Each TNC will be required to draw up policy statements both for employees (including employees in subsidiary companies), and for countries in which the TNC has operations of significant scale. The former to include specification of employment conditions and rights for all types of employees. The latter policy statement to be subject to approval by a consultative body representing the TNC, the national electorate in the 'headquarter' country and the governments of the countries from which overseas profits are derived (one third representation each).

15. **Further democratisation of the UN.** Representation of populous countries, and of the poorest 100 countries, to be increased on UN committees, especially powerful economic and social committees. The objective will be to progress in stages to equal representation of regions by population size.

16. **To establish strong regional policy alliances.** Collaborative working relationships between regional or global non-government organisations (NGOs) and governments must be introduced and strengthened, as part of improved democratisation. The UN must play a leading role, and the provision of a legal framework is one option.

17. **To agree an international poverty line.** An international poverty line that defines a threshold of income (including the value of income in kind) – ordinarily required in different countries to surmount material and social

deprivation – must be a priority. The defined line will be subject to demonstrable scientific, not politically convenient, consensus.

18. **To monitor the success of anti-poverty policies.** Further steps to be taken to fulfil the agreements of the Copenhagen World Summit for Social Development of 1995, and to regularise the publication of annual anti-poverty reports by governments, but also by the UN and the other principal international agencies. This process must involve regular evaluation of the quantitative contribution of different national and cross-national policies to reduce poverty.

Peter Townsend and David Gordon (July 2002)

Index of material and social deprivation: national (UK) and cross-national

UK

Material deprivation

I. Dietary deprivation

I   At least one day in last 14 days with insufficient to eat

2   Short of food on at least one occasion in last 12 months to meet needs of family

3   No fresh meat or fish most days of week (alternative formulation for vegetarians)

4   No special meal or roast most weeks

5   No fresh fruit most days

Cross-national (including developing countries

Material deprivation

Ia. Dietary deprivation

I   Hungry or short of food at least one day in last 30 days

2   Hungry or short of food three days or more in last 30 days

3   No substantial meal in last seven days

4   Short of food on at least one day in last 12 months to meet needs of family

5   No special meal most weeks

6   No fresh fruit most days

7   No reserve food chest/food store to supply basic food needs of family

8   No fresh meat and/or fish and/or vegetarian dish on at least four days of last seven

9   Difficulties getting sufficient staple food eg maize, rice, cassava, potatoes

Ib. Deprivation of health facilities

I   Free medicines not available

2   No health care professional (doctor, nurse, pharmacist, optician) within 30-minute journey

3   No doctor to visit when sick

4   No health centre, hospital, pharmacy within one hour's journey time

5   Cannot afford medicines/medical care when needed

2. Clothing deprivation

I   Inadequate footwear for all weathers

2   Inadequate protection against heavy rain

2. Clothing deprivation

I   Inadequate footwear for all weathers

2   Inadequate protection against heavy rain

3   Inadequate protection against severe cold

4   Fewer than three pairs of socks/stockings in good repair

5   No dressing gown for cold

6   No clothing bought second-hand in last 12 months

3   Inadequate protection against severe cold

4   Less than two pairs shoes in good repair

5   No blanket/dressing gown for cold nights

6   No external clothing bought/made in last 12 months

7   No 'best outfit' for job interview/weddings/other celebrations or formal occasions

3. Housing deprivation

1   No exclusive use of indoor WC and bath

2   No electricity

3   Housing not free of damp

4   Housing not free of infestation

5   Poor access to accommodation

6   Fewer beds than there are adults (and counting couples or pairs of children under seven years of age or same sex under 11 per bed)

7   External structural defects

8   Internal structural defects

9   Not every room heated winter evenings

10 Poor state internal and/or external paint work and decoration

11 No spare room/bed for visitor to sleep

3. Housing deprivation

1   No flush toilet indoors or immediately accessible outdoors

2   No piped water to home or immediately accessible outdoors

3   No source of water within 100 paces (metres)

4   No electricity in household

5   No electricity for collective benefit nearby

6   Housing not free of infestation

7   Poor access to accommodation

8   Fewer beds than there are adults (and counting couples or pairs of children under seven years or same sex under 11 per bed)

9   Shortage of storage space

10 Too dark, not enough light

11 Leaky roof

12 Damp walls, floor, foundations, and so on

13 Mould or rot in walls, floors, windows, and so on

14 No room heating when cold

15 No spare room/bed for visitor to sleep

16 No separate quarters/stall/kennel for family animals

4. Deprivation of home facilities

1   No easy access to transport/car

2   No television

3   No radio

4. Deprivation of home facilities

1   No television

2   No radio

3   No washing machine

4	No washing machine	4	No refrigerator
5	No refrigerator	5	No freezer
6	No freezer	6	No electric iron
7	No electric iron	7	No gas or electric cooker
8	No gas or electric cooker	8	No car/motorbike
9	No vacuum cleaner	9	No bicycle
10	No central heating	10	No easy access to transport
11	No telephone	11	Insufficient chairs, tables for all members of household
12	Lack of carpeting in main rooms	12	Insufficient cooking utensils for all members of household
		13	No electric fan/air-conditioning when hot
		14	No vacuum cleaner
		15	No central heating/ fuel for fire
		16	No telephone
		17	Lack of carpeting/matting in main rooms

5. Deprivation of environment

1. Nowhere for children under five to play safely outside
2. Nowhere for children aged five to ten to play safely nearby
3. Risk of road accidents around home
4. No garden
5. Industrial air pollution
6. Other forms of air pollution
7. Problem of noise from traffic, aircraft, building works

5. Deprivation of environment

1. Nowhere for children to play safely outside
2. Risk of road accidents around home
3. No garden/smallholding for h'hold
4. Problems of air pollution
5. Problems of water pollution
6. Problem of noise from traffic, aircraft, building works
7. No land/shamba/garden large enough to grow vegetables and flowers and for household to sit outside
8. Land sufficient for subsistence but insufficient machinery to plough or harvest, or insufficient fertiliser for next crop to make a living
9. Land sufficient for household subsistence, but insufficient facilities/vaccines/shelter/stalls for animals

6. Deprivation of location

1. No public open space (like park or heath) within easy walking distance
2. No shops to buy ordinary household goods within a ten-minute journey

6. Deprivation of location

1. No public open space (like park or heath) within easy walking distance
2. No shops to buy ordinary household goods within a ten-minute journey

3 Problem of litter in local streets
4 Doctor's surgery or hospital outpatients department not within a ten-minute journey
5 No recreational facilities for young people or older adults nearby

3 Problem of litter in local streets
4 No school within 30-minute journey distance
5 No recreational facilities for young people or older adults nearby
6 No post office
7 No bank
8 Place of worship (for example, church or mosque)

7. Deprivation at work
1 Poor working environment (polluted air [5+], dust, noise, vibration and high or low temperature – maximum score = 9)
2 Stands or walks about more than three-quarters of the working day
3 Works 'unsocial hours'
4 Either poor outdoor amenities of work or poor indoor amenities at work (maximum score = 10)

7. Deprivation at work
1 Poor working environment (polluted air, dust, noise, vibration and high or low temperature)
2 Stands or walks about more than three quarters of the working day
3 Works 'unsocial hours'
4 Either poor outdoor amenities of work or poor indoor amenities at work
5 Inadequate provision for disabled workers
6 No appropriate clothing/overalls for work

Social deprivation

Social deprivation

8. Lack of rights in employment
1 Unemployed for two weeks or more during previous 12 months
2 Subject to one week's termination of employment or less
3 No paid holiday
4 No meals paid or subsidised by employer
5 No entitlement to pension at end of working life or other benefits if sick or disabled
6 Not entitled to pay in sickness
7 Worked 50 or more hours previous week
8 Experiences discrimination at work on grounds of race, sex, age, disability or sexual orientation

8. Lack of rights in employment
1 Unemployed for two weeks or more during previous 12 months
2 Subject to one week's termination of employment or less
3 No paid holiday
4 No meals paid or subsidised by employer
5 No entitlement to old age pension or other benefits if sick or disabled
6 Not entitled to pay in sickness
7 Worked 50 + hours previous week
8 Experiences discrimination at work on grounds of race, sex, age, disability or sexual orientation

9. Deprivation of family activity
1 Difficulties indoors for child to play
2 Child (if present) has not had holiday away from home in the last 12 months
3 Child (if present) has not had outing during the last 12 months
4 No days staying with family or friends elsewhere in previous 12 months
5 Problem of caring for someone in family with ill health/disability
6 Has care of disabled or elderly relative

9. Deprivation of family activity
1 Difficulties indoors for child to play
2 Child (if present) has not had holiday away from home in last 12 months
3 Child (if present) has not had outing during the last 12 months
4 No days staying with family or friends in previous 12 months
5 Problem of caring for someone in family with ill health/disability
6 No toys for children
7 No books for children
8 Family members separated for six months or more of year because of work
9 Cannot afford to attend religious/ national festivals/weddings/funerals
10 Insufficient resources for marriage/ funerals/other expensive ceremonies in life (for example, a coming of age)

10. Lack of integration into community
1 Being alone and isolated from people
2 Relatively unsafe in nearby streets
3 Discrimination experienced because of race/sex/age/disability or sexual orientation
4 In illness no expected source of help
5 No source of care or help from or to others outside the home
6 Moved accommodation three or more times in last five years

10. Lack of integration into community
1 Being alone and isolated from people
2 Relatively unsafe in nearby streets
3 Discrimination experienced because of race/sex/age/disability or sexual orientation
4 In illness no expected source of help
5 No source of care or help from or to others outside the home
6 Moved accommodation three or more times in last five years

11. Lack of formal participation in social institutions
1 Did not vote at last election
2 No participation in trade union, educational courses, sporting or other clubs, or political parties
3 No participation in any 'organised' (for example, church, neighbourhood, regional or national) activities

11. Lack of formal participation in social institutions
1 Did not vote at last general (including presidential) election
2 No participation in trade union, educational courses, sporting or other clubs, or political parties
3 No participation in any 'organised' (for example, church, neighbourhood, regional or national) activities

12. Recreational deprivation

1   No holiday away from home in last 12 months
2   Fewer than three hours a week of specified range of leisure activities

12. Recreational deprivation

1   No holiday away from home in last 12 months
2   Fewer than three hours a week of specified range of leisure activities
3   No opportunity to follow pastime/ hobby

13. Educational deprivation

1   Fewer than ten years of education (people under 60 years of age)
2   No formal qualifications from school or subsequent educational courses or apprenticeships

13. Educational deprivation

1   Fewer than ten years of education (adults aged 18-60 years)
2   Fewer than five years education (people 15+ years)
3   No formal qualifications from school or subsequent educational courses or apprenticeships
4   Cannot read or write/has great difficulty reading/writing
5   No school books for children
6   No dictionary in school
7   Child absent/withdrawn from school because of insufficient parental resources
8   Newspapers not regularly available for family members

Total score on indicators of material and social deprivation

Total score on indicators of material and social deprivation

Source: UK survey questionnaire, Townsend (1993); Cross-national survey questionnaire: research proposal prepared by editors, 1999.

Index

A

Aaberge, R. 27
Abbey, Dr J.L. 208
absolute poverty 59-60, 381, 414
  definition of 67, 70*tab*, 71, 359
  eradication of 366
  measurement of 66
abuse to older people 330, 339-41
access to labour market 131, 136-8, 364
access to resources and services 73*tab*,
    134, 135, 138-40
  in Bangalore 284, 285
  health and nutrition 72-3
  law 123
  in South Africa 341-2
  in Surat 285
  time limits on 134
  water and sanitation 254, 256
active labour market policies 124
adjustment theory 198-9, 200
administration of services and benefits
    182-6
AFDC (Aid to Families with Dependent
    Children) 86-8, 89-91
Africa 9, 54, 197, 238, 280, 424
  see also North Africa; South Africa;
    sub-Saharan Africa
African National Congress 342
age discrimination 330
ageing populations *see* older people
AGETIPS (Public Works and
    Employment Agency) 235, 236, 237,
    238, 245
aggregate growth 385, 387
agriculture 11
  in Ghana 202, 212, 214, 215, 225
  South Africa, role of women in 336
  in sub-Saharan Africa 246
Aid to Families with Dependent
    Children, US 86-8, 89-91
Akerlof, G.A. 37, 38
alternative poverty line 366-7
America *see* US
Amin, S. 211, 352, 354
anti-poverty strategies 386, 387
  constructing 413-27
  of the European Union 54-8, 120
  of the IMF 3, 5-6, 15, 53-4, 57

international 53-4
of Ireland 128
of the World Bank 3, 5-6, 15, 53-4, 57
apartheid 256-60, 329, 330
Apt, Nana 328
Argentina 13
Armed Forces Revolutionary Council of
    Ghana 204
Asamoah, Dr Obed 205
Asia 280, 424
  Central Asia 236
  East Asia 378
  South Asia 378, 379, 423
  Southeast Asia 9
asset management 279
Atkinson, A.B. 5, 177, 182, 408, 422
Australia 8, 67
Austria 178
autonomy 238
average income 385

B

Bangalore 284, 285-6
Bangladesh 380
basic needs 209, 216-17
basic non-food expenditure equation
    321-2
basket of goods measure 58, 320, 321,
    380, 381
Baulch, B. 277
Bauman, Zygmunt 420
Beall, Jo 424
Beenstock, M. 177
Belgium 7, 57, 121, 136, 137, 138
benchmarks 358, 380
benefit line *see* poverty line
benefits
  benefit/wages ratio 151*tab*
  child 104, 156, 164
  and fraud 179
  Netherland recipients of 152, 153*tab*,
    154
  non take-up of 135, 175, 178, 181-6
  perceptions of 162, 163
  sickness 150, 164
  suspension of 90, 98, 137
  unemployment benefits 149, 153*tab*,
    163, 164